Information Systems Research Methods, Epistemology, and Applications

Aileen Cater-Steel
University of Southern Queensland, Australia

Latif Al-Hakim
University of Southern Queensland, Australia

INFORMATION SCIENCE REFERENCE

Hershey · New York

Director of Editorial Content:	Kristin Klinger
Director of Production:	Jennifer Neidig
Managing Editor:	Jamie Snavely
Assistant Managing Editor:	Carole Coulson
Typesetter:	Jeff Ash
Cover Design:	Lisa Tosheff
Printed at:	Yurchak Printing Inc.

Published in the United States of America by
Information Science Reference (an imprint of IGI Global)
701 E. Chocolate Avenue, Suite 200
Hershey PA 17033
Tel: 717-533-8845
Fax: 717-533-8661
E-mail: cust@igi-global.com
Web site: http://www.igi-global.com

and in the United Kingdom by
Information Science Reference (an imprint of IGI Global)
3 Henrietta Street
Covent Garden
London WC2E 8LU
Tel: 44 20 7240 0856
Fax: 44 20 7379 0609
Web site: http://www.eurospanbookstore.com

Library of Congress Cataloging-in-Publication Data

Information systems research methods, epistemology, and applications / Aileen Cater-Steel and Latif Al-Hakim, editors.

    p. cm.

Summary: "The book deals with the concepts and applications of information systems research, both theoretical concepts of information systems research and applications"--Provided by publisher.

Includes bibliographical references and index.

ISBN 978-1-60566-040-0 -- ISBN 978-1-60566-041-7 (ebook)

1. Management information systems. 2. Electronic information resource searching. 3. Research--Methodology. I. Cater-Steel, Aileen, 1954- II. Al-Hakim, Latif, 1946-

T58.6.I4865 2009

658.4'03--dc22

                                2008017753

British Cataloguing in Publication Data
A Cataloguing in Publication record for this book is available from the British Library.

All work contributed to this book set is original material. The views expressed in this book are those of the authors, but not necessarily of the publisher.

Table of Contents

PART 1
Information Systems Research Concepts

Section 1.1
Methodology

Chapter I

Panagiotis Kanellis, Athens University of Economics and Business, Greece
Thanos Papadopoulos, University of Warwick, UK

Chapter II

Francis Chia Cua, University of Otago, New Zealand & Otago Polytechnic, New Zealand
Tony C. Garrett, Korea University, Republic of Korea

Section 1.2
Guidelines

Chapter III

John Loonam, Dublin City University, Ireland
Joe McDonagh, University of Dublin, Trinity College, Ireland

Section 2.4
e-Marketing

Detailed Table of Contents

PART 1
Information Systems Research Concepts

Section 1.1
Methodology

Chapter I
Panagiotis Kanellis, Athens University of Economics and Business, Greece
Thanos Papadopoulos, University of Warwick, UK

In the first chapter of this section, Panagiotis Kanellis and Thanos Papadopoulos offer a journey through the spectrum of epistemological and ontological perspectives in Information Systems, offering the necessary background to the researcher who has to explore diligently the research methods toolkit available and then make a choice. It does not attempt to solve any problems in existing paradigms or present any new ones, but systematically examines and clarifies the underlying set of ontological and epistemological assumptions that underpin every research activity. After a brief discussion on ontology and epistemology, the Information Systems field and its underlying paradigms are discussed and, what follows is an analysis of positivism, interpretivism, and a presentation of selected interpretive approaches. Hence, this chapter serves as a guide to be followed by researchers who would like to clarify and evaluate their views regarding epistemological and ontological assumptions, initiating a philosophical enquiry of their own. Consequently, it contributes in aiding the researcher to build a solid background upon which valid and rigorous research in the Information Systems field should be anchored.

Chapter II

Francis Chia Cua, University of Otago, New Zealand & Otago Polytechnic, New Zealand
Tony C. Garrett, Korea University, Republic of Korea

Ontological and epistemological elements in information systems research are introduced by Francis Cua and Tony Garrett. This chapter argues that ontology, epistemology, and methodology intertwine in a dynamic way. Ontology, as well as epistemology, is both an antecedent and a consequence of methodology. This complex relationship has an impact on the methodology which will affect the outcome later on. Understanding how these three elements can be related to each other can help researchers develop better methodologies for information systems research.

Section 1.2
Guidelines

Chapter III

John Loonam, Dublin City University, Ireland
Joe McDonagh, University of Dublin, Trinity College, Ireland

John Loonam and Joe McDonagh discuss the application of a Grounded Theory Methodology (GTM) in addressing enterprise systems (ES) implementation within the Irish health services. In particular, this chapter will be of benefit to researchers and practitioners endeavouring to focus on ERP implementation within health care organisations. There is a lack of empirical literature to explain the application of GTM for IS inquiry within health care organisations. This empirical vacuum is even more lacking when we turn our attention to ES implementations. This chapter will be comprised of two main sections. The first section introduces GTM, clearly illustrating its benefits to IS inquiry. The second section provides the reader with an application of GTM in practice. The chapter concludes with reflections on GTM as an approach for IS empiricism.

Chapter IV

Khalid Al-Mabrouk, University of Southern Queensland, Australia
Kieran James, University of Southern Queensland, Australia

This chapter by Khalid Al-Mabrouk and Kieran James is a polemic which aims to draw attention to the problems associated with use of Western economic rationalist and positivistic worldviews when studying IT Transfer issues in the developing world. In particular, the authors challenge the extensive use of the term "success" in the extant mainstream IT Transfer literature, arguing that it is problematic for several reasons. Mainstream IT Transfer research portrays IT Transfer as primarily linear, incremental, and progressive in line with the economic rationalist belief that a "rising tide lifts all boats." They suggest Marx's theory of dialectical materialism as an alternative to the dominant hegemony and encourage researchers in IT Transfer to accept the fact that internal contradictions are part of a dialectic system. IT Transfer researchers are encouraged to view local resistance more sympathetically. Concerted efforts should be made to understand and dialog with the other. Recommendations are made for more inter-view-based case study research in preference to mass-mail out surveys which may prove ineffective in reaching a broad segment of the population in non-Western locations. It is suggested that the existing literature's preoccupation with educated urban elites and transnational corporations may also prove to be a hindrance to both our increased understanding and radical social change.

Chapter V

    João Porto de Albuquerque, University of Sao Paulo, Brazil
    Edouard J. Simon, University of Hamburg, Germany
    Jan-Hendrik Wahoff, University of Hamburg, Germany
    Arno Rolf, University of Hamburg, Germany

João Porto de Albuquerque and colleagues from Hamburg explain that research in the Information Systems (IS) field has been characterised by the use of a variety of methods and theoretical underpinnings. This fact recently raised concerns about the rigor of scientific results of IS research and about the legitimacy of the IS academic field. On the other hand, a number of IS researchers have argued for a view that values diversity as a strength of the IS field. This chapter supports this viewpoint and analyses the relation between IS research and concepts originating from theoretical debates around transdisciplinarity. The authors present results from a group of researchers of various disciplinary backgrounds towards an integrative platform for the orientation of transdisciplinary IS research. The Mikropolis platform provides researchers with a common language, allowing the integration of different perspectives through exchange of experiences and mutual understanding. They also discuss some practical issues that arise from the transdisciplinary cooperation in IS research.

Section 1.3
Epistemology

Chapter VI

    Paul D. Witman, California Lutheran University, USA
    Kapp L. Johnson, California Lutheran University, USA

This chapter by Paul Witman and Kapp Johnson provides a set of guidelines to assist information systems researchers in creating, negotiating, and reviewing nondisclosure agreements, in consultation with appropriate legal counsel. It also reviews the use of nondisclosure agreements in academic research environments from multiple points of view, including the perspectives of both public and private sectors. Active academic researchers, industry practitioners, and corporate legal counsel all provided input into the compiled guidelines. An annotated bibliography and links are provided for further review.

Slinger Jansen and Sjaak Brinkkemper are concerned that although information systems is a maturing research area, information systems case study reports generally lack extensive method descriptions, validity defense, and are rarely conducted within a multicase research project. This reduces the ability to build theory in information systems research using case study reports. In this chapter, they offer guidelines, examples, and improvements for multicase studies. If information system researchers conform to these guidelines, more case study reports may be published, improving the rapidly maturing research area of information systems.

This chapter by Erja Mustonen-Ollila and Jukka Heikkonen gives important methodological, theoretical, and practical guidelines to the information system (IS) researchers to carry out a historical study. This study shows how a new theory can be discovered inductively from historical studies using a methodological guideline from previous researchers; using multiple data collection methods, such as semi-structured interviews, archival files, and published news; and using novel data analysis methods from learning and intelligent systems, such as the Self-Organizing Maps (SOMs), SOMs combined with U-matrices, and the Bayesian network modeling. The chapter also outlines the benefits, the main problems, the characteristics, and the implications of historical research in the information system field. Finally some research directions are provided for historical research.

PART 2
Information Systems Research Applications

Section 2.1
Software Development

Large-scale systems development is a complex activity involving number of dependencies that people working together face. Only a few studies concentrate on the coordination of development activities in their organizational context. Paivi Ovaska's research study tries to fill at least part of this gap by studying how systems development process is coordinated in practice. The study uses a multimethodological approach to interpret coordination of systems development process in a contemporary software organization in Finland. The methodology is based on the empirical case-study approach in which the actions, conceptions, and artefacts of practitioners are analyzed using within-case and cross-case principles. In all the three phases of the study, namely multisite coordination, requirement understanding, and working with systems development methods, both the qualitative and quantitative methods were used to an understanding of coordination in systems development. The main contribution of this study is to demonstrate that contemporary systems development is very complex and more driven by opportunity than is currently acknowledged by researchers. The most challenging part of the research process was the combination of qualitative and quantitative methods, because of the lack of multimethodological work done in IS discipline.

Chapter X

Judith Symonds, AUT University, New Zealand
Andrew Connor, AUT University, New Zealand

Usability Evaluation Methods are plentiful in the literature. However, there appears to be a new interest in usability testing from the viewpoint of the industry practitioner and renewed effort to reflect usability design principles throughout the software development process. In this chapter, Judith Symonds and Andrew Connor examine one such example of usability testing from the viewpoint of the industry practitioner and reflect upon how usability evaluation methods are perceived by the software developers of a content driven system and discuss some benefits that can be derived from bringing together usability theory and usability evaluation methods protocols used by practitioners. In particular the authors use the simulated prototyping method and the "Talk Aloud" protocol to assist a small software development company to undertake usability testing. They propose some issues that arise from usability testing from the perspectives of the researchers and practitioners and discuss their understanding of the knowledge transfer that occurs between the two.

Chapter XI

Ivan Ka-Wai Lai, Macau University of Science and Technology, China
Joseph M. Mula, University of Southern Queensland, Australia

Soft Systems Methodology (SSM) has been employed to increase the effectiveness of organizational requirement analysis in software development in recent years. Various forms of SSM for software development have been developed and examined in different environments by different researchers. There is little research or application that can be identified of the use of SSM in software maintenance. Ivan Lai and Joseph Mula develop an SSM model for software maintenance so that further research can be undertaken using this conceptual model.

Chapter XII

Raul Valverde, Concordia University, Canada

Mark Toleman, University of Southern Queensland, Australia

Aileen Cater-Steel, University of Southern Queensland, Australia

Recently, many organisations have become aware of the limitations of their legacy systems to adapt to new technical requirements. Trends towards e-commerce applications, platform independence, reusability of prebuilt components, capacity for reconfiguration, and higher reliability have contributed to the need to update current systems. Consequently, legacy systems need to be re-engineered into new component-based systems. This chapter by Valverde and colleagues shows the use of the design science approach in information systems re-engineering research. In this study, design science and the Bunge-Wand-Weber (BWW) model are used as the main research frameworks to build and evaluate conceptual models generated by the component-based and traditional approaches in re-engineering a legacy system into a component-based information system. The objective of this evaluation is to verify that the re-engineered component-based model is capable of representing the same business requirements as the legacy system.

Section 2.2
ICT Adoption

Chapter XIII

Shaligram Pokharel, Nanyang Technological University, Singapore

Carman Ka Man Lee, Nanyang Technological University, Singapore

Logistics activities in a company consist of a wide scope of processes ranging from planning and implementing material flow and storage, services, and information starting from the point of origin and ending at the point of consumption. If ICT could be used to support these activities, logistics cost would decrease over the long term and the efficiency of logistics activities would increase substantially. In this chapter, Shaligram Pokharel and Carman Ka Man Lee explain a method to study the impact of ICT in logistics companies. This type of study is useful to devise a long term business process improvement policy in a country or a region. The authors suggest methods for collection of data and presenting them through descriptive and statistical analysis. They suggest the use of T-statistic method to test relationship between various variables and ICT implementation. They provide a hypothetical case study to show the steps in the analysis. The chapter would be useful to researchers conducting studies on the impact and suitability of information and communication technologies in logistics and other service providing sector. The results obtained from this type of study can help the decision makers to understand the opportunities and hurdles in achieving greater efficiency in the organizational processes through the use of modern information technology.

Chapter XIV

William Yeoh, University of South Australia, Australia
Jing Gao, University of South Australia, Australia
Andy Koronios, University of South Australia, Australia

Engineering asset management organisations (EAMOs) are increasingly motivated to implement business intelligence (BI) systems in response to dispersed information environments and compliance requirements. However, the implementation of a business intelligence (BI) system is a complex undertaking requiring considerable resources. Yet, so far there are few defined critical success factors (CSFs) to which management can refer. Drawing on the CSFs framework derived from a previous Delphi study, William Yeoh and colleagues use a multiple-case design to examine how these CSFs could be implemented by five EAMOs. The case studies substantiate the construct and applicability of the CSFs framework. These CSFs are: committed management support and sponsorship; a clear vision and well-established business case; business-centric championship and balanced team composition; a business-driven and iterative development approach; user-oriented change management; a business-driven, scalablem, and flexible technical framework; and sustainable data quality and integrity. More significantly, the study further reveals that those organisations which address the CSFs from a business orientation approach will be more likely to achieve better results.

Chapter XV

Ping Li, ROC Consulting International, Singapore
Joseph M. Mula, University of Southern Queensland, Australia

A review of the literature showed that there appears to be very little research undertaken on EDI adoption by SMEs, particularly in Singapore. The study by Ping Li and Joseph Mula is a preliminary attempt to quantify this area. Using a survey-based methodology, the research examined EDI adoption. Results indicate that Singapore SMEs confirm finding by some researchers that EDI adoption is significantly associated with a firm's annual sales but is not significantly associated with employee size as other studies have shown. This study is at odds with previous single-dimension EDI adoption studies indicating a significant relationship between firm size (annual sales) and EDI depth. Organization size showed a significant relationship with the volume and diversity of EDI use but not with the depth and breadth. The most important reason for Singaporean SMEs to adopt EDI was pressure from their EDI-capable trading partners, treating pressure from their competitors as the least important.

Section 2.3
Web Services

Chapter XVI

Hatem F. Halaoui, Haigazian University, Lebanon

Using geographical information systems (GIS) has been of great interest lately. A lot of GIS applications are being introduced to regular and noncomputer- expert people through their everyday used machines such as cars (GPS), mobile (location systems), Internet (locating systems and direction guiders), and others. Google Earth, a free online application, is one of those online geographical systems that provide users with a variety of functionalities towards exploring any place on the earth. The software uses Internet to connect to the online world database and travel in seconds between cities. In this chapter, Hatem Halaoui briefly explores Google Earth and presents a possible future view and an extension of this GIS application by adding a time feature that gives Google Earth the ability to store the history of the geographical information that leads towards a new Google Earth: A History of Earth Geography. For this purpose, the chapter presents storage and indexing approaches to be used for the storage, indexing, retrieval, and manipulation of geographical data used by the geographical database of the world used by Google Earth.

Web technologies are being even more adopted for the development of public and private applications, due to the many intrinsic advantages. Due to this diffusion, estimating the effort required to develop Web applications represents an emerging issue in the field of Web engineering since it can deeply affect the competitiveness of a software company. To this aim, in the last years, several estimation techniques have been proposed. Moreover, many empirical studies have been carried out so far to assess their effectiveness in predicting Web application development effort. In this chapter, Sergio Di Martino and colleagues report on and discuss the results of the most significant empirical studies undertaken in this field.

Section 2.4
e-Marketing

Recently, cellular phones capable of accessing to the Internet are prevailing rapidly in Japan. First, Kazuhiro Takeyasu examines their functions and features. The chapter considers classification of the services offered, the characteristics of cyberspace communication tools and their comparisons with mobile instruments, and strengths and weaknesses of mobile phones. Mobile marketing is then discussed from various perspectives including the ability to use real-time marketing, online coupon marketing, ease of customer navigation, seamless purchase procedures, and retrieval and utilization of information without time and spatial restriction. The author analyzes the differences in meaning between the so-called four Ps in real commerce marketing and those in cyberspace marketing. Finally, several cases using cellular phones are analyzed.

Online auctions are an increasingly popular avenue for completing electronic transactions. Many online auction sites use some type of reputation (feedback) system—where parties to a transaction can rate each other. However, retaliatory feedback threatens to undermine these systems. Retaliatory feedback occurs when one party in a transaction believes that the other party will leave them a negative feedback if they do the same. Ross Malaga examines data gathered from E-Bay in order to show that retaliatory feedback exists and to categorize the problem. A simple solution to the retaliatory feedback problem—feedback escrow—is described.

Foreword

Some people think I am an alien.

If you have picked up a book with a title like this one (*Information Systems Research Methods, Epistemology, and Applications*), some people may think you are an alien too.

Aliens, of course, are creatures from another world. Why should we be characterized as aliens? Perhaps it is because, as researchers, we exist somewhere other than the "real world." We speak of "real world" case studies, grounding our theory in the "real world," doing our fieldwork out in the "real world." This viewpoint holds that information systems practice occurs out there in the real world, whilst researchers observe and reflect from outside the real world, some otherworldly place of another dimension. Perhaps this other world is academia; perhaps it is a division of research and development (R&D) within a larger organization.

It strikes me that I have existed in "non-real worlds," ever since I was six. This was the age at which I entered school followed much later by university. We all thought that our schools and universities were not the real world, but prepared us for the real world. My earliest professional career was in television broadcasting. That world was constructed of bright lights, visual and sound effects, and artificial backdrops. Of course, we realized that the world of our studios, sets, and control rooms was quite separate from the real world. Much of my information systems practical experience was associated with the military and defense industries. Here again, these large institutions created a perception that the military was isolated and distinct from "the world." My work has also allowed me to collaborate with members of large, global, commercial organizations. Members of those companies also tend to regard their corporate environment as something distinct from the real world. It seems as if members of institutions will always regard themselves and their colleagues as existing apart from the real world. From this perspective, "research" seems to be an institution of its own, one existing apart from the "real world."

I am beginning to suspect that, if this "real world" exists, it is actually a rather narrow, imaginary place populated mostly by family farmers and the owners and employees of small businesses. Perhaps instead, the real world is actually composed of many "non-real worlds" each supporting the grand illusion of separation.

The distinction between the researchers' world and the real world may be part of this grander illusion. Do not imagine that academic research is somehow different from corporate R&D. Universities are certainly organizations in the real world. As any academic administrator will admit, these are normal organizations with buildings, budgets, staff, and products. Academia is a very real part of our native planet. Researchers are not aliens who visit the world to collect their data and return to their own planets for analysis of their discoveries. Like any other profession, researchers practice their profession. Researchers practice research.

We construct our distinction between information systems research and information systems practice as a means to distinguish the researcher from the subject. But somehow in this process we can easily forget that research is a profession and a practice itself. But it is indeed a little more complex to consider the practice of information systems research in the context of research into information systems practice.

The problem with such consideration is that it most commonly unfolds in textbook style studies of research methodology. Such studies can be abstract and prescriptive. These studies present the research principles independently from their application, although illustrations of applications may follow, almost as a consequence of the principles. Perhaps it is more useful to study the application of research principles in real studies and to develop the abstractions as a consequence of the application. In this sense we reverse the roles of the research principles: the research principles become a consequence of the context in which we must develop knowledge from research.

This book provides the opportunity for just such a reversal. Many chapters offer insight into principles of information systems research by demonstrating how these develop principles of information systems practice. Others illustrate how well planned information systems research can uncover why the application of such information systems principles succeeds or fails in specific contexts.

Information Systems Research Methods, Epistemology, and Applications provides a book with its own unique, and very pragmatic, treatment of information systems research as a practical outcome of professional researchers exploring their chosen subject. Overall, this book delivers us to the intersection of two realms of practice: research practice and information systems practice. This intersection is a collision between these two very real worlds with very real tasks at hand. This is excellent learning ground.

There are no aliens, only very human researchers engaged in the professional practice of research, who encounter equally human practitioners engaged in the professional practice of information systems. What follows is the real world of information systems research.

Richard Baskerville
Atlanta, Georgia
April 2008

Richard L. Baskerville *is a professor of Information Systems at Georgia State University. His research and authored works regard security of information systems, methods of information systems design and development, and the interaction of information systems and organizations. He is a chartered engineer, holds a BS summa cum laude, from The University of Maryland, and the MSc and PhD degrees from The London School of Economics, University of London.*

Preface

ABSTRACT

This Preface introduces the book *Information Systems Research Methods, Epistemology, and Applications.* The book deals with the concepts and applications of information systems research. The book comprises 19 chapters organised into two main parts. The first part considers the theoretical concepts of information systems research and the second part deals with applications.

INTRODUCTION

Within the information systems discipline, there is a strong tradition of using empirical research to conduct relevant and rigorous studies. It is recognised by many academics and practitioners that it is vital to evaluate the methods, frameworks, processes, and systems implemented in organisations. In practical settings covering many different industry sectors, evidence, in the form of surveys or multiple case studies, is accumulated to confirm existing theories and also to develop new models.

This collection features recent high-quality theoretical and empirical studies related to the concept, development, implementation, operation, and maintenance of information systems in organisations. The book includes both qualitative and quantitative studies of small, medium, and large organisations from both the public and private sectors and from a broad range of industries. The contributions include cases of innovative approaches to evaluation, as well as examples of effective approaches for analysing, summarizing, and presenting sets of empirical data and conclusions. This book provides a valuable contribution as it highlights innovative applications of information systems in organisations, and furthermore provides practical, rather than theoretical, discussion of factors which contribute to success and failure of information systems.

This book is a valuable resource for information systems and information technology (IS/IT) researchers, business managers, IS/IT professionals, and IS/IT students who are interested in empirical research, and/or evaluative studies of information systems in organisations.

In our own research and supervising students, we have found that there was little published research on these topics and felt that there was a need for a collection of recent research. The motivation for this book came from our attendance at various conferences such as the European Conference on Information Systems and the Australasian Conference on Information Systems, and international conferences of Information Resources Management Association (IRMA). We contacted authors we had met at these conferences and encouraged them to extend their research as a contribution to this collection. The call for chapters was also promoted through the ISWorld and L-IRMA mailing lists and this approach resulted in contributions from an international cohort of authors.

STRUCTURE OF THE BOOK

This book is comprised of 19 chapters organised into two main parts; information systems research concepts and information systems research applications.

Part 1: Information Systems Research Concepts

This part includes eight chapters organised into three sections: methodology, guidance, and epistemology.

Section 1.1: Methodology

This section features three chapters. In the first chapter of this section, Panagiotis Kanellis and Thanos Papadopoulos offer a journey through the spectrum of epistemological and ontological perspectives in Information Systems, offering the necessary background to the researcher who has to explore diligently the research methods toolkit available and then make a choice. It does not attempt to solve any problems in existing paradigms or present any new ones, but systematically examines and clarifies the underlying set of ontological and epistemological assumptions that underpin every research activity. After a brief discussion on ontology and epistemology, the Information Systems field and its underlying paradigms are discussed and what follows is an analysis of positivism, interpretivism, and a presentation of selected interpretive approaches. Hence, this chapter serves as a guide to be followed by researchers who would like to clarify and evaluate their views regarding epistemological and ontological assumptions, initiating a philosophical enquiry of their own. Consequently, it contributes in aiding the researcher to build a solid background upon which valid and rigorous research in the Information Systems field should be anchored.

Chapter II

Ontological and epistemological elements in information systems research are introduced by Francis Cua and Tony Garrett. The chapter argues that ontology, epistemology, and methodology intertwine in a dynamic way. Ontology, as well as epistemology, is both an antecedent and a consequence of methodology. This complex relationship has an impact on the methodology which will affect the outcome later on. Understanding how these three elements can be related to each other can help researchers develop better methodologies for information systems research.

Section 1.2: Guidelines

The next four chapters provide guidance for specific research approaches. John Loonam and Joe McDonagh to discuss the application of a Grounded Theory Methodology (GTM) in addressing enterprise systems (ES) implementation within the Irish health services. In particular, this chapter will be of benefit to researchers and practitioners endeavouring to focus on ERP implementation within health care organisations. There is a lack of empirical literature to explain the application of GTM for IS inquiry within health care organisations. This empirical vacuum is even more lacking when we turn our attention to ES implementations. This chapter will be comprised of two main sections. The first section introduces GTM, clearly illustrating its benefits to IS inquiry. The second section provides the reader with an application of GTM in practice. The chapter concludes with reflections on GTM as an approach for IS empiricism.

The chapter by Khalid Al-Mabrouk and Kieran James is a polemic which aims to draw attention to the problems associated with use of Western economic rationalist and positivistic worldviews when studying IT Transfer issues in the developing world. In particular the authors challenge the extensive use of the term "success" in the extant mainstream IT Transfer literature, arguing that it is problematic for several reasons. Mainstream IT Transfer research portrays IT Transfer as primarily linear, incremental, and progressive in line with the economic rationalist belief that a "rising tide lifts all boats." They suggest Marx's theory of dialectical materialism as an alternative to the dominant hegemony and encourage researchers in IT Transfer to accept the fact that internal contradictions are part of a dialectic system. IT Transfer researchers are encouraged to view local resistance more sympathetically. Concerted efforts should be made to understand and dialog with the Other. Recommendations are made for more interview-based case study research in preference to mass-mail out surveys which may prove ineffective in reaching a broad segment of the population in non-Western locations. It is suggested that the existing literature's preoccupation with educated urban elites and transnational corporations may also prove to be a hindrance to both our increased understanding and radical social change.

João Porto de Albuquerque and colleagues from Hamburg explain that research in the Information Systems (IS) field has been characterised by the use of a variety of methods and theoretical underpinnings. This fact recently raised concerns about the rigour of scientific results of IS research and about the legitimacy of the IS academic field. On the other hand, a number of IS researchers has argued for a view that values diversity as a strength of the IS field. This chapter supports this viewpoint and analyses the relation between IS research and concepts originating from theoretical debates around transdisciplinarity. The authors present results from a group of researchers of various disciplinary backgrounds towards an integrative platform for the orientation of transdisciplinary IS research. The Mikropolis platform provides researchers with a common language, allowing the integration of different perspectives through exchange of experiences and mutual understanding. They also discuss some practical issues that arise from the transdisciplinary cooperation in IS research.

Section 1.3: Epistemology

This section includes three chapters focused on Epistemology. The chapter by Paul Witman and Kapp Johnson provides a set of guidelines to assist information systems researchers in creating, negotiating, and reviewing nondisclosure agreements, in consultation with appropriate legal counsel. It also reviews the use of nondisclosure agreements in academic research environments from multiple points of view, including the perspectives of both public and private sectors. Active academic researchers, industry practitioners, and corporate legal counsel all provided input into the compiled guidelines. An annotated bibliography and links are provided for further review.

Slinger Jansen and Sjaak Brinkkemper are concerned that although information systems is a maturing research area, information systems case study reports generally lack extensive method descriptions, validity defense, and are rarely conducted within a multicase research project. This reduces the ability to build theory in information systems research using case study reports. In this chapter they offer guidelines, examples, and improvements for multicase studies. If information system researchers conform to these guidelines, more case study reports may be published, improving the rapidly maturing research area of information systems.

The chapter by Erja Mustonen-Ollila and Jukka Heikkonen gives important methodological, theoretical, and practical guidelines to the information system (IS) researchers to carry out a historical study. This study shows how a new theory can be discovered inductively from historical studies using a methodological guideline from previous researchers; using multiple data collection methods, such as semistructured interviews, archival files, and published news; and using novel data analysis methods from learning and intelligent systems, such as the Self-Organizing Maps (SOMs), SOMs combined with U-matrices, and the Bayesian network modeling. The chapter also outlines the benefits, the main problems, the characteristics, and the implications of historical research in the information system field. Finally some research directions are provided for historical research.

Part 2: Information Systems Research Applications

The second part of the book includes research related to information systems applications divided into four sections: software development, ICT adoption, Web services, and e-marketing.

Section 2.1: Software Development

This section comprises four chapters. Large-scale systems development is a complex activity involving number of dependencies that people working together face. Only a few studies concentrate on the coordination of development activities in their organizational context. Paivi Ovaska's research study tries to fill at least part of this gap by studying how systems development process is coordinated in practice. The study uses a multimethodological approach to interpret coordination of systems development process in a contemporary software organization in Finland. The methodology is based on the empirical case-study approach in which the actions, conceptions, and artefacts of practitioners are analyzed using within-case and cross-case principles. In all the three phases of the study, namely multisite coordination, requirement understanding and working with systems development methods, both the qualitative and quantitative methods were used to an understanding of coordination in systems development. The main contribution of this study is to demonstrate that contemporary systems development is very complex and more driven by opportunity than is currently acknowledged by researchers. The most challenging part of the research process was the combination of qualitative and quantitative methods, because of the lack of multimethodological work done in IS discipline.

Usability Evaluation Methods are plentiful in the literature. However, there appears to be a new interest in usability testing from the viewpoint of the industry practitioner and renewed effort to reflect usability design principles throughout the software development process. In this chapter, Judith Symonds and Andrew Connor examine one such example of usability testing from the viewpoint of the industry practitioner and reflect upon how usability evaluation methods are perceived by the software developers of a content driven system and discuss some benefits that can be derived from bringing together usability theory and usability evaluation methods protocols used by practitioners. In particular the authors use the simulated prototyping method and the "Talk Aloud" protocol to assist a small software development company to undertake usability testing. They propose some issues that arise from usability testing from the perspectives of the researchers and practitioners and discuss their understanding of the knowledge transfer that occurs between the two.

Soft Systems Methodology (SSM) has been employed to increase the effectiveness of organizational requirement analysis in software development in recent years. Various forms of SSM for software development have been developed and examined in different environments by different researchers. There is little research or application that can be identified of the use of SSM in software maintenance. Ivan Lai and Joseph Mula develop a SSM model for software maintenance, so that further research can be undertaken using this conceptual model.

Chapter XII

Recently, many organisations have become aware of the limitations of their legacy systems to adapt to new technical requirements. Trends towards e-commerce applications, platform independence, reusability of prebuilt components, capacity for reconfiguration and higher reliability have contributed to the need to update current systems. Consequently, legacy systems need to be re-engineered into new component-based systems. This chapter, by Valverde and colleagues, shows the use of the design science approach in information systems re-engineering research. In this study, design science and the Bunge-Wand-Weber (BWW) model are used as the main research frameworks to build and evaluate conceptual models generated by the component-based and traditional approaches in re-engineering a legacy system into a component-based information system. The objective of this evaluation is to verify that the re-engineered component-based model is capable of representing the same business requirements as the legacy system.

Section 2.2: ICT Adoption

Three chapters are included in this section addressing diverse adoptions such as supply chain logistics, business intelligence, and EDI.

Logistics activities in a company consist of a wide scope of processes ranging from planning and implementing material flow and storage, services and information starting from the point of origin and ending at the point of consumption. If ICT could be used to support these activities, logistics cost would decrease over the long term and the efficiency of logistics activities would increase substantially. In this chapter, Shaligram Pokharel and Carman Ka Man Lee explain a method to study the impact of ICT in logistics companies. This type of study is useful to devise a long term business process improvement policy in a country or a region. The authors suggest methods for collection of data and presenting them through descriptive and statistical analysis. They suggest the use of T-statistic method to test relationship between various variables and ICT implementation. They provide a hypothetical case study to show the steps in the analysis. The chapter would be useful to researchers conducting studies on the impact and suitability of information and communication technologies in logistics and other service providing sector. The results obtained from this type of study can help the decision makers to understand the opportunities and hurdles in achieving greater efficiency in the organizational processes through the use of modern information technology.

Engineering asset management organisations (EAMOs) are increasingly motivated to implement business intelligence (BI) systems in response to dispersed information environments and compliance requirements. However, the implementation of a business intelligence (BI) system is a complex undertaking requiring considerable resources; yet, so far there are few defined critical success factors (CSFs) to which management can refer. Drawing on the CSFs framework derived from a previous Delphi study, William Yeoh and colleagues use a multiple-case design to examine how these CSFs could be implemented by five EAMOs. The case studies substantiate the construct and applicability of the CSFs framework. These CSFs are: committed management support and sponsorship; a clear vision and well-established business case; business-centric championship and balanced team composition; a business-driven and iterative development approach; user-oriented change management; a business-driven, scalable and flexible technical framework; and sustainable data quality and integrity. More significantly, the study further reveals that those organisations which address the CSFs from a business orientation approach will be more likely to achieve better results.

Chapter XV

A review of the literature showed that there appears to be very little research undertaken on EDI adoption by SMEs particularly in Singapore. The study by Ping Li and Joseph Mula is a preliminary attempt to quantify this area. Using a survey-based methodology, the research examined EDI adoption. Results indicate that Singapore SMEs confirm finding by some researchers that EDI adoption is significantly associated with a firm's annual sales but is not significantly associated with employee size as other studies have shown. This study is at odds with previous single-dimension EDI adoption studies indicating a significant relationship between firm size (annual sales) and EDI depth. Organization size showed a significant relationship with the volume and diversity of EDI use but not with the depth and breadth. The most important reason for Singaporean SMEs to adopt EDI was pressure from their EDI-capable trading partners, treating pressure from their competitors as the least important.

Section 2.3: Web Services

The focus of this section is on the development and use of Web Services. Using geographical information systems (GIS) has been of great interest lately. A lot of GIS applications are being introduced to regular and noncomputer-expert people through their everyday used machines such as cars (GPS), mobile (location systems), Internet (locating systems and direction guiders), and others. Google Earth, a free online application, is one of those online geographical systems that provide users with a variety of functionalities towards exploring any place on the earth. The software uses Internet to connect to the online world database and travel in seconds between cities. In this chapter, Hatem Halaoui briefly explores Google Earth and presents a possible future view and an extension of this GIS application by adding a time feature that gives Google Earth the ability to store the history of the geographical information that leads towards a new Google Earth: A History of Earth Geography. For this purpose, the chapter presents storage and indexing approaches to be used for the storage, indexing, retrieval and manipulation of geographical data used by the geographical database of the world used by Google Earth.

Web technologies are being even more adopted for the development of public and private applications, due to the many intrinsic advantages. Due to this diffusion, estimating the effort required to develop Web applications represents an emerging issue in the field of Web engineering since it can deeply affect the competitiveness of a software company. To this aim, in the last years, several estimation techniques have been proposed. Moreover, many empirical studies have been carried out so far to assess their effectiveness in predicting Web application development effort.

In the chapter, Sergio Di Martino and colleagues report on and discuss the results of the most significant empirical studies undertaken in this field.

Section 2.4: e-Marketing

The final section of the book concentrates on e-marketing and comprises two chapters related to cellular phones and online auctions.

Recently, cellular phones capable of accessing to the Internet are prevailing rapidly in Japan. First, Kazuhiro Takeyasu examines their functions and features. The chapter considers classification of the services offered, the characteristics of cyberspace communication tools and their comparisons with mobile instruments, and strengths and weaknesses of mobile phones. Then, mobile marketing is discussed from various perspectives including the ability to use real-time marketing, online coupon marketing, ease of customer navigation, seamless purchase procedures, and retrieval and utilization of information without time and spatial restriction. The author analyzes the differences in meaning between so-called four Ps in real commerce marketing and those in cyberspace marketing. Finally, several cases using cellular phones are analyzed.

Online auctions are an increasingly popular avenue for completing electronic transactions. Many online auction sites use some type of reputation (feedback) system—where parties to a transaction can rate each other. However, retaliatory feedback threatens to undermine these systems. Retaliatory feedback occurs when one party in a transaction believes that the other party will leave them a negative feedback if they do the same. Ross Malaga examines data gathered from E-Bay in order to show that retaliatory feedback exists and to categorize the problem. A simple solution to the retaliatory feedback problem—feedback escrow—is described.

BOOK DEVELOPMENT PROCESS

A double-blind review process was used for all chapters submitted to the editors. Authors of selected chapters were invited to act on the reviewers' comments and resubmit their chapters to the editors. Chapters were checked and final revisions applied.

We have enjoyed the process of compiling this book and in particular working with the contributors who provided such wide-ranging contributors on the topic of information systems research. It is up to you, the readers, to decide whether the perspectives offered here are relevant to your research or to the practical application of the concepts in your organisations. We would be delighted to hear your feedback on the usefulness of this collection.

DISCLAIMERS

No product or service mentioned in this book is endorsed, nor are any claims made about the capabilities of such product or service. All trademarks are copyrighted to their respective owners.

Aileen Cater-Steel and Latif Al-Hakim
Editors

Acknowledgment

The authors who contributed to this book deserve our heartfelt thanks for their contribution, patience, and cooperation throughout the long and complex process of compiling this book. All the contributors are listed with biographical sketches in a section near the end of the book.

The reviewers also played an essential role and we know the authors were very appreciative of the valuable comments provided by the reviewers. We sincerely thank the reviewers for taking the time to read and comment on the original submissions. Their contribution was an essential ingredient necessary to improving the content and presentation of the chapters.

Thanks also to Professor Richard Baskerville for providing the thought provoking Foreword for the book. Professor Baskerville's contribution to the world of Information Systems Research is widely acclaimed.

A special note of thanks to the staff at IGI Global who provided the necessary process, templates, reminders, and project management of the entire process from our first proposal to this final publication. In particular we wish to express our thanks to Dr. Mehdi Khosrow-Pour, executive editor, and Julia Mosemann, assistant development editor.

Finally, we dedicate this book to Aileen's children, Emily and Declan, and Latif's grandchildren, Zahra, Mustafa, Ibrahim, and Yasamin.

PART 1
Information Systems Research Concepts

Section 1.1
Methodology

Chapter I
Conducting Research in
Information Systems:
An Epistemological Journey

Panagiotis Kanellis
Athens University of Economics and Business, Greece

Thanos Papadopoulos
University of Warwick, UK

ABSTRACT

This chapter offers a journey through the spectrum of epistemological and ontological perspectives in IS (IS), offering the necessary background to the researcher who has to explore diligently the research methods toolkit available and then make a choice. It does not attempt to solve any problems in existing paradigms or present any new ones, but systematically examines and clarifies the underlying set of ontological and epistemological assumptions that underpin every research activity. After a brief discussion on ontology and epistemology, the IS field and its underlying paradigms are discussed and what follow is an analysis of positivism, interpretivism, and a presentation of selected interpretive approaches. Hence, this chapter serves as a guide to be followed by researchers who would like to clarify and evaluate their views regarding epistemological and ontological assumptions, initiating a philosophical enquiry of their own. Consequently, it contributes in aiding the researcher in building a solid background upon which valid and rigorous research in the IS field should be anchored.

INTRODUCTION

Any research activity seeks valid knowledge. This validity stems from community acceptance, that is, an agreement on a set of values which have produced knowledge claims that have withstood the test of time. This set of values is referred to as a "research paradigm." Paradigms do mutate, evolve, or get discarded completely. However, this does not happen overnight due to the already existing cumulative tradition, which sets a pace in their evolution (Kuhn, 1970).

In the IS field, research paradigms and research, although already established through the last 10 years (e.g., Benbasat & Weber, 1996; Klein & Myers, 1999; Wade & Hulland, 2004), are still being under scrutiny and dispute, continuing to be haunted by feelings of inadequacy, and even leading many IS researchers to the lament that the IS field lacks a theoretic core, and thereby to the so-called "crisis" (Benbasat & Weber, 1996; Benbasat & Zmud, 2003; Ciborra, 1998a; Markus & Lee, 1999; Stowell & Mingers, 1997). Numerous research methodologies and approaches for analysing, summarizing, and presenting sets of empirical data and conclusions have been proposed within these paradigms (Becker & Niehaves, 2007; Chen & Hirschheim, 2004; Orlikowski & Baroudi, 1991). However established these may be, the lack of systematic analysis regarding their epistemological assumptions is apparent (e.g., Becker& Niehaves, 2007; Fitzgerald, Hirschheim, Mumford, & Wood-Harper, 1985; Mingers, 2001a), leading the researcher to question, at least, their applicability in the context of his own research purpose and context.

Should we, then, as seekers of valid knowledge and parts of fast changing organizational realities embrace teleology and strive to seek for "written-in-stone" cause-effect relationships and universal truths that underpin positivism's deterministic notions? Or should we not, instead, be looking for epistemological frameworks (or applied epistemologies) which in a given context through the acquisition and systematisation of knowledge, induce awareness to those very changing realities and enable us to make connected statements that are valid and might act as stimulants for corrective action?

The purpose of this chapter is to offer a sound epistemological base to the research methods toolset available to IS researchers, addressing the largest possible spectrum of epistemological issues relevant to the field. This is important for any research endeavour, whether it is placed within a social or applied science domain; even so in the case of IS due to the multidisciplinary nature of the field. The plethora of methodological choices and tools that the new researcher will have to choose from may at times result to confusion and make an otherwise interesting and challenging task, rather daunting and dull. In this vein, this chapter does not attempt to solve any "problems" in existing research paradigms, or to offer a "new" paradigm simply because there are not any "old" ones; rather, it takes the reader to an epistemological journey, systematically examining and clarifying the underlying set of ontological and epistemological assumptions which underpin every IS research paradigm. It touches areas and unearths these paradigms, by critiquing their already existing assumptions. Moreover, it supports a move away from the conventional positivist notions, which seem to dominate the IS field. It does so by considering the ever-changing nature of IS and holding the assumption that as a successful business is constantly adapting to change, so should its IS.

The proposed epistemological journey has a twofold goal: it is useful as an example to any aspiring IS researcher who is faced with the task of having to clarify and form conclusions and views as to what constitutes valid knowledge. Additionally, it offers the opportunity to the researcher to compare and evaluate existing research paradigms, initiating a dialectic process, or in other words a philosophical inquiry. Hence, the contribution of this chapter lies in drawing points/challenges that must be taken into account in order to conduct valid and rigorous research in IS, contributing to the need for evaluating research methods and frameworks within their paradigms' assumptions during the study of IS. The structure of the chapter is as follows: after a discussion on ontology and epistemology, we look into the IS field and its paradigm evolution, characteristics and "workings." Considering the notion of relativism, we analyse the interpretive stance for IS research, followed by a presentation of selective research approaches that fall under interpretivism. We conclude the chapter by presenting our thoughts regarding future IS research.

FUNDAMENTAL EPISTEMOLOGICAL /ONTOLOGICAL QUESTIONS

The ontological and epistemological assumptions one makes drive any subsequent scientific inquiry. These assumptions are the outcome of reflection on reality and its nature. The persistence to find out what reality is has given rise to a number of questions that have remained a casus beli amongst seekers of knowledge for centuries. As one would expect, they remain unresolved in a sense that there is not an "across the board" acceptance. The only feature that seems to be shared by all schools of thought is their untamed individuality. With so many of them in existence and with their numerous projected assumptions and doctrines, even a simple review can be confusing. However, a basic knowledge of the main schools of thought is necessary for the researcher who wants to understand his discipline, clarify his thoughts, and formulate his own epistemological assumptions.

In the IS field, several endeavours have been made in order to classify different research paradigms, while taking into account their different epistemological assumptions. The most prevalent can be found in Burrell and Morgan (1979), who classify research into four distinct paradigms, namely functionalism, interpretivism, radical

structuralism and radical humanism. In doing so, they use different ontological, epistemological, and methodological criteria, which have been discussed in the IS literature (Hirschheim & Klein, 1989). The ontological, epistemological, and methodological choices IS researchers make constitute their underpinning paradigm which is defined as "the most fundamental set of assumptions adopted by a professional community which allow them to share similar perceptions and engage in commonly practices" (Hirschheim & Klein, 1989, p. 1201).

Hence, we set to provide an essentially brief review by structuring it around three philosophical questions in an attempt to understand why some paradigms are followed and some are not. Different paradigms can contribute to the birth of new ideas and insights (Benbasat & Weber, 1996; Hirschheim & Klein 1989). Three diverging paradigms commonly adhered to in IS research are: the positivistic (or conventional), constructivist (or interpretive), and critical paradigm.

Is There an Objective Reality?

This question addresses the existence of a "real world" and is studied by ontology, which analyzes "what is" and "how it is" (Falconer & Mackay, 1999; von Foerster, 1996, in Becker & Niehaves, 2007; Walsham, 1995a, 1995b, 1995c; Weber, 2004). One of the major philosophical schools that deal with this question is idealism, which is opposed to the existence of any objective reality. There are two streams of thought here: subjective idealism (Descartes 1596-1650; Berkeley 1685-1753) and objective idealism (Plato 427-347 BC, Hegel, 1770-1831. See also Grayling (1998), Hegel (1977), Janaway (1998), Rosen (1998), and Scruton (1998). Descartes, the main proponent of subjective idealism, proposed in his Method of Doubt: not to accept anything as true if he could give a reason for thinking it may be false, believing that we could be deceived even in that which seems to us most evident (Grayling, 1998). Descartes required a global doubt about everything, but agreed on the existence of an ultimate and perfect reality whose source is God (Grayling, 1998). Berkeley's idealism is more absolute. According to him, the outside world consists of a number of states in the mind and is a group of "ideas" that we have. Everything that we touch, hear, or feel is not objective realities but "ideas." Thus, objects exist only to the extent that they can be perceived: esse est percipi (Grayling, 1998). The fact that there is a common view of the world shared by many is the result of Divine Intervention. Objective idealism on the other hand, accepts the "real" dimension of objects. The dimension of the substance of Beings, "ideas," the "Being itself," is objective (Grayling, 1998). As Plato believed, the ideas are not a product of the subconscious but exist outside it and over it at a higher ontological domain (Janaway, 1998). According to Hegel (1977) and Rosen (1998), the reality of separate objects should be rejected, but there exists an all-embracing unity, the absolute, which is rational and real. By drawing attention to the particular, we are separating it from the whole; and so the particular is only partial true (Gregory, 1987).

Realism is contrasted with idealism. To the question as to whether reality is objective and exists outside the mind, realism gives a positive answer. But at the core, every realist's perspective as to "what is real" depends largely upon a philosophy of existence. "Matter" and "mind" can both be accepted as real by different persons. For example, Platonists and Scholastic thinkers believed that the "real" consisted of universals that existed absolutely independently of people's minds, while the opposite is advocated by the Cartesians of the seventeenth century who believed that one can only be certain of the reality of mind, matter, and the existence of God (Janaway, 1998; Kohl, 1992). Another form of realism believes in the existence of the physical world independent of our sense experience—the view help by physicists and other scientists "who are not tortured by philosophical paradoxes" (Kohl, 1992, p. 73).

Phenomenologists share the sane view with Immanuel Kant (1724-1804)—who attempts to overcome the differences between realism and idealism (Gardner, 1998; Scruton, 1998)—suggesting that objects exist outside the mind, but they can only be known as phenomena rather than as entities per se. The reason for this is that any empirical fact is subjected to certain a priori conditions that exist, and largely determine the working of the mind. It is those that "alter" the knowledge that we have about things, making us to recognize them only as phenomena. The identity and properties of the objects as are will remain unknown. According to Kant, there exist two types of entities: noumena, which exist independently from human consciousness, and phenomena, that is, constructs that depend on human consciousness. However, we can only acquire knowledge about the phenomena, as the things themselves (noumena) are unknowable. Kant supports the view that the mind shapes the way one understands the world, in accordance with the fundamental principles of phenomenology.

Phenomenology (which must not be confused with phenomenalism) is quite unique with respect to the philosophical tradition, because it refuses to take a position regarding the existence or not of an objective reality, but rather concentrates on providing a new method for seeking knowledge (Introna & Ilharco, 2004). Edmund Husserl (1859-1938), the founder of this movement, distinguished between an experiencing subject (the researcher) and the objects of the world, but he concentrated on establishing the nature of the relationship between the two. Husserl argued for the importance of a conscious person who at the same time is conscious of being unconscious. This awareness is central to phenomenological analysis, as it enables a person to reflect and distance himself from the experience of the world of objects that he has (phenomenological reduction). By doing that, experience is described without presuppositions, and the fundamental structures of consciousness and the "life-world" (Lebenswelt) of people are uncovered (Kohl, 1992). Phenomenology recognizes that a person has values, feelings, and moral beliefs, and that he makes judgments about things in the world thereby giving them meaning. The formation of meanings is called intentionality and is a natural process of experiencing the world. To understand intentionality, one has to distance himself from experience by using phenomenological reduction and "reflect upon the fullness of the experienced moment" (Kohl, 1992, p. 68). Phenomenology's contribution to contemporary thought is the "appreciation of the density of every person's experience and the consequent refusal to simplify experience, or try to fit it to some pre-established theoretical construct" (Kohl, 1992, p. 68). In IS research, phenomenology has been widely followed in various studies (e.g., Boland, 1983, 1985, 1993; Ciborra, 1998b; Ilharco, 2002; Introna, 1997; Introna & Ilharco, 2004; Mingers, 2001b; Zuboff, 1988).

Each philosophical doctrine presented in this brief overview could be criticized on its own merits but, an extensive critique, is inappropriate to the purpose of this chapter. We shall finish this section by simply stating our position in respect to the first question, that is, the existence of an objective reality. Following phenomenologists, we advocate towards the existence of an objective physical reality; however, we differentiate it from social reality. If we concentrate our attention on the difference between our conception of a physical object and our perception of it, we can understand better the existence of the real world in relation to our consciousness. To grasp better the distinction, we use "The Oxford Mini Dictionary," which defines "perceive" as: "to become aware of, see or notice." "Conceive" is defined as: "to form (an idea, etc) in the mind, think." Hence, a perception is a sensory experience of something and its "interpretation" from our conscience, whereas a conception (or "permanent" representation) is what remains when the sensory experience ceases. Whereas a conception that we hold for a specific physical object belongs to

us and only us as the experiencing subjects and can be modified at will, the perception that one holds for an object is more or less the same with the perception the majority of the members of a social community have, regarding the same object. In a sense, a perception is imposed upon us and is not subjected to permutations caused by will, but remains stable; every time we see the same physical object, for example, a river, we form the same perception about it. Social reality is different. It is more complex and, it is constantly changing because it is both created and observed by human beings. It is not about physical objects like a river is; it is about social systems. IS for example, are to large extent social systems.

System requirements and constraints are socially constructed and they change as perceptions change (Hirschheim, Klein, & Lyytinen, 1995). In this case, perceptions themselves are neither static nor are dictated to us by the physical world. They do change through social interaction and learning, as well as through the evolution of language and culture. Thus, although with the physical world there can possibly be a single account of reality, with social systems there can only be different perceptions of it.

Is Knowledge about the Physical/Social Reality Attainable?

Is knowledge about the physical/social reality attainable? And if it is to what degree? This forms the second philosophical question, which, if answered, constitutes the core of epistemology (Becker & Niehaves, 2007; Burrell & Morgan, 1979; Hirschheim et al., 1995; Sturgeon, Martin, & Grayling, 1998; Weber, 2004). Those who aspire to a set of beliefs, hold them as absolute, and do not set them under question, are said to be followers of a dogma. Such people adhere to a position that the possibility of knowledge is an undisputed fact (Sturgeon et al., 1998). According to Kant, a dogmatist is one who develops an adamant view on a philosophical subject, without any preceding critical examination (Gardner, 1998; Scruton, 1998). All the great philosophers such as Plato, Descartes, and Spinoza, have been dogmatists to one extent or another (Grayling, 1998; Janaway, 1998). Scepticism is not comfortable with dogmas, and its followers unless they provided with a satisfactory reason as to why they should do otherwise, doubt any proposition, belief or history. The use of skeptical arguments belongs to epistemology, and in one sense they might be said to define it (Sturgeon et al., 1998). At the extreme, skepticism defies the validity of any knowledge, claiming that we always perceive things in relation to others, which stops us from knowing about their nature as it is. To this, moral beliefs are added, which turn this into an impossible task. Skepticism however, is better understood as a challenge, not as a claim that we can, or cannot know and/or learn. The best way to respond to skepticism is "by not attempting to refute it on an argument-by-argument basis, but by showing how we know" (Sturgeon et al., 1998, p. 57).

Rorty (1982) articulates the essence of pragmatism very successfully by stating:

This theory says that truth is not the sort of thing one should expect to have a philosophically interesting theory about it. For pragmatists, "truth" is just the name of a property which all true statements share [such as 2 plus 2 is 4] (p. xiii).

For the pragmatists, the argument is not whether or not we can achieve valid knowledge, but whether the knowledge we have come to, is useful in a practical sense; that is, does it make our life better? Hence, truth, which can be found only through experiment, and validated through evidence of the senses, lies in action in the real world and not in some eternal realm (Kohl, 1992). If, however, truth can only be associated with the common good, how and with what criteria do we define such good? Do we accept the various opin-

ions of the general public or do we follow one that has been expressed by a single particular person? Pragmatism has been criticized on the strength of this argument, which shows that truth is not what is in the best interest of the human being; rather, it is the other way around (Darke, Shanks, & Broadband, 1998; Marshall, Kelder, & Perry, 2005; Rorty, 1982; Wicks & Freeman, 1998).

Auguste Comte (1798-1858), a French philosopher and sociologist, is credited as being the founder of positivism, but the Sophists and Francis Bacon (1561-1626) preceded him by claiming that knowledge is and is not possible (Grayling, 1998; Janaway, 1998). Metaphysical knowledge is impossible. Positivism postulates that all knowledge can be expressed in statements of laws and facts that are positively corroborated by measurement (Hirschheim et al., 1995). In a sense, Bacon tries to distance philosophy from science, but in doing so he prohibits us to look further than any empirical facts that we may have deduced; but those should only be seen as the beginning of an understanding of complex phenomena, and not as en end in themselves (Hirschheim et al., 1995). Kant and his followers also argued for the importance of having empirical—a posteriori—material extensively, but also stressed that their interpretation is subjected to a priori intellectual and perceptual capabilities (see phenomenology), that disfigure the physical objective reality as is (Gardner, 1998; Scruton, 1998).

Can Knowledge about the Physical/Social Reality be Achieved by a Particular Method?

What is the source of knowledge? The dialectic method? The experience? Or a combination of both? With regard to his question, which refers to the methodological aspect of epistemology, a clear distinction between the various schools of thought is not possible, as most adopt a middle ground. Any differences being portrayed emanate from their ranking or importance regarding the dialectics or experience as primary factors for valid knowledge. Philosophers like Plato and Aristotle, and later Descartes and Hegel, believed to a lesser or greater extent that the source of knowledge is the dialectic method and, the intellect per se—an intellect that operates according to its own laws and capabilities, irrespectively of any empirical facts and what exists out there; for instance, Descartes asserted that certain mathematical axioms and "ideas" we have about God, are ingrained in the human mind and are not the result of experience (Grayling, 1998; Janaway, 1998; Lawson-Tancred, 1998; Rosen, 1998).

Based solely on those pre-existing axioms and ideas, we can learn about the truth by either not using experience at all, or by only using it to an extent so as to awaken our a priori intellectual capabilities. This line of thinking seems to involve two "domains": a conceptual one and the real world. If we take this to the extreme, that is, that concepts shape more or less the world we experience, we cannot compare between the two. If concepts come first, a comparison of the conceptual models with the real world is self-confirming (Hirschheim et al., 1995). Hegel's (1977) dictum "experience only confirms what the concept teaches," sums up an essential aspect of the interpretivist position, which is looked at in more detail later in this chapter. At the opposite end lies positive empiricism—a view associated with John Locke (1632-1704), David Hume (1711-1776), and Berkeley (1685-1753) (Grayling, 1998). According to Kohl (1992), Empiricism is the theory that all knowledge is derived from experience rather than reason. Empiricists claim that reality can be known only through the experience of the senses, and that rationality alone has no ability to provide insight into the nature of the world (p. 60).

The intellect plays an a posteriori role by processing only what is passed to it by the senses. Empiricism is synonymous with pragmatism, which was described previously.

Experience and intellect are inseparable from each other and this would be our position to the third question posed. Kant showed that each on its own is of little value for the acquisition of knowledge, which is the product of the two combined. With social reality in particular, it is obvious that the numerous, fluid, and contradictory perceptions which are imposed on the intellect via the senses, do not constitute knowledge themselves. Somehow all this material must be ordered, structured and classified on the basis of certain criteria, leading eventually to conception. The contribution of empiricism is that it pushed the theory of knowledge towards the understanding of an objective reality, but made the mistake of depending solely on the real world on its own as the provider of truth, becoming a victim of absolutism (Gardner, 1998; Grayling, 1998; Scruton, 1998).

What can, however, be said about the IS field itself? What are the predominant epistemological assumptions shared by the majority of IS researchers? It seems obligatory to know its characteristics and paradigms as well as their limitations. This awareness should enable us through a critical analysis to position our own research better with respect to its philosophical underpinnings.

A LOOK INTO THE INFORMATION SYSTEMS FIELD

To say that the IS field is akin to controversy is perhaps an understatement. Controversy generally emanates from challenging the status quo by the proposition of something new, and most of the time radical—an idea, product, method, act, or, indeed, anything that could achieve that. The resolution of controversy comes only by acceptance from the majority of the members of the social group that has been challenged. With IS, this is the wider academic community, or even better, the "scientific" community and its reluctance to accept the IS researcher and his endeavours, by dismissing them as "pseudo-science" (Klein, Hirschheim, & Nissen, 1991), as field in crisis (Benbasat & Weber, 1996; Benbasat & Zmud, 2003; Ciborra, 1998; Markus & Lee, 1999; Stowell & Mingers, 1997), and as reference discipline (Baskerville & Myers, 2002). It can be argued that those academics that aspire to conduct research into IS with the ultimate aim to achieve tenure are faced with two choices. They either adhere to the established paradigms for acquiring "valid" knowledge (without questioning whether or not they are appropriate for the nature of the objects they wish to study) or, become sceptics and challenge them by arguing their case as best as they can. As any choice, this clearly poses a dilemma, which is essentially an epistemological one. Proven avenues for the acquisition of scientific knowledge exist and can be borrowed from a number of disciplines. Their adoption could lead to publishable research and of course in the long term, tenure. Following the other path is obviously more risky—acceptance, if ever achieved, will take much longer. At the outset this sounds like an ethical question facing the researcher. Is there a "right" and "wrong" epistemology in IS? Why is it that a physics researcher for example, may not have to face this question? By looking into the IS field and, by a consideration of the research thematic and the ways and methods of inquiry, an understanding of its nature as it stands as present can be achieved.

Dickson and DeSanctis (1990) note that publication activity started to blossom after 1979. They distinguish two types of research—scientific, that is, that which is empirical in nature and puts collected data through the rigour of scientific analysis, and that, which comprises of descriptive or conceptual material. They advocate that after 1985 any research aspiring to be termed "IS research" must be of the first type. The main themes up until 1978 exhibit a descriptive nature; the majority of the published work offers guide-lines or step-by-step cookbook approaches around topics like IS planning, evaluation, and technology implementation. Nolan (1973) is credited with introducing the hypothetico-deductive (or scientific) method to the field, by being the first to formally articulate hypotheses with respect to the ways computing evolves in organizations. His *State Hypothesis Model* set the grounds for a predominant empirical flavour that the field acquired and still holds today.

Dickson and DeSanctis (1990) cite a study undertaken by Powers and Dickson (1973) as representative of empirical and scientific IS research. This study was undertaken in 14 organizations with the aim of identifying factors associated with project success and failure. Having agreed on one successful and one unsuccessful project in each one of them, they then chose and related *objective measures* of project management such as user participation, to objective measures of project success such as meeting costs and time budgets, in an attempt to discover *statistically significant correlations*. By doing that, *formal hypotheses* were thus articulated and consequently tested. Powers and Dickson were members of the Management IS Research Centre at the University of Minnesota's Carlson School of Management. This centre—the first of its kind—that included eminent scholars such as Gordon Davis and James Wetherbe amongst others, is credited with the first concentrated attempts to research IS. Their working paper series set a paradigm for the vast majority of IS research that followed there and elsewhere. Their subsequent launch of the Management IS Quarterly (MISQ) in 1977, which quickly established itself as the field's flagship journal, secured their leading position regarding research, and shaped the field for the next 20 years by the advocation of certain epistemologies (e.g., Dickson, Senn, & Chervany, 1977; Ives et al., 1980). This influence was widened by the fact that "Minnesota indoctrinated" graduates, were quickly finding employment in the fast emerging new IS departments in other universities, thus spreading this tradition.

From 1979 to 1988 12 thematics were identified by Dickson and DeSanctis (1990) relevant to the management of IS: Data Resource Management, Administration of Computer Centres, Hardware Resource Management, Software Resource Management, Project Management, Planning, Organising IS, Staffing, Evaluation, Control, Security and Management Issues. Three hundred and two papers were categorised, published in major journals such as *MIS Quarterly, Communications of the ACM, Sloan Management Review* and *Decision Sciences.* They concluded that despite the much larger volume of published material, most of it "is still not empirically based [in the sense of a strict hypothetico-deductive method], and that the trend has been to evolve existing themes rather than to introduce radically different topics or methods into the management of IS area" (p. 52).

Swanson and Ramiller (1993) performed the same activity by analysing the 397 manuscripts submitted to the IS Research (ISR) journal during the period 1987 to 1992. Their aims in performing this task were different from Dickson and DeSanctis whose primary objective was to see how "scientific" the field has become by the scrutinisation of each published paper as to how much or how less empirical it is. Having identified 37 thematic categories, one of their primary aims was to comment on the development of IS as a discipline in its own right. They thus noted,

The view through ISR's window reveals what Banville and Landry (1989) have called a "fragmented adhocracy." That is, the field continues to be topically diverse and to be based on appeals to significantly different and partly incommensurate reference disciplines. Reviewers essentially agreed, interpreting the scattering of research over many different topics, as indicating a lack of major paradigms or foundations particular to IS (p. 325).

More recently, Chen and Hirschheim (2004), confirming partially the aforementioned study,

and examining 1893 papers published in the American or European journals, revealed that at the paradigmatic level, the vast majority (89%) of the U.S. publications are characterized by a positivist paradigm, whereas European journals also mainly publish research based on positivist principles (66%), but they tend to be much more receptive to interpretivist research (34%) than U.S. journals. Although this fragmentation may at first seem to defy any attempt to impose any thematic structure or order, according to Swanson and Ramiller (1993), there are four distinct intellectual traditions that give it some sort of a shape. They characterise them as (1) engineering and design, (2) decision processes, (3) social processes, and (4) economic efficiency and business performance. These parallel what they recognise as the key reference disciplines for IS: *computer science, management science, organisation science* and *economics.*

Is this research diversity harmful for the IS field? What does this natural defiance for the establishment of an IS paradigm[1] in the Kuhnian sense really mean? Is it that the field is too young to achieve one, or is it that its very nature will make any such monistic attempt impossible? And if this is the case, shouldn't we start worrying and increase our efforts to control to the best of our abilities this dispersion?

Benbasat and Weber (1996) suggest that IS needs both paradigms and diversity in the discipline. Their view is justified on the fact that a paradigm can offer coherence to the IS discipline and characterize the phenomena that differentiate it from other disciplines. On the other hand, any paradigms cannot account for all phenomena that are properly the concern of IS researchers, in the light of the multiple tasks of developing, implementing, operating, maintaining, and managing IS. The specific field has to rely on diversity brought by reference disciplines for the different perspectives they provide in studying Information Systems. However, diversity should be controlled and therefore cannot be an excuse for not building theories to account for phenomena that distinguish the Information Systems field from others.

However, Banville and Landry (1989) argue that a field should be accepted for what it is. They conjecture that any scientific field is to be judged relative to its aims, social importance, and degree of fulfilment and argue that IS has made significant contributions in many domains of knowledge such as psychology, computer science, and management practice by being exactly what it is. They conclude that we should not be forgetting what Herbert Simon—the Nobel laureate—has said: "Science, like all creative activity, is exploration, gambling, and adventure. It does not lend itself very well to neat blueprints, detailed roadmaps, and central planning. Perhaps that's why its fun!" (p.51).

What can perhaps be stated about the IS field in its present state is that (a) it is established, at least as a reference discipline (Baskerville & Myers, 2002) (b) although over the last years there has been a move from the dominating positivistic paradigm of the 1980s and early 1990s, positivism is still being used as a research paradigm, especially in research conducted so as to be published in non-European academic journals (Dube & Pare, 2003). Given this view, what are then the points/challenges that must be taken into account with respect to producing good research? We summarise them under six headings. They are:

- *Understanding of the socio-technical nature of IS:* The point here is to be aware of this duality that IS exhibit and the implications it holds for research. We say this because as is often the case, researchers treat IS as a natural science stressing precise mathematical and technical criteria at the expense of logical rigor and theoretical and applied significance that social sciences emphasise. Indeed, such is the complexity of certain phenomena associated with IS that the scientific method of inquiry into them may be too simplistic and produce no significant results with respect to understanding them.

- *Understanding the applied nature of IS:* The highly vocational character of IS should not be ignored. Not only research should be of relevance to industry and commerce, but it should also be presented in such a way that its practical value should be made clear and understood by the practitioner. Thomas Davenport made this point clear as a plenary speaker for the Inaugural Americas Conference on IS, held in 1995 in Pittsburgh, when he said that he finds it impossible to read, let alone understand, a large proportion of the articles published in *M-IS* because of the inaccessible academic language they employ. Because of that, he noted, any practical value that there may be goes largely unnoticed.

- *Understanding of the importance and use of theory:* Differentiating from the recent past, when theory did not appear to be an important consideration for good research in IS (Straub, Ang, & Evaristo, 1984), there are calls for good theory in IS (Watson, 2001) and the development of its "own" theory (Weber, 2003). If theory, however, is to be "borrowed" from any discipline with the purpose of anchoring the research to be undertaken, this theory should be extensively examined and if needed re-evaluated with respect to the focus and objective of the research. Gregor (2006), considering the questions that arise about the bodies of knowledge or theories encompassed in a discipline, that is, domain, structural or ontological, epistemological, and sociopolitical ones, suggests that "there is limited discussion in IS forums of what theory means in IS and what form contributions to knowledge can take" (p. 611). However, blind adoption could have a negative effect by essentially constraining the researcher and not allowing him to "see" beyond a range that this theory allows the researcher to.

- *Clearly stated philosophical stance/episte-mological assumptions:* The IS field allows one the freedom to adopt any epistemological position if he wishes to do so. However, the rationale behind any choice should be explained and made clear as it is those assumptions which underline the treatment of any borrowed theory, research design, and the subsequent reporting and analysis of the results.

- *Research Design:* The research design is a technical plan that attempts to link the beginning and ending of a study (Yin, 2003). Technically, it also refers to a consideration of the various research methods available to a researcher, and how any of those (or a combination) can be employed so as to collect the data required. Numerous methods exist such as case studies, field experiments, field studies, and laboratory experiments, but any choice is dependent upon the epistemological stance adopted.

- *Awareness of the standards required in conducting research:* In conducting research, each method has a set of standards and procedures and an effort should be made in order for those to be reached at the highest level possible. Awareness would ensure that when the results are reported, the researcher is able to comment simultaneously on the limitations of his execution of the research that might have a direct effect on those.

However, the first step in order to conduct IS research and to proceed in the selection of appropriate methods is to decide regarding the dilemma of adopting a positivist or antipositivist epistemological stance. In this vain, the section that follows aims to present the limitation of positivism in the context of fast-changing organizational and social realities that IS as research objects are integrated parts.

THE LIMITATIONS OF POSITIVISM

We defined positivism previously, but we provide below its five main pillars as identified by Hirschheim (1992). Positivism is characterised by:

- *The unity of the scientific method.* Scientific method refers to the hypothesis—thesis—synthesis/antithesis process for acquiring knowledge. By unity is meant that this process is held as valid for all forms of inquiry and domains of study. As such, no distinctions are made between, for example, human and plant life and physical and nonphysical phenomena. Hence, social sciences should emulate the natural sciences (Lee, 1989).

- *The search for human causal relationships.* Cause and effect and the attempts to discover the relationships and regularities between the two in order to make generalisable statements define positivist science. These relationships, which constitute the basis for generalized knowledge, can predict patterns of behavior across situations (Dube & Pare, 2003). Any knowledge acquisition that is not based on this axiom is considered to be "pseudo-science."

- *The belief in empiricism.* This translates to the conviction that the only valid data is that which is experienced from the senses. Subjective perception, for example, is not considered acceptable.

- *Science and its process are value-free.* The experiencing subject, that is, the researcher, and his cultural, social, and moral beliefs as well as his past experience have no role whatsoever to play in the acquisition of knowledge. His or her world simply does not mix with the real world that is being researched. Thus, the subject is seen to play a passive, neutral role and does not intervene in the phenomenon of interest (Dube & Pare, 2003).

- *Logic and mathematics mostly provide the foundation of science.* Those provide the formality needed for determining causal relationships through quantitative analysis—the approach seen as best suited for doing so.

As IS are sociotechnical systems, what gives birth to information are the concerns of the perceiver, that is, the user of the information system. Such a definition of information emphasises the social dimension of the system that is supposed to provide it; it also prohibits us from forgetting the distinctive nature of the social in contrast to natural phenomena. However, positivism denies this distinction. Fuelled by a desire to represent a closure on reality, it frequently involves "an unreflexive use of methods (e.g., experiments, hypothesis testing, quantification) assumed to be successful in the natural sciences and readily transferable to the domain of the social sciences" (Knights, 1992, p. 514). Over the last years, considering the volume of IS literature, works that question positivist notions such as determinism and objectivity either implicitly (Hirschheim, Klein, & Newman, 1991; Klein & Myers, 1999; Robey & Newman, 1996) by demonstrating the social side of IS; or explicitly (Orlikowski & Baroudi, 1991) have grown with exponential rates, although there are still many cases of positivistic research (Dube & Pare, 2003) and of conventional views, justifying the rather cynical view of Mowshowitz (1981): "After one has become habituated to the odours in a room, one ceases to notice them" (p. 154).

However, positivism has institutionalised criteria of validity, replicability, and rigor in the context of scientific research, and has produced models that have enhanced our understanding about the development and use of IS (Orlikowski & Baroudi, 1991). What is to criticize, though, is the notion advocated by many that positivist research is the only way to the acquisition of valid knowledge. If this is not erroneous, it certainly is limiting. For example, Turner, Bikson, Lyytinen, Mathiassen, and Orlikowski (1991) call this one-sided view that there exists a traditional IS research paradigm an oxymoron, in addition to holding it responsible for stopping us in "[doing] the basic descriptive work; developing taxonomies and testing their reliability; and building and validating widely shared conceptual frameworks." She concludes: "In short, we now lack much of the apparatus of traditional science" (Orlikowski, 1991, p. 721). Furthermore, for positivist techniques to be employed, one has to believe that the relationships underlying his phenomena of interest are determinate and one-dimensionally causal; that research is value-free; and that people are not active makers of their social reality. Markus and Robey (1988) elucidate that there is no reason or substantive evidence to suggest that this is the case with information technology and human affairs.

But reality is overwhelmingly complex and, most importantly, it does not remain stable so as to allow oneself to study it by taking snapshots in time—it moves too fast for that (Drucker, 1994). All organizations operate on a set of assumptions which represent their views of reality and include assumptions about markets, about identifying customers/competitors and their values and behaviour, and about technology and its dynamics. Drucker calls those assumptions a company's theory of business and observes that "reality has changed, but the theory of the business has not changed with it" (1994, p. 98). The fact that these assumptions are failing is because the cause-effect relationships that underline them do not hold good for long in the face of continuous change. Handy (1980) identified three sets of spiral and assumed relationships as examples that no longer work, and argues that one cannot control or attempt to plan and determine with certainty for discontinuity. Conditions such as those reigning within contemporary environments should be approached "as experimental opportunities, seeing them as open-ended, not closed problems—divergent, not convergent" (Handy, 1980, p. 121). Such criticisms, reflecting our inabilities to account for a fast-changing reality, have serious implications on the adequacy of the existing knowledge that claims to inform us so as to deal better with it. It also has implications for the dominant methods available for the acquisition of such knowledge.

In this vein, Freedman (1992), with his article entitled "Is Management Still a Science?" supports our scientific predisposition, that is, to search for general laws or rules in a world that often appears to be unpredictable, uncertain and, even uncontrollable for those to have any lasting effect. Freedman draws heavily on chaos theory to argue that the behaviour of even relatively physical systems is fundamentally unpredictable. He remarks:

In a sense, managers are in a position rather similar to that of perhaps natural scientists. They think they understand the relationships between cause and effect in their organizations. But in fact, the links between actions and results are infinitely more complicated than most managers suspect. As a result managers are prisoners of the very systems they are supposed to manage. They understand neither the underlying dynamics of these systems nor how to influence those dynamics to achieve organizations goals. Indeed, the idea of the manager as omniscient scientific planner is fundamentally misguided (Freedman, 1992, p. 33).

The reductionist tradition of trying to break down a system into a number of parts and analyse their behaviour independently in order to predict and control is becoming fast obsolete. Managers who long believed in determinism are finding themselves losing their faith. So what could be the antidote to those seemingly stagnating theories and perspectives? The answer is simple. Epistemologies need to be re-examined. The emphasis should be not on compiling lists of guidelines as to how to control an objective social reality, but on providing useful new ways of thinking about and, looking at the world.

Tsoukas (1994) identifies the three main positivist ontological assumptions as follows:

- Organizations are viewed as orderly entities by design;
- A social system is assumed to be independent of a manager and, thus, the relationship between the two is ignored or construed as external;
- The orderly nature of social systems enables a manager to accumulate explanatory and predictive knowledge about them.

By arguing against such assumptions, Tsoukas advocates that a fresh perspective is needed that places *interpretation* right at the centre of management. Such new thinking in organization theory conceives of management as an open-ended process of co-ordinating purposeful individuals whose actions stem from applying their unique interpretations to the particular situations confronting them. These actions give rise to often unintended and ambiguous circumstances, the meaning of which is open to further interpretations and further actions, and so on. (Tsoukas, 1994, pp. 1-2)

Although Tsoukas's field is organizational behaviour, such ontological and epistemological assumptions are equally attractive to IS. To a large extent, they themselves are social systems that are supposed to model the organization they reside within. Antipositivist assumptions have proven their viability by informing successful applied IS research (e.g., Klein & Myers, 1999; McGrath, 2002; Ormerod, 1996; Thomas, 1996), including special issues in journals like *EJIS* (Bhattacharjee & Paul, 2004) and *M-IS Quarterly* (Markus & Lee, 2000, 1999). After demonstrating the limitations of positivism in the context of a fast-changing IS reality, we illustrate how our understanding about IS could be enriched by conducting research that falls under the interpretivist tradition. The perceptive reader would have noticed and possibly questioned the absence of any mention of relativism in relation to IS. We think that this is the right moment to do so.

RELATIVISM AND IS

According to Bernstein (1983), relativism is a stream of philosophy of the past 200 years that began as a trickle and swelled in recent times into a roaring torrent. Relativism is better explained and understood in relation to objectivism. We base this treatise mainly on points developed in Bernstein (1983) and Williams (1995). Extended discussions can also be found in Rorty (1982), Pratt (1978), and Myrdall (1970).

Something can be called "objective" if it is independent of the individual mind and its validity can be checked by a socially agreed-upon paradigm such as those developed for example in science or mathematics. It is the belief of the objectivist that unless knowledge, language, and indeed, for that matter, philosophy, are grounded in a rigorous manner, we cannot avoid radical scepticism. The search for this rightness or goodness is based on a conviction that there is, or must be, some sort of a permanent and historical framework or model to which researchers can appeal to determine it. Whatever positive claims thus the objectivist can make, the relativist not only refutes them, but goes a step further. In its strongest form, as Bernstein observed:

relativism is the basic conviction that when we turn to the examination of those concepts that have to be taken to be the most fundamental – whether it is the concept of rationality, truth, reality, right, the good, or norms – we are forced to recognise that in the final analysis all such concepts must be understood as relative – a specific conceptual scheme, theoretical framework, paradigm, form of life, society or culture (1983, p. 8).

Relativism has been criticised as being naïve and self-referentially paradoxical, because if one

claims that his position is true and at the same time insists that truth is relative, then what is taken as true may also be false. The result is that at any time, relativism itself may be true *and* false.

The relativist reaction however to objectivism concerns mostly the difference "fixed" and "nonfixed" theorem thinking: objectivism includes the former, whereas relativism completely rejects it, having a twofold aim: first, not to provide us with any "definitive" theories resulting from the identification and exploration of cause-effect relationships; second, *to remind us* that what is supposed to be fixed, ultimate, necessary, or permanent is mistaking what is at best historically or culturally stable. A point should be made here before proceeding further—the distinction between relativism and subjectivism. We have to remember that relativism is a reaction and not a doctrine as such (Williams, 1995). A relativist need not be a subjectivist (a person who accepts that any knowledge claims that he makes is based to a large extent on personal experience, values and feelings), and a subjectivist is not necessarily a relativist. Accordingly, a relativist need not be an objectivist either. Thomas Kuhn—one of the most "famous" objectivists—has been regarded as a relativist from his notion of the evolution of scientific paradigms; although he never agreed to it himself (Bernstein, 1983).

But is relativism not hinging to absolutism in the way extreme objectivism (e.g., positive empiricism) and subjectivism (e.g., idealism) do? Is not the fact that all "knowledge" and "philosophy" themselves are given up in favour of "philosophising," an absolute? If the primary advantage of the nonfixed relativistic position lies in keeping us aware at all times of the relative and changing nature of organizational reality, what would the implications for the applied nature of our focal point—the information system be? Does adopting such a position mean that we should abandon all hope with respect to ever achieving any knowledge that can be practically adequate? Does that mean that our role as researchers is confined to us being passive and discouraged spectators of social change? Relativism by definition can contribute nothing to a social process such as the development of IS. As every process is a negotiating process amongst the disparate streams of knowledge, views and, beliefs that each and every participant brings along, it seems that all relativism has to say is that *there is no basis for any negotiations.*

Bernstein thinks otherwise. Conflict to him is a natural occurrence that is grounded in human plurality; but ultimately it does not mean that "we are limited to being separate individuals with irreducible subjective interests. Rather it means that we seek to discover some common ground to reconcile differences through debate, conversation, and dialogue" (Bernstein, 1983, p. 223). What is implicit here is that for this common ground to be achieved, shared understandings and experience, intersubjective practices and a sense of affinity and solidarity *must already exist.* It can be safely assumed that an organization's common purpose and goals, together with a common culture and values shared by its members, provide the background for the negotiations and subsequent resolution of conflict. If this prerequisite exists, then we may have indeed moved from any fallibilistic absolute to a social process being guided by dialogue. When such prerequisites are not present, the modern response is the idea that we engineer and impose a form of collective will to form such communities—but this is precisely what cannot be done. As such, the use of any knowledge or information—however objective or subjective it might be—should not be used as a form of disciplinary technique. Most IS development approaches are such disciplinary techniques. We seek for the objective and rational—the one whose validity cannot be questioned—and we use such techniques as formalism and reductionism to elicit sets of system requirements from the users. One might argue that this is not the case with certain participatory design methods. However, even those that portray their elicited requirements

as absolute, good, and right, are fixed in time, and because of that, they certainly do not represent the changing reality. They are, however, the will of the designers and information system managers imposed upon the user community in the face of the information system to be implemented.

This is where the practical (but hidden) facet of relativism unfolds. By *thinking* in relativist terms, we are in effect at the same time moving away from it in the sense that "it becomes all the more imperative to try again and again to foster and nurture those forms of community life in which dialogue, conversation, practical discourse, and judgement are concretely embodied in our everyday activities" (Bernstein, 1983, p. 230). This movement is not just a theoretical problem, as the task of establishing the conditions that are founded in dialogical communities *is a practical task.* In short, by keeping a relativistic view we are always reminded that nothing should be conceptualised as being linear, permanent, or fixed.

INTERPRETIVE APPROACHES TO INFORMATION SYSTEMS RESEARCH

It is easy to observe the common thread that runs through any positivist notion. It can be summed up in one word: determinism. Is positivism and determinism applicable however to human and social sciences, where the object of research is or includes the human element? The awareness of the notion of subjectivity that the human element introduces gave rise to the antipositivistic epistemologies and doctrines. The major theme of antipositivism as introduced by Wilhelm Dilthey (1833-1911) is the view that as individuals do not exist in isolation, they need to be studied and understood in the context of their cultural and social life. In addition, the possibility of positive and observer-independent knowledge is denied. Instead, the emphasis is placed upon sympathetic reason in understanding phenomena and attributing meanings through 'understanding (*Verstehen)* methods rather than seeking causal connections and universal laws via the employment of "explanation" methods (Hirschheim, 1992; Hirschheim et al., 1995). Early examples of anti-positivist thinking can be found in the writings of Kant and Hegel (Gardner, 1998; Rosen, 1998; Scruton, 1998).

The point towards antipositivism is therefore our acknowledgement of the fact that it is not viable to understand and explain the nature, or the rationale behind the actions for the human element, as it is impossible to collect complete and objective sets of data that cover *all* the biological, social, and, most importantly, psychological drivers that give rise to them. Proponents of antipositivism argue, consequently, that the scientific ethos is misplaced in social scientific research because of *inter alia* (Galliers, 1992):

- The possibility of many different interpretations of social phenomena;
- The impact of the social scientist on the social system being studied;
- The problems associated with forecasting future events concerned with human activity [given the fact that] there will always be a mixture of intended and unintended effects and the danger of self-fulfilling prophecies or the opposite.

Klein and Myers (1999) propose a set of principles for evaluation of interpretive field research in IS, which lie in the practice of anthropological research and the underlying philosophy of phenomenology and hermeneutics. These principles are the following:

1. *The Fundamental Principle of the Hermeneutic Circle:* this principle suggests that all human understanding is achieved through the iterative consideration of the parts and the whole that they form and is fundamental to all the other principles.

2. *The principle of Contextualization:* this principle deals with the critical reflection of the social and historical background that should be incorporated in the research analysis, so that the audience can be informed about the way that the current situation emerged.

3. *The Principle of Interaction between the Researchers and the Subjects:* this principle has to do with reflecting in a critical way how the interaction between the researcher and the participants determined the social construction of data.

4. *The Principle of Abstraction and Generalization:* this principle relates idiographic details that came to light during data analysis through the application of principles one and two to the "theoretical and general concepts that describe the nature of human understanding and social action" (Klein & Meyers, 1999, p.72).

5. *The Principle of Dialogical Reasoning:* this principle places importance to the sensitivity required so as to trace possible contradictions between any theoretical propositions or preconceptions which guide the research design and the actual findings with subsequent cycles of revision.

6. *The Principle of Multiple Interpretations*: this principle places importance to the sensitivity required so as to trace possible differences in interpretations between the participants in the study, which are usually expressed in multiple narratives or stories of the same event or sequence of events under study.

7. *The Principle of Suspicion:* this principle places importance to the sensitivity required so as to trace possible "biases" and systematic "distortions" in the narratives collected from the participants

As interpretive research is regarded as a valid and important approach to IS research, justified by its acceptance by most mainstream IS journals

(Klein & Myers, 1999; Mingers, 2004; Walsham, 2006), these principles—although they cannot be applied mechanistically and are based on hermeneutics as a foundation for doing interpretive research—contribute to improving interpretive field research methodology from a practical point of view. Also researchers can defend their research based on principles firmly based to one major direction of interpretive research. Even more, this set of principles encourages researchers to consider and make sure each one has not been left out arbitrarily. Walsham (1995, 2006) provides a set of nonprescriptive directives for conducting interpretive fieldwork and, more specifically, he focuses on choosing a style of involvement (that is, gaining and maintaining access, collecting field data, working in different countries) and analysing data (that is, theory choosing and theory building), as well as constructing and justifying a contribution; furthermore, he focuses on the ethical research issues, such as confidentiality and anonymity. He advocates the view that "Interpretive research is here to stay in the field of IS" (Walsham, 1995, p. 329).

Being interested in interpretive techniques such as case studies, textual analysis, ethnography, and participant observation (Walsham, 2006), case studies, textual analysis, and participant observation are now examined in detail. For a comprehensive coverage on ethnography, the interested reader should consult Fetterman (1989), Hammersley and Atkinson (1994), or Van Maanen (1995) and for Grounded theory Glasser and Strauss (1967) and Macredi and Sandom (1999). We should state, though, that the word "interpretive" is not in all cases a synonym for qualitative—qualitative research may or may not be interpretive, depending upon the underlying philosophical assumptions of the researcher (Myers, 1997). Qualitative research can either be conducted in a positivist, interpretive and critical stance (Chua, 1986).

Case Studies

The flexibility of the case study as a research approach allows it to be equally promising from a positivist stance (Dube & Pare, 2004; Yin, 1989), or interpretivist one (Hartley, 2004; Walsham, 1995a, 1995b, 1995c, 2006). Galliers (1992), for example, included it under the scientific (positivist) heading of his taxonomy because the majority of its exponents classify it as such. Ultimately, the utilisation of the case study method depends on the philosophical stance of the researcher and the research objective. Benbasat, Goldstein, and Mead (1987) although approaching the issue of case studies from a positivist perspective, provide a useful "neutral" definition:

A case study examines a phenomenon in its neutral setting, employing multiple methods of data collection to gather information from one or a few entities (people, groups, or organisations). The boundaries of the phenomenon are not clearly evident at the outset of the research and no experimental control or manipulation is used (p. 370).

They identify the key characteristics of case studies as follows:

- Phenomenon is examined in a natural setting.
- Data are collected by multiple means.
- One or few entities (person, group, or organisation) are examined.
- The complexity of the unit is studied intensively.
- Case studies are more suitable for the exploration, classification, and hypothesis development stages of the knowledge building process; the investigator should have a receptive attitude towards exploration.
- No experimental controls or manipulations are involved.

- The investigator may not specify the set of independent and dependent variables in advance.
- The results derived depend heavily on the integrative powers of the investigator.
- Changes in site selection and data collection methods could take place as the investigator develops new hypotheses.
- Case research is useful in the study of "why" and "how" questions because these deal with operational links to be traced over time rather than with frequency or incidence.
- The focus is on contemporary events.

In trying to understand and derive what a case study is, one should be careful not to confuse types of evidence (e.g., qualitative data), types of data collection methods (e.g., ethnography), and research strategies (e.g., case studies) (Yin, 1981). Case studies can use either qualitative or quantitative evidence, or even a mixture of both. The case study does not imply a particular type of evidence nor does it imply the use of a particular data collection method. What the case study does represent is a "research strategy to be likened to an experiment, a history, or a simulation, which may be considered alternative research strategies" (Yin, 1981, p. 59). The main criticism that is made regarding case studies is that they are problematic with respect to generalisability. As their application is restricted to a single organisation, generalisations cannot be made easily if at all. But for antipositivism, generalisability is not of concern. Let us explain.

In interpretive IS research, the validity of the case study approach becomes clear once it is realised that one seeks to understand "the context of the information system and the process over time of mutual influence between the system and its context" (Walsham, 1993, p. 14). To this end, the case study is not merely a technique or even a means of obtaining data; for the interpretivist it is a method for organising data and the selection of a case for study will not as a consequence therefore,

rest on how typical (for example) the case may be, but on its explanatory power (Smith, 1990). It is noted elsewhere that epistemology and research methods are interrelated and a conscious effort must be made by the IS researcher to establish and communicate the extent of this relationship. Hence, if one adopts a positivist epistemological stance, statistical generalisability is the key goal (Walsham, 1993). For an interpretivist, generalisability is irrelevant; his focus is instead on "the plausibility and cogency of the logical reasoning used in describing the results from the cases, and in drawing conclusions from them" (Walsham, 1993, p. 15). Walsham adopts the view that case studies provide the main vehicle for research in the interpretive tradition. He illustrates this point by summarising and commenting on case studies conducted by Boland and Day (1989), Zuboff (1988), and Markus (1983), as representative examples of the interpretivist approach.

In conducting positivistic case studies, Dube and Pare (2004), based on the work of Devers (1999), of Lincoln and Guba (1985), and of Orlikowski and Baroudi (1991), identified criteria to classify a theoretically-grounded case study as being positivist. These criteria, in opposition to interpretive and critical case studies, have to do with the traditional validity and reliability tests conducted in the natural sciences (Yin, 1994) and in primary terms include the following:

- The adoption of the positivistic stance, which has to be clearly stated in the study.
- Evidence of formal research hypotheses.
- Stating explicitly whether the purpose of the study is theory testing of theory building.
- Validity and reliability checking as used in the natural sciences.

More specifically, Dube and Pare, using Benbasat et al. (1987), Eisenhardt (1989), Lee (1989), and Yin (1994), have developed a check-list including three basic areas of concern, namely design, data collection, and data analysis. In the first area, issues are categorized into design, data collection, and data analysis areas. They involve, for instance, the identification of research questions, rational for case selection, as well as the choice of alternative theories so as to increase their validity and predictive power. Furthermore, they include the provision of detailed information with respect to the data collection methods and the triangulation of data to increase internal validity and to provide clear descriptions of analytic methods and procedures followed. In this vein, they make greater use of preliminary data analysis techniques, provide sufficient quotes and compare findings with extant literature so as to increase the confidence in the findings.

Textual Analysis (Hermeneutics)

What DeSanctis (1993) implies by "textual analysis" is the process whereby one attempts to elicit and understand the meaning of "texts" via their interpretation. Any such activity is termed *hermeneutic*. *Hermeneutics* can be seen as a key strand of phenomenology since the act of interpretation of any text or indeed any cultural expression is an important part of the search for meaning and the essence of experience.

First introduced for interpreting the Bible, Hermeneutics is used for translating any "text" or text-analogue" (Butler, 1998; Myers, 2004; Walsham, 1995a, 1995b, 1995c). "Text-analogue" refers not only to written documents, but in a broad sense to "conversations and even no-verbal communications such as gestures or facial expressions" (Diesing 1991, p. 105 in Myers, 2004). Thus, Hermeneutics can play an important role in understanding "textual data."

The fundamental concepts of Hermeneutics in the IS field—extensively studied by Myers (2004)—are summarized as follows:

- *Historicity*: our thoughts are situated in a historical context; thus, previous historical experiences are the means to interpret any is-

sue in the present, or maybe in the future.

- *The hermeneutic circle* (Heidegger, 1976): the interpreter views the text first in parts, then as a whole and then, "from a global understanding of the whole context back to an improved understanding of each part, that is, the meanings of the words" (Klein & Myers, 1999).

- *Prejudice*: the interpreter's prior knowledge plays an important role, as without it, the interpreter cannot understand the text. According to Gadamer (1976), "prejudices" are positive and necessary in order to understand the meaning of a text.

- *Autonomization and Distanciation*: Once a text is written, it has its own autonomous objective existence, independent of its author; in addition, there exists a distance between the author, his text and the readers.

- *Appropriation and Engagement*: the interpreter needs to understand the deeper underpinnings of the text under study. As time goes by and the interpreter engages with the text, both interpreter and interpreted are changed.

With respect to IS, Boland (1985) argues that their use, design, and study, is best understood as a hermeneutic process. He explains:

In using an information system, the available output is a text that must be read and intercepted by people other than its author. In designing an information system, the designer reads the organisation and its intended users as a text in order to make an interpretation that will provide the basis for a system's design. This is also a hermeneutic task. In studying IS, social scientists read the interaction during systems design and use in order to interpret the significance and potential meanings they hold. Hence, doing research in information system is another hermeneutic task. (pp. 195-196)

Boland (1985) draws on the work of Gadamer (1976), who argues that the problem of interpretation is fundamental to our everyday activities, because the world must be interpreted by us first, in order for our intentional actions to become possible. The basic idea is to make explicit possible ways of appreciating different life-worlds (a set of phenomena that wait for our meaning projections) (Hirschheim et al., 1995) and this distinguishes a hermeneutic study from a positivistic and analytical case study.

Hermeneutics as an approach to the understanding of reality, is asserting that all knowledge is necessarily a social construction and thus subjective. Gadamer (1976) provides an in-depth explanation of the basic elements of the act of interpretation in his Philosophical Hermeneutics where he states that any such act is made possible by the pre-understanding of the interpreter action as a "horizon." Horizon is used as a metaphor to connote two things. One is related to the new, distant, and unexplored that lies ahead of us (the horizon possessed by the originator of the text), whilst the other refers to things that are closer and are thus clearer and easier to understand and extract their meaning (the interpreters' horizon). For Gadamer (1976), interpretation is not possible without prejudice, which "narrows" and gives structure to our horizon. Prejudice refers to the assumptions and the pre-understanding that the interpreter has, and as the basis for our ability to experience the world, it is a positive and not a negative thing.

According to hermeneutic theory, this pre-understanding provides the basis and, initiates an interaction between the creator's and interpreter's horizons that will ultimately bring them to the same level. Hirschheim et al. (1995) explain:

While reading the text, the interpreter will form some responses to his or her initial questions thus leading to an understanding of the test. This reading, in turn, will lead them to ask a new set of questions which arise from the first interpre-

tation of the test. This, in turn, will change the interpreter's pre-understanding through the fusion of horizons to understanding which in turn forms a new pre-understanding, is called a hermeneutic cycle. (p. 153)

Participant Observation/Action Research

The primary endeavour of hermeneutics is the description, interpretation, analysis, and understanding of the social world from the perspective of the participant (Orlikowski & Baroudi, 1991). Two research approaches that can be termed interpretivist are *participant* observation and Action Research. Becker and Geer (1969) define participant observation as the

method in which the observer participates in the daily life of the people under study, either openly in the role of researcher or covertly in some disguised role, observing things that happen, listening to what is said and questioning people over some length of time. (p. 322).

Here the role of the researcher is but a passive one. In contrast, the core idea of Action Research—as originally proposed by Lewin (1951) and influenced by work at the Tavistock Institute (Rapoport, 1970; Trist, 1976)—is that the researcher does not remain just a passive observer outside the subject of investigation, but becomes an active participant influencing the relevant human group and, in turn, being influenced by it. By being actively involved in the problem definition and solution generation and implementation, the researcher becomes a participant in the action itself, and the process of change becomes the subject of the research (Checkland, 1981).

According to Baskerville and Myers (2004), the underlying philosophy of Action Research is pragmatism, which although on its own does not have explanatory power, it provides a method of explaining "why things work and why they do not work" (p. 331). Four basic principles stem from pragmatism. The first expresses the fact that all human concepts are defined referring to their consequences, meaning that in order to clarify any concept, human beings have to determine its purpose and consequences. The second is that truth can only be revealed through human action and practice, whereas the third reveals the use of controlled inquiry as crucial in interspersing rational thought into action. The fourth refers to the social contextualization of human action, and views human action as being socially reflective.

The aim of Action Research is to contribute to both the practical concerns of people in an immediate problematic situation, and to the goals of science by the joint collaboration of the researcher and practitioner within a mutually acceptable ethical framework. This duality makes Action Research considerably more demanding than other approaches where the researcher has only to prove the scientific rigor of his research and his contribution to the theoretical development of his subject. The Action Researcher has to produce new knowledge that is of direct practical value and relevance to the professionals with whom the action researcher interacts. For that to be achieved, one must be both a management consultant and an academic researcher at the same time. It is interesting to note that with IS, the issue of relevance vs. rigor has always been the subject of intense debate (see Keen, 1991; Turner et al., 1991). Action Research seems to be a promising approach for reconciling the two sides and so it deserves our careful attention as IS researchers.

It is easy to see how the hermeneutic cycle exemplifies Action Research with two or more stakeholders projecting their compelling but probable incompatible views in trying to describe aspects of organizational reality. The continuous testing and reconciliation of those views will ultimately lead to some form of acceptance and enhanced understanding. It is an iterative and cyclical process of mutual learning resulting in the development of higher competencies through communication. For this to materialize, the researcher must be flexible and willing to change

his original research design, which should not be fixed. Consequently, it is obvious that the demands of a positivist hypothetico-deductive formula are not applicable to interpretivist Action Research that seeks to achieve a holistic understanding of a particular phenomenon or situation. When such phenomena under study are social interactions, the researcher will find it almost impossible to stay outside them. In this case the research aims can only be expressed as hopes, as they cannot be designed with certainty into a form of experiments (Checkland, 1981). In addition, claims to generalisability that may be made across local contexts, are unlike the "covering laws" to which normal science aspires. Relationships are not described by deterministic cause-effect relationships between groups of dependent and independent variables. Any generalizations that an Action Researcher makes tend to describe thematic patterns derived from inquiring in one setting. The valid transfer to other settings requires and depends on confirmation there by further experiment (Argyris & Schon, 1978).

Gummesson's (1991) description of the role of the Action Researcher summarizes eloquently our discussion thus far in addition to providing further insight. He states:

On the basis of their paradigms and pre-understanding and given access to empirical data via their role as change agent, action scientists develop an understanding of the specific decision, implementation, and change process in the cases with which they are involved. They generate a specific (local) theory, which is then tested and modified through action. The interaction between the role of academic researcher and the role of management consultant within a single project as well as between projects, can also help the scientist to generate a more general theory which in turn becomes an instrument for increased theoretical sensitivity and an ability to act in a social context, a theory that is never finalized but is continually transcedended. (Gummesson, 1991, p. 179)

Baskerville and Myers (2004), as editors of a special issue on Action Research in MIS Quarterly, "see no reason why Action Research should not be accepted in the field of IS." They suggest the view that the Action Researcher is concerned to create organizational change and simultaneously to study the process. Hence, the characteristics of Action Research emanate from collaboration and change, involving both the researcher and the subject of research, the iteration of the process and capitalization on learning by both the researcher and the research subject within the context of the subject's social system. They have also clarified four essential premises for the conduct of Action Research. First, during the diagnostic stage, a collaborative analysis of the social situation by the researcher and the research subject takes place, in which theories regarding the research subject and its nature are expressed. Second, during the therapeutic stage, collaborative change takes place, in which changes are introduced and the effects are studied. For the conduct of Action Research, Baskerville and Myers (2004) identified four essential premises. The first of those states that it is necessary to establish beforehand the purpose of any action whilst the second underlines that there must be practical action in the problem setting. The third premise of Action Research is that practical action must inform the theory, and the final premise is that both the reasoning and the action must be socially situated. These premises imply the fact that there should be a clear contribution to practice (the action) and research (the theory), whereas there should be criteria by which Action Research is judged. Examples of Action Research in IS can be found in the literature (e.g., Avison, Lau, Myers, & Nielsen, 1999; Avison, Baskerville, & Myers, 2001; Baskerville & Wood-Harper, 1996; Checkland, 1981; Iversen, Mathiassen, & Nielsen, 2004; Lindgren, Henfridsson, & Schultze, 2004; Martensson & Lee, 2004; Street & Meister, 2004).

Design Science Research and Information Systems

In addition to positivism and interpretivism, over the last years, Design-Science Research (DR) has emerged as a paradigm for performing research in IS, drawing on design science (Arnott, 2006; Carlsson, 2006; Hevner, March, Park, & Ram, 2004; Hirschheim & Klein, 2003; Iivari, 2003; March & Smith, 1995; Purao, 2002; Walls, Widmeyer, & El Sawy, 2004). DR entails an alternative to the natural/behavioural science—a body of knowledge about some class of things (objects or phenomenon) in the world (nature or society) that describes and explains how they behave and interact with each other—that is dominant to IS research (Arnott, 2006; Carlsson, 2006; March & Smith, 1995; Purao, 2002; Simon, 1996). In DR, the researcher "creates and evaluates IT artefacts intended to solve identified organizational problems" (Hevner et al., 2004, p. 77). Such artefacts include, but certainly are not limited to, algorithms (e.g., for information retrieval), human/computer interfaces, and system design methodologies or languages (Vaishnavi & Kuechler, 2005); hence, they can have the form of a construct, a model, a method, or an instantiation (Henver et al., 2004). DR is relevant to the IS community, as it addresses the role of IT artefact in IS research (Orlikowski & Iacono, 2001) and the low level of professional relevance of many IS studies (Benbasat & Zmud, 1999). These controversies are addressed by "by making systems and methods the unit of analysis and by evaluating research outcomes in an organizational context, preferably in a real IT application" (Arnott, 2006, p. 57).

According to Takeda, Veerkamp, Tomiyama, and Yoshikawam (1990), the design of a DR process involves the following phases (Figure 1): first, there should be awareness of a problem; suggestions follow, abductively drawn from the existing knowledge/theory base for the problem area (Pierce, 1931); in development, an attempt to implement the artefact according to the suggested theory takes place; it follows an evaluation phase, in which partially or fully successful implementations are compared to theory, following the functional specification in the suggestion phase; the outcome of evaluation is feed back to development, and the Development, Evaluation and further Suggestion are iteratively performed in the course of the DR. The flow from partial completion of the cycle back to Awareness of the Problem is indicated by the Circumscription arrow. Conclusion indicates termination of a specific design project.

New knowledge is produced through Circumscription and Operation and Goal Knowledge. Circumscription has to do with gaining understanding through the act of construction and detection and analysis of contradictions, where the researcher finds out that certain theoretical concepts do not work in reality as they were supposed to in theory. However, this is not attributed to misunderstandings of the theory per se; rather, it is due to the incomplete nature of any knowledge base (Vaishnavi & Kuechler, 2005). Hence, going back to the "awareness of a problem" phase, is useful in the sense that it adds constraint knowledge to the understanding of the theories that underpin the suggestion and development (Vaishnavi & Kuechler, 2005).

The DR researcher engages in the design of visual artefacts in order to create new realities (Purao, 2002). In this vein, by creating new realities, DR changes the state-of-the-world through the introduction of new and novel artefacts, which are not natural, neutral, or given; rather, they are shaped by the interests, values, and assumptions of the researchers (Orlikowski & Iacono, 2001). This contrasts the typical view of positivistic ontology where a sociotechnical system is taken for granted and is the typical unit of analysis (Vaishnavi & Kuechler, 2005). Nevertheless, DR is contrasting interpretive ontology as well: DR researchers may possess multiple world-states, but are not embedded into different and multiple

realities, as interpretivism advocates; reality for DR is stable, and places constraints on the multiplicity of world-states (Gregg, Kulkarni, & Vinze, 2001; Purao, 2002). For instance, the abductive phase of DR (Figure 1) requires the suggestion of an artefact with intended problem solving; this can be achieved by adhering to a fixed grounding reality (Vaishnavi & Kuechler, 2005).

From an epistemological perspective, DR is claimed to lack a clear articulation in contrast to Positivism and Interpretivism (Purao, 2002). Gregg et al. (2002) claim that information is factual and its meaning is deciphered through the process of construction, whereby artefacts come into being. The behaviour of artefacts is the outcome of interactions between components. Information describes interactions and to the degree the behaviour of an artefact can be predicted, this information is true. Therefore, the meaning of an artefact is the functionality it provides to the system and "what it means is what is does" (Vaishnavi & Kuechler, 2005). The DR researcher can thus be classified as a pragmatist (Cole, Purao, Rossi, & Sein, 2005; Hevner et al., 2004; Marshall et al., 2005; Pierce, 1931; Rorty, 1982; Wicks & Freeman, 1998). Additionally to pragmatism, DR can be instrumental (Hendry, 2004, in Vaishnavi & Kuechler, 2005), due to its dependence on an artefact that is predictable in respect to its functioning (instrument); DR resembles natural-science research more closely than positivist or interpretive research (Vaishnavi & Kuechler, 2005). Therefore, DR can be characterised as "knowing through making" (Purao, 2002), unlike Interpretivism and Positivism, for which knowing is the result of observing or participating (Guba & Lincoln, 1989).

Apart from ontology and epistemology, DR is distinct regarding the values of the researchers and attempts to address the question of "what values does an individual or group hold and why?" that is, axiology (Vaishnavi & Kuechler, 2005). Design researchers pursue the truth or understanding, but, contrasting positivism, they must

Figure 1. Design research process (adopted from Takeda et al., 1990)

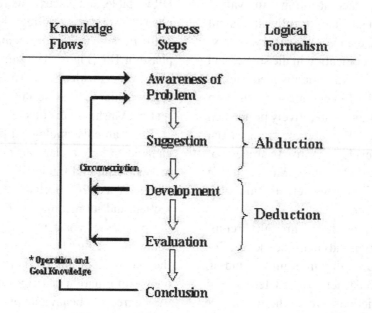

have a higher tolerance for ambiguity; although the outcome of design research effort cannot be fully understood, it can still be perceived as successful (Hevner et al., 2004). In this vein, the value of DR is proven where it can contribute to an addition to an area of knowledge, making an addition which can be further explored, shedding, thereby, light upon conflicting or theoretical bases (Vaishnavi & Kuechler, 2005; March & Smith, 1995). Here we need to state that the values of the design researcher may change as progress is made iteratively through the DR phases. From creating a reality through the construction of artefacts, the researcher then becomes a positivist observer, comparing the behaviour of an IS to theory that was set out in the previous phase. The observations are interpreted, and become the basis for a new theory which sets out to be "tested" and a new circle begins. Ultimately, one could argue that DR resembles Action Research methodology and interpretivism; however, the time frame of DR is shorter than the one of Action Research (Purao, 2002; Vaishnavi & Kuechler, 2005).

Despite its popularity in IS research (e.g., Albert et al., 2004; Arnott, 2006; Carlsson,

2006; Hevner et al., 2004; Hirschheim & Klein, 2003; Iivari, 2003; Van Aken, 2004; Walls et al., 2004), DR must identify its underlying beliefs and assumptions to gain legitimacy. In particular, Carlsson (2006) claims that "there is too little discussion about what IS design science research should include and what should be excluded" (p. 193), expressing a need for IS design research frameworks to include a broader view on IS and IS design knowledge. In this vein, DR in IS will develop more practical knowledge for the design and implementation of new IS initiatives—that is, socio-technical systems where IT artefacts play an important role for achieving the purpose of IS—used in improving already existing IS (Carlsson, 2006). Second, there is little discussion about philosophical assumptions in the IS design science research literature (Carlsson, 2006; Fleetwood & Ackroyd, 2004; Purao, 2002). Without adequate exploration of its underlying philosophical assumptions, DR has suffered from being considered as a pure technological application of the outputs of pure science, following "the lure of design and construction" (Webber, 1997, in Purao, 2002). Current research frameworks interpret DR differently, such as Systems Development Research (Nunamaker, Chen, & Purdin, 1991), Design Theories (Walls, Widmeyer, & El Sawy, 1992), Design Science (March & Smith, 1995), and Software Engineering Research (Gregg et al., 2001). However, the majority of these studies, apart from Gregg et al. (2001), do not seem to state explicit the philosophical and world-views (Purao, 2002); rather, they present a tapestry of different ontological views, depending on either positivism or pragmatism (Carlsson, 2006). Furthermore, DR should be positioned in respect to the clarification of the nature of knowledge it produces in terms of theory-building or theory testing (Purao, 2002). DR can be linked to theory building in two ways (Vaishnavi & Kuechler, 2005): first, by providing a methodological construction of an artefact (in theory), including its experimental proof, that is, an experimental exploration of a theoretical method; second, by making more visible the underlying relationships between an artefact (or IS) and its elements during either the construction or evaluation phase of the artefact and falsifying or elaborating on previously theorized relationships (ibid). However, unlike Positivism and Interpretivism where visible outputs can be theories, facts, laws, and assertions, the most visible output of DR is the artefact itself (Gregg et al., 2001; Purao, 2002).

Ultimately, in order for DR to be fruitful as a new and emerging paradigm in IS research, the above challenges should be met; otherwise, DR "will remain subject to and unable to meet methodological mandates from competing research IS paradigms or supervisory disciplines" (Purao, 2002, p. 7).

CONCLUSION

The purpose of this chapter was to offer, in the words of Smith (1990), "a sound epistemological base to the research methods" (p. 126). Of course this is important for any research endeavour, whether it is placed within a social or applied science domain. Even more so with the IS field due to its multidisciplinary nature. The plethora of methodological choices and tools that the new researcher will have to choose from, may at times result to confusion and make an otherwise interesting and challenging task rather daunting and dull.

Our aim was to embark on a journey of discovery in order to define an epistemological roadmap that will provide a sound basis for researching IS that live and breathe, constantly changing in unison with the changing organizational realities. We started by initiating a philosophical debate asking three fundamental epistemological/ontological questions, through which we aimed to present an overview of contemporary thought, and thus to set a context for what was to follow. Keeping in mind that IS are sociotechnical systems, positivism was explained and its limitations were identified. We also identified what in interpretive terms the practical task is; to provide frameworks that through interpretation, and in the light of fundamental propositions of tested validity, can be used to stimulate an individual's, or a group's interactive thinking, leading to a rational reconsideration of certain fallacious assumptions currently held. We provided a summary of the main points for a selection of interpretive research approaches, namely case studies, hermeneutics and participant observation/Action Research and finally, we explored Design Research as an emerging paradigm in IS.

The epistemological journey does not necessarily stop here. Further inquiries may look into the possibility of bridging the gap between research paradigms and finding appropriate research tools and methods that may support this pluralism and support multimethod research across different paradigms. Additionally, emphasis should be placed to the consequences of choosing a specific paradigm on research evaluation. Thus, the application of a specific framework for directly analyzing the epistemological implications of research methods is another avenue that the epistemological journey may take; but is it a feasible and enjoyable one. The journey to gain an understanding and seek answers for our *own* epistemological questions has left a trail that we hope it will be useful as an example to *any* aspiring researcher—with positivist or antipositivist inclinations—who is faced with the task of having to clarify and form his very own conclusions and views as to what constitutes valid knowledge.

Future Research Directions

The epistemological journey does not necessarily stop here. Future research should be conducted in terms of bridging the gap between research paradigms and finding appropriate research tools and methods that may support this pluralism and support multimethod research across different paradigms. For instance, Mingers (2004a) has suggested a cease of fire in the epistemological battle between positivism and interpretivism, and the emergence of epistemological stability, partly due to the emergence of the critical paradigm in IS. Hence, further development needs to occur, especially in the area of critical approaches to IS, using the critical realism paradigm. Critical realism (e.g., Archer et al., 1998; Bhaskar, 1978) and its application to the IS field (e.g., Heinz et al., 2004; Rooke, 2002) is still in its infancy. However, it can provide a useful grounding for IS research, building a transitive and intransitive dimension to reality, allowing researchers to bridge the dualism between subjective and objective views of reality. Additionally, emphasis should be placed to the consequences of choosing a specific paradigm on research evaluation. Thus, the application of a specific framework for directly analysing the epistemological implications of research methods is another avenue that the epistemological journey may take; but is it a feasible and enjoyable one.

Moving from the paradigm to the method level, attention should be placed on the emerging DR method to IS. We are yet to see more studies

in IS in using this perspective and evaluating its usefulness and applicability. Additionally, a new approach for studying IS and IT artefacts in context, that is, Action Design (Cole et al., 2005; Jarvinen, 2007), has started to emerge in the IS field. This approach aims to combine Action Research and Design Research to develop knowledge about building innovative IS and IT for problem solving in the organisational context, intending to help researchers provide and produce knowledge to support IS practitioners in solving current and anticipated problems in IS development by simultaneously intervening in an organisation through the development of an IS. Knowledge in this case will be built in the contexts where it is put to use and its products will contribute to further theoretical advances. Further research should be placed on Action Design in terms of reviewing its applicability in the IS field.

However, the task of choosing a research paradigm can indeed be a topic of further research. Having gone through this journey in the epistemological foundations of IS, the researcher should clarify his own epistemological and ontological assumptions and choose the appropriate paradigm which reflects the researcher's own conclusions as to the existence of an objective reality, the attainment of knowledge about the physical and social reality, and, finally, to the achievement of knowledge about the physical and social reality by particular methods.

REFERENCES

Albert, T.C., Goes, P.B., & Gupta, A. (2004). GIST: A model for design and management of content and interactivity of customer-centric Web sites. *MIS Quarterly 28*(2), 161-182.

Archer, M., Bhaskar, R., Collier, A., Lawson, T., & Norrie, A. (Eds.). (1998). *Critical realism: Essential readings*. London: Routledge.

Argyris, C., & Schon, D.A. (1978). *Organizational learning: A theory of action perspective.* Reading, MA: Addison-Wesley.

Arnott, D. (2006). Cognitive biases and decision support systems development: A design science approach. *Information Systems Journal, 16*(1), 55-78.

Avison, D.E., Baskerville, R., & Myers, M. (2001). Controlling action research projects. *Information Technology & People, 14*(1), 28-45.

Avison, D., Lau, F., Myers, M., & Nielsen, P.A. (1999). Action research. *Comm. of the ACM, 42*(1), 94-97.

Banville, C., & Landry, M. (1989). Can the field of m-IS be disciplined? *Communications of the ACM, 32*(1), 48-61.

Baskerville, R., & Myers, M. (2002). IS as a reference discipline. *M-IS Quarterly, 26*(1), 1-14.

Baskerville, R., & Myers, M. (2004). Special issue on action research in IS: Making IS research relevant to practice – foreword. *M-IS Quarterly, 28*(3), 329-335.

Baskerville, R.L., & Wood-Harper, A.T. (1996). A critical perspective on action research as a method for IS research. *Journal of Information Technology, 11*(3), 235-246.

Becker, H., & Geer, B. (1969). Participant observation: A comparison. In G.J. McCall & J.L. Simmons (Eds.), *Issues in participant observation.* New York: Random House.

Becker, J., & Niehaves, B. (2007). Epistemological perspectives on IS research: A framework for analysing and systematizing epistemological assumptions. *IS Journal, 17*(2), 197-214.

Benbasat, I., Goldstein, D.K., & Mead, M. (1987). The case research strategy in studies of IS. *M-IS Quarterly, 11*(3), 369-386.

Benbasat, I., & Weber, R. (1996). Research commentary: Rethinking diversity in information system research. *IS Research, 7*(4), 389-399.

Benbasat, I., & Zmud, R.W. (2003). The identity crisis within the IS discipline: Defining and communicating the discipline's core properties. *M-IS Quarterly, 27*(2), 183-194.

Bernstein, R.J. (1983). *Beyond objectivity and relativism.* Oxford, UK: Basil Blackwell.

Bhaskar, R. (1978). *A realist theory of science.* Hemel Hempstead: Harvester.

Bhattacharjee, A., & Paul, R. (2004). Special issue on interpretive approaches to IS and computing. *European Journal of IS, 13*(3), 166.

Boland, R.J. (1983). The in-formation of IS. In R.J. Boland & R.A. Hirschheim (Eds.), *Critical issues in IS research* (363-394). NY: John Wiley & Sons.

Boland, R.J. (1985). Phenomenology: A preferred approach to research on IS. In E. Mumford, R. Hirschheim, G. Fitzgerald, & T. Wood-Harper (Eds.), *Research methods in IS.* New York: North-Holland.

Boland, R.J. (1993). Accounting and the interpretive act. *Accounting, Organisations and Society, 18*(2/3), 125-146.

Boland, R.J., & Day, W.F. (1989). The experience of system design: A hermeneutic of organizational action. *Sc&inavian Journal of Management, 5*(2), 87-104.

Burrell, G., & Morgan, G. (1979). *Sociological paradigms & organizational analysis.* London, UK: Heinemann Educational Publishers.

Butler, T. (1998). Towards a hermeneutic method for interpretive research in IS. *Journal of Information Technology, 13*(4), 285-300.

Carlsson, S.A. (2006, February). *Towards an IS design research framework: A critical realist perspective.* Claremont, CA: DESRIST.

Checkland, P. (1981). *Systems thinking, systems practice*. Chichester, UK: Wiley.

Chen, W., & Hirschheim, R. (2004). A paradigmatic and methodological examination of IS research from 1991 to 2001. *IS Journal, 14*, 197-235.

Chua, W.F. (1986). Radical developments in accounting thought. *The Accounting Review, 61*(4), 601-632.

Ciborra, C.U. (1998a). Crisis and foundations: An inquiry into the nature and limits of models and methods in the IS discipline. *Journal of Strategic IS, 7*, 5-16.

Ciborra, C.U. (1998b). From tool to gestell. *Information Technology and People, 11*(4), 305-327.

Cole, R., Purao, S., Rossi, M., & Sein, M.K. (2005). Being proactive: Where action research meets design research. In *Proceedings of the Twenty-Sixth International Conference on IS* (pp. 325-336).

Darke, P., Shanks, G., & Broadbent, M. (1998). Successfully completing case study research: Combining rigour, relevance and pragmatism. *IS Journal, 8*(4), 273-289

DeSanctis, G. (1993). Theory and research: Goals, priorities and approaches. *M-IS Quarterly, 17*(1), 6-7.

Devers, K.J. (1999). How will we know "good" qualitative research when we see it? Beginning the dialogue in health services research. *Health Services Research, 34*(5), 1153-1188.

Dickson, G., & DeSanctis, G. (1990). The management of IS: Research status and themes. In A.M. Jenkins, H.S. Siegle, W. Wojtkowski, & W.G. Wojtkowski (Eds.), *Research issues in IS: An agenda for the 1990s*. WMC Brown Publishers.

Dickson, G., Senn, J.A., & Chervany, N.L. (1977). Research in management IS: The Minnesota experiments. *Management Science, 23*(9), 913-923.

Diesing, P. (1991). *How does social science work? Reflections on practice*. Pittsburgh, PA: University of Pittsburgh.

Drucker, P.F. (1994, September-October). The theory of business. *Harvard Business Review*, 95-104.

Dube, L., & Pare, G. (2003). Rigor in IS positivist case research: Current practices, trends, and recommendations. *M-IS Quarterly, 27*(4), 597-635.

Eisenhardt, K.M. (1989). Building theories from case study research. *Academy of Management Review, 14*(4), 532-550.

Falconer, D.J., & Mackay, D.R. (1999). *Ontological problems of pluralist research methodologies*. Paper presented at Americas' Conference on IS.

Fetterman, D.M. (1989). *Ethnography step by step*. London, UK: Sage Publications.

Fitzgerald, G., Hirschheim, R., Mumford, E., & Wood-Harper, A.T. (1985). Information research methodology: An introduction to the debate. In E. Mumford, G. Fitzgerald, R. Hirschheim, & A.T. Wood-Harper (Eds), *Research methods in IS* (pp. 3-9), Proceedings of the IFIP (International Federation for Information Processing), WG 8.2 Colloquium, Manchester Business School.

Fleetwood, S., & Ackroyd, S. (Eds.). (2004). *Critical realist applications in organisation and management studies*. London: Routledge.

Freedman, D.H. (1992, November-December). Is management still a science? *Harvard Business Review*, 26-38.

Gadamer, H. (1976). *Philosophical hermeneutics*. Berkeley, CA: University of California Press.

Galliers, R.D. (1992). Choosing IS research approaches. In R.D. Galliers (Ed.), *IS research: Issues, methods & practical guidelines* (pp. 144-162). Oxford, UK: Blackwell Scientific Publications.

Gardner, S. (1998). Kant. In A.C. Grayling (Ed.), *Philosophy 2: Further through the subject* (pp. 574-662). Oxford, UK: Oxford University Press.

Glasser, B., & Strauss, A. (1967). *The discovery of grounded theory*. Chicago: Adeline.

Grayling, A.C. (1998). Modern philosophy II: The empiricists. In A.C. Grayling (Ed.), *Philosophy 1: A guide through the subject* (pp. 484-543). Oxford, UK: Oxford University Press.

Gregg, D.G., Kulkarni, U.R., & Vinze, A.S. (2001). Understanding the philosophical underpinnings of software engineering research in IS. *IS Frontiers, 3*(2), 169-183.

Gregor, S. (2006). The nature of theory in IS. *M-IS Quarterly, 30*(3), 611-642.

Gregory, R.L. (1987). *The Oxford companion to the mind*. Oxford, UK: Oxford University Press.

Guba, E., & Lincoln, Y. (1989). *Fourth generation evaluation*. Newbury Park, CA: Sage Publications.

Gummesson, E. (1991). *Qualitative methods in management research*. London, UK: Sage Publications.

Hammersley, M., & Akinson, P. (1994). *Ethnography: Principles in practice* (2nd Edition). London, UK: Routlege.

Handy, C. (1980, January-February). Through the organizational looking glass. *Harvard Business Review*, 115-121.

Hartley, J. (2004). Case study research. In C. Cassell & G. Symon (Eds.), *An essential guide to qualitative research methods in organizations* (pp. 323-333). London: Sage.

Hegel, G.W.F. (1977). *Phenomenology of spirit*. Oxford: Oxford University Press.

Heidegger, M. (1976). *The piety of thinking* (translated by J. G. Hart and J. C. Maraldo). Bloomington: Indiana University Press.

Hevner, A.R., March, S.T., Park, J., & Ram, S. (2004). Design science in IS research. *M-IS Quarterly, 28*(1), 75-105.

Hirschheim, R. (1992). IS epistemology: A historical perspective. In R.D. Galliers (Ed.), *IS research: Issues, methods & practical guidelines*. Oxford, UK: Blackwell Scientific Publications.

Hirschheim, R., & Klein, H.K. (1989). Four paradigms of IS development. *Communications of the ACM, 32*, 1199-1216.

Hirschheim, R., & Klein, H.K. (2003). Crisis in the IS field? A critical reflection on the state of the discipline. *Journal of the Association for IS, 4*(5), 237-293.

Hirschheim, R., Klein, H.K., & Lyytinen, K. (1995). *IS development and data modelling: Conceptual and philosophical foundations*. Cambridge, UK: Cambridge University Press.

Hirschheim, R., Klein, H.K., & Newman, M. (1991). IS development as social action: Perspective and practice. *Omega, 19*(6), 587-608.

Iivari, J. (2003). The IS core -VII towards IS as a science of meta-artifacts. *Communications of the Association for IS, 12*, 568-581.

Ilharco, F. (2002) *Information technology as ontology*. Unpublished Ph.D. thesis. London School of Economics, London, UK.

Introna, L. (1997) *Management, information and power*. London: Macmillan.

Introna, L., & Ilharco, F. (2004). Phenomenology, screens and the world: A journey with Hursell and Heidegger into phenomenology. In L. Willcocks & J. Mingers (Eds.), *Social theory and philosophy for IS* (pp. 56-102). Chichester: John Wiley & Sons.

Iversen, J.H., Mathiassen, L., & Nielsen, P.A. Managing risk in software process improvement: An action research approach. *MIS Quarterly, 28*(3), 395-433.

Ives, B., Hamilton, S., & Davis, G.B. (1980). A framework for research in computer-based management IS. *Management Science, 26*(9), 910-934.

Janaway, C. (1998). Ancient Greek philosophy I: The pre-Socratics and Plato. In A.C. Grayling (Ed.), *Philosophy 1: A guide through the subject* (pp. 336-397). Oxford, UK: Oxford University Press.

Keen, P.G.W. (1991). Relevance and rigor in IS research: Improving quality, confidence, cohesion and impact. In H.E. Nissen, H. Klein, & R. Hirschheim (Eds.), *IS research: Contemporary approaches and emergent traditions* (pp. 27-49). Amsterdam, The Netherlands: Elsevier.

Klein, H.K., Hirschheim, R., & Nissen, H.E. (1991). A pluralist perspective of the IS research arena. In H.E. Nissen, H. Klein, & R. Hirschheim (Eds.), *IS research: Contemporary approaches and traditions*. Amsterdam, The Netherlands: Elsevier.

Klein, H.K., & Myers, M.D. (1999). A set of principles for conducting and evaluating interpretive field studies in IS. *M-IS Quarterly, 23*(1), 67-94.

Klein, H. K., & Huynh, M. (2004). The critical social theory of Jurgen Habermas and its implications for IS research. In J. Mingers & L. Willcocks (Eds.), *Social theory and philosophy for information systems* (pp. 157-237). Chichester: John Wiley & Sons.

Knights, D. (1992). Changing spaces: The disruptive impact of a new epistemological location for the study of management. *Academy of Management Review, 17*(3), 514-536.

Kohl, H. (1992). *From archetype to zeitgeist.* NewYork: Little Brown.

Kuhn, T.S. (1970). *The structure of scientific revolutions.* Chicago, IL: University of Chicago Press.

Lawson-Tancred, H. (1998). Ancient Greek pilosophy II: Aristotle. In A.C. Grayling (Ed.), *Philosophy 1: A guide through the subject* (pp. 398-439). Oxford, UK: Oxford University Press.

Lee, A.S. (1989). Case studies as natural experiments. *Human Relations, 42*(2), 117-137.

Lewin, K. (1951). Field theory in social science; selected theoretical papers. In D. Cartwright (Ed.). New York: Harper & Row.

Lincoln, Y., & Guba, E. (1985). *Naturalistic inquiry.* New York: Sage.

Lindgren, R., Henfridsson, O., & Schultze, U. (2004). Design principles for competence management systems: A synthesis of an action research study. *M-IS Quarterly, 28*(3), 435-472.

Macredi, R.D., & Sandom, C. (1999). IT-enabled change: Evaluating an improvisational perspective. *European Journal of IS, 8,* 247-259.

March, S.T., & Smith, G. (1995). Design and natural science research on information technology. *Decision Support Systems, 15*(4), 251-266.

Markus, M.L. (1983). Power, politics and m-IS implementation. *Communications of the ACM, 26*(6), 430-445.

Markus, M.L., & Lee, A.S. (1999). Special issue on intensive research in IS: Using qualitative, interpretive, and case study methods to study information technology. *M-IS Quarterly, 23*(1), 35-38.

Markus, M.L., & Lee, A.S. (2000). Special issue on intensive research in IS: Using qualitative, interpretive, and case study methods to study information technology (2nd installment; foreword). *M-IS Quarterly, 24*(1), 1.

Markus, M.L., & Robey, D. (1988). Information technology and organizational change: Causal structure in theory and research. *Management Science, 34*(5), 583-598.

Marshall, P., Kelder, J-A, & Perry, A. (2005). Social constructionism with a twist of pragmatism: A suitable cocktail for IS research. In *16ᵗʰ Australasian Conference on IS,* Sydney.

Martensson, P., & Lee, A.S. (2004). Dialogical action research at omega corporation. *M-IS Quarterly, 28*(3), 507-536.

McGrath, K. (2002). The golden circle: A way of arguing and acting about technology in the London ambulance service. *European Journal of IS, 11*(4), 251-266.

Mingers, J. (2001a). Combining IS research methods: Towards a pluralist methodology. *IS Research, 12,* 240-259.

Mingers, J. (2001b). Embodying IS: The contribution of phenomenology. *Information and Organization, 11*(2), 103-128.

Mingers, J. (2004). Real-izing IS: Critical realism as an underpinning philosophy for IS. *Information & Organization, 14,* 87-103.

Mowschowitz, A. (1981). On approaches to the study of social issues in computing. *Communications of the ACM, 24*(3), 146-155.

Myers, M. (1997). Qualitative research in IS. *M-IS Quarterly, 21*(2), 241-242

Myers, M. (2004). Hermeneutics in IS research. In J. Mingers and L. Willcocks (Eds.), *Social theory and philosophy for IS* (pp. 103-128). Chichester: John Wiley & Sons.

Myrdall, G. (1970). *Objectivity in social research.* London, UK: Gerald Duckworth & Co. Ltd.

Nolan, R.L. (1973). Managing the computer resource: A stage hypothesis. *Communications of the ACM, 16*(7), 399-405.

Nunamaker, J., Chen, M., & Purdin, T. (1991). System development in IS research. *Journal of Management IS, 7*(3), 89-106.

Orlikowski, W.J., & Baroudi, J.J. (1991). Studying IT in organizations: Research approaches and assumptions. *IS Research, 2*(1), 1-28.

Ormerod, R.J. (1996). IS strategy development at Sainsbury's Supermarkets: Using soft OR. *Interfaces, 26*(1), 102-130.

Pierce, C.S. (1931). Collected papers. In C. Harshorne & P. Weiss (Eds). Cambridge, MA: Harvard University Press.

Powers, R., & Dickson, G.W. (1973). M-IS project management. *California Management Review, 15*(3), 127-56

Pratt, V. (1978). *The philosophy of the social sciences.* London, UK: Methuen & Co. Ltd.

Purao, S. (2002). *Design research in technology and IS: Truth or dare.* Unpublished paper, School of Information Sciences and Technology, The Pennsylvania State University, University Park, State College, PA.

Rapoport, R.N. (1970). Three dilemmas of action research. *Human Relations, 23*(6), 499-513.

Ritzer, G. (1975). *Sociology: A multiple paradigm science.* Boston, MA: Allyn & Bacon.

Robey, D., & Newman, M. (1996). Sequential patterns in IS development: An application of a social process model. *ACM Transactions on IS, 14*(1), 30-63.

Rorty, R. (1982). *Consequences of pragmatism.* Brighton, UK: Harvester Press.

Rosen, M. (1998). Continental philosophy from Hegel. In A.C. Grayling (Ed.), *Philosophy 2: Further through the subject* (pp. 663-704). Oxford, UK: Oxford University Press.

Scruton, R. (1998). Modern philosophy I: The rationalists and Kant. In A.C. Grayling (Ed.), *Phi-*

losophy 1: A guide through the subject (pp. 440-483). Oxford, UK: Oxford University Press.

Smith, N.G. (1990). The case study: A useful research method for information management. *Journal of Information Technology, 5*, 123-133.

Stowell, F., & Mingers, J. (1997). Introduction. In J. Mingers, & F. Stowell (Eds.), *IS: An emerging discipline?* London: McGraw-Hill.

Straub, D.W., Ang, S., & Evaristo, R. (1984, February). Normative standards for IS research. *Database,* 21-34.

Street, C., & Meister, D.B. (2004). Small business growth and internal transparency: The role of IS. *M-IS Quarterly, 28*(3), 473-506.

Sturgeon, S., Martin, M.G.F., & Grayling, A.C. (1998). Epistemology. In A.C. Grayling (Ed.), *Philosophy 1: A guide through the subject* (pp. 7-60). Oxford, UK: Oxford University Press.

Swanson, E.B., & Ramiller, N.C. (1993). IS research thematics: Submission to a new journal, 1987-1992. *IS Research, 4*(4), 299-329.

Takeda, H., Veerkamp, P., Tomiyama, T., & Yoshikawam, H. (1990, Winter). Modeling design processes. *AI Magazine,* 37-48.

Thomas, P. (1996). The devil is in the detail: Revealing the social and political processes of technology management. *Technology Analysis & Strategic Management, 8*(1), 71-84.

Trist, E. (1976). N-gaging with large-scale systems. In A. Clark (Ed.), *Experimenting with organizational life: The action research approach* (pp. 43-75). New York: Plenum.

Tsoukas, H. (1994). From social engineering to reflective action in organizational behaviour. In H. Tsoukas (Ed.), *New thinking in organizational behaviour* (pp. 1-22). Oxford, UK: Butterworth-Heinemann.

Turner, J.A., Bikson, T.K., Lyytinen, K., Mathiassen, L., & Orlikowski, W. (1991). Relevance vs. rigor in IS research: An issue of quality. In H.E. Nissen, H.K. Klein, & R. Hirschheim (Eds.), *IS research: Contemporary approaches & emergent traditions* (pp. 715-745). Amsterdam, The Netherlands: Elsevier

Vaishnavi, V., & Kuechler, W. (2005). Design research in IS. Retrieved May 29, 2008, from http://www.Vaishnavi and Kuechler, 2005.org/Researchdesign/drisVaishnavi and Kuechler, 2005.htm

Van Aken, J.E. (2004). Management research based on the paradigm of design sciences: The quest for field-tested and grounded technological rules. *Journal of Management Studies, 41*(2), 219-246.

Van Maanen, J. (1995). *Representation in ethnography.* London, UK: Sage Publications

Wade, M., & Hulland, J. (2004) Review: The resource-based view and information system research: Review, extension, and suggestions for future research. *M-IS Quarterly, 28*(1), 107-142.

Walls, J.G., Widmeyer, G.R., & El Sawy, O.A. (1992). Building an IS design theory for vigilant e-IS. *IS Research, 3*(1), 36-59.

Walls, J.G., Widmeyer, G.R., & El Sawy, O.A. (2004). Assessing information system design theory in perspective: How useful was our 1992 initial rendition? *Journal of Information Technology Theory and Application, 6*(2), 43-58.

Walsham, G. (1993). *Interpreting IS in organizations.* Chichester, UK: Wiley.

Walsham, G. (1995a). Interpretive case studies in IS research: Nature and method. *European Journal of IS, 4*, 74-81.

Walsham, G. (1995b). The emergence of interpetivism in IS research. *IS Research, 6*(4), 376-394.

Walsham, G. (1995c). Interpetive case studies in IS research: Nature and method. *European Journal of IS, 4,* 74-81.

Walsham, G. (2006). Doing interpretive research. *European Journal of IS, 15,* 320-330.

Watson, R. (2001). Research in IS: What we haven't learned. *M-IS Quarterly, 25*(4), 5-15.

Weber, R. (2003). Editor's comment: Theoretically speaking. *M-IS Quarterly, 27*(3), 3-13.

Weber, R. (2004). The rhetoric of positivism vs. interpretivism. *M-IS Quarterly, 28*(1), 3-12.

Wicks, A.C., & Freeman, R.E. (1998). Organization studies and the new pragmatism: Positivism, anti-positivism, and the search for ethics. *Organization Science, 9*(2), 123-140.

Williams, B. (1995). Ethics. In A.C. Grayling (Ed.), *Philosophy.* Oxford UK: Oxford University Press.

Yin, R.K. (1981, March). The case study crisis: Some answers. *Administrative Science Quarterly, 26,* 58-65.

Yin, R.K. (1989). Research design issues in using the case study method to study management IS. In J.I.a.L. Cash (Ed.), *The IS research challenge: Qualitative research methods* (pp. 1-6). Boston MA: Harvard Business School Press.

Yin, R.K. (1994). *Case study research, design and methods* (2nd ed.). Newbury Park: Sage Publications.

Yin, RK (2003). *Applications of case study research.* Thousand Oaks, CA: Sage Publications.

Zuboff, S. (1988). *In the age of the smart machine.* New York: Basic Books.

FURTHER READING

Alvesson, M., & Willmott, H. (Eds.). (1992). On the idea of emancipation in management and organization studies. *Academy of Management Review, 17*(3), 432-464

Benbasat, I., & Zmud, R.W. (1999). Empirical research in IS: The practice of relevance. *MIS Quarterly, 23*(1), 3-16.

Cecez-Kecmanovic, D., Klein, H., & Brooke, C. (2008). Exploring the critical agenda in IS research. *IS Journal, 18*(2), 123-135.

Chiasson, M., & Davidson, E. (2005). Taking industry seriously in IS research. *MIS Quarterly, 29*(4), 591-605.

Christensen, C.M., & Raynor, M.E. (2003). Why hard-nosed executives should care about management theory. *Harvard Business Review, 81*(9), 66-74.

Cole, M., & Avison, D. (2007). The potential of hermeneutics in IS research. *European Journal of IS, 16*(6), 820-833

Desanctis, G. (2003). The social life of IS research. *Journal of the Association for IS, 4,* 360

Doherty, N.F., Coombs, C.R., & Loan-Clarke, J. (2006). A re-conceptualization of the interpretive flexibility of information technologies: Redressing the balance between the social and the technical. *European Journal of IS, 15*(6), 569-582.

Durkheim, E. (1938). *The rules of sociological method.* New York: Free Press.

Foth, M., & Axup, J. (2006). Participatory design and action research: Identical twins or synergetic pair? In *Participatory Design Conference (PDC),* Trento, Italy.

Gerson, E.M., & Star, S.L. (1986). Analyzing due process in the workplace. *ACM Transactions on Office IS , 4(3),* 257-270.

Goles, T., & Hirschheim, R. (2000). The paradigm is dead, the paradigm is dead... long live the paradigm: The legacy of Burrell and Morgan. *Omega, 28*, 249-268.

Hevner, A.R., March, S.T., Jinsoo, P., & Ram, S. (2004). Design science in IS research. *MIS Quarterly, 28*(1), 75-105.

Iivari, J., Hirschheim, R., & Klein, H. (1998). A paradigmatic analysis contrasting IS development approaches and methodologies. *IS Research, 9*(2), 164-193.

Lee, A. (1991). Integrating positivist and interpretivist approaches to organizational research. *Organization Science, 2*, 342-365.

Markus, M.L. (1989). Case selection in a disconfirmatory case study. In *The IS Research Challenge* (pp. 20-26). Harvard Business School Research Colloquium, Boston, MA: Harvard Business School.

Mingers, J. (2004). Paradigm wars: Ceasefire announced who will set up the new adminstration? *Journal of Information Techology, 19*, 165-71.

Niehaves, B., Klose, K., Knackstedt, R., & Becker, J. (2005). Epistemological perspectives on IS-development – a consensus-oriented approach on conceptual modeling. Springer/Berlin: Heidelberg. (LNCS).

Pare, G., & Elam, J.J. (1997). Using case study research to build theories of IT implementation. In A.S. Lee, J. Liebenau, & J.I. DeGross (Eds), *IS and qualitative research* (pp.542-568). London: Chapman and Hall.

Pettigrew, A. (1985). Contextualist research and the study of organizational change processes. In E. Lawler & S. Fransico (Eds.), *Doing research that is useful for theory and practice*. San Francisco: Jossey-Bass.

Richardson, H., & Robinson, B. (2007). The mysterious case of the missing paradigm: A review of critical IS research 1991–2001. *IS Journal, 17*(3), 251-270.

Rosemann, M., & Vessey, I. (2008). Toward improving the relevance of IS research to practice: The role of applicability checks. *MIS Quarterly, 32*(1), 1-22.

Walsham, G. (2005). Learning about being critical. *IS Journal, 15*(2), 111-117.

Weber, R. (2004). The rhetoric of positivism vs. interpretivism: A personal view. *MIS Quarterly, 28*(1), 1.

Wilson, F. (1999). Flogging a dead horse: The implications of epistemological relativism with IS methodological practice. *European Journal of IS, 3*(1), 161-169.

Chapter II
Understanding Ontology and Epistemology in Information Systems Research

Francis Chia Cua
University of Otago, New Zealand
Otago Polytechnic, New Zealand

Tony C. Garrett
Korea University, Republic of Korea

ABSTRACT

This chapter introduces ontological and epistemological elements in information systems research. It argues that ontology, epistemology, and methodology intertwine in a dynamic way. Ontology, as well as epistemology, is both an antecedent and a consequence of methodology. This complex relationship has an impact on the methodology which will affect the outcome later on. Understanding how these three elements can be related to each other can help researchers develop better methodologies for information systems research.

INTRODUCTION

A thorough understanding of the research process is needed in any study. One approach consists of three hierarchical steps. It involves using a specific framework (theory, ontology), identifying the research questions (epistemology), and determining the research strategy (methodology; Burrell & Morgan, 2005; Denzin & Lincoln,

2005b; Grix, 2002, Hay, 2002; Nelson, Treichler, & Grossberg, 1992).

Researchers should at least have a good grasp of the philosophical assumptions of the complex phenomenon they want to study as well as the methods of investigating it. That discipline mandates explicit articulation of the research process by thoroughly understanding, acknowledging, and defending their ontological, epistemological and methodological assumptions (Burrell & Morgan, 2005; Grix 2002). It is that explicit articulation that will infuse *quality* into the research process and interpret them in the *context* of the phenomenon under study. Therefore, all research is interpretive, according to Denzin and Lincoln (2005b).

The contextual setting or the natural setting makes the case study a distinct research methodology. The richness of the context generates the particulars and complexities of the experiential knowledge and legitimises the case study (Benbasat, Goldstein, & Mead, 2002; Flyvbjerg, 2001; Franz & Robey, 1984; Patton, 1990; Snow & Anderson, 1991; Stake, 1995, 2005; Yin, 1993, 1994).

The understanding of ontology and epistemology in this chapter will be in the context of a large public sector entity. The complex phenomenon concerns the replacement of enterprise systems.

The research problem theory is the Diffusion of Innovations (DOI) theory of Rogers (2003). Like the philosophical assumptions that is composed of certain basic beliefs, a paradigm is a set of assumptions that can never be absolute true knowledge (Denzin & Lincoln, 2005c, p 183; Guba, 1990). It guides and interprets the study. "Each interpretive paradigm makes particular demands on the researcher, including the questions the researcher asks and the interpretations he or she brings to them," explain Denzin and Lincoln (2005b, p 22). The paradigm provides a means for the theory to meet the practice. Information systems research relies heavily on theories derived from complementary disciplines including Accounting, Computer Science, Economics, Innovation, Management, Marketing, Psychology, Sociology, and Mathematics. Information systems research utilises theories to examine themes like the adoption and implementation of enterprise systems, communications, strategy, and political, economic and environmental, social, and technological (PEST) factors. One of the 56 theories used in the information systems research in www.istheory.yorku.ca is the DOI Theory.

In the DOI, a process model (Rogers, 2003) consists of an initiation phase and an implementation phase. The initiation phase is composed of the awareness stage, the matchmaking stage, and the business case stage. Rogers calls the third stage the decision stage. For a large public sector entity, it is more appropriate to call it the business case stage. Here, the executive sponsor makes a business case to sell the innovation (e.g., the replacement of enterprise systems) to upper management. This ends in an accept-reject decision which takes place after initiation phase and before the implementation phase. If the accept-reject decision is favourable, then the implementation phase will follow this stage.

The literature review shows that the diffusion research has certain realities and research gaps. Any stage is a potential source of unexpected and undesirable consequences. In fact, Rogers (2003, p 198) finds that diffusion studies have a clearer perspective of the evidences at the awareness and decision stages as compared to those found at the matchmaking stage. Because every stage serves as an antecedent to a subsequent stage, the decision stage will lack clarity if the prior matchmaking stage is ambiguous. Unfortunately, the literature review also states that there are only a few studies about the business case stage. In diffusion research, the study on the business case stage does not even exist. If evidences of the decision stage are clear, then Rogers could probably be referring to studies about the decision-making (e.g., strategic investment decision) that occurs immediately after the third stage instead of being the third stage itself. Undeniably, there is a dire need to study both the matchmaking stage and the business case stage.

This chapter contains a good theoretical base that provides a sound evidence of the theoretical and practical arguments of the complex relationship of epistemology, ontology, and methodology. It can be used to instruct PhD students in a "philosophy of science" course or enlighten anyone who is interested in researching ontology, epistemology, and methodology. It commences with an introduction to explain a discipline that infuses quality into a research. That discipline emphasises the explicit articulation of ontological and epistemological assumptions while developing a research methodology. The second section provides broad definitions and discussions of ontology and epistemology. The third section deals with the controversy, confusion, and other grey areas surrounding ontology and epistemology. It links the discussion to a single case study which concerns a replacement of enterprise systems by a large public sector entity. The research problem theory is the Diffusion of Innovations. The fourth section is the conclusion. The fifth section deals with future research in context of that case study.

BACKGROUND

Ontology, the Theory of Reality

Ontology concerns questions about the being (Blaikie, 2000). Take, for example, the initiation and the implementation (Rogers, 2003) of new enterprise systems (hereinafter referred to as the process or a process as the case may be). The innovation process involves interactions primarily with people and secondarily with technology (Bloomfield, Coombs, Knights, & Littler, 2000). How is the phenomenon defined? How is the reality perceived? Who are the key stakeholders? What are the crucial components, that is, the change drivers, antecedents, stages, phases, decision points, consequences, of the process? How do these components interact with each other? What constitutes the process? How can it be differentiated from another process? Why and how do organisations undertake the process? What constitutes success or failure in the process? The answers to these questions depend on one's interpretation of the reality, affecting the way he defines a phenomenon.

According to Burrell and Morgan (2005), a reality consists of subjective and objective components. To understand a reality, individuals need to interpret it as either something cognitive in the mind or an external physical object. If the reality is internal to the individuals, then that subjective (or soft) reality exists inside their minds. The individuals ought to have awareness of that reality. If the reality is external to the individuals, then that objective (or hard) reality can impose itself into the awareness of individuals from without. It does not need a name nor does it require awareness of its existence. The distinction between the subjective reality and objective reality is akin to black and white. Some authorities including Heidegger (1962), Kant (1934), and Weber (2004) argue that *awareness is a prerequisite to all existence, regardless of whether the reality is subjective or objective.* Bryman (2001) adds that awareness is a key to interpreting a reality. Gilbert (2006) argues that awareness, perceptions, and feelings fill up the details of reality in the mind. Names, concepts, or labels generally describe that reality (Burrell & Morgan, 2005). The cognitive or existential element of a reality creates the fundamental confusion in ontology. Does a reality need to be present in the minds of individuals or does it simply need to exist even without awareness? What really constitutes a reality? How is it interpreted? How does the interpretation influence a reality?

The distinction between the subjective and objective components of a reality is rather unclear. According to Weber (2004), individuals reflect their subjective reality through their objective perception of that reality. Their subjective perceptions of the reality intertwine with their objective experience. Their objective observations likewise intertwine with their subjective experience. This makes separating the subjective and objective components of a reality difficult. Perceptions give meaning to the reality. At the same time, their experiences can affect the way the interactions and events are defined. Likewise, Kant (1934) argues that thoughts without content are void and intuitions without conceptions are blind. In fact, there is no proof that reality exists independent of the mind (Kant, 1934). Heidegger (1962) points out that the pseudo-problem keeps on popping up again and again because many authorities insist on describing a reality as subjective or objective. Adding to the confusion is the presence of a defensive mindset. According to Chris Argyris (2004), illogical and irrational behaviours and actions are logical and rational behaviours and actions in disguise.

Indeed, the essence of ontology is difficult to explain. Kant (1934) and Wyssusek and Schwartz (2003) refer to realism as the objective reality where that reality exists independently of that which has been perceived by the individuals. However, one should take note that realism concerns the perception of the objective reality which pertains to the external reality independent of the individual perception. This subtle difference implies that realism and objective reality are somewhat similar but not the same. Subjective reality, on the other hand, is best described by the common terms: idealism (Kant, 1934), nominalism (Wyssusek & Schwartz, 2003), and constructivism (Bryman, 2001).

Epistemology, the Theory of Processed Knowledge

Epistemology can be defined as processed knowledge. It comes from the Greek words *episteme* (knowledge) and *logos* (argumentation or reason). Knowledge without argumentation (or reasoning) is not processed knowledge. The observation of a phenomenon and the process of conducting an in-depth interview are forms of *episteme* but both cannot be considered as *epistemology*. They merely illustrate methods of the knowledge-gathering process (Grix, 2002) where the outcome of that process is assumed to contribute to the processed knowledge. Both knowledge-gathering processes can only be considered as epistemology if they include argumentation.

That knowledge-gathering process consists of three essential components: access, reflection, and argumentation. Kant (1934) argues that the individuals must have access to the reality. At the same time, they must have the faculties to (reflect on and) structure their experiences. [The access is a fundamental premise that relates ontology to epistemology]. What exists or is perceived to exist (ontology) can be known (Blaikie, 2000).

The concept of [absolute] truth cannot apply to [processed] knowledge (Wyssusek & Schwartz, 2003). Instead, the concept of consensus is more appropriate. The truth of a reality must be consensual to be a true knowledge (Wyssusek & Schwartz, 2003). There is no absolute true knowledge. Instead, there is consensual true knowledge. Plato imposes a further condition. A consensual truth cannot constitute processed knowledge unless it is a "justified true belief" (Myles, 1990). Unknown facts cannot be considered as processed knowledge because its belief element does not exist. Likewise, a belief that cannot be justified as true cannot constitute processed knowledge unless argumentation is present. Therefore, a statement is processed knowledge if the argumentation makes that statement true. The community believes that that statement is true and that the argumentation is valid. This is called true knowledge. Likewise, a statement becomes processed knowledge if a community falsifies it as being false. This is known as false knowledge. The verification and falsification of information are the sources of propositional knowledge. Both types of knowledge constitute processed knowledge. Another type of knowledge is the experiential knowledge of the participants in case study research (Geertz, 1983; Polanyi, 1962; Rumelhart & Ortony, 1977; von Wright, 1971). The narrative truth (that is, the narrations and situational descriptions) in the case study report convey the evidences and experiences of the observers and participants. It enhances the reader's experience when they study the case (Stake, 2005, p. 454). Effectively, there is a transfer of knowledge from the participants to the observers and from the observers to the readers.

Empiricists and rationalists give conflicting answers. To the empiricists, empirical evidences including experiences are the sources of knowledge (Wyssusek & Schwartz, 2003). The evidences are the objective components while the experiences are the subjective components of a reality. Both components are sources of knowledge. To rationalists, reasoning is also considered a source of knowledge. Plato compares epistemology or the knowledge-gathering process to a journey through a dark cave, walking through the long tunnel and coming out into the open to view objects under the bright light of day (Melling, 1987; Santas, 2006). The individuals inside the cave can only see the illusions on the wall. They are ignorant of the reality outside the cave. If they successfully walk out into the open and be exposed to the sun for the first time, they will realise the reality outside the cave. They will be enlightened. They will discover a *higher realm* of reality through a long challenging intellectual journey. The reality outside the cave as well as the illusions that they have experienced while inside the cave are both their sources of knowledge. Multiple sources of knowledge could make the processed knowledge better. For instance, in a case study, Stake (2005) suggests drawing all the information from multiple sources at the same time to learn about the case and to answer the epistemological questions of the case.

Inconsistencies of Theory and Practice

Taleb (2007) warns of the confusion on the evidences of knowledge. This confusion can work both ways (Figure 6). A theoretical problem can be understood in theory but not in practice. Similarly, a practical problem can be understood in practice but not when it is elevated to theory. Bhaskar (2002), Smaling (1987), and Smith (2006) have the same opinion on the disparity between theory and practice. This conflict comes from the debate between the objective view vs. the subjective view of reality or, rather, from the constraints and limitations of human knowledge (Smith, 2006) and positivism vs. interpretive (Weber, 2004). Smith (2006) emphasises a critical examination of ontological assumptions because a point of inconsistencies is located between the ontological assumptions and the methodology which affects the result of the research. Resolving that point of inconsistencies, Taleb (2007, p. 51) advises putting the evidence (ontology) into context. "We react to a piece of information not on its logical merit, but on the basis of which framework [e.g., the Diffusion of Innovations theory] surrounds it, and how it registers with our social-emotional system."

Take this case in context. Vendor ABC submits a response to a Request for Information (RFI). Because the third-party change agent in charge of the short-listing of the vendors for the Request for Proposal (RFP) is aware that many of its new staffs come from the now defunct XYZ entity, the corporate culture of that second entity is an issue. The response of ABC to the RFI contains many objective evidences about the vendor's profile and the attributes of the enterprise systems. Yet the executive sponsor has reacted to a piece of industry knowledge (a subjective reality), originally an absence of evidence despite of the presence of substantial evidence indicated in the response. The concepts of absence of evidence and the evidence of absence as well as the presence of evidence and evidence of presence are similar but not identical. Embedded in those concepts are possible inconsistencies of theory and practice.

Rather than gathering further positive evidence associated with ABC entity and its enterprise systems, that one single "falsified" evidence (i.e., the subjective evidence) could invalidate other positive verifiable evidences presented by the ABC entity in its response to the RFI. One perceived weakness by the executive sponsor could invalidate multiple perceived strengths. One "black swan" is unexpectedly one rare observation amidst the verification of a million white swans. Finding one opposite instance gets closer to the truth and certainty. That one instance makes the data become more meaningful than the many opposing instances. Popper argues that people who believe in falsification hold that "falsified" evidence is wrong with full certainty (Popper, 1965; Ruddin, 2006).

UNDERSTANDING ONTOLOGY

Objective and Subjective Components of a Complex Phenomenon

A complex phenomenon is a complicated web of interrelationships. Take for instance the initiation phase of replacing enterprise systems. That complex phenomenon contains a request for information (RFI) substage. The entity (that is, the host organisation) requests for information from the prospective vendors of enterprise systems, receives their responses, appraises them, and develops a short list of qualified vendors for request for proposal (RFP), a subsequent substage. The RFI document, the responses received by the entity from the prospective vendors, the e-mails or phone conversations for clarifications, the RFP document, and the formal proposals are examples of objective (physical or hard) evidences. Imagine a mind map with the innovation process at the middle with the initiation phase and its objective evidences linked to it. The result is a complex web of interrelationships. By extending the mind map to include the implementation phase and its objective evidences, the web of interrelationships becomes even more complex. The executive sponsor and his project team members will examine the responses to the RFI to determine the strengths and weaknesses of each response. Each response contains allegedly real evidences, such as: the functionality of the enterprise systems,

the reporting tools available, the entities using the enterprise systems, the number of sites in the country, the number of staffs, the number of technical support, the operating systems and database, software cost, cost of concurrent and additional users, maintenance cost, implementation cost, and expansion cost. Is the attribute a weakness or strength? How significant or insignificant is the attribute? How do the individuals involved with the examination of the responses perceive the attributes?

Perception is another layer fused to that complex web of interrelationships. Awareness, perceptions, and feelings are subjective components of that second layer. According to Webster's dictionary, awareness is the conscious knowledge of something. When a single unified awareness is derived from sensory processes and triggered by a stimulus then it becomes perception. Feeling, on the other hand, is the function or the power of perceiving by touch. By adding this layer, the resulting web of interrelationships becomes much more complex. When the executive sponsor and his project team members appraise the prospective vendors and their enterprise systems, the strengths and weaknesses of each response to the RFI and RFP will be considered. This does not mean that the actual strengths and weaknesses that they will perceive can be considered significant attributes. Because actual strengths or weaknesses exist even when there is no awareness of their existence or perception of their relevance and significance, they are irrelevant unless the individuals are aware of them and perceive them to be important. Of course, the strengths and weaknesses of the chosen enterprise systems and the vendor supporting them will have an implication on the host organisation after the adoption and implementation. However, that is another matter.

Figure 1 can be used to examine the response to the RFI and evaluate its attributes. Imagine a matrix of two variables with four boxes. In the left box of the horizontal axis, perception = "no." In the right box, perception = "yes." In the lower

Figure 1. Objective and subjective components of examining the responses to RFI

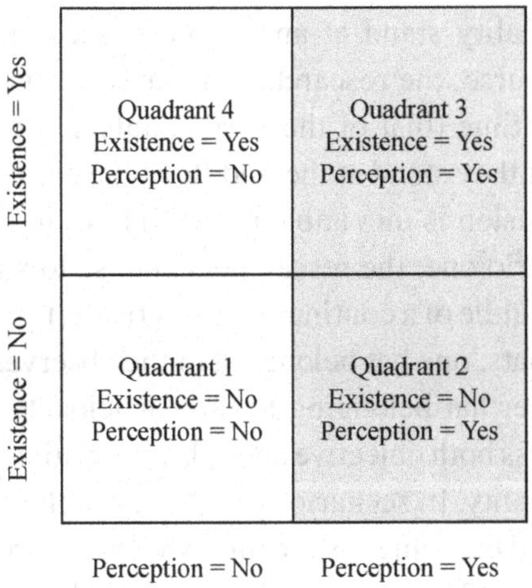

box of the vertical axis, existence = "no." In the upper box, existence = "yes." Two boxes, the Quadrant 2 and Quadrant 3 in Figure 1, have the perception = "yes." In Quadrant 3, the attribute is real because it exists. However, the attribute in Quadrant 2 is equally relevant even if it does not exist.

Subjective Components as Prerequisites of Objective Components of Reality

Awareness is needed to understand the inherent strengths and weaknesses of the enterprise systems. It illustrates a crucial antecedent to the understanding of the objective component of that reality. Because awareness is a subjective component, the subjective components can therefore be considered antecedents of the objective components of that reality:

subjective components ⇨ objective components

Awareness, perceptions, and feelings are subjective components of a reality. Without awareness, perceptions are not possible. Without perceptions,

feelings cannot function. Each is a necessary condition for the other to exist. The feelings are derived from personal feelings influenced by cultures, experiences, opinions, beliefs, preferences and biases (e.g., pro innovation or anti innovation biases). No wonder, feelings and not facts fill up the details in the brain (Gilbert, 2006).

(awareness ⇨ perceptions ⇨ feelings) = subjective components

Reality is complex because it embodies two interrelated concepts. The first concept concerns the hierarchical order of awareness, perceptions, feelings as well as the subjective and objective reality. The second concept is the complex web of interrelationship among the subjective and objective components. There are three sets of interrelatedness: (a) among the subjective components, (b) among the objective components, and (c) among the subjective and objective components. Simply, the ontological components and the concept of ontological hierarchy looks like the following:

(awareness ⇨ perceptions ⇨ feelings) ⇨ objective components

subjective reality ⇨ objective reality

Notwithstanding the web of interrelatedness among the subjective and objective components, the complex reality can be known (Blaikie, 2000) only if there is access, awareness, and reflection of the reality. Once individuals have awareness of and access to the reality, then it is possible to know the reality, its subjective components, its objective components, and their relationships. The individuals who own the perceptions and feelings must be able to interpret, reflect, and express in order to know the reality. Thus, reality can be known only if certain conditions are present, namely: awareness, access, and reflection.

(access ⇔ awareness) ⇨ reflection

Continuum and Interactions

Given that a reality cannot exist without the intertwining subjective and objective components, it is possible to reflect ontologically using the concept of continuum with a hundred percent subjectivity at one end and a hundred percent objectivity at the other end. The subjective and objective realities at these two ends are distinct and clear-cut like oranges and apples. The objective realities can be defined by the keyword, existence. The subjective realities, on the other hand, can be defined by using the keyword awareness, which is the way humans interpret and construct their reality in the mind. The orange and apple are, however, not the only reality. There is the orange-apple juice containing more or less of orange and less or more of apple. Unless the participants and observers stand at the extreme ends of the continuum, their perception and interpretation of reality will vary depending on their position in the continuum.

Another important concept is that of interactions. It differentiates active participants from objective observers. The concept of a continuum is in itself not easy to understand. The concept of interactions is more difficult to understand if the two concepts are fused together. In Figure 2, the terms participants and observers seem to associate the former with the subjective reality and the latter with the objective reality. At the extreme ends of the continuum, the participants are presumed to be always subjective. They cannot be objective. At the other end, the observers are naturally objective, not biased and subjective. The "real world" is not like that. With the concept of continuum, the individuals concerned with the reality stand at any point in a continuum. Of course, the researchers wear two hats at the same time (that of the participants and observers) if they stand at the middle of the continuum. Confusion is inevitable in the four scenarios. In scenario one, the researchers choose to stand at the middle of a continuum. Effectively, they wear two hats, one hat belonging to the observers and another hat belonging to the participants. They possess both objective and subjective mindsets of the reality. In scenario two, the researchers walk toward the subjective reality where they are more concerned about the subjective mindset despite of their role as observers. In the third scenario, we can see the researchers as active participants that can be found in the middle of the continuum. They try to be objective despite their participation. In scenario four, the researchers are active participants who stand toward the end of the objective reality. Given the four scenarios, how do you describe the researchers? Are they observers, participants, neither of the two, or both of the two? The confusion occurs because of the labels associated to them. This is precisely the problem with terminologies.

The initial scenario and the subsequent four scenarios bring forward the complex essence of reality. Many people differentiate reality by putting a clear division between objective or subjective reality. To them, dividing the two is simple and

Figure 2. The initial and the subsequent four scenarios of understanding a reality

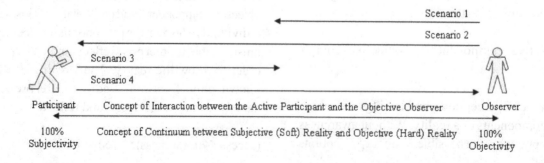

elementary. All research requires interpretation and therefore all research is interpretative (Denzin & Lincoln, 2005b, p. 22). Moreover, reality cannot exist independent of the mind (Kant, 1934; Weber, 2004). The essence of ontology lies in an interpretation of reality that requires awareness even if the study focuses on objective reality. In short, the essence of ontology demands interpretation of the reality and that reality encompasses both the subjective and objective components.

Dominant Logic of Ontology

The dominant logic of ontology is interactions. In the context of the case presented, the executive sponsor interacts with the third party change agent, his project team members, the prospective vendors, and other stakeholders. He utilises government electronic tendering service (GETS) to announce the request for information (RFI). A required functionality of the enterprise systems is its capability of interacting with the banking systems and credit card technology using the Internet technology. Those interactions include interactions between people and people, people and technology, and technology and technology. Understanding that the phenomenon requires an understanding of the innovation process, the interactions involved in that process, the social and psychological mindsets, the host organisation and its extended value chain, and the soft or hard technology. The interactions capture the underlying "why" questions and reaffirms the importance of meanings, interpretations, and context without denying the existence of the causal influences (Smith, 2006, p. 207).

Irrational Subjective Reality Disguised as Rational Objective Reality

Authorities, like Weber (2004) and Kant (1934), favour the dualism of reality. The objective side of ontology indicates the presence of human,

organisational, and/or technological issues in the process even if the researchers, including the stakeholders, are not aware of their existence. The subjective side of ontology indicates the implications of interactions of people and people, of people and technology, and of technology and technology. Unavoidably, the initiation and implementation of new information systems are tainted with grey, neither black nor white. Grey, the dualism of black and white, results in irrational subjective behaviours being perceived as rational objective behaviours.

UNDERSTANDING EPISTEMOLOGY

Complex Relationships of Ontology, Epistemology, and Methodology

The term epistemology embodies a premise and a relationship. Because *what exists or is perceived to exist (ontology) can be known* (Blaikie, 2000), therefore epistemology enables the understanding of a reality, making it a prerequisite to understanding a reality (that is, ontology ⇦ epistemology). However, understanding a reality provides *a priori* knowledge to contribute to the knowledge of the reality (that is, ontology ⇨ epistemology). Thus, ontology affects epistemology and vice versa. Two-dimensional relationships exist between ontology and epistemology (that is, ontology ⇔ epistemology).

A good example of the epistemology (knowledge) of a reality (ontology) is the innovation process of replacing enterprise systems which demands designing an appropriate knowledge-gathering process. Without a methodology, epistemology is not possible (that is, epistemology ⇦ methodology). The methodology encompasses gathering, validating, analysing the data, and crafting the argumentation. Presumably, the research contributes to epistemology. Thus, methodology follows epistemology in a study (that is, epistemology ⇨ methodology). Similar to the relationships between ontology and epistemology, epistemology and methodology also have a two-dimensional relationship (that is, epistemology ⇔ methodology).

The relationship between methodology and ontology are likewise two-dimensional: methodology ⇔ ontology. Without the knowledge-gathering process, it is not possible to understand a reality (that is, methodology ⇨ ontology). But, the pluralism aspect of the reality dictates triangulation of methods and other disciplines in designing the research (that is, methodology ⇦ ontology).

The hierarchy concept of ontology to epistemology to methodology (that is, ontology ⇨epistemology ⇨ methodology) is common in the research literature. It makes it easy to understand their relationships. However, the concept of two-dimensional relationships helps to clarify the complexity in their relationships (that is, ontology ⇔ epistemology ⇔ methodology ⇔ ontology). It embeds the concept of antecedent and consequence. For example, when developing a research strategy (a methodology), we must take into account the complex relationships. The three theories of being, knowledge, and research are inseparable.

Access and Reflection (Perception) Revisited

Individuals reflect their reality through the perception of that reality (Weber, 2004). Perception implicates the awareness and existence of that reality. Objective reality exists even if stakeholders do not have the awareness of its existence. That reality could be relevant in reality. However, it is not relevant from their viewpoints. Take the context of the case, the executive sponsor and his project team members examine the responses to the RFI for the strengths and weaknesses of the vendor and the enterprise systems. These strengths and weaknesses exist even if the response to the RFI does not mention them. These attributes are relevant when the prospective vendors mention

them in their responses to the RFI and the executive sponsor and his project team members perceive them as strengths or weaknesses. Without access to the response documents, it is not possible to determine the physical evidences. Without reflection, it is not possible to classify them as strengths or weaknesses or as significant or insignificant. Existence is a prerequisite of access. Access is a prerequisite of reflection. Thus, existence ⇨ access ⇨ reflection. Reflection is a part of the realism that Wyssusek and Schwartz (2003) gave a subtle distinction from the objective reality. Kant (1934) adds in the faculties to do the reflection. Access to the reality and faculties to do reflection are antecedents of a research process. The faculties implicate the role of *a priori* knowledge and emphasise reflection in the knowledge-generating process. The access to the objective reality makes knowledge hard while the reflection of the reality makes it soft.

What Constitutes Knowledge?

What makes up knowledge? That is a fundamental question in epistemology. An observation of a phenomenon, such as the examination of the responses to Request for Information (RFI), could lead to knowledge. Yet it lacks the quality of epistemology. Because epistemology = episteme + logos, the missing link is the reasoning.

Imagine a diagram. A box, called "claim," contains a statement that says "not all perceived weaknesses from the responses to the RFI are insignificant." To support that claim, an "evidence" box on the left side of the "claim" box states that "the project staffs of a prospective vendor ABC compose of individuals from the now defunct XYZ entity." Between those two boxes is an arrow drawn from the "evidence" box on the left to the "claim" box on the right. That arrow infers that the evidence is a reason for the claim (Figure 4). The significant weakness perceived by the executive sponsor and his team members is a reason for that claim.

Bearing in mind the concepts of absolute true knowledge, consensual true knowledge, and justified true belief discussed in the background section (Myles, 1990; Wyssusek & Schwartz, 2003), a claim is deemed a consensual true knowledge to a community only if the community gives a consensus that the statement is true. For example, the villagers in Los Molinas stubbornly drank water from a canal floated with dead monkeys instead of a nearby tap with the clean drinking water. To combat the infections caused by the contaminated water, the Peruvian government and health authorities instructed the villagers to boil the water. Even after 2 years of communicating the new idea to the villagers (e.g., getting the clean water from the tap, boiling the water, and drinking the boiled water), a majority continued to drink from the filthy river. The diffusion process ignored the culture of Peruvian villagers (Rogers, 2003, pp. 1-5). The Peruvian villagers believed a consensual true knowledge that healthy people do not drink boiled water and that only sick people do. Absolute truth cannot exist to those villagers who did not believe in drinking clean water from the faucet. What constitutes knowledge depends on where the individuals are (inside or outside the cave) and how they understand their reality. The enlightened individuals may regard both empirical evidences and reasoning as their sources of knowledge. The unenlightened individuals may regard the consensual beliefs as their sources of knowledge. Wherever the individuals stand (inside or outside the cave) and whatever is the true knowledge (consensual or absolute true knowledge), three critical issues (deemed knowledge, diversity of knowledge, and argumentation) remain.

Deemed Knowledge

Deemed knowledge is a key point in Plato's parable of a cave. It depends on where the individuals are at the stage of their journey and what their perceptions are. Individuals who have walked out the cave differ from individuals who are at the different stages of their journey inside the cave. The enlightened individuals, belonging to the former group, have added a stack of knowledge, the higher realm of knowledge, on top of the lower realm of knowledge. They look at knowledge with a pluralistic mindset. The essence of the deemed knowledge is the realisation of the complex combination of the subjective and objective reality as well as the diversity of that knowledge which is bounded by certain hard and soft norms.

Diversity of Knowledge

Diversity of knowledge is another key point of the cave parable. As mentioned in the background section, individuals have different levels of awareness, perceptions, and feelings of their reality. They are bound by their prior higher and/or lower realm of knowledge. In fact, some individuals have more diversified knowledge than others do. Their multiple sources of knowledge give them more information which is an advantage of a case study research. Many sources may be drawn all at once to learn about a phenomenon (Stake, 2005). Such optimises the understanding of that phenomenon and "gains credibility by triangulating the descriptions and interpretations, not just in a single step but continuously throughout the period of study" (Stake, 2005, p. 443).

Argumentation, Verification, and Falsification

Eight statements originate from Figure 3. Which statement constitutes deemed knowledge, consensual true knowledge, or absolute true knowledge? The number of staffs in ABC entity, including those from XYZ entity, is an objective reality. However, a piece of industry knowledge about the new staffs from XYZ entity is perceived as a significant weakness. It is a subjective reality. If the executive sponsor accepts it to be true, then that knowledge is a deemed knowledge. It is also a consensual true knowledge. It could be an objective reality if the executive sponsor verifies it to be true. Then that piece of knowledge becomes an absolute true knowledge insofar as the number of staffs from XYZ entity is concerned. Regardless of whether that knowledge pertains to objective reality or subjective reality, a deemed knowledge is a complex realisation of what the individuals perceived as true knowledge. Between the number of staffs in ABC entity (a perceived strength) and the number of staffs in ABC entity coming from XYZ entity (a perceived weakness), both perceptions are deemed knowledge.

Statement 1. There is a *presence of evidence* of perceived significant weakness from the responses to the RFI.

Statement 2. There is an *evidence of presence* of perceived significant weakness from the responses to the RFI.

Statement 3. There is an *absence of evidence* of perceived significant weakness from the responses to the RFI.

Statement 4. There is an *evidence of absence* of perceived significant weakness from the responses to the RFI.

Figure 3. A logical mistake of assertion is inevitable

	Weakness = No	Weakness = Yes
Significance = Yes	Quadrant 4 Significance = Yes Weakness = No (Strength = Yes)	Quadrant 3 Significance = Yes Weakness = Yes (Strength = No)
Significance = No	Quadrant 1 Significance = No Weakness = No (Strength = Yes)	Quadrant 2 Significance = No Weakness = Yes (Strength = No)

Statement 5. All perceived weaknesses from the responses to the RFI are significant.

Statement 6. All perceived weaknesses from the responses to the RFI are insignificant.

Statement 7. Not all perceived weaknesses from the responses to the RFI are significant.

Statement 8. Not all perceived weaknesses from the responses to the RFI are insignificant.

Statement 1 is similar but not identical to the evidence presented in Statement 2. Statement 1 asks for the presence of evidence of at least one perceived significant weakness. The perceived significant weakness should cause the exclusion of the enterprise systems or their vendor in the short-list for RFP. The verification should look for the awareness or unawareness of that significant weakness. In the first instance, awareness of a significant weakness whether it exists or not should supposedly lead to the exclusion of it in the short-list. In the second instance, the unawareness of a real weakness expectedly causes a possible exclusion. The evidence present in Statement 2 is more complicated. If all the other three quadrants are false (that is, "not Quadrant 1" and "not Quadrant 2" and "not Quadrant 4"), then Quadrant 3 is right. In effect, Statement 2 looks at Quadrant 3 indirectly.

With Statement 3, the absence of evidence refers to "not Quadrant 3." It demands proving Quadrant 3 to be false. In so doing, Quadrant 1, Quadrant 2, or Quadrant 4 becomes true. Thus, "not Quadrant 3" somehow refers indirectly to quadrants 1, 2, and/or 4. Statement 4 indicates the evidence of absence of perceived significant weakness. It refers directly and collectively at Quadrant 1, Quadrant 2, and Quadrant 4.

The confusions of those four statements are due to how individuals react and infer them into their socio-emotional context of the theory and the practice. Taleb (2007) attributes those confusions to the "domain specificity of reactions and inferences." It means understanding a reality (*ontology* or the theory) involves knowledge and reasoning (*epistemology*) which necessarily involves the context (*techne* or the practice).

Which statement constitutes the absolute true knowledge? Assuming that Statement 1 or Statement 2 is true, are all the perceived weaknesses significant (Statement 5)? Likewise, if Statement 3 or Statement 4 is true, are all the perceived weaknesses insignificant (Statement 6)? Statement 5 and Statement 6 cannot be the absolute true knowledge. If there is at least one insignificant perceived weakness, then it is with certainty that not all weaknesses are significant and Statement 7 becomes the absolute true knowledge. If there is one significant perceived weakness found, then not all perceived weaknesses are insignificant. Statement 8 becomes the absolute true knowledge. Effectively, an insignificant perceived weakness results to the assertion that not all perceived weaknesses are significant. Likewise, a significant weakness results to the assertion that not all perceived weaknesses are insignificant. Effectively, one single falsified observation invalidates the many verified observations.

PHILOSOPHICAL ASSUMPTIONS

Between that evidence and that claim in Figure 4 are some hidden philosophical assumptions (Table 1). Replacing enterprise systems is a problem-solving intervention with expected consequences in mind (Assumption 1). It embodies physical evidences (e.g., the responses to RFI), shared meanings (e.g., the staff coming from XYZ entity), and defensive reasoning (e.g., the undesirable company culture of XYZ entity). Those evidences are not necessarily the source of absolute truth (Assumption 2). However, they can cause large unexpected consequence (Assumption 3). The perception of that weakness may be irrational. Yet the defensive reasoning and decision to exclude the vendor from the short-list disguise the irrational behaviour (Assumption 6).

Imagine a point of intersection of two lines called theory and practice (Sjoberg, Williams, Vaughn, & Sjoberg, 1991, p. 29). That point embeds the complex phenomenon (ontology) of choice to be studied (Stake, 2005, p. 438), a knowledge base (theory), the research questions to be answered (epistemology), and the research strategy (methodology). The last component in that point identifies the data to be gathered and

Figure 4. Hidden assumptions in argumentation

Hidden assumptions
• Replacing enterprise systems is a problem-solving intervention with expected consequences (Assumption 1)
• That technological innovation embodies physical evidences (eg, the responses to RFI), shared meanings, and defensive reasoning. Those evidences are not necessarily the source of absolute truth (Assumption 2).
• A small weakness may cause large unexpected consequence (Assumption 3).
• The perception of weakness may be irrational. Yet the defensive reasoning and decision to exclude the vendor from the short-list disguises the irrational behaviour (Assumption 6).

⇩

Evidence		Claim
The project staffs of ABC entity is composed of individuals from the now defunct XYZ entity.	⇨	Not all perceived weaknesses from the responses to the RFI are insignificant.

how they will be gathered, analysed, argued, and presented so that the audience (the "community") will acknowledge consensually that the study or the outcome of that study constitutes knowledge. This point embodies a premise that the right methodology will lead to gathering the right data to answer the research questions, ensure quality in research, and eventually contribute to the knowledge. Without the right methodology, the contribution to the knowledge is not possible.

Table 1. Ontological assumptions (1 to 8) and epistemological assumptions (9 to 12)

Assumption 1

Replacing enterprise systems is a problem-solving intervention (Thull, 2005) with expected consequences. That complex phenomenon is a choice of research interest (Stake, 2005). The intervention moves from one stage to another and from one state to another.

Assumption 2

Replacing enterprise systems embodies physical evidences and documentations, complex interactions (Note 1), shared meanings, and defensive reasoning (Argyris, 2004; Bryman, 2001, pp 16-18; Burrell & Morgan, 2005, pp 1-20; Gilbert, 2006; Heidegger, 1962, p 249; Kant, 1934; Weber, 2004). The physical evidences and documentations are hard realities. Bounded by experience, culture, and social norms, the shared meanings and defensive mindsets are soft realities existing inside the minds.

Assumption 3

Built into the systems, unexpected consequences are always in perpetual motion and change (Ormerod, 2005; Rogres, 2003). A large unexpected consequence may have very small causes (Ormerod, 2005).

Assumption 4

The purpose of technological innovations is seamless alignment (Note 2). That expected consequence concerns (a) value proposition and performance, (b) information availability, (c) value chain or network linkages, and (d) transactional efficiencies. The innovation comes with a VALUE orientation (strategic vision). The gatekeepers expect to configure the enterprise systems, align business processes, and extend the value chain toward a strategic vision (Canals, 2000, p 158).

Assumption 5

Understanding how to solve problems, make decisions, and act under conditions of incomplete information are the highest and most urgent human pursuit (Taleb, 2007, p 57).

Assumption 6

Because of the possible presence of defensive reasoning and behaviours, a rational behaviour may be an irrational behaviour in disguised (Argyris, 2004; Luhmann, 2006).

Assumption 7

Designing a research (methodology) takes into account the threats of inconsistencies between theory and practice. It is difficult to understand a theory in practice or to understand a practical problem in theory (Baskar, 2002; Smaling, 1987; Smith, 2006; Taleb, 2007). It is not possible to align perfectly theory and practice.

Assumption 8

Because evidences available for studying a phenomenon are generally incomplete and not necessarily the source of truth, the knowledge derived from the study should relate to the context where the phenomenon happens. At least, this minimises the risk of inconsistencies to theory and practice.

Assumption 9

The complex interactions (eg, business processes), the shared meanings including the experience, culture, and social norms of the stakeholders, and their defensive mindset are sources of hard and soft knowledge.

Assumption 10

Many sources may be drawn all at once to learn about the phenomenon (Stake, 2005).

Assumption 11

What constitutes knowledge depends on the thorough understanding of the researchers and the participants involved with the phenomenon and the nature of the empirical evidence and reasoning required.

Assumption 12

A single piece of information can be more meaningful than a lot of data. The merit of such information does not rely on the logical merit. Rather it relies on how it forms part of a chain of evidence, how it functions in the context, and how it is reflected in the social-emotional systems.

Note 1. The interaction is what Pennings and Buitendam (1987, p xiv) have referred to as meshing new enterprise systems with organisation design, business process, strategy, and external relationships. It involves (a) people to people, (b) people to organisation, (c) people to technology, (d) organisation to other organisations, (e) organisation to technology, and (f) technology to technology.

Note 2. To satisfy the needs of its customers (Principle 1), the entity must put together all processes (Principle 2). Superior process performance is a requirement (Principle 3) and its pre-requisite is to undertake process design or redesign in order to foster an environment that inspires people to work productively (Principle 4). These are four principles (Hammer, 1996, pp 97-105) to seamless alignment

---

Borrowing from the critical theory of Habermas (1970, 1974), that same point of intersection embodies three cognitive interests that individuals direct their attempts to acquire knowledge, namely: technical interest, practical interest, and emancipatory interest. Technical and practical interests derive from, and at the same time are dependent on, work, and interaction. Work depends upon "mastery over the environment of action" while interaction requires "intersubjective understanding among those [stakeholders] involved" (Jackson, 1992, p. 12). Embedded into those two interests, work, and interaction is a third interest, the emancipatory interest stems from the exploitation of opportunities (eg, innovation) and systemic distorted communication.

That systemic distorted communication is an outcome whenever individuals filter information (Habermas, 1970, 1974; Luhmann, 2006). That statement is a philosophical assumption in a diffusion research. According to Luhmann (2006), social systems are systems of communication. Society is the most encompassing social system. It comprises all and only communication. The boundary between the system and its surrounding complex environment defines a system. It affords the system to filter the information into the system through communication from the outside. Distorted communication is a result of such filtering into the system from the outside. Argyris (2004) tackles a similar challenge: defensive reasoning prevents individuals from understanding their own incompetence.

Diffusion is a form of communication. It involves communicating a new idea or innovation to the targeted audience. Replacing existing enterprise systems is an example of a new idea. The idea itself does not have to be new. However, the audience in which the diffusion is directed to has to perceive it as new. Diffusing a replacement of enterprise systems passes through an initiation phase and implementation phase. Those two phases are parts of the innovation process. That innovation process involves the social system, communications, and interactions. In the initiation phase, the executive sponsor has a perception of a gap and explores options of competing enterprise systems. Matchmaking the options with the expectations in mind depends on a risk mindset. Generally, a risk-averse organisation has a procurement policy that requires formal request for information (RFI), request for proposal (RFP), and a business case. The premise is that the rigour embedded into these requirements minimises the risks of unexpected undesirable consequences and fosters achievement of expected desirable consequences.

In the inferential arrow between the evidence box and the claim box in Figure 4 are hidden statements. Table 1 explicitly states twelve hidden philosophical assumptions. Those statements are claims acceptable to "the community." Evidences to support them are not necessary. Those assumptions facilitate in designing the research methodology, interpreting and evaluating the data collected, and minimising threats of theory-practice inconsistencies. They put quality into the research.

Ontological assumptions have implications to epistemology and methodology. The information needed to study the phenomenon come from many sources. There are therefore many ways to study and understand a complex phenomenon. For researchers who delimit their scope to make the study manageable and decide to temporarily focus on the delimited phenomenon by using available methods (Stake, 2005), an appropriate approach is a case study. Figure 5 shows the implications of the philosophical assumptions on methodology because of the contribution of knowledge. The ontological assumptions help articulate the epistemological assumptions and draw attention to the research questions of what can be learned about the case. Those questions represent the drive to design the methodology in order to optimise understanding of the case rather than to generalise beyond it (Stake, 2005, p. 443).

Figure 5. Implications of assumptions on methodology and contribution to knowledge

Ontological assumptions
Replacing enterprise systems is a problem-solving intervention to foster seamless alignment.

⇩

Epistemological assumptions
Business processes, complex interactions, shared meanings, and defensive mindset may be drawn all at once to learn hard and soft knowledge.

⇩

Research design (methodology)
The many sources of rich contextual and empirical evidences such a s archival documents, in-depth interviews, and observations could and would be drawn all at once to learn about the phenomenon. One evidence of exception can be more meaningful than a lot of data.

⇩

Epistemology (argumentation)
The contribution to knowledge depends on hard and soft experiential knowledge, understanding of the rich contextual phenomenon, and the argumentation based on the chain of evidences.

RESOLVING THREATS OF INCONSISTENCIES

Quality in articulating the ontological and epistemological assumptions influences the quality when designing a methodology of research. In turn, the quality of the methodology affects the quality of the research outcomes. Figure 6 reiterates the complex two-dimensional relationships of ontology, epistemology, and methodology.

There are at least three possible sources of inconsistencies (Figure 6): one being methodology which affects the understanding of the reality and the contribution to knowledge. Note how the methodology affects the outcomes, which in turn affect the ontology and epistemology. Likewise, the way the philosophical assumptions are interpreted affects how the methodology is designed. There is a backward link from the outcome to the methodology. The outcome of the research goes back to methodology in the case of action research. Another threat of inconsistencies originates from the confusion between theory and practice.

CONCLUSION

To conclude, a complex phenomenon consists of subjective and objective components. The subjective components are awareness, perceptions, and feelings of and about the reality. They exist in the mind of individuals who have at least a vague idea of what it is if a name is not available. Objective components do not need awareness in order to exist. However, without the awareness, perceptions, and feelings, how can a reality be relevant? What is the colour of reality?

The hierarchy of ontology, epistemology, and methodology makes it simple to understand the research process, to articulate the philosophical assumptions, and to defend the unique paradigm that drives the study. However, that process is not hierarchical and one-directional. It is complex. Their relationships are two-directional. Thus, ontology is both an antecedent and consequence of epistemology and methodology. In addition, epistemology is both an antecedent and consequence of methodology and ontology. Likewise, methodology is both an antecedent and consequence of ontology. Understanding the ontology of a phenomenon implicitly takes into account epistemology and methodology. Articulating the epistemology implicitly involved the consideration of the methodology and ontology. Designing the methodology has the ontology and epistemology in mind. Articulating a unique set of philosophical assumptions naturally integrates the three into one.

The notion of the researchers (objective observers) and the others (subjective participants)

Figure 6. The threats of inconsistencies are bountiful in research

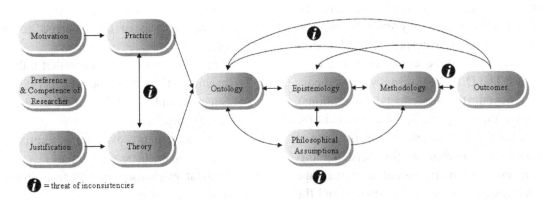

is always controversial. Many assume that the researchers must, can, and should be objective observers while the others are active participants. In reality, this clear-cut scenario is an illusion. Qualitative research accepts the scenario where the researchers can travel from the objective end of a continuum toward the subjective end. The premise is that the subjective components of the reality (the awareness, perceptions, and feelings) are prerequisite of understanding the objective components of that reality.

Interactions constitute the dominant logic of ontology (the complex phenomenon). In replacing enterprise systems, those interactions are the diffusion of a technological innovation. The interactions are complex because of the involvement of people, organisation, and technology (e.g., people to people, people to organisation, people to technology, organisation to other organisations, organisation to technology, and technology to technology). Pennings and Buitendam (1987, p. xiv) refer to those interactions as the meshing of the enterprise systems with organisation design, business process, strategy, and external relationships. The complex interactions together with the shared meanings and defensive reasoning implicate on business processes, mindsets of the stakeholders, and extended value chain of the host organisation adopting the enterprise systems.

A fundamental question in epistemology is what constitutes knowledge? Some individuals

would consider the answers to the questions about the reality constitute knowledge. Other individuals would consider the answers and the reasoning that comes with them to constitute consensual knowledge that is justifiable and believable. That deemed knowledge is a key point of Plato's parable of the cave. What constitutes knowledge depends on where the individuals are inside or outside the cave and how they interpret their reality. There are many sources of knowledge bounded by higher or lower realm of knowledge, experiences, cultures, and other norms.

There is a weakness of a deemed knowledge. It depends on mindset. It is not necessarily the absolute truth. In argumentation, a claim relies on the evidence to support that claim. Four possibilities are the presence of evidence, the evidence of presence, the absence of evidence, and the evidence of absence. The examination of the evidence leads to eight possible statements (Table 1). Of those statements, only the eighth statement, if proven true, will result to assertion. Effectively, that last statement is a falsification. One single falsification invalidates much verification.

FUTURE RESEARCH DIRECTIONS

This chapter represents an explicit reflection to designing single-case diffusion research about replacing enterprise systems by a large public sector entity. The focus of the study is about the business case stage. Extensive literature review indicates that there is no study about the business case stage of replacing enterprise systems. There are, however, some studies concerning other business cases. The Diffusion of Innovations theory takes into account the antecedents (or conditions), the process including the decision points in the process, and the consequences. One direction of future research is to examine the decision points in the process, particularly the matchmaking stage and business case stage, and to understand the impact of each decision point. Another direction is to understand the performance metrics, control systems, and implications of innovations to the business case stage including the matchmaking stage prior to that business case stage (Figure 7). The cocreation of total value requires management to understand the full implications of the innovation to all strategic and ethically critical stakeholders. The diffusion of an innovation to the stakeholders fosters creation of value and relationships.

The study of the business case stage (Stage III in Figure 7) and making the accept-reject decision preferably includes:

- Examination of the conceptual basis of the study
- Sound analysis of the business environment
- Analysis of strategic factors that influence in general the innovation process (Stage I to Stage V) and specifically the business case stage (Stage III)
- Critical evaluation of the innovation process and/or the business case stage
- Critical evaluation of the techniques to design the study
- Critical evaluation of the output of the innovation process and/or the business case stage to organizational goals, strategies, and management practices
- Reflexive reflection on the experience of designing a case study and of studying the case
- Reflection on meeting the challenge of the industry, entity, and/or the chosen field

Future research may:

- Articulate more than a set of philosophical assumptions and engage the paradigms in a dialogue (Denzin & Lincoln, 2005c, p. 189);

Figure 7. The innovation process of replacing enterprise systems

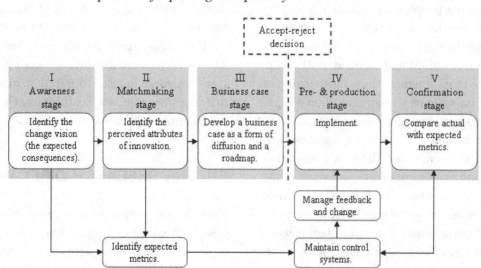

- Challenge the old to new contested methodology (Denzin & Lincoln, 2005a) and everything that is pregiven (Bauman, 2005);
- Test and validate those arrows in Figure 6 which have been argued but not tested;
- Explore issues such as the interactive nature of the inquiry, ethics and values (praxis), [power and] empowerment, foundations of truth, validity, and voice (single or multivoiced), reflexivity, and representation (Denzin & Lincoln, 2005c; Lincoln & Guba, 2000);
- Critically argue issues, such as collaborations, politics, uneven distribution or depth of knowing, the changing nature of the phenomenon, the grounding of abstract relations, and the culture that operates within a continuously unfolding contemporary (Holmes & Marcus, 2005);
- Conduct critical conversations about the community, global society in transition, democracy, and other issues (Denzin & Lincoln, 2005a, 2005b, 2005c);
- Examine more than one theory using the same set of "facts" (Denzin & Lincoln, 2005c, p. 184);
- Look beyond the business case and innovation towards a broader conception of knowledge management (Grant, 1997). The study may look into exploring what constitutes knowledge to the entity, identifying the knowledge available within the entity, and assessing how the expertise and the know-how of employees has directed the innovation process.
- Explore the relationships between the vendors of enterprise systems and the entity, build a distinction between knowledge generation (knowledge exploration) and knowledge application (knowledge exploitation), and distinguish the strengths and weaknesses of accessing which is different from acquiring the knowledge (Grant & Baden-Fuller, 2004).

REFERENCES

Argyris, C. (2004). *Reasons and Rationalizations: The Limits to Organizational Knowledge.* Oxford: Oxford University Press.

Bauman, Z. (2005). Afterthought: On writing; On writing sociology. In N. K. Denzin & Y. S. Lincoln (Eds.), *Handbook of Qualitative Research* (3rd ed., pp. 1089-1098). Thousand Oaks, CA: Sage Publications.

Benbasat, I., Goldstein, D. K., & Mead, M. (2002). The case research strategy in studies of information systems. In M. D. Myers & D. Avison (Eds.), *Qualitative Research in Information Systems: A Reader* (pp. 79-99). London: Sage Publications.

Bhaskar, R. (2002). *From Science to Emancipation: Alienation and the Actuality of Enlightenment.* Delhi: Sage Publications India Pvt Ltd.

Blaikie, N. (2000). *Designing Social Research.* Cambridge: Polity.

Bloomfield, B. P., Coombs, R., Knights, D., & Littler, D. (2000). *Information Technology and Organisation.* Oxford University Press.

Bryman, A. (2001). *Social Research Methods.* Oxford: Oxford University Press.

Burrell, G. & Morgan, G. (2005). *Sociological Paradigms and Organisational Analysis: Elements of the Sociology of Corporate Life.* Ardershot: Ashgate Publishing Limited.

Canals, J. (2000). *Managing Corporate Growth.* Oxford: Oxford University Press.

Denzin, N. K. & Lincoln, Y. S. (2005a). The eight and ninth moments: Qualitative research in/and the fractured future. In N. K. Denzin & Y. S. Lincoln (Eds.), *Handbook of Qualitative Research* (3rd ed., pp. 1115-1126). Thousand Oaks, CA: Sage Publications.

Denzin, N. K. & Lincoln, Y. S. (2005b). Introduction: The discipline and practice of qualitative research. In N. K. Denzin & Y. S. Lincoln (Eds.), *Handbook of Qualitative Research* (3rd ed., pp. 1-32). Thousand Oaks, CA: Sage Publications.

Denzin, N. K. & Lincoln, Y. S. (2005c). Paradigms and perspectives in contention. In N. K. Denzin & Y. S. Lincoln (Eds.), *Handbook of Qualitative Research* (3rd ed., pp. 183-190). Thousand Oaks, CA: Sage Publications.

Flyvbjerg, B. (2001). *Making social science matter: Why social inquiry fails and how it can succeed again* (S. Sampson, Trans.). Cambridge: Cambridge University Press.

Franz, C. R. & Robey, D. (1984). An investigation of user-led system design: Rational and political perspectives. *Communications of the ACM, 27*(12), 1202-1217.

Geertz, C. (1983). *Local knowledge: Further essays in interpretive anthropology.* New York: Basic Books.

Gilbert, D. (2006). *Stumbling on happiness.* New York: Random House, Inc.

Grant, R. M. (1997). The knowledge-based view of the firm: Implications for management practices. *Long Range Planning, 30*(3), 450-454.

Grant, R. M. & Baden-Fuller, C. (2004). A knowledge accessing theory of strategic alliances. *Journal of Management Studies, 41*(1), 61-84.

Grix, J. (2002). Introducing students to the generic terminology of social research. *Politics, 22*(3), 175-186.

Guba, E. G. (1990). The alternative paradigm dialog. In E. G. Guba (Ed.), *The paradigm dialog* (pp. 17-30). Newbury Park: California: Sage Publications.

Habermas, J. (1970). Knowledge and interest. In D. Emmet & A. MacIntyre (Eds.), *Sociological Theory and Philosophical Analysis* (pp. 36-54). London: Macmillan.

Habermas, J. (1974). *Theory and practice.* London: Heinemann.

Hammer, M. (1996). *Beyond reengineering: how the process-centered organization is changing our work and our lives.* New York: HarperCollins Publishers, Inc.

Hay, C. (2002). *Political analysis: A critical introduction.* Basingstoke: Palgrave.

Heidegger, M. (1962). *Being and time* (J. Macquarrie & E. Robinson, Trans.). New York: Harper.

Holmes, D. R. & Marcus, G. E. (2005). Refunctioning ethnography: The challenge of an anthropology of the contemporary. In N. K. Denzin & Y. S. Lincoln (Eds.), *Handbook of Qualitative Research* (3rd ed., pp. 1099-1113). Thousand Oaks, CA: Sage Publications.

Jackson, M. C. (1992). *Systems methodology for the management sciences.* New York: Plenum Press.

Kant, I. (1934). *The critique of pure reason* (J. M. D. Meiklejohn, Trans.). London: J M Dent.

Lincoln, Y. S. & Guba, E. G. (2000). Paradigmatic controversies, contradictions, and emerging confluences. In N. K. Denzin & Y. S. Lincoln (Eds.), *Handbook of Qualitative Research* (2nd ed., pp. 163-188). Thousand Oaks, CA: Sage Publications.

Luhmann, N. (2006). System as difference. *Organization, 13*(1), 37-57.

Melling, D. (1987). *Understanding Plato.* New York: Oxford University Press.

Myles, B. (1990). *The Theaetetus of Plato* (M. J. Levett & M. Burnyeat, Trans.). Indianapolis: Hackett Publishing Company, Inc.

Nelson, C., Treichler, P. A., & Grossberg, L. (1992). Cultural studies: An introduction. In L. Grossberg, C. Nelson & P. A. Treichler (Eds.), *Cultural Studies* (pp. 1-16). New York: Routledge.

Ormerod, P. (2005). *Why most things fail: Evolution, extinction and economics*. London: Faber and Faber Limited.

Patton, M. Q. (1990). *Qualitative Evaluation and Research Methods* (2nd ed.). Newbury Park, CA: Sage.

Pennings, J. & Buitendam, A. (Eds.). (1987). *New technology as organizational innovation*. Cambridge, Massachusetts: Ballinger.

Polanyi, M. (1962). *Personal knowledge*. London: Routledge and Kegan Paul.

Popper, K. (1965). *Conjectures and refutations*. New York: Harper and Row.

Rogers, E. M. (2003). Diffusion of Innovations (5th ed.). New York: Free Press/Simon & Schuster, Inc.

Ruddin, L P. (2006). You Can Generalize Stupid! Social Scientists, Bent Flyvbjerg, and Case Study Methodology. *Qualitative Inquiry, 12*(4), 797-812.

Rumelhart, D. E., & Ortony, A. (1977). *The representation of knowledge in memory*. In R. C. Anderson, R. J. Shapiro & W. E. Montague (Eds.), (pp. 99-135). Hillsdale, NJ: Erlbaum Publishing.

Santas, G. X. (Ed.). (2006). *The Blackwell Guide to Plato's Republic*. Malden, MA: Blackwell Publishing Ltd.

Sjoberg, G., Williams, N., Vaughn, T. R., & Sjoberg, A. F. (1991). The case study approach in social research: Basic methodological issues. In J. R. Feagin & A. M. Orum (Eds.), *A Case for the Case Study* (pp. 27-79). Chapel Hill: University of North Carolina Press.

Smaling, A. (1987). *Methodological objectivity and qualitative research*. Lisse, the Netherlands: Swets & Zeitlinger.

Smith, M. L. (2006). Overcoming theory-practice inconsistencies: Critical realism and information systems research. *Information and Organization, 16*, 191-211.

Snow, D. A., & Anderson, L. (1991). Researching the homeless: The characteristic features and virtues of the case study. In G. R. Ferris & A. M. Orum (Eds.), *A Case for the Case Study* (pp. 143-173). Chapel Hill: University of North Carolina Press.

Stake, R. E. (1995). *The art of case study research*. London: Sage Publications, Inc.

Stake, R. E. (2005). Qualitative case studies. In N. K. Denzin & Y. S. Lincoln (Eds.), *The Sage Handbook of Qualitative Research* (3rd ed., pp. 443-466).

Taleb, N. N. (2007). *The Black Swan: The impact of the highly improbable*. London: Penguine Books Ltd.

Thull, J. (2005). *The Prime Solution*. Dearborn Trade Publishing.

von Wright, G. H. (1971). A new system of deontic logic. *Danish Yearbook of Philosophy, 1*, 173-182.

Weber, R. (2004). The rhetoric of positivism versus interpretivism: A personal view. *MIS Quarterly, 28*(1), iii-xii.

Wyssusek, B. & Schwartz, M. (2003). *Towards a sociopragmatic-constructivist understanding of information systems*. Hershey, PA: IRM Press.

Yin, R. K. (1993). *Applications of case study research*. Newbury Park: Sage Publications.

Yin, R. K. (1994). *Case Study Research: Design and Methods* (2nd ed.). London: Sage Publications.

ADDITIONAL READINGS

Denzin, N & Lincoln, Y (Eds.). (1994). *Handbook of Qualitative Research*. Thousand Oaks, California: Sage Publications.

Denzin, N K & Lincoln, Y S (Eds.). (2005). *Handbook of Qualitative Research (3rd ed.)*. Thousand Oaks, California: Sage Publications.

Dietz, J L G. (2006). *Enterprise Ontology: Theory and Methodology*. Berlin, Germany: Springer-Verlag.

Lewis, D K. (1999). *Papers in Metaphysics and Epistemology: Volume 2*. Cambridge, United Kingdom: Cambridge University Press.

Section 1.2
Guidelines

Chapter III
A Grounded Theory Study of Enterprise Systems Implementation:
Lessons Learned from the Irish Health Services

John Loonam
Dublin City University, Ireland

Joe McDonagh
University of Dublin, Trinity College, Ireland

ABSTRACT

Enterprise systems (ES) promise to integrate all information flowing across the organisation. They claim to lay redundant many of the integration challenges associated with legacy systems, bring greater competitive advantages to the firm, and assist organisations to compete globally. However, despite such promises these systems are experiencing significant implementation challenges. The ES literature, particularly studies on critical success factors, point to top management support as a fundamental prerequisite for ensuring implementation success. Yet, the literature remains rather opaque, lacking an empirical understanding of how top management support ES implementation. As a result, this study seeks to explore this research question. With a lack of empirical knowledge about the topic, a grounded theory methodology was adopted. Such a methodology allows the investigator to explore the topic by grounding the inquiry in raw data. The Irish health system was taken as the organisational context, with their ES initiative one of the largest implementations in Western Europe.

INTRODUCTION

The objective of this chapter is to discuss the application of a Grounded Theory Methodology (GTM) in addressing "enterprise systems (ES) implementation within the Irish health services." In particular, this chapter will be of benefit to researchers and practitioners endeavouring to focus on ERP implementation within health care organisations. There is a lack of empirical literature to explain the application of GTM for IS inquiry within health care organisations. This empirical vacuum is even more lacking when we turn our attention to ES implementations. This chapter will be comprised of two main sections. The first section will "introduce GTM," clearly illustrating its benefits to IS inquiry. The second section will provide the reader with an "application of GTM in practice." The chapter will conclude with reflections on GTM as an approach for IS empiricism.

INVESTIGATIVE FOCUS

Since the 1950s, organisations have sought to increase effectiveness and efficiency through the use of computers. During the 1970s and 1980s, IS was recognised as a means to creating greater competitive advantages for implementing organisations. Today, IS has permeated to the very core of many firms, often determining their success, or indeed failure. As a consequence of the escalated growth and interest in IS, huge emphasises has been placed on integrating various systems throughout the organisation. Such integration gives the organisation a single view of the enterprise. To this end, enterprise systems (ES) began to emerge in the early 1990s. These systems promised "seamless integration" of organisations business processes, throughout its value chain (Davenport, 2000). In other words, these systems allow the organisation to unite all its business processes under the umbrella of a single system. According to Parr and Shanks (2000), ES's have two important features, firstly they facilitate a casual connection between a visual model of business processes and the software implementation of those processes, and secondly they ensure a level of integration, data integrity and security, which is not easily achievable with multiple software platforms. Kraemmergaard and Moller (2002, p. 2) note that the real benefits of ES are their potential to integrate beyond the organisations own value chain, delivering inter-enterprise integration. This form of integration allows a single organisation to integrate with customers and suppliers along its value chain and to other organisations with similar areas of interest (Davenport, 2000). Finally, Brown and Vessey (1999, p. 411) believe that ES implementations provide "total solutions" to an organisation's information systems needs by addressing a large proportion of business functions. These "off the shelf" packages allow an organisation to improve their current business processes and adopt new best practices (Al-Mashari, 2000).

Consequently, many organisations have moved to implement enterprise systems. The adoption of these systems is expected to bring significant benefits to the organisation. The case literature illustrates this point, with the Toro Co. saving $10 million annually due to inventory reductions, while Owens Corning claims that their ES software helped it to save $50 million in logistics, materials management, and sourcing (Umble, Haft, & Umble, 2003, p. 244). Similarly, other cases reveal large savings in costs and increased levels of organisational effectiveness after ES implementation. Companies such as Geneva Pharmaceuticals (Bhattacherjee, 2000), Lucent Technologies (Francesconi, 1998), Farmland Industries (Jesitus, 1998), and Digital Equipment Corporation (Bancroft, Seip, & Sprengel, 1998), have had significant reductions in costs and increased organisational performance as a result of ES adoptions. The literature highlights notable advantages and benefits for the implementation of these systems.

However, despite such promises, implementation results revealed significant failures. Some studies have cited up to 90% failure rates for the implementation of such systems (Sammon, Adam, & Elichirigoity, 2001). Considering that these systems are enterprise-wide, can often cost millions of euro and take between 1-3 years to install (Markus & Tanis, 2000c), their failure can have devastating consequences on an organisation. For example, in the case of FoxMeyer Drug, a $5 billion pharmaceutical company, the firm filled for bankruptcy after major problems were generated by a failed enterprise system (Helm, Hall, & Hall, 2001).

It, therefore, becomes important to ask why: why are ES implementations delivering such poor performances, and in some cases complete failure. According to Sammon et al. (2001, p. 2), "the main implementation risks associated with ES initiatives are related to change management and the business reengineering that results from integrating an organisation." According to a study by Deloitte and Touche (2001), the main reasons for poor ES performance after implementation range from people obstacles (which according to the study contributed to 68% of the problem), to business processes (which were at 16%), and information systems issues (which were at 12%) (cited in Crowe, Zayas-Castro, & Vanichsenee, 2002, p. 3). As a consequence, empirical investigations have focused on factors that are critical to ES success, that is, critical success factors (CSF). In particular, top management support was identified as the most important factor for ensuring success (Somers & Nelson, 2001; Umble et al., 2003).

However, there was a lack of empirical depth within the literature as to how top management support ES implementation. An empirical inquiry was called for. This research, therefore, sought to investigate the topic within the Irish health services. In conducting such a study, the investigation would need to build an empirical explanation, that is, theory. However, before building any theory, the investigator must first align their philosophical views with the demands of the research question. The outcome will decide the methodological choices available to the investigator and the investigation.

A CALL FOR INTERPRETIVISM

Before discussing the merits and application of a grounded theory methodology, it is first important to provide the reader with a preliminary review about the nature of empirical inquiry. Prior to commencing any inquiry, the investigator must address their ontological and epistemological views and indeed how such views fit with their research question and the methodological choices made to conduct the study. Essentially, ontology describes the reality, while epistemology is the relationship between reality and the investigator, with the methodology being the technique used to discover such reality (Perry, Riege, & Brown, 1999). Hirschheim (2002) provides an historical overview of the relationship between the investigator and reality since the 17th Century, that is, an explanation of the epistemological status of science. In effect, two epistemological paradigms have preoccupied scientists' view of reality, that is, the positivist and interpretivist perspectives. Briefly explained, the positivist perspective is based on the ontological assumption that there exists an objective social reality that can be studied independently of the action of the human actors in this reality. "The epistemological assumption following from this is that there exist unidirectional cause-effect relationships that can be identified and tested through the use of hypothetic-deductive logic and analysis" (Khazanchi & Munkvold, 2000, p. 34). In contrast, the interpretivist perspective is based upon the ontological assumption that reality and our knowledge thereof are social constructions, incapable of being studied independent of the social actors that construct and make sense of reality. Instead of seeking unidirectional cause-effect relationships, the focus is to understand the actors' view of their social world (Khazanchi & Munkvold, 2000, p. 34).

As this study seeks to "explore" how top management support ES implementation, an interpretivist epistemology is required. This investigation focuses on understanding an enterprise system within a specific organisational setting. Skok and Legge (2002, p. 74) note that when examining any ES project, the situation becomes complex because of the variety of associated stakeholders and the inter-relationships between them. In such a world of multiple perspectives and "interpretations," there is a need to provide an abstraction of the situation.

In other words, it is important that the investigator remain open to interpretation when exploring the nature of enterprise systems. However, multiple perspectives are not only applicable to enterprise systems but indeed to all information systems. Greatbatch, Murphy, and Dingwall (2001, p. 181), for example, note that "many of the social processes which surround the implementation of computer systems over time in real-world settings are not amenable to quantitative (or positivistic) analysis because they resist treatment as discrete, static entities."

In order to remain open to interpretation, it is critical that the investigator adopts a suitable methodological approach. Choice of methodology is important as it needs to align with the empirical orientation of the study, that is, for this investigation that is interpretivism, while also providing the investigator with appropriate tools and techniques to collect and analyse data. As many interpretivist inquiries seek to explore a new topic, current empirical knowledge is often limited. Therefore, it is important that the investigator chooses a methodology that remains flexible during theory building. Such methodological approaches must first start research with a "considerable degree of openness to the field data" (Walsham, 1995, p. 76). Eisenhardt (1989, p. 536), in dealing with case studies, states that attempting to approach this ideal is important because preordained theoretical perspectives or propositions may bias and limit the findings. Investigators should formulate a research problem and possibly specify some potentially important variables, however they should avoid thinking about specific relationships between variables and theories as much as possible, especially at the outset of the process.

Walsham reiterates the importance of avoiding formal theoretical predispositions, stating that while "theory can provide a valuable initial guide, there is a danger of the researcher only seeing what the theory suggests, and thus using the theory in a rigid way which stifles potential new issues and avenues of exploration" (199, p. 76). It, therefore, becomes important for the investigator to choose a methodology that remains flexible during data collection and analysis. For this investigation, a grounded theory methodology (GTM) offered such an approach. The objective of GTM is to ground data that are systematically gathered and analysed. The theory emerges during the research process and is a product of the continuous interplay between analysis and data collection (Glaser & Strauss, 1967).

A GROUNDED PERSPECTIVE

The grounded theory methodology (GTM) first emerged in the 1960s with Glaser and Strauss publishing studies based on the method. In 1967 both authors published an extended exposition of the method and this text[1] of origin has remained the main reference point for researchers working with GTM. Its origins lie with the principles of symbolic interactionism, which basically prescribe to the belief that researchers must enter the world of their subjects in order to understand the subjects' environment and the interactions and interpretations that occur. Symbolic interactionism is both a theory of human behaviour and an approach to enquiry about human conduct and group behaviour. A principle tenet is that humans come to understand social definitions through the socialisation process (Goulding, 2002).

Using the principles of symbolic interactionism, Glaser and Strauss set out to develop a more systematic procedure for collecting and analysing qualitative data (Goulding, 2002). The basic premise of grounded theory grew largely out of the protest against the methodological climate in which the role of qualitative research was viewed as preliminary to the "real" methodologies of quantitative research (Charmaz, 1983). Grounded theory therefore was intended as a methodology for developing theory that is grounded in data that are systematically gathered and analysed. The theory evolves during the research process and is a product of continuous interplay between analysis and data collection (Strauss & Corbin, 1990). The method is most commonly used to generate theory where little is already known, or to provide a fresh slant on existing knowledge (Turner, 1983). This is the fundamental difference between GTM and quantitative methods of inquiry, which normally aims to "explore" (interpretivism) rather than to "test" (positivism) theory. Glaser and Strauss saw this imbalance between "theory generation and verification" and set about developing processes for theory generation as opposed to theory generated by logical deduction from a priori assumptions (Bryant, 2002, p. 28). This gave rise to the grounded theory method.

The fundamental objective of GTM is to develop theory from exploratory research. One of the major challenges, however, facing GTM is also experienced by other qualitative approaches, namely the dominance of positivism within general research studies. This is particularly evident within IS research, where the majority of studies have focused upon positivistic criteria that aim to test theory. This, of course, is a result of how IS has been viewed within practice, and unfortunately academia, that is, as a separate technical systems-based entity. However, many recent IS studies have illustrated the importance of understanding wider organisational, social and cultural aspects and this in turn has elevated the importance of qualitative methods within IS research.

Until relatively recently, the method had something of a peripheral, if not pariah, status in many areas; but in recent years it has enjoyed a resurgence, and there is a growing body of literature that attests to its range of application in IS research. (Bryant, 2002, p. 28).

According to Myers and Avison (2002, p. 9), grounded theory approaches are becoming increasingly common in IS research literature because the method is extremely useful in developing context-based descriptions and explanations of the phenomenon (2002, p. 9). It is also a general style of doing analysis that does not depend on particular disciplinary perspectives (Strauss, 1987) and therefore lends itself to information systems research, which can be described as a hybrid discipline (Urquhart, 2000). One of the better examples of a grounded theory approach in IS research is Orlikowski's paper on CASE[2] tools as organisational change (1993). She states that

the grounded theory approach was useful because it allowed a focus on contextual elements as well as the action of key players associated with organisational change-elements that are often omitted in IS studies that rely on variance models and cross-sectional, quantitative data. (Orlikowski, 1993, p. 310)

Similarly, GTM was appealing to this investigation as it sought to explore the field of enterprise systems.

THE APPLICATION OF GTM

In adopting a GTM approach to inquiry, the Irish health system was selected as the organisational context for this investigation. Preliminary inquiry revealed that this organisation was implementing an enterprise system (using SAP), which had commenced in 1995, was one of the largest ES implementations in Western Europe, and had an estimated €130 million spent on the initiative. In order to explain the application of GTM in practice, Pandit's (1996) five stage model is adapted by this investigation. However, before discussing these stages, let us first briefly reflect on the workings of grounded theory as a methodology.

Using a grounded theory method, both secondary and primary data are collected and analysed, using three coding techniques, namely open, axial, and selective coding. GTM inquiry begins by theoretically sampling emerging data, where future directions and decisions concerning data collection and analysis are based upon prior knowledge and understanding. In GTM, both data collection and analysis occur in tandem with one another. While theoretical sampling assists with data collection, the investigator also deploys the three coding techniques to analyse the data. Open coding moves data from general phenomenon into emerging trends and concepts. In effect, data concepts are the building blocks of GTM. During open coding the investigator is "comparing" all data and assigning concepts with specific codes. The next stage involves axial coding, where the emergent concepts are classified into higher order concepts or categories. This process involves reassembling data that were fractured during open coding. Finally, selective coding takes place, where data are refined and core categories selected. These categories form the rudimentary elements of a "grounded theory." As data collection and analysis occurs in tandem, coding is complete once the investigator reaches theoretical saturation. Saturation occurs when no new data has emerged in the field and only the same data concepts keep appearing.

In order to illustrate the above cited workings of GTM in practice, five stages are now presented. While these stages are ranked from one to five, it is important to note that they are iterative and often the investigator must move systemically from one to the other throughout the investigation. The stages begin with a research design phase, followed by data collection, data gathering, and data analysis. Finally, the investigator moves to compare and contrast the extant literature to the

new emergent grounded theory. Each of these phases will now be highlighted in more detail.

1. **Research design:** The objective of this phase is to develop a research focus, which is then narrowed to become a research question. According to Strauss and Corbin (1998), there are a number of methods for assisting the investigator in developing a research focus. These include: (1) the investigator can identify problems in their workplace, (2) speaking with academic faculty, where the investigator can synthesis their ideas, (3) identify problems and gaps in the literature, and (4) by entering the research field and developing a research question.

Of particular relevance to this investigation was the identification of gaps in preliminary literature. A preliminary review of the enterprise systems literature revealed that the implementation of these systems was not easy. Some studies cited up to 90% failure with such systems, primarily because organisational issues were ignored or bypassed. In particular, top management support was identified as one of the most important critical factors for ensuring the successful implementation of an enterprise system. Anecdotal evidence emanating from experiential knowledge had informed the investigator as to the importance of top management support; now the academic literature was further supporting such beliefs. Consequently, a research question was formed.

2. **Data collection:** In a GTM inquiry, the data collection phase begins when the study commences. All data is applicable and relevant to GTM. An important feature of GTM is the simultaneous collection and analysis of data. Upon entry into the field, the investigator begins to also analyse the data, looking for emerging trends. This process is referred to as "theoretical sampling" by the original authors.

Theoretical sampling is the process of data collection for generating theory whereby the analyst jointly collects, codes, and analyses his data and decides what data to collect next and where to find them, in order to develop his theory as it emerges. This process of data collection is "controlled" by the emerging theory. (Glaser & Strauss, 1967, p. 45)

In addition to theoretical sampling, another feature of grounded theory is the application of the "constant" comparative method (Goulding, 2002). Constant comparison involves comparing like with like in order to look for emerging patterns and themes across the data. According to Glaser and Strauss there are four stages to the constant comparative method. These include (1) comparing incidents applicable to each category, (2) integrating categories and their properties, (3) delimiting the theory, and (4) finally writing the theory (Glaser & Strauss, 1967, p. 105).

In applying data collection techniques, this investigation separated this stage into two steps. Strauss and Corbin refer to these two steps as (a) technical literature collection and (b) non-technical literature collection. Technical literature refers to the current body of knowledge about the research topic, for example, the extant literature. As a result, this investigation conducted an initial preliminary review of the ES literature. Such a review seeks to sensitise the investigator with the emergent data.

The nontechnical literature refers to the organisational evidence, that is, meeting minutes, interviews, consulting reports, observations, memo writing, and so forth. This is often referred to as "secondary" data within other qualitative methodologies, for example, case study. The nontechnical literature played a pivotal role in this investigation. As this study was engaged in a 10 year long SAP implementation, there was a huge reservoir of non-technical literature for the investigator to collect. This included consultancy reports, steering meeting minutes, project presentations, government reports, progress reports, vendor reports, and general project specifications. On top of the huge reservoir of nontechnical literature already gathered, the investigator also conducted a series of interviews. The interview style remained unstructured, that is, questioning tended to emerge during the interview rather than leading the interview in a structured format. Each informant was therefore afforded greater scope to discuss and develop ideas during the session. Preliminary interview questions were developed from the data collected and already analysed. The approach of collecting and analysing data simultaneously greatly aided the process of data sampling and the pursuit of constant data comparisons. In GTM, each interview honed the questioning and format of the next, until finally theoretical saturation had been achieved.

Initially, prior to interview commencement, key informants were informed, via e-mail, as to the nature of the research inquiry and the forthcoming interview. After interviewing key informants, theoretical sampling of the data selected future informants. Permission to use a dictaphone to record interview sessions was also sought. If informants were uncomfortable with the use of a recording mechanism, the investigator would keep notes. All interviews were written up directly after each session. This allowed the investigator to follow up on any outstanding or unclear points with the interviewee. With unstructured interviews, it was difficult to know their specific length until afterwards. However, each informant was scheduled for a 1 hour interview. If more time was required it could be arranged to follow-up with another interview, or over the phone at a later date. Upon conclusion of the interview, informants were thanked for their participation and given the investigator's contact details. This allowed informants to gain access to the recorded material if they so wished or to follow-up with further comments and/or suggestions. Interviews were then transcribed directly after each meeting. The investigator also kept memos of each meeting, which in turn assisted with the process of probing and questioning the data. Such an approach greatly facilitated with sharpening and focusing future interview sessions.

3. **Data ordering:** Data ordering acts as a bridge between data collection and analysis. As this study was focusing on a complex organisation, which was implementing a system that affected the entire organisation, data management was critical. GTM inquiry also involves many approaches to data collection, which increases the need to order data. In particular, the vast array of nontechnical literature (secondary field data) available to this study meant that the investigator needed to create a systematic order for the data. Folders were created to give a hierarchical structure to the data. In all, the field data was divided into five core folders: (1) Data Analysis, (2) Diary of research, (3) Health care reports, (4) Interviews, and (5) Secondary data. The data analysis folder focused on the data analysis process, that is, open, axial, and selective coding. The diary of research folder allowed the investigator to record study memos, meeting minutes, and scheduling appointments. The third folder focused on health care reports, which provided knowledge about health care in Ireland. Interview transcripts and meetings were recorded in the fourth folder. Finally, the secondary data was placed in the fifth core folder. This folder included project reports, consultant reports, and steering committee minutes and presentations. Data ordering played an important part in assisting the investigator to analyse the data. As data collection and data analysis occur in tandem with one another, that is, theoretical sampling drives data collection, data ordering also occurs in tandem with these two phases.

4. **Data analysis:** In tandem with data collection and ordering, the researcher is also analysing the data. Data analysis starts upon entering the field, without it theoretical sampling will not take place. GTM has devised a number of methods for analysing data. With GTM the idea is to look for patterns and reoccurring events in the data through comparing data against each other. This process is called "coding," where interview, observational, and other data forms are broken down into distinct units of meaning which are then labelled to generate concepts. These concepts are then clustered into descriptive categories, which are later re-evaluated for their interrelationships and through a series of analytical steps are gradually subsumed into higher order categories, or a single core category, which suggests an emergent theory (Goulding, 2002).

Theoretical coding involves breaking down the data into specific "units of analysis." Each unit represents a step on the road to developing an emerging theory. In effect data are arranged in a hierarchical manner, with the eventual emergence of a grounded theory. Strauss and Corbin (1998) give us examples of the hierarchy language used for data analysis.

*   **Phenomena:** Central ideas in the data represented as concepts.
*   **Concepts:** Involves moving from just describing what is happening in the data, to explaining the relationship between and across incidents.
*   **Categories:** These are higher order concepts. Grouping concepts into categories enables the analyst to reduce the number of units with which they are working.
*   **Properties:** These are the characteristics or attributes of a category. The delineation of which gives the category greater meaning.

These data analysing terms are explained better when we look briefly at the coding techniques available to the analyst. Three coding procedures have been identified; these include open, axial, and selective coding (Strauss & Corbin, 1998). The fundamental objective of using these coding techniques is to arrive at a situation where the data is "saturated," thus giving rise to a grounded theory. Each of these coding techniques is now briefly discussed providing examples of its application from this investigation.

1. **Open coding:** Open coding involves breaking down the data into distinct units of meaning. Such a process allows the researcher to place specific "phenomenon" into groups, therefore giving rise to early concept development for the emerging theory. This classification of concepts into specific groups is referred to as "conceptualising" the data (Strauss & Corbin, 1998, p. 103). Following on from this the process of "abstraction" takes place, where descriptive codes and concepts are moved to a higher abstract level. Abstraction involves collapsing concepts into higher order concepts, known as categories. According to Strauss (1987) abstraction involves constantly asking theoretically relevant questions. To assist the process of abstraction, the researcher moves beyond open coding and towards axial coding techniques.

With the application of open coding within the Irish health services, the investigator used two steps. First, the investigator moved through the data line-by-line, italicising, bolding, highlighting, and underling both hardcopy and electronic documents alike. This process fits with the rudimentary elements of what open coding is about. The approach proved arduous and time-consuming, but revealed a vast array of data imagery, events, words, incidents, acts, and ideas, that greatly assisted with the development of an understanding towards the research phenomenon under inquiry. Strauss and Corbin

(1998) refer to these factors as the block work to building sound data concepts. The second step involved building a "library" in Microsoft Excel. This process allowed the investigator to order data systematically (Pandit, 1996), moving data to a state of higher order concepts, or as Glaser and Strauss (1967) refer to it as, data conceptualisation. A comments column was also created in the database to allow the investigator to write notes and make comments on emerging data. Glaser and Strauss (1967) encourage investigator commentary and question raising throughout coding, believing that it aids with the process of constant comparison and theoretical sampling.

2. **Axial coding:** Axial coding involves moving to a higher level of abstraction and is achieved by specifying relationships and delineating a core category or construct around which the other concepts revolve. It relies on a synthetic technique of making connections between subcategories to construct a more comprehensive scheme (Orlikowski, 1993, p. 315). In other words, the purpose of axial coding is to begin the process of reassembling data that were fractured during open coding. Higher level concepts known as categories are related to their subcategories to form more precise and complete explanations about phenomenon (Strauss & Corbin, 1998, p. 124). Subcategories are the same as categories except instead of standing for a phenomenon it asks questions of the phenomenon, such as when, where, who, how, and with what consequences. Such an approach gives the category greater explanatory power, therefore fitting with the idea of developing theoretical abstraction from the data (Strauss & Corbin, 1998).

In applying axial coding, Strauss and Corbin support the use of story-maps or network diagrams (1998). Similarly, this investigation design a story-map to tell the story of the SAP implementation within the Irish health services. Specifically, the story-map used illustrated the strategies taken, conditions that shaped these strategies, the actions taken because of these conditions, and the consequences and outcomes of such actions. In story-mapping, axial coding reconstructs concepts "fractured" during open coding, and unites them through data abstraction. Strauss and Corbin found that story-mapping greatly assisted in data abstraction (1998). Abstraction involves grouping "concepts" to form higher order concepts or "subcategories." After mapping the story, the investigator is able to abstract "concept groups" or "subcategories." In effect, a number of key trends are beginning to emerge from the story under investigation. These key trends will form the bases for an emergent theory.

3. **Selective coding:** Selective coding is the final data analysis technique. The fundamental premise of selective coding is to "refine and integrate categories" having reached a point of theoretical saturation (Strauss & Corbin, 1998, p. 143). Emerging data no longer presents any new ideas or concepts and is a repeat of data already collected and categorised. Understanding the causal relationship between data, as identified from axial coding, the researcher is able to place data concepts and subcategories into higher order emerging categories. Selective coding now refines and integrates these "emerging categories." Data are "selected" or pulled up out of concepts and categorised. The application of selective coding revealed a number of key patterns to explain how top management support ES implementation. In effect, these key patterns tell the story of ES implementation within the Irish health services.

5. <u>**Literature comparison:**</u> Finally, the literature comparison phase is the last stage in GTM inquiry. The objective at this stage is to compare the "emergent theory" to the extant literature, that is, the technical literature in the areas domain. At this stage the researcher can compare and contrast their theory with various frameworks or macro theories from the literature. There are two distinct advantages with tying the emergent theory to the extant literature, namely (1) it improves construct definitions and therefore "internal" validity, and (2) it also improves "external" validity by establishing the domain to which the study's findings can be generalised with Pandit (1996).

REFLECTIONS ON GTM IN PRACTICE

This section seeks to illustrate some practical issues relating to GTM inquiry. These reflections highlight the investigators key observations after using a GTM approach. First, the importance of maintaining ethical standards is highlighted. This is followed by addressing investigator bias, the challenge of conceptualisation, and highlighting the role of literature in theory formation.

Throughout this inquiry, it was vital that certain *ethical* standards were adhered to. Ethics are best described as the set of values or principles the investigator maintains during the investigation (Goulding, 2002). Examples of ethical considerations include client/investigator confidentiality, including people in the research who have given of their consent, only recording interviews when permitted, not considering documents unless they have been initially cleared by informants, limiting "surprise" questions within interviews by forwarding interview structure to all informants beforehand, and finally regularly communicating the research projects integrity and confidentiality when dealing with informants at all times. Once the Irish health services had agreed to this investigation, a liaison officer was appointed to assist the study. This individual played a pivotal role in ensuring all prospective informants were notified as to the nature of the study and what was expected from them.

Similarly, to ensure ethical considerations are adhered to, the *investigator* plays an important role in interpretivist inquiry. In fact, they are the primary means for collecting, ordering, and analysing data, therefore the investigator can never assume a value neutral stance in the relationship between theory and practice and is always implicated in the phenomenon being studied (Orlikowski & Baroudi, 1991). It is, therefore, critical that the investigator acknowledge their role in interpretivist inquiry and try to control individual bias. For this study, GTM provided the investigator with a means to overcoming challenges associated with particular biases. Through "constant comparison" of data, the investigator is able to state their assumptions about the data, which in turn can be compared and contrasted to emerging data. This process allows individual biases to be either validated or rejected by the data. As a result, investigator biases are minimised through empirical rigor and constant comparison of data.

However, while investigator biases can be minimised, it is worth noting that GTM inquiries involve considerable *conceptualisation* of data (Strauss & Corbin, 1998). This process, as the original authors note, requires a considerable degree of openness to the data (Glaser & Strauss, 1967), which is best fostered through a "creative theoretical imagination" (Strauss & Corbin, 1998). Essentially, the investigator is moving data "concepts" to higher order concepts, which in turn become "categories." Categories form the rudimentary elements of a "grounded theory." However, in order to derive categories, the investigator must conceptualise data. Herein lies the challenge for GTM inquiries, which may be accused of lacking scientific (deductive) rigor, based instead around subjective (inductive) assumptions. Yet, Strauss and Corbin (1998) note that the constant interplay of data in GTM involves both deductive and inductive approaches

to inquiry. By "constantly comparing" emergent data, the investigator is deductively conceptualising data, whereas "theoretical sampling" is inductively selecting data deduced from earlier constant comparison. Furthermore, this study found Strauss and Corbin's (1998) approach to GTM quite systematic and rigorous in its approach to data analysis. This point is further evidenced by Smit and Bryant's (2000) study, where their findings revealed a majority preference for Strauss and Corbin's approach rather than Glaser's approach to GTM within the IS literature. Similarly, the authors note the systematic and thorough nature of Strauss and Corbin's approach to GTM. However, reflecting on GTM in practice, this study believes that Strauss and Corbin's (1998) approach to GTM could be further enriched by the use of multiple methodologies to generate deeper insights into the emergent theory. This point is supported by Gasson (2004), who noted that a holistic view of any research question requires multiple approaches, as the selection of a research strategy entails a trade-off: the strengths of one approach overcome the weaknesses in another approach and vice versa. This in itself is a powerful argument for pluralism and for the use of multiple research approaches during any investigation. (Gasson, 2004, p. 99)

Examples of other methods of inductive coding include, "discourse analysis, soft systems conceptual models, process modelling, and inductive categorisation" (Gasson, 2004). These tools would sharpen analysis allowing the investigator to further compare and contrast data.

Finally, reflecting on the role of extant *literature* with the emergent theory, this investigation disagrees with Glaser's (1992) refusal to review current knowledge when conducing GTM inquiry. Instead, this investigation concurs with Strauss and Corbin's (1998) view that the literature can greatly assist the investigator in shaping their understanding of the research phenomenon. In fact, the authors view the literature as another form of empirical data; therefore isolating review until primary data collection has occurred does little to advance knowledge and theoretical development. For this investigation, while a lack of empirical knowledge existed within the extant literature, preliminary review prior to field data collection greatly assisted the investigator in understanding data concepts.

FUTURE RESEARCH DIRECTIONS

Future research will seek to extend the current study in a number of directions. First, as this investigation seeks to build a "grounded theory," the emergence of such will need further empirical validation and elaboration. Exploratory studies build "substantive theories," that is, theories that are substantial to the case under inquiry. These theories require further exploration and eventual generalisation. Consequently, future investigations might conduct more quantitative or positivistic inquiries, using multiple case studies or survey instruments, to refine and test this "emergent" theory.

Second, this study was focused on the Irish health system. Future inquiries could examine other health systems internationally. This would allow for a comparative analysis of results, which in turn would enable practitioners to broaden their knowledge. Similarly, this study could also be extended to other public and private sector organisations within Ireland, and indeed internationally. Questions such as how other private/public sector industries shape top management support could be asked.

Finally, future research needs to focus on all critical success factors for enterprise systems implementation. This study focuses on top management support, but studies have identified other factors that are also important for project success. For example, future investigations could focus on issues such as project team competence, the role of the project champion, the role of management and technical consultants during implementation,

change management perspectives throughout implementing organisations, relationship management between vendors and their clients, and data integrity and conversion to new system.

CONCLUSION

Reflecting on GTM as an approach to empirical inquiry, the investigator must be clear as to their ontological worldview and their corresponding epistemology. These views, in turn, will determine their methodological choice. As this study sought to explore the field of enterprise systems, an interpretivist stance was adopted. Such a stance seeks to build theory by interpreting the world through the words and behaviours of the social actors in it. While initially much of the language of scientific endeavour belonged to the world of positivism, many IS investigations are now acknowledging the depth and applicability of interpretivist inquiry, particularly for studies focusing on complex systems, social, and organisational issues. Such inquiry is particularly suited to IS initiatives in complex organisations such as health care. Finally, in describing how this investigation conducted its GTM inquiry, five stages are outlined. The chapter first begins by explaining the research design process. The data collection, ordering, and analysis phases are then explained. Finally, the comparison of literature to the emergent theory is considered. While many of these phases occurred in tandem, they are separated in this chapter for explanatory purposes only. The grounded theory method allows the investigator to deploy a multitude of techniques for data collection, for example memo-taking, secondary data collection, and interviewing. Data are analysed via constantly comparing and theoretically sampling all emerging concepts. Strauss and Corbin (1998) outline three coding techniques for data analysis. Following these three coding techniques, the investigation allows data concepts to emerge. These concepts, as Strauss and

Corbin (1998) stated, form the "building blocks of a grounded theory." In turn, these concepts are developed during coding and selected to form an emergent theory grounded in data.

REFERENCES

Al-Mashari, M. (2000). Constructs of process change management in ERP context: A focus on SAP R/3. In *Americas Conference on Information Systems,* Long Beach, California.

Bancroft, N., Seip, H., & Sprengel, A. (1998). *Implementing SAP R/3: How to introduce a large system into a large organisation.* Greenwich, CT: Manning Publications.

Bhattacherjee, A. (2000). Beginning SAP R/3 implementation at Geneva Pharmaceuticals. *Communications of the AIS.*

Brown, C. V., & Vessey, I. (1999). ERP implementation approaches: Toward a contingency framework. In *International Conference on Information Systems (ICIS),* Charlotte, North Carolina.

Bryant, A. (2002). Re-grounding grounded theory. *Journal of Information Technology Theory and Application, 4*(1), 25-42.

Charmaz, K. (1983). The grounded theory method: An explication and interpretation. In R. Emerson (Ed.), *Contemporary field research: A collection of readings.* Boston, MA: Little Brown.

Crowe, T. J., Zayas-Castro, J. L., & Vanichsenee, S. (2002). Readiness assessment for enterprise resource planning. In *the 11th International Conference on Management of Technology (IAMOT2002).*

Davenport, T. H. (2000). *Mission critical: Realizing the promise of enterprise systems.* Boston, MA: Harvard Business School Press.

Deloitte & Touche (2001, June). *Value for money audit of the Irish health system.* Government of Ireland.

Eisenhardt, K. M. (1989). Building theories from case study research. *Academy of Management Review, 14(*4), 532-550.

Francesconi, T. (1998). Transforming Lucent's CFO. *Management Accounting, 80*(1), 22-30.

Gasson, S. (2004). Rigor in grounded theory research: An interpretive perspective on generating theory from qualitative field studies. In M. E. Whitman & A. B. Woszczynski (Eds.), *The handbook of information systems research* (pp. 79-102). Idea Group Publishing.

Glaser, B. G., & Strauss, A. (1967). *The discovery of grounded theory: Strategies for qualitative research.* New York: Aldine de Gruyter.

Goulding, C. (2002). *Grounded theory: A practical guide for management, business, and market researchers.* Thousand Oaks, CA, London: Sage Publications.

Greatbatch, D., Murphy, E., & Dingwall, R. (2001). Evaluating medical information systems: Ethnomethodological and interactionist approaches. *Health Services Management Research, 14*(3), 181-191.

Helm, S., Hall, M., & Hall, C. (2003). Pre-implementation attitudes and organisational readiness for implementing an ERP system. *European Journal of Information Systems, 146.*

Hirschheim, R., & Newman, M. (2002). Symbolism and information systems development: Myth, metaphor, and magic. In M. D. Myers & D. Avison (Eds.), *Qualitative research in information systems: A reader.* Thousand Oaks, CA, London: Sage Publications.

Jesitus, J. (1998). Even farmers get SAPed. *Industry Week, 247*(5), 32-36.

Khazanchi, D., & Munkvold, B. (2000). Is information systems a science? An inquiry into the nature of the information systems discipline. *The Database for Advances in Information Systems, 31*(3), 24-40.

Kraemmergaard, P., & Moller, C. (2000). *A research framework for studying the implementation of enterprise resource planning (ERP) systems.* IRIS 23. Laboratorium for Interaction Technology, University of Trollhattan Uddevalla.

Markus, M. L., & Tanis, C. (2000). The enterprise systems experience-from adoption to success. In R. W. Zmud (Ed.), *Framing the domains of IT research: Glimpsing the future through the past* (pp. 173-207). Cincinnati, OH: Pinnaflex Educational Resources, Inc.

Myers, M. D., & Avison, D. (Eds.). (2002). *Qualitative research in information systems: A reader.* London: Sage Publications Ltd.

Orlikowski, W. J. (1993). CASE tools as organisational change: Investigating incremental and radical changes in systems development. *Management Information Systems Quarterly, 17*(3), 309-340.

Orlikowski, W. J., & Baroudi, J. J. (1991). Studying information technology in organisations: Research approaches and assumptions. *Information Systems Research 2*(1), 1-28.

Pandit, N. (1996). The creation of theory: A recent application of the grounded theory method. *The Qualitative Report, 2*(4).

Parr, A., & Shanks, G. (2000). A model of ERP project implementation. *Journal of Information Technology, 15,* 289-303.

Perry, C., Riege, A., & Brown, L. (1999). Realism's role among scientific paradigms in marketing research. *Irish Marketing Review, 12*(2).

Sammon, D., Adam, F., & Elichirigoity, F. (2001b). ERP dreams and sound business rationale. In *Seventh Americas Conference on Information Systems.*

Skok, W., & Legge, M. (2002). Evaluating enterprise resource planning (ERP) systems using an interpretive approach. *Knowledge and Process Management, 9*(2), 72-82.

Smit, J., & Bryant, A. (2000). Grounded theory method in IS research: Glaser vs. Strauss. Research in Progress Working Papers, 2000-2007.

Somers, T., & Nelson, K. (2001). The impact of critical success factors across the stages of enterprise resource planning implementations. In *Hawaii International Conference on Systems Sciences.*

Strauss, A. L., & Corbin, J. (1990). *Basics of qualitative research: Grounded theory procedures and techniques.* Newbury Park, CA: Sage Publications.

Strauss, A. L., & Corbin, J. (1994). Grounded theory methodology: An overview. In N. K. Denzin & Y. S. Lincoln (Eds.), *Handbook of qualitative research.* Thousand Oaks, CA: Sage Publications.

Strauss, A. L., & Corbin, J. (1998). Basics of qualitative research: Techniques and procedures for developing grounded theory (2nd ed.). London, Thousand Oaks, CA: Sage Publications.

Turner, B. (1983). The use of grounded theory for the qualitative analysis of organisational behaviour. *Journal of Management Studies, 20,* 333-348.

Umble, E. J., Haft, J., & Umble, M. (2003). Enterprise resource planning: Implementation procedures and critical success factors. *European Journal of Operational Research, 146,* 241-257.

Urquhart, C. (2000, January). Strategies for conversion and systems analysis in requirements gathering: Qualitative view of analyst-client communications. *The Qualitative Report 4*(1/2).

Walsham, G. (1995). Interpretive case studies in IS research: Nature and method. *European Journal of Information Systems, 4*(2), 74-81.

ENDNOTES

[1] The Discovery of Grounded Theory (Glaser, & Strauss, 1967).

[2] Computer-aided software engineering

Chapter IV
A Critical Theory Approach to Information Technology Transfer to the Developing World and a Critique of Maintained Assumptions in the Literature

Khalid Al-Mabrouk
University of Southern Queensland, Australia

Kieran James
University of Southern Queensland, Australia

ABSTRACT

This chapter reviews some of the existing Information Technology Transfer (ITT) literature and suggests that it has fallen victim to the well-known limitations of an economic rationalist and positivist world-view. In particular we challenge the extensive use of the term "success" in the ITT literature, arguing that it is problematic for several reasons. Mainstream ITT research portrays ITT as primarily linear, incremental, and progressive in line with the economic rationalist belief that a "rising tide lifts all boats." We suggest Marx's theory of dialectical materialism as an alternative to the dominant hegemony and encourage researchers in ITT to accept the fact that internal contradictions are part of a dialectic system. We encourage ITT researchers to view local resistance more sympathetically. Concerted efforts should be made to understand and dialog with the Other. Overall we recommend more interview based case study research in preference to mass-mail out surveys which may prove ineffective in reaching a broad segment of the population in non-Western locations. The existing literature's preoccupation with educated urban elites and Transnational Corporations may also prove to be a hindrance to both our increased understanding and radical social change.

INTRODUCTION

This chapter is written in the form of a polemic which aims to highlight limitations and problems associated with accepting uncritically an economic rationalist and positivist worldview when researching Information Technology (IT) Transfer in the developing world. A polemic is a style of writing which is deliberately unbalanced and provocative; the aim is to highlight weaknesses and limitations in established thought so as to create radical social change. The Free Dictionary at Farlex (available online at www.freediction-ary.com) defines "polemic" as "a controversial argument, especially one refuting or attacking a specific opinion or doctrine." Our aim is for our readers to reflexively challenge their own maintained assumptions consistent with Michel Foucault's (1986, 1987) late-period writings on ethics where he presents an "ethics of the self" according to which one creates and forms oneself reflexively as an ethical subject. Because this chapter is written as a polemic, we are not bound to follow conventional rules associated with other forms of writing such as a need for completeness and balance. Famous polemics of the past include Karl Marx's many newspaper articles written in the 1850s for the *New York Tribune* and his later "Critique of the Gotha Program" (Marx, 1994), Friedrich Nietzsche's *Beyond Good and Evil* (1973) and *Twilight of the Idols* (1990), Herbert Marcuse's *One-Dimensional Man* (1964), and the recent philosophical work by Australian author Tamas Pataki entitled *Against Religion* (Pataki, 2007).

This chapter investigates and explores, from a neo-Marxist/Critical Theory perspective, some of the key issues that arise when we consider IT Transfer to countries in the developing world. We also critique two generally well-regarded articles in the recent mainstream (i.e., noncritical) IT Transfer literature, Straub, Loch, and Hill (2001) and Nahar, Lyytinen, Huda, and Muravyov (2006), with a view to highlighting

how these articles, whilst commendable in many ways, reflect the dominant hegemony of Western technological rationality (Adorno, 1994a; Bapat, 2005, p. 171; Marcuse, 1964; Weber, 1968). It is important to remember that we are *not* reviewing these papers from within the confines of a mainstream worldview. To do so would mean that we would be forced to focus on points of methodology. Instead we critique these papers from a radical sociopolitical perspective. Our critique is holistic and integrated and may bring to readers' consciousness issues that they may have not previously considered. It is hoped that this chapter will prove to be especially useful for early-career and higher-degree researchers who see merit in an integrated and sociopolitical approach to researching IT Transfer issues.

We conclude that research in this emerging and important field should take cues from Marx and the Critical Theory of the Frankfurt School, so as to best extract oneself from a positivist worldview that detracts from the ability to meaningfully engage with members of a cultural Other. We discourage the continued use of value-laden Western technological-rational concepts borrowed in many cases from the natural sciences such as "ranking of success factors" (Nahar et al., 2006, p. 669), "rival hypotheses" (Straub et al., 2001, p. 17), "scientific hypotheses" (Straub et al., 2001, p. 20), "success or failure of the adoption process" (Straub et al., 2001, p. 9), and so forth. This terminology reflects and perpetuates the limited and limiting cultural worldview of its originators (see Tinker, Merino, & Neimark, 1982 in the critical accounting literature). Many cultures in the developing world, such as most South, East, and South-East Asian (both Confucian-influenced and ethnic Indo-Malay), Pacific Island, and Australian Aboriginal cultures value cooperation more highly than competition (Heitmeyer, 2004; Hofstede, 2001; James & Otsuka, 2007; Otsuka & Smith, 2005; Singh, 2004). They also tend to value *achievement through (shared, cooperative) effort* more highly than *achievement through ability* (Chen & Stevenson, 1995; Hess & Azuma, 1991; Otsuka & Smith, 2005; Yee, Otsuka, James, & Leung, 2007). For example, whilst Westerners perceive ability to be largely fixed, East-Asians for regard effort as an important moderating factor which interacts with ability to determine achievement (Chen & Stevenson, 1995; Hess & Azuma, 1991; Otsuka & Smith, 2005; Yee et al., 2007). Furthermore, Westerners, influenced by Aristotle, insist on classifying things according to binary opposites: hot/cold, day/night, success/failure, profit/loss, rich/poor, black/white, and so forth. By contrast, writes the Japanese-Australian educational psychology researcher Setsuo Otsuka (2006), East-Asians, influenced by Zen Buddhism, are much more able and willing to view objects from an integrated and holistic perspective. East-Asians tend to have a much reduced urge to measure and to classify everything that moves (and many things that do not) compared to Westerners.

Within non-Western worldviews, interview and case-based studies (e.g., Alawattage & Wickramasinghe, 2006; Efferin & Hopper, 2007; Otsuka, 2005; Sian, 2006; Uche, 2002; Wickramasinghe & Hopper, 2005; Yee et al., 2007), designed to add insight rather than prove/disprove hypotheses, hold much more promise than "one-size-fits-all" large-sample surveys. Anonymous mass-mailed surveys are likely to be particularly ineffective in cultures that value personal friendships and co-operation much more highly than competition and where an outsider/insider distinction is important. Only Westernized urban elites are likely to be the recipients of such surveys and are also likely to be the only group which is willing to take the time to respond. The reason is that these surveys are produced and disseminated by community "outsiders" to whom no traditional, culture-infused reciprocal obligations are owed.

We strongly encourage future IT Transfer researchers to take into account normative Critical Theory-based arguments (see, e.g., Boyce, 2006; Cordoba, 2007; Jones & Fleming, 2003;

Reid, 2002) which maintain that the process of globalization has increased income inequality both between nations (in Boyce's (2006) words, the Global North and Global South) and within nations (the foreign and indigenous elites vs. the rest; the urban vs. rural populations). Future IT Transfer research should acknowledge a shared commitment to spread around the economic benefits of globalization in a more equitable manner rather than relying implicitly on naïve economic rationalist beliefs such as "a rising tide lifts all boats" (Boyce, 2006). IT Transfer research must move beyond the study of Transnational Corporations (TNCs) (e.g., Nahar et al., 2006) and educated urban indigenous elites (e.g., Nahar et al. 2006; Straub et al., 2001) since these groups are the first to participate in the benefits of IT Transfer and their participation says nothing at all about IT participation rates experienced by either urban nonelites or rural dwellers.

Instead of a positivist quasiscientific research program of hypothesis development and testing (Cordoba, 2007; Klein & Lyytinen, 1985), we urge a plurality of research methods and more extensive use of compassionate, context-anchored qualitative interview and case-based research. A good example within the IS literature of a worldview and research design that we fully support is the pilot case study presented by Cordoba (2007) where focus groups of stakeholders joined the research team to express their views as to how the planned IS system at Colombia's Javeriana University could help to best meet *personal* stakeholder goals and needs. Another relevant example is the paper Al-Mabrouk & Soar (in press) which assesses the viewpoints of various stakeholder groups about how they perceive IT Transfer issues involving the Arab world. In terms of theory (another of the extant IT Transfer literature's weaker points), we recommend Marx's theory of dialectical materialism (Udo & Edoho, 2000, p. 331), which avoids both the need to choose between "rival" hypotheses purely based on statistical outcomes (since a dialectical "system" can quite well accommodate internal contradictions) and the "political quietism" (Tinker, Neimark, & Lehman, 1991) of middle-of-the-road positions.

DIALECTICAL MATERIALISM, GLOBALIZATION, AND IT TRANSFER

Marx introduced many important concepts to the philosophical and economics literatures, and along with Max Weber, is regarded as one of the founding fathers of the modern discipline of sociology (Wallace & Wolf, 2006). Contemporary authors, writing from both neoliberal and post-modern perspectives, have found it very difficult to extinguish what Jacques Derrida famously termed the "spectres of Marx." Others, such as the French philosopher Michel Foucault, much more wisely, have acknowledged their intellectual debt to Marx (Foucault, 1980a, pp. 52-53) and have used his concepts freely (without always acknowledging the source so as to distance themselves from the oppressive definitions of Marx and Marxism found in the discourses of "Marxist journals"). As Foucault (1980a, pp. 52-53) points out, many of Marx's ideas are so an integral to an understanding of society that contemporary writers should and must rely upon them in the same way that a contemporary physicist relies upon Einstein without quoting him by name. Foucault (1980b, pp. 80-81) regards "totalitarian theories" (citing Marxism and psychoanalysis as examples) as providing "useful tools for local research" (even for postmodernists). In fact, Foucault cited heavily from Volume 1 of Marx's *Capital* to develop his argument in *Discipline and Punish* (1979) that the capitalist factory, as a disciplinary and normalizing institution, had come to rely heavily even by Marx's day on professional managers and supervisors to regulate, discipline, and control labour. Two of Marx's most important theories are *historical materialism* and *dialectical materialism*. The focus of this section of our chapter

is the relevance of dialectical materialism to IT Transfer research.

Marx's dialectical materialism, which transforms the concept of the dialectic found in the writings of G.W.F. Hegel, is the cornerstone to a proper exposition and understanding of Marx (Althusser, 2007; Tinker, 2005). Dialectical materialism is based on the thesis-antithesis-synthesis model (Althusser, 2007; Tinker, 2005). Any field of struggle at any point in time has a "thesis" (its most obvious characteristic or manifestation) and its internal, contradictory opposite or "antithesis" and both exist in the whole simultaneously. The internal contradiction posed *within the system* (this is the key point) by the thesis and anti-thesis lead on to the "synthesis" which fuses elements of the thesis and antithesis together and remedies (at least to a certain degree) the original contradiction. In Marxian theory, the ever-increasing production and economic wealth created by capitalism (the thesis) is contrasted with the increasing exploitation and pauperization of the proletariat (antithesis). In original Marxian analysis, the synthesis was presented as being increased working-class consciousness leading to socialism and (through the withering away of the State) communism. Under the re-formulated dialectic of the Frankfurt School (as represented by the work of Theodor W. Adorno, Max Horkheimer, and Herbert Marcuse), the *synthesis* became the incorporation of the proletariat (who suffer from *false consciousness* (Adorno, 1994b) as to the current state of their exploitation) within the existing economic and social mainstream and the entrenchment of consumer capitalism in the West.

Whilst IT Transfer research has very happily expounded upon Marx's thesis (the prospects of using IT to create efficiency and wealth) it has failed to adequately address his antithesis (increasing exploitation of the proletariat associated with capitalism and its power technologies such as IT). The negative effects of IT on income inequality, structural unemployment, poverty, alienation, cultural hegemony and domination, disenfranchisement, and environmental degradation have rarely been explored within the mainstream IT Transfer literature. As such, much of its arguments and conclusions are hopelessly one-sided and unbalanced. More generally, the advantage of a dialectic as opposed to an economic rationalist worldview is that multiple and contradictory insights into the workings of the "system" are permitted, that is, there is not always a pressing need to put "rival hypotheses" to the test using elaborate statistical methods. A researcher using a Critical Theory perspective thus learns to develop the ability to *accept the existence of contradictions*; all that the Critical Theory researcher hopes to achieve is to gain additional insight.

An important method used by Marx in the writing of his magnum opus, Volume 1 of *Capital* (Marx, 1976; Tinker, 1999; Wheen, 2006) can be seen by his decision to begin Chapter 1 of Volume 1 not at the macro, abstract level of (say) "the factory," "surplus value," or "society" but at the microlevel, concrete form of the commodity. Only in Chapter 7 of Volume 1 does Marx move on to consider the pressing issue of the creation of surplus value through unpaid labour time (Bryer, 1999, 2006) within the capitalist production process which some regard as his key theoretical "discovery." However, we should not ignore Tinker's (1999) argument that our focus nowadays should not be so much on the "labour theory of value," which marginalist economists reject, but on the "value theory of labour." Why start with the commodity? There are several reasons. First, Marx's concept of "commodity fetishism" is a refinement of his earlier theory of capitalist-created "alienation" (wrongly claimed by Louis Althusser to be a "left-over" from Marx's early period as a humanist idealist; Althusser, 2005a, 2005b, 2005c). Second, the commodity represents a microcosm of the whole capitalist system: contained within it are the dialectic of use-values (which consumers need for their own well-being) and exchange-values (which capitalists relentlessly pursue) and the dialectic of the wealth creation

of capitalism and the increasing pauperization of the proletariat. Contained within the commodity are both capitalism's greatest achievement and, in Marx's view, the seed of its own ultimate destruction. The commodity contains *within itself* the essence of both capitalism's thesis and antithesis. Everything in *Capital* Volumes 1 to 3 which Marx would later derive is already there within the commodity.

Marx's emphasis on the dialectic of the commodity has relevance for IT Transfer research. We should not be afraid to find internal contradictions in real-world IT Transfer scenarios nor should we be afraid of failures and setbacks regarding IT Transfer in the real world. Localised dialectics of IT Transfer need to be grasped in all of their infuriating complexity. Arguably, case study methods are best equipped to achieve this (although we do not claim that mass mail-out surveys should never be used).

A pressing issue that many authors, both accounting academics (e.g., Boyce, 2006; Everett, 2003; Graham & Neu, 2003) and those from other disciplines (e.g., Held & McGrew, 2002; Hoogvelt, 1997; Jones & Fleming, 2003; Korten, 2001; Nederveen Pieterse, 2002; Reid, 2002; Worthington, 2000) are presently grappling with is globalization, or (as we should say) the dialectic of globalization. Many authors on IT Transfer (e.g., Kahen, 1995, 1996; Straub et al., 2001) assume, however, that globalization is nonproblematic, that is, it is essentially linear, incremental, and progressive, and it creates economic and other benefits for those fortunate enough to be touched by it (the "rising tide lifts all boats" theory of Boyce, 2006). As alluded to above, the costs of globalization are rarely acknowledged by these authors. Important costs of globalization that many authors outside the IT Transfer field are increasingly recognising include environmental degradation (Diamond, 2005); the spread and encouragement of oppressive and unsafe working conditions (Fishman, 2006; Schlosser, 2002); and the increased income inequality which globalization often contributes to, both between and within nation-states (Boyce, 2006; Diamond, 2005; diFazio, 1998; Esposito, Aronowitz, Chancer, diFazio, & Yard, 1998; Jones & Fleming, 2003; Reed, 2002; Schlosser, 2002).

Globalization (of which IT Transfer is but one aspect) is thus full of internal contradictions (i.e., it is dialectical). It is not ambiguously "good" (as many IT Transfer researchers appear to believe) nor is it unambiguously "bad." Quantitative mass-mail surveys *used in isolation* are unlikely to yield researchers sufficiently rich insights into the complexity of the globalization dialectic as it relates to IT Transfer. Intensive case studies using both interviews and archival data are encouraged. Interviews must be conducted with a wide range of individuals, both elite and nonelite, both those working at TNCs and those working at domestic public companies, domestic private companies, and nonprofit organizations. In the words of Bapat (2005, pp. 163-168), Alawattage and Wickramasinghe (2006), Otsuka (2005), and Wickramasinghe and Hopper (2005), "local narratives" are important. Power relations must be understood and critiqued. Human empowerment, human emancipation, and radical social change should be our goals (Cordoba, 2007, pp. 912, 918; James, 2007; Kellner, 1991; Marcuse, 1964, 1968, pp. 28-29; Marcuse & Neumann, n.d.; Tinker, 2005, p. 101; Udo & Edoho, 2000, p. 332). IT Transfer is a worthwhile research area to explore, and it may prove to be a focus of analysis, like the commodity form was for Marx, which will attract the interest of globalization researchers from outside the IT/IS discipline. Non-IT/IS researchers may come to view IT Transfer as a compressed concrete site in which to explore and unpack globalization issues. IT/IS academics need to take the lead in IT Transfer research but, for this research to have a wider impact outside the narrow traditional boundaries of our discipline, researchers must be willing to grapple with the complex issues of the globalization dialectic. There will be no perfect solutions to any problem

no matter how high the R^2 and how significant the t-statistics of any given empirical study may happen to be!

IT Transfer researchers must consider (although it might prove distasteful for some) whether in some localised contexts and from some perspectives *resistance to* IT Transfer might not be a justifiable or even laudable course of action. In the critical accounting literature, using a Foucauldian approach, McPhail (1999) argues that resistance should be expected and even encouraged in particular localised struggles for empowerment and for social change. McPhail (1999) demonstrates that whilst it is true that the mid-period Foucault of *Discipline and Punish* (1979) and *The History of Sexuality Volume 1* (1981) believed that power/knowledge can be a positive force on occasion (e.g., it may lead to improved health care provision), there are often situations which do appear to merit localised resistance. Kahen (1995, 1996, p. 6) talks about localised resistance in Kenya to IT Transfer based on a Kenyan perception that "IT will reduce employment." However, Kahen (1995, 1996) unfortunately regards such a state of affairs only in the negative rather than as a localised struggle that may well be justified (or at the very least needs to be engaged with and understood, through respectful dialogue and detailed interview-based research). Such Kenyan concerns should not be so easily dismissed. Kahen (1996) and similar authors are advised to understand the internal contradictions of the dialectic: IT Transfer is not, and should not be viewed as being, always linear, incremental, and progressive. A rising tide may well *not* lift all boats. IT Transfer is a contested site (Tinker et al., 1991) where a multitude of backgrounds, life and work experiences and cultural beliefs may encounter one another and where some form of clash may be inevitable and often even desirable. In addition, a Critical Theory-based normative version of Stakeholder Theory, which accepts Reed's (2002) proposition that TNCs operating in developing countries have *additional normative ethical obligations* to stakeholders, is recommended as a way to disentangle and address conflicting views and better meet pressing stakeholder needs (Cordoba, 2007).

CRITIQUE OF THE MAINTAINED ASSUMPTIONS OF TWO PAPERS FROM THE MAINSTREAM IT TRANSFER LITERATURE

This last section of our chapter critiques articles by Nahar et al. (2006) and Straub et al. (2001) so as to highlight some emerging issues with, and limitations of, the typical "mainstream" approach to IT Transfer research and its rarely challenged maintained assumptions. These two articles were not selected by us because they are "worse" than any others but because their approach is typical of our field. Critique on these two papers will provide a focus for our discussion in this section. Since our chapter is written as a polemic, a complete literature review of the IT Transfer area is not necessary.

Nahar et al. (2006) claim to identify success factors for IT-supported information technology transfer. Whilst, commendably, these authors regard IT Transfer as both "complex" and "risky" (p. 663), they quickly fall back on the naïve economic rationalist maintained assumption that IT Transfer "provides benefits for all parties" (p. 663). What about the costs? Do the authors mean benefits net of all costs? Surely we must go beyond mere assertion here. If only parties legally contracting with the firm are being considered, what about other stakeholders and society's disadvantaged? Why assume that even those who enter into legal contracts only do so if the expected outcome is favourable? What about members of the proletariat who are forced to sell their labour power on the market-place in order to survive? We are reminded here also of such people as the 15-20% of American Wal-Mart customers discussed in Fishman (2006) who despise the corporation but shop there

anyway due to limited alternative options and the constraints imposed by their budgets. Wal-Mart may provide these people with (net financial) "benefits" as consumers but as human beings they hate the corporation with a passion. Nahar et al.'s (2006) untested maintained assumption of "benefits to all parties" puts a halt on further discourse (who can argue with benefits?); ignores the social, economic and political context (Bapat, 2005; Boyce, 2006; Jones & Fleming, 2003; Sy & Tinker, 2006); and amounts to a justification for the sociopolitical status quo (Adorno, 1994a, pp. 78, 164).

The Nahar et al. (2006, p. 664) paper gives us readers the usual, unsubstantiated marketing-speak about the claimed benefits of IT. However, the marketing-speak presented could have been copy-pasted from the first chapter of a first-year undergraduate text. It reveals nothing but such discussions appear to be par for the course for the first few pages of any IT Transfer paper (e.g., see also Udo & Edoho, 2000, pp. 329-331). To cite Nahar et al. (2006, p. 664):

Information technology can increase capacity as well as decrease costs of information storage, processing, and communication. IT adds value to an organization by providing support to the administrative infrastructure, business processes, and the operational skills of the staff. IT increases global connectivity, overcomes distance, decreases time barriers, reduces communication costs, cuts cost through automation, facilitates information sharing, and facilitates access to the advice of remote experts.

Numerous sources are cited to back up these assertions, but we have to wonder why the authors bother. Since when do platitudes need to be referenced? The only thing that matters, according to the authors, is "value to the organization," presumably meaning maximized share market price. Surely a more sophisticated model, which incorporates effects on diverse stakeholders, is warranted here (Cordoba, 2007). For their part, labour process theorists Kala Saravanamuthu and

Tony Tinker (2003) went far beyond Nahar et al. (2006) when they argued that senior management have a complicated dual obligation to *both* capital and labour. Nahar et al. (2006) unfortunately make no attempt to grapple with such issues (and neither does fellow IT Transfer researcher Kahen, 1995, 1996). We are in urgent need of a holistic and integrated Critical Theory inspired "critical IT literature" and "critical IT Transfer literature."

Nahar et al.'s (2006) study is not specifically concerned with the impact of cultural factors on IT Transfer "success." However, some comments are in order on this point. The very notion of "successful implementation" reveals substantial hidden cultural baggage. The focus on "success" as though it were an objective, out-there, verifiable reality, separate from our perceptions, reflects the importance that Anglo-American culture, as seen in its love for professional sports, places on competitive notions such as "winning" and "success." We observe the word "success" and its variants littered throughout the Nahar et al. (2006) paper from the Abstract right through to the Conclusions (Section 7, commencing on p. 672). But isn't the whole notion of "success" culturally determined? We have seen the confusion created by analogies taken from the sports field in the discourse on the "War on Terror" led by the "Coalition of the Willing." (How would President George W. Bush define "success" in Iraq? How would anyone even know what success should look like in such a context?) Returning to the IT Transfer literature, does "success" include a healthier environment, improved working conditions, more supportive and nurturing family relationships, more community recognition of the arts, and more funding for education, health, and disadvantaged groups? If not, why not? If not, why not just replace the word "success" with less value-laden, less misleading, and less culturally-bound terminology such as "market share increase," "share price maximization," or "profit maximization"? This is unlikely to happen in the IT Transfer literature,

unfortunately, because quite frankly we Westerners like the word success.

The use of the word "success" we argue is one of the primary marketing tools that the IT Transfer literature has used to sell, justify, and reproduce itself. Writing instead "share price maximization" just would not cut it. These words are too dry. Why does the word "success" appeal so much to us as Westerners? Let us just admit it. We *want* to be successful. We think we know what the word means and we do not object to its use in the slightest. Visions of gleefully lifting up a championship trophy for first place in a swimming race or basketball tournament, backed by the cheer of an adoring crowd, fills our minds at the mere mention of the word. Through primary school sports days and similar mechanisms, we are culturally indoctrinated from a very early age about the crucial importance of winning and success. As Adorno (1994a, p. 81) in his penetrating sociological analysis of the astrology column in the *Los Angeles Times* points out, the clear message of that column to its audience of trained dependents is that "the only thing that really counts [in life] is success". Equally importantly, focus by Nahar et al. (2006) on the word "success" obscures for us two key questions: "successful *from whose perspective*?" and "successful *for* which social actors?" (If you think that we have just written the same question twice, please re-read carefully.)

Although Nahar et al. (2006) present an Appendix A entitled "Ranking of success factors by recursive branch and bound method: a description" designed to suitably impress those who have never thought to question the prevailing dominant hegemony of Western technological-rationality (Adorno, 1994a; Marcuse, 1964; Weber, 1968), we are provided with zero information as to the identities and backgrounds of focus group participants and interviewees. We had to check the paper several times to make sure we were not in error here. Amazingly, the very detailed and verbose Section 4 (pp. 665-667) entitled "Research design and methods" does not provide any information about who the focus group and interview participants actually were. No doubt they were part of the sophisticated urban elite, our cherished "in-group" (Adorno, 1994a, p. 22). Were they MBA students and/or business leaders? Were they from the major corporations? We might think so if "success" is what we love most and if we define "success" in the standard Anglo-American way. However, what will the views of such ruling educated elites tell us of the views and experiences of our most marginalized citizens—the poor, African Americans, Native Americans, Hispanics, Australian Aboriginals, western Sydney Lebanese Muslims; in Emmanuel Levinas' (1969; Everett, 2007; Stratton, 1998) words, "The Other" or, as Bauman (1989; Crook, 1994, p. 10) put it, our "conceptual Jew," that is, our "defining and threatening Other?" Why are such groups excluded from the dominant discourse in IT journals? Maybe they could share with us (if only we were interested to listen) valuable insights as to why our IT Transfer "success rate" is as low as we seem to think it is (Bapat, 2005, chap. 7). Even the four fictional case studies presented to the study participants in the Nahar et al. (2006) study are exclusively "large" companies (pp. 667-669) and/or "multinationals" (pp. 667-668). Why? Surely these are the companies most proficient in IT who are able to ensure widespread standardization of technologies and processes within group member companies (Quattrone & Hopper, 2005; Yee et al., 2007). IT Transfer is less likely to suffer major implementation problems in these companies and, if it does, surely the companies bear the attached responsibility due to their inefficiency and clumsiness.

Case studies of small companies, not-for-profit organizations, and traditional communities would surely provide additional useful insight into why IT Transfer is *most uneven* and *difficult to achieve* in the real-world. It would allow us to see clearly one major, as yet largely unacknowledged, inhibitor to IT Transfer in developing countries: *Not everyone works for a TNC!* (This sentence should be re-read slowly to ensure that it sinks in.) Not even everyone (although admittedly many do) spend as much as a year of their working lives at a TNC during which time they can learn IT and transfer it to their later (smaller) workplaces.

We now move on to discuss the Straub et al. (2001) paper. Straub et al. (2001) entire focus is on (perceived) "successful outcomes" of IT Transfer projects (their sole dependent variable in all their tests). The unashamed success focus reflects the American cultural bias of the all-American author team (indeed a "multidisciplinary" author team, they proudly tell us, but not a multi-national or multi-ethnic one since all three of the authors are listed as being affiliated with US institutions and all have European sounding family names). Firmly entrenched in the Anglo-American mind is ingrained dichotomous "win/loss" thinking. It is the worldview and language of American sports. The authors should realise that they are constraining the world to fit their Western technical-rational worldview (Adorno, 1994a; Marcuse, 1964; Weber, 1968), which is all the more problematic since they are specifically aiming to assess the impact of one claimed feature of Arab culture on the perceived "success" of IT Transfer. There is a literature in educational psychology (e.g., Hein & Lehman, 1999) which argues that members of some ethnic groups tend to be more self-critical of their own abilities and their own achievements than members of other ethnic groups (e.g., East-Asians more critical, Westerners much less so). This is an established research finding in the educational psychology literature. To illustrate this point, a Japanese student scoring 61% on a test might self-report her performance after-the-fact as "poor" whereas a Westerner scoring the same 61% might classify her performance after-the-fact as "fair" or even as "good." The findings of this literature, of which Straub et al. (2001) appear unaware, renders the self-reporting of perceived implementation success by Straub et al. (2001) Arab respondents somewhat problematic. Self-reporting of success outcomes may not be as objective and reliable as Straub et al. (2001) and like-minded researchers assume. As Nietzsche (1994, section 32) writes:

The gauge by which we measure, our own nature, is no unchangeable quantity; we have moods and vacillations; yet we would have to know ourselves to be a fixed gauge if we were to evaluate fairly the relationship of any one thing to ourselves.

Incidentally, Straub et al. (2001, p. 19) conclude by saying that their "findings generally support the contemporary critical theory literature." However, it is hard to know exactly which "critical theory" they are referring to since the names Adorno, Habermas, Horkheimer, and Marcuse are missing from their (extensive) Reference list. Terms such as Critical Theory have precise technical meanings in the sociology discipline (as the term IT Transfer has in ours) and should not be used by IT Transfer researchers in an ad-hoc fashion.

To conclude the discussion in this section, we argue that extensive use of the word "success" in the IT Transfer literature is problematic for several reasons: (a) the notion of success is culturally determined; (b) even if all cultures agree on what success is, members of some cultural groups are more self-critical of their own achievements than those of other social groups; and (c) it obscures the vital questions: "successful *from whose perspective*?" and "successful *for* which social actors?"

We close this section by recommend the following:

a. Use context-anchored, compassionate qualitative case study research as well as or in place of mass mail-out surveys so as to fully capture the richness and complexity of dialectical real-world settings;

b. Use Western dichotomous notions of "success" and "successful implementation" only with extreme caution, after due self-reflection, and after banning oneself from

watching, listening to, or reading about any professional sporting match for at least a three-week period;

c. Team with co-researchers from other ethnic backgrounds and/or nationalities so as to provide alternative perspectives and a safeguard against unreflexively applying dominant culture worldviews to members of non-dominant and/or non-Western cultures;

d. Teach oneself some introductory sociology and philosophy (focus on key authors and texts) so as to bring a socially and culturally informed worldview to the research project and so that one does not "re-invent the wheel" (after studying these disciplines one is much less likely to routinely separate the "economic" from the "social" in any given setting); and

e. If IT Transfer researchers want to continue to strictly adhere to "win/loss" thinking, then using numbers extracted from published financial statements and/or internal cost accounting reports might be a way around the self-reporting bias problem. Joint research with accounting academics offers promise in this regard.

CONCLUSION

This chapter critiques some of the existing Information Technology (IT) Transfer literature and suggests that it has fallen victim to the well-known limitations of an economic rationalist and positivist worldview. In particular we challenge the extensive use of the term "success" in the IT Transfer literature, arguing that it is problematic for several reasons: (a) the notion of success is culturally determined; (b) even if all cultures agree on what success is, members of some cultural groups are more self-critical of their own achievements than those of other social groups; and (c) it obscures the vital questions: "successful *from whose perspective?*" and "successful *for which social actors?*" Mainstream IT Transfer research portrays IT Transfer as primarily linear, incremental and progressive in line with the economic rationalist belief that a "rising tide lifts all boats" (Boyce, 2006). We suggest Marx's theory of dialectical materialism as an alternative to the dominant hegemony and encourage researchers in IT Transfer to accept the fact that internal contradictions are part of a dialectic system. We also encourage IT Transfer researchers to view local resistance more sympathetically. Concerted efforts should be made to understand and dialog with the Other. In Bapat's (2005) words, "local narratives" are important. Overall we recommend, in the spirit of Major and Hopper (2005) and Wickramasinghe and Hopper (2005) in the critical accounting literature and Otsuka (2005) in the sociology of education literature, more interview-based case study research in the IT Transfer area. Interview based research is preferable to mass-mail out surveys, not only because of the richness and depth of insight they provide the researcher but also that they are a more culturally appropriate research tool in non-Western countries where personal friendships and the concept of an "in-group" are so important. This chapter also presents a view that the extant mainstream IT Transfer literature's preoccupation with educated urban elites and TNCs may prove to be an additional hindrance to both our increased understanding of localised struggles and radical social change.

ACKNOWLEDGMENT

We would like to thank Dr. Setsuo Otsuka (Charles Sturt University, Australia) for his sincere collegiality and the many insights he has shared with us regarding Japanese and East-Asian cultural characteristics and ways of looking at the world. We also gratefully acknowledge the helpful comments of two anonymous reviewers for this chapter and the editors of this book (Dr. Aileen Cater-Steel and Dr. Latif Al Hakim).

REFERENCES

Adorno, T. W. (1994a). The stars down to earth. In S. Crook (Ed.), *The stars down to earth and other essays on the irrational in culture* (pp. 46-171). London and New York, NY: Taylor & Francis Group Routledge Classics.

Adorno, T. W. (1994b). Theses against occultism. In S. Crook (Ed.), *The stars down to earth and other essays on the irrational in culture* (pp. 173-180). London and New York, NY: Taylor & Francis Group Routledge Classics.

Alawattage, C., & Wickramasinghe, D. (2006). Appearance of accounting in a political hegemony. *Critical Perspectives on Accounting.* Retrieved June 1, 2008, from www.sciencedirect.com

Al-Mabrouk, K., & Soar, J. (in press). A Delphi study on issues for successful information technology transfer in the Arab World. *The International Arab Journal of Information Technology.*

Althusser, L. (2005a). On the young Marx. In *For Marx* (Chapter 2, pp. 49-86). London and New York, NY: Verso.

Althusser, L. (2005b). The 1844 manuscripts of Karl Marx. In *For Marx* (Chapter 5, pp. 153-160). London and New York, NY: Verso.

Althusser, L. (2005c). Marxism and humanism. In *For Marx* (Chapter 7, pp. 219-248). London and New York, NY: Verso.

Althusser, L. (2007). *Politics and history: Montesquieu, Rousseau, Marx.* London and New York, NY: Verso.

Bapat, J. (2005). *Development projects and critical theory of environment.* New Delhi, India: Sage Publications.

Bauman, Z. (1989). *Modernity and the holocaust.* Cambridge: Polity Press.

Boyce, G. (2006). The social relevance of ethics education in a global(ising) era: From individual dilemmas to systemic crises. *Critical Perspectives on Accounting. Retrieved June 1, 2008, from* www.sciencedirect.com

Bryer, R. A. (1999). A Marxist critique of the FASB's conceptual framework. *Critical Perspectives on Accounting, 10*(5), 551-589.

Bryer, R. A. (2006). Accounting and control of the labour process. *Critical Perspectives on Accounting, 17*(5), 551-598.

Chen, C., & Stevenson, H. W., with Hayward, C., & Burgess, S. (1995). Culture and academic achievement: ethnic and cross-national differences. In M. L. Maehr and P. R. Pintrich (Eds.), *Advances in motivation and achievement: Culture, motivation and achievement* (Volume 9, pp. 119-151). Greenwich, CT: JAL Press.

Cordoba, J.-R. (2007). Developing inclusion and critical reflection in information systems planning. *Organization Connexions, 14*(6), 909-927.

Crook, S. (1994), Introduction: Adorno and authoritarian irrationalism. In S. Crook (Ed.), *The stars down to earth and other essays on the irrational in culture* (pp. 1-45). London and New York, NY: Taylor & Francis Group Routledge Classics.

Diamond, J. (2005). *Collapse: How societies choose to fail or survive.* Camberwell: Penguin.

diFazio, W. (1998). Poverty, the postmodern and the jobless future. *Critical Perspectives on Accounting, 9*(1), 57-74.

Efferin, S., & Hopper, T. (2007). Management control, culture and ethnicity in a Chinese Indonesian company. *Accounting, Organizations and Society, 32*, 223-262.

Esposito, D., Aronowitz, S., Chancer, L., diFazio, W., & Yard, M. (1998). The (in)spectre returns! Global capital and the future of work. *Critical Perspectives on Accounting, 9*(1), 7-54.

Everett, J. (2003). Globalisation and its new spaces for (alternative) accounting research. *Accounting Forum, 27*(4), 400-424.

Fishman, C. (2006). *The Wal-Mart effect: How an out-of-town superstore became a superpower.* New York: Allen Lane.

Foucault, M. (1979). *Discipline and punish: The birth of the prison.* London: Penguin Books.

Foucault, M. (1980a). Prison talk: An interview with J.-J. Brochier. In C. Gordon (Ed.), *Power/Knowledge: Selected interviews and other writings, 1972-1977* (Chapter 3, pp. 37-54). New York: Random House.

Foucault, M. (1980b). Two lectures. In C. Gordon (Ed.), *Power/Knowledge: Selected interviews and other writings, 1972-1977* (Chapter 5, pp. 78-108). New York: Random House.

Foucault, M. (1986). *The care of the self: The history of sexuality volume 3.* London: Penguin Books.

Foucault, M. (1987). *The use of pleasure: The history of sexuality volume 2.* London: Penguin Books.

Graham, C., & Neu, D. (2003). Accounting for globalization. *Accounting Forum, 27*(4), 449-471.

Hein, S. J., & Lehman, D. R. (1999). Culture, self-discrepancies, and self-satisfaction. *Personality & Social Psychology Bulletin, 25*(8), 915-925.

Heitmeyer, D. (2004). It's not a race: Aboriginality and education. In J. Allen (Ed), *Sociology of education: Possibilities and practices* (3rd ed.) (Chapter 10, pp. 220-249). Southbank: Social Science Press.

Held, D., & McGrew, A. (2002). *Globalization/ anti-globalization*. Cambridge: Polity.

Hess, R. D., & Azuma, H. (1991). Cultural support for schooling: Contrasts between Japan and the United States. *Educational Researcher, 20*(9), 2-8, 12.

Hofstede, G. (2001). *Culture's consequences: Comparing values, behaviors, institutions and organizations across nations* (2nd ed.). Thousand Oaks, CA: Sage Publications.

Hoogvelt, A. (1997). *Globalisation and the post-colonial world; The new political economy of development*. London: Macmillan.

James, K. (2007). A critical theory and postmodernist approach to the teaching of accounting theory. *Critical Perspectives on Accounting*. Retrieved June 1, 2008, from www.sciencedirect.com.

James, K., & Otsuka, S. (2007). International Chinese graduates and the Australian public accounting industry. Working Paper, University of Southern Queensland, Australia.

Jones, M. T., & Fleming, P. (2003). Unpacking complexity through critical stakeholder analysis: The case of globalization. *Business & Society, 42*(4), 430-454.

Kahen, G. (1995). Assessment of information technology for developing countries: Appropriateness, local constraints, IT characteristics and impacts. *International Journal of Computer and Applications Technology, 8*(5/6), 325-332.

Kahen, G. (1996). Building a framework for successful information technology transfer to developing countries: Requirements and effective integration to a viable IT transfer. *International Journal of Computer and Applications Technology, 9*(1), 1-8.

Kellner, D. (1991). Introduction to the second edition. In *One-dimensional man: Studies in the ideology of advanced industrial society* (pp. xi–xxxix). Boston, MA: Beacon Press.

Klein, H., & Lyytinen, K. (1985). The poverty of scientism in information systems. In E. Mumford, R. Hirschheim, B. Fitzgerald, & A. T. Wood-Harper (Eds.), *Research methods in information systems: Proceedings of the IFIP colloquium* (pp. 131-161). Amsterdam: New Holland.

Korten, D. (2001). *When corporations rule the world*. Bloomfield: Kumarian Press and Berrett-Koehler.

Major, M., & Hopper, T. (2005). Managers divided: Implementing ABC in a Portuguese telecommunications company. *Management Accounting Research, 16*, 205-229.

Marcuse, H. (1964). *One-dimensional man: Studies in the ideology of advanced industrial society*. Boston, MA: Beacon Press.

Marcuse, H. (1968). The struggle against liberalism in the totalitarian view of the state. In *Negations: Essays in Critical Theory* (Chapter 1, pp. 3-42). London: Allen Lane The Penguin Press.

Marcuse, H., & Neumann, F. (n.d.). *A history of the doctrine of social change*. Unpublished manuscript in the Marcuse Archive.

Marx, K. H. (1976). *Capital: A critique of political economy volume 1*. London: Penguin Books.

Marx, K. H. (1994). Critique of the Gotha Program. In L. H. Simon (Ed.), *Selected writings* (pp. 315-332). Indianapolis, IN: Hackett Publishing.

McPhail, K. (1999). The threat of ethical accountants: An application of Foucault's concept of ethics to accounting education and some thoughts on ethically educating for the other. *Critical Perspectives on Accounting, 10*(6), 833-866.

Nahar, N., Lyytinen, K., Huda, N., & Muravyov, S. V. (2006). Success factors for information technology supported information technology transfer: Finding expert consensus. *Information & Management, 43,* 663-677.

Nederveen Pieterse, J. (2002). Globalization, kitsch and conflict: Technologies of work, war and politics. *Review of International Political Economy, 9*(1), 1-36.

Nietzsche, F. (1973). *Beyond good and evil.* London: Penguin Books.

Nietzsche, F. (1990). *Twilight of the idols.* London: Penguin Books.

Nietzsche, F. (1994). *Human, all too human.* London: Penguin Books.

Otsuka, S. (2005). *Cultural influences on academic performance in Fiji: A case study in the Nadroga/Navosa Province.* Unpublished doctoral dissertation, University of Sydney, Australia.

Otsuka, S. (2006). Multicultural classroom in the 21st Century: A case of cross-cultural interaction between Australians and Japanese. In J. Zajda (Ed.), *Equity, access and democracy in education.* Melbourne, Australia: James Nicholas Publishers.

Otsuka, S., & Smith, I. D. (2005). Educational applications of the expectancy-value model of achievement motivation in the diverse cultural contexts of the west and east. *Change: Transformations in Education, 8*(1), 91-109.

Pataki, T. (2007). *Against religion.* Melbourne, Australia: Scribe Publications.

Quattrone, P., & Hopper, T. (2005). A time-space odyssey: Management control systems in two multinational organizations. *Accounting Organizations and Society, 30*(7/8), 735-764.

Reid, D. (2002). Employing normative stakeholder theory in developing countries. *Business & Society, 41*(2), 166-207.

Saravanamuthu, K., & Tinker, T. (2003). Politics of managing: The dialectic of control. *Accounting, Organizations and Society, 28*(1), 37-64.

Schlosser, E. (2002). *Fast food nation: What the all-American meal is doing to the world.* London: Penguin Books.

Sian, S. (2006). Inclusion, exclusion and control: The case of the Kenyan accounting professionalisation project. *Accounting, Organizations and Society, 31*(3), 295-322.

Singh, M. (2004). Enabling Australia: Responsive education and global movements of people. In J. Allen (Ed), *Sociology of education: Possibilities and practices* (3rd ed.) (Chapter 9, pp. 197-219). Southbank: Social Science Press.

Stratton, J. (1998). *Race daze: Australia in identity crisis.* Annandale: Pluto Press.

Straub, D. W., Loch, K. D., & Hill, C. E. (2001, October-December). Transfer of information technology to the Arab world: A test of cultural influence modelling. *Journal of Global Information Management,* 6-28.

Sy, A., & Tinker, T. (2006). Bury Pacioli in Africa: A bookkeeper's reification of accountancy. *Abacus, 42*(1), 105-127.

Tinker, T. (1999). Mickey Marxism rides again! *Critical Perspectives on Accounting, 10*(5), 643-670.

Tinker, T. (2005). The withering of criticism: A review of professional, Foucauldian, ethnographic, and epistemic studies in accounting. *Accounting, Auditing & Accountability Journal, 18*(1), 100-135.

Tinker, A. M., Merino, B. D., & Neimark, M. D. (1982). The normative origins of positive theories: ideology and accounting thought. *Accounting, Organizations and Society, 7*(2), 167-200.

Tinker, T., Neimark, M., & Lehman, C. (1991). Falling down the hole in the middle of the road: political quietism in corporate social reporting. *Accounting, Auditing & Accountability Journal, 4*(2).

Uche, C. U. (2002). Professional accounting development in Nigeria: Threats from the inside and outside. *Accounting, Organizations and Society, 27,* 471-496.

Udo, G. J., & Edoho, F. M. (2000). Information technology transfer to African nations: An economic development mandate. *Journal of Technology Transfer, 25,* 329-342.

Wallace, R. A., & Wolf, A. (2006). *Contemporary sociological theory: Expanding the classical tradition* (6th ed.). Upper Saddle River, NJ: Pearson Prentice-Hall.

Weber, M. (1968). *Economy and society, volumes I, II and III.* New York: Bedminster.

Wheen, F. (2006). *Marx's das kapital: A biography.* Crows Nest: Allen & Unwin.

Wickramasinghe, D., & Hopper, T. (2005). A cultural political economy of management accounting controls: A case study of a textile mill in a traditional Sinhalese village. *Critical Perspectives on Accounting, 16*(4), 473-503.

Worthington, R. (2000). *Rethinking globalization: Production, politics, actions.* New York: Peter Lang.

Yee, C. S.-L., Otsuka, S., James, K., & Leung J. K.-S. (2007). *How does Japanese culture affect budgeting? A pilot study and research agenda.* Working Paper, University of Southern Queensland, Australia.

Chapter V
The Challenge of Transdisciplinarity in Information Systems Research:
Towards an Integrative Platform

João Porto de Albuquerque
University of Sao Paulo, Brazil

Edouard J. Simon
University of Hamburg, Germany

Jan-Hendrik Wahoff
University of Hamburg, Germany

Arno Rolf
University of Hamburg, Germany

ABSTRACT

Research in the Information Systems (IS) field has been characterised by the use of a variety of methods and theoretical underpinnings. This fact recently raised concerns about the rigour of scientific results of IS research and about the legitimacy of the IS academic field. On the other hand, a number of IS researchers have argued for a view that values diversity as a strength of the IS field. This chapter supports this viewpoint and analyzes the relation between IS research and concepts originating from theoretical debates around transdisciplinarity. We present results from a group of researchers of various disciplinary backgrounds towards an integrative platform for the orientation of transdisciplinary IS research. The Mikropolis platform provides researchers with a common language, allowing the integration of different perspectives through exchange of experiences and mutual understanding. We also discuss some practical issues that arise from the transdisciplinary cooperation in IS research.

INTRODUCTION

Research on Information Systems (IS) is constantly faced with the challenge of addressing the complexity of sociotechnical systems. As a problem-oriented field of study, IS research is concerned with the interplay between information and communication technologies (ICTs) and the organisational and societal contexts in which technologies are used, generally under the assumption that the outcomes of technology use depend as much on characteristics of the technology as on organisational and social actions that shape them (Avgerou, 2000).

While this common epistemic interest demarcates and to some extent unifies the IS field, a great variety of research approaches and methods have been used in IS research. This theoretical and methodological diversity can be traced back to the manifold disciplinary origins of IS from computer science and applied social sciences like organisation studies, management science, and organisational psychology. Thus, in addition to the traditional theoretical paradigm of *organisational rationalism* originated from concepts of the management and organisational sciences (Avgerou, 2000), recent IS sociotechnical research also builds upon theories from social sciences such as structuration theory (Orlikowski, 2000), critical theory (Ngwenyama & Lee, 1997), and actor-network theory (Monteiro & Hanseth, 1996).[1] Several corresponding research methods from the social sciences are used in IS research, both of *quantitative* (e.g., surveys) and *qualitative* nature (e.g., case study, ethnomethodology). Indeed, a recent survey (Glass, Ramesh, & Vessey, 2004) supports the picture of IS as an applied discipline that applies concepts of other disciplines.

The diversity of approaches and methods and the consequent lack of a unified theoretical core has generated concerns about the legitimacy of IS as an academic discipline (Benbasat & Zmud, 2003). Countering this viewpoint, a number of authors regard pluralism rather as necessary for the IS research to cope with the complex and multidimensional issues studied (Mingers, 2001). Following this line, Lyytinen and King (2004) propose the metaphor for the IS discipline as a "market of ideas in which scholars and practitioners exchange their views regarding the design and management of information and associated technologies in organized human enterprise"(p. 221). As such, the theoretical and methodological diversity of IS is seen as a valuable resource for the plasticity of the research in response to changes in ICT and organisation forms (Lyytinen & King, 2004).

Therefore, to fulfil its mission and address the complexity of IS and social practices, IS research should not harden and restrict itself to a theoretical "core" orthodoxy (Benbasat & Zmud, 2003), but rather dare the challenge of developing strategies for dealing with multiple research approaches, integrating different methods of inquiry, and articulating diverse theoretical backgrounds. Facing this challenge means replacing the hierarchical and homogeneous mode of scientific practice by a new form characterised by complexity, hybridity, nonlinearity, reflexivity, heterogeneity, and transdisciplinarity—the Mode 2 knowledge production described by Gibbons, Limoges, Nowotny, Schwartzman, Scott, and Trow (1994). Thus, a transdisciplinary approach to IS does not strive for a one-dimensional synthesis of the object IS around a unified theory at the centre, but assumes that the complex and intertwined relations between ICTs and human practices must be approached in multiple ways. Each of these perspectives sheds a different light to the understanding of the multidimensional object studied.

This chapter[2] argues for the relevance of transdisciplinarity for IS research by contrastively analysing the theoretical underpinnings of transdisciplinarity and IS, and thereafter reporting about practical experiences towards a transdisciplinary approach to IS research. This approach builds upon multidisciplinary collaboration, in which a group of practitioners and researches with diverse disciplinary backgrounds (psychology, political science, IS, computer science, sociology) works together on related themes. To enable communication and articulation among the different perspectives involved, we use the *Mikropolis* platform (Krause, Rolf, Christ, & Simon, 2006; Simon, Janneck, & Gumm, 2006) that provides us with a common exchange language and a unifying research concern, thereby allowing us to transpose disciplinary boundaries. Nevertheless, each researcher uses the researcher's own methods and has additional particular research interests. We press the argument that this approach has the advantage of producing results enriched by the multiple perspectives, whilst also providing a critical feedback to the theoretical basis.

The rest of the chapter is organised as follows. First, we discuss the meaning of the interrelated terms interdisciplinarity and transdisciplinarity and their relation to IS research. We then briefly present the main concepts and perspectives of the *Mikropolis* platform. Thereafter, we describe our experience of transdisciplinary work using Mikropolis, analysing difficulties, challenges, and lessons learned. Finally, we present our concluding remarks and prospects for future work.

BACKGROUND

Inter- and Transdisciplinarity

Transdisciplinarity and the related term interdisciplinarity are generally opposed to pluri- or crossdisciplinarity. The latter two refer to a form of cooperation among different scientific disciplines that does not change the existing disciplinary and theoretical structures. Thus, the result of pluri- or crossdisciplinary research can be characterised as a juxtaposition or uncoordinated collage of pieces stemming from diverse disciplinary traditions. Interdisciplinarity, in turn, involves collaboration and cross-fertilisation among disciplines, so

that concepts and methods perceived as useful that originate from different disciplines are put together to achieve common problem definitions, terminologies and methods. The research results are thus a unified whole, and this process can indeed yield new disciplines (For more details about different forms of interdisciplinary practice and terminology variations see, for instance, Balsiger, 2005; Jantsch, 1972).

The term *transdisciplinarity* was coined in the 1970s, and it was defined in the first international seminar on interdisciplinarity as "a common system of axioms for a set of disciplines" (Klein, 2004). Meanwhile, the term has broadened its meaning and has been related to a mode of knowledge production called *Mode 2*, which is distinct from the traditional mode, or Mode 1 (Gibbons et al., 1994). The Mode 1 of knowledge production is characterised by being a discipline-based form of research, which therefore adheres to the values and principles of a specific scientific discipline. On the other hand, Mode 2 transcends disciplinary borders. In Mode 2, it is no longer a specific discipline that drives knowledge production, but rather the search for solutions to real-world problems taken out of mutually defined problem settings in the application context. Therefore, in Mode 2 it is not academia alone which produces and then redistributes knowledge, but the processes of knowledge production cut across the domains of academia and application context. Accordingly, Mode 2 may be characterised as being complex, hybrid, nonlinear, reflexive, heterogeneous, and transdisciplinary (Gibbons et al., 1994). As such, transdisciplinarity is the privileged form of knowledge production in Mode 2, corresponding to "a movement beyond disciplinary structures in the constitution of the intellectual agenda, in the manner in which resources are deployed, and in the ways in which research is organised, results communicated and the outcome evaluated" (Gibbons et al., 1994, p. 27).

In contrast with interdisciplinarity, a characteristic of transdisciplinary research is that the problems to be researched originate from nonscientific application contexts, and they are formulated in these contexts independently of scientific theories and disciplinary definitions (Balsiger, 2005). In this manner, the philosopher Mittelstraß places transdisciplinarity in the interface between the two systems "science" and "society" (Balsiger, 2005). Differently from a mere applied research though, transdisciplinarity does not proceed by segmenting a predefined problem into smaller parts each to be solved by a specific discipline or method (as usual in applied research), but involves a genuine integration and communication among researchers with different disciplinary perspectives, and among these and the people of the application context (Balsiger, 2005).

Klein (2004) adds to these features of transdisciplinarity the acknowledgement of multidimensionality. Based on the works of the physicist Basarab Nicolescu, she argues that "transdisciplinarity requires deconstruction, which accepts that an object can pertain to different levels of reality, with attendant contradictions, paradoxes and conflicts" (Klein, 2004, p. 524). According to this view, a transdisciplinary approach should not strive to achieve a one-dimensional theory or methodology—for such a procedure would imply the creation of yet another discipline. Instead, transdisciplinarity is capable of taking into account the "flow of information circulating between various branches of knowledge," and achieving a coherent whole that preserves the multidimensional aspect of the object of study (Klein, 2004). Thus, transdisciplinarity call into question disciplinary thinking, while pluri-, cross-, and interdisciplinarity do not.

But what is the position of the IS field in this picture? The next section explores this relation.

IS Research and Transdisciplinarity

As regards the definition of the object of study and the relation of IS to the so-called "reference" disciplines (Keen, 1987), we may infer that IS has an interdisciplinary nature. Indeed, the IS field has drawn on concepts and methods from a number of different disciplines and research traditions, putting them together to address issues that arise in the interplay between ICTs and social and organisational practices. Were we to accept the demands of Benbasat and Zmud (2003) for the establishment of a well-defined and constant disciplinary "core" for IS, research in the IS field would be "disciplined"; that is, fixed boundaries would be defined for the undertaking of IS research on the basis of a limited number of chosen concepts, methods, and concerns. We would see here the birth of a new interdisciplinary discipline, similarly to what happened to other fields like for example socio-biology arising from sociology and biology.

Such unification could only be achieved at the expense of expurgating from the plural body of research in the IS field works that are not aligned with the proposed "core"—for Benbasat and Zmud (2003) the strict adherence to topics "closely related" to the IT artefact and to organisations—and preventing future research that uses alternative thematic, concepts, and approaches to be accepted in the IS field. In fact, the proposal of a narrow focus for computing disciplines is not new and has a parallel in the positions of formalists like Dijkstra (1989), who defended the setting up of a firewall between the problems of formal *correctness*—to be explored by computing researchers—and that of *pleasantness* of use—to be addressed by other disciplines like psychology.[3]

Nevertheless, there are many researchers that question the underlying premise of the argument of Benbasat and Zmud (2003) which see diversity as a threat for the scientific rigour of the IS field—for instance, the earlier work of Keen (1987), and, more recently, responding directly to Benbasat and Zmud (2003), Lyytinen and King (2004), and Galliers (2003). For these authors, diversity of methods and topics is not only convenient to deal with the complex set of relations that arise from the encounters of technology and human practices, but also a real necessity for the field if it is going to stand the pace of the changes in the object of study.

As Galliers (2003) points out, accepting diversity implies moving from a concept of IS as a discipline with fixed boundaries and theoretical core to that of IS as a transdisciplinary field of studies. Indeed, the praxis-based core of IS (Lyytinen & King, 2004) is directly related to the problem-solving orientation of transdisciplinary research mentioned in the previous section. And if we consider methods used in IS such as participatory approaches to IS design (e.g., Floyd, 1993) and action research (e.g., Baskerville & Myers, 2004), we can see that many of the problems addressed by IS research originate from practitioners' demands, and are solved in interaction with the views of people in the context of technology use. As claimed by Keen (1987), an important goal of IS research is to improve practice through research. That corresponds directly to the problem-solving orientation of research in Mode 2 described by Gibbons et al. (1994, Sect. 2).

The multidimensional nature of the object of study of IS research—a main tenet of transdisciplinary research as explained in Section 2—is also acknowledged in a number of works in the IS community. For instance, Land and Kennedy-McGregor (1981) include in the notion of information systems:

1) the informal human system comprising the system of discourse and interaction between individuals and groups (...); 2) the formal, human system comprising the system of rules and regulations, of departmental boundaries and defined roles (...); 3) the formal computer system (...); 4) the informal computer system epitomised by personal computing and the possibility of using the formal systems and computer networks as means of holding unstructured information and passing informal messages (...); 5) the external system, formal and informal. (Galliers, 2003, p. 341)

In this manner, the challenge for the IS field is considering diversity as a strength, and developing means for the integration of different approaches and perspectives in order to achieve an enrichment of the research results. Following the indications of theoretical works on transdisciplinarity mentioned in the previous section, this integration should not intend to reduce the object of inquiry to a particular theory nor to a certain type of causal principles (for instance, the precedence of technological issues over the social concerns or vice-versa). It rather implies acknowledging the multidimensionality of the object of study and the necessity of using diverse methods and approaches to deal with the different facets of an information system, while striving to achieve a dialogue among the different perspectives and theoretical constructs.

After analysing experiences of transdisciplinary research cooperation, Balsiger (2005) argues for the need of establishing an *integrative framework* for each transdisciplinary research project, adapting the idea of a "generalised axiomatic system" contained in the early work of Erich Jantsch (1972) on transdisciplinarity. This integrative framework should not only make clear the part of each different disciplinary perspective in the context of the research project as a whole, but also allow the different participants to communicate and to understand results and concerns from the other viewpoints in relation to their own research.

Due to the unique character of each transdisciplinary project, there can hardly be something like a universal approach that one would be able to use in all different projects. Nevertheless, we believe that a common conceptual platform for understanding socio-technical phenomena can be achieved on an appropriately high level of abstraction. This platform can in turn be used as a template in the establishment of an integrative framework for particular projects. The next section thus presents an approach towards the development of such a conceptual platform that can be used for transdisciplinary IS research.

THE MIKROPOLIS PLATFORM

The *Mikropolis* platform described here was originated as a didactical instrument in higher education aimed at explaining the interplay among computing activities, human beings, and the global society within the same systemic context. As a didactical model, *Mikropolis* has been used in the last 10 years as an orientation model for students of Computer Science and Business Informatics courses at University of Hamburg. It has been also adopted by a number of scholars in Germany and was recently published by the German Federal Agency for Civic Education (Rolf, 2004). The name *Mikropolis* is derived from the German term "Mikroelektronik" (microelectronics) and the Greek word *polis* (which refers to a city or a body of citizens), thus emphasising the necessity to consider not only technical aspects of ICTs but the interplay between social and technological implications.

Based on the didactical model, the Mikropolis platform is being developed by a multidisciplinary network of researchers, which includes people with backgrounds in information systems, computer science, environmental and business informatics, political science, psychology, and sociology. We share a common understanding that designers and developers of software and information technology must take into account the social and organisational conditions as well as the consequences of technology use.

The Mikropolis platform does not have the explanatory power of a theory, nor is it meant to replace or complement existing theoretical approaches to socio-technical phenomena. It is rather to be understood as a heuristic framework that allows the integration of different disciplinary perspectives and theoretical approaches by providing a common language in which sociotechnical

phenomena may be described. As such, as argued above, this can only be achieved at a high level of abstraction.

The platform makes an analytical distinction between the *micro-* and *macro-context* of socio-technical interplay, referring to the societal and organisational level respectively. This affords a view of organisational aspects of computerisation and the wider societal influence, as well as the social relations that emerge from ICT-related organisational change in respect to economy, society, culture, and politics. Furthermore the platform distinguishes a *structural* and a *temporal* perspective from which we should interpret these contexts. The following sections examine each of these distinctions in turn.

Micro and Macro Contexts

At the microcontext, we look at how the shaping of human behaviour and technological artefacts is interwoven, both in development and use of ICT. The focus here lies on the interplay between ICTs and their embedding into organisational contexts. At an interorganisational level, we distinguish those organisations using and those developing ICT. This distinction is merely an analytical one, since many organisations using information technology develop or at least customise the products they use in-house, and those developing are themselves users of ICT. Therefore we accent the complex system of different actors that are involved in advancing information technology, for example globally operating software vendors, publicly funded research institutions, or ICT-related research and development sections of larger organisations. The relation between these actors can be characterised as a sectional system of innovation (Malerba, 2004). The interaction between organisations using ICT and the ICT-related sectoral innovation system is used for the analysis of the interplay between development and use of ICT, which can be characterised as either demand-driven or technology-driven.

Regarding the implications of ICT for the society at large, we take a look at the interplay between technological innovation and social change. Thus, at the societal level of analysis of computerisation the focus lies on the sociopolitical and socio-economic context in which the organisations are themselves embedded, comprehending social and political norms, cultural habits and values, and the economic pressures of a globalised world. At this level, social patterns, standards, and guiding ideals and principles (*Leitbilder*) are thus considered, as well as social and cultural values, norms, and regulations. In this manner, the macrocontext enables the description of specific factors and conditions that are relevant to the actor's actions in the microcontext, that is, to ICT production and consumption. Further, the structures in the microcontext can thereby be observed in the perspective of their significance for bringing forth transformations to the social sphere as a whole.

Structural and Temporal Perspectives

The structural perspective used in our platform comprises the transformation processes from social actions to the technical information format. ICT is used and developed in specific contexts of interaction, where people work together and communicate, consisting of a specific set of rules, tradition, and history from which the previous elements emerged. In terms of individual ICT development and use, this involves, on the one hand, the interrelated processes of formalising human action, and of "translating" it into computer executable routines. On the other hand, it means reintroducing those formalised routines into the organisational context, triggering social changes and unexpected uses of the technology produced. Since this process involves a generalised description of context-specific action, which is then somehow transferred back into a social context, we call it the interplay between *decontextualisation* and *recontextualisation*.

For the sake of better visualisation, Figure 1—adapted from (Krause et al., 2006)—offers a pictorial representation of the platform elements presented so far. At the centre, the structural perspective is placed between the two systems of which the microcontext is composed: the organisations that use ICT (at the left-hand side) and the IT sectoral innovation system (at the right-hand side). These elements are then embedded in the wider social context of the macrocontext, represented in Figure 1 by the viewpoint of the global society.

The last element of the platform adds a temporal dimension to the previous ones by means of a historical analysis of technological developments based on the theory of path dependency (e.g., Schreyögg, Sydow, & Koch, 2003). These *technology utilisation paths* reflect paradigms, guiding principles, standards, methods, products, and tools that were developed in the lifetime of a technology in the society, in organisations and in the IT system. As such, the temporal perspective of our approach involves the historical development and establishment process of certain sociotechnical structures until reaching their actual state; that is, the history of the social interactions among the actors that were involved in and affected by the development of a technology, of the actors' conflicts and consequent power losses and wins, and of the guiding principles and the supporting technical paradigms. This historical analysis thus adds value to the previous perspectives by examining the conditions that led to the success or failure of certain alternatives, and enabling one to use them as lessons for future technology development.

TRANSDISCIPLINARITY IN PRACTICE

The platform presented in the previous section is both the provisional result of and an enabling instrument for the cooperation of a group of

Figure 1. A pictorial representation of the elements of the Mikropolis platform

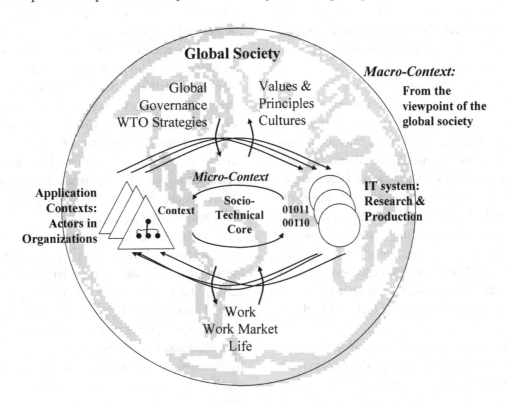

researchers with different perspectives over the same commonly defined problem. Mikropolis was profitably applied in various settings for examining the inter-relation between human action and IT design in research projects on sociotechnical design of virtual organisations. In the following section, we summarise results from a case study of the development of a collaboration software for a network of freelancers[4] in order to exemplify how Mikropolis can be used as an integrative platform for transdisciplinary IS research that can inform one about the social issues involved in the design and use of IT.

Example Application

The example application presented here is concerned with the development of a groupware application for a network of about 15 freelancers working in the field of IT and management

consulting. The network was established in 1997 with the goal of fostering the exchange of work experiences, knowledge, and work results. Furthermore, the intention was providing the members with vocational training and with the opportunity for networking, that is, for finding new partners for large projects and acquiring new clients through other network members. The network is completely self-organised by its members. Lacking formal hierarchies or predefined roles, the network heavily relies on intrinsic motivation for participation, involvement, and commitment of its individual members.

To better organise the network, several project management systems had been tested by its members in the past years. However, with each of the systems tested, the usage turned out to be unsatisfactorily low. The network members blamed this on the respective software, which they regarded as unsuitable for their tasks. Thus, the decision was made to develop a new groupware system. This system was to be developed using participatory and evolutionary design methods, so as to be continually adapted to the organisational needs of the network.

A systematic evaluation was carried out to investigate the requirements of the organisation in respect to software support. For this purpose, semistructured interviews were conducted both with groups and individual members. Furthermore, the system usage was observed while working with two core members (acting as representatives) in order to discuss their usage experiences, to analyse problems during system use, and to plan further developments for about 18 months. Regular workshops were organised every 2 or 3 months with the network representatives for the elaboration of design ideas (Finck, Janneck, & Rolf, 2006).

After a year and a half of development, the evaluation results pointed to a positive resonance: the network members emphasised that online communication was indeed generally needed, and that the developed groupware tool was adequate to their needs. However, in spite of the widely positive feedback from the users, the actual usage of the system turned out to be notably low. This could be verified by the low frequency of new content being fed into the system, among other indicators.

To understand this paradoxical situation, the Mikropolis platform was used as an analytical instrument. As a first step, the members of the network were conceptualised as actors in the *microcontext*. We analysed the design process with regard to these actors and their inter-relations to one another, as well as the relationship that they established with the developer team. This analysis brought into light the fact that, in respect to the development process, there were actually two distinct kinds of actors in the network. On the one hand, there were a small number of actors who actively participated in the development process with ideas and suggestions, whilst on the other

hand, there were many others who were only passive involved. This lead us to the conclusion that the network as whole was rather heterogeneous than homogeneous. Two groups of actors had been formed within the network, and power was unevenly distributed between these groups. As opposed to the ideal image of a self-organising network of equals, a powerful informal hierarchy had in fact been established. The analysis of the actors' interests, actions, and motives showed us a clear area of conflict between the propagated ideal of equal, nonhierarchical cooperation and the actual development practice.

Nonetheless, the usability tests on the achieved software resulted satisfactory for all members of the network, regardless of whether they had or not actively taken part in the development process. Indeed, there were no obvious reasons to assume that the development process—which was heavily influenced by only a subgroup of the actors in the network—could not lead to a satisfactory result for the not-directly-involved actors as well. However, by tracing the *technology utilisation path* we were able to see that previous decisions regarding IT support had seldom been discussed with a substantial number of network members, but rather been made by the same group of few individuals who were especially competent with and interested in IT. Since several project management tools had been unsatisfactorily tested beforehand, the introduction of yet another software caused confusion amongst the actors less involved in the decision making process, making them insecure about the continuity of software use (will the new software be replaced after a short time just like all the others?). This fact reduced their motivation to spend time learning about the new tool and using it.

The next step was to look at the *macrocontext*. Here we could establish the economic situation and its perception by the individual actors as the decisive factor for the low system usage. Since the actors saw each other as competitors in the same market, there was no incentive to share information that could benefit the other actors in the network. Consequently, information about work experience and contacts to potential clients were better withheld by the actors.

In this manner, using the Mikropolis platform, we could disentangle the apparent paradox in the initial situation—namely, how come a system that was developed with participatory methods and that had good results in usability tests has such a low usage? We concluded that the discrepancy between the stated goals, ideals, and motives of the network on the one hand, and the daily practices of the freelancers on the other, were responsible for the low intensity of utilisation of the network platform observed. Despite the actors' common belief in the need for a collaboration tool, concrete occasions and tangible incentives for system use were rare. Furthermore, due to the economic pressures that the freelancers were facing in the market, it was rather sensible to be especially careful when sharing economically relevant content.

Discussion

In the exemplary research described above, the Mikropolis platform was used to structure the problem at hand. The setting in which a problem was identified was mapped to the Mikropolis platform. More specifically, actors, groups of actors, organisations, the socio-economic situation, and their inter-relations where identified and related to the elements of the Mikropolis platform. In doing so, the complexity of a high-level problem (low system usage) could be managed and the underlying problems could be brought into light. The initial problem was thus broken down and described in a manner that offers fresh insights and allows the derivation of possible solutions.

Furthermore, the platform enabled the initial perspective centred on design to be complemented by more comprehensive social and organisational considerations achieved by an analytical perspective. Using the Mikropolis platform, designers were thus able to make sense of and draw conclusions from the analysis for future sociotechnical

development. One of these conclusions was the importance of considering the diversity of interests of actors and groups of actors inside the organisation arenas in the microcontext. Regarding software support, they inferred the need to check whether functionalities supporting equal and intense cooperation are truly compatible with the organisation's structure and its insertion in the wider societal context.

During our experiences, another major advantage of our approach to transdisciplinarity was to help overcome the cognitive constraint mentioned by Heintz and Origgi (2004): it is indeed very difficult to become an expert in more than one field. Through the multidisciplinary collaboration enabled by the Mikropolis platform, though, each researcher contributes to the whole with particular expertise on research methods and approaches according to disciplinary background. However, each researcher also uses the researcher's own methods and has additional particular research interests. The results of the common research process are thus brought back to question the original theories, avoiding in this way a mechanical application of theories from other disciplines to the IS context—as pointed out by Monteiro (2004) with respect to actor-network theory—by providing a critical feedback to the theoretical basis. As such, as pointed out by Gibbons et al. (1994) "some outputs of transdisciplinary knowledge production, particularly new instruments may enter into and fertilise any number of disciplinary sciences" (p. 9).

CONCLUSION

In this chapter, we argued for a transdisciplinary approach to IS research. The underlying assumptions of this argument are in consonance with a view of diversity in the IS field as beneficial and necessary to cope with the sociotechnical imbrications in which ICT are involved in our society nowadays. Like other researchers, we see the IS field as a transdisciplinary forum—or *market of ideas* in the words of Lyytinen and King (2004)—where research results using different approaches, methods, and theoretical foundations come together in dialogue.

Furthermore, our approach extends the use of transdisciplinarity from the level of the IS community to particular research projects by means of transdisciplinary collaboration. This collaboration is enabled by means of the Mikropolis platform, which offers a common conceptual framework for the analysis of socio-technical phenomena.

The Mikropolis platform offers a sociotechnical structural perspective of IS development, which is integrated into the microcontext of the relations between ICT producers and ICT consumers. These two perspectives are also contrasted against the backdrop of the globalised society in the macrocontext, and they are put into a historical perspective by means of the technological development paths. The analytical differentiation among these perspectives thus adds clarity to the different aspects of the ICT system design task that, in fact, always takes place simultaneously in the "seamless web" of sociotechnical relations (Hughes, 1983). In this manner, the platform affords a better understanding of the relations and dependencies among those different perspectives, thereby helping one to apprehend how complex and multifaceted the transformation process is that results from the interplay among ICT, organisations, individuals, and social actors in a globalised world.

As such, Mikropolis offers a common language for communication and articulation of perspectives from researchers with multiple disciplinary backgrounds. On the other hand, the platform reflects itself the provisional results of multidisciplinary interactions. For, as pointed out by Klein (1994), "interlanguages develop from acts of integration, not prior to them" (p. 5). The learning platform so far obtained is to be taken neither as a theoretical instrument to substitute other sociotechnical theories, nor as a fully-fledged universal construct. It is rather a provisional pidgin[5] to facilitate dialogue and cooperation of

different perspectives, without striving to dissolve the particularities of the perspectives involved, but rather acknowledging multidimensionality and preserving idiosyncrasies. The platform is thus in a state of permanent evolution.

FUTURE RESEARCH DIRECTIONS

Transdisciplinary research in Information Systems should strive to integrate various disciplines as well as to cross over the domains of academia and practical application, thus constantly alternating between theoretical research and field work. Relying upon the framework presented in this chapter, we may conceptualise transdisciplinary research as a dialectical process of doing research both *on* and *with* the Mikropolis platform.

In terms of empirical research, the Mikropolis platform is being currently used as a basis for analysing complex problem settings in ICT development for the public health sector. Additionally, an action research project is also using Mikropolis to accompany the institution-wide introduction of an educational software into a higher education institution. In this manner, research projects like these provide real-life problems to be analysed relying upon the Mikropolis platform, whilst at the same time give important feedback of which new directions for further development of the platform may emerge.

Notwithstanding the uniqueness of each transdisciplinary project, further research shall focus on developing a concept on how to support transdisciplinary IS projects with the use of the Mikropolis platform, thus making the platform available for a wider range of practitioners. By incorporating these new viewpoints, we believe to step forward into the direction of improving dialogue with both scientific and nonscientific contexts and thus better addressing relevant issues for the society as a whole.

Another interesting direction for transdisciplinary research in IS is the theoretical development of the Mikropolis platform. In this context, work is due to relate the components of the platform more closely to different social theories, like, for instance, neo-institutionalism, micropolitics, and actor-network theory. At a more abstract level, the epistemic underpinnings of the Mikropolis platform should also be a focus of research, aiming not only at further developing Mikropolis itself, but also at gaining insight regarding the epistemic foundations of transdisciplinarity as a research modus for IS.

ACKNOWLEDGMENT

We are most indebted to Paul Drews and Roman Langer for the fruitful discussions in which some of the ideas of this chapter were born. We also thank the members of the Mikropolis network for our insightful discussions in the group, and the anonymous reviewers for their helpful suggestions. However, the authors take full responsibility for the chapter's content.

REFERENCES

Avgerou, C. (2000). Information systems: What sort of science is it? *Omega, 28*(5), 567-579.

Avgerou, C., Ciborra, C., & Land, F. (Eds.). (2004). *The social study of information and communication technology: Innovation, actors, and contexts.* Oxford: Oxford University Press.

Balsiger, P. W. (2005). *Transdisziplinarität: Systematisch-vergleichende untersuchung disziplinenübergreifender wissenschaftspraxis.* München: Fink.

Baskerville, R., & Myers, M. D. (Eds.). (2004). Special issue on action research in information systems: Making is research relevant to practice. *MIS Quarterly, 28*(3).

Benbasat, I., & Zmud, R. W. (2003). The identity crisis within the IS discipline: Defining and communicating the discipline's core properties. *MIS Quarterly, 27*(2), 183-194.

Djikstra, E. W. (1989). On the cruelty of really teaching computing science. In P. J. Denning (Ed.), A debate on teaching computing science. *Communications of ACM, 32*(12), 1397-1404.

Finck, M., Janneck, M., & Rolf, A. (2006). Techniknutzung zwischen kooperation und konkurrenz: Eine analyse von nutzungsproblemen. In F. Lehner, H. Nösekabel, & P. Kleinschmidt (Eds.), *Multikonferenz wirtschaftsinformatik 2006 - MKWI 2006, Buch 1, teilkonferenz collaborative business* (pp. 20-22, 363-376). Passau.

Floyd, C. (1993). STEPS - a methodical approach to participatory design. *Communications of the ACM, 36*(6), 83.

Galliers, R. D. (2003). Change as crisis of growth? Toward a trans-disciplinary view of information systems as a field of study: A response to Benbasat and Zmud's call for returning to the IT artifact. *Journal of the Association for Information Systems, 4*(6), 337-351.

Gibbons, M., Limoges, C., Nowotny, H., Schwartzman, S., Scott, P., & Trow, M. (1994). *The new production of knowledge: the dynamic of science and research in contemporary societies.* London: Sage Publications.

Glass, R. L., Ramesh, V., & Vessey, I. (2004). An analysis of research in computing disciplines. *Communications of ACM, 47*(6), 89-94.

Heinz, C., & Origgi, G. (2004). Rethinking interdisciplinarity. Emergent Issues. Seminar Rethinking Interdisciplinarity. Retrieved June 1, 2008, from http://www.interdisciplines.org/interdisciplinarity/papers/11/

Hugues, T. P. (1983). *Networks of power: Electrification in western society, 1880-1930.* Baltimore, MD: Johns Hopkins University Press.

Janneck, M., & Finck, M. (2006). Making the community a hospitable place - identity, strong bounds, and self-organisation in Web-based communities. *International Journal of Web Based Communities, 2*(4), 458-473.

Jantsch, E. (1972). Towards interdisciplinarity and transdisciplinarity in education and innovation. In L. Apostel, G. Berger, A. Briggs, & G. Michaud (Eds.), *Interdisciplinarity. Problems of teaching and researching in universities* (pp. 97-121). Paris: Center for Educational Research and Innovation, Organization for Economic Cooperation and Development.

Keen, P. G. W. (1987). MIS research: Current status, trends and needs. In R. A. Buckingham, R. A. Hirschheim, F. F. Land, & C. J. Tully (Eds.), *Information systems education: Recommendations and implementation* (pp. 1-13). Cambridge: Cambridge University Press.

Klein, J. T. (1994). Notes toward a social epistemology of transdisciplinarity. In *Communication au Premier Congrès Mondial de la Transdisciplinarité*. Retrieved June 1, 2008, from http://nicol.club.fr/ciret/bulletin/b12/b12c2.htm

Klein, J. T. (2004). Prospects for transdisciplinarity. *Futures, 36*(2), 515-526.

Krause, D., Rolf, A., Christ, M., & Simon, E. (2006). Wissen, wie alles zusammenhängt – das mikropolis-modell als orientierungswerkzeug für die gestaltung von informationstechnik in organisationen und gesellschaft. *Informatik Spektrum, 29*(4), 263-273.

Land, F. F., & Kennedy-McGregor, M. (1981). Information and information systems: Concepts and perspectives. In R. D. Galliers (Ed.), *Information systems research: Issues, methods and practical guidelines* (pp. 63-91). Oxford: Blackwell.

Lyytinen, K., & King, J. L. (2004). Nothing at the center? Academic legitimacy in the information systems field. *Journal of the Association for Information Systems, 5*(6), 220-246.

Malerba, F. (Ed.). (2004). *Sectoral systems of innovation: Concepts, issues and analyses of six major sectors in Europe*. Cambridge: Cambridge University Press.

Mingers, J. (2001). Combining IS research methods: Towards a pluralist methodology. *Information Systems Research, 12*(3), 240-259.

Monteiro, E. (2004). Actor network theory and cultural aspects of interpretative studies. In C. Avgerou, C. Ciborra, & F. Land (Eds.), *The social study of information and communication technology: Innovation, actors, and contexts* (pp. 129-139). Oxford: Oxford University Press.

Monteiro, E., & Hanseth, O. (1996). Social shaping of information infrastructure: On being specific about technology. In W. J. Orlikowski, G. Walsham, M. J. Jones, & J. I. DeGross (Eds.), *Information technology and changes in organizational work* (pp. 325-343). London: Chapman & Hall.

Myers, M. D. (1997). Qualitative research in information systems. *MIS Quarterly, 21*(2), 241-242. Retrieved June 1, 2008, from http://www.misq.org/discovery/MISQD_isworld/

Ngwenyama, O. K., & Lee, A. S. (1997). Communication richness in electronic mail: Critical social theory and the contextuality of meaning. *MIS Quarterly, 21*(2), 145-167.

Orlikowski, W. (2000). Using technology and constituting structures: A practice lens for studying technology in organizations. *Organization Science, 11*(4), 404-428.

Orlikowski, W. J., & Baroudi, J. J. (1991). Studying information technology in organizations: Research approaches and assumptions. *Information Systems Research, 2*(1), 1-28.

Porto de Albuquerque, J., & Simon, E.J. (2007). Dealing with socio-technical complexity: Towards a transdisciplinary approach to IS research. In O. Hubert, J. Schelp, & R. Winter (Eds.), *Proceedings* of the 15th European Conference on Information Systems (ECIS 2007) (pp. 1458-1468).

Rolf, A. (2004). Von der theoriearbeit zur gestaltung. In H.-D. Kübler & E. Elling (Eds.), *Wissensgesellschaft. Neue medien und ihre konsequenzen.* Bonn: Bundeszentrale für politische Bildung.

Rolf, A., Janneck, M., & Finck, M. (2006). Soziotechnische gestaltung von freelancer-netzwerken – eine exemplarische analyse mit dem mikropolismodell. *WISU – Das Wirtschaftsinformatikstudium, 9*(06), 1089-1095.

Schneberger, S., & Wade, M. (Eds.). (2006). Theories used in IS research. Retrieved June 1, 2008, from http://www.istheory.yorku.ca

Schreyögg, G., Sydow, J., & Koch, J. (2003). Organisatorische pfade — von der pfadabhängigkeit zur pfadreaktion? In G. Schreyögg & J. Sydow (Eds.), *Managementforschung 13: Strategische prozesse und pPfad* (pp. 257-294). Wiesbaden: Gabler.

Simon, E., Janneck, M., & Gumm, D. (2006, September 21-23). Understanding socio-technical change: Towards a multidisciplinary approach. In J. Berleur, M. I. Nurminen, & J. Impagliazzo (Eds.), *Social informatics: An information xociety for all?* In *Remembrance of Rob Kling, Proceedings of the Seventh International Conference on Human Choice and Computers (HCC7), IFIP TC 9,* Maribor, Slovenia (pp. 232-243). New York: Springer.

ADDITIONAL READING

Castells, M. (1996). *The rise of the network society (The information age: Economy, society and culture, volume 1)*. Malden, MA: Blackwell Publishers, Inc.

Checkland, P. (1981). *Systems thinking, systems practice*. Chichester: John Wiley & Sons.

Checkland, P., & Holwell, S. (1998). *Information, systems and information systems: Making sense of the field*. Chichester: John Wiley & Sons.

Dittrich, Y., & Floyd, C., & Klischewski, R. (2002). *Social thinking - software practice*. Cambridge, MA: MIT Press.

Giddens, A. (1984). *The constitution of society: Outline for a theory of structuration*. Cambridge: Polity Press.

Hirschheim, R., & Klein, H. K. (2003). Crisis in the IS field? A critical reflection on the state of the discipline. *Journal of the Association for Information Systems, 4*(5), 237-293.

Jantsch, E. (1970). Inter- and transdisciplinary university: A systems approach to education and innovation. *Policy Sciences, 1*(4), 403-428.

King, J. L., & Lyytinen K. (2004). Reach and grasp. *MIS Quarterly, 28*(4), 539-551.

Klein, J. T. (1996). *Crossing boundaries: Knowledge, disciplinarities, and interdisciplinarities*. Charlottesville, VA: University Press of Virginia.

Kling, R. (1994). Organizational analysis in computer science. In C. Huff & T. Finholt (Eds.), *Social issues in computing* (pp. 18-37). New York: McGraw-Hill, Inc.

Kocka J. (Ed.). (1987). *Interdisziplinarität. Praxis – herausforderung – ideologie*. Frankfurt a. M.: Suhrkamp.

Kröber, G. (1983). Interdisziplinarität – ein aktuelles erfordernis der gesellschafts- und wissenschaftsentwicklung. *Deutsche Zeitschrift für Philosophie, 31*(5), 575-589.

Latour, B. (1987). *Science in action: How to follow scientists and engineers through society*. Cambridge, MA: Havard University Press.

Latour, B. (2005). *Reassembling the social: An introduction to actor-network-theory*. Oxford: Oxford University Press.

Lenk, H. (1980). Interdisziplinarität und die rolle der philosophie. *Zeitschrift für Didaktik der Philosophie, 2*(1), 10-19.

Mingers, J., & Willcocks, L. (2004). *Social theory and philosophy for information systems.* Chichester: Wiley & Sons.

Mittelstraß, J. (2003). *Transdisziplinarität – wissenschaftliche zukunft und institutionelle wirklichkeit.* Konstanz: UVK.

Möller, A., & Bornemann, B. (2005). Kyoto ist anderswo. *Informatik Spektrum, 28*(1), 15-23.

Nicolescu, B. (2006). Transdisciplinarity – past, present and future. In B. Haverkort & C. Reijntjes (Eds.), Moving worldviews - reshaping sciences, policies and practices for endogenous sustainable development (pp. 142-166). Holland: COMPAS Editions.

Noble, D. (1984). *Forces of production: A social history of industrial automation.* New York: Knopf.

Nowotny, H., Scott, P., & Gibbons, M. (2001). *Rethinking science. Knowledge and the public in an age of uncertainty.* Cambridge: Polity Press.

Orlikowski, W. J. (1992). The duality of technology: Rethinking the concept of technology in organizations. *Organization Science: A Journal of the Institute of Management Sciences, 3*(3), 398-427.

Orlikowski, W., & Iacono, S. (2001). Desperately seeking the IT in IT research. *Information Systems Research, 7*(4), 400-408.

Powell, W. W., & Dimaggio, P. J. (1991). *The new institutionalism in organizational analysis.* Chicago: University of Chicago Press.

Rolf, A. (1998). *Grundlagen der organisations- und wirtschaftsinformatik.* Berlin, Germany: Springer.

Voßkamp, W. (1984). Von der wissenschaftlichen spezialisierung zum gespräch zwischen dn disziplinen. In H. Wendt & N. Loacker (Eds.), *Kindlers enzyklopädie* (pp. 445-462). Zürich: Kindler.

Wahoff, J.-H. (2005). *Das mikropolis-modell als ausgangspunkt für eine transdisziplinäre wirtschaftsinformatik* (Fachbereichsbericht 266). Hamburg, Germany: Universität Hamburg.

Williams R., & Edge, D. (1996). The social shaping of technology. *Research Policy, 25,* 865-899.

ENDNOTES

[1] For a more comprehensive cover see Avgerou, Ciborra, and Land (2004), Orlikowski and Baroudi (1991), Myers (1997), and the online resource Schneberger and Wade (2006).

[2] An earlier version of this paper appeared as Porto de Albuquerque, J., & Simon, E.J. (2007). Dealing with socio-technical complexity: Towards a transdisciplinary approach to IS research. In O. Hubert, J. Schelp, & R. Winter (Eds.), *Proceedings of the 15th European Conference on Information Systems (ECIS 2007)* (pp. 1458-1468).

[3] The outcome of the debate in which the position of Dijkstra (1989) was presented has in the end broadened the field of computing, which includes today areas that explicitly address the human use of technologies like human-computer interaction.

[4] For further details on the software developed and on the case study see Janneck and Finck (2006), and for more detailed accounts of the analysis presented as follows see Rolf, Janneck, and Finck (2006) and Finck et al. (2006).

[5] This metaphor was proposed by Klein (1994) in analogy with the term *pidgin* from linguistics, which means an interim language with simplified vocabulary and grammar, based in partial agreement on the meaning of shared terms.

Section 1.3
Epistemology

Chapter VI
A Guide to Non–Disclosure Agreements for Researchers Using Public and Private Sector Sources

Paul D. Witman
California Lutheran University, USA

Kapp L. Johnson
California Lutheran University, USA

ABSTRACT

This chapter provides a set of guidelines to assist information systems researchers in creating, negotiating, and reviewing nondisclosure agreements, in consultation with appropriate legal counsel. It also reviews the use of nondisclosure agreements in academic research environments from multiple points of view, including the perspectives of both public and private sectors. Active academic researchers, industry practitioners, and corporate legal counsel all provided input into the compiled guidelines. An annotated bibliography and links are provided for further review.

INTRODUCTION AND OBJECTIVES

Nondisclosure Agreements (NDAs) are an important and necessary tool for researchers when dealing with a research subject which wants to contractually protect its confidential informa-

tion, or when the researcher's own confidential information needs to be protected. Research subjects may require agreement to a NDA before allowing researchers access to data, to protect the research subject's proprietary data, procedures, and identity. Likewise, researchers may require agreement to a NDA to protect the creation of intellectual property as a result of the research. Failure to execute a proper NDA could result in legal disputes, fees, and liability, as well as an inability to use the data collected for research purposes.

The objective of this chapter is to provide the reader with a set of guidelines and observations about NDAs that are specific to the needs of the academic community. Most NDAs are executed between commercial and/or public-sector enterprises, and as a result it is difficult to find reference material that provides guidance appropriate to information security researchers on this critical topic.

Nondisclosure agreements are often used in the larger context of intellectual property policies and management. These policies may be created by universities or other sponsoring organizations, or may be created by outside organizations. A full discussion of intellectual property policies is beyond the scope of this chapter.

BACKGROUND

These guidelines were developed as the result of a research project to seek out information about academic NDAs. The research was conducted as an e-mail-based survey, using open-ended questions. A request for suggested guidelines went to the ISWorld distribution list, an e-mail distribution delivered to a global community of Information Science (IS) researchers, students, and faculty members. The request was not country-specific, nor specific to any particular segment of IS.

The 11 contributors, including 10 in academia, were self-selected and responded to the initial request. Of those 10, at least 2 had some industry experience as well; 1 contributor is a corporate legal counsel who provided significant reviews and provided guidance both from the corporate perspective and what academics should consider.

Of the 11 contributors, 9 were based in the United States, 1 in the United Kingdom, and 1 in Canada. Of the 10 in academia, 8 were faculty members, and 2 were students.

This research is exploratory in nature, and is not intended as an exhaustive guide to the topic. The chapter focuses primarily on United States legal definitions and practices, but we anticipate that many of the guidelines and principles may apply in other jurisdictions.

Different research methods may, of course, have different impacts on the need for nondisclosure agreements. The key question, of course, is whether your research will either expose you to intellectual property that needs to be protected, or will create intellectual property that needs to be protected. Comments on key methods used in most recent IS research (Chen & Hirschheim, 2004) follow. In all cases, if new intellectual property is to be created by the research and needs to be protected from disclosure, a nondisclosure agreement is an appropriate consideration.

- **Case study:** Case studies often look at organizational activities that may well expose the researcher to intellectual property. Multiple case studies may further expose the researcher to similar intellectual property at competing organizations, and, as such, it may be in the researchers' best interest to be clear about how they will protect that property.
- **Survey:** This method seems somewhat less likely to call for a nondisclosure agreement, unless the questionnaires address (or might address) intellectual property.
- **Laboratory experiment:** May call for a nondisclosure in cases such as when the experiment will leverage intellectual property belonging to the researcher, partner, or research subject that needs to be protected.
- **Field experiment:** Similar to laboratory experiments, but may also call for special consideration if the field location will put

either the researcher's or their partner's or research subject's intellectual property at greater risk.

- **Action research:** Given the nature of action research, where researchers actively try to influence a phenomenon, it is possible that intellectual property might be created as a result of that research, and as such might give rise to need for a NDA.

- **Longitudinal studies**, which by definition take place over a period of time, may warrant special consideration in terms of how the NDA is structured. A NDA that relies on a particular individual for research or publication approval may be risky given that organizational roles and employment change over time.

LEGAL OVERVIEW

A Nondisclosure Agreement is an "agreement restricting the use of information by prohibiting a contracting party from divulging data" (Beyer, 2001). NDAs arise out of a relationship whereby one or both parties to the agreement seek to contractually articulate the respective rights and responsibilities of the parties with regard to some kind of intellectual property. Generally speaking, Intellectual Property is any property that can be protected by law including copyrights, ideas, inventions, and other forms of the intellect that has independent commercial value and is not generally known.

For the researcher, it is very important to determine what rights apply to the work to be produced—that is, the researcher's results, papers, and products. The researcher should ask the question as to whether the property is primarily functional or aesthetic. Functional elements are protected by utility patents and trade secrets. Nonfunctional or aesthetic elements are protected by trademarks, copyrights, and patents. The researcher may ask the question: "Does this

creation accomplish a task or goal or is it done primarily to appeal to the senses or provide information or entertainment?" (Milgrim, 2006a, Chapter 9.04).

Thus, courts apply property rules when it comes to intellectual product. Because intellectual product is considered property, the issue for the researcher is to identify who is the "owner" of the property. This is critical because the owner of intellectual property has the right to use it and disclose it to others or restrict its use and disclosure as the case may be (Milgrim, 2006b, Chapter 2.01).

Consequently, the identification of the type of intellectual property law applicable to the researcher's activity is very important. Intellectual property law involves several distinct legal disciplines which at times overlap (Milgrim, 2006a, Chapter 9.02). There are four types of Intellectual Property laws which are generally applicable to the activities of researchers: Patent Law, Copyright Law, Trademark Law, and Trade Secret Law.

Briefly, patents are of two types of interest to security researchers: utility and design. The most common patent is utility patents and is granted to the inventor of a new, nonobvious invention. A design patent is granted for a new but nonfunctional design (USPTO, 2006b).

Copyrights are granted to authors of "original works of authorship" that include dramatic, musical, artistic, computer programs, and certain other intellectual works, both published and unpublished. Copyrights protect the form of expression rather than the subject matter of the writing that is, copyrights do not protect ideas and facts, only the manner in which the ideas and facts are expressed (USPTO, 2006a).

Trademark or Servicemark law protects a word, name, symbol, or device that is used in trade with goods to indicate the source of the goods, as distinguished from the goods of others (USPTO, 2006c).

Lastly, which will be of most interest to researchers, Trade Secret law protects any confidential information that gives the creator or holder of the secret a competitive advantage, that is, the information has independent economic value derived from the fact that it is secret. By definition, trade secrets are confidential information, and the owner of the trade secret can prevent others from using the information (NCCUSL, 1985, Section 1(4)).

As is often the case, Intellectual Property overlaps and the researcher should be aware that patent, copyright, trademark/servicemark, and trade secrets can overlap with regard to a particular product, service, or information. For instance, it is very difficult, if not impossible, to pursue a patent application, while at the same time keeping the invention as a trade secret. In addition, it is not unheard of for a product to be protected under both trademark and copyright law. Finally, patent law can intersect with copyright and trademark/servicemark law in the manner or appearance of an item as well as its design and nonobvious functionality (Milgrim, 2006b, Chapter 9.04).

Researchers must also be aware that it is the nature of confidentiality that creates the need for a nondisclosure agreement. While confidentiality may be implied from the relationship of the parties or the nature of the communication between the parties, express nondisclosure agreements are the safest means for a researcher to protect himself from violating a confidential duty as well as protecting intellectual interests which arise out of the relationship. Therefore, NDAs can differ in the nature and scope of the disclosure, but NDAs must include a clear description of the information held to be confidential, how the confidential information may or may not be used, the duty of confidentiality, choice of law and venue, remedies for breach including injunctive relief, duration of the agreement, scope of activities, who owns the confidential information, and protection of marginal matter, as well as post employment activities.

Finally, it must be noted that nondisclosure agreements are contractual. In other words, the law of contracts controls the analysis and the rules a court (whether state or federal) will apply in the case of a breach. Because commercial agreements are in the domain of state law, state law will apply, even if one party is allowed to bring the cause of action in federal court; the federal court will apply the applicable state law (Milgrim, 2006b, Chapter 4.01).

Thus, as a matter of law, NDAs are very important in protecting the rights of the owner of the confidential information as to its disclosure and use in a public way.

The significance of *not* having an NDA when it is appropriate cannot be underestimated. NDAs are designed to protect the parties to the agreement. On the one hand, an NDA is designed to protect the party making the disclosure of confidential information. Because of its proprietary nature, the disclosing party wants to make certain that the use of the information is consistent with that party's expectations. On the other hand, an NDA is also designed to protect the receiving party's expectations of the permitted use of the proprietary confidential information. For both parties, the NDA creates contractual rights that are enforceable and compensation when those contractual rights have been breached. Finally, an NDA facilitates the development of research and new knowledge by creating a robust environment for researchers where the rights and responsibilities of the parties are clearly expressed.

LITERATURE REVIEW

The literature review provides a framework for other researchers to consider as they review their own needs for confidentiality agreements. While little in the way of concrete guidelines exists in the literature, much is published on the topics of industry-university research collaboration, intellectual property, and the impact of confidentiality agreements on various parts of the research community.

At least since the mid-1980s, universities struggled with how to balance the needs of openness and proprietary control (GUIRR, 1997). This dilemma came about because of the 1980 change in U.S. federal law that made copyright the primary protection for computer software (Peterson, 1985), with its somewhat less rigorous protection for ideas rather than embodiment (Oppedahl & Larson LLP, 1995). The issues that arise generally center on the classic tension between the academy's desire for open, free sharing of information, and the commercial world's desire to maintain trade secrecy of certain information for commercial purposes.

The reality, however, is rarely so clear cut. Academics also need to keep certain information secret (e.g., confidentiality of the identity of research subjects, delays to allow patent filing). Commercial researchers are sometimes motivated to publish and make a name for themselves or for their employer, both in academic and in trade journals (Newberg & Dunn, 2002). An institution that wishes to commercialize the results of its research may impose publication restrictions both to allow time for patent filings and to allow establishing spin-off business units to bring an idea or invention to market.

Newberg and Dunn (2002) documented several organizational models for Industry-University Research Collaboration, each of which may impact the need for and use of nondisclosure agreements. These include:

1. University to Industry Technology Licensing, where the university clearly owns and is selling or licensing a technology to industry for commercialization
2. Industry-Sponsored University Research, where it is important to establish intellectual property ownership, given that industry is sponsoring and paying for the research

3. Spin-off Companies, often with lead researchers and students taking academic research into the commercial domain, that require appropriate confidentiality and intellectual property ownership agreements; and
4. Idea Labs, such as MIT's Media Lab (Newberg & Dunn, 2002, p. 205), where ongoing cutting-edge research is conducted in an established organizational setting.

Each of these organizational models carries with it potentially different implications about the ownership of intellectual property, and the level of protection that must be accorded to its information. As such, the organizational context of the research must be considered as an aspect of the design of any nondisclosure agreement.

In the case of a formal research consortium inside the university, it may be appropriate to require separate NDAs between the consortium and its researchers, employees, and visitors (Newberg & Dunn, 2002). This approach simplifies relationships with organizations (their NDA could be with the consortium), and may serve to enable free exchange of information among the researchers within the consortium.

The process of establishing ownership of intellectual property is one that can be dealt with in an ad hoc fashion, or can be a very structured part of the campus research environment. Carnegie Mellon University (CMU) is often cited for its highly structured approach. CMU (2001) uses a detailed model identifying the various ways in which intellectual property can be created, and who contributes to that process. From this model, the policy then dictates the ownership of the property. It further prescribes how any economic benefits from that property are to be shared between the researchers, the university, and the sponsors. A detailed review of intellectual property policy is beyond the scope of this chapter. Nondisclosure agreements, however, will need to consider the intellectual property policies of all parties to the agreement.

Confidentiality agreements may impair the researcher's ability to publish—either by constraining what can be published, by delaying the publication, or by preventing it entirely. NDAs may also impact the researcher's legal right to do the ethically correct thing (e.g., publish results of a study showing impact of chemicals on public health) (GUIRR, 1997).

It is also important for the researcher to understand that even data that is provided under a NDA may lose its confidential status in a number of ways. For example, information that is generally known in the industry of the provider of the information, or information that is generally available to the public, may not be need to be treated as confidential by the researcher (Volonino, 2005). These conditions may vary based on the applicable laws; therefore, it is important to seek appropriate legal counsel.

At least one study out of the dot-com era also identified potential negative impacts to students. Based on confidentiality agreements signed with one professor, students were in some cases unable to complete assignments given by another professor due to the overlap in the assignment vis-a-vis the confidential information (Marcus, 1999). There remains some dispute about the cause of this issue; it has been represented that the assignment was given as a deliberate form of industrial espionage against another professor. Whatever the facts may be in this case, the potential remains for this problem to occur.

Figure 1 shows a sample of the various entities and constraints that may need to be considered as a nondisclosure agreement is negotiated (modeled after Newberg & Dunn, 2002, p. 225).

Figure 1. Factors to consider in negotiating a nondisclosure agreement

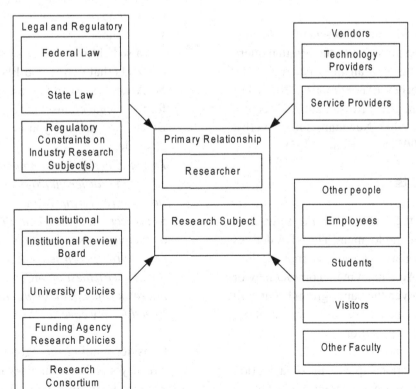

Legal and regulatory factors impact both the researcher and the organization, and may drive some aspects of the nondisclosure agreement, particularly related to the level of protection required. Institutional requirements impact the researcher as well (e.g., intellectual property creation and ownership policies).

Vendors may provide technology and services for a project, and the researcher needs to consider, before launching the project, how and whether any confidential data may be shared with them. Lastly, other people may be exposed to confidential data through participation in the project in a variety of roles, and it may be appropriate to establish constraints around what may or may not be shared with them. Students involved in the research project should also sign an NDA. Stim and Fishman (2001) provide a sample NDA to be used with students to protect confidential information held by a professor.

GUIDELINES

The following guidelines represent the collective wisdom of the respondents to the original query to ISWorld, along with an informal review by a corporate attorney (Anonymous, 2005; Clay, 2005; Edgington, 2005; Kaiser, 2005; Kitchens, 2005; McLaren, 2005; Newman, 2005; Overby, 2005; Straub, 2005; Westerman, 2005).

Starting Points

1. Note that the NDA is not the same as a contract for employment. The NDA defines what each party can and cannot disclose to others. An employment contract may or may not cover the same ground, but will also cover such issues as compensation, deliverable expectations, and ownership of intellectual property.

2. Treat the relationship with the organization as a relationship, not as a transaction (Gross-

man, 2004, pp. 35-38). Take the time to build relationships with your sponsor and with other key participants, so that the NDA is more of a natural part of the process, rather than being the very first step in a relationship.

In other words, don't view the NDA as a contract for a single transaction by which you get some data, publish something, and then move on. Develop a relationship in which you provide interesting analysis and insight to the organization, help them understand some questions, and so forth. If you develop a group of organizations that enjoy working with you and will share data over time, what a great asset to have as a researcher! (Overby, 2005)

3. Expect to work from the organization's standard NDA. In general, that will make the process simpler than asking them to sign yours. However, if the organization is small and does not have a standard NDA, having one of your own as a template is to your advantage.

4. It is also helpful to create standard wording elements that you would like to see in the NDA so that you can suggest specific clauses for their legal counsel to respond to.

5. Be clear about why you need changes: for example,

    I want to make these changes because our situation is different from the typical situation covered by this NDA. Of course, I need to protect your confidentiality. But, as an academic, I also need to be free to use my research outputs in teaching and publishing. So, let's see if these changes can protect your interests while also giving me the freedom I need for my career. (Westerman, 2005)

6. Consider making the agreement only between yourself and the organization, and exclude your university. This separation

also simplifies the process. That said, it is important to understand your university's policies and ensure that they are not liable by implication for your work, and that its policies do not require any specific clauses or process.

7. Consider whether the relationship might become one of mutual disclosure, and whether your own, or your university's confidential information needs to be protected as well, possibly for commercialization. Particularly in this latter case, the Bayh-Dole Act of 1980, which affects ownership of intellectual property developed under federal funding, should be factored into the language of the NDA (Foley, 2004).

8. Avoid vague language in the agreement, and gain an understanding of such common legal terms as "prorated" and "reasonable."

Time Limits

9. If possible, obtain permission to publish freely after 3 years (this is the standard timeframe, though it can be negotiated). Some organizations will have difficulty with such a clause. Even though technology does move quickly, legacy systems often do not, and you could still be in possession of information of value to the organization which could be detrimental if freely disseminated.

10. The organization may view a time limit as unacceptable, but it is still worth asking.

Approval Requirements

11. If you can, avoid a requirement for explicit approval by the organization. It will certainly simplify the publication process. Many respondents were more vociferous than that. Approval requirements were, in their minds, something to be avoided at all costs. Alternatively, you might seek agreement that the organization has a right to review

how they are identified (or disguised), and will have the opportunity to comment (for correctness, within a reasonable timeframe) on any other part of the work. That would be a reasonable compromise.

12. A planned review of the findings by the organization can both strengthen your validity as well as improve the possibility of approval by your local Institutional Review Board.

13. Consider an annotation in the NDA that you retain the right to publish your research, with the exception of the organization's right to retain anonymity and prevent publication of proprietary information, and that both parties will work in good faith to make that possible.

14. Consider offering to co-author with an organization employee if you will be publishing in a trade journal as one of your outlets. This option could help build their stature in the market, and motivate them to participate.

15. Be careful that any approvals language does not require a new approval each time you speak or write about the research you conducted with this data.

Courts and Jurisdictions

16. Note that laws vary from state to state and from country to country. You will need to be sure that your agreement is appropriate for the laws that govern it.

17. Some respondents indicated that courts will often rule against the party that drafted the agreement. However, the corporate counsel who participated in this study indicated that this assumption is generally a myth, and that courts in general will rule against the party that wrote the agreement only in the case of an ambiguity in the terms that is material to the dispute. It is also worth noting that the party with the burden of proof is more likely to lose the case.

18. The agreement should specify both what laws apply (generally, in the U.S., which state's laws), and in which court system (generally, in the U.S., which county's courts).

Original Documents

19. It is commonplace to be asked to return originals. It is also reasonable for the organization to request return, especially if the relationship sours for any reason. Do not offer this option in the NDA if it is not requested.
20. Be careful to define clearly what needs to be returned, as your derivative works need to be retained to document your work.
21. Do not allow either an implication or an explicit statement that everything coming from the organization is proprietary. Consider asking for proprietary documents and works to be explicitly labeled as such.
22. If your research data includes personal information, try to get that data "anonymized" before you take possession. Anonymization helps protect the organization and you from liability.
23. Ensure that you understand and adhere to any regulatory requirements that apply to the industry or governmental agency under research (e.g., health care and banking privacy regulation, government meeting disclosure requirements, etc.).

Disguising the Organization

24. To help smooth the process of obtaining publication approval, consider disguising the name of the organization(s). Even if the financials and other demographics might make it identifiable, you might be able to reduce those numbers by some factor. If there are multiple organizations involved, reducing all numbers by the same factor for all subject organizations might achieve the same result.

25. It is likely the organization would view this request as reasonable. However, you need to ensure that the disguising you provide is real and permanent.

DERIVATIVE WORKS[1]

26. Make sure you own your work product and all derivative works, unless you are being paid for the work, in which case ownership should be defined by the contract for the work.
27. You need to establish your right to create research papers and derivative works based on those papers from the information obtained from the organization.
28. The organization will likely take the position that they own your work product and derivative works from those, so you'll need to establish that ownership explicitly.

A model nondisclosure agreement, for reference purposes only, may be found in the Appendix to this chapter. The model is designed to provide an example of clauses in an agreement that a researcher might expect to see from a research subject, along with specific clauses that the researcher would like added or modified to be more amenable to their needs.

FUTURE TRENDS

While the foundations of intellectual property law are long-standing, it is reasonable to anticipate changes in such laws as they are interpreted both across national boundaries, and as the impact of new technologies continues to be felt. For example, Grossman (2004) notes issues such as the potential invisible violation of trademark via meta-tags on HTML pages. Such issues may seem to have an obvious answer, but will likely take years to work through the courts and legislatures and be embodied in updated legislation.

Globalization is affecting intellectual property rights. Globalization is creating cross-border research and development. To date, there is no international patent, which means that a patent is enforceable only in the jurisdiction where it is granted. To exacerbate the problem, United States patent law does not include extraterritorial effect and generally does not restrict potential infringement outside the boarders of the United States. However, this issue is before the U.S. Court of Appeals (*Voda v. Cordis Corp.*). Here the court is being asked to consider whether patent matters arising under foreign law maybe heard under U.S. jurisdiction. Until this matter is heard, practitioners may have to be careful in the important freedom-to-operate and infringement clauses of their agreements. Where these clauses reference foreign activities, they may want to assess the impact of an adjudication by a forum other than that originally contemplated.[2]

CONCLUSION

This set of guidelines has been used in multiple negotiations, and its parameters provided useful guidance to help structure the discussion with counsel. For example, the need to provide the right to publish anonymized data was not one that was initially acceptable to the research subject, but with appropriate attention to the relationship (Guidelines 2 and 5) with the subject, and by communicating the reason for the need (Guideline 13), an acceptable clause was created and agreed upon.

While finalizing a nondisclosure agreement clearly is an event that warrants the attention of qualified legal counsel, the element required in NDAs that meet the needs of the academic community is not apparently well known in the legal community. As such, we believe it is helpful for researchers to be armed with guidance that can help inform their discussions with counsel, resulting in agreements that appropriately protect all the parties involved.

The aim of this chapter is to provide researchers with a background on nondisclosure agreements so that they may be better able to know when such an agreement might be appropriate. There are risks involved in not using a nondisclosure agreement when it is appropriate, and there are risks in using a poorly designed nondisclosure agreement. It is incumbent upon the researcher to engage legal counsel appropriately to help mitigate these risks.

LIMITATIONS AND DIRECTIONS FOR FUTURE RESEARCH

Contributors to this set of guidelines were not country-specific in their suggestions. This research could be extended to look more closely at laws and regulations outside the United States, and to the effects of cross-border research teams (Shippey, 2002). The Wiki containing the living version of this chapter is shown in Appendix I, and other researchers may contribute to the knowledge base residing there. Formal review by representative legal counsel from the university and corporate settings would be valuable to strengthen the validity and reliability of the data.

A data base of best practice clauses, accessible based on the characteristics that the researcher is seeking, might be built to provide a robust collection of material from which to craft future agreements. A survey of the users of these guidelines might also be conducted to evaluate their value to the community, and to further enhance and build on the collected expertise.

NOTE

A portion of this material is drawn from Witman's (2005) article, which first appeared in the *Communications of the Association for Information Systems*. A previous version of this chapter appeared in *Handbook of Research in Information*

Security and Assurance, edited by Jeet Gupta and Sushil Sharma.

ACKNOWLEDGMENT

The authors greatly appreciate the contributions of Paul Clay, Theresa Edgington, Kate Kaiser, Fred L. Kitchens, Tim McLaren, Julian Newman, Eric Overby, Terry Ryan, Detmar Straub, and George Westerman, as well as the helpful comments from Nathan Garrett and Rich Burkhard.

REFERENCES

Anonymous. (2005). Review of NDA guidelines. Personal communication via e-mail. Simi Valley, CA.

Beyer, G. W. (2001). *Modern dictionary for the legal profession* (3rd ed.). Buffalo, NY: William S. Hein & Co., Inc.

Chen, W. S., & Hirschheim, R. (2004). A paradigmatic and methodological examination of information systems research from 1991 to 2001. *Information Systems Journal, 14*(3), 197-235.

Clay, P. (2005). Response to NDA query. Personal communication via e-mail. Simi Valley, CA.

CMU. (2001, November). IP policy mark-up, including changes proposed by the University Research Council. Retrieved June 1, 2008, from http://www.andrew.cmu.edu/org/fac-senate/docsDec01/markedIPPol.pdf

Edgington, T. (2005). Response to NDA query. Personal communication via e-mail. Simi Valley, CA.

Foley, J. (2004). Bayh-Dole Act bad for computing research? *Computing Research News, 16*(1), 4, 7.

Garner, B. A. (2004). *Black's law dictionary* (Vol. 1). St Paul, MN: Thomson/West.

Grossman, M., Esq. (2004). *Technology law: What every business (and business-minded person) needs to know.* Lanham, MD: The Scarecrow Press, Inc.

GUIRR. (1997, October). *Openness and secrecy in research: Preserving openness in a competitive world.* Retrieved June 1, 2008, from http://www7.nationalacademies.org/guirr/Openness_and_Secrecy.html

Kaiser, K. (2005). Response to NDA query. Personal communication via e-mail. Simi Valley, CA.

Kitchens, F. L. (2005). Response to NDA query. Personal communication via e-mail. Simi Valley, CA.

Marcus, A. D. (1999). Class struggle: MIT students, lured to new tech firms, get caught in a bind--they work for professors who may also oversee their academic careers--homework as nondisclosure. *Wall Street Journal (Eastern Edition)*, p. A1.

McLaren, T. (2005). Response to NDA query. Personal communication via e-mail. Simi Valley, CA.

Milgrim, M. R. (2006a). *Milgrim on trade secrets* (Vol. 2). New York: Matthew Bender & Company.

Milgrim, M. R. (2006b). *Milgrim on trade secrets* (Vol. 1). New York: Matthew Bender & Company.

NCCUSL. (1985, August 9). Uniform Trade Secrets Act with 1985 Amendments. Retrieved June 1, 2008, from http://www.law.upenn.edu/bll/ulc/fnact99/1980s/utsa85.htm

Newberg, J. A., & Dunn, R. L. (2002). Keeping secrets in the campus lab: Law, values and rules of engagement for industry-university R&D partnerships. *American Business Law Journal, 39*(2), 187-240.

Newman, J. (2005). Response to NDA query. Personal communication via e-mail. Simi Valley, CA.

Oppedahl & Larson LLP. (1995, June 29). Comparing patents and copyrights. Retrieved June 1, 2008, from http://www.patents.com/patents.htm#compare-copyright

Overby, E. (2005). Response to NDA query. Personal communication via e-mail. Simi Valley, CA.

Peterson, I. (1985). Bits of ownership: Growing computer software sales are forcing universities to rethink their copyright and patent policies. *Science News, 128*(12), 189-190.

Shippey, K. C. (2002). *A short course in international intellectual property rights: Protecting your brands, marks, copyrights, patents, designs, and related rights worldwide.* Novato, CA: World Trade Press.

Stim, R., & Fishman, S. (2001). *Nondisclosure agreements: Protect your trade secrets and more* (1st ed.). Berkeley, CA: Nolo Press.

Straub, D. (2005). Response to NDA query. Personal communication via e-mail. Simi Valley, CA.

USPTO. (2006a, November 6, 2006). General information concerning patents - what is a Copyright? Retrieved June 1, 2008, from http://www.uspto.gov/web/offices/pac/doc/general/index.html#copyright

USPTO. (2006b, November 6, 2006). General information concerning patents - what is a patent? Retrieved June 1, 2008, from http://www.uspto.gov/web/offices/pac/doc/general/index.html#patent

USPTO. (2006c, November 6, 2006). General information concerning patents - what is a trademark or servicemark? Retrieved June 1, 2008, from http://www.uspto.gov/web/offices/pac/doc/general/index.html#mark

Volonino, L. (2005). Editing feedback on manuscript. Personal communication via e-mail. Simi Valley, CA.

Westerman, G. (2005). Response to NDA query. Personal communication via e-mail. Simi Valley, CA.

Witman, P. (2005). The art and science of nondisclosure agreements. *Communications of the AIS, 16*(11), 260-269.

ADDITIONAL SOURCES

Sample Nondisclosures from Institutions

- From the University of Wisconsin – Milwaukee's Center for Industrial Mathematics. Commentary on nondisclosures and a sample NDA: http://www.uwm.edu/Dept/CIM/indmath8.html
- From the University of Connecticut's Office of Sponsored Research. Provides three forms of NDA, including one-way disclosure in each direction, and mutual exchange: http://www.osp.uconn.edu/nondisclosure.html

Sample Intellectual Property Policies

- From Carnegie Mellon University. Broad coverage of intellectual property policy, well beyond the topics of nondisclosure agreements: http://www.cmu.edu/policies/documents/IntellProp.html
- From Johns Hopkins University Technol-

ogy Transfer. Starting point for initiating agreements with the university: http://www. techtransfer.jhu.edu/initiateAgreement

Sample Nondisclosures from the View of Researcher as Discloser

- NDA from Columbia University's Science and Technology Ventures. Assumes that the University is disclosing *its* confidential information to a third party: http://www.stv. columbia.edu/guide/agreements/nondisclosure
- NDA from Southern Methodist University, Focusing on the researcher's work as an "Inventor": http://www.smu.edu/research/ Limited%20Use%20and% 20Nondisclosu re%20Agreement.doc

Sample NDA for Clinical Trials

- University of Minnesota's Research Services Organization guidelines. Focuses to some extent on clinical trials, but basic guidelines are provided that could be applicable to other fields: http://www.ahc.umn.edu/research/rso/information/sponsors/instructions/home.html

KEY TERMS

Confidentiality: Restrictions on the dissemination of information (Garner, 2004, p. 318).

Copyright: "A property right in an original work of authorship ..., giving the holder exclusive right to reproduce, adapt, distribute, perform, and display the work" (Garner, 2004, p. 361).

Intellectual Property: "A category of intangible rights protecting commercially valuable products of the human intellect," including but not limited to trademark, copyright, patent, and trade secret rights (Garner, 2004, p. 824).

Nondisclosure Agreement: A contract promising "not to disclose any information shared by or discovered from a trade secret holder" (Garner, 2004, p. 1079).

Patent: "The right to exclude others from making, using, marketing, selling, ..., or importing an invention for a specified period" (Garner, 2004, p. 1156).

Trade Secret: "A formula, process, device, or other business information that is kept confidential to maintain an advantage over competitors" (Garner, 2004, p. 1533).

Trademark: "A word, phrase, logo, or other graphic symbol used ... to distinguish a product... from those of others" (Garner, 2004, p. 1530).

ENDNOTE

[1] A derivative work, for copyright purposes, is a new work that is created substantially from an original work (Radcliffe & Brinson, 1999). Examples might be a translation of a book into another language, or in research terms, reusing a large portion of an existing paper to create a new paper with theoretical extensions.

[2] Voda v. Cordis Corp., Appeal No. 05-1238, 2005 WL 2174497 at *11 (Fed. Cir. June 6, 2005).

APPENDIX

Nondisclosure Agreement

AGREEMENT made this [*specify day*] day of [*specify month and year*] between [*name of first party*], and [*name of second party*].

1. Addresses. [*name of first party*] is a [*specify whether individual or business entity*] located at [*identify address*]. [*name of second party*] is a [*specify whether individual or business entity*] located at [*identify address*].

2. Purpose. [*name of first party*] wishes to engage the services of [*name of second party*] (the "Engagement") and in connection with such services, [*name of first party*] may disclose to [*name of second party*] certain confidential technical and business information which [*name of first party*] desires [*name of second party*] to treat as confidential.

3. Definition. "Confidential Information" as used in this Agreement means information or material that is not generally available to or used by others, or the utility or value of which is not generally known or recognized as standard practice whether or not the underlying details are in the public domain, including without limitation: (a) Information or material that relates to [*first party's*] inventions, technological developments, "know how", purchasing, accounting, merchandising or licensing; (b) Trade secrets; (c) Software in various stages of development (source code, object code, documentation, diagrams, flow charts), drawings, specifications, models, date and customer information; and (d) Any information of the type described above that [*first party*] treats as proprietary or designates as confidential, whether or not owned or developed by [*first party*].

4. Nonuse and Nondisclosure of Confidential Information. During the term of this Agreement, [*second party*] will have access to and become acquainted with various propriety information of Employer, including discoveries, developments, designs, formulas, patterns, devices, secret inventions, processes, software programs, technical data, customer and supplier lists, and compilations of information, records, and specifications , and other matters consisting of trade secrets, all of which are owned by [*first party*] and regularly used in the operation of [*first party's*] business. [*Second party*] may also have access to the confidential information of third parties that has been provided to [*first party*] subject to a Confidential Disclosure Agreement.

    All proprietary information and all files, records, documents, drawings, specifications, equipment, computer files, computer records, computer programs, and similar items relating to the business of [*first party*], whether they are prepared by [*second party*] or come into [*second party's*] possession in any other way and whether or not they contain or constitute trade secrets owned by [*first party*], are and shall remain the excusive property of [*first party*] and shall not be removed from the premises of [*first party*], or reproduced or distributed in any manner, under any circumstances whatsoever without the prior written consent of [*first party*].

    [*second party*] promises and agrees that [*she or he*] shall not misuse, misappropriate, or disclose any proprietary information or trade secrets described herein, directly or indirectly, or use them in any way, either during the term of this agreement or at any time thereafter, except as required in the course of the Agreement.

5. Obligations of Confidentiality not Applicable. Obligations of Confidentiality imposed by this Agreement will not apply to confidential information that (a) Is or has been generally available

to the public by any means, through no fault of [*second party*], and without breach of this Agreement; (b) Is or has been lawfully disclosed to [*second party*] by a third party without an obligation of confidentiality being imposed on [*second party*]; (c) Has been disclosed without restriction by [*first party*] or by a third party owner of confidential information.

6. <u>Academic Use of Confidential Information</u>. Notwithstanding anything above, [*second party*] may use the above identified Confidential Information for not for profit educational or research activities ultimately leading to publication in academic or trade journals (the "Academic Activities"). If the Confidential Information is used for the Academic Activities, [*second party*] shall protect the anonymity of the Confidential Information as well as the source of the Confidential Information. [*Second party*] shall not publish or otherwise disseminate in writing or otherwise the result of the Academic Activities without the prior consent of [*first party*], such consent to be withheld only as necessary to ensure the anonymity of the Confidential Information. The parties agree that the [*second party*] has the right to produce derivative publications subject to this Agreement.

7. <u>Ownership of Work Product</u>. The parties agree that any and all intellectual properties, including, but not limited to, all ideas, concepts, themes, inventions, designs, improvements, and discoveries conceived, developed, or written by [*second party*], either individually or jointly in collaboration with others, pursuant to this Agreement, shall belong to and be the sole and exclusive property of [*first party*].

   Notwithstanding the above, the parties agree that the ownership of derivative work product shall belong to and be the sole and exclusive property of [*second party*]. A "derivative work" is herein defined as a new work based upon an original work to which enough original creative work has been added so that the new work represents an original work of authorship.

8. <u>Term</u>. The obligations of [*second party*] under this Agreement shall survive until such time as all Confidential Information disclosed under this Agreement becomes publicly known and made generally available through no action or inaction of the [*second party*].

9. <u>Return of Materials</u>. [*second party*] agrees to deliver to [*first party*], promptly on request, or thirty days from the date of termination of this Agreement, all confidential material herein identified, in the possession of [*second party*] pertaining to the business of [*first* party] and originating with [*first party*] that came into the possession of [*second party*].

10. <u>Remedies</u>. The parties to this Agreement acknowledge and agree that it is impossible to measure in money the damages which will accrue to the [*first party*] if [*second party*] shall breach or be in default of any of [*second party's*] representations or agreements set forth in this Agreement. Accordingly, if [*second party*] breaches or is in default of any of the representations and agreements set forth above, will cause irreparable injury to [*first party*] and that, in addition to any other remedies that may be available, in law, equity or otherwise, [*first party*] shall be entitled to obtain injunctive relief against the threatened breach of this Agreement or the continuation of any such breach, without the necessity of proving actual damages.

11. <u>Non-interference</u>. For the period of one (1) years after the termination of this Agreement, with or without cause, [*second party*] shall not interfere with the relationship of [*first party*] and any of its customers, employees, agents, representatives or supplier.

12. <u>Non-solicitation</u>. For the period of one (1) years after the termination of this Agreement, with or without cause, [*second party*] shall not solicit, operate, be employed by or otherwise participate in the business or operations of any of the [*first party's*] clients.

13. <u>Miscellaneous</u>. This Agreement shall bind and inure to the benefit of the parties and their successors and assigns. This Agreement supersedes any and all other agreements, either oral or in writing, between the parties with respect to the services provided under this Agreement, and contains all of the covenants and agreements between the parties with respect to the services provided herein. Each party to this agreement acknowledges that no representations, inducement, promises, or agreements, orally or otherwise, other than those set forth herein, have been made by any party, or anyone acting on behalf of any party, and that no other agreement, statement, or promise not contained in this agreement shall be valid or binding. Any modification of this agreement shall be effective only if it is in writing signed by the party to be charged. This agreement shall be governed by and construed in accordance with the laws of the state of [*state*]. If any provision in this agreement is held by a court of competent jurisdiction to be invalid, void, or unenforceable, the remaining provisions shall nevertheless continue in full force without being impaired or invalidated in any way.

FIRST PARTY

_____[*signature*]

SECOND PARTY

_____[*signature]*

Chapter VII
Applied Multi-Case Research in a Mixed-Method Research Project:
Customer Configuration Updating Improvement

Slinger Jansen
Utrecht University, The Netherlands

Sjaak Brinkkemper
Utrecht University, The Netherlands

ABSTRACT

Even though information systems is a maturing research area, information systems case study reports generally lack extensive method descriptions, validity defense, and are rarely conducted within a multi-case research project. This reduces the ability to build theory in information systems research using case study reports. In this chapter we offer guidelines, examples, and improvements for multicase studies. If information system researchers stick to these guidelines, case study reports and papers will get published more often, improving the rapidly maturing research area of information systems.

MULTIPLE CASE STUDY RESEARCH

It is our belief that IS research is quickly getting more mature and deserves more attention in the area of methods and practices. In this chapter, we report on our experiences (Jansen & Brinkkemper, 2007; Jansen et al., 2006; van de Weerd, Brinkkemper, Souer, & Versendaal, 2006; van de Weerd, Brinkkemper, & Versendaal, 2007) with multicase studies in the area of Information Systems (IS) research. We believe that case study evidence is fundamental for building theories in this rapidly maturing field (Darke, Shanks, & Broadbent, 1998). Case studies encourage students and researches to train themselves in understanding large complex systems (for system maintenance) and organizations. Furthermore, case studies are generally appreciated by practitioners, and provide a popular method in IS research to disseminate and explain phenomena in the field. These case studies are, however, often reported without much validation. This chapter provides a detailed description of a multicase research project to help researchers to document their research methods, compare their research approach, and provide them with helpful experience reports. We believe such descriptions will improve the overall quality of multicase study research and reports, thus contributing to IS research at large.

Case Study Context

The experiences reported in this chapter concern a multicase research project that lasted from 2003 until 2006 and concerns the customer configuration updating practices of product software vendors.

To date, product software is defined as a packaged configuration of software components or a software-based service, with auxiliary materials, which is released for and traded in a specific market (Xu & Brinkkemper, 2005). One area that is specific to product software vendors is the fact that they have to release, deliver, and deploy their products on a wide range of systems, for a wide range of customers, in many variations. Furthermore, these applications constantly evolve, introducing versioning problems. An increasingly important part of product software development thus is customer configuration updating (CCU). CCU is "the combination of the vendor side release process, the product or update delivery process, the customer side deployment process, and the activation and usage processes" (Jansen et al.,

2006). The release process describes how products and updates are made available to testers, pilot customers, and customers. The delivery process describes the method and frequency of update and knowledge delivery from vendor to customer *and* from customer to vendor. The deployment process describes how a system or customer configuration evolves between component configurations due to the installation of products and updates. Finally, the activation and usage process concerns license activation and knowledge creation on the end-user side.

Product software vendors encounter particular problems when trying to improve these processes because vendors have to deal with multiple revisions, variable features, different deployment environments and architectures, different customers, different distribution media, and dependencies on external products. Also, there are not many tools available that support the delivery and deployment of software product releases that are generic enough to accomplish these tasks for any product. Case studies have shown (Ballintijn, 2007; Jansen, 2005; Jansen, 2006a, 2006b; Jansen, Ballintijn & Brinkkemper, 2004; Jansen, Brinkkemper, Ballintijn et al., 2005) that many issues remain unsolved. Large parts of the CCU process are still performed manually, such as quick fix distribution and deployment, license file creation, and error feedback reporting. Next to this, surveys have shown that up to 15% of deployments of products are unsuccessful due to missing components and configuration errors by the deployers. System administrators for large networked environments, too, experience many problems with respect to deployment, caused by heterogeneous environments, faulty configuration update tools, and lack of knowledge about system and software constraints. These problems require attention due to their large overhead costs (implementation, testing, configuration evolution, etc) and due to the fact that no quality guarantees can be given at deployment or update time.

To solve the problems stated above, a model to improve the CCU process of a software vendor has been developed. This model is based on a number of theories which, when applied correctly, improve the CCU process for any product software vendor and its customers (Roberts, Cater-Steel, & Toleman, 2006). Over the last 4 years we have conducted mixed-method research to evaluate these theories. The methods that have been applied are case studies, tool evaluations, prototype building, design research, and two surveys. The different methods were used to confirm or refute the theories. Case study research proved particularly useful where "research and theory are at their early formative stages" (Benbasat, Goldstein, & Mead, 1987). We would like to address the role of case studies in mixed-method research.

The CCU improvement model, although intuitively addressing the right issues with the right amount of attention, needed to be evaluated and validated. The model consists of a process model and maturity measures in each of the mentioned process areas. Since 2003, Utrecht University and CWI[1] have performed a number of case studies to establish problems in CCU and to test the model for improvement of CCU on the software vendor, system administrator, and end-user sides. These case studies led to successful research output (Ballintijn, 2007; Jansen & Brinkkemper, 2007; Jansen & Rijsemus, 2006; Jansen et al., 2006) and contributed to the area of IS research and, more specifically, software product management. To further confirm conclusions and observations drawn in the case studies and make a stronger claim for generalisability, a survey was been undertaken during February of 2007 (Jansen & Brinkkemper, 2008). The case studies were performed with care and rigor, using Yin's (2003) case study method and guidelines. To avoid common pitfalls, we have used guidelines and pointers from Kitchenham, Pickard, and Pfleeger (1995) and Flyvbjerg (2006).

Contributions and Structure

The main aims of this chapter are to encourage researchers in IS to more explicitly define and describe their research methods in publications. Second, we wish to encourage both industrial and scientific researchers to publish case study reports in case study databases. Finally, we wish to encourage researchers to do more emperical research and rigorously apply validity criteria to their research.

The chapter reports on a multicase research project that lasted from 2003 until 2006 and concerns the customer configuration updating practices of product software vendors. In the next section, the research methods and validity criteria are described. Furthermore, we provide a detailed overview of the used research methods, the case study protocols, databases, and reports are described in detail, an experience report is provided on the case studies and the strong points of this research and its findings are highlighted, the cases are discussed and some of the points for improvement are stated, and we describe the conclusions of this research and discuss the future of case studies in education and IS research.

THE RESEARCH AND ITS METHOD

The aims of these case studies were to determine the state of the practice of CCU, to explore what problems were still open, and to test the hypothesis that the CCU model potentially efficiently and cost-effectively improves the CCU processes. At the time of conception, we were already aware of the fact that this was a mixed-method research project, where the team would be doing tool prototyping and surveys as well as the case studies. To make sure the case studies would follow rigorous methods, we extensively used Yin (2003). This research followed positivistic principles wherein we believe that there are pre-existing regularities

Figure 1. Process-deliverable diagram example

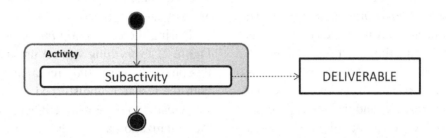

that can be discovered, investigated, and characterized relatively unproblematic using constructs devised by us (Orlikowski & Baroudi, 1991). We did attempt to closely guard the principles of validity by explicitly using the same case study protocol, case study database structure, and case study report structure.

The units of study of the cases were product software vendors, and, more specifically, the CCU processes of different product teams within these product software vendors. The case studies had the specific aims to uncover problems that were potentially of interest to the research community, to establish the state of the practice by documenting the practices and processes of product software vendors, and to find potential points for improvement for the participating product software vendors. The deliverables of each case study are the case study report (listing potential points for improvement), the case study database, and a list of publishable results. We find that our work is similar to the work of Gable (1994). Gable (1994), however, does not elaborate on the specific methods on how data was gathered for his study and does not provide the same level of detail as in this chapter. Furthermore, Gable (1994) defined his first study as a pilot project because no dependent variables had been specified. In another multiple-case study, which has strong survey elements, Radford and Kern (2006) only briefly describe their data collection and analysis.

The Method

As IS research is rapidly maturing, we are eager to present our research method for future reference, usage, and criticism. It is our firm belief that a further standardization and documentation of IS research methods contributes to the field as a whole and enables better research. To document the research method, we use process-deliverable diagrams, a technique taken from the field of method engineering (Saeki, 1994). Method engineering enables a method developer to take parts of a method called method fragments from a method base and compose them into new methods that are applicable to the developer's situation. With our work, we wish to contribute to such a method base for IS research.

The process-deliverable diagrams define activities, sub activities, and deliverables from the activities. The left-hand side is a metaprocess model based on UML activity diagrams and the right-hand side is a meta-data model based on UML class diagrams. The dotted arrows indicate which concepts (deliverables) are created or adjusted in the corresponding activities. Please see van de Weerd et al. (2006) for a more detailed overview of this modeling technique.

The case studies have all been conducted using the same method, consisting of four activities: case study invitation, case study initiation, research execution, and case study finalization. The main deliverables of each case study were the case study protocol, case study database, and case study report. We now describe each activity and each deliverable in detail.

During the *case study invitation* activity, we attempted to find as many interested participants as possible by contacting our professional and personal networks. The e-mail sent out to different mailing lists described the motivation behind the research, the research and case study process, and the possibilities for cooperation. We invited interested parties to reply. Once a number of suitable candidates had replied, we contacted them by phone to further establish the details and to make an appointment with the initiator (usually someone from higher management) and the potential *project champion* for an introductory presentation. At these meetings we would generally also introduce the Nondisclosure Agreement (NDA), to clarify that we would treat results as confidential but had the intention to publish interesting results. After the introductory presentation, both the research

group and the product software vendor had 2 weeks to consider the possibilities for cooperation and initiate further contact.

During the *case study initiation phase* (see Figure 2), everything was set up such that after this phase the case study researcher could start with the research undisturbed. First a protocol was created to demonstrate potential impact on the organization and to show that the intention was a win-win situation for both the company, in the form of advice and publicity, and the research team, in the form of the results of the case study and the opportunity to (anonymously) publish the results of the research. As part of the protocol, the NDA was finalized and signed together with the project champion. The project champion also played a part in determining the scope of the research within the company (who to interview, access to which systems, documentation, access to the intranet, etc.) Finally the first documents

Figure 2. Invitation and initiation activities

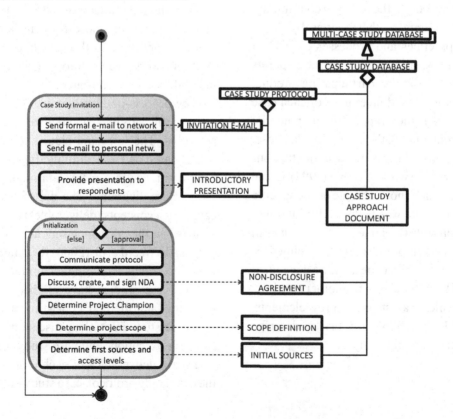

Figure 3. Research execution activity

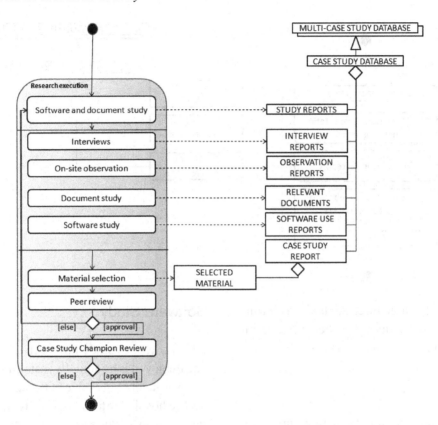

were shared and discussed with the project champion to get the researcher started. These activities generally provided the researcher with a running start once the researcher moved its working place to the company for the case study period.

Once the researcher arrived at the site, the *case study research execution phase* was formally started. The case study database was set up (both a digital folder and a paper binder) and the peer reviewer was assigned. The researcher would then start by studying mostly documents and software that was available on the intranet. After the researcher had built a database of assumptions (mostly in the form of schematic process pictures and lists of facts), the first phase of the interviews was started. After most of the interviews and observations were done, the researcher would, while still at the product software vendor's site, write up a draft of the case study report. This report would be extensively reviewed by the peer

researcher and after his approval the report would be reviewed by the project champion. The project champion's approval of the case study report indicated the end of the research execution phase. The researcher would then return to its research institute to finalize the case study report.

The *finalization phase,* of the case study was usually started after the case study project champion had approved of the report. Final changes would be made by the researcher at his home institute where a final presentation was also prepared. Both the report and the presentation contain advice, based on CCU literature for the product software vendor on how to improve their CCU practices. As a final step the case study report was published as a technical report within the research organization, the database was added to the large multicase database, possibilities for further cooperation were discussed, and publishing opportunities for the research were considered.

Figure 4. Case study finalization activity

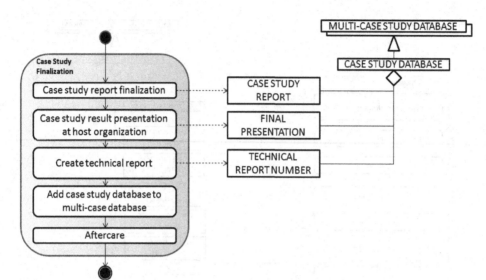

The researcher used three methods to find answers to the research questions, being document study, software study, and interviews.

Document Study

The project champion would generally supply the researcher with a number of relevant documents before the research was started. These documents would not only provide insights into the CCU processes of a software vendor but, more importantly, would provide an understanding of the terminology used in the company. The researcher would write down terms that were confusing and bring them up during the first interviews. We noticed that development documentation is often out of date and frequently presents a vision instead of the truth. Document study was the second most powerful but also time consuming method. Documents were very helpful in supporting both software study (manuals, mostly) and the interviews. During the interviews documents were often used to provide a foundation for discussion. Typical documents were implementation manuals, deployment manuals, development instructions, and implementation/sales presentations.

Software Study

An easy way to study how software is delivered and deployed is by actually installing the product on a workstation. For five of the cases (the sixth is a large hospital information system), we actually installed the products locally. This type of research provides deep insight into the deployment process (dependencies, minimum requirements, etc.) and more importantly proved to the interviewees that the researcher had sufficient knowledge about the delivery, licensing, and deployment processes. The software vendors freely provided licenses for research purposes.

Interviews

Interviews consisted of two sessions of approximately one hour. The first interview consisted of three parts. First, the interviewee was interviewed for approximately 15 minutes with predefined questions. After the short round a longer round of 45 minutes followed, during which the researcher and the interviewee would discuss different aspects of the CCU process. During the last 5 minutes, time was taken to see who else was of importance to the researcher. Approximately 1 week after the first round with an interviewee, a second interview was arranged to double check the facts distilled from different sources, such as software study, documentation study, and material from other interviews. We found the two round system powerful, especially when sources seemed to disagree. After gathering a new list of potential interviewees the researcher would generally call or visit that person to arrange a new interview. In about 10% of the interviews, the conversation was ended prematurely, mostly because the person did have any knowledge of interest to the researcher. Special forms were created for the interviews on which the researcher could make notes and write down standard answers, such as the person's name and job position. Furthermore, the interview notes were written up within 24 hours after doing the interview (mostly immediately after the interviews) (Walsham, 1993).

We found that e-mail discussions are only useful before interviews. If an e-mail discussion becomes too detailed, it is best to call or meet that person, even after the interviews have been completed. We also noticed that a good researcher brings a notebook and pen to lunch.

Data Analysis

During the process of analyzing the data gathered through software study, document study, and the interviews, we found that a concrete scope, triangulation, and a strong belief in the CCU model were most necessary to create valuable deductions in the case study reports. During the first case study, the scope of the research had only been vaguely defined, leading to a case study project without boundaries. By re-evaluating the scope of the case study during the project, a final list of to do items could be made, enabling the researcher to define when enough data had been gathered. Scoping enabled us to clearly define the boundaries of the research, especially after seeing what results were interesting to the community at that time.

One large part of data analysis was theory shaping, where the different descriptions and facts were modeled in different process diagrams. By triangulating these diagrams with data from interviews, software, and internal documents, these models were changed until they represented the practice of an organization fully. This method of data analysis is described by others as constant comparative analysis (Hewitt-Taylor, 2001).

It was hard to identify weaknesses within the product software vendor's practices without having a clear view of what we considered mature CCU. As the project progressed more knowledge became available about good and bad CCU practices. As the researchers became more knowledgeable on the subject the quality of our data analysis improved. We found the length of the first case study contributing in this aspect, because it enabled us to explore the case study practice.

Validity

There exist four validity criteria for emperical research (Eisenhardt, 1989; Flyvbjerg, 2006; Yin, 2003;) and we have attempted to satisfy all. They are the following:

Construct Validity. Construct validity is satisfied when concepts being studied are operationalized and measured correctly. A glossary of terms was created before actually starting the multicase research. Furthermore, we attempted to identify and compare different constructs within the case. Also, the same protocol was applied to each case study. To gain correct and consistent facts for the case study database, we did double interviews and cross checked our results from the document and software study with these. Periodic peer review of the case study database ensured that the right information was being collected and stored. Finally, to minimize personal bias the case study reports were reviewed by fellow project members, the researcher was required to stay at the site, and the researcher had to inform participants of the exact aims of the project.

Internal Validity. Internal validity is defined as establishing a causal relationship and distinguishing spurious relationships. To make sure we correctly extracted facts from the case study database the case study report was reviewed extensively by informed outsiders, the project champion, and one other employee from the product software vendor. We mostly used explanation building for establishing causal relationships (Stake, 2005). To make sure the facts and relationships in the case study reports were complete, towards the end of the case study we would formally invite the project champion to make suggestions to complete and prioritize lists, process overviews, and the list of improvements.

External Validity. External validity is defined as establishing the domain to which a study's findings can be generalized. The cases are found to be representative for the Dutch product software vendor market domain because the vendors have come from a list of the Platform for Productsoftware,[2] an organization that aims to share knowledge between research institutes and product software vendors in The Netherlands, with over 100 members. The list shows that the cases are typical for the Dutch software industry with respect to size, number of customers, and income.

Empirical Reliability. Empirical reliability is defined as the ability to demonstrate that the study can be repeated with the same results. A lot of work has been put into defining the procedures of the research (the case study protocol), the case study databases, and the case study report. We expect that the cases and the results can be repeated if the circumstances are at least similar (same interviewees, same documents, etc).

We found these validity criteria guiding beacons in designing the research and would advise others to discuss them frequently during the progress of the research.

THE CASE STUDY PROTOCOL, DATABASE, AND REPORT

In this section, the case study protocols, databases, and reports are described in detail.

The Protocol

The case study protocol serves three purposes. First, the aim of the case study protocol is to clearly define the aims of the case study so as to avoid confusion and conflict in the future. Second, we use the protocol to convince the participants of the usefulness of the research. Third, the case study protocol is a useful document to instruct different researchers at different sites and enabled us to reuse the results from the different cases. The protocol has been specifically adjusted for each case but only to change the company details in each. The peer-reviewer and the researcher must agree on the protocol during the initiation process. This document is kept deliberately short to enable product software vendors to quickly decide whether or not to cooperate.

The document consists of four parts, the introduction, the description of the research, the description of this specific case, the conclusions, and a summary and related work of the case study. In the first two parts, the research was described nonspecific to the product software vendor. The research description consists of a description of the different participants, the conceptual model and terminology used, the CCU model on which this research is based, the research questions, the applied research methods, and potential participants. In the third part was explained how we would go about our research and what confidentiality aspects would be taken into account. In the fourth part, the research is summarized and related work is provided.

The document, generally no longer than seven pages, needed to take away any doubts that we would be wasting the product software vendor's time. To do so, the research aim is stated in short, a short description is given of the overall research, and a lot of attention is given to the description of the CCU model. We also note that product software vendors spent the most time over the list of potential participants (in the form of job titles, since we had no inside information on the company itself yet) and the list of used research methods (software study, document study, and interviews). Some of the job titles are *configuration manager, developer, supportdesk employee*, and *development manager*. The document was used as a checklist once the project was ending to determine whether points had been missed.

The Database

At the end of each of the case studies, the researcher was responsible for delivering his case study database. The case study database, as depicted in Figure 5, was structured similarly for each case and consisted of four parts. During the case study, documents and materials were obtained from the product software vendor on which the researcher had had no influence. These were either available on paper or available digitally. The third and fourth parts of the case study database consist of materials created by the researcher, such as interview and observation notes and screenshots and captures. Because the case study databases never grew over approximately 150 items, the documents were kept in two digital folders and two binders. We had the largest problem storing e-mails and digital discussions, due to the many different formats in which they were delivered. We also found that meticulous record keeping (Benbasat, Goldstein, & Mead, 1987) is essential for storing items in the case study databases. Due to the fact that the researchers are not at their normal working place and were travelling by public transport or car documents were indeed lost. Also, due to insufficient record keeping a lot of duplication was found in the databases, especially among the digital folders and paper binders.

The Report

Please see Figure 6 for the template outline of a case study report. The aim of the case study report is to provide future researchers with concise mate-

Figure 5. Case study database

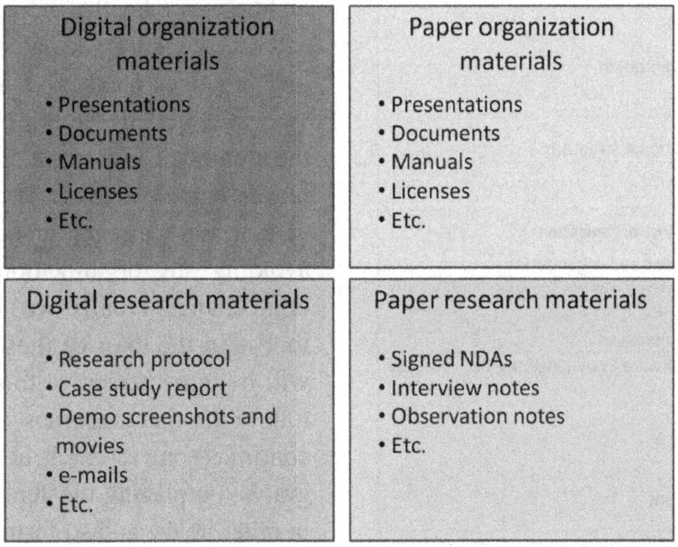

Digital organization materials	Paper organization materials
• Presentations • Documents • Manuals • Licenses • Etc.	• Presentations • Documents • Manuals • Licenses • Etc.
Digital research materials	Paper research materials
• Research protocol • Case study report • Demo screenshots and movies • e-mails • Etc.	• Signed NDAs • Interview notes • Observation notes • Etc.

rial about the case studies done. The case study reports, varying from 18 to 50 pages, all adhering to this outline, thus using a uniform method to present the varying results and observations of the different researchers.

CONDUCTING THE RESEARCH

We found that the research took approximately 24 weeks per case study. Of these 24 weeks, only a small part was done at the companies (see Table 1). The other weeks we were waiting for responses from software vendors or writing up reports and processing material. We found that it generally took product software vendors one week to send an answer to the invitations. It then took another week for them to respond to our formal invitation letter by mail. Putting the NDA together took between one and four weeks. After the NDA had

Figure 6. Case study report outline

---

1. **Introduction** – describing the case study and motivation in short

2. **Research** – describing the research questions, method and vision

  2.1 Research project
  2.2 Conceptual model and terminology
  2.3 CCU model description
  2.4 Research questions
  2.5 Research methods

3. **Description of the host organization**

  3.1 Short description
  3.2 Main product(s)
  3.3 Employees and organizational structure
  3.4 Customers
  3.5 The market

4. **Description of CCU at the host organization**

  4.1 Development management and organization
      4.1.1 Versioning
      4.1.2 Documentation
      4.1.3 Software architecture
      4.1.4 The host's software knowledge mgmt processes
  4.2 Release process
  4.3 Delivery process
  4.4 Deployment process
  4.5 Usage and activation

5. **Observations and Conclusions**

6. **Potential Improvements**

---

been signed, we generally gained access immediately to the product software vendor's resources. The research itself took between 3 and 10 ten weeks and became progressively shorter as we gained more experience. Once the first phase of research had been done, the writing of the case study report took an average of 2 to 4 weeks. Getting it approved, however, took between 1 and 10 weeks, depending on the quality of the report, the sensitivity of the data, and the detail of process descriptions. In general, we would present our results to the case study participants approximately 2 weeks after the case study report had been approved.

Finding the Best Fitting Case

A strong point of this research was the selection procedure for case study participants. This research project was supported by the Platform for Productsoftware, providing us with an excellent case selection source. At first, the project was mostly opportunity driven where we would grasp any organization prepared to share their experience. As the results of our research were spread, however, we were soon invited by a larger number of product software vendors than we could handle. This enabled us to pick software vendors with different products, practices, and technologies. Furthermore, it enabled us to pick software vendors who had very mature processes and practices (Jansen et al., 2006) and others who were actually looking for improvements in the area of CCU (Jansen, 2006a). Screening is a powerful tool when selecting a product software vendor and we recommend being selective and avoiding any organization that is undergoing rapid change. Finally, we noticed that once your foot is in the door of these organizations, they will be more receptive to new initiatives. With four of the six companies we dealt with, we have continued our research in the form of research grants, outplacing master students, case studies in other fields, and so forth.

Table 1. Case studies overview

Identification Code	Time	Formal interviewees	Informal interviewees	Organization size	Duration at the host
ERPComp	Early 2004	15	24	1504	10 weeks
OCSComp	Early 2005	4	8	114	7 weeks
HISCComp	Mid 2005	7	12	107	6 weeks
FMSComp	Late 2005	8	8	164	4 weeks
CMSComp	Early 2006	4	8	65	3 weeks
TDSComp	Mid 2006	4	5	62	3 weeks

The Publications

The work led to a number of publications. The best case was the research conducted at a large bookkeeping product software firm, which had already implemented many different aspects of the CCU model. The research conducted there led to two papers being accepted at a leading conference (Jansen, Brinkkemper, Ballintijn et al., 2005) and in a journal (Jansen et al., 2006). The research from the third case study was published in the industrial forum of a large conference (Ballintijn, 2007). Finally, an overview paper of all the cases was published at a leading conference by Jansen and Brinkkemper (2007).

From Protocol to Theory

The multicase research was conducted to determine the state of the practice in CCU, to define the scope of CCU, and to contribute new findings to this field. The underlying hypothesis was that proper knowledge management over the distributed locations where a product is being used and developed (at the vendor, end-user, system administrator, etc.) can reduce deployment failures and enable quicker fault location in a software product.

To find new contributions, four methods were used. First, we formulated long lists of hypotheses, stating such things as "a software vendor cannot support more than 1000 end-users without tool support for updates and deployments," "software vendors are unaware of the hardware that is used by customers," and "vendors with more than 100 customers automatically release their software." Second, we performed cross-case comparison, taking different CCU processes and trying to abstract similarities and differences between the cases (Jansen & Brinkkemper, 2007). Also, we labeled findings in the case study databases in relation to the formulated theories. Finally, a tool evaluation framework was created (Jansen, Brinkkemper, & Ballintijn, 2005) and applied to the various tools found during the cases to see whether and how these tools supported the processes.

The processes defined in the CCU model were validated (proved to be similar to those of each subject of study) by the case studies, for the first time providing us with a validated overview of the CCU processes and practices, that is, all the processes involved with knowledge creation and distribution around a software product. The CCU model enabled the linking of each process to best practices from the different cases. Finally, those hypotheses that had not yet been accepted or refuted were processed (where possible) by comparing and contrasting the different case studies.

Findings

During the case studies we found a number of factors contributing positively, and in some cases even essential, to the end results of the case studies.

To begin with, *the elevator pitch is your introduction to the company*; especially the first couple of days you will have to explain why you are visiting the company. If you can clearly and shortly convey the message of why you are there to random people, we found it was much easier getting access to unexpected sources. In one case, it even lead us to the packaging department where only a couple of years ago batches of up to 20 floppies were formatted, printed, wrapped, and sent off to customers at 5 packages per minute.

A good relation with the project champion is essential for a successful case study. We noticed that the success of the case studies was greatly dependent on a project champion within the company who was responsible for the success of the case study within the product software vendor. For each case study performed, we noticed that the project champion would perform as an intermediary between the vendor's organization and the research institute. Furthermore, the project champion would reconfirm the importance of the research to interviewees and remove information blockades. During the case studies there were six project champions guiding us through the process of conducting the research at their product software vendors. Among these six were five development managers and one product manager. These people were generally hands-on professionals who had spent between 5 and 10 years at the company. We found that the project champions had to support the project above all else. Their motivation to approve of our research was mostly that we would propose improvements to their processes and compare them to those of others. We also found that project champions, after signing the NDA, gave complete openness and were not afraid to show weaknesses of the organization.

After the cases were complete, we *organized meetings for practitioners to report on the results of our research*. A working group that meets four times per year was started to share experiences and knowledge about the CCU processes. The companies are willing to share their knowledge of these processes because their strategic value lies in the fact that they build great bookkeeping software or content management systems (for example) and not in their development and CCU processes. Currently, two of the product software vendors still participate in the working group and we maintain strong ties with the other four.

CCU Conclusions and End Products

Here we give examples to the reader of some of the contributions of the research to show the types of deliverables that can come from multicase research. The research has been undertaken with two main research questions in mind: "What are the concepts and is the state of affairs of customer configuration updating for product software?" and "Can customer configuration updating be improved by explicitly managing and sharing knowledge about software products?"

The first research question was answered providing an overview of the current state of the art (research), and the practice (multicase project). Also, the CCU model has been created, providing practitioners with a method to evaluate its processes, tools, and practices. The second research question was answered by stating the methods used by product software vendors to explicitly manage and share knowledge. Furthermore, a tool was developed (currently under validation at one of the case study participants) that enables a product software vendor to share all types of knowledge in a software supply network with its customers (Jansen, 2007b). Besides the tools, CCU model, and publications, one of the main deliverables of this research was a Ph.D. thesis (Jansen, 2007a).

DISCUSSION

As can be seen in Table 1, the duration of the case study projects became progressively shorter. As the experience of the researchers grew, so did their ability to quickly get to the point; unfortunately, so did their sloppiness. We found that towards the final two cases, the study had become a fairly straightforward assignment in filling in the standard structure for case study reports found in Figure 6. This did, however, lead to longer periods of discussion with the peer reviewer (who was essential for the quality of this process) and the project champion.

Some of these discussions were extensive and lengthy. The NDAs stated that we would not publish anything without the product software vendor's explicit permission. In one case we were given the choice to remove sensitive details or to fully anonymize the report. Obviously we chose to anonymize the report, but that lead to other problems. The company is quite unique in The Netherlands and already the report stated that the vendor was a member of the 100 members of the Platform for Product Software, enabling further identification (and even if we had removed that fact the informed reader would know, since we are the founders of the Platform). Fortunately, as the discussion went into its sixth week, the project champion gave up and approved the report. In the future, we would not change the NDA, however, since the vendor's approval of all outgoing publications was a key selling point for the case studies.

To deal with the issue of self-selection, where the results from the cases are influenced by the fact that vendors respond to an invitation and thus find the research questions relevant, we took two measures. First, the invitation stated explicitly that we were looking for both product software vendors who found their own processes mature and those who really wished to improve their CCU processes. The second measure is that we actively approached two software vendors who initially had not replied to the invitational e-mail.

During the research, a list of hypotheses was formulated. Not all hypotheses were accepted or refuted using the multicase project. A large part could only be processed with the results from the survey, and some challenges still remain, such as determining the "ideal" moment for a product release (encompassing both CCU and requirements engineering), applying the CCU model to software vendors selling their applications in a Web service model, and so forth.

According to Eisenhardt (1989), 4 to 10 cases appear to be a sufficient amount for theory building. However arbitrary this suggestion may sound, the presented six cases fall into this range nicely.

Case Studies in Mixed-Method Research

The multicase study has been the larger part of a mixed-method research project into the CCU practices of software vendors. The research furthermore consists of prototype tool building (Jansen, 2007b; van der Storm, 2007) and a survey done at the beginning of 2007. Gable (1994) states that mixed-method research is not new, but underappreciated in the IS community. Some journals even specifically target one type of research, encouraging further polarization of research methods. In Klein's five fundamental attitudes towards research methods we identify ourselves as pluralists, that is, we believe that different approaches can be brought to bear on the same problem domain and that there exists no single universally valid way to delineate objects of study or to match the strengths and weaknesses of research approaches with contingent features of the object of study (Klein, Nissen, & Hirschheim, 1991).

While using mixed-methods to establish empirical evidence for theories within our model, we noticed that case studies were responsible for the larger part of the success of our research. These cases confirmed hypotheses, provided anecdotal evidence and counterarguments, and strengthened the applicability of the research work in practice. Furthermore, the multicase study project uncovered problems of interest to the scientific community. The case studies certainly delivered in that respect and we hope to validate the claims about our prototype tools in production environments of the case study participants. Furthermore, the case study subjects were brutally honest about limitations to and feasibility of the CCU model. On the other hand, the case studies were lacking in two areas. The feasibility of certain tools and protocols within the model could never be proven until a prototype was built. Second, it was hard to generalize conclusions from the case studies to other organizations. This research was undertaken as mixed-method project, where different hypotheses were tested using different methods. This is different from method triangulation, where one hypothesis is tested using different methods.

Due to the limited use of rival hypotheses and the fact that we were studying a relatively small subset of software vendors to validate the CCU improvement model, we encountered problems in generalizing our conclusions (Gable, 1994). To further validate our research, a benchmark survey was launched in February of 2007. The benchmark survey takes a "double survey" approach, where the results from the first survey are published in a report (including improvement advice) to the submitter. A second survey is attached to the report to see whether it was of use to the software vendor. The cases were the source for all improvement advice given in the survey reports. Both the advice and the reports were deemed useful and informative by the survey submitters. We find the use of different methods extremely useful to test hypotheses and become experts in the field of CCU. Furthermore, the use of mixed-method research has enabled us to generalize the conclusions from our multicase research.

Multiple vs. Single Case Study Research

The research project was always intended to consist mostly of multicase research. There are three reasons for this. To begin with, we wanted to find out the current state of the practice in CCU, not the one company that does things differently (Yin, 2003, calls these "black sheep" cases). Second, we needed a solid base to launch other research from, such as surveys. This was reached through multicase research, which is considered to deliver more "robust" results than a single case study (Herriott & Firestone, 1983). Finally, we needed measurable constructs and a conceptualized overview of the CCU research field. Such constructs had hardly been defined in previous research by others (Jansen, 2007a), enabling us to take a green fields approach. In a single case study, we potentially had not been able to define constructs as well, simply because one study would not have provided a full overview of the different concepts.

In practice, the different case studies unearthed much more than a single one would have. The multiple cases enabled the discovery of one particular exotic case (Jansen et al., 2006), more theory building, and the definition of similarities and differences between the different CCU processes of the organizations. The exotic case is described further in another section of the chapter. Some of our early hunches, such as the fact that the number of customers a vendor has is detrimental to the process of license management, could only be confirmed by looking at multiple case studies. The same holds for product complexity: a more complex product leads software vendors to having a more elaborate CCU process with more manual steps, leading to our conclusion that such complexity comes at a price.

The identification of differences and similarities between the cases enabled us to define processes and best practices that are standard in regards to the CCU process for software vendors.

For example, all companies use the major, minor, and bugfix release model, where major releases happen every 1 to 3 years, minor releases happen every 6 months to a year, and bug fix releases are released anywhere between one per day to one per 6 months. Another find was that all cases used a release scenario to make sure that on the day of a release the product was released in full without any missing parts (documentation, languages, libraries, etc.) An interesting sidebar to this find is that later in the survey we uncovered that this holds only for those organizations with more than 5 employees (all organizations from the cases had 62 employees or more). Similarly, differences were found between the cases. Some of the organizations had strict well-planned release schedules set up to map out the different versions that would be released over the following 3 year period, whereas others had vague targets and flexible dates. Also, when it comes to license management of their software products, all vendors used different mechanisms and support tools. One final reason to do multicase research was that we wished to give something back to the organizations from previous experiences and from some of the research on CCU in academia, in the form of advice and consultancy.

Yin (2003) states that one should try to avoid to put "all eggs in one basket," that is, one should always attempt to get more case studies or be ready to defend the choice for that specific case fiercely. The one downside that we did find in this research was that a lot of work is involved in doing six case studies. If one is going to do such research, our advice is to distribute the work over different researchers. Also, in the future, we hope to combine different forms of research to get more data from one organization in different research fields. Finally, the selection of the cases deserves at least as much attention as with one case because a case study in a multicase project must at all times contribute to the data. We have provided an example of a case that contributed only marginally to our work in another section of the chapter.

The Best Case

In 2003, when this research started, there were no reports on how the industry performed in the area of CCU. To establish whether there were new and innovative practices in this area, an invitation was sent out for case study participants with either a mature or immature process. One organization, Exact Software, contacted us immediately. They believed their practices were innovative and industry leading. They had, for example, their own updater that kept customers up to date, maintained a customer base of 160.000 with low overhead, and had several product lines. The last founder of the company, which presently has 2,644 employees, was leaving the organization and wished to contribute to the research community. This put the organization in an extraordinary position, where in the past the company was well known to reject any type of scientific cooperation, the company was now open for our research.

Within 5 weeks, our researcher started at Exact to study the processes. The product manager at that time facilitated the research completely. The researcher obtained a login ID for the intranet from any location and started work at the development department in Delft, the Netherlands. The case study did bring forward new and innovative ideas and these results were published in two papers (Jansen, Brinkkemper, Ballintijn et al., 2005; Jansen et al., 2006) (the founder is a co-author of one of these). The case study was a success for three reasons. First, the company was undergoing changes and was open to research and new ideas. Second, the company displayed novel phenomena worth reporting. Finally, the company wished to provide openness to the outside world making the publication process much easier.

The Worst Case

In 2004 a software vendor providing an online statistics package responded to our invitation for case studies. The vendor had three products, with

100,000, 1,000, and 100 customers respectively. One of these products was a pure software product with a full delivery and deployment process and was of interest to our research. The other two products were provided as an online service and were thus less interesting. The management of the organization was undergoing changes, but the case study champion proved to be a reliable character with strong interests in our research. At face value, we approved of the case study and would start, due to the fact that the research team was busy in 2005.

When the case study began, all seemed well. Unfortunately the smallest product (100 customers) was the product of interest, which we only discovered in 2005. Furthermore, the project champion was away a lot, making it hard to get access to all sources. As the case study progressed, the product with the largest amount of customers was sold to another company and the project champion left the company. These changes made the employees wary of changes and thus were reluctant to participate in a case study. Fortunately the project champion was replaced by a new equally competent project champion, but the results proved to be only marginally relevant. These problems could have been avoided by better screening of the organization before the initiation of the case study.

Case Studies in Education, Industry, and Research

The case studies undertaken contribute to our educational program, to our industrial partners, and to our research initiatives. In the research methods course for our information systems students, the multicase example is discussed in 1 out of 20 2-hour lectures. Many of our students do projects with industrial partners and we find that case study education is essential for these students. Case study education has proven fruitful, since many of the student projects have lead to publications (Bakhshi, Versendaal, van den Berg, & van den Ende, 2007; Brinkkemper, van Soest, & Jansen, 2007).

The multicase research project would have been much harder without the Platform for Productsoftware. The Platform enabled us to handpick case study participants, organize expert meetings, and the Platform provided us with an outlet to the industry when there were best practice findings. The research we have undertaken in the multicase project has created credibility with the software vendors in the Platform. The credibility has lead to software vendors approaching us when encountering fundamental problems, creating long-lasting relations between our research group and some of the industrial parties that participated in the case studies.

With regards to research, the multicase research project now serves as an example to new Ph.D. students and starting researchers in our research group. We advise new Ph.D. students to start with a practical case study, as to gain an understanding of the problems in industry, compared to the problems and challenges these students gather from literature. We caution them, however, that what is interesting to an organization is frequently not aligned with our interests.

CONCLUSION

Case studies are a useful tool for IS and technology (IS/IT) research and improvement projects. More and more of our students are joining large consultancy firms after they obtain their Master's Degree. The use of case studies will improve a student's value in research and in the consultancy industry. We therefore encourage educational institutes to put case studies on the curriculum as one of the main drivers of IS/IT research. Case studies can also be of vital importance in new (Ph.D.) research projects to give the researchers a feel for the problems and terminology used in the particular field of IS research.

There are three reasons for reporting on the research conducted in a multicase study project in this chapter. First, we wish to propagate that case studies must be centrally stored to enable further theory building in the field of IS. Second, we want to formally report on our research methods, in a structured and fragmented fashion, to enable re-use and comments on our methods. Finally, we wish to share our experiences in case study research to improve future case study research.

FUTURE RESEARCH DIRECTIONS

Case study research undoubtedly contributes to the field of IS. All too often, however, case studies are published as mayflies. There should be a collaborative research database in which teaching cases and research case studies reside and can be retrieved through a simple interface. A good example is the eXperience (http://en.experience-online.ch) e-business case study database. Such databases enable IS practitioners and researchers to learn from others and to extract theories from literature research.

This work is only a first attempt at formally documenting research methods. In the future, we hope to contribute to the method base in other forms so that IS researchers can develop a research method toolkit. We found the mixed-method approach for this research successful and hope to repeat it in different projects to further evaluate mixed-method research.

ADDITIONAL READINGS

For the beginning case study scientist, we recommend reading Yin's (2003) case study method and guidelines. Common fallacies and pitfalls are described in regards to information system case studies in Kitchenham et al. (1995) and Flyvbjerg (2006). Describing research with method engineering techniques enables re-use and discussion

about research methods. This requires comprehensive descriptions (van de Weerd et al., 2006) of method engineering techniques. In regards to CCU, we recommend reading more on the benchmark survey for Dutch product software vendors (Jansen & Brinkkemper, 2008) and the changing product software industry (Brinkkemper, Soest & Jansen, 2007).

REFERENCES

Bakhshi, N., Versendaal, J., van den Berg, J., & van den Ende, D. (2007). Impact of the extensible business reporting language on the administrative burden of organizations: A case study at the Dutch water boards. In *Proceedings of the 4th International Conference on Enterprise Systems, Accounting & Logistics.*

Ballintijn, G. (2007). A case study of the release management of a health care information system. In *Proceedings of the IEEE International Conference on Software Maintenance, ICSM2005, Industrial Applications track.*

Benbasat, I., Goldstein, D. K., & Mead, M. (1987). The case research strategy in studies of information systems. *MIS Q., 11*(3), 369-386.

Brinkkemper, S., van Soest, I., & Jansen, S. (2007). Modeling of product software businesses: Investigation into industry product and channel typologies. In *The Inter-Networked World: ISD Theory, Practice, and Education, Pproceedings of the Sixteenth International Conference on Information Systems Development (ISD 2007).* Springer-Verlag.

Darke, P., Shanks, G. G., & Broadbent, M. (1998). Successfully completing case study research: Combining rigour, relevance and pragmatism. *Information Systems Journal, 8*(4), 273-290.

Eisenhardt, K. M. (1989). Building theories from case study research. *Academy of Management Review, 14*, 532-550.

Flyvbjerg, B. (2006). Five misunderstandings about case-study research. *Qualitative Inquiry, 12*(2), 219.

Gable, G. G. (1994). Integrating case study and survey research methods: An example in information systems. *European Journal of Information Systems, 3*(2), 112-126.

Herriott, R. E., & Firestone, W. A. (1983). Multisite qualitative policy research: Optimizing description and generalizability. *Educational Researcher, 12,* 14-19.

Hewitt-Taylor, J. (2001) Use of constant comparative analysis in qualitative research. *Nursing Standard, 15,* 42, 39-42.

Jansen, S. (2005). Software release and deployment at Planon: A case study report. In *Technical Report SEN-E0504.* CWI.

Jansen, S. (2006a). *Software release and deployment at a content management systems vendor: A case study report* (Tech. Rep. No. UU-CS-2006-044). Utrecht University: Institute of Computing and Information Sciences.

Jansen, S. (2006b). *Software release and deployment at Stabiplan: A case study report* (Tech. Rep. No. UU-CS-2006-041). Utrecht University: Institute of Computing and Information Sciences.

Jansen, S. (2007a). *Customer configuration updating in a software supply network.* Ph.D. Thesis, Utrecht University.

Jansen, S. (2007b). Pheme: An infrastructure to enable any type of communication between a software vendor and an end-user. In *International Conference on Software Maintenance 2007, tool demonstration.*

Jansen, S., Ballintijn, G., & Brinkkemper, S. (2004). *Software release and deployment at exact: A case study report* (Tech. Rep. No. SEN-E0414). CWI.

Jansen, S., Ballintijn, G., Brinkkemper, S., & van Nieuwland, A. (2006). Integrated development and maintenance for the release, delivery, deployment, and customization of product software: A case study in mass-market ERP software. In *Journal of Software Maintenance and Evolution: Research and Practice, 18,* 133-151. John Wiley & Sons, Ltd.

Jansen, S., & Brinkkemper, S. (2007). Definition and validation of the key process areas of release, delivery and deployment of product software vendors: Turning the ugly duckling into a swan. In *Proceedings of the International Conference on Software Maintenance (ICSM2006, Research track).*

Jansen, S., & Brinkkemper, S. (2008). A benchmark survey into the customer configuration processes and practices of product software vendors in The Netherlands. In *Proceedings of the 7th IEEE International Conference on Composition-Based Software Systems (ICCBSS).* IEEE.

Jansen, S., Brinkkemper, S., & Ballintijn, G. (2005). A process framework and typology for software product updaters. In *Ninth European Conference on Software Maintenance and Reengineering* (pp. 265-274). IEEE.

Jansen, S., Brinkkemper, S., Ballintijn, G., & van Nieuwland, A. (2005). Integrated development and maintenance of software products to support efficient updating of customer configurations: A case study in mass market ERP software. In *Proceedings of the 21st International Conference on Software Maintenance.* IEEE.

Jansen, S., & Rijsemus, W. (2006, September.). Balancing total cost of ownership and cost of maintenance within a software supply network. In *Proceedings of the IEEE International Conference on Software Maintenance,* Philadelphia, PA, USA.

Kitchenham, B., Pickard, L., & Pfleeger, S. L. (1995). Case studies for method and tool evaluation. *IEEE Software, 12*(4), 52-62.

Klein, H. K., Nissen, H.-E., & Hirschheim, R. (1991). A pluralist perspective of the information systems arena. *Information Systems Reserch: Contemporary Approaches and Emergent Traditions,* 1-20.

Orlikowski, W. J., & Baroudi, J. J. (1991). Studying information technology in organizations. *Information Systems Research, 2,* 1-28.

Radford, M. L., & Kern, M. K. (2006). A multiple-case study investigation of the discontinuation of nine chat reference services. *Library and Information Science Research, 28*(4), 521-547.

Roberts, D., Cater-Steel, A., & Toleman, M. (2006). Factors influencing the decisions of SMEs to purchase software package upgrades. In *Proceedings of the 17th Australasian Conference on Information Systems (ACIS 2006).*

Saeki, M. (1994). Software specification and design methods and method engineering. *International Journal of Software Engineering and Knowledge Engineering.*

Stake, R. E. (2005). *Multiple case study analysis.* The Guilford Press.

van der Storm, T., (2007). The Sisyphus continuous integration system. In *Proceedings of the Conference on Software Maintenance and Reengineering.* IEEE Computer Society Press.

van de Weerd, I., Brinkkemper, S., Souer, J., & Versendaal, J. (2006). A situational implementation method for Web-based content management system-applications: Method engineering and validation in practice. *Software Process: Improvement and Practice, 11*(5), 521-538.

van de Weerd, I., Brinkkemper, S., & Versendaal, J. (2007). Concepts for incremental method evolution: Empirical exploration and validation in requirements management. In *Proceedings of the 19th Conference on Advanced Information Systems Engineering.*

Walsham, G. (1993). *Interpreting information systems in organizations.* New York: John Wiley & Sons, Inc.

Xu, L., & Brinkkemper, S. (2005). Concepts of product software: Paving the road for urgently needed research. In *First International Workshop on Philosophical Foundations of Information Systems Engineering* (LNCS). Springer-Verlag.

Yin, R. K. (2003). *Case study research - design and methods* (3rd ed.). SAGE Publications.

ENDNOTES

[1] http://www.cwi.nl
[2] http://www.productsoftware.nl/

Chapter VIII
Historical Research in Information System Field:
From Data Collection to Theory Creation

Erja Mustonen-Ollila
Lappeenranta University of Technology (LUT), Finland

Jukka Heikkonen
Helsinki University of Technology, Finland

ABSTRACT

This chapter gives important methodological, theoretical, and practical guidelines to the information system (IS) researchers to carry out a historical study. This study shows how a new theory can be discovered inductively from historical studies using a methodological guideline from Mason, McKenney, and Copeland (1997b), using multiple data collection methods, such as semistructured interviews, archival files, and published news, and using novel data analysis methods from learning and intelligent systems, such as the Self-Organizing Maps (SOMs), SOMs combined with U-matrices, and the Bayesian network modeling. It also outlines the benefits, the main problems, the characteristics, and the implications of historical research in the information system field. Finally this chapter gives future some research directions of historical research.

INTRODUCTION AND BACKGROUND

The goal of this chapter is to outline how a new theory can be discovered inductively using histori-cal research approach. Historical research is difficult to carry out because its nature is interpretive, the research of which has been largely ignored so far (Bannister, 2002). There are studies outlining the importance of historical research in the area of information systems (IS) (Ein-Dor & Segev, 1993; Locker, Miller, Richardson, Tebeaux, & Yates, 1996; Mustonen-Ollila, 2005; Sandberg, 2005), studies involving single or multiple time periods and being longitudinal in its nature (Barley, 1990; Heiskanen, 1994; Pettigrew, 1989, 1990), and a study of the historical evolution of information system and time generation categories' development (Friedman & Cornford, 1989). Historical research can be characterised as longitudinal research from the past, because both longitudinal research and historical research are characterised by the measurement of differences or change in a variable from one time period to another, and longitudinal data analysis permits insights into the processes of change (Davies, 1994; Menard, 2002). In the historical studies, the research begins far away in the past when the distant causes for the events did not mean anything to each other, but later on effected to the current effects.

The fundamental assumptions of the historical research are as follows. First, in historical research, several simultaneously used data collection methods are needed. If the bulk of the gathered data is qualitative, consisting of interviews and archival material, historical research methods should be adopted (Copeland & McKenney, 1988; Mason, McKenney, & Copeland, 1997a, 1997b; McKenney, Mason, & Copeland, 1997) such that the suggestions of Pettigrew (1985) should be followed mostly when gathering and organising the data.

Pettigrew (1985) studies the management of organisational change, which is the phenomena in its real context. Pettigrew (1985) points out the aspects of continuity and change, and his study illustrates how change as a continuous incremental process can be interspersed with radical periods of change. These major decisions are associated with major changes in business market conditions (Dawson, 2003).

Second, the terminology and concepts between the historical research and the other forms of over time dependent research, such as longitudinal research and time series research are interchangeable, because they all study the phenomena of change and patterns over time but from different perspectives.

Third, data collection in historical studies is often problematic, because the access to the research objects is difficult since the time has passed. Longitudinal historical data gathering poses special problems, because attrition of cases can be serious for the reasons as follows. The lost individuals, interviewees not remembering or not wanting to remember the past events, the secondary or some other sources are the only available sources, researcher is not able to maintain contact with the research subjects, or some other attrition of data can have happened (Bannister, 2002; Buckland, 1998; Menard, 2002; Rutter, Maughan, Pickles, & Simonoff, 1998; Sandberg, 2005). Historical research takes place over a long time period, typically more than 10 or 20 years, and researchers of history are not present at the time of the historical events being studied (Bannister, 2002). Historical research generally considers events in retrospect including oral histories and life and work histories (Bannister, 2002; Ruspini, 1999). The historical studies generally use many primary and secondary sources of evidence (Mason at el., 1997b) which can be both qualitative and quantitative in nature (Eisenhard, 1989; Venkatesh & Vitalari, 1991). Primary historical and longitudinal sources are the key sources of evidence, such as written material (e.g., notes, diaries, internal documents generally, and stories), and eye witnesses at a single time period for several time periods (Bannister, 2002; Mustonen-Ollila, 2005; Sandberg, 2005; Venkatesh & Vitalari, 1991). Secondary data needs pre handling, and interpretation to generate understandable results. Data collection of the past events is dependent on existing transcriptions and their interpretation to discover the historical patterns is based on researcher's own intuition (Bannister, 2002; Buckland, 1998; Kieser, 1994). Studying historical change needs the use of longitudinal data, which is certainly not a cure for a weak research design and data analysis (Menard, 2002).

Fourth, in quantitative longitudinal research, the data analysis is used to give a parsimonious summary of patterns of relations between variables in the survey dataset (Lambert & Gayle, 2004). On the other hand, data analysis and interpretation of the results in historical studies needing quantitative longitudinal data is very complex and requires considerable sophistication. The preferred analysis strategy is partly determined by the shape of the data set in terms of number of cases and periods. The choice of a particular data analysis approach must depend on the objectives of the research (Venkatesh & Vitalari, 1991), but, unfortunately, historical research is lacking proper data analysing methods, which may influence the trustworthiness of the research (Sandberg, 2005). Even if modern analysing methods are now easily implemented, longitudinal empirical research and thus historical research do lag behind for such reasons such as the reviewers' are not aware of the moderns analysis methods (Willett & Singer, 2006), and a shortage of researchers with skills appropriate for longitudinal data analysis (Lambert & Gayle, 2004). Specifically, if the purpose of the historical study is to find out the unique patterns from the data, to discover changes over time, to build up different categories, to discover relationships and dependencies between the concepts and categories, to find out internal or external factors from the past, and to find out causal chains and path dependencies (Kieser, 1994; Mason et al., 1997b), then new analysing tools and methods are needed, such as Self-Organizing Maps (SOM) (Kohonen, 1989), SOM combined with Unified distance matrices (U-matrix) (Ultsch & Siemon, 1990), and Bayesian networks (Heckerman, 1996). Use of SOM, U-matrix, and Bayesian networks is rare in the information systems field (Ein-Dor & Segev, 1993; Mustonen-Ollila & Heikkonen, 2002, 2003), even if they can give several advantages to the historical research as described in this chapter.

Fifth, suitable methodological guidelines to carry out historical studies are needed in IS literature. Mason et al. (1997a, 1997b) present the only methodological guideline, which is based on organisation theory by Kieser (1994), and is close to that described by Yin (1994) for case study research (Bannister, 2002). When analysing longitudinal historical qualitative data, one ought to begin by putting it in a chronological order because the time line can help in the organisation of the large amount of empirical data (Mustonen-Ollila, 2005; Mustonen-Ollila & Lyytinen, 2003, 2004; Sandberg, 2005). In the interpretation phase, the data should be organised according to the themes based on the developed framework. This kind of analytical data organisation helps to understand the patterns in the data and to establish sequences across levels of analysis (Pettigrew, 1997; Sandberg, 2005; Yin, 1981). The theoretical framework of the study should be linked to the cases via pattern-matching logic (Yin, 1994), because the goal is to find patterns and themes in the progression of organisations over time (Pettigrew, 1997). This is in line with Pettigrew's (1992) and Lambert and Gayle's (2004) claims that longitudinal research is not only describing the change, but also involves the identification of patterns, and the search for the underlying mechanisms that shape the patterns.

Even if the historical studies are difficult to carry out, they are important to the IS society. Therefore, the main objective of our study is to describe how IS research could improve by using historical research methods. Our study outlines the main problems, the characteristics, the benefits, and the implications of historical research in the IS field, and it shows how historical case studies can be used to create a new theory. The second objective of our study is to give important methodological, theoretical, and practical guidelines to IS researchers to carry out a historical study, and it hopefully will effect positively the future of historical research in IS field.

The rest of the chapter is organised as follows. We first present the main thrust of the chapter by presenting data collection procedures for historical studies, outlining new analysing methods and tools, and presenting how to use historical research to discover a new theory inductively. We then make some conclusions, present future directions, and give additional readings of the research area.

RESEARCH METHODOLOGY IN HISTORICAL STUDIES

Issues, Controversies, Problems

The data collection in historical studies should be handled with care due to its direct effect to the research results achieved. In the historical data collection, the reconstruction of the past events and processes is achieved by interviewing the key persons of the different organisations. Even if the limitations of such data are understood, the collected data set in a form of a manuscript in a logical order over time is the strength of a historical study. Qualitative research tends to produce a large amount of data which must be manipulated and data reduction must also be used. Unfortunately, collecting a representative data set by following a time dependent vertical research design that involves several organisations is difficult to carry out due to resource and access limitations. Therefore, the sample should be limited to the number of organisations that are possible to study. By doing this, there is a control over the dependent variables, such as time, the organisations, and the concept categories (Mustonen-Ollila, 2005).

The definition of past events will form the basis for interviews and collecting data. Also archival files must be explored and system handbooks, system documentation, and minutes of meetings should be collected. The archival data must encompass several time periods representing a secondary source of data (Järvenpää, 1991). Other empirical data can contain tape-recorded semistructured interviews dealing with the experiences of the past events and main concepts in the study, the processes, and changes in the concepts. The interviews should be carried out both with people in charge in the organisations and with some people who have worked at those organisations at that time. The interviewees ought to be involved in multiple situations and events, and their working careers should extend at least over a period of 10 to 30 years in the studied organisations if possible.

Also published news about changes in the organisations' environments and examined documentation of the relevant issues to the study must be gathered. Owing to the data being qualitative and consisting of interviews and archival material, historical research methods must be adopted.

In our research (Mustonen-Ollila, 2003, 2004, 2005; Mustonen-Ollila & Heikkonen, 2002, 2003; Mustonen-Ollila & Lyytinen, 2003, 2004), a qualitative case study with a replication logic (Curtis et al., 1988; Johnson, 1975; Laudon, 1989; Yin, 1994) was chosen to address our research questions. We collected data using a longitudinal vertical research design that involved multiple organisations. Our study was a descriptive case study (Yin, 1994) in that it embodied history and the context of ISPI adoptions (Pettigrew, 1985, 1989, 1990) and emulated Friedman and Cornford's (1989) by covering several generations of computing. Because the bulk of the gathered data was qualitative and covered both primary and secondary sources (Järvenpää, 1991), we adopted historical methods of generalizing from context (Copeland & McKenney, 1988; Mason et al., 1997a, 1997b).

Triangulation should be used by checking simultaneously different data sources, such as archival material to improve the reliability and validity of the data. The triangulation by multiple data collection techniques provides stronger substantiation of constructs and hypotheses (Denzin,

1978; Mustonen-Ollila, 2005; Sandberg, 2005; Yin, 1994). Collecting different types of data by different methods from different sources produces a wider scope of coverage and may result in a fuller picture of the phenomena under study, and both quantitative and qualitative data should be used in any study (Eisenhardt, 1989).

All research being qualitative or quantitative is based on underlying philosophical assumptions about the appropriate research methods and valid research. The underlying epistemology guides the research and philosophical assumptions and according to Hirschheim (1992) epistemology refers to the assumptions about knowledge and how the knowledge can be obtained. There are several paradigms for qualitative research, such as positivism, critical theory, and constructivism (Cuba & Lincoln, 1994). However, in the practical social research the paradigms are not so far away from each other. Qualitative research can be positivist, interpretive, or critical. Thus, the choice of a specific qualitative research method is independent of the underlying philosophical assumptions (Myers, 1997).

The main weaknesses of qualitative and quantitative studies are that there may be a lack of rigor in the study, the studies may provide little basis for scientific generalisation, and they can often take too long time, and result in massive, unreadable documents. (Carr, 1994; Huber & Van de Ven, 1995; Eisenhardt, 1989; Mustonen-Ollila, 2005, 2007; Sandberg, 2005).

Triangulation (Yin, 1994) facilitates the combination of various data-collection methods, and whereas interviews may provide depth and personal feeling, secondary sources may provide factual information (Forster, 1994; Pettigrew, 1990). Therefore triangulation is seen as a powerful means to increase the reliability, such as the ability to replicate results from one period to the next (Sandberg, 2005).

The gathered data set should be arranged in a manuscript, which includes descriptions of all the important events, their decision-makers, the

participating companies, their organisational structures, and the relevant changes in the organisations. These events must be arranged in chronological order, such as according to time and themes and written into a baseline description that identifies all the important issues of the main phenomena in the companies. To increase reliability of the information a logical chain of evidence of the data is needed (Yin, 1994). Since this base line history manuscript does not always include any analysis of phenomena and events, no explanation of these events or phenomena is necessary. This is done to minimise bias in interpretation of the data. The manuscript must be corrected for multiple omissions. If the analysis contains several important omissions, more data should be gathered and a second version of the manuscript should be written. This new manuscript can be divided into several parts in order to retain confidentiality of some of the data, if necessary. The new manuscript must be again corrected for omissions (Mustonen-Ollila, 2003, 2004, 2005; 2007; Mustonen-Ollila & Heikkonen, 2002, 2003; Mustonen-Ollila & Lyytinen, 2003, 2004).

The problem formulation can be done in favour of a particular research method. In historical studies both the conceptual (Swanson & Ramiller, 1993), and the empirical (Miles & Huberman, 1984) research approaches should be applied.

Conceptual research is research on concepts, and it examines the role of the concept in its context without defining research methods. In empirical research empirical observations or data are collected in order to answer particular research questions. Empirical research is also useful in answering practical questions. Empirical case studies are interpreted and analysed using qualitative research methods. The selected research approach includes practice orientation and inductive theory creation (Miles & Huberman, 1984). Wolfe (1994) argues that the third stream of research of organisational innovation is the process theory (PT) models: "Process theory research of organisational innovation investigates the nature of the innovation process, how and why innovations emerge, develop, grow and terminate." The unit of analysis is the innovation process. PT studies tend to be inductive, in-depth longitudinal examinations of how innovations develop over time. Research methods employed include historical analyses of the archival data, and published reports, interviews, questionnaires, and real-time, field observation.

The research questions must be studied empirically, but the concepts derived from the data are studied both conceptually and empirically. In the conceptual part, the literature of phenomena domains should be analysed, and the main concepts must be related to the present theories.

SOLUTIONS AND RECOMMENDATIONS

The reconstruction of histories is a feature of retrospective research making it possible to identify changes, relationships between the variables, and patterns in their context (Mason et al., 1997b; Sandberg, 2005). When the purpose of the data analysis is to find out the unique patterns and changes in the organisations, and to discover a new theory from the empirically found concepts, categories, and factors then the Self-Organizing Maps (SOMs) (Kohonen, 1989, 1995), SOMs combined with U-matrices (Ultsch & Siemon, 1990), and the Bayesian networks (Heckerman, 1996) are suitable statistical tools for the tasks as discussed below. SOM is a statistical method for clustering the data and combined with U-matrix representation it can give hints about the hindered concepts, categories, and factors on the data, but also can visualize the data to give new insights to the complex data. Bayesian network is a tool for relieving and visualizing the statistical dependencies among the data variables. Both SOM and Bayesian networks have been used in many data analyzing and data mining applica-

tions, see, for example, Heckerman (1996) and Kohonen (1995).

The SOM is a vector quantization (clustering) method to data samples from an input space onto a typically lower dimensional space of a map such that the topological relationships between the samples are preserved. This means that the input samples, which are close to each other, tend to be represented by the units (codebooks, weight vectors) close to each other on the map space which typically is a one or two dimensional discrete lattice of codebooks. The codebooks are weight vectors with the same dimensionality as the input vectors.

Figure 1 illustrates the use of SOM and its topology preserving ability.

The training of the SOM is based on so called unsupervised learning, meaning that the data used for learning does not contain any information about the desired output for the given input, but instead the unsupervised learning scheme tries to capture the emergent collective properties and regularities in the data. This makes the SOM especially suitable for the type of data where the main characteristics emerging from the data are of interest (such as concepts, categories, and factors), and the topology-preserving tendency of the map allows easy visualisation and analysis of the data. The SOM has been used especially successfully in such explorative data analysis where the dimensionality of the data is large and the characteristics like conditional probabilities between the variables are needed to be explored.

The SOM training algorithm is either iterative or batch based. In the iterative approach, a sample, input vector $x(n)$ at step n, from the input space V_P, is picked and compared against the weight vector w_i of the unit with index i in the map V_M. The best matching unit b (bmu), that is, the closest unit, for the input pattern $x(n)$ is then searched using some metric based criterion such as Euclidean vector norm. The weights of the best matching and the units in its topologic neighborhood are then updated towards $x(n)$. In batch training the

Figure 1. A simple example of 2D SOM that represents the original 3D data of the three variables. After mapping the data from 3D space to 2D map space the potential data clusters (groups) can be observed and further analysed

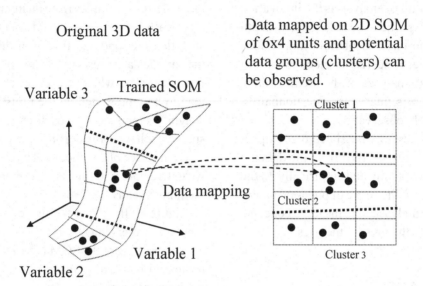

Original 3D data

Data mapped on 2D SOM of 6x4 units and potential data groups (clusters) can be observed.

bmus are computed for all data samples and the map is updated toward the estimated optimum for the set. When using batch training, usually few iterations over the training set are sufficient for convergence. In our experiences we used batch learning scheme. The mathematical properties of the SOM have been considered by several authors (e.g., Cottrel, 1998; Kohonen, 1989, 1995; Luttrell, 1989). Briefly, it has been shown that learning the units of the map tend to approximate closely the probability density function of the training data, which is desired a property in the case of clustering.

Historical studies in information systems research have many characteristics that support the use of SOM. The gathered data has typically rather high dimensionality, that is, each sample consists of several independent variables, such as factors, and the data itself in a table form does not easily show its contents. For analysing and visualization of this data 2D SOM of certain number of units (codebooks) is one of the most convenient tools. The number of units may vary from 25 up to a couple of hundred depending on

the number of training samples and the characteristics of the data. After training, the SOM divides the data into clusters and the weight vectors of the units represent the centers of the clusters. The distribution of the data on the SOM units is examined by projecting the data on a map (i.e., when searching for the best matching unit for each data sample). The number of hits from the data to each map unit is counted to each of the varying factors, such as organisations, time, and the concept categories, which may be the dependent variables. The hit distribution, the weight vector values of the units, and their correlation is analysed and interpreted. Furthermore, the relationships between variables can be studied. To find out the relationships, possible significant correlations, and conditional probabilities between variables should be analysed. An interesting finding can be that variables are related to each other, and the results can show linear or nonlinear relationships between the variables (Mustonen-Ollila & Heikkonen, 2003).

A popular way of using SOM is to utilise its component planes and U-matrix representations

(Kohonen, 1989, 1995; Ultsch & Siemon, 1990). Also, in historical studies of information systems, the variation in the concepts and categories over time can be further investigated with these representations. In component plane plotting (Kohonen, 1995), the components of codebook vectors are drawn in the shape of the map lattice; each component plane visualizes the corresponding variation of the weight vector. By looking at the component planes of two or more codebook variables, it is possible to observe the dependencies between the variables. The plotted component planes can be then qualitatively or even quantitatively analysed by experts. The results naturally depend on the data, but in the cases where there are clear similarities and regularities in the data, these can be observed by the formed pronounced clusters of units on the map. These observable clusters can provide clues to the experts on the dependencies and characteristics of the data, and some data clusters of particular interest can be picked for further more detailed analysis even if a correlation or a linear relationship between

the concepts and categories is not immediately quantitatively measured.

The visual U-matrix representation of the SOM (Ultsch & Siemon, 1990) shows the distances between the units and their neighbouring map units, that is, codebooks, and helps to see the emerging higher level clusters of the data consisting of one or more SOM units. This U-matrix visualization is typically based on a colouring scheme in a way that the units belonging to the same clusters are indicated by uniform areas of low intensity values whereas the cluster boundaries are represented by high intensities. This intensity map is based on calculated average distances between the adjacent units of the SOM; the higher the distance and thus a more probable gap between the units is represented by a higher intensity whereas dark colouring between the units signifies that the codebook vectors are close to each other in the input space. This is illustrated in Figure 2. Of course, U-matrix does not provide definite answers about the clusters, but it gives clues as to what similarities (clusters) there may be in the

Figure 2. A simple example of how 2D SOM of 10x10 units with the U matrix can find three clusters of data. In the left the original samples as red dots, the units of the trained SOM as black dots, and the topology is represented as gray lines are seen. In the right is the U matrix representation of the trained SOM: Those units that within their own clusters have darker colour (shorter distances to adjacent units) whereas the units that are between the clusters have whiter colour (longer distances to adjacent units)

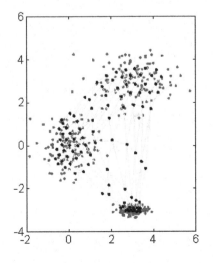
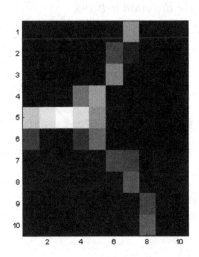

data by revealing possible cluster boundaries on the map. Teaching SOM and representing it with the U-matrix offers, thus, a fast way to get insight on the data. If several dependencies between the concepts and categories exist, the dependencies can be seen visually from the output U-matrix intensity map even if a correlation or a linear relationship between the concepts and categories is not measured. The U-matrix representation is descriptive in its nature and different development paths can be discovered, such as analysing processes and studying the phenomena over time. The U-matrix representation is a novel statistical analysing method in the area of IS (Mustonen-Ollila & Heikkonen, 2008a, 2008b).

For the modelling of the probabilistic dependencies between the concepts or categories, the Bayesian network approach (Heckerman, 1996) is appropriate. Founded on the Bayesian modelling framework and Bayesian dependency modelling, the Bayesian network is based on directed graphs where the variables of interest are represented as nodes and those nodes (i.e., variables), which are dependent are connected by arcs. In simple, the variables A and B are dependent on each other if from the known values of A it is possible to guess the values of variable B. By observing the independencies of the variables, which are suggested by the network structure, the full probability distribution for a set of variables can be simplified for the purposes of data analysis. If the analysis shows that the derived dependency graphs for each time generation over time, then they could be used as models for the studied phenomena over time. For example, consider a simple graph in Figure 3 with four variables A, B, C, and D. By using the chain rule of probability, the joint probability of all variables is $P(A,B,C,D)=P(A) \times P(C|A) \times P(B|A,C) \times P(D|A,B,C)$. By using conditional independency relations relieved by the graph structure, this can be simplified as $P(A,B,C,D)=P(A) \times P(C|A) \times P(B|A) \times P(D|B,C)$ where the single probability terms can be easily determined from the data. With the Bayesian rule, the condition probabilities can be expressed in the form $P(X|Y) = P(Y|X)P(X)/P(Y)$. For Bayesian network construction, the B-course software (CoSCo, 2000) can be easily used, but also many other commercial and non-commercial software exist.

The discovery of using Bayesian modelling, which sought the proper model to use and to describe the dependencies between the different concepts and categories over a million of possible models is a rather novel statistical analysing method in the area of IS (Mustonen-Ollila & Heikkonen, 2002). Both the dependencies between the concepts and categories and their variation over

Figure 3. A simple Bayesian network

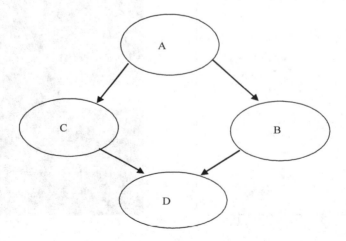

time can be studied with the help of the resulting network structure. One of the main focuses of the longitudinal historical studies is to observe changes in the main processes over time and the longitudinal historical data is important because a horizontal survey research would not have given answers to the research questions.

Theories can be discovered in different ways, such as by the empirical results, discovering the relationships between the concepts and categories, and developing conceptual frameworks. The above statistical methodologies when used efficiently are valuable tools for this. The theories can also be created by some laws (Webster & Watson, 2002). The final product of creating a theory from the case studies may be concepts, a conceptual framework, or propositions or possible mid-range theory (Eisenhardt, 1989). According to Markus and Robey (1988), theories are established by using a process or a variance theory. Process theory tries to understand the phenomena in terms of the cause-effect events leading to an outcome. Variance theory explains phenomena in terms of the relationships that are the linking hypotheses between the dependent and independent variables. A new theory can be presented by viewing both the variance theory and the process theory. The emergent theory, which can be a conceptual framework, the various concepts, the concept categories, and their relationships and dependencies with each other, offers a new type of theoretical constructs for understanding the studied phenomena in different perspectives. It can be argued that the discovered theory reflects the phenomena in the multiple organisational contexts better than the earlier fragmented theories in the literature about the phenomena. The discovered theory can cover more concepts and related categories and also an organisational view of the phenomena over time.

Thus, a new theory can be presented in the form of conceptual framework and classes of concepts which are called information system process innovations denoted as ISPIs, ISPI cat-egories, ISPI development generations, three organisational units, decision-maker categories, and relationships between the concepts. In the study, both the viewpoints of variance theory and the process theory can be applied. An example of such theory creation can be seen from studies from Mustonen-Ollila and Lyytinen (2003, 2004), Mustonen-Ollila and Heikkonen (2002, 2003), Mustonen-Ollila (2003, 2004, 2005, 2007).

The research process can indicate that understanding the role of the phenomena in organisations would not suffice, and extraction of the historical study from the interpretive research approach, organisational research approach, and practice oriented research approach to inductive theory creation (Miles & Huberman, 1984) during the research process is needed.

One limitation of the historical studies concerns the comprehensiveness and thus reliability of the data: despite the efforts to obtain, through in-depth interviews, and extensive use of archival material and all relevant facts that affect to the phenomena, we have to accept the limitation of a historical method. Historical studies try to interpret the situations and events happened a long time ago in the organisations, the data collected is empirical, and thus the study is a practice oriented research approach. However, historical study approach may not be enough to understand the issues happened a long time ago in the past. Therefore, we have to expand our research to inductive theory creation in order to understand the role of the phenomena in the organisations.

Finally, our obtained results (Mustonen-Ollila, 2003, 2004, 2005; Mustonen-Ollila & Heikkonen, 2002, 2003; Mustonen-Ollila & Lyytinen, 2003, 2004) may not be applicable to other organisations because the phenomena studied in our studies can be atypical.

Instead of having a single contribution and suggestion, the results may provide many implications to both practitioners and researchers. When building up a new theory from the historical data, the grounded theory (Glaser &

Strauss, 1967) approach and descriptive case study approach embodying time, history, and context are useful. The cases should be selected so that they either predict similar results (literal replication) or produce contrasting results but for predictable reasons (theoretical replication) (Yin, 1994). Replication is not always successful, and evidence of changes in strength or patterns of relationships over time may alert the researcher to real changes in relationships or unreliability of measurement (Menard, 2002). The credibility can be increased in the study by familiarising the researcher with the theoretical background and forming a theoretical framework before entering the field (Miles & Huberman, 1994; Sandberg, 2005). Theory triangulation can be used where multiple perspectives are used to interpret a single set of data, and methodological triangulation where multiple methods have employed in the research problem (Denzin, 1978).

According to Eisenhardt (1989), the combination of case study with grounded theory (GT) approach has three major strengths: it produces a novel theory, the emergent theory is testable, and the resultant theory is empirically valid. In GT approach, the theory emerges from the data. In our case studies, we used the theoretical framework to clarify the concepts and phenomena before entering the field which is not always in the done in GT approach. We used also GT approach because the collected data validated the major concepts and relationships of the framework and therefore the theory emerged from the data. Some concepts in the framework however were not validated from the field data.

According to Glaser (1992) there is no need to review any literature of the studied area before entering the field. This is in line with our research because we started collecting the data before developing our theoretical framework. On the other hand, in some of our case studies, the theoretical framework guided our inquires in the field. GT is used in interpretive case studies. Our case studies (Mustonen-Ollila, 2003, 2004,

2005; Mustonen-Ollila & Heikkonen, 2002, 2003; Mustonen-Ollila & Lyytinen, 2003, 2004) were interpretive in their nature even if we had to expand them to inductive theory creation on later stages of the research.

In historical studies, a conceptual framework of the studied processes must be developed, and the concepts must be grounded on empirical evidence and theories reflecting the findings from the field study over time. The most fundamental components in this conceptual framework of the processes are its concepts, and categories, and the relationships between the concepts over time. The concepts should be sharpened by building evidence which described the concepts. Constant comparison between the data and concepts must be done so that accumulating evidence converges on simple and well defined concepts (constructs). This new theory integrates present theories and literature. By analysing the environment, the factors explaining the phenomena of certain concepts' creation can be explained. With the help of these findings, a general theory is inductively created by which factors generally explain what the concepts are. A special status in theory building is given to dependent variables, such as time, organisations, and categories, which are the focal concepts in the theory. The ancillary concepts, such as factors and mechanisms in the theory, are the independent variables which are associated with changes in the value of the dependent variables. The conceptual framework tries to explain the changes in the values of these concepts over time. The boundary conditions in the theory creation have to be taken into account, because the phenomenon is normally so atypical that it holds only in specific contextual organisational environments. In the studies, the results of testing can validate the conceptual framework, which will become the discovered theory for the phenomena (Mustonen-Ollila, 2005, 2007). The conceptual framework should be cut into the sub frameworks, denoted as the research models according to the research questions. The research questions are the basis in the development of the sub frameworks in order to study the phenomena. The sub frameworks must be compared with the various theories, because possibly there is no single theory, which could explain the different aspects of the conceptual framework. The sub frameworks and related research must be therefore integrated together. However, the conceptual framework and the sub frameworks are only attempts to describe the reality and use of the models as methodological tools for scholars and practitioners in research work. These frameworks and concepts grounded on empirical data can be used in other studies to visualise the complexity of the historical research in the organisational studies. The data which confirms the emergent relationships enhanced confidence in the validity of the relationships (Mustonen-Ollila, 2003, 2004, 2005; Mustonen-Ollila & Heikkonen, 2002, 2003; Mustonen-Ollila & Lyytinen, 2003, 2004). The data which disconfirms the relationships provides an opportunity to expand end refine the emerging theory (Mustonen-Ollila, 2005). In a historical study, various perspectives of the phenomena can be emphasized which form a rich, even contradictory theoretical basis. Some of the conflicting results with the present literature can result in a more creative and new way of thinking. The non conflicting results can strengthen the definitions of the concepts and the conceptual framework. The past studies with similar findings are important because they tie together the underlying similarities in phenomena not associated with each other. Stronger internal validity is achieved. The results, however, may not be readily applicable to other organisations since the phenomena can be atypical. Thus, generalisation of the results can be difficult, but not necessary impossible.

The data should be categorised under several themes over time, which can be discovered from the data, including the major changes in the organisations, influencing people working inside or outside the organisations, and so forth. These themes can also form the main categories or the concepts in the data. This is the selective way of finding the concepts and categories from the data and it is based on researchers' own intuition and knowledge. The concepts must be categorised according to relevant terminology and theories, which are the most refereed work of categorising concepts in the studied research area. After the categories are discovered, the amount of the categories must be decided. The problem of the categories is: are there enough proofs found from the data to make the categories and concepts valid and reliable, and whether the categories and concepts discovered are the correct ones. Some other concepts and categories can emerge from the data later. If the concepts and categories are not proper, the researcher must go back to the data again and discover new concepts. After the abstract concepts are found, they can be coded according to the instructions of Glaser and Strauss (1967) using selective coding in searching the data categories. The abstract concepts can also be found with the content analysis approach (Järvinen, 2004; Krippendorff, 1980). Content analysis is text analysis method (Krippendorff, 1980; Järvinen, 2004). The approach requires a researcher to construct a category system, code the data, and calculate the frequencies or percentages that are used to test hypotheses about the relationships among the variables of interest. It is assumed that the meaning of text data is objective in the sense that a text corresponds to an objective reality. The text is interpreted and understood without extraneous contextual knowledge. In our case studies the purpose of the analysis was to find out the unique patterns of the organisations. The concepts were sharpened by building evidence which described the concepts. Constant comparison between the data and concepts was made so that accumulating evidence converges on simple and well defined concepts (constructs).

The selected reference theories must be in the same contextual area as the subject of study. In some cases theoretical models in the research can be lacking, and also the classification does not take into account the most important issues in the area. In this case the researcher must expand the present theories and models by emphasising the missing issues. If the goal of the study is to discover a new theory of change trying to improve the present concept categories, then the researcher must test the concepts of the present theories of change in the studied organisations. This has to be done in order to find out if the discovered concepts of the new theory were similar or different from the concepts of the past theories. The findings can indicate that some of the concepts of the past theories are confirmed and some of the concepts were disconfirmed.

One of the most important requirements to study changes in phenomena in other organisations is that their findings are based on the past theories categorisation over time. If this requirement is fulfilled, the tested hypotheses in the study could be tested in any organisation. On the other hand, the hypotheses discovered should be tested separately in every organisation under study. Some of the research questions should also be formulated differently.

In our study, the boundary conditions of the theory had to be taken into account because the phenomenon was so atypical that it holds only in these specific contextual organisational environments. The primary focus in the theory building was the dependent and independent variables and their relationships with each other. Sometimes there is limited knowledge of the context because access to secondary sources is allowed alone. The limited number of studied companies affects to the findings, which can be generalised across a set of organisations with care (Mustonen-Ollila, 2005).

CONCLUSION

This chapter gives important methodological, theoretical, and practical guidelines to the information system (IS) researchers to carry out a historical study. This study shows how a new theory can be discovered inductively from his-

torical studies using a methodological guideline from Mason et al. (1997b); using multiple data collection methods, such as semi-structured interviews, archival files, and published news; and using novel data analysis methods from learning and intelligent systems, such as the Self-Organizing Maps (SOMs), SOMs combined with U-matrices, and the Bayesian network modeling. It also outlines the benefits, the main problems, the characteristics, and the implications of historical research in the information system field. Finally this chapter gives future some research directions of historical research in the IS field.

Our study shows one example of creating a theory inductively from empirical historical case studies by building up a conceptual framework and discovering concepts and categories from the theories and empirical data. An example where a theory has been derived using this methods can be found from Mustonen-Ollila (2005). Mustonen-Ollila's (2005) study examines the history and evolution of information system process innovation (ISPI) processes (adoption, adaptation, and unlearning) within the information system development (ISD) work in an internal information system (IS) department and in two IS software house organisations in Finland over a 43-year time-period. The study offers insights into influential actors and their dependencies in deciding over ISPIs. The research uses a qualitative research approach, and the research methodology involves the description of the ISPI processes, how the actors searched for ISPIs, and how the relationships between the actors changed over time. The existing theories were evaluated using the conceptual models of the ISPI processes based on the innovation literature in the IS area. The main focus of the study was to observe changes in the main ISPI processes over time. The main contribution of the thesis was the new theory. The term theory should be understood as (1) a new conceptual framework of the ISPI processes, (2) new ISPI concepts and categories, and the relationships between the ISPI concepts inside the ISPI processes.

In this study, we have outlined how to use a methodological guideline to carry out historical studies, and how qualitative, and quantitative research methods, a multiple case study approach, historical data collection methods, and learning and intelligent systems' data analysing methods and tools can be used to discover a new theory inductively from empirical historical case studies (Mustonen-Ollila, 2003, 2004, 2005, 2007; Mustonen-Ollila & Heikkonen, 2002, 2003; Mustonen-Ollila & Lyytinen, 2003, 2004). We focused on creating a theory by inductively developing a conceptual framework, and deriving concepts and categories from the data and the past theories. We derived the concepts both from the theory and practice using content analysis; the SOM (Mustonen-Ollila & Heikkonen, 2002, 2003) and the SOM with U-matrix can be utilized to classify the concepts into the concept categories and the patterns (Mustonen-Ollila & Heikkonen, 2008a, 2008b); with the Bayesian network approach one can find out the relationships and the dependencies between the concepts, variables, and concept categories (Mustonen-Ollila & Heikkonen, 2002); and with the SOM component plane plotting of the factors, and their variation over time can be discovered (Mustonen-Ollila & Heikkonen, 2003).

In our study, we have also outlined the characteristics, problems, benefits, and implications of historical studies by presenting new issues in the historical research. Studying historical research problems over time is very complex and covers studies of changes over time, finding patterns over time, studying relationships and dependencies between the variables over time, and discovering variation in different factors. The significance of applying new research methods to historical research is evitable, but it needs a close cooperation between the IS researchers and researchers from learning and intelligent systems science.

FUTURE RESEARCH DIRECTIONS

There are several new interesting research directions to investigate in the historical longitudinal research. The first direction would be to study the development of the main Information System Process Innovation (ISPI) concepts and categories looking at the prism of sociology of knowledge (Berger, 1963; Berger & Luckmann, 1966). Berger (1963) argues that to understand the organisations one must look behind the official mechanisms regulating the power in the community.

In this study the information system process innovation (ISPI) is defined as a new way of developing, implementing, and maintaining information systems in an organisational context. ISPIs play a major role in changing the information system development (ISD) process in organisations, and they can improve the process and outcomes of information systems. ISPIs affect the ISD processes, and their study can provide a useful framework to understand the complex nature of ISD.

A second direction would be to find out the actors' behaviour mechanisms in using and implementing ISPIs. In such a study Actor-Network Theory (ANT) could be used to find out answers on how a diverse group of actors can reach agreement with each other (Latour, 1991). According to Latour (1991) and Riihimaa (2004), the ANT looks at the innovation process from the viewpoint of the artifact (which may be a product or a process) and the networks needed concurrently when the artifact is created and delivered. At the beginning, there is a project to create a product. When a network is created, it is a process of mobilisation, organisation, and persuasion. The key position is held by an innovator who succeeds in directing, mobilizing, or changing the interest of other actors according to the innovator's own visions (Mustonen-Ollila & Heikkonen, 2008c).

The third research direction of the future could be to investigate what are the reasons for failures or successes in infusion processes or how they vary between different concepts and categories over time (Swanson & Ramiller, 1997). In our study, the concepts are defined as ISPIs and the categories are defined as ISPI categories. ISPIs can be classified into four categories based on their scope, purpose and content in how they align with technological and administrative innovations. These are project management and control procedures, (M) (Administrative Innovation); description methods, (D) (Administrative Innovation); development tools, (TO) (Technological Innovation); and base line technology innovation called technology innovation (T). The first category includes rules and administrative procedures that help control, manage, and coordinate development activities. Examples of type M innovations are project management guidelines or organisational arrangements like chief programmer teams (Swanson, 1994). Innovations of type D include notational systems and standards, which help to describe the development product or process and/or its relationship to the environment. Such innovations include the well known standardised modelling techniques like Data Flow Diagrams, Unified Modelling Method (UML) and process modelling approaches. The innovations of type TO include all "productivity tools" for system development covering application generators, Computer Aided Software Engineering (CASE) tools, documentation tools, data dictionaries, or tools to configure, or manage software components. Innovations of type T consist of (externally) developed technical platforms like programming languages, database management systems and middleware components (Mustonen-Ollila, 2003, 2004, 2005; Mustonen-Ollila & Heikkonen, 2002, 2003; Mustonen-Ollila & Lyytinen, 2003, 2004).

Based on Friedman and Cornford (1989) ISPIs can be classified into several generations. Friedman and Cornford (1989) point out- based on an extensive empirical analysis of the historical evolution of IS development—that the four types of innovations discussed above are often closely "horizontally" related, and they can be accordingly classified into a set of evolutionary generations. They point out that the changes in these generations are driven by: (1) technological changes in hardware and software (Type T innovation), (2) changes in the types of systems being developed, and (3) changes in the types of users. The two latter are thus external demand factors that drive the ISPI. They are outcomes of attempts to harness the new computing capabilities into new organisational domains and tasks (what Swanson 1994 calls type II and type III innovations) (Mustonen-Ollila, 2003, 2004, 2005; Mustonen-Ollila & Heikkonen, 2002, 2003; Mustonen-Ollila & Lyytinen, 2003, 2004).

Four generations of ISPIs can be recognised. The first generation (from the late 1940s until the mid 1960s) is largely hampered by "hardware constraints," that is, hardware costs and limitations in its capacity and reliability (lack of T innovations). The second generation (from the mid 1960s until the early 1980s), in turn, is characterised by "software constraints," that is, poor productivity of systems developers and difficulties of delivering reliable systems on time and within budget (lack of D, M, and TO innovations). The third generation (early 1980s to the beginning of the 1990s), is instead driven by the challenge to overcome "user relationship constraints," that is, system quality problems arising from the inadequate perception of user demand and the resulting inadequate service (lack of M, D, and TO innovations). Finally, the fourth generation (from the beginning of 1990s) is affected by "organisational constraints" (lack of M, and D innovations) (Publication I). In the latter case the constraints arise from complex interactions between computing systems and specific organisational agents including customers and clients, suppliers, competitors, cooperators, representatives, and public bodies (Friedman & Cornford, 1989; Mustonen-Ollila, 2003, 2004, 2005; Mustonen-Ollila & Heikkonen, 2002, 2003; Mustonen-Ollila & Lyytinen, 2003, 2004).

The fourth new research direction could be the task of describing the evolution paths of the main categories and concepts, which are based on predecessor and successor relationships over time. Changes in concepts and categories are developed through many stages of evolution over time. A study of the antecedents, and consequences of the evolution paths, and the utilisation of other reference literature such as the organisation theory to discover how the organisation changed due to shift to new evolution paths would be an interesting subject of study. The task of describing the modification processes of the concepts and categories would be also one of the new research directions (Mustonen-Ollila & Heikkonen, 2008a, 2008b).

The main design choice of the observations and research questions regarding longitudinal historical studies is the use of diverse research methods at the same time, and one of the main characteristics of historical longitudinal research is its long time span. We do not know, however, what would be the ideal and optimal research period to study history and changes over time. One of the issues is also to find a suitable site where to collect the data. Multiple data collection points raise a special problem how to compare the different observations with each other. The main research goals in the longitudinal historical studies are to capture changes over time, to discover dependencies between the concepts and categories, to find out the patterns over time, and finally to discover a new theory by using longitudinal historical research design (Mustonen-Ollila, 2003, 2004, 20052007; Mustonen-Ollila & Heikkonen, 2002, 2003; Mustonen-Ollila & Lyytinen, 2003, 2004).

REFERENCES

Bannister, F. (2002). The dimension of time: Historiography in information systems research. *Electronic Journal of Business Research Methods, 1*(1), 1-10.

Barley, S. R. (1990). Images of imaging: Notes on doing longitudinal field work. *Organization Science, 1*(3), 220-247.

Berger, P.L. (1963). *Invitation to sociology: A humanistic perspective.* USA: Doubleday&Co. Hunt Barnard Printing Ltd. Great Britain: Aylesbury.

Berger, P.L., & Luckmann, T. (1966). *The social construction of reality: A tretise in the sociology of knowledge.* USA.

Buckland, M. (1998). *Overview of the history of science information systems.* Paper presented at the meeting of the American Heritage Foundation Conference on History and Heritage of Science information systems, Pittsburgh, PA. Retrieved June 3, 2008, from http://www.sims.berkeley.edu/~buckland/chfintr.htm

Carr, L.T (1994). The strengths and weaknesses of qualitative and quantitative research; what method for nursing? *Journal of Advance Nursing, 20*(4), 716-721.

Copeland, D.G., & McKenney, J.L. (1988). Airline reservations systems: Lessons from history. *MIS Quarterly, 12*(3), 353-370.

CoSCo. (2000). *B-cource service.* Complex Computation Group, Department of Computer Science, University of Helsinki, Finland. Retrieved June 3, 2008, from http://b-cource.cs.helsinki.fi/

Cottrell, M. (1998). Theoretical aspects of the SOM algorithm. *Neurocomputing, 21,* 119-138.

Curtis, B., Krasner, H., & Iscoe, N. (1988). A field study of the software design process for large systems. *Communications of ACM, 31*(11), 1268-1287.

Davies, R.B. (1994). From cross-sectional to longitudinal analysis. In A. Dale & R.B. Davies (Eds.), *Analyzing social & political change, a casebook of methods.* Sage Publications.

Dawson, P. (2003). *Reshaping change: A processual perspective. Understanding organizational change*. Routledge, Taylor and Francis Group.

Denzin, N.K. (Ed.). (1978). *The research act: A theoretical introduction to sociological methods*. New York: McGraw-Hill.

Ein-Dor, P., & Segev, E. (1993). A classification of information systems: Analysis and interpretation. *Information Systems Research, 4*(2), 166-204.

Eisenhardt, K.M. (1989). Building theories from case study research. *Academy of Management Review, 14*(4), 532-550.

Friedman, A., & Cornford, D. (1989). *Computer systems development: History, organization and implementation*. New York: Information Systems Series; John Wiley & sons.

Glaser, B.G. (1992). *Emergence vs. forcing: Basics of grounded theory*. Mill Valley, CA: Sociology Press.

Glaser, B., & Strauss, A. (1967). *The discovery of the grounded theory: Strategies for qualitative research*. London: Wiedenfeld and Nicholson.

Guba, E.G., & Lincoln, Y.S. (1994). Competing paradigms in qualitative research. In N.K- Denzin & Y.S. Lincoln (Eds.), *Handbook of qualitative research. Thousand Oaks, CA:* Sage.

Heckerman, D. (1996). A *tutorial on learning with Bayesian networks* (Tech. Rep. No. MSR-TR-95-06). Redmond, WA: Microsoft Research: Advanced Technology Division.

Heiskanen, A. (1994). *Issues and factors affecting the success and failure of a student record system development process: A longitudinal investigation based on reflection-in-action*. Doctoral dissertation, University of Helsinki, Yliopistopaino, Helsinki.

Hirschheim, R. (1992). Information systems epistemology: An historical perspective. In R. Galliers (Ed.), *Information systems research: Is-* sues, methods and practical guidelines. Oxford: Blackwell Scientific Publications.

Huber, G.P., & Van de Ven, A.H. (1995). *Longitudinal field research methods: Studying process of organizational change*. Thousand Oaks, CA: Sage Publications.

Järvenpää, S. (1991). Panning for gold in information systems research: Second-hand data. Information Systems research Arena in the 90's: Information Systems research: contemporary approaches and emergent traditions. In *Proceedings of the IFIP TC/WG 8.2 Working Conference*, Copenhagen, Denmark, (pp. 63-80).

Järvinen, P. (2004). *On research methods*. Opinpaja: Tampere.

Johnson, J.M. (1975). *Doing field research*. New York: The Free Press.

Kieser, A. (1994). Why organization theory needs historical analyses - and how this should be performed. *Organizational Science, 5*(4), 608-620.

Kohonen, T. (1989). *Self-organization and associative memory*. Berlin: Springer-Verlag, Heidelberg.

Kohonen, T. (1995). *Self-organized maps*. Berlin, Germany: Springer-Verlag.

Krippendorff, K. (1980). *Content analysis: An introduction to its methods*. Beverly Hills, CA: Sage Publications.

Lambert, P., & Gayle, V. (2004). Quantitative approaches to longitudinal research. *Session 2 of RCBN Training Workshop Longitudinal Research in Education*, University of York, England. Retrieved June 3, 2008, from http://www.cf.ac.uk/socsi/capacity/Activities/Themes/Secondary/Lambert.ppt

Latour, B. (1991). Materials of power: Technology is society made durable. In *A Sociology of Monsters: Essays on Power, Technology, and Domination, Sociological Review Monograph, 38,* 103-131.

Laudon, K. C. (1989). Design guidelines for choices involving time in qualitative research. In J. Cash & P. Lawrence (Ed.), *The Information systems research challenge: qualitative research methods* (pp. 1-12). Cambridge, MA: Harvard Business School.

Locker, K., Miller, S., Richardson, M., Tebeaux, E., & Yates, J. (1996). Studying the history of business communication. *Business Communications Quarterly, 59*(2), 109-138.

Luttrell, S. P. (1989). Self-organization: A derivation from first principles of a class of learning algorithms. In *Proceedings of the IJCNN'89 International Joint Conference on Neural Networks* (Vol. 2. pp. 495-498).

Markus, K.L., & Robey, D. (1988). Information technology and organisational change: Causal structure in theory and research. *Management Science, 34*(5), 583-598.

Mason, R., McKenney, J., & Copeland, D.G. (1997a). A historical method for MIS

research: Steps and assumptions. *MIS Quarterly, 21*(3), 307-320.

Mason, R., McKenney, J., & Copeland, D.G. (1997b). Developing an historical tradition in MIS research. *MIS Quarterly, 21*(3), 257-276.

McKenney, J.L., Mason, R.O., & Copeland, D. (1997c). Bank of America: The crest and trough of technological leadership. *MIS Quarterly, 21*(3), 321-353.

Menard, S.W. (2002). Longitudinal research. In *Series: Quantitative Applications in the Social Sciences.* USA: Sage Publications.

Miles, M., & Huberman, A. (1984). *A qualitative data analysis: A sourcebook of new methods.* Beverly Hills, CA: Sage Publications.

Miles, M.B., & Huberman, A.M. (1994). *Qualitative data analysis.* Thousand Oaks, CA: Sage Publications.

Mustonen-Ollila, E. (2003). How outsourcing impacts to decision-making over IS process innovations. In *Proceedings of the Computer Supported Scientific Collaboration (CSSC) Workshop, ECSCW'03 8th European Conference of Computer-Supported Cooperative Work,* Helsinki, Finland. (pp. 1-4).

Mustonen-Ollila, E. (2004). IS process innovation unlearning in organisations. In *Proceedings of the European Conference on Information Systems (ECIS), The European IS Profession in the Global Networking Environment,* Turku, Finland (pp. 1-12).

Mustonen-Ollila, E. (2005). *Information system process innovation adoption, adaptation, learning, and unlearning: A longitudinal case study.* Doctoral dissertation. Acta Universitatis Lappeenrantaensis 216, Lappeenranta University of Technology: Digipaino, Finland.

Mustonen-Ollila, E. (2007, December). Information system process innovation life cycle model. *Journal of Knowledge Management: In the Knowledge Garden, 8*(4), 1-12.

Mustoen-Ollila, E., & Heikkonen, J. (2002). Gatekeepers in information system process innovation adaptation: A longitudinal case study. In T. Terano & M.D. Myers (Ed.), *Proceedings of the 6th Pacific Asia Conference on Information System: The Next E-What? for Business and Communities* (pp. 1043-1047). Tokyo, Japan.

Mustonen-Ollila, E., & Heikkonen, J. (2003). IS process innovation knowledge acquisition and information distribution mechanisms. In *Proceedings of the United Kingdom Academy for Information Systems (UKAIS2003) Conference, Coordination and Coopetition: The IS role,* Warwick, England, (pp. 1-16).

Mustonen-Ollila, E., & Heikkonen, J. (2008a). IS process innovation evolution in organizations. *The Academy of Information and Management Sciences Journals* (AIMS), (Forthcoming).

Mustonen-Ollila, E., & Heikkonen, J. (2008b). Information System process innovation evolution paths. Submitted for a review to the *10th International Conference on Enterprise Information Systems (ICEIS2008)*, 12-16 June, 2008, Barcelona, Spain.

Mustonen-Ollila, E., & Heikkonen, J. (2008c). *Actors' behaviour mechanisms in using and implementing information system process innovations: A longitudinal case study using actor-network theory and structuration theory.* (Under work).

Mustonen-Ollila, E., & Lyytinen, K. (2003). Why organisations adopt information system process innovations: A longitudinal study using diffusion of innovation theory. *Information Systems Journal, 13*, 279-297.

Mustonen-Ollila, E., & Lyytinen, K. (2004). How organizations adopt information system process innovations: A longitudinal analysis. *European Journal of Information Systems, 13*, 35-51.

Myers, M.D. (1997, June). Qualitative research in information systems. *MIS Quarterly, 21*(2), 241-242.

Pettigrew, A. (1985). *The wakening giant, continuity and change in ICI.* Oxford and New York: Basil Blackwell.

Pettigrew, A. (1989). Issues of time and site selection in longitudinal research on change. *The Information Systems Research Challenge: Qualitative Research Methods, 1*, 13-19. Boston, MA.

Pettigrew, A.M. (1990). Longitudinal field research on change: Theory and practice. *Organization Science, 1*(3), 267-292.

Pettigrew, A.M. (1997). What is a processual analysis? *Scandinavian Journal of Management, 13*(4), 337-348.

Riihimaa, J. (2004). *Taxonomy of information and communication technology system innovations adopted by small and medium sized enterprises.*

Doctoral dissertation, University of Tampere, Tampere University Press, Tampere.

Ruspini, E. (1999). Longitudinal research and the analysis of social change. *Quality & Quantity, 33*(3), 219-227.

Rutter, M., Maughan, B., Pickles, A., & Simonoff, E. (1998). Retrospective recall recalled. In R.B. Cairns, L.B. Bergman, & J. Kagan (Ed.), *Methods and models for studying the individual* (pp. 219-242). Thousand Oaks, CA: Sage Publications.

Sandberg, B. (2005). *The hidden market-even for those who create it? Customer-related proactiveness in developing radical innovations.* Publications of the Turku School of Economics and Business Administration Series, doctoral dissertation, Turku, Finland.

Swanson, E.B. (1994). Information systems innovation among organizations. *Management Science, 40*(9), 1069-1088.

Swanson E.B., & Ramiller, N.C. (1993). Information systems research thematics: Submissions to a new journal, 1987-1992. *Information Systems Research, 4*(4), 299-330.

Swanson, E.B., & Ramiller, N.C. (1997). The organizing vision in information systems innovation. *Organization Science, 8*(5), 458-274.

Ultsch, A., & Siemon, H.P. (1990) Kohonen's self organizing feature maps for exploratory data analysis. In *Proceeding of the INNC'90, Internal Neural Network Conference* (pp. 305-308). Dordrecht, Netherlands: Kluwer.

Venkatesh, A., & Vitalari, N.P. (1991). Longitudinal surveys in information systems research: An examination of issues, methods, and applications. In K. Kramer (Ed.), *The information systems challenge: Survey research methods* (pp. 115-144). Harvard University Press.

Webster, J., & Watson, R.T. (2002). Analyzing the past to prepare for the future: Writing a literature review. *MIS Quaterly, 26*(2), xii-xxii.

Willett, J.B., & Singer, J.D. (2006). *In longitudinal research: Present status and future prospects.* Harvard University, Graduate School of Education. Retrieved June 3, 2008, from http://www. ats.ucla.edu/stat/seminars/alda/alda.ppt

Wolfe, R.A. (1994). Organizational innovation: Review, critique and suggested research directions. *Journal of Management Studies, 3.* University of Alberta.

Yin, R.K. (1981). Life histories of innovations: How new practices become routinized. *Public Administration Review, 41,* 21-28.

Yin, R. (1994). *Case study research – design and methods.* London: Sage Publications.

ADDITIONAL READING

Allison, G.T. (1971). *Essence of decision, explaining the Cuban Missile Crisis.* Boston, MA: Brown and Company.

Attewell, P. (1992). Technology diffusion and organizational learning: The case of business computing. *Organization Science, 3*(1), 1-19.

Berger, J. (1985). *Statistical decision theory and Bayesian analysis.* New York: Springer-Verlag,

Bloomfield, B.P., Coombs, R., Cooper, D.J., & Rea, D. (1992). Machines and manoeuvres: Responsibility accounting and the construction of hospital information systems. *Accounting, Management & Information Technology, 2*(4), 197-219.

Brandt, S. (1976). *Statistical and computational methods in data analysis.* North-Holland Publishing Company.

Buntine, W. (1996). A guide to the literature on learning graphical models. *IEEE Transactions on Knowledge and Data Engineering, 8,* 195-210.

Clark, P., & Staunton, N. (1989). *Innovation in technology and organization.* London: Routledge.

Cottrell, M. (1998). Theoretical aspects of the SOM algorithm. *Neurocomputing, 21,* 119-138.

Curtis, B., Krasner, H., & Iscoe, N. (1988). A field study of the software design process for large systems. *Communications of the ACM, 31*(11), 1268-1287.

Denzin, N.K. (1978). *The research act: A theoretical introduction to sociological methods.* New York: McGraw-Hill.

Fichman, R.G., & Kemerer, C.F. (1997). The assimilation of software process innovations: An organisational learning perspective. *Management Science, 43*(1), 1345-1363.

Fitzgerald, B. (1997). The use of systems development methodologies in practice: A field study. *Information Systems Journal, 7,* 201-212.

Giddens, A. (1984). *The constitution of society.* East Sussex, UK: Polity Press.

Hedberg, B.L.T., Nyström, P.C., & Starbuck, W.H. (1976). Camping on seesaws- prescriptions for a self-designing organization. *Administrative Science Quaterly, 21*(1), 41-65.

Hedberg, B. (1981). How organizations learn and unlearn. In P.C. Nyström & W.H. Starbuck (Ed.), *Handbook of organizational design* (pp. 3-27). Oxford University Press.

Huber, G.P. (1991). Organizational learning: The contributing processes and the literatures. *Organization Science, 2*(1), 88-115.

Huff, S., & Munro, M.C. (1985, December). Information technology assessment and adoption: A field study. *MIS Quarterly,* 327-339.

Jensen, F. (1996). *An introduction to Bayesian network.* London: UCL Press.

Johnson, J.M. (1975). *Doing field research.* New York: The Free Press.

Kimberly, J.R. (1981). Managerial innovation. In P.C. Nyström & W.H. Starbuck (Ed.), *Handbook of organizational design: Adapting organizations to their environments.* Oxford University Press.

Kimberly, J.R. (1985). *The organisational context of technological innovation, implementing advanced technology.* Jossey-Bass.

Kwon, T.H., & Zmud, R.W. (1987). Unifying the fragmented models in information systems implementation. In R. Boland & R. Hirschheim (Ed.), *Critical Issues in Information Systems Research* (pp. 227-251). New York: John Wiley & Sons.

Laudon, K.C. (1989). Design guidelines for choices involving time in qualitative research. In J. Cash & P. Lawrence (Ed.), *The information systems research challenge: Qualitative research methods* (pp. 1-12). Cambridge, MA: Harvard Business School.

Luttrell, S.P. (1989). Self-organization: A derivation from first principles of a class of learning algorithms. In *Proceedings of the IJCNN'89 International Joint Conference On Neural Networks* (Vol. 2, pp. 495-498).

March, J.G., & Simon, H. (1958). *Organizations.* New York: John Wiley & Sons.

Monteiro, E., & Hanseth, O. (1995, December). Social shaping of information infrastructure: On being specific about the technology, information technology and changes in organizational work. In *Proceedings of the IFIP WG8.2 Working Conference on Information Technology and Changes in Organizational Work* (pp. 325-342).

Newell, S., Swan, J.A., & Galliers, R.D. (2000). A knowledge-focused perspective on the diffusion and adoption of complex information technologies: The BPR example. *Information Systems Journal, 10*(3), 239-259.

Nilakanta, S., & Scamell, R.W. (1990). The effect of information sources and communication channels on the diffusion of innovation in a data base development environment. *Management Science, 36*(1), 24-40.

Orlikowski, W. (1991). Integrated information environment or matrix of control? The contradictory implications of information technology. *Accounting, Management, and Information Technologies, 1*(1), 9-42.

Pfeffer, J. (1981). *Power in organisations.* Massachusetts: Pitman Publishing.

Prescott, M.B., & Conger, S.A. (1995). Information technology innovations: A classification by IT [Special issue of Technological Diffusion of Innovations; Special double issue: of Diffusion Technological Innovation]. *The Data Base for Advances in Information Systems, A Quarterly publication of SIGMIS, 26*(2-3), 20-41.

Rogers, E.M. (1995). *Diffusion of innovations.* New York: The Free Press.

Sarason, S.B. (1972). *The creation of settings and the future societies.* Jossey Bass: Brookline Books.

Sauer, C., & Lau, C. (1997). Trying to adapt systems development methodologies- a case-based exploration of business users' interests. *Information Systems Journal, 7,* 255-275.

Terreberry, S. (1968). The evolution of organisational environments. *Administrative Science Quaterly, 12,* 590-613.

von Hippel, E., & Katz, R. (2002). Shifting innovation to users via toolkits. *Management Science, 48*(7), 821-834.

PART 2
Information Systems Research Applications

Section 2.1
Software Development

Chapter IX
A Multi–Methodological Approach to Study Systems Development in a Software Organization

Paivi Ovaska
South Karelia University of Applied Sciences, Finland

ABSTRACT

Large-scale systems development is a complex activity involving number of dependencies that people working together face. Only a few studies concentrate on the coordination of development activities in their organizational context. This research study tries to fill at least part of this gap by studying how systems development process is coordinated in practice. The study uses a multimethodological approach to interpret coordination of systems development process in a contemporary software organization in Finland. The methodology is based on the empirical case-study approach in which the actions, conceptions, and artefacts of practitioners are analyzed using within-case and cross-case principles. In all the three phases of the study, namely multi-\site coordination, requirement understanding, and working with systems development methods, both the qualitative and quantitative methods were used to an understanding of coordination in systems development. The main contribution of this study is to demonstrate that contemporary systems development is much more complex and more driven by opportunity than is currently acknowledged by researchers. The most challenging part of the research process was the combination of qualitative and quantitative methods, because of the lack of multimethodological work done in IS discipline.

INTRODUCTION

Large-scale systems development is a complex activity involving number of dependencies that people working together face. Furthermore, in distributed and multiparty information systems projects, there is even a larger number of stakeholders involved, and a great number of dependencies. These dependencies create a need for coordination that requires continuous effort by developers. Broadly defined, coordination is management of interdependencies between activities (Malone & Crowston, 1994). This definition assumes that if there are no interdependencies, there is nothing to coordinate. The activities can be activities or objects; everything that has dependencies requires coordination (Malone & Crowston, 1994). Coordination is an inherent aspect of work in any organization and takes place in the form of meetings, scheduling, milestones, planning, and processes.

To systematize coordination, many methods and process models have been proposed over the years. These models mainly focus on the sequence of steps used by developers to develop information systems. The status of methods as a whole has been described as a "method jungle," as "an unorganized collection of methods more or less similar to each other" (Jayaratna, 1994). Though these methods and process models have helped companies to gain certification and attain global standards, they do not take into account interpersonal interactions and various other social aspects of development organizations. The development of new methods has tended to be more technology driven, often being influenced by the introduction of improved techniques and software tools (Nandhakumar & Avison, 1999).

Only a few studies concentrate on the process of systems development and coordination of development activities in their organizational context. Kraut and Streeter (1995) found that coordination becomes much more difficult as project size and complexity increases. Apparently,

complexity increases when the project is located in multiples sites. Communication is a salient part of coordination, and it has been observed (e.g., Allen, 1977) that distance affects the frequency of communication. Communication delays and breakdowns taking place in software development projects are discussed in several studies (Curtis, Krasner, & Iscoe, 1988; Kraut & Streeter, 1995; Herbsleb et al., 2000).

Systematic surveys of the existing literature in both Information Systems (Wynekoop & Russo, 1997) and Software Engineering (Glass, Vessey, & Ramesh, 2002) fields revealed that most of the research papers in these fields consist of normative research in which concept development is not based on empirical grounding or theoretical analysis, but merely upon the author's opinions. Because of that, many researchers (e.g., Curtis et al., 1988; Orlikowski, 1993) call for more empirical studies in order to understand how information systems are developed in today's organizations and how development work is coordinated in various types of organizations before development of new methods.

This research study tries to fill at least part of this gap by further clarifying how systems development process is coordinated in practice. This objective is reached by conducting a series of empirical studies of two systems development projects in a contemporary organization that competes in the information technology business. We study the early systems development, which we consider to be most important phases in development process: requirement elicitation and architecture design. In this study, the actions, conceptions, and artefacts of practitioners are interpreted and analyzed using multimethodological approach. By multimethodological approach is meant research approach that uses different research methods structured as a set of guidelines or activities to assist in generating valid and reliable research results (Mingers, 2001). The objective for this research is twofold: (1) to understand how practitioners coordinate the systems development process and (2) to make a contribution to the theory and practice of systems development.

The rest of this chapter is structured as follows. First we describe the other research using multiple research methods and then the research framework is created and the research process used is explained. After that, the research findings are summarized. The discussion of using this methodology by comparing it to framework proposed by Mingers (2001) as well the general experiences in using the methodology is given in the sixth section. Finally, we summarize the used methodology and research findings and give direction for future research.

RELATED RESEARCH

Combining different research methods has been the subject of much debated after 1990s. Mingers (2001) advocated multimethodological research on the grounds that both the target of the research and the research process were complex and multidimensional, requiring range of different approaches.

There have been numerous reviews of the information system research literature, each with different purpose, but few of them specifically considered combining methodologies. Mingers (2003) reviewed systematically the six IS top journal published in the time period from the year 1993 to 2000 and studied the extent of multimethodological research. The results of this study clearly show a lack of multimethodological research published within IS. In the following table is shown the proportion of multimethodological research papers in these journals.

Mingers also looked at the particular combinations of methods used. He found that the vast majority (70%) involve only observation, survey, case study, and interview. In these studies, the mixture of hard (quantitative) and soft (qualitative) methods were rare.

Example of studies in IS discipline using multimethodological approaches are Markus (1994), Ngwenyama and Lee (1997), Trauth and Jessup (2000), and Ormerod (1995), but the literature around the theme is quite scarce.

In relation to IS field, in the area of Management Science, a research of Munro and Mingers (2002) showed that the use of multimethodological methods were very common among practitioners within organizational interventions and was driven by the demands of complex real-world

Table 1. Proportion of multimethodological papers (1993, 2000) adapted from Mingers (2003)

Year	ISR (%)	ISJ (%)	MISQ (%)	EJIS (%)	AMIT (%)	JIT (%)	Average (%)
1993	40	0	50	0	-	21	22
1994	13	20	35	29	-	13	25
1995	0	11	7	18	33	8	13
1996	28	14	18	15	60	0	23
1997	18	27	19	7	63	17	25
1998	0	0	20	18	25	16	13
1999	0	22	24	21	56	21	24
2000	10	31	13	0	33	33	20

Note: Information Systems Research (ISR); Information Systems Journal (ISJ); MIS Quarterly (MISQ); European Journal of Information Systems (EJIS); Accounting, Managements and Information Technology (AIMT); Journal of Information Technology (JIT)

problem situations. According to this study, practitioners used two, three or even more methods together in this area.

DEVELOPING THE METHODOLOGY

Studied Organization

The research study was carried out in a software development department of an international ICT company. The software development department was an internal partner for the company's business units. The development of applications and services was assigned to an in-house software development unit (Internal Development Unit, later referred as IDU) or outsourced companies. The use of IDU for development of new services was mandated by the company's top management. IDU had approximately 150 employees that had formerly focused on R&D work in the company. During the past few years, it had tried to improve its software skills and processes in order to make its development more effective and also to prove its capability to other business units. All the business units of the company did not agree with IDU's processes and did not trust in its software development capability. Their attitudes towards IDU competencies in software development were quite suspicious, mainly because of IDU's history as an R&D department. Quite often business units preferred outsourcing instead of developing in-house.

The projects, called here the "DS project" and the "EC project" respectively developed mobile services to both the global and domestic telecommunication markets. A major goal of both projects was the renewal of old platform architecture to allow the services to be better and easier modifiable, maintainable, and scalable.

The DS project developed a directory service platform for international markets. The project was partitioned into two subprojects to facilitate easier management. Partitioning was carried out on the basis of the architecture and technology: one subsystem had a highly distributed, component-based architecture (Server) and the other was a centralized subsystem (Client), which handled authentication, authorization and user interfaces. The functionality of the services required subsystems to communicate only through an extensible and configurable interface.

The goal of the EC project was to develop an Electronic Commerce mobile service platform. The system was intended to enable organizers or their sponsors to promote their products in all kinds of events, such as ice hockey and football games. The system was composed of two subsystems: the platform in which the services are run (Platform subsystem) and the toolbox (Tool subsystem). The Tool subsystem allowed adding, configuring and simulating of services to run in a Windows PC and with a service platform in an UNIX environment.

The actual systems development projects took place in IDU during the year 2001 and they were planned and organized according to a traditional waterfall model with distinct requirement elicitation, analysis, software design, implementation, and testing phases.

Shaping the Research Problem

The basic notion of systems development, namely systems development as a process that involves real people in real environments (e.g., Lyytinen, 1987), formed the ground for constructing our research methodology. To truly understand systems development, it is imperative to study people-systems development practitioners as they solve real development problems in real environments. Therefore, as

Rosen (1991) puts it, "to understand social process one must get inside the world of those generating it." This kind of goals favoured interpretive approach that enables researcher to understand human thought and action in social and organizational contexts (Walsham, 1995).

Systems development in organizational environment arouses different kinds of dependencies. The structure of the software system itself creates dependencies between software elements, while the structure of the development process creates dependencies between software developers. Each of these both shapes and reflects the development process; therefore, the other objective of selecting the research methodology to this study was to focus on different aspects of systems development (both technical and social dependencies) and therefore to get richer understanding of the dependencies.

Yet another goal was also to be more convinced of information accuracy also discussed in Yin (1994). Quantitative evidence can indicate relationships which may not be salient to the researcher. It also can keep researchers from being carried away by vivid, but false impressions in qualitative data, and it can bolster findings when it corroborates those findings from qualitative evidence (Eisenhardt, 1989).

Above objectives favoured selecting the interpretive approach (Walsham, 1995) and integrating different methods according to multimethodological approach (Eisenhardt, 1989; Mingers, 2003). Used methods are described in another section along with description of research process. In the following, the basic principles of the shaping the research methodology are explained in more detail.

Phases Adopted in Research

The research included three phases: studies on how architecture affects a multi site development project, studies on how requirements were shaped and interpreted during the systems development and how this process is to be estimated, and a study on how practitioners work with systems development methods. It is briefly explained how these three phases shaped the research problem:

Phase One: Multisite Coordination

The objective of this phase was to clarify the systems development problems related to software architecture and investigate how practitioners cope with these problems in systems development. This phase consisted of two parts: a qualitative study about social complexities and a quantitative analysis of technical complexities. During the phase, the problems found in the qualitative study evolved more to coordination and communication problems for which architecture provided a tool. In the quantitative study, the understanding of the architecture as a size predictor in the project cost estimation got its basic shape. The results from this phase of study are given in another section.

Phase Two: Requirement Understanding Process

In the beginning of phase two, we tried to find coordination problems or problems related to software architecture, but observed that the problems were more related to requirement understanding and organizational conflicts. This observation shaped the research problem towards the interpretation of the requirement understanding process and how this could be measured to get better estimates of the project timetable along with the architecture measures from phase one. The results from this phase are given in another section. At the end of this phase, the observations so far suggested that methods in the organization played an important role in the case study projects. This led us to shape the study towards the interpretation of the role of methods and their use in the studied organization.

Phase Three: Working with Systems Development Methods

In this phase, the comparisons of the results of phase one and phase two according to their similarities and differences (cross-case analysis). During this analysis, it appeared that the coordination and the requirements understanding in the projects were the result of using and adapting methods based on the practitioner's background, experience and the development situation at hand. The results from this phase are given in another section.

RESEARCH PROCESS

In this section, the research process is explained. Figure 1 explains the flow of research phases and tasks. After that the process is explained in a more detailed level.

Preparing for the Study

The beginning of our research study included an initial definition of the research question, a selection of cases and crafting instruments and protocols.

Each of the phases of the study had the research questions of its own. Table 2 summarizes the research questions of each three phases.

The selection of cases relied on the theoretical sampling principle (Glaser & Strauss, 1967), in which cases are chosen as extreme situations and polar types in which the process of interest is "transparently observable." The sampling strategy of the current study was designed to be built around projects displaying problems in systems development, big problems that caused delays to the project's timetable. Within these projects in the studied organization, we chose projects of polar types: one project had problems inside the project, the other problems with the customer; one was smaller and the other one bigger; they both produced service platforms for different business areas. The analysis revealed that the projects had even more different features, such as the orientation, attitudes, and experience of the participants, and the communication between participants that extended the emergent theory (Eisenhardt, 1989). To facilitate iteration and comparison, which is an

Figure 1. Research process

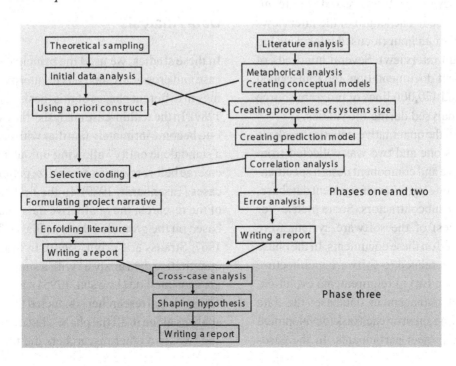

Table 2. Research questions in each three phases of the study

Phase one	Phase two	Phase three
What kind of coordination problems related to software architecture was present during the systems development?	How were software requirements shaped and interpreted during systems development?	How practitioners use systems development methods in projects?
How did these problems differ in the same-site and multi-site environments?		How methods support systems development practitioners in projects?

inevitable feature of the grounded theory method (Locke, 2003), these two projects were analyzed one by one.

Data Collection

During the study, most of the data was collected from project extensive documentation (see Table 3) based on the dynamic process of data collection (Glaser & Strauss, 1967), where samples were extended and focused according to the emerging needs of the theoretical sampling. In both case projects, the project documentation data was complemented with interviews among project participants (customer, project managers, designers, etc.).

The interviews were all tape-recorded and completely transcribed. The length of the interviews varied from half an hour (focused interviews) to 2 hours (group interview). Several hundreds of pages of project documentation, the transcribed interviews, and 170,000 lines of program source codes were analysed during the studies.

The data for the quantitative statistical analysis in both phases one and two was collected from the architecture and component design specifications, source code, project management database, and bills from subcontractors. Some metrics (or property values) of the software system were calculated based on these documents. In the phase this metric was related to software architecture and in the phase two to requirements evolution. In the project management database, the data included the time spent on each task (development effort) by the project participants. In the cases

where foreign consultants were involved in the development work, the development effort data was taken from the subcontractors' bills.

Seed Categories

Specification of a priori constructs (Eisenhardt, 1989) or also called seed categories (Miles & Huberman, 1984) can help research. In phase one, a notion of the common object from Malone and Crowston's coordination theory (Malone & Crowston, 1990, 1994) was used to interpret the coordination in the project. In phase two, the concept of a technology frame of reference (Orlikowski & Gash, 1994) was used to interpret the requirement understanding in the project.

Data Analysis

In these studies, we used the principle of within-case and cross-case analysis to interpret the findings in different phases of this thesis (Eisenhardt, 1989). In the within-case analysis "the overall idea is to become intimately familiar with each case as a standalone entity" allowing unique patterns to emerge before trying to generalize patterns across cases (Eisenhardt, 1989). In the first two phases of the research, the qualitative data analysis was based on the grounded theory (Glaser & Strauss, 1967; Strauss & Corbin, 1990). In those phases, quantitative data analysis with a simple linear regression method (Lawson, 1995) was carried out. The principal researcher conducted the qualitative analysis alone in all the phases, but, in phases one and two, two other researchers did the quantita-

Table 3. Data available from the case projects

Data/Document/Artifact DS project	Data/Document/Artifact EC project
15 Progress Report (from Project Manager)	15 Progress Reports (from Project Manager)
Project management Software: Plan vs. Actual costs	Project management Software (Niku Workbench): Plan vs. Actual costs, development effort
11 Project Steering Group Meeting Minutes	16 Project Steering Group Meeting Minutes
46 Project Group Meeting Minutes	26 Project Group Meeting Minutes
Project Plan	Project Plans
Functional Specifications	Requirement Specification document
Requirement Catalogue	Project Quality Criteria document
Risk analysis document	Architecture Specification
Project Quality Criteria document	26 Module Specifications
Architecture Descriptions	22 Tool subsystem UI specifications
Module Specifications	Kick-off presentation, Steering Group kick-out meeting minutes
Group Interview with project participants	Focused interviews of three BU members (development manager, team leader, designer)
Group interview slides	Focused interviews of four IDU members (steering group representative, project architect, 2 project designers)
Source code (Lines of Codes) 138,000 LOC	Source code (Lines of Codes) 32,000 LOC

tive data analysis and provided complementary insights (Eisenhardt, 1989) into the qualitative analysis in our discussions. As outsiders of the qualitative data collection, they were able to look at the data more with greater objectivity (Nandhakumar & Jones, 1997), which facilitated a more reliable data analysis as a whole.

In the first and second phase of the study, the qualitative data analysis started quite early, right after the data on the project meeting minutes was collected. In the first phase, data collection continued with design specifications simultaneously with the analysis of the data on the project meeting minutes. In phase two, the collection of requirement specification data started while the analysis of the data on the project meeting minutes was still being performed. The quantitative data collection started as soon as some initial findings of the qualitative data analysis were made. Such overlap of data collection and analysis is strongly recommended by Eisenhardt (1989) and Strauss

and Corbin (1990). To help manage the quite extensive amount of information and the analysis process, the Atlas.ti (Scientific Software, 2001) tool was used. It helped in the analysis process, for example in the retrieval of categories, memo making and recording of semantic relationships.

The quantitative data analysis was hypotheses testing in nature and naturally used a priori constructs. Both hypotheses were based on the initial findings of the corresponding qualitative studies. To the statistical data analysis, we used the Matlab Optimization Toolbox (MathWorks Inc., 2003).

In the following we describe the data analysis process in the three phases of the study.

Phase One

Data analysis started with open coding according to Miles and Huberman (1984). In open coding, a researcher tries to find relevant categories based on research questions. Open coding started with the finding of problems and deviations related to coordination and software architecture (relevant categories in this study) in the project progress, using mainly project meeting minutes and the group interview as a data source. We further used architecture and design specifications to help pinpoint the problems. We observed in total 329 deviations and problems related to software architecture and coordination.

Data analysis continued with the axial coding, in which categories found in open coding were refined, developed further, and related. In this phase, we used a notion of common object as a seed category based on Malone and Crowston's coordination theory (Malone & Crowston, 1990, 1994) to help in the interpretation of coordination problems in the project. We identified two types of common objects from the study, namely component and development activity. The following

example (Figure 2) shows a translated excerpt of a transcript after axial coding. This example shows how common objects were interpreted from the project material.

In the selective coding phase, where the "core category," or central category that ties all other categories in the theory together, was identified and related to other categories (Glaser & Strauss, 1967). The identification of common objects helped in finding the interdependencies between activities that caused coordination problems in the project. We identified three interdependencies between components and three interdependencies between development activities. These interdependencies are explained in another section.

After finding the interdependencies, we tried to find an answer to the research question of how the problems in coordination differed in multisite and same same-site environments (cross-case analysis). To find these differences, we compared

Figure 2. Translated excerpt of a transcript after axial coding in the phase one

"On the Server side, we gained experience from new technologies, like XML, XSL and CORBA"

Technical orientation of the Server
Common object: development activity

"We had a lot of problems with Client and Server synchronization. The Client was first and the Server was behind, it should be wice versa "

"The Client-Server interface was dependent on core resources"

Interface and interdependence problems
Common object: component

"AA and MS&LB need communication with architect and designer"

Communication problems
Common object: development activity

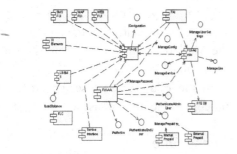

Interface problems
Common object: component

"The second actual build was made 24th August, FFE not ready for testing"

Assembly order problems
Common object: development activity

the two subprojects and analyzed the differences in the coordination processes between them.

In the quantitative analysis, we used metaphorical analysis (Frost & Morgan, 1983; Lakoff & Johson, 1980; Schultze & Orlikowski, 2001) to help understand the architecture of the system. According to our metaphor of architecture drawing, we identified three categories that described the architecture of our case study system best. Within these categories, we attempted to select the properties, which were simple and could be calculated based on project design specifications. We chose the simple linear prediction model to analyze the correlation between architecture properties and systems development effort. From these 7 property values for six components, a total of 42 property values were calculated. From these property values, we calculated coefficient values using Matlab Optimization toolbox. In the end of this quantitative process, we calculated the model errors to determine the quality of our cost effort estimation model and analyzed the results based on coefficient values.

Phase Two

Phase two started with the identification of problems and deviations in the project progress. During the development, these were issues that were brought to the project meetings for discussion and decision-making. The steering and project group meeting minutes were the main sources for problem and change identification. We observed in total 150 problems and deviations related to project progress. Most of the concerns brought to the steering group were related to the other subsystem and its requirements. Also the system development styles and strategies caused concerns.

To better understand the requirements of the system, we investigated in more detail the requirements specification document. We were able to extract only four initial requirements that were related to the other subsystem. Our analysis

continued as we used three conceptual models of both subsystems developed in the qualitative study.

Through these models, we were able to grasp how the subsystems evolved through different phases of systems development. The content of these conceptual models suggested to us that the other subsystem's requirements changed considerably during the process. This led us into investigating further why this subsystem's requirements changed so much, while the other subsystem's requirements remained stable.

To answer this question, we made focused interviews among the project participants to identify the reasons for these changes. Project participants were asked to reflect on the project's history by showing the analysis and implementation models of the system and to describe their understanding of what happened in the project between the requirement analysis and implementation phases. Four of the interviewed project participants were from the development side and three from the business side. Business side representatives were also asked about the competences and processes of development side during the time the project was running and how these competences and processes had evolved after that. The interviews were audio taped and fully transcribed to preserve all the details.

Based on the interviews, we observed that requirements did not change that much during the project, but the understanding of them changed. The open coding proceeded in parallel, treating each interview as confirmation or further development of results from earlier findings. During this process, the categories developed gradually. First, we identified quite concrete concerns of system development. In further analysis, we found more subtle contextual attitudes and expectations about how systems development should be performed. These attitudes and expectations were so strongly visible in the data that we could interpret them as technology frames (Orlikowski & Gash, 1994). In further analysis, we used technology frames as a priori construct or lenses to the data. This further analysis consisted of group analysis, cross-group analysis and re-examination of the categories. This iterative examination of the data yielded five categories of technology frames, which were used as a basis for the next phase, axial coding.

During the axial coding, we identified four processes of stereotypical "tensions" between these attitudes and expectations, which affected how project participants emphasized these frames of understanding in different phases of the project. These tensions and explained in another section.

In the selective coding phase, the causal relationships between categories were recorded with Atlas.ti's (Scientific Software, 2001) semantic network capability. Figure 3 shows an example of such a network diagram. In Figure 3, the boxes represent categories, the arrows the interpreted causalities between them, and the lines simple associations between the categories. The abbreviations business value of system development (BVSD), system development strategy

(SPS), system development capability (SDC), and system development resource allocation (SDRA) correspond to the categories of frames of understanding.

Based on project material, interviews, and analysis, we formulated the project narrative to trace how the participants' attitudes and expectation influenced the systems development process. In the end of the research process, the project narrative was sent by e-mail to the project manager to get her opinion on the correspondence of the narrative with the reality. She adjusted some details, which did not affect the main findings.

In the quantitative analysis, we formulated the metric describing the identified requirement evolution in the project. The metric was quite simple: it calculated the concepts found during the analysis and implementation models of the system. These analysis and implementation models were formed based on the project specifications. In the statistical analysis, we used the same simple prediction model as in phase one of the study. The other metrics needed were chosen

Figure 3. An example of semantic network diagram using Atlas.ti (Scientific Software, 2001)

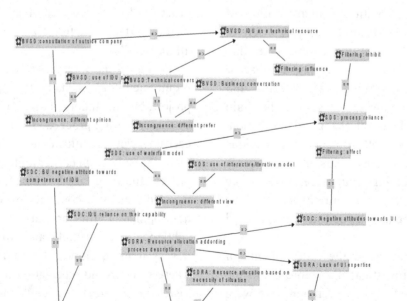

based on simplicity and wide usage. Using this prediction model, we calculated the correlation between metrics chosen and the development effort. In the end of the process, we formulated the model errors to determinine the reliability of our prediction model and analyzed the results.

Phase Three

In phase three, we used cross-case analysis to interpret the final results in this thesis (Eisenhardt, 1989). We searched for cross-cased patterns to compare the multi-site and same-site development by listing their similarities and differences (Eisenhardt, 1989). We selected pairs of cases and listed similarities and differences between each pair. In this phase, the number of cases was actually three because one of the case projects consisted of two subprojects. The cross-category table produced in this process is shown in Table 4.

Shaping the Hypothesis

From the within-case analysis, the cross-case analysis and overall impressions, tentative tenses and concepts and their relationships begin to emerge, which is called hypothesis shaping (Eisenhardt, 1989). The idea is that researchers constantly compare emergent theory and "raw" data—iterating towards a theory with closely fit data (Eisenhardt, 1989).

In the hypothesis shaping, we used the semantic network diagram capability of Atlas.ti software (Scientific Software, 2001). This semantic network is shown in Figure 2. This network shows the relationships between the core categories used to interpret the role of methods.

Finishing and Reporting the Studies

Eisenhardt (1989) distinguishes the phase "enfolding literature." By this phase, Eisenhardt means the comparison of the findings with similar and conflicting literature. The aim of this phase is to raise confidence, creative thinking, and the validity, generalizability, and conceptual level of the findings. Yin (Yin, 1994) refers to this as "analytic generalization" to distinguish it from the more typical statistical generalization that generalizes from a sample to a population. In phase one, the main comparisons were done with Malone and Crowston's (Malone & Crowston, 1990, 1994) coordination theory and cost estimation literature. The comparisons of phase two were made with traditional requirement engineering approaches and existing sociotechnical approaches to requirement elicitation, especially the concept of a technological frame. All these provided conflicting and similar concepts and patterns, which all provided an alternative and more creative view to our findings. In phase three, the findings were compared to a few empirical studies of the role of methods in systems development.

SUMMARY OF FINDINGS

Phase One: Multisite Coordination (Ovaska & Bern, 2004; Ovaska, Rossi, & Marttiin, 2004)

In phase one, we discovered six different coordination processes to explain most of the coordination problems related to software architecture in the case studies. These six processes can be summarised as follows:

1. *Interfaces*: Managing interfaces between system components
2. *Integration*: Managing the assembly of system components, enabling their integration into a full, working system architecture
3. *Interdependence*: Managing the interdependencies between system components
4. *Communication*: Managing the communication processes between development participants
5. *Responsibility*: Managing the allocation of responsibilities for key decisions related to

Table 4. Cross-category table between projects in the studies

Category	Case Project 1 subproject A	Case Project 1 subproject B	Case Project 2
Adaptation to method	yes	no	yes
Problems	minor technical inside project	inside project, coordination and architecture understanding	conflicts with client, requirement understanding
Timetable estimation	no major problems	problems	problems
Orientation and attitudes	Architect's technical orientation	Architect's business orientation	Designer's positive attitude towards UI and windows
Experience	Experienced project group	Unexperienced project group	Unexperienced project group
Communication	good	bad	in the beginning bad, later good
Understanding the system	fairly good	not very good	in the beginning no, learning to understand
Understanding the development situation	yes	no	in the beginning no later yes
Method purpose	communication and coordination	method use failed	communication and learning
The most meaning metric (relative to development effort)	Coupling (NIC)	-	Requirements Creep

the software architecture and subsystem designs

6. *Perspectives*: Managing the different perspectives development participants brought to the project and managing negotiations related to these perspectives

This phase suggest that technical dependencies among software components (interfaces, integration, and interdependence) create social dependencies (communication, responsibility, perspectives) among the software developers implementing those components. It also supports the Malone and Crowston's coordination theory by highlighting the importance of the coordination of interdependencies between activities instead of purely coordinating activities in systems development.

Phase Two: Rrequirement Understanding
(Ovaska, 2004; Ovaska, Rossi, & Smolander, 2005)

In phase two of the research process four categories of technology frames were identified that could explain attitudes and expectations that affected people's understanding of requirements and which were directly related to the ISD process. These categories can be summarised as follows:

1. *Business value of systems development*: attitudes and expectations about the relationship between business and system development.
2. *Systems development strategy*: attitudes and expectations about the system development lifecycle model and associated ISD processes.
3. *Systems development capability*: the assumptions, attitudes and expectations surrounding the various competencies of project participants in different areas of system development
4. *Systems development resource allocation*: the assumptions, attitudes and expectations as regards scheduling, budgeting, and prioritisation of systems development activities

Within these four frames it was possible to identify stereotypical "tensions" which emerged as the projects unfolded. These tensions and the processes associated with them had important effects on how the project participants emphasized various technology frames during the different phases of the project:

1. *Incongruence*: this tension emerged when understanding, attitudes, or expectations differed among the stakeholders, causing conflicts and misunderstanding
2. *Filtering*: this tension surfaced when a stakeholder of the development process left something out of scope because of his/her particular perspective, attitude, series of expectations, or experience of ISD
3. *Negotiation*: this refers to tensions associated with the various negotiations between project participants and took place in order to resolve incongruities
4. *Shifting*: this emerged when the understanding of a frame changed (called a "frame shift"). After a frame shift, the parties involved achieved an understanding of a frame that was more aligned and suitable for the current situation than before the shift.

In this phase, we observed that preconceptions, attitudes, and expectations about systems development among project participants filtered the understanding of software requirements, negotiating between project participants resolved the issues caused by filtering and shifts in these attitudes and expectations facilitated changes in the understanding of requirements. In spite of this observed filtering, shifting, and negotiation, the developed system exceeded the customer's needs and expectations even though it was delivered late. The results of this phase suggest that the current conceptions regarding requirement elicitation do not correspond with the needs of practice. The traditional requirement engineering research concentrates on detecting and representing requirements and ensuring that they are complete and consistent. It sees requirements mainly in a system context assuming that they already exist somewhere ready to be picked in the requirement elicitation phase. Our study has consequences beyond such a view. It suggests that requirement elicitation is in practice an ad-hoc and iterative process involving political, cognitive and social aspects that affect the interpretation of requirements during the whole project lifetime.

Phase Three: Working with Methods (Ovaska, 2005)

During the cross-case analysis in phase three of the research process, we discovered the five categories which summarised various ways in which methods were used in the target projects:

1. *Methods used as tools*: rather than following predefined phases and tasks practitioners used ISD methods as if they were a set of tools which could be variously deployed or discarded as the need arose
2. *Methods used to coordinate*: practitioners primarily used methods to coordinate systems development
3. *Methods used a communication language*: methods were used to provide common communication language between various project participants, and the methods thus helped to set the agenda for many discussions
4. *Methods as a means to aid understanding of the system and its requirements*: methods were used to help develop an understanding of the system in terms of requirements and expectations of users and align these with various technical and nontechnical issues which arose
5. *Understanding the development context*: methods were used by participants to make sense of the development situation as it shifted over time

This phase suggests that working with methods is complex social interaction and a mutual understanding process between project participants. The methods were used in our case study as a tool for communication and learning and as a resource in project planning among system development participants, not as a list of phases to be followed in detail. Method use requires communication between project participants to adopt the method to the development situation. Without commu-

nication, methods use failed. When participants gained common understanding of the appropriate development strategy and method, the method use became a learning process. In this learning process, system development participants changed their understanding of the system, according to changing development situations. Without the common understanding of the system between project participants, the estimation of project timetable and resources did not succeed. Based on the observations of our study, we argue that methods are used more as support and guide the development than strict phases to be followed in detail.

DISCUSSION

In this section the multimethodological approach used in this study is discussed related to the multimethodological guidelines set out by Mingers (2001). The guidelines suggest that in designing research one should consider the following domains:

- *The context of the research*—in particular the relationships between the research situation and task, the methods and theories available, and the researchers' own competencies and commitments
- *The dimensions of the research situation*—in particular, the material, social, and personal aspects

In the following, these domains are explained in more detail along with the comparison our multimethodological approach to it. Finally, we summarize the general experiences of using the methodology and its limitations.

The Context of the Research

The multimethodology used in this study lies on the most close to dominant type of design in which one method is the main approach with contributions from the others. The qualitative methods were our main method in all phases contributed from qualitative statistical analysis. The reasons for such a design were formed from the nature of systems development as a social process.

The professional and scientific background of principal researcher provides some explanations for understanding the selection of the research method and also the role of the researcher in the interpretive research process. Because of her educational background in engineering, she also wanted to get some "hard evidence" of the projects, maybe to become more assured of the reliability of the research. She wanted to carry out some statistical, quantitative calculations that would support the qualitative work. During the learning process in the research work, the quantitative calculations faded into the background and shifted more towards an interpretive approach.

Although the principal researcher did not work on the chosen projects, she acquired "deep familiarity" (Nandhakumar & Jones, 1997) with the research context and its actors during the 5 years working in that company. During the observation period, she was fully involved in the activities of the company. During the analysis period, she was not involved in the activities, but had full access to all project documents gaining access to information that would not otherwise have been divulged. The used data in the study was mainly documents gathered during the projects. Without her personal experience in the company, it would have been difficult to interpret the local meanings, dominant perceptions, tacit knowledge, and non-verbal communication (Nandhakumar & Jones, 1997) from the documentation. Without the deep familiarity with the research context and its actors, it would not be possible to gain additional insight in the actors' interpretations, their motivation, and perspectives (Nandhakumar, Jones, 1997) in the focused interviews carried out during the study. Her role as a researcher was somewhere between an outside observer and involved researcher (Walsham, 1995); it can be called an "involved observer" participating in the work of the company before the analysis period.

The Dimensions of the Research Situation

According to Mingers (2001), each research situation is the combination of three worlds: the material world, the social world, and the personal world. Each domain has different modes of existence and different epistemological possibilities as followed:

- *The material world* is outside and independent of human beings characterized as objective in the sense that it is independent of the observer although our observations and descriptions of it are not. Our relationship to this world is one of *observation*.
- *The personal world* is the world of our own individual interpretations, experiences, thoughts, and beliefs. We do not observe it, but *experience* it.
- *The social world* is the world that we share with others in a particular social system and *participate* in it.

In comparing our research situation and methodology to this framework, all these worlds were present to the following extent. The study covered material aspects, such as architecture as a predictor of system size or requirement creep as a measure of requirement evolution. The interpretive analysis of documentation and interviews explored the meaning of coordination and requirements understanding for particular individuals; and group interviews and their interpretations revealed the social aspects of coordination and requirements understanding.

General Experiences

In general, we experienced the methodology highly iterative learning process, in this process the research themes and questions changed during its phases.

The most challenging part of the research was the combination of quantitative and qualitative methods, mainly because of the lack of the empirical frameworks to guide the work; therefore the frameworks would be helpful in designing and developing this kind of research.

Limitations of the Methodology

A critical issue for researchers concerns the generalizability of the results of their work, and Yin (1994) notes that this issue is often rose with respect to case studies. Different arguments for the generalizability of case study research have been given (Dutton & Dukerich, 1991; Eisenhardt, 1989; Walsham, 1995; Yin, 1994). It is argued that in case study research, the identified concepts and categories are compared to theoretical concepts and patterns, unlike in statistical generalization from a sample to a population. Still, due to the nature of this study in which the understanding of method use was interpreted on the basis of separate phenomena found in one organization, the generalization of the use of methods may be limited. Therefore, the understanding gained in these studies provides a basis for understanding similar phenomena in the same settings rather than enabling the understanding of phenomena in other contexts.

SUMMARY AND FUTURE WORK

This chapter has described the multimethodological approach to study coordination of systems development process. We used the principle of within-case and cross-case analysis to interpret the findings in different phases of the study. In all these three phases, we used both qualitative and quantitative methods to get richer and more reliable understanding from coordination phenomena.

The three phases of the study have provided a rich picture of different aspects of systems development in the software organization. In the first phase of the study, we examined the role of architecture in coordination and cost estimation in a multisite software development from quantitative and qualitative viewpoints. The second phase involved two studies, one qualitative and the other quantitative, on the evolving requirement understanding process and the measurement of this process. The third phase was a study based on the first two studies on the role of methods and how practitioners work with them using principle of cross-case analysis. The research process of these phases was explained.

We experienced the methodology highly iterative and adaptive learning process, in which the research themes and questions evolved during its phases. The study covered material aspects, such as architecture as a predictor of system size as well as personal and social aspects. Highly interpretive analysis of documentation and interviews covered aspects of particular individuals whereas the group interviews and their interpretation revealed the social aspects of coordination of systems development work.

The main contribution of this study is to demonstrate that contemporary systems development is very complex and more driven by opportunity than is currently acknowledged by researchers. We need more knowledge of the current and emerging business and organizational contexts in which and for which these systems are developed. This study suggests that further rich, multimethodological research is urgently needed in order to build a picture of how communities of practice make sense of systems development. Only in this way we can begin to find ways to understand and address the problems in systems development.

The most challenging part of the research process was the combination of qualitative and quantitative methods because of the lack of multimethodological work done so far; therefore the frameworks would be helpful in designing and developing multimethodological approaches.

In the future, our multimethodological framework needs deeper work towards a theory-building approach, especially related to analysis process in the phase three. Also, the replication of our study in other contexts and redefinition of the framework based on experiences is necessary.

REFERENCES

Allen, T. (1977). *Managing the flow of technology*. Cambridge, MA: MIT Press.

Curtis, B., Krasner, H., & Iscoe, N. (1988). A field study of the software design process for large systems. *Communications of the ACM, 31*(11), 1268-1287.

Dutton, J., & Dukerich, J. (1997). Keeping an eye on the mirror: Image and identity in organizational adaptation. *Academy of Management Journal, 34*, 517-554.

Eisenhardt, K.M. (1989). Building theories from case study research. *Academy of Management Review, 14*(4), 532-550.

Frost, P.J., Morgan, G. (1983). Symbols of sensemaking: The realization of the framework. L. R. Pondy, P.J. Frost, G. Morgan & R.T.C. Dandrike (Eds.), *Organizational Symbolism* (pp. 419-437). New York: Wiley.

Glaser, B., & Strauss, A.L. (1967). *The discovery of grounded theory: Strategies for qualitative research*. Chicago, Adline.

Glass, R., Vessey, I., & Ramesh, V. (2002). Research in software engineering: An analysis of the literature. *Information and Software Technology, 44*(8), 491-506.

Jayaratna, N. (1994). *Understanding and evaluating methodologies: NIMSAD a systematic framework*. New York, McGraw-Hill.

Hersleb, J.D., Mockus, A., Finholt, T.A., & Grinter, R.E. (2000). Distance, dependencies and delay in a global collaboration. *ACM Conference on Computer-Supported Cooperative Work*. Philadelphia (p. 319, 328), December 2-7.

Kraut, R.E., & Streeter, L.A. (1995). Coordination in software development. *Communications of the ACM, 38*(3), 69-81.

Lakoff, G., & Johson, M. (1980). *Metaphors we live by*. Chicago: The University of Chicago Press.

Lawson, C.L. (1995). *Solving least squares problems*. Society of Industrial and Applied Mathematics.

Lee, A (1997). Integrating positivist and interpretivist approaches to organizational research. *Organization Science, 2*, 342-264.

Locke, K. (2003). *Grounded theory in management research*. London: Sage.

Lyytinen, K. (1987). Different perspectives on information systems: Problems and solutions. *ACM Computing Surveys, 19*(1), 5-46.

Malone, T.W., & Crowston, K. (1990, October 7-10). What is coordination theory and how can it help design cooperative work systems? In *Conference on Computer Supported Cooperative Work (CSCW '90)*, Los Angeles, (pp. 357-370). ACM Press.

Malone, T.W., & Crowston, K. (1994). The interdisciplinary study of coordination. *ACM Computing Surveys, 26*(1), 87-110.

Markus, I. (1994). Electronic mail as the medium of managerial choice. *Organizational Science, 5*(4), 502-527.

Mathworks Inc. (1995). Matlab. Retrieved August 20, 2008 from http://www.mathworks.com

Miles, M.B., & Huberman, A.M. (1984). *Qualitative data analysis: A sourcebook of a new methods.* Beverly Hills, CA: Sage.

Mingers, J. (2001). Combining IS research methods: Towards a pluralist methodology. *Information Systems Research, 12*(3), 240-259.

Mingers, J. (2003). The paucity of multimethod research: A review of the information systems literature. *Information Systems Journal, 13,* 233-249.

Munro, I., & Mingers, J. (2002). The use of multimethodology in practice—Results of a survey of practitioners. *Journal of Operational Research Society, 53,* 369-378.

Nandhakumar, J., & Avison, D. (1999). The fiction of methodology development: A field study of information systems development. *Information Technology & People, 12*(2), 176-191.

Nandhakumar, J., & Jones, M. (1997). Too close for comfort? Distance and engagement in interpretive information systems research. *Information Systems Journal, 7*(2), 109-131.

Ngwenyama, O., & Lee, A. (1997). Communication richness in electronic mail: Critical social theory and the contextuality of meaning. *MIS Quarterly, 21,* 145-167.

Orlikowski, W.J. (1993). Case tools as organizational change: Investigating incremental and radical changes in systems development. *MIS Quarterly, 17*(3).

Orlikowski, W.J., & Gash, D.C. (1994). Technological frames: Making sense of information technology in organizations. *ACM Transactions on Information Systems, 12*(2), 174-207.

Ormerod, R. (1995). Putting soft OR methods to work: Information systems strategy development at Sainsbury's. *Journal of the Operational Research Society, 46*(3), 277-293.

Ovaska, P. (2004, April 14-17). Measuring requirement evolution – a case study in the e-commerce domain. In *6th International Conference on Enterprise Information Systems (ICEIS(3)),* Porto, Portugal, INSTICC (pp. 669-673).

Ovaska, P. (2005). Working with methods: Observations on the role methods in systems development. O. Vasilegas, A. Capinskas, W. Wotjowski, W.G. Wotjowski, J. Zupneic, & S. Wrycza (Eds.), *Information systems development, advances in theory, practice and education, ISD 2004* (pp. 185-197). Springer.

Ovaska, P., & Bern, A. (2004, June 7-11). Architecture as a predictor of system size – a metaphor from construction projects. In *16th International Conference on Advanced Information Systems Engineering (CAISE '04 Forum),* Riga, Latvia, Riga Technical University (pp. 193-203).

Ovaska, P., Rossi, M., & Marttiin, P. (2004). Architecture as a coordination tool in multi-site software development. *Software Process Improvement and Practice, 8*(4), 233-248.

Ovaska, P., Rossi, M., & Smolander, K. (2005). Filtering, negotiating and shifting in the understanding of information systems requirements. *Scandinavian Journal of Information Systems, 17*(1), 31-66.

Rosen, M. (1991). Coming to terms with the field: Understanding and doing organizational ethnography. *Journal of Management Studies, 28,* 7-24.

Schultze, U., & Orlikowski, W.J. (2001). Metaphors of virtuality: Shaping an emergent reality. *Information and Organization, 11*(1), 45-77.

Scientific Software. (2001). Atlas.ti-the knowledge workbench. Retrieved June 3, 2008, from http://www.atlasti.de/

Strauss, A., & Corbin, J. (1990). *Basics of qualitative research: Grounded theory procedures and applications.* Newbury Park, CA: Sage.

Trauth, E.M., & Jessup, L. (2000). Understanding computer-mediated discussions: positivist and interpretive analyses of group support system use [Special issue on intensive research]. *MIS Quarterly, 24*(1), 43-79.

Walsham, G. (1995). Interpretive case studies in IS research. *European Journal of Information Systems, 4,* 74-81.

Wynekoop, J., & Russo, N. (1997). Studying system development methodologies: An examination of research methods. *Information Systems Journal, 7*(1), 47-65.

Yin, R.K. (1994). *Case study research: Design and methods* (2nd ed.). Newbury Park: Sage.

ADDITIONAL READINGS

Andersson, S., & Felici, M. (2001, September 10-13). Requirements evolution: From process to product oriented management. In *Proceedings of the 3rd International Conference on Product Focused Software Process Improvement,* Kaiserslautern, Germany (pp. 27-41). Springer Verlag.

Andersson, S., & Felici, M. (2002, August 26-29). Quantitative aspects of requirement evolution. In *Proceedings of the 26th Annual International Conference on Computer Software and Applications Conference (COMPSAC 2002),* Oxford, England (pp. 27-32). IEEE Society

Baskerville, R., Travis, J., & Truex, D.P. (1992). Systems without method: The impact of new technologies on information systems development projects. In J.I. DeGross (Ed.), *Transactions on the impact of computer supported technologies in information systems development* (pp. 241-260).

Boehm, B. (1987). Improving software productivity. *IEEE Computer, 20*(8), 43-58.

Brodner, P. (2006). Behind the IT productivity paradox: The semiotic nature of IT artefacts. In F. Meyer (Ed.), *2006 International Federation of Automation and Control (IFAC) Conference on Automation Based on Human Skill* (ABoHS), Nancy, France.

Brooks, F.P.J. (1995). *The mythical man-month - 20th anniversary edition.* Boston, MA: Addison-Wesley.

Benbasat, I., D. Goldstein & Mead M. (1987) The case study research strategy in studies of information systems. *MIS Quarterly,* 11(3),369-386.

Benbasatam, I. & Weber, R. (1996) Rethinking 'diversity' in information systems research. *Information Systems Research.*7(4): 389-399.

Calloway, L.J., & Ariav, G. (1991). Developing and using qualitative methodology to study relationships among designers and tools. In E. Nissen, H. Klein, & R. Hirschheim (Eds.), *Information systems research: Contemporary approaches and emergent traditions* (pp. 175-193). Amsterdam, North-Holland.

Fitzgerald, B. (1998). An empirical investigation into the adoption of systems development methodologies. *Information & Management, 34*(6), 317-328.

Galliers, R. (1993). Research issues in information systems. *Journal of Information Technology, 8*(2), 92-98.

Gersick, C. (1988). Time and transition in work teams: Toward a new model of group development. *Acade.*

Iivari, J., & Maansaari, J. (1998). The usage of systems development methods: Are we stuck to old practices? Information and Software Technology, *40*(9), 501-510.

Jick, T.D. (1983). Mixing qualitative and quantitative methods: Triangulation in actions. In J. Van Maanen (Ed.), *Qualitative methodology* (pp. 135-148). Beverly Hills, CA: Sage.

Kidder, T. (1982). *Soul of a new machine*. New York: Avon.

Landry, M., & Banville, C. (1992). A disciplined methodological pluralism for MIS research. *Accounting, Management & Information Technology, 2*(2), 77-97.

Mintzberg, H. (1979). An emerging strategy of direct research. *Administrative Science Quarterly, 24*(4), 582-589.

Munro, I., & Mingers, J. (2002). The use of multimethodology in practice & results of a survey of practitioners. *J Opl Res Soc., 53,* 369-378.

Orlikowski, W.J. (1993). Case tools as organizational change: Investigating incremental and radical changes in systems development. *MIS Quarterly, 17*(3), 309-340.

Pinfield, L. (1986). A field evaluation of perspectives on organizational decision making. *Administrative Science Quarterly, 31*(3), 365-388.

Pohl, K. (1994). Three dimensions of requirements engineering: Framework and its application. *Information Systems, 19*(3), 243-258.

Robey, D. (1996). Diversity in information systems research: Threat, promise and responsibility. *Information Systems Research, 7*(4), 400-408.

Suchman, L. (1987). Plans and situated action. Cambridge: Cambridge University Press.

Truex, D.P., Baskerville, R., & Travis, J. (2001). Amethodical systems development: The deferred meaning of systems development methods. *Accounting, Management and Information Technologies, 10*(1), 53-79.

van Lamsweerde, A. (2000). Requirements engineering in the year 00: A research perspective. In *Proceedings of the International Conference on Software Engineering (ICSE 2000)*, Limerick, Ireland (pp. 5-19).

Weill, P., & Broadbent, M. (1998). *Leveraging the new Infrastructure*. Boston, MA: Harvard Business School Press.

Wiegers, K.E. (1999). *Software requirements*. Microsoft Press.

Winograd, T., & Flores, F. (1986). *Understanding computers and cognition*. Norwood, NJ: Ablex.

Wynekoop, J., & Russo, N. (1995). Systems development methodologies: Unanswered questions. *Journal of Information Technology, 10*(2), 65-73.

Chapter X
Usability Evaluation Meets Design:
The Case of bisco Office™

Judith Symonds
AUT University, New Zealand

Andrew Connor
AUT University, New Zealand

ABSTRACT

Usability Evaluation Methods (UEM) are plentiful in the literature. However, there appears to be a new interest in usability testing from the viewpoint of the industry practitioner and renewed effort to reflect usability design principles throughout the software development process. In this chapter we examine one such example of usability testing from the viewpoint of the industry practitioner and reflect upon how usability evaluation methods are perceived by the software developers of a content driven system and discuss some benefits that can be derived from bringing together usability theory and usability evaluation methods protocols used by practitioners. In particular, we use the simulated prototyping method and the "Talk Aloud" protocol to assist a small software development company to undertake usability testing. We propose some issues that arise from usability testing from the perspectives of the researchers and practitioners and discuss our understanding of the knowledge transfer that occurs between the two.

USABILITY EVALUATION METHODS

Usability is a multidisciplinary field that falls under the larger umbrella of Human-Computer Interaction (HCI) where there are essentially two camps: design and evaluation (Wania, Atwood, & McCain, 2006). In their bibliographic citation analysis of the HCI literature, Wania et al. (2006) suggest that the two camps can learn from each other implying that they are separate and noninclusive. But, in industry, are usability design and evaluation really so far apart? Even relatively early research (Sullivan, 1989) called for usability to be considered throughout the entire software design process and suggested that considering only usability evaluation or testing is a "narrow conception" of usability. More recently, a study of Dutch IT companies found that in the software industry and the IT industry in general, there is variance in whether design is a consideration throughout the development process. In the study it was found that the usability of the system is often only addressed in the latter stages of the process (Gemser, Jacobs, & Ten Cate, 2006). The study also showed that developers of content-driven systems were more likely to consider usability throughout the whole design process. The authors suggest that this is related to the amount of influence customers have over the design process.

Hartson, Andre, and Williges (2003) conducted a thorough review of User Evaluation Methods (UEMs) for usability and even went so far as to establish a criteria for selection of a most suited UEM and provide guidance on the number of tests needed to ensure the reliability of the process. Carter (2007) advocates the simplicity of usability testing and suggests that the academic community have become too wrapped up in the protocols of UEMs and have lost sight of the usefulness of usability testing. The expectations of the practitioner and the usability expert differ. Certainly, away from the theory, there is an interest in how usability testing can be undertaken in the field (Waterson, Landay, & Matthews, 2002).

The three most widely used, robust, easy-to-use UEMs are cognitive walkthrough (CW), heuristic evaluation (HE), and thinking aloud (TA) (Hertzum & Jacobsen, 2003). The thinking (or talking) aloud (TA) verbal protocol analysis has been widely used, for example, in health care Web site design (Zimmerman, Akerelrea, Buller, Hau, & Leblanc, 2003) and in software development (Hohmann, 2003). Roberts and Fels (2006) extend the think aloud protocol to include procedures to follow when the participant is deaf. Krahmer and Ummelen (2004) in their comparison of the think aloud protocols developed by Ericsson and Simon

(1998) and Boren and Ramey (2000) argue that the correct use of a UEM is important for two reasons. First, if UEMs used in practice are not reliable and valid, it becomes difficult to compare and replicate studies and therefore to redesign or improve previous versions. However, this reason pales into significance with the second reason which is simply that if UEMs used in practice are not reliable and valid, it becomes difficult to identify problems signalled by the test user from those that might be evoked by the test setting or indeed other intervening factors. Given these implications for incorrect use of the protocols and a reported lack of understanding between the groups, we wanted to understand the knowledge transfer process better.

KNOWLEDGE TRANSFER

In recent years, there has been significant research focus on knowledge transfer which has led to several models of the process. The "science push" or knowledge-driven model assumes that a unidirectional flow of information from researchers to practitioners exists. The "demand pull" or problem-solving model views the process as occurring through the commissioning of information from researchers with the intent of addressing a well-defined practical problem (Landry, Amara, & Lamari 2001; Weiss, 1979). A third model, the interactive model, suggests that knowledge transfer as a reciprocal and mutual activity, one that involves researchers and practitioners in the development, conduct, interpretation, and application of research and research-based knowledge (Landry, Amara, & Lamari 2001). Whilst each of these models are equally applicable in different circumstances, active engagement between researchers and practitioners is required to ensure that the exchange, synthesis, and application of research based knowledge is effective (Huberman, 1990; Lomas, 2000). This observation is consistent with the view of Dougherty, who argues that "Knowledge transfer is about connection not collection, and that connection ultimately depends on choice made by individuals" (Dougherty, 1999, p. 262). Despite these assertions, a great deal of research has identified that there is a significant gap between research and practice (Rynes, Bartunek, & Daft, 2001).

The research-practice gap is so significant that some researchers have commented that its origins are a result of differences in the most basic assumptions and beliefs of researchers and practitioners (Shrivastava & Mitroff, 1984; Thomas & Tymon, 1982). Similarly, others have observed that there are notable differences between researchers and practitioners with respect to the goals they seek to influence, the social systems in which they operate, the variables they attempt to manipulate, and acceptable time frames for addressing problems (Johns, 1993; Powell, & Owen-Smith, 1998; Thomas & Tymon, 1982).

An early study of usability engineering practices in European companies (Dillon, Sweeney, & Maguire, 1993) identified many issues with the implementation of usability evaluation methods. These authors go on to comment that

It is worth pointing out that formal, user-based evaluations carried out in fully equipped usability laboratories by dedicated, trained staff are an ideal of the human factors profession. That companies rarely meet this ideal in practice is not a criticism but a statement of fact. (Dillon et al., 1993, p. 92)

The research described in this chapter has two key elements, namely the environment in which it was conducted was one where interaction of the practitioners and researchers was facilitated by being embedded in a technology incubator business park. Second, the purpose of the research was not to conduct a formal usability study and publish data related to the software being assessed. In stead, the purpose was:

- To build a better understanding of the differing goals and time frames of the researchers and practitioners involved,

- To provide opportunities for bidirectional transfer of both knowledge and technology
- To enhance the case study organisations software product, and
- To lead to a better understanding of the knowledge transfer process between researchers and practitioners.

This chapter presents the experience of a group of researchers with expertise in usability testing working with a small software development company inexperienced with formal usability testing processes to provide technical guidance on how to undertake usability testing on their product.

METHOD

This study uses a qualitative inquiry research approach within the *Verstehen* (Patton, 2002) tradition of understanding the meaning of behaviour through fieldwork. To achieve this, we designed an experiment using a single case study to tell a story contrasting the researcher's experience of usability testing and that of a software development company undertaking formal usability testing for the first time. The experiment was designed to allow the researchers to observe interaction between experts and industry people to try to understand the process of knowledge transfer while also sharing useful usability testing knowledge with the software developer. Data was collected using observation and qualitative interview techniques with a special interest in issues that arose during the transfer of knowledge between the researchers and the software development organisation. Although usability data was collected about the software product and the testing process itself, this in not the focus of this particular chapter. Next, we describe the case study organisation to provide a context for the discussion.

CASE DESCRIPTION

Building Integration Software Company Limited (*bisco*) was started by two Carter Holt Harvey (CHH) employees who had been researching integrated building design systems with the ultimate objective of improving timber usage. After a period of consideration, Nick Alexander (NA) and Nick Clements (NC) (both former CHH employees) decided that there was a sufficiently large market to support a dedicated product suite in the area of integrated construction information management.

The *bisco* concept case was accepted into the AUT Technology Park Incubator program in February 2005, and *bisco* was incorporated as a company in March 2005. At the time of this study, *bisco* employed five full-time software developers and were supporting a number of collaborative research projects with a team of dedicated researchers.

Their product—*bisco Office*™—is designed to revolutionise building by changing the way information flows through the building industry. Automatically unlocking the information currently held in three dimensional (3D) Computer Aided Design (CAD) models is the key to exchanging and sharing information efficiently throughout the building industry supply chain. The key industry issues in this area are:

1. Most residential houses are designed in 3D CAD packages but then are manually re-entered into other applications to complete the process.
2. Typically plans are printed out and then manually surveyed to determine material quantities. Quantity specification documents are also manually created.
3. The designs will be manually recreated in other applications like Frame and Truss design, roofing, or windows, and
4. Reprocessing of building information is slow, expensive, and error prone when completed manually.

The *bisco* solution for providing more accessible and reusable building industry information is to develop a software solution that extracts information from 3D CAD models and automatically reprocess them for other uses. Such automatic reprocessing requires tools to be developed to extract the data then transform it into the formats required by the other processes. The structure of information exchange in the building industry is shown in Figure 1.

To achieve wide acceptance, the system has to be capable of working with all leading CAD applications (something not achieved before). In addition to this, *bisco Office*™ manages all the business information in a way that ensures it is easily located, stored securely, and is available to a network of mobile users.

Usability Testing the bisco Office™ Product

The *bisco Office*™ tool set manages information throughout the building industry supply chain from concept, through planning, construction, and completion. As a result, it needs to organise and manage very large amounts of specific and complex information in various formats. The tool set will be accessible to a wide variety of actors within the building industry and to be successful, it must be easy to understand and use.

The developers of *bisco Office*™ faced two problems with the usability testing of their software. First, they were unable to objectively analyse the usability of the software user interface from the perspective of the different types of users of the tool set. Second, they had very little experience of usability testing techniques, or understanding of usability best practice and protocols. The developers feared that this lack of knowledge and experience could preclude them from gaining an objective and complete assessment of the usability of their software product.

The software developers at *bisco* sought out usability expertise from AUT University to help

*Figure 1. Information exchange using **bisco** Office™ software*

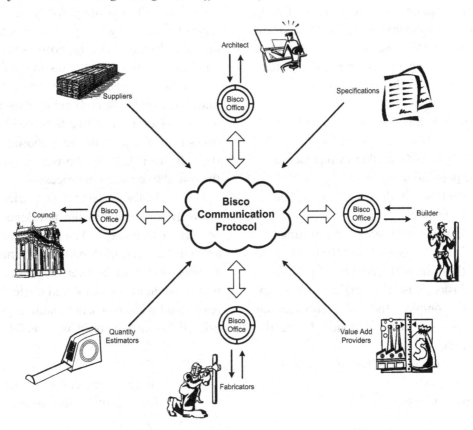

them learn about usability testing. **Bisco** employed the services of a postgraduate student studying software usability to do some of the initial planning and assist with the assessment process with the assistance of a technology infrastructure New Zealand government grant. The postgraduate student had completed a course in software usability and the project also benefited from the input of usability experts from the School of Computing and Mathematical Sciences at AUT University, New Zealand.

The problem was one of balance between the objectives of the practitioners and the researchers in this study. There was incongruence between how much data to collect and how closely to follow the protocols. One aspect of contention was how many "observers" to allow at the testing sessions given that there was no one-way mirror or specialised usability testing facility.

THE EXPERIMENT

In order to be able to observe and understand the knowledge transfer process between the researchers and the practitioners, usability testing of the **bisco Office™** software was undertaken. Although extensive usability data was collected and analysed, it is not reported in this chapter as the focus is to understand the knowledge transfer process that occurred between the researchers and the practitioners. The usability testing itself is the vehicle for such transfer. However, for the reader to be able to understand the issues discussed, the context of the experiment is important; therefore, we describe the method used for the usability testing.

The simulated prototyping usability testing method (Hohmann, 2003) was used for the **bisco Office™** usability testing. This method was chosen because it is designed for use by practitioners and is clearly explained for the purpose of users not familiar with usability testing. Using this technique, a representative user attempts to complete assigned tasks using a prototype of the system. The process involves the following:

1. Assign developer roles and responsibilities
2. Carefully select users that are representative of the population
3. Develop tasks for the users to complete
4. Run the test
    a. Explain of the goal of the testing
    b. Have the user attempt the tasks while the observer records any signs of confusion, misunderstanding or inability to complete the task—encouraging the user to "talk aloud" during the process.
    c. Discuss the results of the test with the user and
5. Compile the results.

As a part of the integral process, we ran two consultation sessions with a usability expert from the University with several years experience running a usability laboratory. The first session was an information session. In the second session, the developers undertook the usability evaluation process with the consultant acting as the user. The second session was most beneficial in terms of both researchers and practitioners learning what was required and understanding the extent of the current knowledge of the other party.

In our testing experiment, we assigned three of the main roles of the five identified by Hohmann (2003) of leader/greeter, facilitator, and observer. We wrapped the roles of leader and greeter into one role as this suited the actual role of the person involved. We did not need a computer role as the interface was already in a fully functional mode and there was no need for a person to simulate the operation of the software user interface. The

leader/greeter was also the codirector of *bisco*, but not the chief developer. The facilitator was a part-time employee experienced with training and the observer was the postgraduate student employed for the usability testing project.

The task of selecting representative users was undertaken of by the codirector of *bisco* who had a close relationship with a test-site builder. Five users from the test-site were chosen as well as two "dry-run" testers who were used to pretest the usability evaluation process.

The tasks for the testing were selected by the bisco group including the developers and the postgraduate student. The tasks were focused around the navigation patterns of the software and ease of completing every day tasks. The tasks were written as scenarios add context and were read aloud with the users as well as provided in printed format. The tasks were as follows.

1. Scenario 1
    a. find a customer contact details
    b. find a contract (document)
2. Scenario 2
    a. find a document name "Sherrock House Detail"
    b. find out who is the supplier of this project and find out contact detail
    c. delete a contact and then add a new one for "Northern Concrete Cutters"
3. Scenario 3
    a. Find a supplier and add a document.

During the testing, one personal computer with a second visual display attached was used as recommended by Krahmer and Ummelen (2004)—one for the user and facilitator and one for the observer and the team. This was especially important so that the observer could sit opposite the user and observe body language as well as have full view of what was happening on the computer screen. The observer also used preset sheets to help with logging of the observations. There was also a developer and a researcher present at the testing. The team used screen-capture software and a personal VCR to record each test so that the software team were able to preserve the screen and the audio from each test. During the testing users were encouraged to "Think Aloud."

Usability testing was carried out at one of the planned sites for installation of the *bisco Office*™ software. At the end of the usability testing experiment, the researchers interviewed *bisco's* codirector using an open interview style. The focus of the interview was the codirectors experiences and reflections of learning and carrying out usability testing. The opportunity to interview the codirector, himself an experienced software developer, also allowed the researchers to explore any issues that arose during their involvement in the usability testing process. An open-coding data analysis technique was used to analyse the interview data.

ISSUES ARISING

Many of the points raised in the literature also occurred in this study such as the information intensive nature of *bisco Office*™ and the need and interest for usability evaluation. However, the researchers also found the *bisco* software development team were very interested in the validity and reliability of the usability evaluation method. First, some usability evaluation environmental issues observed in this study are discussed.

System Reliant on Client Satisfaction

The *bisco* team members were very open to the idea of usability testing. Based on their past experience, they understood the importance of developing usable software and were very willing to learn. The following outlines the level of awareness at *bisco* around the importance of building usability features into the software to ensure the overall success of the project.

NC: The previous ones, [software development projects] we sort of said, "oh well, we will get the thing working first and then we will come back and do the user interface." So, we basically didn't worry about the user interface at all, we made it functional, but that was all, we didn't really try and address much in the way of usability, and often, users would get lost as to where they were in the system. Or if they wanted to get back to where they were, they wouldn't know how to get back. Umm, and so, we realised, it just made it, the whole thing that bit more difficult. It made training that little bit harder because each time they had to do something, they would get lost and then you would have to tell them how to get back again, and then next time they weren't so confident to go and do something because they weren't sure if they were able to get back again.

One motivator for *bisco's* interest in usability evaluation is the complexity of their system. They are striving to have the base navigation and user interface reasonably intuitive and usable without extensive training.

In this discussion, three key themes arise. They are:

1. The trade-off between needing to train users more and inherently good usability,
2. The way that usability testing brings software developers closer to the customer perspective, and
3. The important link between incorporating usability into the software and customer uptake of software.

At the end of this discussion, we link these three themes back to how some of the knowledge was transferred and what was learned.

Training Compensating for Good Usability

At the outset, there was a very blurred understanding of what might be a "training" issue and what might be a "usability" issue. For example, in one part of the software, the words used on a particular button meaningfully describe the function of that button to the developer. Usability testing revealed that the function of the button was not intuitive to the user. This issue could be addressed through either documentation or training. This trade-off was apparent, but the implications were not evident to the *bisco* developers until they witnessed the usability tests on their software.

NC: ...and quite often it happened that, you would have them doing a task and they would be hovering over what they should be clicking on, and they would almost click on it and then they would say "no, I'm lost, I don't know what to do." And, that was purely a terminology thing.

If the function of a particular button is not intuitive, it can easily be taught and documented in the training manuals. However, what is learned can easily be forgotten. The *bisco* team tried to balance the usability testing feedback with a reality check to identify aspects of the software that users could be taught and aren't an issue and then aspects that are a usability issue in the software and should be intuitive.

During the usability testing process, the team, and in particular the facilitator had to resist the urge to train the user to use the software as shown in the following quote:

NC: so you are not actually trying to teach them how to use it, you are holding back to see what they stumble on and then you make a decision when they stumble on something, are they stumbling because that is something that they would have

had in the training or are they stumbling because it isn't quite as obvious as it should be?

This was partly because the facilitator had user training experience, but was also something that the whole software development team grappled with. The UEM and particularly the protocol used helped to guide the team in their roles and to ensure the process was followed so that the results were reliable.

Evaluation Influencing Design

The *bisco* team were very quick at responding to many of the action points raised by the usability testing and in many cases, they were aware of the problem but did not realise the importance of it until they saw the user interact with the software.

NC: I think it is going to change our thinking a little bit, just in terms of how we approach things. And, umm, help reinforcing thinking about things from a customer perspective.

In particular, *bisco* talked of changing future software development to emphasise the customer perspective more as shown in the following comment.

NC: ... and if we are able to continue with that thinking so when we develop the next thing, we are actually thinking through, well while this might be how we describe it or how we expect to see it, but how would a customer expect to see it? And sort of being able to think back to this is how it happened when you actually saw it in the usability test and sort of looking at how could we use the software from that perspective, I think it sort of helps thinking about things a bit differently.

Therefore, the involvement with the UEM and the resulting learning is now informing future design and reinforcing good software design.

Testing with Actual Users

The *bisco* team members have an excellent relationship with their final end-users and therefore they had the opportunity to test with actual users. This could be risky given that there is always a danger in showing the software to users before it is ready and alienating the potential buyers of the software in the process. However, *bisco* sought to turn this risk of alienation around into a process of gaining "buy-in" for potential users of the software as shown in the codirectors comments when asked about the risk of usability testing with actual users.

NC: No, I think it has helped for a couple of reasons, it has helped them to buy in to what we are doing. I think it has, and hopefully they will see that we have made some changes as a result of the feedback, so they will see that we are listening to them.

The codirector refers to the usability process as one of engagement with the users and a way to provide a positive perception of the system and a good introduction to the system as a concept.

NC: I think it has helped engage them with what we are looking to do. So, I think it has almost part of the sales process. Selling it in to them as a concept and what the system will do for them, and so I think it is quite a good soft start to get them hooked into the whole system.

However, *bisco* were careful to manage the delicate process of managing user expectations by communicating very clearly with the users and making sure that they were aware that all suggestions would not be implemented.

NC: We won't have made all of the things that they have asked for, but I have said to them that we wouldn't be. So, I said that we would try. So I think they will some changes to it as a result, so hopefully they will see that the product has moved forward from where it was with the usability testing.

Testing Environment

During the testing, the team of researchers were interested in feedback regarding the usability experience. In particular, issues that arose around the testing environment, the composition of the testing team, and the transfer of knowledge within the team.

Unrealistic Experience

The usability testing was a fairly artificial test of the users' experience with the software because the users were not at their own desk using the software in their own time. During testing, testers were under a fair amount of intense scrutiny from a team of six people representing the software product.

The relationship between *bisco* and the people doing the testing was very close, and therefore it was straightforward to reflect on whether the test environment worked well. The software development team at *bisco* felt that although the users were influenced by the number of people sitting at the table, they were soon comforted by the instructions and the design of the tests.

Developer Involvement Good

There was room in the team to allow for a developer to observe the tests. The bisco team regarded this as a very valuable opportunity as it helped to inform the developers.

NC: ...we did have some of developers there and it was worth them seeing how people got around and seeing, coz when you are creating something, you are completely intimate with and you will be working it with it for months, so you take so many things for granted.

The researchers' observations revealed that by allowing developers to see the user reaction to the software helped to point out problems with the functionality that the developers did not originally like, but had become accustomed to. When the developers saw the user struggling with the functionality, they remembered their initial feelings and quickly addressed the problem.

The *bisco* team felt that the testing environment was the best compromise between expense and value.

NC: So, I think that they found it a little bit off-putting, sort of having so many people intently watching them, but most of them seemed to get over that pretty quickly and umm, certainly, all the people that were there got value out of it. I think the way that, Phil, was saying that when they used to have the usability lab where they used to have the developers being able to watch on camera, I guess that would be the ideal scenario, you know, we are not going to get to the point where we have a usability set up like that. With one way glass or cameras or whatever.

However, NC adds that the testing environment is going to be a relatively unrealistic situation, unless you were testing at their desk, in their office environment, and install an unobtrusive camera. He concludes that usability testing is always going to be unrealistic, it is just a matter of how much impact the lack of realism actually has.

Inclusion of the developers in the process is a departure from the protocol. However, it is a very useful tactic to have the UEM inform usability design and to influence the work practices of the developer.

Knowledge Transfer

The codirector of *bisco* appreciated the opportunity to learn about the protocol and process of usability testing and the opportunity to learn from people who had planned usability studies previously. In particular, the codirector mentioned that without the guidance that they received from the researchers they would have been more likely to have run the session like a training session and not found out what the real usability issues were.

NC: Yeah, it has been a really worthwhile exercise for us and I think that the real benefit for us has been learning the skills of how to structure the test and sort out what is a usability test. So, without any of us having any sort of formal training, in it, I'd heard of it, but didn't really know how you went about doing. So, I think the time with Phil and being able to get his experiences short-cut things a lot for us. We probably could have fumbled through, but I think that we would have tended to make it, more like a training session so I think that we would have missed a lot and I think we would have helped them out too soon and not necessarily seen where we got to and really sort of seen which bits they struggled. So, the biggest thing for me is that we now have the skills and how to structure the approach and structure in such a way that we are going to derive the benefits from it, which is how we are going to make the software easier to use.

There were several benefits to this project (see Table 1). The protocol imparts the rigor whereby the actors in the process are guided to collect the data in a reliable and valid way. The postgraduate student was also given valuable industry experience having first learned about usability evaluation methods from the researchers and then given the opportunity to assist the practitioners to undertake the usability evaluation methods as well as involvement in the planning

*Table 1. Benefits of the project from the perspective of **bisco***

Actor Involvement	Benefit
User Involvement	Influence user perceptions
Developer Involvement	Influence development practices and attitudes
Researcher Involvement	Identify critical success points in the usability evaluation protocol

and execution of the usability testing undertaken. The researchers were given a unique opportunity to impart valuable usability testing knowledge and experience as well as evaluate the effectiveness of their own usability training of postgraduate students and to add to their practical knowledge of usability testing.

LESSONS LEARNED

From the viewpoint of the researcher, there was value in experiencing the usability testing technique and observing the interactions between testers and users and testers and developers. In particular, the developers observed that it was really difficult to maintain objectivity and to get the user to open up about the experience. It was very important to remain nonjudgemental in the process. The researchers found that even the words "think aloud" as suggested by Hohmann (2003) were too judgemental and a better phase to use was "talk aloud." The researchers also found that more directed questions were better in the discussion of the results of the test with the user, process 4(c), such as "You hesitated at that point, tell me about that," rather than, "Why did you hesitate"—which might suggest to the user that their hesitation was "wrong." The UEM protocol helped the facilitators become aware of this effect and to at least factor it in to their interpretation of the results, if not to strive for ways to improve the process or to better individual practice.

The developers responded positively to seeing how a user might use the software and it opened their mind to options that they had not thought about or gave them more incentive to address problems that they knew existed but they had accepted as part of the environment. Many of the changes in the software were implemented even before the test results were reported. This suggests that the usability evaluation process did have a fairly immediate impact on the usability design process in this instance.

Essentially, our foray into usability testing from the viewpoint of the industry practitioner suggested to us that whilst practitioners were not necessarily aware of the theoretical underpinnings of UEMs (the psychological origins of the "think aloud" protocol, for example), they were able to follow a protocol and saw the benefit of doing so and were very interested in producing reliable and valid results. They knew whether the results they had achieved were reliable and valid by whether they "rung true" even though they were not aware of the underlying reasons for certain aspects of the usability protocol or even the higher capacity to compare and choose between UEMs. This study has shown that in the right environment, with the right level of interaction from research and practitioners, teams undertaking usability testing can start to share common goals and timeframes to achieve useful knowledge transfer. Therefore, it seems important that the practitioners and academics cooperate on this so that the practitioners can be guided on what protocols to use and can be updated with improvements and new understanding of usability theory that can influence software design. In return, academics can receive feedback on how usability protocols work from the viewpoint of the industry practitioner and can therefore contribute to the growing understanding of usability knowledge. In this light, it is difficult to understand how taking an isolated view of UEMs, as suggested by some authors, can contribute to anything but mediocrity leading to a stand-still in the communal (researchers and practitioners included) understanding of usability.

FUTURE RESEARCH DIRECTIONS

Information systems researchers and practitioners can gain much from working together. From the researcher point of view, industry partnership is an important ingredient in gaining external government grants. From a practitioner point of view, researchers and their affiliated universities are an important source of employees and research and development knowledge. Research based funding schemes in countries such as the United Kingdom, Australia, and New Zealand have forced universities and researchers to take notice of commercial opportunities.

However, in our experience, at least, the prospect of researchers and practitioners working together is something akin to a meeting of a turtle and a hare. This is mostly because the researchers (let us say the turtles) and the practitioners (let us say the hares) have very different motivators and goals. Although the university environment is changing, researchers operate in a somewhat insular environment where timelines stretch over years. From the point of planning the research to the point of publication often takes between 2 and 5 years in the university environment. Practitioners are more closely situated to the market and therefore must respond to pressures from competitors and consumers. This position forces practitioners to have a much tighter horizon for projects.

There is great potential for researchers and practitioners to work together to learn more about the usability of software and great potential for learning on both sides. However, few practitioners will wait silently by until September when new projects are sought and then February when work on the projects can begin.

Experience has shown us that timing is very important when working with practitioner teams to achieve research oriented projects. There will always be tensions within the project as universities and industry are governed by different rules of operation. For example, gaining full ethics approval for observation of the testers will be a major hurdle for the researchers. However, the practitioners are much more likely to be worried about issues that will affect their bottom line such as time to market and consumer reaction to their software product. We were able to overcome some of these tensions by working with a business in a technology incubator park sponsored by our University. The environment at the incubator park enabled us to have a closer relationship with a large group of industry people and therefore we could get the timing right for the project. The environment at the incubator park also enabled us to gain access funds to support the students involved in the project much more quickly. The geographic proximity of the incubator park also gave the researchers better access to the projects and the students were able to spend more time with the practitioners.

In conclusion, obviously, university research would be severely deficient if limited to only start-up companies working from a university incubator park. However, incubator parks afford researchers with ready made connections and a relatively safe environment from which to launch information systems research further afield.

REFERENCES

Boren, T., & Ramey, J. (2000). Thinking aloud: Reconciling theory and practice. *IEEE Transactions on Professional Communication, 43*(2), 261-278.

Carter P. (2007). Liberating usability testing. *Interactions*, *14*(2), 18-22.

Dillon, A., Sweeney, M., & Maguire, M. (1993). A survey of usability evaluation practices and requirements in the European IT industry. In. J. Alty, S. Guest, & D. Diaper (Eds.), HCI'93, *People and Computers VII* (pp. 81-94). Cambridge: Cambridge University Press.

Dougherty, V. (1999). Knowledge is about people, not databases. *Industrial and Commercial Training*, *31*(7), 262-266

Ericsson, K.A., & Simon, H.A. (1998). How to study thinking in everyday life: Contrasting think-aloud protocols with descriptions and explanations of thinking. *Mind, Culture, and Activity*, *5*(3), 178-186.

Gemser, G., Jacobs, D., & Ten Cate, R. (2006). Design and competitive advantage in technology-driven sectors: The role of usability and aesthetics in Dutch IT companies. *Technology Analysis & Strategic Management*, *18*(5), 561-580.

Hartson, H.R., Andre, T.W., & Williges, R.C. (2003). Criteria for evaluating usability evaluation methods. *International Journal of Human-Computer Interaction*, *15*(1), 145-181.

Hertzum, M., & Jacobsen, N.E. (2003), The evaluator effect: A chilling fact about usability evaluation methods. *International Journal of Human-Computer Interaction*, *15*(1), 183-204.

Hohmann, L. (2003). Usability: Happier users mean greater profits. *Information Systems Management*, *20*(4), 66-76.

Huberman, A.M. (1983). Improving social practice through the utilization of university-based knowledge. *Higher Education*, *12*, 257-272.

Johns, G. (1993). Constraints on the adoption of psychology-based personnel practices: Lessons from organizational innovation. *Personnel Psychology*, *46*, 569-592.

Krahmer, E., & Ummelen, N. (2004). Thinking about thinking aloud: A comparison of two verbal protocols for usability testing. *IEEE Transactions on Professional Communication*, *47*(2), 105-117.

Landry, R., Amara, N., & Lamari, M. (2001). Utilization of social science research knowledge in Canada. *Research Policy, 30*, 333-349.

Lomas, J. (2000). Connecting research and policy. *ISUMA, 1*(1), 140-144.

Patton, M.Q. (2002). *Qualitative research & evaluation methods* (3rd ed.). London: Sage Publications.

Powell, W.W., & Owen-Smith, J. (1998). Universities and the market for intellectual property in the life sciences. *Journal of Policy Analysis and Management*, 17, 253-277.

Roberts, V.L., & Fels, D.I. (2006). Methods for inclusion: Employing think aloud protocols in software usability studies with individuals who are deaf. *International Journal of Human-Computer Studies, 64*, 489-501.

Rynes, S.L., Bartunek, J.M., & Daft, R.L. (2001). Across the great divide: Knowledge creation and transfer between practitioners and academics. *Academy of Management Journal*, *44*(2), 340-355

Shrivastava, P., & Mitroff, 1.1. (1984). Enhancing organizational research utilization: The role of decision makers' assumptions. *Academy of Management Review, 9*, 18-26.

Sullivan P. (1989). Beyond a narrow conception of usability testing. *IEEE Transactions on Professional Communication*, *32*(4), 256-264.

Thomas, K.W., & Tymon, W.G. (1982). Necessary properties of relevant research: Lessons from recent criticisms of the organizational sciences. *Academy of Management Review, 7*, 345-352.

Wania, C.E., Atwood, M.E., & McCain, K.W. (2006). How do design and evaluation interrelate in HCI research? In *Proceedings of the 6th ACM conference on Designing Interactive Systems,* University Park, PA, USA (pp. 90-98).

Waterson, S., Landay, J.A., & Matthews, T. (2002). In the lab and out in the wild: Remote Web usability testing for mobile devices. In *Conference on Human Factors in Computing Systems (CHI '02 extended abstracts on human factors in computing systems)*, Minneapolis, MN, USA, (pp. 796-797).

Weiss, C.H. (1979). The many meanings of research utilization. *Public Administration Review, 39,* 426-431.

Zimmerman, D.E., Akerelrea, C.Z., Buller, D.B., Hau, B., & Leblanc, M. (2003). Integrating usability testing into the development of a 5 a day nutrition Web site for at-risk populations in the American southwest. *Journal of Health Psychology, 8,* 119-134.

Chapter XI
An Analysis–Form of Soft Systems Methodology for Information Systems Maintenance

Ivan Ka-Wai Lai
Macau University of Science and Technology, China

Joseph M. Mula
University of Southern Queensland, Australia

ABSTRACT

Soft Systems Methodology (SSM) has been employed to increase the effectiveness of organizational requirement analysis in Information Systems (IS) development in recent years. Various forms of SSM for IS development have been developed and examined in different environments by different researchers. There appears to be little research or application that can be identified of the use of SSM in IS maintenance. The objective of this chapter is to develop a conceptual "analysis-form" of SSM for IS maintenance, so that further research can be undertaken in the application of this conceptual model.

BACKGROUND

During the past few decades, many information systems (IS) were developed in a wide range of working environments. There are many reasons for change to an existing IS in an organization. Examples are functionality, flexibility, continuous availability, and correct operation (Lehman, 1989; Lientz & Swanson, 1980). Once an IS has been developed, it is rarely free of errors and occasionally operates in the same way in the changed environment (Leveson, 1995). Literature suggested that IS maintenance is gaining more notoriety because of its increasing cost (Smith,

1999). People are becoming more concerned about how to improve the IS maintenance process so as to reduce IS maintenance costs.

IS maintenance is a knowledge intensive task (Anquetil, de Oliveira, de Sousa, & Batista Dias, 2006). A good understanding of different aspects of IS is needed, to, for example, identify the problems to solve, the software process to adopt, the computer language and system architecture to be used. All these examples consume high levels of human effort as well as costs.

Maintaining software is primarily a cognitive task that has been described in various ways by different investigators (Eioerman & Dishaw, 2007). Lutters and Seaman (2007) suggested the use of documentation for IS maintenance. Von Mayrhauser, Vans, and Howe (1997) focused on the software comprehension process associated with maintenance described as the Integrated Comprehension Model. In this process model, individuals employ a top-down model in which they engage in hypothesis generation and verification, a program model in which they develop a flow of control abstraction of the program, and a situation model in which they develop data-flow/functional abstraction of the program. IS professionals use all three approaches and use them interchangeably.

Based on the literature, human knowledge is a major factor in IS maintenance. Soft Systems Methodology (SSM) is concerned with human activity systems (Platt & Warwick, 1995). SSM should be a very useful tool for IS maintenance as it aims to improve human conditions by understanding and changing the situation (Checkland, 1992).

SSM focuses upon a stage-by-stage process. An early model, which was presented by Checkland (1981), consisted of seven iterative stages. It explained the action devices to improve the problem situation by comparison with the "real world" and "systems thinking about the real world." The classical form of SSM (seven-stage structure),

the developed form of SSM, and the Processes for Organization Meanings (POM) model all do not produce any outputs suitable to satisfy the technical needs of IS users and programmers. Thus a model is required that incorporates both organizational and technical needs.

This chapter describes a review of SSM and the application of SSM to IS development. Then, an "analysis-form" of SSM for IS maintenance is presented with its design and structure. The objective of this chapter is to present a SSM "analysis-form" conceptual model for IS maintenance so that further research can uncover the applicability of this conceptual model through its use.

LITERATURE REVIEW

Problems on IS Maintenance

An understanding of the problems of IS maintenance is critical. IS maintenance problems can be grouped into four categories—psychological, characteristic, practical, and management problems.

Psychological Problems

Higgins (1986) pointed out that the maintenance process involves psychological problems. Reasons why programmers are unlikely to undertake the maintenance process include:

- Program was written by another programmer;
- One programmer may use radically different logic from another programmer;
- It provides ample opportunities for failure other than for success;
- Need to study the whole program even if it requires a small change; and/or
- Users always compare the new system with the old one.

Many IS maintenance problems are organizational in nature, involving issues of, for example, organization design, task definition and assignment, work technique, and policies for coordination and control. Situations in which organizational problems arise have been identified as a set of six relationships (the relational foundations of maintenance) as a basis for its effective management (Swanson & Beath, 1989). The six relationships are: (1) among-systems relationship; (2) among-staff relationship; (3) among-user relationship; (4) systems-staff relationship; (5) systems-user relationship; and (6) staff-user relationship. Problems in maintenance can be viewed as a lack of fit interpretation among these six relationships and can be viewed as psychological problems amongst these parties.

Characteristic Problems

Swanson and Beath (1989) also indicated that the nature of IS is one of the main sources of maintenance problems. They identified four natural characteristic problems in maintenance: (1) IS embody and institutionalize organizational knowledge; (2) IS tend to grow and elaborate over time; (3) IS tend to be long-lived; and (4) IS tend to congregate and develop as families whose members are highly dependent upon one another.

Practical Problems

A study by Lientz and Swanson (1980) pointed out that major sources of problems in practice include: (1) user knowledge; (2) programmer effectiveness; (3) product quality; and (4) programmer time availability. Swanson and Beath (1989) undertook multiple-case studies on IS maintenance and identified 26 potential problem items that contributed to the problems of maintaining IS in the 12 cases. They divided the problems into similar factors and worked out six problem factors as: (1) user knowledge; (2) programmer effectiveness; (3) product quality; (4) programmer

time availability; (5) machine requirements; and (6) system reliability.

Maintenance Management Problems

The study of the practical problems, as explained by Swanson and Beath (1989), was based on an earlier extensive survey conducted by Lientz and Swanson (1980). Other writers have conducted similar surveys, which addressed IS maintenance problems (e.g., Ball, 1987; McClure, 1992; Nosek & Plavia, 1990). Dekleva (1992), undertook his survey, where managerial views were included and categorized. He classified problems into four categories: (1) maintenance management; (2) organizational environment; (3) personnel factors; and (4) system characteristics. The results of the survey concluded that:

a. Maintenance problems rooted in an organizational environment cause maintenance management problems;

b. High maintenance management problems precipitate high personnel problems; and

c. Problems associated with system characteristics cause problems described in the personnel factors category.

Literature points to the problems of IS maintenance being not just computer problems. The problems involve a combination of people, organization, and technology. Based on Deleva's (1992) and Chapin's (1993) surveys, there are two technological problems (maintenance management and systems characteristics) and three nontechnological problems (personnel factors, user relations, and environmental factors) within IS maintenance. However, most IS maintenance studies have focussed on technological problems. Little methodology has been developed in relation to human behavior. But according to Schneidewind's (1987) explanation, a human being is the major factor in IS maintenance cost. There is a lack of an adequate methodology that incorporates human activities; however SSM is an approach designed to study social systems. It could be a useful tool for undertaking IS maintenance.

Soft Systems Methodology and its Applications

SSM was originated in 1972 by Checkland as a means of dealing with complex managerial as opposed to technically defined problem situations. SSM had been developed over the preceding 30 years based on the principle that development can best be undertaken by the interaction between theory and practice (Tsouvalis & Checkland, 1996). Tajino and Smith (2005) reported that SSM has been used in over 200 cases (mainly in the UK and other parts of Europe) that involved a wide variety of management issues in private business enterprises (e.g., Ferrari, Fares, & Martinelli, 2002), nonprofit organizations (e.g., Luckett, Ngubane, & Memela, 2001), and health care services (e.g., Atkinson, Eldabi, & Paul, 2002).

In terms of system thinking, Checkland (1981) distinguished between SSM and hard systems methodology. Checkland argued that SSM starts with an urge to bring about improvement in a social system in which there is felt to be an ill-defined

problem situation. Hard systems methodology starts with an urge to solve a relatively well defined problem which an analyst may, to a large extent, take as given, once a client requiring help is identified.

Checkland (1981) described a seven-stage process (Figure 1) in his earlier work. The seven-stage model consists of two types of activities: real-world activities and systems thinking activities. The seven stages are: the problem unstructured; the problem expressed; root definitions of relevant systems; conceptual models; comparing the expressed problem to the conceptual models; feasible and desirable change; and action to improve the problem situation.

In 1990, Checkland and Scholes (1990) presented the developed form of SSM (Figure 2), which showed the developing nature of the modelling and enquiry processes during a case study. The developed form of SSM is a conceptual model that uses nouns to represent concrete components and arrows to represent interaction between components. SSM is used to promote user participation and identify systems which are appropriate for computerization based on human activity considerations (McDermid, 1990).

Figure 1. The classical form of SSM as a seven-stage structure (adapted from Checkland, 1981)

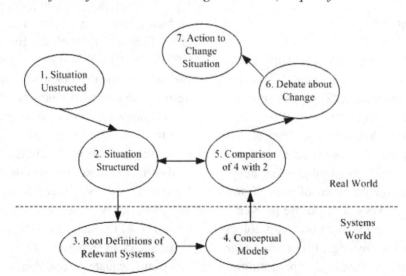

Figure 2. The developed form of SSM (adapted from Checkland & Scholes, 1990)

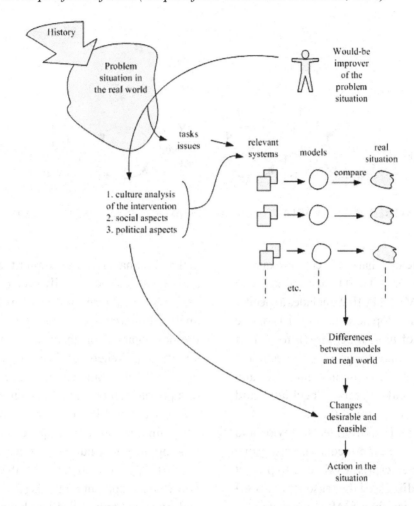

Checkland (1995) used systems concepts as the well-defined theoretical base for model building, and substitutes for the Realist claim that social reality will be explained. However, there is no practical example of the use of the developed form of conceptual model until Checkland and Holwell (1998) first presented their account of IS and IS development. Checkland and Holwell distinguished between data, capta, information, and knowledge (Figure 3). Capta is the selected or created facts that are actually collected from the real world. They developed an elaborated model called Processes for Organization Meanings (POM) model of categories (data, capta, information, and knowledge) in relation to organization activities and their consequent action (Figure

4). The concept implied by the POM model is contrary to the then conventional wisdom about the process of IS development.

More literature emerged after 1990 on the use of SSM in IS projects. Many writers attempted to justify the use of SSM and the combined use of SSM with other existing IS development techniques for IS development. Shafer (1988) presented a Functional Analysis of Office Requirements (FAOR) method that provides a source of general problem-solving and learning heuristics. FAOR consists of four stages: exploration, method tailoring, analysis, and evaluation. FAOR considers the participation of team members and team working critical to understanding complex systems. Avison and Wood-Harper (1990) presented a

Figure 3. The links between data, capta, information, and knowledge (adapted from Checkland & Holwell, 1998)

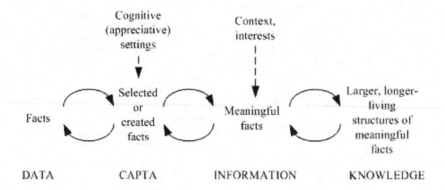

MULTIVIEW method that represents an example of bringing together soft and hard approaches to IS development. MULTIVIEW includes a specific approach for IS development that consists of five stages: analysis of human activity, information analysis, analysis and design of sociotechnical aspects, design of the computer interface, and design of technical aspects. Checkland and Holwell (1998) have justified the use of SSM in large organizational environments. Taylor and DaCosta (1999) have examined a case study in a small to medium enterprise (SME), of IS project using SSM, and discussed the reasons why SSM is just as appropriate in a SME environment as it is in a large organization environment. Taylor and DaCosta (1999) concluded that SSM can help to provide a deeper understanding of information systems-related problems within an SME environment. Lai (2000) proposed a model where SSM and object-oriented methodologies can be used together to increase the effectiveness of organizational requirements analysis for IS development. Lai suggested one of the main benefits that arose from the use of an integrated framework in the IS development project is improved user requirements definition which is important to successful implementation of IS. Rose (2007) proposed an Interact-Transformation-Interaction (ITI) model. This model views the software process as a so-

cial and managerial task, rather than a technical activity. It was successfully used (in conjunction with developed forms of SSM which incorporate analysis based on structuration theory) to structure the development of an intranet in a university department. Wherever, in a large organization or a SME environment, in a public university or a private company, SSM can more effectively uncover the real IS needs by means of seeking "accommodation" of IS requirements and investigating the wider human activity system.

Xu (2000) pointed out that "SSM is one of the new IS development methods (ISDMs) concepts and practice" and "SSM has been successfully applied to ISDMs such as MULTIVIEW, FAOR and other methods through contributing systems ideas" (p. 106). The core idea of SSM is to generate logical systems models that are thought to be a problem situation and then to compare the model and situation in order to structure a debate about change (Ledington & Ledington, 1999). SSM emphasizes the importance of the human participants and the way in which they relate to each other through the work that they perform (McDermid, 1990). A number of researches have used SSM in numerous organizations as a vehicle for establishing organizational requirements for IS projects (Checkland, 1981; Checkland & Scholes, 1990; Taylor & DaCosta, 1999).

Figure 4. The POM model (adapted from Checkland & Holwell, 1998)

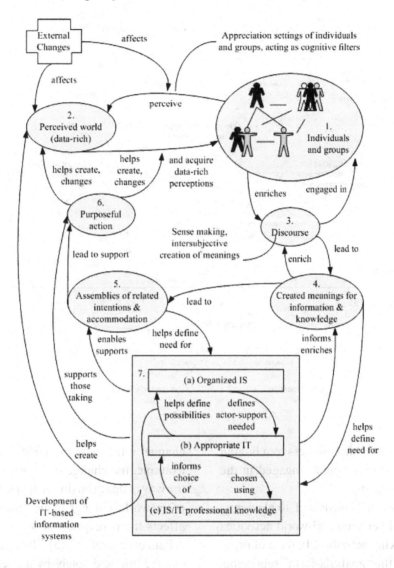

A search of the literature covering the period 1950 to 2007 inclusive was undertaken. All articles identified with the keywords "soft systems methodology" were reviewed. Articles identified as referring to IS maintenance/MIS maintenance/software maintenance were scanned to find those which related to SSM. This search showed that there were no articles identified with respect to the use of SSM as an operational method to assist IS maintenance activities. Thus it was concluded that there appears to be a gap in the literature on the use of the SSM as an operational method to maintain an IS.

ANALYSIS-FORM OF SSM FOR IS MAINTENANCE

Based on concepts derived by Checkland (1981), Checkland & Scholes, 1990), (Checkland & Holwell, 1998), a new form of SSM "analysis-form" was developed by this research for use in IS maintenance (Figure 5). It attempts to model the real world in the same structure as the purposed model. The SSM "analysis-form" is used as a tool to analysis the elements in "real word" and "thinking about the real world," and explains

Figure 5. Analysis-form of SSM for IS maintenance

the "whole" IS maintenance process as a human activities system to participants engaged in the IS maintenance project.

The "analysis-form" consists of 10 elements, which are divided between real-world activities and systems thinking activities. In term of organizational needs, the "analysis-form" represents the ideal type sets of human actions expressed as a system for IS maintenance. This ideal set of human interactions is the ideal actions and reactions between users, owners, and programmers during the IS maintenance process. In term of technical needs, the "analysis-form" produces outputs of a "change requirement" and "real information system."

There are many reasons why users and owners want to change their existing IS. These reasons are due to "external change" (1), "internal change" (2), and "need for improvement" (3). "External

change" is the change outside an organization, for example, the change in technical standards and the way of doing business. It affects people's view of the world. Change in the "perceived world" (4) affects the perception of owners and users of a "client organization" (5). "Internal change" is the change initiated solely by a client organization. It directly affects the perceptions of a client's organization. Based on these perceptions, a client organization will want to modify an existing IS to incorporate change. The need for improvement may be affected by internal and external change, but normally it is a proactive action which aims to make the system better.

Normally, a client organization defines the change in the form of "change requirement" (7), which is somewhat technical in nature. It is hard for nontechnical users and owners to draw up a technical document. Therefore, an "IT organization" (6) will help a client organization to define the change and specify in a technical form. A change requirement outlines the idea for change and draws a picture of the output—"conceptual model" (8). This conceptual model can be described as a purposeful IS. A conceptual model cannot be built from nothing. But by reference to the "benchmarking" (8a) and change techniques (8b), a conceptual model can be built thoroughly and reduce bias.

An IT organization then takes "action" (9) to modify existing IS. After a period of time, a modified IS is released. A client organization will then compare the "real IS" with the purposeful one. Users and owners imagine a purposeful IS based on their change requirement. But programmers develop a real IS which may be different to the purposeful one. This "comparison" (10) may lead a client organization to place another change requirement and start the next cycle of modification.

The activities or elements are defined as follows.

1. **External change:** External change is the change induced by the environment outside an organization and out of its control. Examples are globalization, new government regulation, development of new technology, and terrorist threats.

2. **Internal change:** Internal change is the change within an organization that is within its control, such as change of an organization's structure, change of CEO, and change of production process.

3. **Need for improvement:** Need for improvement may be responsive or proactive. It depends on managerial decision

4. **Perceived world:** Perceived world is what people perceive they will accomplish through their various assumptions. The worldview will be changed due to the external environmental change such as the availability of new technology. For example, the wide use of the Internet leads to a modification of existing IS to be an Internet-enabled application.

5. **Client organization:** This is an organization where the IS is implemented.

6. **IT organization:** This is an organization that undertakes an IS maintenance service for a client organization.

Within an IT organization, there are two different maintenance processes:

- The maintenance process used by an individual software maintainer (programmer) to implement a specific modification request; and

- The process at an organizational level that manages the stream of maintenance requests from users and owners.

7. **Change requirement:** A client organization places a change request and an IT organization makes a request analysis. An IT organization helps a client organization to define which parts of the existing IS should be changed. Then, they draw up a change requirement specification. A change requirement is a technical document that is commonly used in traditional IS maintenance.

8. **Conceptual model:** Conceptual model is the model made after formulating change requirement. By referring to system thinking and benchmarking, the conceptual model is more closely to be from free of bias.

9. **Action to improve IS:** A purposed action of IS maintenance takes place in the form of program design and coding. Programmers modify the original design and build a new version of the IS.

10. **Comparison of IS and conceptual model:** Users and owners compare the real IS and conceptual model. The comparison affects a client organization and leads to the start of the next change to modify the IS.

The change requirement is the main driver for IS maintenance. According to the Lientz and Swanson's (1980) study, approximately 80% of IS maintenance activities are attributed to adaptive and perfective maintenance, both of which relate to a changing requirement. The "analysis-form" focuses on the change requirement and the following areas: (1) planning for requirements change; (2) assessing the impact of change; (3) determining requirements volatility; and (4) assessing client organization and IT origination effectiveness at handling change. A change requirement can be classified into the following types:

1. Screen change—changes to the "interactive forms"
    a. Layout/detail changes—changes to the design of a single form
    b. Style change—changes to the style of a form that will affect many or all forms
2. Report change—changes to the reports generated
    a. Report layout—changes to the layout or design of a report
    b. Query change—changes to the query mechanism used to generate reports
    c. New field change—the addition of one or more new fields to a report
3. Data change—changes to the database structure

The broad features of "analysis-form" are:

1. It purports to be a defensible device with a structure and language, which can be used to make sense of life in real organization.
2. Elements are connected in a particular way to form a structure. The elements define a set of connected processes.
3. The structure of the "analysis-form" is cyclic. The ending element (10) is connected to the starting point; the action cycle is then restarted.

4. The process can encompass different ways of conceptualizing an organization.
5. The "analysis-form" enables the user to define the process to maintain an IS.

DISCUSSION

Literature posits that IS maintenance problems have both technological and nontechnological bases (Chapin, 1985; Dart, Christie, & Brown, 1993; Dekliva, 1992; Lientz & Swanson, 1980; Martin & Osborne, 1983; Swanson & Beath, 1989; Tan & Gable, 1998). Nontechnological problems are mainly human related. For technological problems, maintenance management also involves management activities between people and events. System characteristics are defined by human beings. Therefore, both problems contain human related issues. Any solution to improve the maintenance phase must address these issues. Thus, any model to be applied to IS maintenance must include the human factor.

The "analysis-form" leads to information that supports people's understanding of the ideal set of human actions, which is a two-way relationship between a client organization and an IT organization. It helps the learning process for users, owners, and programmers to improve not only communications but also technical issues. Checkland (2001) stated that SSM is based on a principle that any understanding of the process must be systemic and continual. The cyclic nature of the "analysis-form" implies that IS maintenance can be done continuously.

Flood and Jackson (1991) argued that SSM rested heavily on the issue of participation. Participation is an essential part of the "analysis-form." The interaction between ideals and experiences of the real world leads to a debate; the level of participation in the debate is crucial in defining and implementing the change (Callo & Packham, 1999). The "analysis-form" provides a rich picture for users, owners, and programmers to construct their IS maintenance activities. Those activities are highly participative. The effectiveness of the "analysis-form" depends on the level of participation from participants in a client organization to build their capacity to maintain their IS.

The objective of this study was to extend SSM as an operational model in IS maintenance with the aim of making a contribution to the literature and providing a stimulus for further research. Checkland (1981) suggested that theoretical models consist of extending a familiar theory into a new domain of application; these models draw from some more basic theory or theories, a set of assumptions about an object or system, including its inner structure, composition or mechanism. In this study, the "familiar theory" is SSM and "new domain of application" is the area of maintenance of IS. In order to show that SSM can be used in the process of IS maintenance, a conceptual model was developed. It is proposed that this model be tested in "practice" in further studies.

The study is useful by making a contribution to knowledge in two areas. First, this study makes a contribution by adding to the literature on SSM. It also makes a contribution to the literature on IS maintenance by providing an alternative method to maintain an IS. This research examined the issues contributing to the lack of an organizational methodology in IS maintenance. Second, the research developed a conceptual model as an "analysis-form" of SSM to assist IS maintenance. This study was exploratory so further research could be undertaken on IS maintenance by using this "analysis-form."

CONCLUSION

Literature highlights that the problems of IS maintenance are not just computer problems. The problems involve the combination of people, organization, and technology. Any solution to improve the maintenance phase must address the human related issues. In this chapter, an extended SSM model is developed for improving the human condition by understanding and changing the situation of IS maintenance. The "analysis-form" is used as a tool to increase the effectiveness of organizational requirement analysis in IS maintenance process. Hence, this study provides opportunities for further research that will see this "analysis-form" further validated and refined by collecting and analysing data from organisations during the IS maintenance process.

REFERENCES

Anquetil, N., de Oliveira, K.M., de Sousa, K.D., & Batista Dias, M.G. (2006). Software maintenance seen as a knowledge management issue. *Information and Software Technology, 49*(8), 515-529.

Atkinson, C., Eldabi, T., & Paul, R. (2002). Integrated approaches to health informatics research and development. *Logistics Information Management, 15*(2), 138-152.

Avison, D.E., & Wood-Harper, A.T. (1990). *Multiview: An exploration in information systems development.* Maidenhead: McGraw-Hill.

Ball, R.K. (1987). *Annual software maintenance survey: Survey results* (working paper). Vallejo, CA: Software Maintenance Association.

Callo, V.N., & Packham, R.G. (1999). The use of soft systems methodology in emancipatory development. *System Research and Behavioral Science, 16*(4), 311-310.

Chapin, N. (1985). Software maintenance: A different view. In *AFIPS Conference Proceedings, 54th National Computer Conference* (pp. 509-513).

Chapin, N. (1993). Management problems seen in software maintenance: An empowerment study. In *IEEE 1993 Conference on Software Maintenance* (pp. 329-333).

Checkland, P.B. (1972). Towards a system-based methodology for real-world problem solving. *Journal of Systems Engineering, 3*(2), 87-116.

Checkland, P.B. (1981). *Systems thinking, systems practice.* Chichester, UK: Wiley.

Checkland, P.B. (1992). From framework through experience to learning: The essential nature of action research. In C.J. Bruce & A.L. Russell (Eds.), *Transforming tomorrow today: Proceedings of the Second World Congress on Action Learning.* Nathan, Queensland: Action Learning, Action Research and Process Management Association Incorporated, Griffith University.

Checkland, P.B. (1995). Model validation in soft systems practice. *System Research, 12*(1), 47-54.

Checkland, P.B. (2001). Soft systems methodology in action: Participative creation of an information strategy for an acute hospital. In J. Rosenhead & J. Mingers (Eds.), *Rational analysis for a problematic world revisited: Problem structuring methods for complexity, uncertainty and conflict* (2ⁿᵈ ed.) (pp. 91-113). Chichester, West Sussex: John Wiley and Sons.

Checkland, P.B., & Holwell, S. (1998). *Information, systems and information systems.* Chichester, West Sussex: Wiley.

Checkland, P.B., & Scholes, J. (1990). *Soft systems methodology in action.* Chichester, West Sussex: Wiley.

Dart, S.A., Christie, A.M., & Brown, A.W. (1993). *A case study in software maintenance* (SEI Tech. Rep. No. CMU/SEI-93-TR-08). Pittsburgh PA: Software Engineering Institute, Carnegie Mellon University.

Dekleva, S.M. (1992). Delphi study of software maintenance problems. In *IEEE 1992 Conference on Software Maintenance* (pp. 10-17).

Eioerman, M.A., & Dishaw, M.T. (2007). The process of software maintenance: A comparison of object-oriented and third-generation development languages. *Journal of Software Maintenance and Evolution: Research and Practice, 19*(1), 33-47.

Ferrari, M., Fares, B., & Martinelli, P. (2002). The systemic approach of SSM: The case of a Brazilian company. *Systemic Practice and Action Research, 15*(1), 51-66.

Flood, R.L., & Jackson, M.C. (1991). *Creative problem solving: Total systems intervention.* Chichester, West Sussex: Wiley.

Higgins, A.D. (1986). *Data structured software maintenance: The WARNIER/ORR approach.* New York: Dorset House Publishing Co.

Lai, S.L. (2000). An integration of systems science methods and object-oriented analysis for determining organizational information requirements. *Systems Research and Behavioral Science, 17*(2), 205-228.

Ledington, P.W.J., & Ledington, J. (1999). The problem of comparison in soft systems methodology. *Systems Research and Behavioral Science, 16*(4), 329-339.

Lehman, M.M. (1989). Uncertainty in computer application and its control through the engineering of software. *Journal of Software Maintenance: Research and Practice, 1*(1), 3-27.

Leveson, N.G. (1995). *Safeware: System safety and computers.* Reading, MA: Addison-Wesley.

Lientz, B.P., & Swanson, E.B. (1980). *Software maintenance management.* Reading, MA: Addison-Wesley.

Luckett, S., Ngubane, S., & Memela, B. (2001). Designing a management system for a rural community development organization using a systemic action research process. *Systemic Practice and Action Research, 14*(4), 517-542.

Lutters, W.G., & Seaman, C.B. (2007). Revealing actual documentation usage in software maintenance through war stories. *Information and Software Technology, 49*(6), 576-587.

Martin, J., & Osborne, W.M. (1983). *Guidance on software maintenance.* NBS Special Publication 500-106. Washington, DC: Institute for Computer Science and Technology, National Bureau of Standards.

McClure, C. (1992). *The three Rs of software automation.* Englewood Cliffs, NJ: Prentice Hall.

McDermid, D.C. (1990). *Software engineering for information systems.* Oxford: Blackwell Scientific Publications.

Nosek, J., & Palvia, P. (1990). Software maintenance management: Change in the last decade. *Journal of Software Maintenance: Research and Practice, 2*(3), 157-174.

Platt, A., & Warwick, S. (1995). Review of soft systems methodology. *Industrial Management and Data Systems, 4*(1), 19-21.

Rose, J. (2007). Interaction, transformation and information systems development – an extended application of SSM. *Information Technology & People, 15*(3), 242-268.

Schneidewind, N.T. (1987). The state of software maintenance. *IEEE Transactions on Software Engineering, 13*(3), 303-310.

Shafer, G. (1988). *Functional analysis of office requirements: A multiperspective approach.* Chichester: John Wiley & Sons.

Smith, D.D. (1999). *Designing maintainable software.* Berlin, Heidelberg, New York: Springer-Verlag.

Swanson, E.B., & Beath, C.M. (1989). *Maintaining information systems in organizations.* Great Britain: John Wiley & Sons.

Tajino, A., & Smith, C. (2005). Exploratory practice and soft systems methodology. *Language Teaching Research, 9*(4), 448-469.

Tan, W.G., & Gable, G.G. (1998). Attitude of maintenance personnel towards maintenance work: A comparative analysis. *Software Maintenance: Research and Practice, 10*(1), 59-74.

Taylor, M.J., & DaCosta, J.L. (1999). Software issues in IS projects: Lessons from an SME case study. *System Research and Behavioral Science, 16*(3), 263-272.

Tsouvalis, C., & Checkland, P.B. (1996). Reflecting on SSM: The dividing line between real world and system thinking world. *Systems Research, 13*(1), 33-45.

Von Mayrhauser, A., Vans, A.M., & Howe, A.E. (1997). Program understanding behaviour during enhancement of large-scale software. *Journal of Software Maintenance: Research and Practice, 9*(5), 299-327.

Xu, L.D. (2000). The contribution of systems science to information systems rersearch. *Systems Research and Behavioral Science, 17*(2), 105-116.

Chapter XII
Design Science:
A Case Study in Information Systems Re-Engineering

Raul Valverde
Concordia University, Canada

Mark Toleman
University of Southern Queensland, Australia

Aileen Cater-Steel
University of Southern Queensland, Australia

ABSTRACT

Recently, many organisations have become aware of the limitations of their legacy systems to adapt to new technical requirements. Trends towards e-commerce applications, platform independence, reusability of prebuilt components, capacity for reconfiguration, and higher reliability have contributed to the need to update current systems. Consequently, legacy systems need to be re-engineered into new component-based systems. This chapter shows the use of the design science approach in information systems re-engineering research. In this study, design science and the Bunge-Wand-Weber (BWW) model are used as the main research frameworks to build and evaluate conceptual models generated by the component-based and traditional approaches in re-engineering a legacy system into a component-based information system. The objective of this evaluation is to verify that the re-engineered component-based model is capable of representing the same business requirements as the legacy system.

INTRODUCTION

The objective of this chapter is to show how the design science research approach can be used for applied information systems (IS) research.

Design science in information systems is defined by March and Smith (1995) as an attempt to create things that serve human purposes, as opposed to natural and social sciences, which try to understand reality.

The IS research problem chosen to demonstrate the use of design science is the re-engineering of a legacy system in a financial institution. The vast majority of legacy information systems were implemented using the traditional paradigm. The traditional paradigm consists of modeling techniques used by system analysts including system flow charts and data flow diagrams (DFD) to capture, during the analysis phase, the activities within a system. However, with recent developments, particularly trends towards e-commerce applications, platform independence, reusability of prebuilt components, capacity for reconfiguration, and higher reliability, many organizations are realizing they need to re-engineer their systems. Given the limitations of legacy systems to adapt to these new technical requirements, new component-based systems are required to meet these trends; however, there is a high degree of interest and concern in establishing whether or not a full migration to a more portable and scalable component-based architecture will be able to represent the legacy business requirements in the underlying conceptual model of re-engineered information systems.

To address this concern, the research project re-engineered a sample process to derive a component model from the legacy system and posed the question: Is the resulting component-based model equivalent to the legacy conceptual model?

In order to answer the research question, the project evaluated the conceptual models generated by the component-based and traditional approaches in the re-engineering process in order to verify that the re-engineered component-based model was capable of representing the same business requirements of the legacy system. Design science is used as the central research approach for this project.

The first section provides the background for this chapter. Then, the application of design science in information systems re-engineering is demonstrated by using a case study. Finally, directions of future research are suggested.

DESIGN SCIENCE BACKGROUND

Design Science as an Information Systems Research Approach

The design science approach has a history of providing useful results in the evaluation of constructs and models in information systems (Hevner, March, Park, & Ram, 2004). This is in line with Nunamaker and Chen (1990) who classify design science in IS as applied research that applies knowledge to solve practical problems. March and Smith (1995) define design science as an attempt to create artifacts that serve human purposes, as opposed to natural and social sciences, which try to understand reality (Au, 2001).

Fundamental Concepts of Design Science

March and Smith (1995) outline a design science framework with two axes, namely research activities and research outputs. Research outputs cover constructs, models, methods, and instantiations. Research activities comprise building, evaluating, theorizing on, and justifying artifacts.

Constructs or concepts form the vocabulary of a domain. They constitute a conceptualization used to describe problems within a domain. A *model* is a set of propositions or statements expressing relationships among constructs. In design activities, models represent situations as problem and solution statements. A *method* is a set of steps (an algorithm or guideline) used to perform a task. Methods are based on a set of underlying constructs (language) and a representation (model) of the solution space. An *instantiation* is the realization of an artifact in its environment. Instantiations operationalize constructs, models, and methods.

Concerning research activities, March and Smith (1995) identify *build* and *evaluate* as the two main issues in design science. *Build* refers to the construction of constructs, models, methods, and artifacts demonstrating that they can be constructed. *Evaluate* refers to the development of criteria and the assessment of the output's performance against those criteria. Parallel to these two research activities in design science, March and Smith (1995) add the natural and social science couple, which are *theorize* and *justify*. *Theorise* refers to the construction of theories that explain how or why something happens. In the case of IT and IS research this is often an explanation of how or why an artifact works within its environment. *Justify* refers to theory-proving and requires the gathering of scientific evidence that supports or refutes the theory (March & Smith, 1995).

The use of the design science research framework is justified on three grounds for the chosen research project. First, it provides a framework that can be used for Information Systems applied research. This is in line with Nunamaker and Chen (1990) who classify design science in IS as applied research that uses knowledge to solve practical problems. Second, design science provides a framework for evaluation of models. The objective of this research project is the evaluation of the capacity of component-based models to represent business requirements of legacy conceptual models. This framework seems to be aligned with this objective. Finally, the framework can be used to extend the scope of this research. Although the objective of this research is not to create new theory based on the findings, the framework provides that possibility and could be used for future research.

The objective of the project chosen to demonstrate the design science approach is to use component-based constructs to compare the representation of the same requirements in component-based models with legacy systems modeled with traditional constructs. Very few research frameworks for applied research in information systems have been developed in the past. However, design science is a scientific research method that can be used in developing an evaluation of conceptual models' frameworks (March & Smith, 1995).

For the chosen research problem, the design science approach is used to design an evaluation of conceptual models' frameworks to help IS specialists in the verification of representation of the business requirements in re-engineered component-based models originally represented in legacy conceptual models.

The *building* part of the research uses re-engineering methodologies to generate the conceptual models required for the research. There are many re-engineering methodologies that help to cope with the problem of transforming legacy systems originally developed with traditional methodologies into component-based systems.

APPLICATION OF DESIGN SCIENCE APPROACH

Research Outline

The research project chosen to demonstrate the design science framework covers the *build* and *evaluate* research activities and has a research output of *constructs* and *models*. *Instantiations* are not covered as the scope of this research is limited to conceptual models. Conceptual models do not include any implementation details that can be used for instantiation.

March and Smith (1995) propose a 4 by 4 framework that produces 16 cells describing viable research efforts. The different cells have different objectives with different appropriate research methods. A research project can cover multiple cells, but does not necessarily have to cover them all.

The *build* part of the framework will be used as part of this research since conceptual models need to be created for ontological evaluation. The main activity of the research project will be the *evaluation* phase, as it will allow identification of metrics to compare the performance of constructs and models.

Table 1 illustrates the cells at the intersection of research activities and research outputs of March and Smith's (1995) framework which are discussed in this chapter. Each cell/intersection contains a specific research objective of the overall research. The *build* column covers the recovery of a conceptual model for a legacy system and the generation of a re-engineered component-based model. Construct building is not required as existing constructs for both traditional and component-based are used.

The *evaluate* column in Table 1 includes evaluating the completeness of the component-based constructs (UML) in terms of ontological deficiencies that the constructs could have when modeling traditional constructs. Conceptual models need to be evaluated in order to measure the capacity of the component-based model to represent the same requirements as the legacy model.

Selection of Methodologies Applied to the Design Science Approach

In the previous section we explained the research objectives in the different cells of March and Smith's framework (1995) covered by the research study. However, as March and Smith explain, every cell and research objective may call for a different methodology. This makes it necessary to identify an adequate method for each specific research objective, resulting in an overall method mix. To achieve this, several methodologies were identified as part of the literature review. These methods are listed in Table 2.

The IS research problem chosen to demonstrate the use of design science involves three main parts: conceptual model recovery, system re-engineering, and ontological evaluation.

Methodologies Selected for Conceptual Model Recovery

The conceptual model recovery of the case study is one of the major challenges in the research since most of the legacy systems have very poor documentation in terms of models and technical design. In order to address this problem, the researcher captured the conceptual model of the legacy system by applying a reverse engineering approach as specified in the Jacobson and Lindstrom (1991) methodology. There are many re-engineering methodologies that help to cope with the problem of transforming legacy systems originally developed with traditional methodologies into component-based systems. The Jacobson and Lindstrom (1991) approach for re-engineering of legacy systems was chosen for the following reasons:

- It contemplates cases of a complete change of implementation technique and no change in the functionality, which is the case of this research;

Table 1. Research activities based on design science approach (adapted from March & Smith, 1995)

	Build	Evaluate
Constructs	Not required	Identifying ontological modeling deficiencies of component-based constructs in terms of traditional construct representation
Model	Recovering the legacy conceptual model of the case study Generating the re-engineered component-based model for the legacy system	Evaluating the capacity of the re-engineered component-based for representing the same business requirements embedded in the legacy model

Table 2. Methodologies selected for research project

Methodology	Definition
Case Study	Study of a single phenomenon (e.g., an application, a technology, a decision) in an organization over a logical time frame
Jacobson & Linstrom (1991)	Methodology for information systems re-engineering and legacy system conceptual model recovery
Fettke & Loos (2003)	Methodology for ontological evaluation of conceptual models
Interviews	Research in which information is obtained by asking respondents questions directly
Direct observation	This occurs when a field visit is conducted during the case study
Secondary Data	A study that utilizes existing organizational and business data, that is, document, diagrams, and so forth.
Rosemann & Green (2002)	Meta Models methodology for Normalized Reference Models generation and comparison

- It does not require the use of source code. In the case study used for this research there is no access to the source code used to develop the system;
- It also covers reverse engineering. This is useful for this research given the need to capture the original conceptual model for the legacy system;
- It is relatively simple to use.

Although Jacobson and Lindstrom's (1991) original methodology was proposed for object-oriented systems, it can be easily adapted for component-based systems since components can be viewed as a higher level of abstraction based on object-oriented methodology. The methodology for this project uses data collection methods including interviews, direct observation and secondary data.

Methodologies Selected for System Re-engineering

Once the conceptual models from the legacy system are recovered, the system is re-engineered using the Jacobson and Lindstrom (1991) approach for re-engineering of legacy systems. The output of this step is the re-engineered component-based model as detailed in Valverde and Toleman (2007).

Methodologies Selected for Ontological evaluation

The legacy system and re-engineered models generated as part of the building part of the research are then evaluated based on the ontological evaluation of grammars (Wand & Weber, 1993). As part of the evaluation research, an analysis is done using the Bunge-Wand-Weber (BWW) model. The BWW model is an ontological theory initially developed by Bunge (1977, 1979) and adapted and extended by Wand and Weber (Wand & Weber, 1989, 1995; Weber, 1997).

The BWW model is well founded on mathematical concepts. Prior research on the evaluation of grammars has shown it has been used successfully in information systems research (Evermann & Wand, 2001; Green & Rosemann, 2000; Opdahl & Henderson-Sellers, 2002; Weber & Zhang, 1996).

After developing the re-engineered model, it is necessary to compare both legacy and re-engineered models for equivalency of representation of business requirements. An ontological normalization methodology developed by Fettke and Loos (2003) is used for this activity. The Fettke and Loos (2003) methodology is considered appropriate as it provides a mechanism for the comparison of conceptual models; models can be compared based of their normalized referenced models; and it is simple to use.

In order to generate these normalized reference models in BWW terms, the Rosemann and Green (2002) BWW meta-model is used. This meta-model is based on the original entity relationship specification from Chen (1976) with extensions made by Scheer (1998). Scheer's version is called the extended ER model (eERM).

Once the legacy system and re-engineered models are generated, they can be evaluated based on an ontological evaluation of grammars (Wand & Weber, 1993). An ontological normalization for the original and re-engineered models is generated. The two models are evaluated using the Fettke and Loos (2003) methodology based on their ontologically normalized models generated by the Rosemann and Green (2002) methodology. The result of the comparison reveals that the compared models are equivalent, complementary or in conflict (Fettke & Loos, 2003). Table 3 displays the mapping of the retained methodologies to the activities.

Research Project Procedures

The case study methodology is chosen to evaluate the capacity of the re-engineered component model to represent the same requirements as the legacy traditional model (Benbasat, Goldstein, & Mead, 1987). The case-study system selected is a *Home Loan* information system developed by a consultant company in the Netherlands. The system was customized for a mid-sized home loan bank that specializes in the marketing, sales, and administration of its own home loan products. The information system was designed for use on Unisys A-Series mainframes.

In this chapter, the focus is not on reporting the outputs of the re-engineered business process but on the procedures and frameworks used by the researcher in adopting a design science research approach. Research procedures are divided into build and evaluation procedures. Build procedures are required to accomplish the build objectives of the design science approach while the evaluation procedures accomplish the evaluation objectives.

Data Collection (Build)

Data gathering is an important part of this research as it is required to commence the building part of the research. For this research, observation techniques, interviews, and review of physical artifacts and system documents were used as the sources for data gathering. The most common methods of collecting data within the case study approach are through observation and interviews (Bell, 1992).

The use of observation as a method of data collection is well documented (Bell, 1992; Benbasat

Table 3. Research methodologies selected for the design science approach

	Build	Evaluate
Constructs	Not required	Fettke & Loos (2003)
Model	Case Study	Case Study
	Interviews	Fettke & Loos (2003)
	Secondary Data	Rosemann & Green (2002)
	Direct Observation	
	Jacobson & Linstrom (1991)	

et al., 1987; Stake, 1995) and works well in case research (Yin, 1994).

Before observations were used in the research project, the three minimum conditions set out by Tull and Hawkins (1993) were met: the data were available for observation; the behaviour was repetitive, frequent, or otherwise predictable; and each event covered a reasonably short time span.

According to Jorgensen (1989), observation is appropriate for studies of almost every human existence. Through observation, it is possible to describe what goes on, who or what is involved, when and where things happen, how they occur, and why things happen as they do in particular situations (Jorgensen, 1989). A great deal of time is spent on paying attention, watching, and listening carefully (Neuman, 1994). The observer uses all the senses, noticing what is seen, heard, smelled, tasted, and touched (Neuman, 1994; Spradley, 1979).

In terms of research stance, Neuman (1994) identifies four possible roles for the participant observer:

- **Complete participant:** The researcher operates under conditions of secret observation and full participation;
- **Complete observer:** The researcher is behind a one-way mirror or in an invisible role that permits undetected and unnoticed observation and eavesdropping;
- **Participant as observer:** The researcher and members are aware of the research role, but the researcher is an intimate friend who is a pseudo-member;
- **Observer as participant:** The researcher is a known, overt observer from the beginning, who has more limited or formal contact with members.

In this study, the researcher visited the case study information system's site and observed its functionality as a *complete observer*. The justi-

fication for this role is to avoid intrusion in the normal operation of the information systems and learn the most by observing the users in the natural environment of the information systems.

The technique used to interview users, maintainers, and designers was open-ended interviews. The use of this technique is justified for this research by two main reasons. First, the goal is to elicit the respondent's views and experiences in his or her own terms, rather than to collect data that are simply a choice among pre-established response categories (Anderson, Aydin, & Jay, 1994). Second, the interview is not bound to a rigid interview format or set of questions that would be difficult to establish given the nature of the research and would limit the results (Anderson et al., 1994).

The final goal of the open interview is to interview system users, maintainers, and designers of the legacy systems in order to find out how the system was developed, what are the functions of the system, and the type of documentation used for the system development. The system owners consented to the participation of the developers in the interviews.

System documentation was collected in order to perform the reverse engineering analysis required to recover the conceptual models (Jacobson & Lindstrom, 1991). The legacy information system can be described by using different elements such as requirements specifications, user operating instructions, maintenance manuals, training manuals, design documentation, source code files, and database schema descriptions (Jacobson & Lindstrom, 1991). Information systems documentation is a valuable source of data. Documentation related to the system, including manuals, database schemas, and system architecture diagrams were collected.

Conceptual Model Recovery (Build)

In order to capture the conceptual model of the legacy system, the reverse engineering methodology, as specified in Jacobson and Lindstrom (1991), was applied. The following three steps were used:

- Develop a concrete graph that describes the components of the system and their interrelationship;
- Develop an abstract graph showing the behavior and the structure of the system;
- Develop a mapping between the two, that is, how something in the abstract graph relates to the concrete graph and vice versa.

The abstract graph should be free of implementation details. For example, mechanisms for persistent storage or partitioning into processes should not appear on this graph. The concrete graph must, on the other hand, show these details. The mapping between the two should explain how the abstract graph is implemented by way of the concrete graph (Jacobson & Lindstrom, 1991).

Use cases are an excellent tool for reverse engineering since they provide a sequence of user interactions with the system (Jacobson & Lindstrom, 1991). Their purpose is to define a typical way of using the system and to describe the business process, to document how the business works and what the business goals are of each interaction with the system. In the context of reverse engineering, it is possible to explore a legacy system with use cases (Jacobson & Lindstrom, 1991).

Use cases were developed to create the concrete graph for reverse engineering. These use cases show the interrelationship between manuals, documentation, interviews, source code, and researcher's observation of the system. The abstract graph described in the Jacobson and Lindstrom (1991) methodology is in fact an example of the legacy conceptual model. For this research project, the conceptual model was represented in terms of data flow diagrams (DFDs), a context diagram, and entity relationship (E-R) diagrams.

The description of the business process, business events, and responses is essential in generating a conceptual model (Whitten, Bentley, & Dittman, 2001). The use cases employed to construct the concrete graph document the business processes, events, and responses required to construct this legacy abstract graph. In order to generate the DFDs required to construct the legacy conceptual model, business events to which the system must respond and appropriate responses were identified with the help of the use cases. According to Whitten et al. (2001), there are essentially three types of events:

- **External events:** Are so named because they are initiated by external agents. When these events happen, an input data flow occurs for the system in the DFD;
- **Temporal events:** Trigger processes on the basis of time. When these events happen, an input called *control flow* occurs;
- **State events:** Trigger processes based on a system change from one state or condition to another.

Information systems usually respond to external or temporal events. State events are usually associated with real time systems (Whitten et al., 2001).

Once these events were identified, DFDs were drawn with the help of the list of mapping transformations suggested by Whitten et al. (2001). The concrete graph represented by the use case can be mapped to the abstract graph represented by the DFD. The actor in the use case that initiated the event will become the external agent; the event identified in the use case will be handled by a process in the DFD; the input or trigger in the use case will become the data or control flow in the DFD; all outputs and responses in the use case will become data flows in the DFD.

The data model of the legacy conceptual model is generated by identifying the data stores in the DFD, examining the use cases, and finally documented by using an E-R Diagram.

Component-Based Model Generation (Build)

Once the model was reverse engineered from the legacy system, the legacy system was re-engineered for a complete change in implementation technique but no change in functionality by preparing an analysis model and then mapping each analysis object to the implementation of the old system (Jacobson & Lindstrom, 1991).

In the first step, an analysis model was prepared with the help of the use cases prepared in the reverse engineering process. These use cases already contain the information that was assimilated from the manuals, system architecture documentation, open interviews, and research observations described as description elements in the Jacobson and Lindstom (1991) methodology (Figure 1). Only the analysis model of the re-engineering process was required since the primary objective of the research project was the comparison of conceptual models and not the full implementation of the information systems.

An analysis model only contains the logical aspects and is free of physical implementation details. The logical representation of a component is concerned with its logical abstraction, its relationship with other logical elements, and its assigned responsibilities. The logical representation of a component-based system was modeled by using the UML diagrams: use case diagrams, class diagrams, sequence diagram, and state diagrams (Houston & Norris, 2001).

Actors were identified from the use cases and use case diagrams were constructed to identify the system scope and boundaries. The model should be free of physical implementation details. For the case of components, their logical representation was modeled using UML subsystems and identified inside the use case diagrams as proposed by Houston and Norris (2001). Class diagrams were prepared using the criteria for finding objects as described in Jacobson's (1987) object-oriented method. This step was accomplished by reviewing each use case to find nouns that correspond to business entities or events (Jacobson, 1987). Not all the nouns in the use cases represent valid business objects. A cleansing process removed nouns that represent synonyms, nouns outside of the scope of the system, nouns that are roles

Figure 1. Preparation of the analysis model (adapted from Jacobson & Linstrom, 1991)

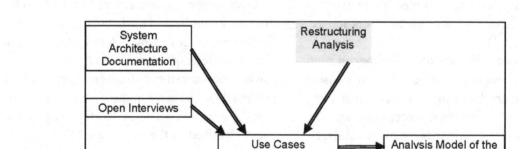

without unique behavior or are external roles, unclear nouns that need focus, or nouns that are really actions or attributes (Whitten et al., 2001). Once objects were identified, their relationships were modeled as part of the class diagrams and interfaces were identified.

Ontological Evaluation (Evaluation)

Once the legacy conceptual model was recovered and the component business analysis model represented with the use of UML diagrams, the Fettke and Loos (2003) methodology was used to evaluate these models for equivalency of representation of business requirements.

As part of this evaluation, the ontological normalization of the legacy and re-engineered component models was generated. The ontological normalization of a reference model consisted of four steps (Fettke & Loos, 2003):

- **Step 1.** Develop a transformation mapping;
- **Step 2.** Identify ontological modeling deficiencies;
- **Step 3.** Transform the models; and
- **Step 4.** Assess the results.

In the first step of this method, a transformation mapping of the traditional and component-based (UML) diagrams used for representing the conceptual models was developed. This transformation mapping allowed converting the constructs of the traditional and component-based (UML) diagrams to the constructs of the BWW model. The first step was based on the method for the ontological evaluation of grammars proposed by Wand and Weber (1993).

The transformation mapping consisted of two mathematical mappings. First, a representation mapping described whether and how the constructs of the BWW model are mapped onto the traditional and component-based (UML) constructs. Second, the interpretation mapping described whether and how the traditional and component-based (UML) constructs are mapped onto the constructs of the BWW model (Fettke & Loos, 2003).

All ontological deficiencies of the conceptual models were identified as part of the second step of the generation of the normalized ontological models. To identify the ontological deficiencies of the recovered model and re-engineered component-based model, all constructs of the models were reviewed. Each construct of the models analyzed was examined with respect to whether the construct was used correctly regarding the interpretation mapping.

Three classifications of deficiencies were used:

- **Adequacy:** The grammatical construct is ontologically adequate. Nevertheless, an ontological deficiency can emerge by applying the grammatical construct to build the reference model. Therefore it must be examined whether the construct of the reference model is used correctly with respect to the interpretation mapping. The construct of the reference model is used adequately if it is used correctly with respect to the interpretation mapping.
- **Excess:** Construct excess is a modeling deficiency in general and needs special handling in the transformation step. Therefore, this construct should be marked as excessive in the reference model.
- **Overload:** Construct overload is a modeling deficiency in general and needs special handling in the transformation step. Therefore, this construct should be marked as overloaded in the reference model (Fettke & Loos, 2003).

Based on the representation mapping, it was decided whether the traditional and component-based grammar are incomplete or redundant. An incomplete grammar suggests that specific facts of reality cannot be adequately represented in the model.

In the third step, the models were transformed to ontological models. The outcome of this step was two ontologically normalized models. The objective of both techniques was to represent the domain of interest in a normalized way by applying specific transformation patterns (Fettke & Loos, 2003).

The two models were compared based on their ontologically normalized models. The result of this comparison was an analysis that revealed whether the compared models are equivalent, complementary, or in conflict. In order to generate these normalized reference models in BWW terms, the Rosemann and Green (2002) BWW meta-models were used.

CONCLUSION

This chapter has discussed how design science can be used for the research of information systems re-engineering. The research activities identified by March and Smith (1995) were fundamental for this study. This framework requires two main activities: build and evaluate, which require the use of several methodologies as the first was used for construction of conceptual and BWW normalized models and the second for the evaluation of these models for equivalency of business requirements using the Fettke and Loos (2003) ontological methodology. The case study methodology was used as the main methodology to build and evaluate conceptual models. The Jacobson and Lindstrom (1991) approach for re-engineering of legacy systems was employed to build the original conceptual model of the legacy system under research and for the building of the component-based re-engineered models. Conceptual models were built with the help of data collected by using interviews, observation techniques, and review of information systems documents.

The methodology by Fettke and Loos (2003) was selected to evaluate the models generated by the reverse engineering (legacy conceptual model) and those generated by the re-engineering process (component model). Traditional and component-based constructs were also evaluated under the same methodology. The Rosemann and Green (2002) metamodels were used as the primary tool to represent the normalized models in BWW construct terms.

FUTURE RESEARCH DIRECTIONS

Future research can be concentrated in the development of automated tools for the re-engineering of information systems based on design science. A software tool could be constructed to build legacy and re-engineered conceptual models and evaluate them based on the methodology proposed. This software tool could translate the legacy and component models into ontological normalized reference models that could be used for comparison.

REFERENCES

Anderson, J.G., Aydin, C.E., & Jay, S.J. (1994). *Evaluating health care information systems: Methods and applications.* USA: Sage.

Au, Y.A. (2001). Design science I: The role of design science in electronic commerce research. *Communications of the Association for Information Systems (CAIS)*, *7*(1).

Bell, J. (1992). *Doing your research project.* Open University Press, Milton Keynes

Benbasat, I., Goldstein, D., & Mead, M. (1987). The case research strategy in studies of information systems, *MIS Quarterly*, *11*(3), 368-386.

Bunge, M., (1977). *Treatise on basic philosophy (Vol. 3): Ontology 1: The furniture of the world.* Boston, MA: Reidel.

Bunge, M., (1979). *Treatise on basic philosophy: Volume 4: Ontology II: A world of systems.* Dordrecht: Reidel.

Chen, P.P.-S., (1976). The entity-relationship model: Toward a unified view of data. *ACM Transactions on Database Systems, 1*(1), 9-36.

Evermann, J., & Wand, Y. (2001). An ontological examination of object interaction in conceptual modeling. In *Proceedings of the 11th Workshop on Information Technologies and Systems, (WITS 2001),* New Orleans, Louisiana.

Fettke, P., & Loos, P. (2003). Ontological evaluation of reference models using the Bunge Wand-Weber-model. In *Proceedings of the Ninth Americas Conference on Information Systems,* Tampa, FL (pp. 2944-2955).

Hevner, A.R., March, S.T., Park, J., & Ram, S. (2004). Design research in information systems research. *MIS Quarterly, 28*(1), 75-105.

Houston, K., & Norris, D. (2001). Software component and the UML. In *Component based software engineering* (Chap. 14, pp. 243-263). Addison-Wesley.

Jacobson. I. (1987). Object oriented development in an industrial environment. In *Proceedings of OOPSLA,* Orlando, FL (pp. 183-191). ACM Press.

Jacobson, I., & Lindstrom, F. (1991). Re-engineering of old systems to an object-oriented approach. In *Proceedings of Conference on Object-Oriented Programming Systems, Languages and Applications OOPSLA 1991* (pp. 340-350).

Jorgensen, D.L. (1989). *Participant observation: Methodology for human studies.* Newbury, CA: Sage.

March, S., & Smith, G. (1995). Design and natural science research on information technology. *Decision Support Systems, 15*(4), 251 - 266.

Neuman, W.L. (1994). Sampling. In W.L. Neuman (Ed.), *Social research methods* (pp. 193-220). Boston, MA: Allyn and Bacon.

Nunamaker, J.F., & Chen, M. (1990). Systems development in information systems research. In *The Proceedings of the Twenty-Third Hawaii International Conference on System Sciences* (pp. 631-640). IEEE Computer Society Press.

Opdahl, A.L., & Henderson-Sellers, B. (2002). Understanding and improving the UML metamodel through ontological analysis. *Journal of Software and Systems Modelling (SoSyM), 1*(1), 43-67. Springer.

Rosemann, M., & Green, P. (2002). Developing a meta model for the Bunge-Wand-Weber ontological constructs. *Information Systems, 27,* 75-91.

Scheer, A.-W. (1998). *ARIS-business process frameworks* (2nd ed.). Berlin, Germany: Springer-Verlag.

Spradley, J.P. (1979). *The ethnographic interview.* New York: Holt, Rinehart and Winston.

Stake, R.E. (1995). *The art of case study research.* CA: Sage.

Tull, D.S., & Hawkins, D.I. (1993). *Marketing research.* New York: McMillan.

Valverde, R., & Toleman, M. (2007). Ontological evaluation of business models: Comparing traditional and component-based paradigms in information systems re-engineering. In R. Kishore, R. Ramesh, & R. Sharman (Eds), *Ontologies in the context of information systems.* Berlin, Germany: Springer-Verlag.

Weber, R. (1997). *Ontological foundations of information systems. Coopers and Lybrand accounting research methodology.* Melbourne, Australia: Monograph No. 4.

Wand, Y., & Weber, R. (1989). An ontological evaluation of systems analysis and design methods. In E. Falkenberg & P. Lindgreen (Eds.), *Proceedings of the IFIP WG8.1 working conference on information systems concepts: An in-depth analysis,* Namur, Belgium (pp.79-107). North-Holland, Amsterdam.

Wand, Y., & Weber, R. (1993). On the ontological expressiveness of information systems analysis and design grammars. *Information Systems Journal, 3*(2), 217-237.

Wand, Y., & Weber, R. (1995). On the deep structure of information systems. *Information Systems Journal, 5*(2), 203-223.

Weber, R., & Zhang, Y. (1996). An analytical evaluation of NIAM's grammar for conceptual schema diagrams. *Information Systems Journal, 6*(2), 147-170.

Whitten, J.L., Bentley, D.L., & Dittman, K.V. (2001). *Systems analysis and design methods.* New York: McGraw-Hill.

Yin, R.K. (1994). *Case study research-design and methods.* In *Applied social research methods series: Vol. 5* (2nd ed.). Newbury Park: Sage.

ADDITIONAL READINGS

Bloor Research. (2001). *Understanding business goals.* Retrieved June 6, 2008, from http://www.it-director.com/business/content.php?cid=2254

Brown, A.W. (2000). *Large-scale, component-based development.* Prentice Hall, NJ.

Carey, J., & Carlson, B. (2001). *Business Components in component based software engineering.* Reading, MA: Addison-Wesley

Davies, L., Green, P., & Rosemann, M. (2002, October 24-26). Facilitating an ontological foundation of information systems with meta models.

In *Proceedings of ACIS International Conference of Computer Science, Software Engineering, Information Technology, E-Business, and Applicaitons (ACIS 2002),* St-Louis, MO.

Evermann, J., & Wand, Y. (2001). An ontological examination of object interaction in conceptual modeling. In *Proceedings of the 11th Workshop on Information Technologies and Systems, (WITS 2001),* New Orleans, LA.

Favre, J.M , Duclos, F., Estublier, J., Sanlaville, R., & Auffret, J.J. (2001, March 14-16). Reverse engineering a large component-based software product. In *Proceedings of the Fifth European Conference on Software Maintenance and Re-engineering (CSMR),* Lisbon, Portugal.

Green, P., & Rosemann, M. (1999). An ontological analysis of integrated process modelling. In *Proceedings of the 11th International Conference on Advanced Information Systems Engineering (CAiSE 99),* Berlin, Germany (pp. 225-240). Springer.

Green, P., & Rosemann, M. (2000). Integrated process modelling: An ontological evaluation. *Information Systems, 25*(2), 73-87.

Green, P., & Rosemann, M. (2005). *Business analysis with ontologies.* New York: Idea Group Publishing.

Heineman, G.T., & Councill, W.T. (2001). Definition of a software component and its elements' in component based software engineering. Boston, MA: Addison-Wesley.

Henderson-Sellers, B. (2001). An open process for component-based development. In G.T. Heineman & W. T. Councill (Eds.), *Component based software engineering* (pp. 243-263). Addison-Wesley.

Henderson-Sellers, B., & Barbier, F. (1999). Black and white diamonds. In R. France & B. Rumpe (Eds.), *Proceedings of the UML 99-The Unified Modeling Language (Beyond the Standard),*

UML 99, (LNCS No. 1723, pp. 550-565). Berlin, Germany: Springer Verlag.

Irwin, G., & Turk, D. (2005). An ontological analysis of use case modeling grammar. *Journal of the Association for Information Systems, 6*(1), 1-36.

Section 2.2
ICT Adoption

Chapter XIII
Analyzing the Use of Information Systems in Logistics Industry

Shaligram Pokharel
Nanyang Technological University, Singapore

Carman Ka Man Lee
Nanyang Technological University, Singapore

ABSTRACT

Information and communication technology (ICT) refer to a family of technologies that facilitate information capturing, storing, processing, disseminating, and providing a supportive role for human activities to enhance organizational efficiency and effectiveness. With the use of ICT, organizations are expected to have better decision-making capabilities and faster execution of activities. Logistics activities in a company consist of a wide scope of processes ranging from planning and implementing material flow and storage, services, and information from the point of origin to the point of consumption. If ICT could be used to support these activities, logistics cost would decrease over the long term and the efficiency of logistics activities would increase substantially. In this chapter, we explain a method for studying the impact of ICT in logistics companies. This type of study is useful to devise a long term business process improvement policy in a country or a region. We suggest methods for collecting data and presenting them through descriptive and statistical analysis. We suggest the use of t-statistic method to test relationships between various variables and ICT implementation. We have provided a hypothetical case study to show the steps in the analysis. We believe that the chapter will be useful to researchers in conducting studies on the impact and suitability of ICT in logistics and other service providing sectors. The results obtained from this type of study can help the decision makers to understand the opportunities and hurdles in achieving greater efficiency in the organizational processes through the use of modern information technology.

INTRODUCTION

Business process efficiency can be enhanced by cutting down or shifting some nonvalue adding processes to automated processing. The pace of development in computer hardware and software and other technologies have enabled many companies to reorganize their business related processes, such as in finance or manufacturing. The use of information and communication technologies (ICT) or information technology (IT) helps to capture, store, process, and disseminate information to provide a supportive role for human activities in order to enhance organizational efficiency and effectiveness (Cohen, Salomon, & Nijkamp, 2002). The decision on the use of ICT is strategic (Huber, 1990) as ICT capabilities significantly influence overall logistics competence (Closs, Goldsby, & Clinton, 1997). ICT can improve an organization's ability to respond and change to a dynamic environment (Monteiro & Macdonald, 1996).

In the remainder of the chapter, we discuss the type of logistics services and their relation with ICT, development of a research framework, development of questionnaires, and finally the collection and analysis of data. The emphasis in this chapter is on the illustration of the method to analyze the use of ICT both in terms descriptive analysis and statistical analysis and then on helping readers draw conclusions based on the analysis. The chapter ends with conclusions and some remarks on possible extension of research work in the area of ICT and logistics.

Logistics Services

Logistics services are generally categorized into four groups: warehousing, freight forwarding, transportation, and depot operations (Andersen Consulting, 1998). Warehousing refers to receiving of goods, keeping their records, storing them in order for easy retrieval, receiving orders for withdrawal, withdrawal of goods from the store,

packaging, and finally preparing documentation for dispatch.

Freight forwarding refers to the coordination of freight movement, carrier selection, cargo clearance and tracking, and documentation of container cargoes. A freight forwarding agency obtains, prepares, and checks customs and insurance documentation to comply with various regulations of different countries. It may also develop appropriate routes for shipment and arrange payments for subsequent services on behalf of the clients.

Transportation refers to material transport from the shipper to the consignee carried out by sea (or river), air, and land. Transportation is an important part of logistics in terms of total logistics costs. Swenseth and Godfrey (2002) mention that the cost of transportation can be as high as 50% of overall logistics costs.

Depot operations refer to obtaining containers, doing major and minor maintenance, container modification, container inspections (to adhere to the standards as per the Institute of International Container Lessors), storing, releasing, and tracking of container movements. Therefore, proper documentation is necessary to manage containers properly.

Logistics and ICT

One study has shown that in the United States, logistics costs amounts to 6-11% of total sales and about 8-9% of a country's GDP can come from logistics activities alone (Langley, Allen, & Colombo, 2003). It is also shown that with the use of ICT, logistics costs could be reduced by as much as 50% (Gattorna & Berger, 2001). The use of ICT can enhance internal communication capabilities, speed and information accuracy (Huber, 1990). However, the adoption of ICT in different companies may be hindered by the size of the company. While large companies may be motivated to invest in ICT because of their long term business focus, smaller companies may not be motivated to adopt a full fledged ICT system due to smaller business volume and higher investment requirements (Pokharel, 2005). Therefore, larger companies might spend more on ICT than the smaller companies (Mitra & Chaya, 1996). Dawe (1994) mentions that companies that shy away from ICT investments generally cite examples such as obsolescence and irrelevance of applications to a firm's particular information needs.

DEVELOPMENT OF METHODOLOGY

The development of research framework to carry out the study, sampling method, and data analysis methods are the focus of this section. We present some hypothetical constructs to establish the relation between various parameters that can be obtained from the survey. It is to be noted that completeness on the response to all questions in survey questionnaire is essential to draw conclusions from this type of analysis.

Research Framework

Development of a research framework to understand the underlying relation between different factors with ICT has been proposed by various authors (see for example, Andersen, 2001; Byrd & Davidson, 2003; Carbonara, 2005; Klein, 2007; Nanang, Pokharel, & Jiao, 2003; Ngai, Lai, & Cheng, 2007; Pokharel, 2005; Spanos, Prastacos, & Poulymenakou, 2002). Andersen (2001) has used a framework that shows relation among six different factors—the use of Internet, organizational performance, strategic planning, decentralized decision making, computer network, and the level of environmental dynamism and complexity. Spanos et al. (2002) have used five factors—structure, strategy, human capital and management systems, and ICT adoption—to pose four research questions. The research framework adopted by Byrd and Davidson (2003) considers five different factors—IT department technical quality, IT plan utilization, top management support for IT, IT impact on supply chain, and firm's performance. Nanang et al. (2003) use a framework to examine the relation of company information, information technology, and warehouse operations with the status of IT use in warehouses. Similarly Carbonara (2005) use nine different factors, Pokharel (2005) use five factors, Klein (2007) use seven factors, and Ngai et al. (2007) use four factors to develop research framework for their studies. Some of these studies have analyzed the research question in relation to one identified factor while others have studied relations with more than one factor mentioned in their research framework.

The effective use of ICT can be described in terms of coordination of internal and external functions by an organization in order to increase the customer service level. The use of ICT in external functions could be influenced by size, ownership, targeted market, and type of products handled by the organization. While the use of ICT in internal function could be influenced by the exposure of the company decision makers or senior level managers (what motivates them and what stops them from adopting it), annual revenues, availability of suitable ICT hardware and software in the market, and the employee expertise in handing ICT functions. Based on the above, a research framework has been proposed in Figure 1 for analyzing the relationship between ICT and different variables. Each of the links (arrows) in Figure 1 poses a research question. For example, the link between the size of the company and ICT use addresses the research question—"is the level of ICT use related to the change in size of an organization?" Similar analysis can be done between the types of industries served and the ICT use.

A good research framework addresses the outlined research questions and leads to the design of a good questionnaire. However, questionnaire should be validated with academics (for clarity suitability of analysis) and with practitioners (for clarity ease in providing the answer). Pretesting for evaluation of questionnaires has also been mentioned by Kitchenham and Pfleeger (2002b).

Two types of questions are generally seen in the survey instruments—open and closed (Kitchenham & Pfleeger, 2002a). While open questions are for respondents to write their own reply, closed questions are for selecting answers from the list of predefined choices. Closed questions are easier to analyze and they can also contain questions on ordinal scale (Kitchenham & Pfleeger, 2002a). Such questions take shorter time to complete than those that are open (Kitchenham & Pfleeger, 2002a). Therefore, methods like preempting the answers and providing a Likert-type scale can provide some relief to the respondents. This type of scale is also adopted by Andersen (2001) to study the potential performance improvements on an organization's communication capability. Nanang et al. (2003) and Pokharel (2005) have also used this type of scale in their surveys.

Sampling Method

Establishing an approximate number of companies in logistics is the first step in conducting the survey. If such information could be obtained,

further sampling can be done. For the number of logistics companies in a region or a country, researchers can seek the information from various associations dealing with logistics sector. Some of the examples of those associations are: Logistics Association of Australia (http://www.laa.asn. au/home), Asian Logistics Directory (http://www. schednet.com/), Singapore Logistics Association (http://www.sla.org.sg/index.shtm), European Logistics Association (http://www.elalog.org/), Hong Kong Logistics Association (http://www. hkla.org.hk/), and Supply Chain & Logistics Association Canada (http://www.sclcanada.org/index. php?id=10). The names of logistics companies in Singapore can also be obtained from http://www. thegreenbook.com.

Selection of sample size for the survey can be done by using probabilistic or nonprobabilistic methods (Kitchenham & Pfleeger, 2002c) as discussed next. In probabilistic methods, such as random sampling, each organization in the large population is assumed to have a probability of being included in the sample. Applicable probabilistic sampling methods for organizational surveys are random sampling, stratified sampling, cluster sampling, and systematic sampling. Random sampling can be used when the population size is too large. In stratified random sampling,

Figure 1. Research on ICT use

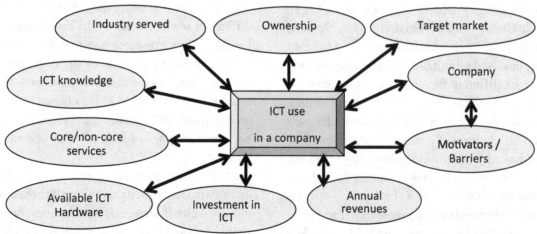

logistics companies can be grouped according to the service that they provide; then a percentage population is selected randomly from each group as sample. In cluster sampling, samples can be chosen from the list of members of associations, like transport associations, dealing with a particular logistics service group. This type of sampling is also used by Kuan and Chau (2001) to study EDI adoption in small businesses. In systematic sampling, every *n*th organization in the list is selected for survey.

The nonprobabilistic sampling methods are good when the population and its size are hard to identify, which is often the case in this type of surveys dealing with services provided by the organizations. Therefore, sample size is based on convenience (for example, time, cost, ease in carrying survey, and resources devoted for the survey) or quota (judgment used for choosing the sample from a stratified sample) or snowballing (referrals from other organizations).

The total number of samples for survey can be obtained through standard sampling methods, for example, by using statistical parameters (such as standard deviation and mean) of similar surveys. However, for the type of survey mentioned in this chapter, sample size can be calculated by using convenience sampling, for example, fixing the number of companies to survey and then using random sampling to choose the companies from the obtained list. Nanang et al. (2003), Pokharel (2005), and Spanos et al. (2002) have chosen convenience sampling method for their study. A combination of stratified (or systematic) sampling and convenience sampling is used by Joshi, Kathuria, and Porth (2003) and Ellram and Zsidisin (2002) for the selection of sample size.

Understanding Survey Response Rate

In this type of surveys, number of respondents becomes an important criterion to make a meaningful inference from the analysis. However, literature search shows that many of this type of surveys get less than 30% response rate—Tay and Kam (2001) report 8.8%; Nanang et al. (2003) report 10.7%; and Sum and Teo (1999) reported 11.1% response rate for their surveys. Augur, Barnir, and Gallaugher (2003) have reported only 15.3% response rate from those companies who initially agreed to complete the surveys. The companies could cite many reasons, for example, lack of time, personnel, data, and other factors for not responding to such surveys.

When the total population size is small (less than 30 organizations) and only a few of these organizations show interest in participating in the surveys, an interview based survey can be conducted. Pan and Pokharel (2007) have used this method to assess the use of ICT in hospital logistics. Citing McCracken (1988), Golicic, McCarthy, and Mentzer (2002) mention that qualitative inference can be made with as little as eight responses for most survey questions. When the response rate is low, the total number of returned questionnaire, as that mentioned by Lancioni, Smith, and Oliva (2000), should be taken into account. Responses from two dozens in a group would be good enough to start the statistical analysis (Motulsky, 1995).

DATA ANALYSIS

Survey data can be analyzed through descriptive and or statistical methods (see for example, Byrd & Davidson, 2003). Descriptive analysis generally refers to the characteristics or profile of companies. For example, Byrd and Davidson (2003) have presented their description analysis in terms of characteristics such as employee size, revenue size and industry group. Similarly, Klien (2007) has given descriptive statistics on the type of client industry, year of client relationship and client employee size to present their result on integrated e-business supply chain relationships. Other characteristics could be the year of operation of the company, budget, types of services provided, ownership of the company, types of ICT hardware and software used for logistics functions, motivators and barriers to use ICT and the mean, and standard deviation of various characteristics. Descriptive analysis method is also used by Davies, Mason, and Lalwani (2007) to study the impact of ICT on haulage industry in UK.

Descriptive Factors for Analysis

Some of the factors that can be used for the analysis of respondents are discussed below.

Company Size

The size of logistics companies is categorized either in terms of employee size or in terms of revenues or initial investments. Attempt should be made to present data table correlating employee size and operating revenues. However, our experience is that companies are reluctant to give their revenue figures; therefore, in such cases, the information on employee size itself might have to be assumed as the key factor to segregate the companies.

ICT Implementation

The survey can identify the types of ICT used in logistics companies. Our experience is that the development of a comprehensive list would help in answering the questions faster. Companies can provide information on additional ICT they use for logistics functions.

ICT Value

The implementation of ICT types may not exhibit the widespread use of ICT in the company. For example, the existence of Internet does not necessarily mean that it is available to all the employees (or for all business activities) in a company.

Therefore, investments made in ICT should also be examined. In general, higher investment means a greater use of technology in logistics functions. Similarly, companies serving a particular type of industry can have higher investment in ICT.

Motivators and Barriers in ICT Implementation

In a survey of EDI adopters, Min and Galle (2003) found that the high cost of investment was a major deterrent for a decision EDI use. However, the authors also noted that recognition of ICT use as a part of corporate policy and a large pool of customers or suppliers using ICT were the motivators for its adoption. The cost for integration of new technology with existing system can be a barrier to ICT implementation (Jakobs, Pils, & Wallbaum, 2001). The lack of management support could also be another major factor in ICT implementation (Proudlock, Phelps, & Gamble, 1999).

Perceived motivators and barriers for ICT adoption can be measured on a Likert-type scale that ranges from "agree" to "disagree" on each motivator and barrier. Identification of these factors can help in improving the use of ICT in logistics sector. For example, the perception of problems of integrating the existing system with new technology could be addressed by ICT vendors.

Statistical Analysis

Statistical analysis refers to quantitative analysis method used to obtain insights on the collected data. Klein (2007) mentions that quantitative analysis methods can focus on structural equation modeling such as partial least squares, or testing relationships between latent variables, or specific construct measures for dependent and independent variables. Some authors have used Pearson correlation tests, chi-square tests, or t-tests for statistical analysis (see for example, Guimaraes, 2000; Nanang et al., 2003; Pokharel, 2005). In statistical analysis, hypothesis testing of relationship between various factors, as shown by arrows in Figure 1, is also conducted.

The choice of a statistical method to analyze the collected data depends on many factors as mentioned by Motulsky (1995). As per the author, if the distribution of the population is assumed as Gaussian, the response rate is not high and the statistical analysis requires comparison of paired and unpaired groups, then Student *t*-tests should be used for quantitative analysis. As the size of response grows, the *t*-distribution approaches normal distribution; therefore, it is a relevant quantitative method for comparison of respondents. Some relevant hypotheses (each is called the null hypothesis) that can be tested with Student *t*-test are given below. Hypothesis tests can be done either by comparing the *t*-stat values with *t*-critical values or in terms of a significance level (α) which is related to the confidence interval. In general, a 95% confidence interval (or α=0.05) is used to accept or reject a null hypothesis. These values, in turn, depend on the degrees of freedom. If the absolute *t*-stat value is greater than the *t*-critical value, then the null hypothesis is rejected and *vice versa*. As a proxy to *t*-stat values, *p*-values are used to reject or accept the null hypothesis. If a *p*-value is smaller than α (for example, *p<0.05* for 95% confidence interval), then the null hypothesis is rejected. An opposite of the null hypothesis is called an alternate hypothesis. For more details on student *t*-tests, readers are advised to refer Motulsky (1995).

Company Size/Revenues and ICT Implementation Level

In general, company size can influence the use of ICT in logistics companies. Annual revenues can also influence the use of ICT. In general, generation of higher annual revenues would require an efficient business process. However, it may not be true in all companies with higher revenues. Therefore, we can test the hypothesis of no significant difference on the use of ICT by companies of different sizes. The two null hypotheses can be written as:

Hypothesis 1a: There is no significant difference in the level of ICT implementation in the companies of different sizes.

Hypothesis 1b: There is no significant difference in the level of ICT implementation in the companies with different annual revenues.

Targeted Market and ICT Implementation

Logistics companies target local, regional or global market. If the market is larger, companies have a larger volume of transaction for which ICT based business process can be used. Therefore, the null hypothesis can be written as:

Hypothesis 2: There is no significant difference in the level of ICT implementation in the companies covering different markets.

Ownership and Level of ICT Implementation

Ownership of the company can have a significant role in the implementation of ICT solutions in logistics companies. For example, branches of multinational companies are more likely to have higher level of ICT implementation due to the requirements from their headquarters. Therefore, the null hypothesis can be written as:

Hypothesis 3: There is no significant difference in the level of ICT implementation in the companies with different ownership.

IT Knowledge and ICT Implementation

If a company has an ICT/IT department, then it can be expected that the staff in that department would have adequate knowledge to operate and maintain ICT infrastructure and functions. We can assume that having an ICT department means more ICT knowledge within the company and therefore, it should have a full fledged use of ICT. However, this may not be necessarily true as ICT services may be outsourced to third parties. Therefore, the null hypothesis can be written as:

Hypothesis 4: There is no significant difference in the level of ICT implementation in companies with and without prevailing ICT knowledge.

Logistics Service and ICT Implementation

Although logistics companies can provide more than one service, companies providing a particular type of logistics service, for example freight forwarding, could have a higher ICT use. However, the complexity in handling more than one logistics service may also require better ICT infrastructure. Therefore, next hypothesis can be written as:

Hypothesis 5: There is no significant difference in the level of ICT implementation in the companies providing one and more types of logistics services.

Types of Industry Served and ICT Implementation

Company servicing one type of products might have to align themselves with their client due to potentially large volume of such materials. However, when more than one type of product is handled, the process to handle inventory, transportation, or custom clearance might be different.

Similarly, companies dealing with industrial goods could differ from companies dealing with consumer products alone. In general, companies dealing with industrial goods might have to implement ICT to align themselves with their parent company and to satisfy the customer demands as soon as possible. Also, companies dealing with

consumer goods might have to track and trace the flow of materials, demand, supplies, and the inventory, which requires better ICT infrastructure. Therefore, the following two hypotheses can be written as:

Hypothesis 6a: There is no significant difference in the level of ICT implementation in the companies serving one or more types of products.

Hypothesis 6b: There is no significant difference in the level of ICT implementation in the companies providing industrial or consumer products.

Motivators and ICT

Statistical analysis could also be done to show the relation between the influencing factors relating to ICT implementation. As shown in Figure 1, there could be a relation between the size of the company and the motivators or barriers for the implementation of ICT. It is generally assumed that larger companies are positive towards ICT implementation. Similarly, smaller companies could have more barriers to ICT implementation. Therefore, the following two null hypotheses can be written as:

Hypothesis 7a: There is no significant difference between the size of the company and the motivation to use ICT.

Hypothesis 7b: There is no significant difference between the size of the company and the barriers of use ICT.

ICT Hardware and Investments and the Level of ICT Implementation

In general, the more the availability ICT hardware in a logistics company, the higher the level of ICT implementation in their business processes. Also, if the value of ICT used is high, the company might be using relevant large scale software and hardware for their business processes. Therefore, the two null hypotheses can be written as:

Hypothesis 8a: There is no significant difference in the level of ICT implementation in the companies with different levels of installed ICT hardware.

Hypothesis 8b: There is no significant difference in the level of ICT implementation in the companies with different values of installed ICT hardware.

CASE STUDY

We have developed a hypothetical case study by assuming four main logistics services—warehousing, transportation, freight forwarding, and depot operations. We assume that the true population of companies providing logistics services cannot be established and, therefore, we have to prepare a list of logistics companies from some published information. The prepared list can be used for random sampling for survey.

Development of Questionnaire

A sample questionnaire that can be used to obtain data for assessing the use of ICT in logistics sector is given in the annex of this chapter. The questionnaire is divided into two parts so that it can be filled by a senior person from the company. The design of questionnaire should take cultural factors into account. Some companies might find the questionnaire easy to respond, while others may find it too time consuming and ambiguous. Therefore, the given set of questions could be taken as the set of base questions for developing questionnaires in different cultural contexts.

Sampling Method

We assume that data is collected from an established source (through the Internet or directory of business associations). We assume that the questionnaire is sent to a list of randomly selected 1,000 companies. It is further assumed that 311 questionnaires are returned, of which 52 are postal return due to nonexistence of the company at the given address and 7 are incomplete returns. This makes the total sample size as 941 and the total response rate as 26.8%. The following analysis is based on the responses prepared for this hypothetical case study.

Descriptive Analysis

The profile of the respondents can be established as given in Table 1. The table shows that among the respondents, only 31 companies have more than 100 employees. It is also found that more than two-fifths of respondents have 50 or fewer employees. Looking at the table, in terms of company size, companies might be grouped as "small" with less than 50 employees and "medium-large" with 50 or more employees. However, researchers can choose two groups as "small" with up to 100 employees and large with more than 100 employees as done by Pokharel (2005). The target here is to adopt a standard prevalent in the study area.

Table 1 further shows that about 60% of the respondents are local companies. In terms of target market, about half of the companies are serving to the global market and less than one third of companies provide services to the local market only. Local market here means the market within a country.

Most of the companies cater to the logistics needs of healthcare and electronics. About 20% of respondents (N=52) provide services to the automotive companies. Data analysis shows that none of the companies provide service to a single industry. It is seen that about 70% of the companies focus only on one logistics service. Further analysis shows that among the companies providing only core service, 32 are from warehousing, 86 are from transportation, 24 are from freight forwarding, and 36 are from depot operations. This shows that among the respondents, the transportation sector forms the largest group and the

Table 1. Characteristics of responding companies

Characteristics	Number
Company size	
• Less than 50	112
• 50-100 employees	109
• More than 100 employees	31
Company Ownership	
• Local	151
• Multinational	101
Target Market	
• Local	77
• Local-Regional	53
• Global	122
Serviced Industries	
• Electronics	171
• Chemical	79
• Healthcare	157
• Precision	48
• Construction	77
• Automotive	52
• Telecommunications	109
• Food and Beverages	105
Logistics activities	
• Only one core activity	178
• More than one activity	74
Annual Revenues	
• Less than $1 million	14
• $1 m-$10m	33
• $10m-$50m	89
• More than $50m	116

freight forwarding is the smallest group. Similar analysis can be done for companies providing more than one logistics service.

In terms of annual revenues, more than 45% of the companies earn more than $50 million annually. Only 14 companies earn $1 million or less. For the purpose of comparison between the mean values of two groups, if necessary, revenues of $50 million can be assumed as the cut off point.

Table 2 provides ICT characteristics of the respondents. Data shows that more than 50%

of the companies have an ICT department. The examination of the value of ICT in the company shows that more than 65% of the companies have ICT hardware and software worth more than $100,000. The response showed that none of the companies reported as having equipment worth less than $50,000.

Data shows that, on an average, each responding company has more than five types of ICT hardware. All of the responding companies had computers and fax machines and about 60% of them also had a computer scanner. Similarly, about 40% of the companies had image capturing devices. Although all the companies have computers, only 159 respondents mentioned that they have Internet facilities; therefore, not all the companies having computer use Internet

Table 2. Characteristics of the respondents related to ICT

Characteristics	Number
ICT knowledge	
• Have ICT Department	136
• Do not have ICT Department	116
ICT Hardware	
• Computer and fax	252
• Internet	159
• Scanner	145
• Image capture (video/digital image)	99
• Automated Guided Vehicle	87
• EDI	83
• Bar code scanner	67
• Handheld computer	56
• Sorting device	47
• Voice Recognition	43
• RFID	28
• Wireless data transmission	19
• Automated storage and retrieval system	10
ICT Value	
• Less than $100,000	83
• $100,000 or more	169

or Web-based processing of logistics functions. These companies can be promoted to use wireless access, if not land line, of Internet facilities to increase their processing efficiency.

Table 3 gives the average values for different influencing factors for ICT implementation in logistics companies. A Likert-type 3-scale is used (as given in the questionnaire) to assess the status

Table 3. Factors influencing ICT use

Factors	Mean±Std
Implementation Status	
• Order Processing	3.00±0.00
• Accounting/Financial Processing	2.70±0.40
• Warehouse Management System	2.42±0.79
• Customs Documentation Management System	2.40±0.50
• Transportation Management System	2.25±0.94
• Human Resource Management	2.25±0.43
• Software of Container Packaging or Palleting	1.79±0.91
Motivators	
• Increasing business process efficiency	3.00±0.00
• Reducing data entry error	2.90±0.30
• Reducing order processing time	2.60±0.60
• Decreasing labor cost	2.31±0.48
• Helping clients to reduce inventory costs	2.00±1.00
• Facilitating timely payments	2.00±1.00
• Helping clients to improve customer service level	1.90±0.80
• Aligning with corporate policy	1.60±0.60
Barriers	
• The company does not have sufficient resources to implement ICT	2.94±0.23
• Currently available technology or software do not meet specific requirements	2.87±0.34
• Customers or suppliers' software not compatible	2.78±0.43
• Difficult to justify investment and operation costs	2.73±0.64
• Associated or anticipated problems of computer virus	2.68±0.58
• Management does not perceive the need as yet	2.44±0.59
• Fear of not achieving expected work efficiency	2.30±0.60
• Unaware of software available in the market	2.26±0.44
• Current structure of the organization does not promote the use of ICT	2.03±0.49
• Difficult in finding qualified people to operate the existing system	2.00±1.00
• Improvement in business process is not obvious	2.00±1.00
• Many software available and therefore, difficult to choose one	2.00±0.93
• Perceived continuous investment in technology	1.80±0.90
• Purchase, implementation, and operation takes a long time	1.60±0.84
• The available software does not interface with the company's information system	1.49±0.71

(or level) of ICT implementation, motivators and barriers. Table 3 shows that order processing is used by all the respondents, whereas return material management system is used by only a few of the respondents. Most of the companies have implemented ICT systems at least partially to cater to business processing needs of the companies.

Statistical Analysis

Only four of the hypotheses mentioned earlier will be explained here for the purpose of illustration: the relation between company size and ICT; industries served and ICT; core/noncore service offered and ICT; and finally, motivators and ICT. In terms of motivators, relationship will be tested between large and small logistics companies. We use two sided test by assuming unequal variances between the samples in two groups being compared. The testing pattern and way of drawing inferences would be similar for other relationships as well.

Company Size and Level of ICT Implementation

As mentioned earlier, respondent companies can be grouped into small (N=112; implementation level mean = 2.42 ± 0.21) and medium-large (N=140; implementation level mean =2.41± 0.31) companies. Statistical test gives a t-stat value of 0.181 and (p=0.856). From *t*-distribution table or from the statistical software, the *t*-critical value is obtained as 1.969. As *t*-critical is greater than absolute *t*-stat for this test, the null hypothesis is accepted. Alternatively, the two tail *p>0.05* also indicates that the null hypothesis has to be accepted. From this, we conclude that there is no significant difference in the perception of small and medium-large companies on the implementation of ICT although smaller companies generally tend to focus on specific items and on local/regional markets. The lack of difference in the implementation level also shows that there

might be a competitive business environment in logistics and, therefore, all companies tend to implement ICT to the best extent possible.

Industries Served and ICT Implementation Level

Companies servicing to only one type of industry can have a different level of ICT requirements to suit their specific logistics functions. Therefore, another test is to examine the level of ICT implementation between industries providing service to one and more type of products. Data analysis shows that the average level of ICT implementation is 2.44±0.33 *(N=49)* for companies providing services to only one type of industry and 2.40±0.25 *(N=203)* for companies providing more than one service. On absolute terms, the mean is not that different between the two groups. Statistical analysis gives a *t*-stat value of 0.762 (p=0.45). Therefore, as in the earlier case, as *p>0.05*, it can be concluded that there is no significant difference between the perception on ICT implementation by logistics companies providing services to one or more types of industry. When companies provide services to only one type of industry, there might be a need to increase business process efficiency to meet the specialized customers. However, when the companies are providing services to more than one type of industry, integration of business processes could be difficult but implementation of ICT can help in achieving integration and efficiency in business processes.

Core Service and ICT Implementation

Due to the nature of business, companies providing a particular type of service may perceive the need for higher level of ICT than those providing more than one service. To examine this, the respondents are grouped into companies providing only one service (N=178) and companies providing more than one service (N=74) in addition to the core service. The mean value for the two groups is

2.32±0.21 and 2.63±0.26. This shows a slightly high importance given to ICT by companies providing more than one service. However, statistical analysis gives a *t*-stat of 9.07 (p<<0.01). As p<<0.05, it can be said that the perception on the level of ICT implementation significantly differs between the companies providing only one or more logistics services. The companies providing more than one service perceive a higher level of ICT need in their business than the companies providing only one service.

Motivators for Companies with Different Sizes

Another analysis is done to find out the difference in the perception of motivators between small and medium-large companies. Table 4 shows the average value of perceived motivators. The analysis shows that small companies consider increasing efficiency and reducing data entry error as their main motivators for ICT implementation. Alignment with corporate policy is not considered as the prime factor, possibly because of the nature of business, which might require at least some inclusion of ICT in their logistics functions. In medium-large companies, efficiency and reduction in data entry errors are the two main motivators. Alignment of corporate policy is the least concerned feature in these companies as well. Compared to small companies, helping clients to reduce inventory costs and increasing service levels are not featured as important motivators in medium-large companies.

Statistical analysis shows that none of the company groups show significant difference in their perception on the motivators, when 95% confidence interval is considered. However, for 90% confidence interval, the perception of the companies is changed for decreasing labor cost and improving customer service level. Smaller companies might be putting more importance on these factors (due to a positive *t*-stat value) than their larger counterparts. Decreasing labor costs for internal economic efficiency and increasing customer service level for clients' satisfaction could be emphasized more in smaller companies due to their need to attract more business from clients and their referrals.

Table 4. Perceived motivators in different sized companies

Perceived Motivator	Average values		Significant values
	Small companies	Medium-large companies	
Aligning with corporate policy	1.6±0.6	1.5±0.6	0.506
Decreasing labor cost	2.3±0.5	2.3±0.5	0.902*
Increasing efficiency	3.0±0.0	3.0±0.0	0.023
Reducing data entry error	2.9±0.3	2.9±0.3	0.157
Reducing order processing time	2.0±1.0	2.6±0.6	0.224
Helping clients to reduce inventory cost	2.0±0.8	1.8±0.8	0.854
Helping clients to improve customer service level	3.0±1.0	2.0±1.0	0.905*
Facilitating timely payment	2.0±0.0	2.0±0.0	0.478

*significant at p<0.1 level

CONCLUSION

This chapter has provided a broad methodology to assess the use of ICT in logistics companies. The specific nature of logistics service used in the survey is highlighted in the descriptive analysis. The statistical analysis shows the relation between various company characteristics and their objectives.

The framework and the method proposed in this chapter are portable for use in similar kind of surveys where comparison of one group of respondents with the other group is required to understand their statistical significance. The use of *t*-statistics in this chapter is to show how a simple statistical method can be used to obtain important insights from the responses. However, as in all sample surveys, the basic assumption here is that the collected samples represent the larger population and the information obtained genuinely represent the facts.

The examination of four different types of perceptions in statistical analysis section of the case study is to show the insight of numerical results. Similar techniques can be used to test other hypothesis. The perception could be between the dependent (level of ICT implementation in this chapter) and one independent variable or between the two independent variables if they are known to influence each other.

FUTURE RESEARCH DIRECTIONS

This chapter is prepared to help the readers to understand the value of surveys in ICT or in logistics industry. Extension of the analysis can be done to test the hypotheses between the small and large companies within a group in service, for example, the difference in perception on ICT between large and small warehousing companies or the difference in perception on ICT between large warehouse and large transportation companies. Pokharel (2005) has shown this type of

analysis and has developed further insights on the use of ICT.

Analysis of survey data by using factor analysis to a group of variables could be an extension of this study. This will help in simplifying the influence of various factors on the use of ICT.

One of the elements that can be used to establish the use of ICT could be to find out how the company is currently communicating with their clients or business partners. Similarly, study can also examine the impact of outsourcing the logistics functions in terms of business efficiency. The required IT skills of the staff, for example, knowledge on word processing, spreadsheet, database management, or knowledge on particular software can also help in assessing ICT penetration in the companies.

REFERENCES

Andersen, T. J. (2001). Information technology, strategic decision making approaches and organizational performance in different industrial settings. *Journal of Strategic Information Systems, 10*(2), 101-119.

Andersen Consulting. (1998). *Logistics information system (LIS) study* (No. 4). Singapore National Computer Board.

Asian Logistics Directory. Retrieved June 8, 2008, from http://www.schednet.com/

Augur, P., Barnir, A., & Gallaugher, J. M. (2003). Strategic orientation, competition, and Internet-based electronic commerce. *Information Technology and Management, 4*(2-3), 139-164.

Byrd, T. A., & Davidson, N. C. (2003). Examining possible antecedents of IT impact on the supply chain and its effect on firm performance. *Information & Management, 41*(2), 243-255.

Carbonara, N. (2005). Information and communication technology and geographical clusters:

Opportunities and spread. *Technovation, 25*(3), 213-222.

Closs, D. J., Goldsby, T. J., & Clinton, S. R. (1997). Information technology influences on world class logistics capability. *International Journal of Physical Distribution and Logistics Management, 27*(1), 4-17.

Cohen, G., Salomon, I., & Nijkamp, P. (2002). Information-communication technology (ICT) and transport: Does knowledge underpin policy? *Telecommunications Policy, 26*, 31-52.

Davies, I., Mason, R., & Lalwani, C. (2007). Assessing the impact of ICT on UK general haulage companies. *International Journal of Production Economics, 106*(1), 12-27.

Dawe, R. L. (1994). An investigation of the pace and determination of information technology use in the manufacturing materials logistics system: A case study of Northern California's electronics manufacturers. *Journal of Business Logistics, 15*(1), 229-259.

Ellram, L. M., & Zsidisin, G. A. (2002). Factors that drive purchasing and supply management's use of information technology. *IEEE Transactions on Engineering Management, 49*(3), 269-281.

European Logistics Association. Retrieved June 8, 2008, from http://www.elalog.org/

Gattorna, J. L., & Berger, A. J. (2001). E-synchronized supply chain. *Supply Chain Management Review Global Supplement, 5*(1), 22-28.

Golicic, S. L. Davis, D. F., McCarthy, T.M., & Mentzer, J.T. (2002). The impact of e-commerce on supply chain relationships. *International Journal of Physical Distribution and Logistics Management, 32*(10), 851-871.

The Green Book, Singapore. Retrieved June 8, 2008, from http://www.thegreenbook.com

Guimaraes, T. (2000). The impact of competitive intelligence and IS support in changing small business organizations. *Logistics Information Management, 13*(3), 117-125.

Hong Kong Logistics Association. Retrieved June 8, 2008, from http://www.hkla.org.hk/

Huber, G. P. (1990). A theory of the effects of advanced information technologies on organizational design, intelligence, and decision making. *Academy of Management Review, 15*, 47-71.

Jakobs, K. Pils, C., & Wallbaum, M. (2001). Using the Internet in transport logistics- the example of a track and trace system. *Lecture Notes in Computer Science, 2093*, 194-203.

Joshi, M. P., Kathuria, R., & Porth, S. J. (2003). Alignment of strategic priorities and performance: An integration of operations and strategic management perspectives. *Journal of Operations Management, 21*(3), 353-369.

Kitchenham, B., & Pfleeger, S. L. (2002a) Principles of survey research part 3: Constructing a survey instrument. *ACM SIGSOFT Software Engineering Notes, 27*(2), 20-24.

Kitchenham, B., & Pfleeger, S. L. (2002b) Principles of survey research part 4: Questionnaire evaluation. *ACM SIGSOFT Software Engineering Notes, 27*(3), 20-23.

Kitchenham, B., & Pfleeger, S. L. (2002c) Principles of survey research part 5: Populations and samples. *ACM SIGSOFT Software Engineering Notes, 27*(5), 17-20.

Klein, R. (2007). Customization and real time information access in integrated e-business supply chain relationships. *Journal of Operations Management, 25*(6), 1366-1381.

Kuan, K. K. Y., & Chau, P. Y. K. (2001). A perception-based model for EDI adoption in small businesses using a technology-organization-environment framework. *Information and Management, 38*(8), 507-521.

Lancioni, R. A., Smith, M. F., & Oliva, T. A. (2000). The role of the Internet in supply chain management. *Industrial Marketing Management, 29*(1), 45-56.

Langley, C. J., Allen, G. R., & Colombo, M. J. (2003). *Third party logistics study results and findings of the 2003 eighth annual study.* Georgia: Georgia Institute of Technology, Cap Gemini Ernest and Young, and FedEx Corporate Services.

Logistics Association of Australia. Retrieved June 8, 2008, from http://www.laa.asn.au/home

McCracken, G. (Ed.). (1988). *The long interview.* Beverly Hills, CA: Sage Publications.

Min, H., & Galle, W. P. (2003). E-purchasing: profiles of adopters and nonadopters. *Industrial Marketing Management, 32*(3), 227-233.

Mitra, S., & Chaya, A.K. (1996). Analyzing cost-effectiveness of organizations: The impact of information technology spending. *Journal of Management Information Systems, 13*(2), 29-57.

Monteiro, L., & Macdonald, S. (1996). From efficiency to flexibility: The strategic use of information in airline industry, *Journal of Strategic Information Systems, 5*(3), 169-188.

Motulsky, H. (Ed.). (1995). *Intuitive biostatistics.* New York: Oxford University Press.

Nanang, D. D., Pokharel, S., & Jiao, J. (2003). Strategic use of information technology in warehouses: A Singapore case. *Conradi Research Review, 2*(1), 5-25.

National Computer Board, Gintic Institute of Manufacturing Technology and Singapore Confederation of Industries. (1996). *Survey on Information Technology in Supporting Supply Chain Management.* Singapore.

Ngai, E. W. T., Lai, K. H., & Cheng, T. C. E. (2007). Logistics information systems: The Hong Kong experience. *International Journal of Production Economics.* Retrieved June 8, 2008, from doi:10.1016/j.ijpe.2007.05.018

Pan, Z. X. (Thomas), & Pokharel, S. (2007). Logistics in hospitals: A case study of some Singapore hospitals. *Leadership in Health Services* (Accepted for publication).

Pokharel, S. (2005). Perception on information and communication technology perspectives in logistics: A study of transportation and warehouses sectors in Singapore. *The Journal of Enterprise Information Management, 18*(2), 136-149.

Proudlock, M., Phelps, B., & Gamble, P. (1999). IT adoption strategies: Best practice guidelines for professional SMEs enterprise development. *Journal of Small Business and 6*(3), 240-252.

Singapore Logistics Association. Retrieved June 8, 2008, from http://www.sla.org.sg/index.shtm

Spanos, Y. E., Prastacos, G. P., & Poulymenakou, A. (2002). The relationship between information and communication technologies adoption and management. *Information and Management, 39*(8), 659-675.

Sum, C. C., & Teo, C. B. (1999). Strategic postures of logistics service providers in Singapore. *International Journal of Physical Distribution and Logistics Management, 29*(9), 588-605.

Supply Chain & Logistics Association Canada. Retrieved June 8, 2008, from http://www.scl-canada.org/index.php?id=10

Swenseth, S. R., & Godfrey, M. R. (2002). Incorporating transportation costs into inventory replenishment decisions. *International Journal of Production Economics, 77*(2), 113-130.

Tay, B. S., & Kam, B. C. (2001). Information technology in logistics: Issues and development. In *Proceedings of the first International Conference on Integrated Logistics: Logistics 2001.* Singapore: Nanyang Technological University.

ADDITIONAL READING

Bharadwaj, A. (2000). A resource based perspective on information technology capability and firm performance: An empirical investigation. *MIS Quarterly, 24*(1), 169-196.

Bourque, L., & Fielder, E. (1995). *How to conduct self-administered and mail surveys.* Sage Publications.

Bowersox, D. J., & Closs, D. J. (Ed.). (1996). *Logistics management: The integrated supply chain process.* New York: McGraw-Hill Companies, Inc.

Brynjolfsson, E., & Hitt, L. M. (2000). Beyond computation: Information technology, organizational transformation and business performance. *The Journal of Economic Perspectives, 14*(4), 23-48

Chang, E., Dillon, T., Gardner, W., Talevski, A., Rajugan,R., & Kapnoullas,T. (2003). A virtual logistics network and an E-hub as a competitive approach for small to medium size companies. *Lecture Notes in Computer Science, 2713,* 265-271.

Chang, K. C., Jackson, J., & Grover, V. (2003). E-commerce and corporate strategy: An executive perspective. *Information and Management, 40*(7), 663-675.

Der, G. (2002). (Ed.). *A handbook of statistical analyses using SAS.* New York: Chapman & Hall/CRC.

Eng, T. Y. (2006). An investigation into the mediating role of cross-functional coordination on the linkage between organizational norms and SCM performance. *Industrial Marketing Management, 35*(6), 762-773.

Groves , R. M., Fowler, F. J., Couper, M. P., Lepkowski, J.M., Singer, E., & Tourangeau, R. (Eds.). (2004). *Survey methodology* (Wiley Series in Survey Methodology) Hoboken, NJ: J. Wiley.

Gutiérrez, G., & Durán, A. (1997). Information technology in logistics: A Spanish perspective. *Logistics Information Management, 10*(2), 73-79.

Handfield, R. B., & Nichols, E. L. (Ed.). (1999). *Introduction to supply chain management.* New Jersey: Prentice Hall.

Hsu, C., & Tsai, I. (1999). Logistics costs, consumer demand and retail establishment density. *Papers in Regional Science, 78*(3), 243-263.

Huang, C. Y., & Nof, S. (1999). Enterprise agility: A view from the PRISM lab. *International Journal of Agile Management Systems, 1*(1), 51-61.

Ju, T. L., Chen, S. H., Li, C. Y., & Lee, T. S. (2005). A strategic contingency model for technology alliance. *Industrial Management & Data Systems, 105*(5), 623-644.

Lai, K. H., Ngai, E. W. T., & Cheng, T. C. E. (2004). An empirical study of supply chain performance in transport logistics. *International Journal of Production Economics, 87*(3), 321-331.

Lee, H. G., Clark, T., & Tam, K. Y. (1999). Can EDI benefit adapters? *Information Systems Research, 10*(2), 186-195.

Lee, T. S., & Tsai, H. J. (2005). The effects of business operation mode on market orientation, learning orientation and innovativeness. *Industrial Management & Data Systems, 105*(3), 325-348.

Lek, C. L., & Al-Hawamdeh, S. (2001). Government initiatives and knowledge economy: Case of Singapore. *Lecture Notes in Computer Science, 2105,* 19-32.

Lesjak, D., & Vehovar, V. (2005). Factors affecting evaluation of e-business projects. *Industrial Management & Data Systems, 105*(4), 409-428.

Ofori, G. (2003). Preparing Singapore's construction industry for knowledge-based economy: practices and performance. *Construction Management and Economics, 21*(2), 113-125.

Peck, R., Olsen, C., & Devore, J. L. (2005). *Introduction to statistics and data analysis.* Belmont, CA: Thomson-Brooks/Cole.

Rayner, B. (1995). The premier 100. *Computer World (The 100 Supplement), 29*(41), 41-47.

Schuman, D. H., & Presse, D. S. (Ed.). (1996). *Questions and answers in attitude surveys: Experiments on question form, wording, and context.* California: SAGE Publication.

Tay, B. S. (2002). *Information and technology in logistics: A study in investment behaviour.* M.Sc. thesis, Nanyang Technology University.

Turner, T. J., Mendibil, K., Bititci, U. S., Daisley, P., & Breen, T. H. J. (2002). Improving the reliability of the customer order fulfillment process in a product identification company. *International Journal of Production Economics, 78*(1), 99-107.

Yang, S. M., Yan, M. H., & Wu, J. T. B. (2005). The impacts of establishing enterprise information portals on e-business performance. *Industrial Management & Data Systems 105*(3), 349-368.

Yazici, H. J. (2002). The role of communication in organizational change: An empirical investigation. *Information and Management, 39*(7), 539-552.

ANNEX

Sample Questionnaire

PART 1

COMPANY PROFILE

1. What is the staffing strength in your company?

Persons	Please √ as applicable
Less than 50 persons	
51-100 persons	
101-500 persons	
More than 500 persons	

2. Ownership of your company

Ownership	Please √ as applicable
Local Company	
Multinational Company	

3. Targeted market (or operating market) of your company

Targeted Market	Please √ as applicable
Local market (Country)	
Both local and regional markets	
Global market (can include local/region as well)	

4. The focus of your company's activities

Operations	Place 1 for core and 2 for other(s)
Warehousing	
Transportation	
Freight Forwarding	
Depot Operations	

5. Which of the following industry segments are your customers? (Please √ as many as applicable)

Customers	Industrial goods/ raw materials	Consumer products
Electronics/software		
Chemical/petrochemical		

Healthcare/biomedical		
Precision/ nano-technology		
Construction		
Hospitality		
Exposition		
Automotive		
Telecommunication		
Food & Beverage		

6. What was the total annual gross revenue of your company? (Please √ as applicable).

Revenues	(Please√ as applicable)
Less than S$ 1 million	
Between S$ 1 and 10 million	
Between S$ 11 and S$ 50 million	
More than S$ 50 million	

PART 2

INFORMATION AND COMMUNICTIONS TECHNOLOGY (ICT)

7. Is there an IT/ICT department in your company? Yes/No (delete as applicable).

8. Do you have the following ICT hardware in your company? (Please√ as many as applicable).

ICT hardware	(Please√ as many as applicable)
Computer	
Fax machines	
Computer Scanner	
Video Camera (including CCTV)	
Digital Imaging	
Internet/Extranet	
Bar Code Scanner	
Electronic Data Interchange (EDI)/E-Commerce	
Automated Guided Vehicles (AGV)	
Hand-held/On Board Computers	
Sorting Devices	
Voice Recognition System	
Wireless or Radio Frequency System	
Automated Storage and Retrieval System	
Radio-frequency Identification (RFID)	
Geographical Positioning System (GPS)	

9. What is the status of ICT implementation in following logistics functions in your company? (1= "not implemented"; 2: implemented partially"; 3: "fully implemented").

Logistics Activities	Status (1-3)
Order Processing	
Warehouse (or inventory) Management	
Transportation Management (Vehicle Routing/Scheduling)	
Accounting/Financial Processing	
Customs documentation Management System	
Human Resource Management	
Software of Container Packaging or Palleting	
Others, please specify:	

10. How much is the cumulative investment in ICT (hardware/software) in your company?

Investment	(Please√ as applicable)
Less than S$ 100,000	
More than S$ 100,000	

11. In your opinion, how would you rate the following expected motivators for adopting ICT in your company (1= "disagree"; 2="neither agree nor disagree"; 3= "agree").

Motivators	Rating (1-3)
Aligning with corporate policy	
Decreasing labor cost	
Increasing business process efficiency	
Reducing data entry error	
Reducing order processing time	
Helping clients to reduce inventory cost	
Helping clients to improve customer service level	
Facilitating timely payment	
Other motivators, please specify_____	

12. If you were to implement ICT, what barriers do you think would you have to face? (1= "disagree"; 2="neither agree not disagree"; 3= "agree").

Anticipated Barriers	Rating (1-3)
The company does not have sufficient resources to implement ICT	
Currently available technology or software do not meet specific requirements	
Customers or suppliers' software not compatible	
Difficult to justify investment and operation costs	
Associated or anticipated problems of computer virus	

Management does not perceive the need as yet	
Fear of not achieving expected work efficiency	
Unaware of software available in the market	
Current structure of the organization does not promote the use of ICT	
Difficult in finding qualified people to operate the existing system	
Improvement in business process is not obvious	
Many software available and therefore, difficult to choose one	
Perceived continuous investment in technology	
Purchase, implementation and operation takes a long time	
The available software does not interface with the company's information system	
The company does not have sufficient resources to implement ICT	

Chapter XIV

Empirical Investigation of Critical Success Factors for Implementing Business Intelligence Systems in Multiple Engineering Asset Management Organisations

William Yeoh
University of South Australia, Australia

Jing Gao
University of South Australia, Australia

Andy Koronios
University of South Australia, Australia

ABSTRACT

Engineering asset management organisations (EAMOs) are increasingly motivated to implement business intelligence (BI) systems in response to dispersed information environments and compliance requirements. However, the implementation of a business intelligence (BI) system is a complex undertaking requiring considerable resources. Yet, so far, there are few defined critical success factors (CSFs) to which management can refer. Drawing on the CSFs framework derived from a previous Delphi study, a multiple-case design was used to examine how these CSFs could be implemented by five EAMOs. The case studies substantiate the construct and applicability of the CSFs framework. These CSFs are: committed management support and sponsorship, a clear vision and well-established business case, business-centric championship and balanced team composition, a business-driven and iterative develop-

ment approach, user-oriented change management, a business-driven, scalable and flexible technical framework, and sustainable data quality and integrity. More significantly, the study further reveals that those organisations which address the CSFs from a business orientation approach will be more likely to achieve better results.

INTRODUCTION

Background

Engineering asset management organisations (EAMOs), such as utilities and transportation enterprises, store vast amounts of asset-orientated data (Lin, Gao, Koronios, & Chanana, 2007). However, the data and information environments in these organisations are typically fragmented and characterised by disparate operational, transactional, and legacy systems spread across multiple platforms, diverse structures, and different data formats (Haider, 2007; Haider & Koronios, 2003). The plethora of different systems makes it very difficult, even impossible, for a system in one functional unit to communicate with systems in other units. This lack of integration of information systems, together with the large volumes of transactional data which might be spread in different pools across the enterprise, can lead to increased difficulties in analysing, summarising, and extracting actionable information resulting in suboptimal management performance (Ponniah, 2001). Moreover, heightened competition resulting from market deregulation as well as increased regulatory compliance and governance requirements, such as the Sarbanes-Oxley ordinance in the U.S. and the CLERP 9 Acts in Australia, have demanded greater accountability for decision making within such organisations (Logan & Buytendijk, 2003; Mathew, 2003).

On the other hand, existing management information systems are no longer adequate for EAMO's modern business needs and not always meeting the expectations of decision makers at all hierarchical levels (Olszak & Ziemba, 2007). These systems were unable to handle the integration of different, dispersed, and heterogenic data within such enterprises. Nor could they effectively interpret such data in any broader contexts or discover new data interdependencies (Bui, 2000, cited in Olszak & Ziemba, 2007; Gray & Watson, 1998), due to improper techniques of data acquisition, analysis, discovery, and visualisation (Olszak & Ziemba, 2007). Therefore, in response to these pressing challenges of information dispersion and compliance requirements, EAMOs are compelled to improve their business execution and management decision support through the implementation of a contemporary BI system (Olszak & Ziemba, 2007).

According to Negash (2004), "BI systems combine data gathering, data storage, and knowledge management with analytical tools to present complex internal and competitive information to planners and decision makers." Whilst Moss and Atre (2003) state that "it is an architecture and a collection of integrated operational as well as decision-support applications and databases that provide the business community easy access to business data." Stated simply, the main tasks of a business intelligence (BI) system include "intelligent exploration, integration, aggregation and a multidimensional analysis of data originating from various information resources" (Olszak & Ziemba, 2007). Implicit in this definition, data is treated as a highly valuable corporate resource, and transformed from *quantity* to *quality* (Gangadharan & Swami, 2004). As a result, critical information from many different sources of an asset management enterprise can be integrated into a coherent body for strategic planning and effective allocation of assets and resources. Hence, meaningful information could be delivered at the right time, at the right location, and in the right form (Negash, 2004) to assist individuals, departments, divisions, or even larger units for improved decision-making (Jagielska, Darke, & Zagari, 2003).

From an architectural standpoint, a BI system is composed of a set of three complementary data management technologies, namely data warehousing, OLAP, and knowledge discovery (which is aided predominantly by data mining techniques). To be specific, Olszak and Ziemba (2007, p. 138) posit that a BI system is composed of the following components:

- Extraction-Transformation-Load (ETL) tools that are responsible for data transfer from operational or transaction systems to data warehouses;
- Data warehouses to provide some rooms for thematic storing of aggregated and analysed data;
- OLAP analytic tools to let users access, analyse and model business problems and share information that is stored in data warehouses;
- Data mining tools for determining patterns, generalisations, regularities, and rules in data resources;
- Reporting and ad hoc inquiry tools for creating and utilising different synthetic reports; and
- Presentation layers that include customised graphical and multimedia interfaces to provide users with information in a comfortable and accessible form.

In the past few years, the BI market has experienced extremely high growth as vendors continue to report substantial profits (Gartner, 2006a; IDC, 2007). Forrester's recent survey indicated that for most CIOs, BI was the most important application

to be purchased (Brunelli, 2006). The results of the latest Merrill Lynch survey into CIO spending similarly found that the area with the top spending priority was BI (White, 2006). These findings are echoed by Gartner's CIOs priorities surveys in 2006 which revealed that BI ranked highest in technology priority (Gartner, 2006b). In the most recent survey of 1,400 CIOs, Gartner likewise found that BI leads the list of the top ten technology priorities (Gartner, 2007).

While the BI market appears vibrant and the importance of BI systems is becoming more widely recognised, particularly in EAMOs, nevertheless few studies have investigated the implementation of BI systems in general and critical success factors in particular. Although there have been a plethora of guidelines from the IT industry, most rely on anecdotal reports or quotations based on hearsay (Jagielska et al., 2003). This is because the study of BI systems is a relatively new area that has primarily been driven by the IT industry and vendors (Jagielska et al., 2003). Therefore, empirical research to shed more light on those critical factors influencing the implementation of BI systems is desirable because the understanding of critical success factors (CSFs) enables BI stakeholders to optimise their scarce resources and efforts on those significant factors that are most likely to have an impact on the system implementation, and thus increase the chances of implementation success.

Research Motivation

CSFs have been one of the earliest and most prominent topics in the area of IS research (Lu, Huang, & Heng, 2006). Rockart (1979) defines CSFs as "the limited number of areas in which results, if they are satisfactory, will ensure successful competitive performance for the organisation." Whilst Greene and Loughridge (1996) assert that the identification of CSFs can help to clarify the nature and amount of resources that must be gathered to permit the project team to concentrate their efforts on meeting priority issues rather than what the available technologies will allow. Thus, the emphasis here is on "few" and "must go right" (Khandelwal, 2000). For obvious reasons, CSFs are high-level management considerations as distinct from a detailed set of project deliverable specifications.

The IS literature contains many studies that investigate the factors that impact the implementation of an information system. As a result of such research efforts, a number of critical factors have been investigated and identified; for instance, top management commitment and adequate sponsorship (Lu et al., 2006). However, while these studies are helpful, the complexity involved in the implementation of BI systems is arguably different from traditional systems development efforts (Bischoff & Alexander, 1997; Fuchs, 2006; Han & Kamber, 2001; Ponniah, 2001; Power, 2002). The implementation of a BI system is not a conventional application-based IT project (such as an operational or transactional system), which has been the focus of many CSF studies (Wixom & Watson, 2001). Instead, it shares similar characteristics with other enterprise-wide infrastructure projects such as enterprise resource planning (ERP) systems implementation.

That is, a BI system implementation is regarded as a complicated infrastructure project and is defined as a set of shared, tangible IT resources that provide a foundation to enable present and future business applications (Duncan, 1995). It is not a simple activity to purchase a combination of software and hardware, but rather it is a complex undertaking requiring requisite infrastructure and resources; initially it involves various stakeholders several months to develop, and it may possibly take several years to become adopted fully across the enterprise (Moss & Atre, 2003; Moss & Hoberman, 2004; Olszak & Ziemba, 2007; Reinschmidt & Francoise, 2000; Watson & Haley, 1997). Typical expenditure on these systems includes all BI infrastructure, software programs, licenses, training, consulting, and implementation

costs, and may demand seven-digit expenditure (Watson & Haley, 1997). Furthermore, BI stakeholders need to address issues foreign to the conventional systems, and these might include cross-functional data quality and integrity issues, technical complexities such as multidimensional data modelling, cross-organisational needs and socio-politics, and broader enterprise integration and consistency challenges (Shin, 2003).

Specifically, the key infrastructural component—a data warehouse—is a subject-oriented, integrated, time-variant, and nonvolatile collection of data that differ from conventional online transactional processing (OLTP) databases (Inmon, 1994). A complex data structure must be maintained in order to provide an integrated view of the organisation's data so users can query across departmental boundaries for dynamic retrieval of rich decision-support information. Furthermore, the BI system's architecture is highly complex owing to the back-end systems originating from multiple data sources and to the vast volume of data to be processed (Sen & Jacob, 1998). Moss and Atre (2003) reported that a surprisingly high rate of 60% of BI projects end in abandonment or failure due to an assortment of issues. The complexity of BI systems is further exemplified by Gartner's recent study which predicted that more than half of the systems that had been implemented would achieve only limited acceptance (Friedman, 2005). In brief, the implementation of a BI system is associated with many challenges as summarised below (Fuchs, 2006; Moss & Atre, 2003; Watson, Gerard, Gonzalez, Haywood, & Fenton, 1999):

- Lack of recognition of BI projects as cross-organisational business initiatives which differ from typical stand-alone solutions.
- Unengaged or weak business sponsors.
- Inadequate formal involvement from the business side of the enterprise.
- Inappropriate project team structure and dynamics.

- No software release concept (no iterative development method).
- No work breakdown structure (no methodology).
- Ineffective project management (only project administration).
- No business analysis and no standardisation activities (with too much reliance on disparate methods and tools)
- Underlying back-end systems and processes which originally were not adapted for BI applications because the normalised database structures in operational systems are suited to updating data, but not for exporting data to other systems.
- Poor data quality derived from source systems that can often go unnoticed until cross-systems analysis is conducted.
- Inadequate resources needed to keep the system alive and constantly adapted to the needs of users.
- The maintenance process for BI systems that tends to be vague and ill-defined because it is quite difficult to determine how the business users will work with the BI system if they are given such analytical and reporting freedom.

Despite the daunting complexities in implementing BI systems, there has been little empirical research about the CSFs impacting the implementation of BI systems. The gap in the literature is reflected in the low level of contributions to international conferences and journals (Yeoh, Gao, & Koronios, 2006). More importantly, the value of previous CSF studies will obviously decline with age (Little, 1998). As pointed out by Dickson, Leithesier, Wetherbe, and Nechis (1984), "New technologies, economic and legal conditions, and other developments will cause the relative importance of these issues to change and cause new ones to come into existence." Thus the rapid advancement of technology innovation in general, and the pace at which new technologies are being adopted in particular, will apparently influence the state of criticality for such types of CSFs research (Little, 1998). Furthermore, CSFs applicable to other types of information systems may not necessarily apply to a contemporary BI system.

Therefore, the increased rate of adoption of BI systems, the complexities of implementing a contemporary BI system, the scarcity of academic research, and the far-reaching business implications justify a more focused examination of CSFs as well as the associated contextual issues required for implementing BI systems.

BI System vs. Operational System

As the focus of this study is on BI systems, it is critical to understand how they differ from other systems, and especially those for operational and transactional purposes. In general, there are two fundamental types of information systems within the IS literature, namely online transactional processing (OLTP) systems (also known as operational or transactional systems) and online analytical processing (OLAP) systems such as BI systems (Datta & Thomas, 1999; Ponniah, 2001; Power, 2002). There have been numerous successful cases associated with OLTP-based operational systems, but the knowledge required for building these systems is not adequate for successful implementation of OLAP-based BI systems (Fuchs, 2006; Power, 2002). In fact, BI systems differ in many ways from operational systems that process business transactions (Power, 2002), and there is a need for a more sophisticated technical and philosophical understanding of BI systems. A number of researchers have described the differences between BI systems and operational systems (see Datta & Thomas, 1999; Fuchs, 2006; Han & Kamber, 2001; Ponniah, 2001; Power, 2002) and these are summarised in Table 1 below, followed by detailed discussion.

The major difference between operational systems and BI systems is in the general purpose

Table 1. Comparison of BI system with operational system (Adapted from Fuchs, 2006; Han & Kamber, 2001; Ponniah, 2002; Power, 2002)

Attributes	Operational system	BI system
Business purpose	Support the operational business activities in an efficient manner.	Support strategic and tactical activities by giving the right information and new insights to the business.
Characteristic	Operational processing	Informational processing
Orientation	Transaction	Analysis
Function	Day-to-day operations	Long-term informational requirements, decision support
Business	The users often have no choice whether or not to use the system; he or she is not obligated to use the system in order to conduct business.	"Voluntarily," in the sense that users can perform analysis and reporting with other tools (such as spreadsheets), even though it may be less efficient.
Education	Easy to plan, because an operational system often consists of fixed business process that need to be taught.	Difficult to foresee, as most BI systems allow for many nonprocesses based ways to create reports and analyses.
User type	Frontline worker, operational staff	Knowledge worker, managerial staff
IT support	Relatively easy to plan, unless the system suffers from quality problems.	Demands flexibility
Focus	Data in	Information out
Unit of work	Short, simple transaction	Complex query
View	Detailed, flat relational	Summarised, multidimensional
Operations	Index/hash on primary key	Lots of scans
Data content	Current values	Archived, derived, summarised
Data structure	Optimised for transactions	Optimised for complex queries
Database design	Entity relational based, application oriented	Star/snowflake schema, subject oriented
Access frequency	High	Medium to low
Access type	Read/write, update, delete	Mostly read
Usage	Predictable, repetitive	Ad-Hoc, random, heuristic
Number of records accessed	Tens	millions
Priority	High performance, high availability	High flexibility, end-user autonomy
Metric	Transaction throughput	Query throughput, response time
Response time	Sub-seconds	Several seconds to minutes
Number of users	Large number	Relatively small number
Development	Most operational processes are known and taken into account when implementing the system	The BI system develops over time, because it is often difficult to foresee the usage of a new and mostly non-process based system
User reaction in case of system failure	Immediate when the system is not working, because the day-to-day business stops	The user "can wait" in the sense that the business will go on, even though the BI system stops

of each. Operational systems are online transactional processing (OLTP) systems designed to expedite and automate transaction processing, record keeping, and simple reporting of transactions (Datta & Thomas, 1999; Power, 2002). These so-called "bread-and-butter" systems, such as sales order processing, procurement, inventory control, claims processing, billing, and so on, are not designed to provide business intelligence. They are used to run the repetitive, day-to-day core business of an organisation and to support its daily business processing by capturing information about the economic activities of the company (Ponniah, 2001). For example, information processed for each transaction may include a single invoice, a single order, or a single purchase. Hence, an OLTP system records current information and maintains a database of transaction information which is a predictable usage (Corey, Abbey, Abramson, & Taub, 2001) whereas a BI system uses those transaction data for analysis (Power, 2002). In brief, the purpose of operational systems is to record data in the database of computers (Ponniah, 2001).

In contrast, specially designed BI systems are not intended to run the core business processes, but aim to retrieve information from existing computer's databases (Ponniah, 2001). It is an online analytical processing (OLAP) system that is used to support decision-making and thus facilitate better managerial work. In this information environment, summarised and aggregated data are much more critical than detailed records (Datta & Thomas, 1999). As a result, business users are able to scour data for information about the business to provide tactical or even operational decision support (Turban, Sharda, Aronson, & King, 2007). Therefore, a BI system is intended to provide competitive advantages that make an impact on the bottom line of the organisation (Kulkarni & King, 1997). The typical output information consists of summarised reports and consolidated statements that provide a picture of the overall performance of the enterprise, and in so doing they enable insights, new thinking, and new understanding of the business to knowledge workers. The database typically contains long periods of historical data comprising hundreds of gigabytes and terabytes (Chauduri & Dayal, 1997).

An analytical processing using OLAP system is performed through comparisons or by analysing patterns. For instance, sales trends are analysed along with specific marketing strategies to determine the relative success of those initiatives. However, such analysis is difficult to perform with OLTP systems because the data are sourced from different information systems across multiple departmental units (Poe, Klauer, Brobst, 1997). In other words, a BI system can be viewed as market-centric with a shrinking information time window as opposed to an operational system that is customer-centric and time specified (Han & Kamber, 2001).

The differing requirements of OLTP and OLAP systems demand different data models for each type of system (Datta & Thomas, 1999). The relational data model commonly used in OLTP systems is not meant for effective querying and so is unlike the dimensional data model used in OLAP systems (Datta & Thomas, 1999; Goede, 2001). However, the dimensional design of an OLAP system is not suitable for OLTP systems because of redundancy and the loss of referential integrity of the data (Datta & Thomas, 1999; Goede, 2001). Although these two qualities are crucial in every information system, an OLAP system primarily emphasises flexibility in the retrieval of decision-relevant information in conducting analysis (Power, 2002). Also, Eckerson (2003) asserts that the relational design (of an OLTP system) enforces a business process structure which should not be changed regularly, but dimensional design (of an OLAP system) needs to be changed dynamically to meet the ever-changing needs of the business. Thus, an OLAP-based BI system aims to enhance effectiveness of business decision-making rather than increasing efficiency in processing transactional data (Power, 2002).

Moreover, the maintenance process for BI systems differs significantly from operational systems (Fuchs, 2006). Typically, an operational system implementation has a standard project management plan. Usually, the system maintenance and support are not considered as part of the project, but a future process for which a system maintenance team will be held responsible. Unlike BI systems, the maintenance part can be relatively small once the system is put in place. In contrast to operational systems, the overall project management of a BI system implementation takes into account the maintenance process during the outset (Fuchs, 2006). The BI project evolves into a process that turns some of the usual IT project phases into a well-defined repetitive process. In order to optimise the investment, the existing BI application would be measured against certain predefined metrics and overall benefits. Based on this, together with the evolving business and user demands, the system is further modified and improved. This adaptive process model acknowledges that the user's needs change over time and that their way of working with BI applications is often difficult to predict at one single stage. Thus the maintenance process optimises the current BI solution in corresponding to the changing needs leading to a perception of positive benefits (Fuchs, 2006).

Therefore, given the above substantial differences, organisations are compelled to implement two separate types of information systems, one being an OLTP-based operational system and the other an OLAP-based BI system. Whilst there have been a number of studies on CSFs for operational systems, their applicability to contemporary BI systems cannot be taken for granted. The subtle differences warrant rigorous research to specifically address the CSFs affecting the implementation of BI systems.

Research Aim

Given the motivation for this research and drawing on the CSFs framework developed in a previous Delphi study, the authors used multiple case studies to:

- Examine the CSFs and their associated contextual issues that impact the implementation of BI systems in EAMOs

The remainder of this chapter has been structured as follows. The following section describes the research framework and discusses the definition of success criteria in this study before elaborating on the research methodology. The later section then presents the research findings. In the subsequent section the authors discuss the findings of the study and then state their conclusions.

RESEARCH FRAMEWORK

Implementation Success Criteria

A rigorous review of the literature has indicated that it is very difficult to quantify the benefits of a BI system implementation using standard economic evaluation methods. While the cost and timeframe of a BI system implementation can be estimated, assigning monetary value to the benefits is difficult since the benefits can be intangible and transient (Rockart & DeLong, 1988). Instead, the return on investment in a BI should be included in those of the business process as a whole (Liautaud & Hammond, 2001). Therefore, the benefits perceived by business stakeholders in this study should be considered to be qualitative, and dependent upon the particular features of each individual case. Nevertheless, Delone and McLean (1992, 2003) have suggested that the success of an information system could be evaluated against a number of criteria, and other researchers, such as Wixom and Watson (2001) and

Ariyachandra and Watson (2006), have proposed additional criteria that can be used to determine the level of success of a data warehouse-based information system.

Based on their combined suggestions, especially Ariyachandra and Watson's proposition (2006), the implementation success criteria of this research takes into account two key dimensions: *infrastructure performance*, and *process performance*. The infrastructure performance has parallels with the three major IS success variables described by Delone and McLean (1992, 2003), namely system quality, information quality, and system use, whereas process performance can be assessed in terms of time-schedule and budgetary considerations. Specifically, system quality is concerned with the performance characteristics of the information processing system itself, in which the system should be flexible, scalable, and able to integrate data (Ariyachandra & Watson, 2006; Delone & McLean, 1992, 2003). Information quality refers to accuracy, completeness, timeliness, relevance, consistency, and usefulness of information generated by the system (Ariyachandra & Watson, 2006; Delone & McLean, 1992, 2003; Fisher, Lauria, Chengalur-Smith, & Wang, 2006). System use is defined as "recipient consumption of the output of an information system" (Delone & McLean, 1992, 2003). Given that many theoretical and empirical studies have used and tested DeLone and McLean's IS success criteria (albeit with a number of multiple dimensions), it is considered that the success criteria provide a solid foundation for measuring implementation success, and thus are suitable for this study into the related CSFs.

CSF Reviewed

In the previous section, the measure for implementation success was introduced and defined. Those success criteria serve as the operationalisations of this study's dependent variables. The focus will now move on to the dependent variables, the so-called critical success factors.

There is relatively little academic literature on the subject of CSFs for successful BI system implementation. The field of BI systems is driven by industry, and it takes time for a tradition of academic scrutiny and evaluation to develop into a comprehensive literature. Nonetheless, there have been a number of studies which have sought to identify CSFs for the implementation of a data warehouse. Since a data warehouse is a core component of a BI system, their CSF studies are believed to be applicable to BI systems. Specifically, the synthesis of the literature (conducted in an earlier phase of this research, see Yeoh et al., 2006) provides a theoretical platform for this study about CSFs affecting the success of a BI system implementation. Following the literature review, a Delphi study was carried out with a panel of 15 BI system experts in order to identify the relevant CSFs (see Yeoh, Gao, & Koronios, 2007). Based on the Delphi findings, a CSF framework was developed to incorporate those CSFs which were endorsed by the panel.

This research framework outlines how a set of factors contribute to the success of a BI system implementation. It postulates that there is a set of CSFs which determine the quality of the BI system and its information output which, in turn, have a positive effect on the users' attitudes towards the use of the system. In other words, this framework treats the proposed factors as necessary factors for implementation success, whereas the absence of the CSFs would lead to failure of the system. Subsequently, individual users and their respective organisations would assess the benefits of the BI system implementation. This perception of the benefits would then become part of an interactive, business-driven evolutionary continuum to further support evolving business needs for improved BI systems (Arnott, 2004; Arnott & Pervan, 2005). This framework, and its related research issues, are the foci for the data collection and analysis of this research. The framework's components are illustrated in Figure 1. Within the framework, description of

Figure 1. CSFs framework for implementation of BI systems

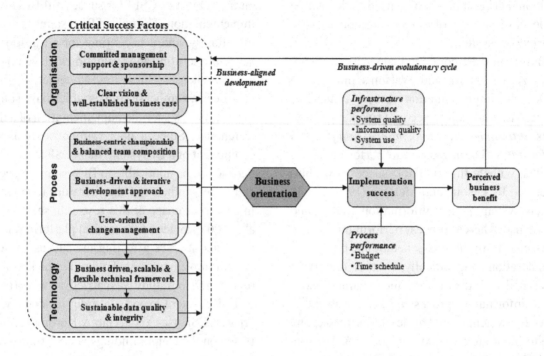

each CSFs identified by the Delphi study (Yeoh et al., 2007) is as follows.

Business orientation (BO) emphasises the business-aligned approach relating to the current and future needs of business intelligence in order to successfully address the CSFs influencing BI systems.

CSF#1: Committed management support and sponsorship. This refers to the commitment and sponsorship of top management to the BI initiative. This commitment is particularly required to overcome organisational challenges, including issues such as: flow of information, data ownership and technical framework development that is cross-functional, people issues, and consistent sponsorship of the initiative from the business side.

CSF#2: Clear vision and well-established business case. This refers to the existence of a strategic business vision with a clear outline of business objectives. In implementing BI systems, a detailed business case is required to describe the BI initiative in qualitative terms, and more

importantly it must be aligned with the business vision. The case should clearly outline the business needs, processes and inadequacies of the existing information infrastructure to address the core decision-support problems of the business.

CSF#3: Business-centric championship and balanced team composition. This refers to a business-centric champion who views the BI system in strategic and organisational terms rather than in technical terms. Ideally the champion possesses strong business acumen, is technically knowledgeable, and committed to the leadership of the BI competency team. The team comprises cross-functional representatives from IT and business. They provide a central location to drive consistent BI deployments, and this ensures ease in coordinating and supporting BI and performance management initiatives that span multiple departments.

CSF#4: Business-driven and iterative development approach. The scope of the BI system implementation is clearly defined at the outset, and an incremental delivery ("iterative") approach is adopted. The project commences in those areas which can readily be impacted in order to get buy-in and where programs can be scheduled to deliver quick wins.

CSF#5: User-oriented change management. Key users and relevant functional managers are involved throughout the entire implementation process, and during the business-driven, iterative maintenance process to develop further improvements. Training, education, and consistent support from the BI competency team are in place to induce individuals to embrace new practices, procedures, and technology throughout the period of the system implementation.

CSF#6: Business-driven, scalable, and flexible technical framework. This refers to the establishment of a strategic, scalable, and flexible technical framework covering both architecture design and data modelling in alignment with short and long-term business requirements, and including additional internal and external data sources. At the initial phase, a pilot prototype is used as proof-of-concept and stable source systems are in place.

CSF#7: Sustainable data quality and integrity. This refers to business-led establishment of common definitions, measures, and classifications that are used across the organisation, and the foundation of high-quality data at source systems, and a data governance framework is in place to monitor the data collection process.

RESEARCH METHODOLOGY

Methodology

This study applied a qualitative case study methodology with multiple-case design and content analysis techniques. The use of this approach is valid for the following reasons.

- As opposed to sampling logic, case study research is an empirical investigation

following *replication* logic that leads to analytic generalisation (Eisenhardt, 1989; Yin, 2003); by

- Investigating a relatively new research area within a real-life context (Eisenhardt, 1989; Yin, 2003); to
- Provide in-depth and rich contextual information which describes an actual situation (Robson, 1993); from
- Rigorous observation and systematic examination using multiple sources (Miles & Huberman, 1994; Yin, 2003).

It should be noted that, unlike sampling logic, replication logic is a purposive selection—it does not aim to generalise the findings to an entire population (Firestone, 1993). Thus multiple case studies in this study should be regarded as multiple experiments and not multiple respondents in a survey (Yin, 2003). That is, relevance rather than representativeness is prioritised in case selection. Within each case, and guided by the research questions, the need for in-depth investigation and richer understanding of critical factors within the organisation's real-life context was the subject of this study. Given the research objectives, case study research with multiple-case design was the appropriate methodology.

Research Site

In order to maintain homogeneity and thus lessening the potential for confounding effects of different industries and IT environments, it was decided that all case organisations should come from the same industry. The engineering asset management organisations (EAMOs), such as electric, gas, water utilities, and railway companies, were selected for three reasons. First, the types of information systems in these asset-intensive organisations are identical. Typically, they are composed of asset operational systems, maintenance systems, condition monitoring, work management, and contract management.

Secondly, due to fierce competition resulting from deregulation, increased regulatory compliance, and governance requirements, many EAMOs are on the verge of implementing large-scale BI systems, yet there is very limited literature to guide such organisations. For instance, a recent BI project introduced by an Australian water utility cost several millions dollars (LeMay, 2006). Third, the experiences of such EAMOs (that are traditionally characterised by its silo information environment) could provide better insights and richer contexts for comprehensive understanding.

Furthermore, fear of a shortage of cases was eliminated because this research was supported and sponsored by the Cooperative Research Centre for Integrated Engineering Asset Management (CIEAM). Hence, the BI system usage in this study focuses on the asset management business rather than the conventional market-centric applications. To assess the importance of the seven previously-identified CSFs, the authors studied five Australian EAMOs that had implemented BI systems. The backgrounds of these case companies are illustrated in Table 2.

Data Collection

Data collection for this study entailed semistructured interviews with key stakeholders of BI projects, and those interviewed included project managers, end users, key project stakeholders (who have been involved directly in either business or IT functions), and in two instances, external consultants/contractors. To facilitate data triangulation, data were also gathered from a number of sources including relevant documents (such as business cases), training documents, presentation slides, and publicly available reports (such as annual reports and financial statements).

In order to maintain consistency of questioning, the authors used the CSF research framework as a basis for the interviews, inviting participants to comment on the proposed CSF framework. After the interview, further clarifications (if any) were made by follow-up phone calls. The authors also observed the BI system in operation and gathered data about the CSFs for BI system implementation. However, the authors were cautious about being over-reliant on key informants, and attempted to seek contrary evidence when possible in order to corroborate findings and issues from other interviewees.

A cross case analysis approach was used in this study to gain better understandings and increase the generalisability of the findings (Miles & Huberman, 1994). In searching for patterns, the authors examined similarities and differences about relationships within the data (Eisenhardt, 1989). Hence, varying the order in which case

Table 2. Background of case organisations

Case	Types of EAM Industry	Annual revenue *	No. of staff **	Total assets #
C1	Rail transport and network access	M	M	L
C2	Rail transport and network access	L	L	L
C3	Builder and maintainer of large engineering asset	M	M	S
C4	Electric and gas utilities	L	M	L
C5	Water, sewage, recycled water utilities	L	M	L

Note: Case descriptions have been disguised slightly to preserve the anonymity of participants.
*Small=<AUD $100 million, Medium=AUD $100 to $1000 million, Large= >AUD$1000 million
** Small = <1000 staff, Medium = 1000-5000 staff, Large = over 5000 staff
#Small=<AUD $1000 million, Medium=AUD $1000 to $5000 million, Large= >AUD$5000 million

data are arrayed enables patterns to become more obvious (Stuart et al., 2002). Moreover, this research did not produce quantitative data. In all cases, the authors were examining the presence or absence of a particular CSF (e.g., were adequate resources provided?), while at the same time ascertaining whether that characteristic was fulfilled in a meaningful way.

RESULTS

Implementation Success

After analysis of the triangulated results for all five organisations, three instances of notable success emerged, together with one moderately successful case and one failure. The three successful cases of BI system implementation described their respective BI systems as stable, easy to use, fully functional, flexible, and responsive within anticipated times. Furthermore, the information generated was considered accurate, timely, complete, consistent, and relevant to most participants. In addition to the encouraging trend of system use among end-users, the project leaders of these organisations confirmed that their implementation projects were completed on time and within bud-

get. However, the moderately successful case was experiencing uncontrollable external factors in its BI system implementation. The key application of its BI system was not identical to those of conventional commercial enterprises. Due to its unique form of business and the peculiar bonus system with its major client, it was more concerned with ensuring on-time delivery of assets and meeting quality and safety standards rather than reducing costs or staffing. The BI system thus enables them to analyse and investigate underlying business activities with ease. Also, auditable reporting can be generated from the system to assist the business meet its strict regulatory requirements.

On the other hand, the firm that experienced BI failure did so because it encountered business issues at the early phase of its implementation process. The business needs and requirements for BI system had not been clearly defined, yet there existed silo information systems with multiple versions of the truth. In that firm the BI initiative was driven mainly by the IT department alone and was viewed as a technological issue, and as a result the management had to suspend the BI initiative. This instance of failure served as a useful contrast case for comparative analysis in this research. Table 3 summarises the findings of implementation success for all cases.

Table 3. Implementation success measure for the five cases (source: developed from field data)

Success measures / Case code		C1	C2	C3	C4	C5
Infrastructure performance						
1	System quality	✓	✓	✓	✓	N/A
2	Information quality	✓	✓	✓	✓	X
3	System use	✓	✓	*N*	✓	N/A
Process performance						
4	Budget	✓	*N*	✓	✓	X
5	Time schedule	✓	✓	✓	✓	X
	Overall	S	S	*N*	S	*U*

Note: ✓ =Good; N =Acceptable; X=Poor; S=Successful; N =Partially successful; U =Unsuccessful

CSFs Observed

To demonstrate how the implementation success compared against the management of the CSFs of the five case organisations, an analysis of the CSFs 1 to 7 was conducted through a cross-case analysis. Table 4 summaries the relevant CSFs performance in matrices recommended by Miles and Huberman (1994), and these were used as an initial step in analysing patterns in the data. For each case, management of each CSF is rated through a summary rating of ✓ (for a CSF that was fully-addressed), N (for a CSF that was partially addressed), or X (for a CSF that was ignored). Moreover, the summary ratings are supported through factual data from field research with each organisation.

OVERALL ANALYSIS AND DISCUSSION

The CSFs identified from a previous Delphi study were examined empirically in five engineering asset management organisations. This section discusses the qualitative results of the case studies. Essentially, the evidence from these studies clearly substantiated the construct and applicability of the multidimensional CSFs framework proposed in the previous Delphi study. More importantly, the studies further reveal the significance of addressing those CSFs through the *business orientation* approach. That is, without a specific business purpose, the BI initiatives rarely produce a substantial impact on business. As a result, the implementation of a BI system has a much greater likelihood for success when business needs are identified at the outset and used as the driver behind the implementation effort. Thus, the entire system implementation must be business-driven and organisation-focussed. It should also have interactive business-side involvement, and be adapted to meet evolving business requirements throughout the lifecycle. Invariably,

a "build it and they will come" approach which overlooks business-focused strategies in system implementation proves to be unsatisfactory and very expensive (Bates, 2000). In other words, this particular metafactor (i.e., a business orientation approach) dictates the commandment of the proposed CSFs, particularly within the following important aspects: business case formation, management commitment, championship, team composition, scoping and development methodology, organisational change management, technical framework development, data model, and data quality issues.

In essence, the three successful cases (C1, C2, and C4) seemed to emphasise the business-oriented approach when addressing the CSFs, while the partially successful case (C3) appeared to comprise a mixture of business and customer-centric approaches. The instance of failure (C5) was not totally business-driven but instead was technology oriented. The three successful cases shifted their focus from the technological view and instead adopted an approach that put their respective business needs first. On the basis of these case studies, it is apparent that the manner in which an organisation addresses those CSFs, whether through a business-oriented, technology-oriented, or customer-oriented approach, will have a substantial impact on the implementation outcome. Having a clearly-defined set of CSFs is important, but it is even more critical to address the CSFs from the right approach. In the case of BI systems implementation, the triangulated data of case studies clearly demonstrates that by placing business needs ahead of other issues an enterprise has a higher likelihood of achieving a useful business information system.

In order to meet the need for systems which provide management with dynamic analytics and business reporting, the findings of these case studies indicate that business stakeholders should involve interactively throughout the implementation process. One explanation is that a BI initiative "provides the users with access to

Table 4. Evaluation of critical success factors in multiple EAMOs

CSF	C1 (Rail company)	C2 (Rail company)	C3 (Large engineering asset builder and maintainer)	C4 (Electric utility)	C5 (Water utility)
Background *Note:* *BIS = BI system*	*Due to new arrangement, the company has acquired a competitor company and is now overseeing a much wider area of rail network. *The BIS success story of the acquired company has inspired the executives to expand the BIS initiative to an enterprise-wide scale. *In order to facilitate "one-stop" planning, reporting and business analysis, the company adopted BIS with great enthusiasm.	*The company has been using BIS for more than a decade initially for its various silo functional needs, such as safety reporting, network access, maintenance and operation. *To better facilitate overall business performance, the organisation has recently been restructured accordingly, and the silos BIS are undergoing amalgamation.	*BIS was implemented as part of its ERP package. The key use of the system is for business reporting, analysis of asset lifecycle performance and supply chain management. *Due to its unique business nature, the BI tool was not meant to cut down the operating cost or for competitive advantage, but rather to meet the strict compliance requirements and bonus system.	*BIS was implemented for advanced analysis, planning and risk management of the vast electricity network. *Due to market deregulation, legislative compliance and auditing requirement, BIS was adopted and widely supported by all stakeholders. *For the BIS, conformance and compliance is more critical than cost saving.	*The BI initiative was mainly driven by its manager of business information system, who is a technology enthusiast. *He has been promoting the advantages of BIS, and organised a number of interactive sessions with BI vendors. *However, the BI effort was not supported by business stakeholder, as they clearly failed to identify their BI needs and requirement.
1. Committed management support and sponsorship	✓ *There was consistent support from the executives, and direct endorsement from the CEO. *Their endorsement of the BIS commanded respect and interest among others. *Budget described as generous.	✓ *The initial BIS development was strongly supported by functional managers. *Now the silos BIS have gained the attention of top executives. *As a result, it involved some degree of organisational restructuring (i.e., an amalgamated BIS is in progress for its major network access and maintenance divisions). *Budget described as adequate.	N *Initially the executives focused more on the benefits of ERP than the BIS. *However, the BIS was gaining momentum as in supporting auditable business reporting and complying with the needs of its key client and strict regulation. *Budget described as adequate.	✓ *Top management support was strong, MD is crucially aware. *Budget described as generous. *Top-down commitment was shown in defining process of business needs and report requirement.	X *Top management was not convinced about the usefulness of a BIS to their business. *The executives rather supported its ERP modules expansion projects.

Note: * *denotes emerging finding from multiple case studies*

continued on following page

Table 4. continued

	✓	✓	N	✓	X
2: Clear vision and well-established business case	* There is clear business vision for the BI system adoption. * A link from the BI system to business objectives is defined. * The current BI initiative spans all functional boundaries of asset management. * The business case was highly endorsed by all relevant stakeholders.	* Initially the business vision was more functionally oriented, but recently an enterprise-wide business vision has been in place. * The recent amalgamated BI initiative was a vision of top management. The actual business case is still in the preparation stage.	* There was some degree of business vision in place, but the business case was mainly driven by its key customer who is still very influential. * The company was initially seen as a purpose-built contractor of the customer (who actually still maintains a large share of ownership with the company).	* The current BI initiative spans all functional boundaries of asset management. * The business case was highly endorsed by top management and supported by all relevant stakeholders, and particularly welcomed by business analysts and general users.	* There is no clear business vision from the senior management. * Business case was driven by technology and thus received little support from the business side.
3. Business-centric championship and balanced team composition	* The team consists of IT manager (champion) and several IS staff in partnership with external consultants. * Particularly, the champion played a successful role as "coordinator" among executives, business stakeholders and key users. * However, the actual construction of the system was developed by external consultants and contractors with the assistance of some internal IS staff. * On-going incremental development was carried out by the internal team.	* Owing to legacy, the two main silo BIS are championed respectively by two individual project managers. However, a "middleman" was recently appointed to coordinate silo BI systems integration issues from business perspective. * All systems were developed in-house and maintained by a large team and contractors. * The team comprises both BIS experts and business personnel. * Though the IT department alone comprises more than 50 competent IS employees, the challenges of silo BIS integration was due to the business issues.	* Initially, the manager of business information system acted as the champion, but the actual implementation was contracted to external consultants and IT vendor. * After the system was in operation, a business analyst was assigned to the role of system owner to oversee the maintenance task. Nonetheless, his role is more like a coordinator between users and service provider.	* The BI initiative was championed by a designated system manager, who was also a senior electrical engineer with strong business acumen. * The system was mainly developed by external contractors and assisted a team of internal IS staff. * For on-going development, a team of internal IS staff in partnership with external contractors acted upon the request of key users during regular review and, occasionally, upon ad-hoc request.	* The BI initiative was championed by manager of business information system, a technology enthusiast. * The BI team comprises IT personnel only with minimal participation from business side.

*Note: * denotes emerging finding from multiple case studies*

continued on following page

Table 4. continued

4: Business-driven and iterative development approach	✓ *Project scope was clearly defined, covering almost the whole enterprise. *Top-down approach for setting report requirements. *Incremental delivery approach was adopted over a number of phases to deliver quick wins. *The project started on area most easily impacted. *The team learnt from the BIS experience of acquired company, and practiced it in parent company.	✓ *Project scope is clearly defined by functional area, but not meant to be enterprise-wide. *For second phase integrated BIS, incremental delivery approach was adopted with the initial focus on business integration issues. *Technical solutions will be introduced later according to the identified business problems.	N *Project scope was limited to those involved in asset management and integrated lifecycle support area. *Top-down approach was adopted as the company had little choice over the system vendor.	✓ *Project scope was clearly defined for engineering side of the business. *Incremental delivery approach was adopted to deliver quick wins. *Reporting requirement was set via top-down approach, but bottom-up implementation was widely practised.	X *Project scope is clearly defined. *The project started on several areas at once, "big-bang" approach. *The team faced communication issues with the business stakeholders.
5: User-oriented change management	✓ *The project manager consulted the CEO and top management individually before making final case. *Key business stakeholders and users were involved with project throughout the implementation process. *Consistent support was in place.	✓ *The users were familiar with and dependent on the BIS, and generally welcomed the integrated BIS effort. *Education was not an issue. *When any new requirement arose from respective functional units, unit manager called-in as local champion. *Consistent support is in place.	X *Users were not consulted but rather asked to use the system, especially in meeting the compliance requirement set by its key customer. *Consistent support is in place.	✓ *Key business analysts/users were involved from outset. *Regular workshops were conducted with user group. *Consistent support was in place.	X *Business stakeholders and key users were not involved in the early phase. *Business side were asked to suggest their BI needs rather than based on genuine, evolving business requirement.

*Note: * denotes emerging finding from multiple case studies*

continued on following page

Table 4. continued

6: Business-driven, scalable and flexible technical framework	✓ *The ERP implementation laid a solid infrastructure foundation for the BIS. *The data model was flexible, scalable and extensible cross all functional areas. *The technical framework was standardised centrally and driven by business needs. *The compatibility of various analytical, reporting and mining tools with the ERP was validated at outset.	N *The silo BIS and ERP implementation had provided adequate infrastructure foundation for the integrated BIS. *Though the data model of silo BIS was adequate and extensible, it was not meant for integrated BIS. *Integrating those silo BIS posed compatibility issues due to different IT vendors. *The team was working on the broader data model and technical framework in order to integrate the silo BIS.	✓ *The ERP implementation laid a good infrastructure foundation for the BIS. *Although the data model was flexible, scalable and extensible, it was limited to certain functional areas only. *There was a standardised technical framework, but with limited extensibility. *There was no compatibility issue for the various analytical and reporting tools as those tools are strategic partners of its ERP system.	✓ *The implementation of integrated asset management system provides a good infrastructure foundation for the BIS. *The data model is flexible, scalable and extensible across all asset management domains. *There was a standardised, scalable and extensible technical framework to accommodate both advanced analytics and mining requirements.	N *The ERP implementation and various silo systems provide somewhat stable foundation for BIS infrastructure. *The data model is flexible and extensible but meant for functional needs. *The technical framework is extensible to accommodate BI requirement. *There is compatibility issues with various IS application.
7: Sustainable data quality and integrity	✓ *Master data management approach was adopted. *A data dictionary framework was in place. It included a data governance committee, corporate coding policy, corporate glossary, and data dictionary. *A corporate data model has been developed, which includes candidate information entities and subject areas and baselines. *In doing so, workshops, interviews and questionnaires were done; corporate systems were reverse engineered. *Transaction systems were aligned to facilitate common hierarchy for management reporting and communication.	N *A functionally-based data dictionary framework was in place, and includes corporate glossary and data dictionary. *To address multiple versions of truth, the newly appointed Integrated BIS champion and the business decision support personnel were preparing a core asset information oriented framework. *These silo BIS are reverse-engineered, high-level steering committee and workshops were in place.	✓ *The quality of data was adequate as most of the glossary and measures had been fully supplied by its key customer. *The role of the data steward was well defined as being the functional steward. *Within the system, there was an automated data quality "watchdog" mechanism to track operational data quality issues. *Data provider will be alerted and asked to solve the issues.	✓ *A data dictionary framework was in place. *Data quality working group, corporate glossary and data dictionary were in place. *There were regular workshops with the key users. *Users were pro-active to report any data quality issues, and actions were taken promptly. *Data cleansing tool was applied.	N *A functional-based data dictionary framework is in place. *Visualisation tool and pictures of assets were incorporated as part of data quality and validation effort. *The data inconsistency was usually validated by long-time experienced personnel.
*Overall business orientation approach	✓	✓	N	✓	X

*Note: * denotes emerging finding from multiple case studies* information that they did not already know that can actually be used to change their actions and decisions" (Hancock & Toren, 2006). In other words, it necessitates the participation of business stakeholders in the development of a process of business analysis and reporting that usually demands practical business experience (Hancock & Toren, 2006). Moreover, due to evolving business needs and ever-changing information requirements, it was found that the respective BI teams had to provide continual high-level maintenance and support not only on tools application, but also at broader data modelling and system scalability issues. The designing of data models and system architecture frameworks needs consistent input from those most familiar with the business needs of the enterprise.

In summary, the three successful cases clearly demonstrated that addressing the CSFs from a business perspective was the cornerstone on which they successfully based the implementation of their BI systems. Conversely, the unsuccessful case failed because it focused primarily on the technology and neglected the core requirements of its business. In order to better address the CSFs, it is essential for an organisation to emphasise the business orientation approach, and in so doing it will gain an advantage over competitors. Indeed, this view was supported by Gartner Research, which stated that, "best in class organisations focus on business objectives and use a business-driven approach to define and scope their people, process, application, technology and/or services strategy" (Burton, Geishecker, & Hostmann, 2006).

Also, it is relevant to note that in implementing a BI system neither data nor technical factors appeared to be as critical as other organisational and process factors. According to most research participants, technological difficulties can be solved by technical solutions. However, it was found that achieving management and organisational commitment for a BI initiative poses the greatest challenge because the BI teams considered them to be outside their direct control. The level of or-

ganisational support is reflected in the attitudes of the business stakeholders; that is, their attitudes to change, time, cost, technology, and project scope. Based on a large-scale survey result, Watson and Haley (1997) similarly pointed out that the most critical factors for successful data warehousing implementations (the antecedent of BI systems) were organisational in nature. Thus, committed management support and adequate resources were found to determine the implementation success because these factors worked to overcome socio-political resistance, address change-management issues, and increase organisational buy-in. This finding was also congruent with Gartner's recent observation that "overcoming complex organisational dynamics will become the most significant challenge to the success of BI initiatives" (Burton et al., 2006). Therefore, organisational and process-related factors must not be taken for granted in the implementation of BI systems.

CONCLUDING REMARK

Implementing a BI system is a costly, resourceful, and complex undertaking. This study examined the CSFs impacting BI systems implementation in EAMOs. Based on a previous Delphi study, it developed a multidimensional CSF framework for understanding those CSF issues. These CSFs are: committed management support and sponsorship, a clear vision and well-established business case, a business-centric championship and balanced team composition, a business-driven and iterative development approach, user-oriented change management, a business-driven, scalable and flexible technical framework, and sustainable data quality and integrity.

Subsequently, the proposed CSFs were then examined empirically in case studies of five engineering asset management organisations. The evidence from these studies clearly confirmed and substantiated the construct and applicability of the CSFs framework. Within the set of

CSFs, an analysis of the findings indicated that nontechnical factors, including organisational and process-related factors, were more influential and important than technological and data-related factors. More importantly, the research suggests that organisations are in a better position to successfully address those CSFs through the *business orientation* approach. Thus this business orientation meta-CSF should be regarded as the most critical factor in determining the implementation success of BI systems.

This research has made a contribution to our understanding of the CSFs that impact on BI systems implementation. The literature review reveals that there is a lack of research on CSFs for successful implementation of BI systems. This study, therefore, fills in the research gap. This research provides thought-provoking insights into multidimensional CSFs that influence the implementation of BI systems. The CSFs which have been identified allow a clear understanding of the pivotal factors that must be addressed. Hence, it focuses attention on those important areas that might otherwise be neglected or taken for granted but are significant for the implementation success. Moreover, the consolidated CSFs framework provides a significant contribution to theoretical understanding of how implementation of BI systems can be improved. More specifically, the findings suggest that in investigating the critical success factors researchers should not only consider the technical context but also focus on organisational and process dimensions to provide a more comprehensive research approach.

Not only does this research contribute to the academic literature on this topic but it also benefits organisations in several ways. The identification of CSFs enables BI stakeholders to gain a comprehensive understanding of those CSFs through a business orientation approach, especially in the planning and management of BI initiatives. Such outcomes will help them to determine those factors to which they should give priority. It also helps to ensure that those CSFs will receive deliberate

and continuous management scrutiny. For senior management, this research finding can certainly assist them by optimising their scarce resources on those key areas that are most likely to have an impact on the implementation of the BI systems. Moreover, the management can concentrate their commitment to monitor, control and support those critical areas of implementation. In short, the CSFs findings represent the best practices of firms that have successfully implemented BI systems. The empirical evidence that was revealed provides insights for BI stakeholders and will significantly increase the chances of implementation success. Those that address the CSFs from a business orientation approach and translate the business needs into a well-managed BI system implementation will likely succeed.

IMPLICATION FOR FUTURE RESEARCH

The results of this study suggest several areas for future research. They include replication of current study, theory testing research, and longitudinal study. First, this research focused on engineering asset management industries that implement BI systems for better managing their asset-intensive business. Thus, further empirical research in other industries or in other countries may shed light on where and how the research findings can impact the success of a BI system implementation. Research on cross-industry or across-country comparisons of CSFs will enrich and complement this research with additional insights, and possibly new understanding of factors.

As it stands, this study was exploratory in nature and hence quantitative research can be conducted using a structured questionnaire with adequate samples. It could provide insight into the correlation between factors identified in the CSFs framework and determine the generalisablity of this study. In addition, a longitudinal study may be useful to further test the theory built in this research. It would be ideal if a researcher could observe a case organisation prior to commencing a BI system implementation project, and then follow the progress of implementation to completion. Nonetheless, a longitudinal research would require a long-term commitment by both the researcher and the participating organisation.

ACKNOWLEDGMENT

This research is conducted through the Cooperative Research Centre for Integrated Engineering Asset Management (CIEAM). The support of CIEAM partners is gratefully acknowledged.

REFERENCE

Ariyachandra, T., & Watson, H. J. (2006). Which data warehouse architecture is most successful? *Business Intelligence, 11*(1).

Arnott, D. (2004). Decision support systems evolution: Framework, case study and research agenda. *European Journal of Information Systems, 13*, 247-259.

Arnott, D., & Pervan, G. (2005). A critical analysis of decision support systems research. *Journal of Information Technology, 20*(2), 67-87.

Bates, A. W. (2000). Chapter ten: Avoiding the Faustian contract and meeting the technology challenge. In T. Bates (Ed.), *Managing technological change*. San Francisco: Jossey-Bass.

Bischoff, J., & Alexander, T. (1997). *Data warehouse: Practical advice from the experts*. Upper Saddle River, NJ: Prentice Hall.

Bui, T. (2000). Decision support systems for sustainable development. In G. Kersten, Z. Mikolajuk, & A. Yeh (Eds.), *Decision support systems for sustainable development: A resource book of methods and applications*. MA: Kluwer Academic.

Burton, B., Geishecker, L., & Hostmann, B. (2006). *Organizational structure: Business intelligence and information management*: Gartner Research.

Chauduri, S., & Dayal, U. (1997). An overview of data warehousing and OLAP technology. *SIGMOD Record, 26*(1), 65-74.

Corey, M., Abbey, M., Abramson, I., & Taub, B. (2001). *Oracle data warehousing*. Osborne: McGraw-Hill.

Datta, A., & Thomas, H. (1999). The cube data model: A conceptual model and algebra for online analytical processing in data warehouses. *Decision Support Systems, 27*(3), 289-301.

Delone, W., & McLean, E. (1992). Information systems success: The quest for the dependent variable. *Information System Research, 3*(1), 60-95.

Delone, W., & McLean, E. (2003). The DeLone and McLean model of information systems success: A ten-year update. *Management Information Systems, 19*(4), 9-30.

Dickson, G. W., Leitheiser, R. L., Wetherbe, J. C., & Nechis, M. (1984). Key information systems issues for the 1980's. *MIS Quarterly, 8*(3), 135-159.

Duncan, N. B. (1995). Capturing flexibility of information technology infrastructure: A study of resource characteristics and their measure. *Management Information Systems, 12*(2), 37-57.

Eckerson, W. (2003). Evaluationg ETL and data integration platforms. *The Data warehouse Institute Report Series*, 1-40.

Eisenhardt, K. (1989). Building theories from case study research. *Academy of Management Review, 14*(4), 532-550.

Firestone, W. (1993). Alternative arguments for generalizing from data as applied to qualitative research. *Educational researcher, 22*(4), 16-27.

Fisher, C. W., Lauria, E., Chengalur-Smith, I., & Wang, R. Y. (2006). *Introduction to information quality*. Cambridge, MA: MITIQ Press.

Friedman, T. (2005). *Gartner says more than 50 percent of data warehouse projects will have limited acceptance or will be failures through 2007*. Retrieved June 9, 2008, from http://www.gartner.com/it/page.jsp?id=492112

Fuchs, G. (2006). The vital BI maintenance process. In B. Sujatha (Ed.), *Business intelligence implementation: Issues and perspectives* (pp. 116-123). Hyderabad: The ICFAI University Press.

Gangadharan, G. R., & Swami, S. N. (2004). *Business intelligence systems: Design and implementation strategies*. Paper presented at the 26th International Conference Information Technology Interfaces ITI.

Goede, R. (2001). *A framework for the explicit use of specific systems thinking methodologies in data-driven decision support system development*. University of Pretoria.

Gray, P., & Watson, H. J. (1998). *Decision support in the data warehouse*. Upper Saddle River, NJ: Prentice Hall.

Greene, F., & Loughridge, B. (1996). Investigating the management information needs of academic heads of department: A critical success factors approach. *Information Research, 1*(3), 1-3.

Haider, A. (2007). *Information systems based engineering asset management evaluation: Operational interpretations*. University of South Australia, Adelaide.

Haider, A., & Koronios, A. (2003). *Managing engineering assets: A knowledge based approach through information quality*. Paper presented at the International Business Information Management Conference, Cairo.

Han, J., & Kamber, M. (2001). *Data mining: Concepts and techniques*. San Francisco: Morgan Kauffmann.

Hancock, J. C., & Toren, R. (2006). *Practical business intelligence with SQL server 2005 (Microsoft Windows server system series)*. NJ: Addison-Wesley.

Inmon, W. H., & Hackathorn, R. D. (1994). *Using the data warehouse*. Somerset, NJ: Wiley-QED Publishing.

Jagielska, I., Darke, P., & Zagari, G. (2003). *Business intelligence systems for decision support: Concepts, processes and practice*. Paper presented at the 7th International Conference of the International Society for Decision Support Systems.

Khandelwal, V. (2000). What the Australian CEOs want from IT. *Research and Practice in Information Technology, 32*(3), 151-167.

Kulkarni, J., & King, R. (1997). *Business intelligence systems and data mining*. SAS Institute.

LeMay, R. (2006). Sydney Water signs business intelligence vendor. Retrieved June 9, 2008, from http://www.zdnet.com.au/news/software/soa/Sydney-Water-signs-business-intelligence-vendor/0,130061733,139268270,00.htm

Liautaud, B., & Hammond, M. (2000). *E-business intelligence: Turning information into knowledge and profit*. New York: McGraw-Hill.

Lin, S., Gao, J., Koronios, A., & Chanana, V. (2007). Developing a data quality framework for asset management in engineering organisations. *International Journal of Information Quality, 1*(1), 100-126.

Little, R. G. (1998). *Identification of factors affecting the implementation of data warehousing*. Auburn University.

Logan, D., & Buytendijk, F. (2003). *The Sarbanes-Oxley Act will impact your enterprise*. Gartner.

Lu, X. H., Huang, L. H., & Heng, M. S. H. (2006). Critical success factors of inter-organizational information systems—a case study of Cisco and

Xiao Tong in China. *Information & Management, 43*(3), 395-408.

Mathew, J. (2003). *CIEAM business plan V1.0.* Brisbane, Australia: Centre for Integrated Engineering Asset Management (CIEAM).

Miles, M., & Huberman, A. (1994). *Qualitative data analysis: An expanded sourcebook.* London: Sage.

Moss, L., & Atre, S. (2003). *Business intelligence roadmap: The complete lifecycle for decision-support applications.* Boston, MA: Addison-Wesley.

Moss, L., & Hoberman, S. (2004). *The importance of data modeling as a foundation for business insight.* Teradata.

Negash, S. (2004). Business iIntelligence. *Communications of the Association for Information Systems, 13*, 177-195.

Olszak, C., & Ziemba, E. (2007). Approach to building and implementing business intelligence systems. *Interdisciplinary Journal of Information, Knowledge, and Management, 2*, 135-148.

Poe, V., Klauer, P., & Brobst, S. (1997). *Building a data warehouse for decision support* (2nd ed.). New Jersey: Prentice Hall.

Ponniah, P. (2001). *Data warehousing fundamentals.* New York: Wiley-Interscience.

Power, D. J. (2001). *Supporting decision-makers: An expanded framework.* Paper presented at the Informing Science and IT Education, Krakow, Poland.

Reinschmidt, J., & Francoise, A. (2000). *Business intelligence certification guide.* San Jose, CA: IBM Corporation, International Technical Support Organization.

Robson, C. (1993). *Real world research.* Oxford: Blackwell Science.

Rockart, J. F. (1979). Chief executives define their own data needs. *Harvard Business Review, 57*(2), 81-93.

Rockart, J. F., & DeLong, D. W. (1988). *Executive support systems: The emergence of top management computer use.* Homewood, IL: Dow Jones-Irwin.

Sen, A., & Jacob, V. (1998). Industrial-strength data warehousing. *Communications of the ACM, 41*(9), 28-31.

Shin, B. (2003). An exploratory investigation of system success factors in data warehousing. *Journal of the Association for Information Systems, 14*(1).

Turban, E., Sharda, R., Aronson, J., & King, D. (2007). *Business intelligence* (1st ed.). New Jersey: Prentice Hall.

Watson, H. J., Gerard, J. G., Gonzalez, L. E., Haywood, M. E., & Fenton, D. (1999). Data warehousing failures: Case studies and findings. *Journal of Data Warehousing, 4*(1), 44-55.

Watson, H. J., & Haley, B. J. (1997). Data warehousing: A framework and survey of current practices. *Journal of Data Warehousing, 2*(1), 10-17.

Wixom, B., & Watson, H. (2001). An empirical investigation of the factors affecting data-warehousing success. *MIS Quarterly, 25*(1), 17-41.

Yeoh, W., Gao, J., & Koronios, A. (2006). *Exploring critical success factors for implementation of business intelligence systems.* Paper presented at the 6th International Business Information Management Conference Bonn, Germany.

Yeoh, W., Gao, J., & Koronios, A. (2007). Towards a critical success factors framework for implementing business intelligence system: A Delphi study in engineering asset management organisations. In L. Xu; A. Tjoa, & S. Chaudhry (Eds.), *IFIP Series Vol. 255, research and practical issues of enterprise information systems II* (Vol. 2). Boston, MA: Springer.

Yin, R. (2003). *Case study research: Design and methods* (3rd ed.). Thousand Oaks, CA: Sage.

ADDITIONAL READING

Adelman, S., & Moss, L. (2000). *Data warehouse project management.* Upper Saddle River, NJ: Addison-Wesley.

Chang, E., Dillon, T. S., & Hussain, F. K. (2006). *Trust and reputation for service-oriented environments.* UK: John Wiley and Sons.

Dresner, H., Linden, A., Buytendijk, F., & Friedman, T. (2002). *The business intelligence competency center: An essential business strategy.* Gartner Research.

Fisher, C. W., Lauria, E., Chengalur-Smith, I., & Wang, R Y. (2006). *Introduction to information quality.* Cambridge, MA: MITIQ Press.

Gangadharan, G. R., & Swami, S. N. (2004). *Business intelligence systems: Design and implementation strategies.* Paper presented at the 26th International Conference Information Technology Interfaces ITI.

Hancock, J.C., & Toren, R. (2006). *Practical business intelligence with SQL server 2005 (Microsoft Windows server system series).* NJ: Addison-Wesley.

Inmon, W. H., Imhoff, C., & Sousa, R. (1997). *Corporate information factory:* New York: John Wiley & Sons.

Inmon, W. H., Welch, J. D., & Glassey, K. L. (1997). *Managing the data warehouse.* New York: John Wiley & Sons, Inc.

Kalakota, R., & Robinson, M. M. (2000). *E-business 2.0: Roadmap for success.* Addison-Wesley Professional.

Kimball, R., Reeves, L., Thornthwaite, W., Ross, M., & Thornwaite, W. (1998). *The data warehouse lifecycle toolkit: Expert methods for designing, developing and deploying data warehouses with CD rom.* New York: John Wiley & Sons, Inc.

Liautaud, B., & Hammond, M. (2000). *E-business intelligence: Turning information into knowledge and profit.* New York: McGraw-Hill.

Moss, L. T., & Atre, S. (2003). *Business intelligence roadmap: The complete project lifecycle for decision-support applications.* Addison-Wesley Professional.

Negash, S. (2004). Business intelligence. *Communications of the Association for Information Systems, 13,* 177-195.

Olszak, C., & Ziemba, E. (2007). Approach to building and implementing business intelligence systems. *Interdisciplinary Journal of Information, Knowledge, and Management, 2,* 135-148.

Ponniah, P. (2001). *Data warehousing fundamentals.* New York: Wiley-Interscience.

Power, D. J. (2002). *Decisions support systems: Concepts and resources for managers.* Westport, CT: Quorum Books.

Turban, E., Sharda, R., Aronson, J., & King, D. (2007). *Business intelligence* (1st ed.). Prentice Hall, NJ.

Vitt, E., Luckevich, M., & Misner, S. (2002). *Business intelligence.* Redmond, WA: Microsoft Press Redmond.

Watson, H.J., Fuller, C., & Ariyachandra, T. (2004). Data warehouse governance: Best practices at Blue Cross and Blue Shield of North Carolina. *Decision Support Systems, 38*(3), 435-450.

Watson, H, & Haley, B. (1998). Managerial considerations. *Communications of the ACM, 41*(9), 32-37.

Watson, H. J., Houdeshel, G., & Rainer Jr., R. K. (1996). *Building executive information systems and other decision support applications.* New York: John Wiley & Sons, Inc.

Chapter XV
Electronic Data Interchange (EDI) Adoption:
A Study of SMEs in Singapore

Ping Li
ROC Consulting International, Singapore

Joseph M. Mula
University of Southern Queensland, Australia

ABSTRACT

A review of the literature showed that there appears to be very little research undertaken on Electronic Data Interchange (EDI) adoption by small to medium sized business (SMEs) particularly in Singapore. This study is a preliminary attempt to quantify this area. Using a survey-based methodology, the research examined EDI adoption. Results indicate that Singapore SMEs confirm findings by some researchers that EDI adoption is significantly associated with a firm's annual sales but is not significantly associated with employee size as other studies have shown (Rogers, Daugherty, & Stank, 1992). This study is at odds with previous single-dimension EDI adoption studies indicating a significant relationship between firm size (annual sales) and EDI depth (Williams, Magee, & Suzuki, 1998). Organization size showed a significant relationship with the volume and diversity of EDI use but not with the depth and breadth. The most important reason for Singaporean SMEs to adopt EDI was pressure from their EDI-capable trading partners, treating pressure from their competitors as the least important.

INTRODUCTION

Electronic Data Interchange (EDI) can be defined as the transmission of standard business documents in a standard format between industrial trading partners (Walton & Marucheck, 1997). Tingle (2000) points out that electronic commerce applications are moving toward EDI by using standards from Extensible Markup Language (XML) applications while EDI is moving toward e-commerce (EC) by becoming Web-enabled. The Internet platform makes the facilitation of cross-border trade documents commercially more feasible. With the problem of security and interoperability being solved, traders have confidence in Internet-based EDI (Tan, Thio, & Wei, 2003).

In addition, many firms that are pursuing electronic commerce with business partners on the World Wide Web are maintaining existing EDI relationships and using the Web to investigate alternative suppliers or buyers. Others have begun to move away from the traditional Value Added Network (VAN)-mediated, proprietary EDI framework to use Web-based EDI. Many believe they will use both VAN-based EDI and Internet-based EDI as e-commerce tools (Jones & Beatty, 2001). Therefore, EDI still has a place in the e-commerce arena, even after more than 20 years of research and use (ASC X12 Group, 2002).

However, Chong, Lim, and Wong (1998) reported that Singaporean small to medium sized businesses (SMEs) were still in the infant stage of EC but they do not explain why SMEs were still at this stage. Most research on EC inhibitors explored EC's usage for all sizes and types of organizations, or investigated issues at a macro multicountry level (OECD, 1998). Furthermore, these researchers have focused on general EC adoption; they have not identified factors that influenced EDI adoption in particular. There appears to be very little research investigating EDI adoption by SMEs and particularly in Singapore. This study, focusing on EDI adoption by SMEs, is a preliminary attempt to quantify this area.

OVERVIEW OF IT AND E-COMMERCE

Information Technology (IT) has been fundamentally changing the way organizations conduct their businesses and compete in the market place. Using IT, firms can link up with their suppliers

and customers located in any part of the world, and employees can consult with each other on a real time basis. IT can expedite responses to customers' orders and queries, reduce inventory, shorten production cycle time, improve quality, enhance the efficiency of delivery of products and services, and strengthen in-company coordination (Takashi, 2001)

Electronic commerce is the use of inter-networked computers to create and transform business relationships. E-commerce can be defined as including any form of commercial transactions of any kind of goods and services, conducted over computer networks, whether they are open or closed networks (Wong & Lam, 1999). In the knowledge-based economy, IT and e-commerce play a vital role in world-class organizations globally, regionally, and in Singapore.

IT and E-Commerce Globally and Regionally

The business environment has changed in the second half of the 20th Century and IT is a key driver. The pace of change continues to accelerate and corporations around the world will seek to revitalize and reinvent their business in the 21st Century. IT has contributed to GDP growth in three ways. The first is the rapid growth of IT-producing industries; the second is the capital deepening of IT facilities to enhance business efficiency in all industries; the third is GDP growth by the creation of new businesses with the use of IT. The adoption of IT should not be imagined merely as a technology issue, but as the propulsive force of a new social revolution or "destructive" constructor (Takashi, 2001).

E-commerce has changed and is changing the way business is conducted around the world. It was estimated that by the year 2005, the value of worldwide electronic commerce will reach U.S. $ 8.5 trillion, while the Asia Pacific region will have electronic commerce revenue of U.S. $ 2.4 trillion (Gartner Group, 2000). Another prediction placed the global e-commerce trade at U.S. $ 9.2 trillion by 2005. Global e-business B2B (business-to-business) was predicted to be U.S. $ 1.41 trillion in 2005 and U.S. $2.4 trillion in 2006. Predictions vary due partly to the lack of global data and no unanimous definition of e-commerce (Yang & Miao, 2005).

In terms of regional distribution of growth in e-commerce, the fastest growing region is expected to be the Asia-Pacific, including Australia and New Zealand. With the exception of Mexico and Israel, all of the top 10 fastest growing countries are from the Asia-Pacific. This region is expected to account for about a quarter of the global e-commerce revenues. Japan is already the second most important nation in the global e-commerce map and is the country with the highest value of e-commerce activities in Asia. South Korea comes next with substantial e-commerce activities already afoot and stunning future growth projections. Hong Kong, Singapore, and Israel form the third rung with India, China, Malaysia, The Philippines, Indonesia, Turkey, and Vietnam forming the next tier (Chakrabarti & Kardile, 2002). Business-to-consumer (B2C) reached U.S. $59.1 billion in five largest[1] Asia-Pacific e-commerce regions in 2006 and is predicted to reach U.S. $168 billion by 2011 (E-Marketer, 2008).

Compared with larger enterprises, SMEs have generally been found to lag behind in exploiting the advantage of IT to improve their productivity and competitiveness. A lack of knowledge of how IT can transform their businesses, nonavailability of expertise and finances, and inadequate training of their manpower are some of the major contributing factors to the slower pace of IT applications among SMEs in comparison with their larger counterparts (Takeaki, 2001).

In China, fewer SMEs have introduced e-commerce in comparison with larger enterprises. Most SMEs in Hong Kong have begun to understand the importance of e-commerce, and are applying it to enhance their competitiveness, though the overall adoption is still at the development stage. Through the newly established Electronic Com-

merce Resource Center, Thailand has formulated a national policy framework and an action plan for the promotion and development of e-commerce in SMEs (Takashi, 2001).

IT and E-Commerce in Singapore

Singapore is a small country with a population of about four million. It has a small market and limited natural resources that make it almost impossible to depend on these resources for its growth. The Singapore Government has recognized the importance of knowledge assets in the new economy and the need to invest in its people to remain competitive. As a result, the government encourages organizations to make use of the available infrastructure to increase productivity and efficiency in their operations (Chan & Hawamdeh, 2002).

The Singapore Government has used information technology to stimulate economic growth and achieve national competitiveness. Launched in 1991, "IT 2000" was as a plan to guide Singapore IT development into the 21st Century. This plan sought to transform Singapore into an intelligent island (National Computer Board, 1992). In September 1998, Singapore's e-commerce master plan was launched, to drive the pervasive use of electronic commerce in Singapore, and to strengthen Singapore's position as an international e-commerce hub. The target was to have S$4 billion worth of products and services transacted electronically through Singapore, and 50% of businesses to use some form of e-commerce by the year 2003 (IDA, 1997).

A survey on Information and Communication Technology (ICT) and e-commerce adoption by businesses in Singapore found that most businesses were planning to implement IT for their business activities at the end of the 20th Century. Over half of the organizations had implemented e-commerce in their businesses (Shapiro, 1999). The Center for Management Innovation & Technopreneurship in the National University of Singapore's (NUS) survey on business-to-business e-commerce in Singapore, found that over 73% of the companies surveyed had corporate access to the Internet, and over one-third of the companies have implemented business-to-business e-commerce (Chan & Hawamdeh, 2002).

In November 1998, in conjunction with the rapid growth of e-commerce in Singapore, the government launched the Local Enterprise E-Commerce Program to build up e-commerce applications and encourage local companies to implement e-commerce in their business operations with a budget of S$9 million providing 50% funding of implementation costs incurred by companies (Chan & Hawamdeh, 2002). One study by PricewaterhouseCoopers found that most SMEs identify e-commerce as an important factor to improve customer services and exchange of information. This study also postulated that more SMEs will adopt e-commerce applications as a result of the Singapore Government's effort to encourage the private sector to adopt e-commerce (Shapiro, 1999).

In January 2000, the Singapore Productivity and Standards Board (PSB) that had been spearheading the development and upgrading of SMEs, released a 10-year strategic plan called the SME 21 Plan to create a community of vibrant and resilient SMEs that will enhance Singapore's competitiveness and economic growth. Under the SME 21 Plan, PSB aims to promote greater use of IT and e-commerce among SMEs. In January 2000 when PSB first started with the e-commerce service providers (ECSPs) there were fewer than 1,000 SMEs subscribers to e-commerce solutions. By 2001, there were approximately 16,000 SMEs subscribers (Gwee, 2001).

DEVELOPMENT AND EVOLUTION OF EDI

E-commerce includes both business-to-business (B2B) and business-to-consumer (B2C) elements. These two streams—business-to-business EDI-

centred electronic commerce, and individual use of the Internet and the WWW—came together in the mid-1990s. A great deal of B2B electronic commerce is still conducted over private networks, using primarily traditional EDI channels and value-added network (VAN) service providers. But EDI can be conducted either over private networks or over the Internet (Huff, Schneberger, & Newson, 2000). It is fair to say that, despite the visibility of the B2C sector, it is the B2B sector that forms the core of the e-commerce revolution (Rajesh & Vikas, 2002). Hence, EDI plays a very important role in this competitive business environment.

The information systems (IS) literature provides examples of the use of IS and IT by organizations to gain a competitive edge (Mackay & Rosier, 1996). EDI is one type of Inter-organizational Systems (IOS). IOS do more than speed the flow of information; they allow closer integration and also affect business relationships (Emmelhainz, 1987). They are often considered to be a prerequisite to doing business in today's competitive environment (Rogers et al., 1992).

Inter-Organizational Systems (IOS)

IOS technology impacts on inter- and intra-firm management and business practices which in turn influence such areas as economic value creation and strategic competitive advantage. Origins of IOS competitive advantage can be traced to two factors; first, comparative efficiency (Bakos & Tracy, 1986) and second, strengthened structural bonding in the relationship which closely ties exchange partners together (Han, 1992). Johnston and Vitale (1998) also believe that perhaps the most significant outcome of IOS adoption is the positive change it brings to buyer-seller relationships.

Definitions of IOSs vary, but all seem to include implicitly or explicitly that two or more organizations use the same system, and that communication takes place through a computerized system (Johnston & Vitale, 1998). Ojala and Suomi (1992) defined an IOS as a system in which two or more independently managed organizations communicated in a computer memory-to-memory fashion without the transfer of physical media. Within this definition, there are three principal uses of these systems: (1) electronic data interchange (EDI), that is, the transmission of standard business documents in a standard format between industrial trading partners (Walton & Marucheck, 1997); (2) electronic mail: transfer of human-initiated messages from one computer to another; and (3) human usage of external databases with computer interfaces (Ojala & Suomi, 1992).

EDI is just one form of IOS. EDI use can expedite inter-organizational transactions, reduce transmission costs, improve the accuracy of the information exchanged, reduce paper flow, and eliminate labour-intensive tasks. In addition, EDI offers the potential for forging new partnerships through the implementation of continuous replenishment and quick response systems (Bamfield, 1994b; Lambert, Emmelhainz, & Gardner, 1996).

Despite dramatic growth in EDI use, there is still some disagreement about what EDI is. Hence, it is important to define explicitly EDI for this study.

EDI Definition

Kimberley (1994) defined EDI as involving the electronic transmission from one computer system to another of any common business information, for example, purchase orders, invoices, payment instructions, schedules, and manifests. Mackay and Rosier (1996) argued that this definition should really be modified to include the terms "application-to-application" rather than simply "computer-to-computer," as potentially the significant benefits of adopting EDI are to be found when both trading partners have fully integrated EDI into their internal application systems. Therefore, Mackay and Rosier (1996) described EDI as the paperless transmission of business documents

between trading partner application systems, via a computer and communications network, in a standard message format.

XML-based EDI, sponsored by UN/FACT and OASIS, is a modular suite of specifications that enables enterprises of any size and in any geographical location to conduct business over the Internet. Using XML, companies now have a standard method to exchange business messages, conduct trading relationships, communicate data in common terms, and register business processes. XML messages are consistent and based upon a well-developed business process, work with clear business semantics, and allow business to be conducted according to standard or mutually agreed upon practices (Lim & Kamarudin, 2002).

Hence, this research defines EDI as the transmission of standard business documents in a standard format between industry trading partners. It includes VAN-based EDI and Internet-based EDI. Note that this definition excludes electronic mail and fax. An understanding of the operation of EDI is essential for effective utilization of modern technology in businesses. The brief description that follows has been shortened from a more detailed one contained in Li (2005).

Operation of EDI

The operation of traditional VAN-based EDI and Web-based EDI is different. VAN-based EDI is conducted by private network using EDIFACT or other standards, but Web-based EDI is conducted via Internet using XML.

VAN-Based EDI

EDI involves three basic processes: (1) directing data to and gathering data from different application programs; (2) converting data from proprietary formats (as used by application programs) to standard formats (as transmitted by the communication network) and reversing this process at the other end; and (3) the actual transmission of data between trading partners over a communication network (Banerjee & Golhar, 1995).

In order to run EDI, five basic components are typically needed: (1) EDI standards such as those developed by the American National Standard Institute (ANSI); (2) EDI software to generate, receive, and interpret transactions with trading partners; (3) a capability to send and receive EDI transactions, a function often provided by value-added networks (VAN), third-party networks or point-to-point configurations; (4) enhancements to applications software to accept or start EDI transactions, and changes to traditional business procedures for strategic advantage; and (5) hardware, including appropriate peripherals such as a printer, modem, and storage device (Colberg, 1990).

Web-Based EDI/XML-Based EDI

To appreciate the usage of XML-based EDI, Figure 1 illustrates how all the components fit together and dynamically interact. Note that Company A and Company B are assumed to be two trading partners that conduct their business transactions via the Internet.

EDI Communication Links

For EDI to function smoothly, companies must establish the required communication links to move information. Previous studies identify four types of communication links—point-to-point configurations, third party networks, value added networks, and XML-based (Lankford & Riggs, 1996). Furthermore, Zwass (1996) pointed out that EDI is moving beyond the VAN-based sphere by leveraging into the Internet using Extensible Markup Language (XML). Point-to-point configurations link manufactures' and suppliers' computers via a communication network. Third party networks serve as electronic data interchange service bureaus, in addition to providing "mailbox" services available from value-

added networks. Value-added networks provide "mailbox" services for the JIT manufacturer and supplier companies. Value-added networks also provide the ability to consolidate EDI transactions, allowing the user to send information to multiple receivers in a single dial-up session (Lankford & Riggs, 1996).

Extensible Markup Language (XML) is open and easy to implement. Participation is free and open to anyone. XML is complimentary, not competitive, with existing standards, such as UN/EDIFACT, X12, thus preserving much of the existing investment in these applications. Much of the focus is on the needs of smaller organizations. In Singapore, value added networks are the most commonly used of these four methods for the communication and transfer of information, but XML-based forms have most recently been used by organizations (Lim & Kamarudin, 2002).

As EDI has evolved so has the variety of message standards—the mutually agreed format or syntax of the "message"—EDI standards (Pfeiffer, 1992). There are different EDI standards used in different industries and different countries at different times.

EDI Standards

Business documentation traded between companies is, in effect, a series of "transactions.". In the parlance of EDI, these "transactions" are often referred to as "messages." Overall, different industry sectors have tended to agree on particular formats of the information to be exchanged electronically. In his study, Robson (1994) introduced the evolution of the EDI Standards in different countries. For example, the USA amalgamated a number of standards into AQNSI ASC X12 (American National Standards Institute Accredited Standards Committee X12). The creation of EDIFACT (Electronic Data for Administration, Commerce and Transportation/Trade) was the most important development. It was originated by the French who considered commerce and

Figure 1. High-level overview of XML-EDI interaction between two companies (Adapted from Lim & Kamarudin, 2002, p. 5)

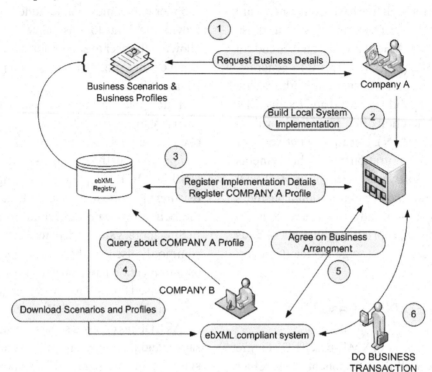

trade to be interchangeable terms. This single standard has emerged as being the only true multi-industry/multinational standard to be embraced throughout the world. On the international front, the United Nations developed a standard known as UN/EDIFACT, which is widely used in Europe (Tingle, 2000).

The Uniform Code Council (UCC) recently published a report on e-commerce emerging technology strategies that are designed to leverage emerging business-to-business interface technologies with traditional UCC supported EDI technologies. To make EDI simpler and cheaper for everyone, the UCC developed a single uniform set of Web Forms or Web-EDI, and a Web-EDI flat file XML interface syntax (Tingle, 2000).

The business processes supported by ebXML[2] are expressed as process models and encoded in XML. All ebXML-developed messages are encoded in XML as well. However, ebXML may

transport any type of data such as binary content or EDI transactions (Lim & Kamarudin, 2002).

In Singapore, EDIFACT is adopted as the national message standards for EDI (Lim & Kamarudin, 2002).

A different EDI standard for different industries and in different countries is one of the problems companies face when considering the adoption of EDI. However, the popularity of EDI in the world is obvious as evidenced below.

STATUS OF EDI

EDI is gradually reshaping business practices and procedures around the world allowing trading partners to exchange information in a standard electronic format (Maingot & Quon, 2001). However, the diffusion of EDI globally, regionally, and in Singapore is disproportionate.

EDI Globally and Regionally

By the time of the 1991 EDICA Conference in Sydney, it was claimed that there were 1,500 corporations using EDI in Australia and New Zealand. This would have compared favourably with the populations variously claimed for the U.S. (50,000), but less so with the UK (12,000) and Singapore (2,000). The transaction volumes in Australia to date were small compared with those countries (Clarke, 2001).

Australia and New Zealand have been active in EDI since 1986. Both countries have well established EDI infrastructures, with national acceptance of ANSI X12 and EDIFACT, multiple domestic service providers, active EDI Associations, and both government and private industry support. Australia is a mature, self-contained EDI market. There were 4,000 – 5,000 EDI users in 1994 (Kimberley, 1994).

Value added network applications thrived in Japan during the 1980s with around 3,000 users of EDI by 1990 all based on private or industry standards. South Korea has been actively planning for EDI since 1987, and has a range of industry VANs offering proprietary EDI solutions where there are around 3,000 to 4,000 private format users. EDI Malaysia is the first EDI service provider for trade facilitation, which began carrying traffic at the end of 1993. Thailand, The Philippines and Indonesia are all at the pilot stage (Kimberley, 1994).

The majority of the software houses in Japan (Hitachi, IBM Japan, and Fujitsu) supported the Web services for B2B by leveraging on the following technology—Simple Object Access Protocol (SOAP), RosettaNet and XML-based EDI. Korea has made substantial progress in the area of XML- and ebXML-based EDI. Taiwan has a Global Logistics Management Project that utilizes the ebXML version 1.0 technology. A test site was set up for the OASIS ebXML Registry version 2.0 reference implementations in Hong Kong. Both these two countries are late starters.

There are merely reporting that their current EDI systems are going to be XML-enabled soon (Lim & Kamarudin, 2002).

In 2002, the total annual value of EDI transactions ranged from U.S. $1.8 trillion to U.S. $3.2 trillion worldwide. Traditional EDI commerce has been predicted to continue to have a compound annual growth rate (CAGR) of 8.4% through 2006, while Internet EDI commerce will have a CAGR of 52.1% through the same period (Drickhamer, 2003).

A study by Chen and Williams (1998) identified three types of SME responses to the use of EDI. First, SMEs may see advantages in using EDI. As a minimum, they may regard EDI as an essential business tool for dealing with large customers as well as enhancing their own operational efficiency. This would be through the integration of EDI into its existing internal information system, making use of the early delivery of machine-processable information. Second, SMEs may be pessimistic and reactive, view EDI as an extra cost for staying in business, and do as little as possible to satisfy customers' requests. Third, SMEs may be conscious of their strengths and opportunities, and develop without yielding to demand from large customers and necessarily participating in EDI. This may result in the loss of its business with these customers. Attention now turns to Singapore SMEs' adoption of EDI.

EDI in Singapore

Since 1986, Singapore's EDI service provider has been a monopoly organization. Operated by Singapore Network Service (SNS), the service is known as TradeNet. All import and export trade declarations are processed by TradeNet which has over 2,000 EDI users. By the end of 1991, processing of paper documents was phased out. SNS, a government owned service, then extended services into higher value added applications such as certificate of assignment presentation for quota control (Kimberley, 1994).

Besides being a clearinghouse for trade declaration documents, TradeNet is linked to other systems that offer trade information services and to computer systems of major banks to allow electronic payment of processing fees, duties, goods and services taxes, and network usage charges. TradeNet represents a significant electronic integration initiative. It took two years to develop at an estimated cost of S$50 million (U.S. $33 million). By the end of 1992, TradeNet had linked the Trade Development Board (TDB) with about 30 public-sector organizations and 2,200 organizations from the trading and banking communities. By the end of 1994, almost 99% of all trade declaration documents had been processed by TradeNet (Teo, Tan, & Wei, 1997). Goods are precleared by U.S. Customs using a dedicated X.25 link especially installed for textile quota approvals. Singapore Airlines, QANTAS, and Air New Zealand preclear passengers via a special EDI manifest transmission (Kimberley, 1994).

Other VAN and EDI services include government tendering, retail ordering, Medinet (for medical benefits and health care claims), Graphnet for CAD/CAM data, Buildnet for the construction industry, Portnet (the Port of Singapore), and Spectrum (an air cargo community system). Portnet, TradeNet, and Spectrum systems ultimately lead to the Total Trade and Transportation System (TTTS), comprising eight major modules. In addition to TradeNet, Medinet and Graphnet, SNS offers a range of information services which include MAINS for sea cargo information, ELVIS for textile visas, Lawnet a legal retrieval systems, and CurrencyNet. Other services include EDIFACT services and a Singapore Post airmail end-to-end tracking system. IVANS is active at present strictly for international connections, include GEIS, Advantis, AT&T, Infonet and SITA. Other arrangements include a connection with Fujitsu's FENIC system to link SNS with Japanese trading partner, INTIS, the Rotterdam port system, ACS, and the U.S. Customs Service (Kimberley, 1994).

The Singaporean EDI committee actively pursued XML-based EDI and spearheaded the transition of VAN-based EDI to XML-based EDI in Singapore. The Pan Asia Alliance project is cited as the main contributor of the current XML-based EDI initiative in the country (Lim & Kamarudin, 2002). According to the Singapore EDI Committee Progress Report (SEC, 2001), there were more than 35,000 EDI users in Singapore. However, it appears that there is no official report on the status of EDI in Singapore SMEs. Before looking at EDI adoption issues, it is necessary to define the term SME in Singapore and determine their significance to its economy.

SMEs in Singapore

In 2003, the Association of Small and Medium-Sized Enterprise (ASME) of Singapore defined a small to medium enterprises (SME) as one which is locally registered with at least 30% local equity; has less than S$30 million total annual turnover; and has a work force of less than 200 workers. For the purpose of this research, the SME definition used by ASME was adopted.

Obviously, government, public, and scientific attention to SMEs has been increasing over time in many countries due to their significant contributions to economies. Local SMEs play a vital role in the economic development of Singapore. Their role is regarded as a key source of entrepreneurship and innovation. Although foreign multinational corporations (MNCs) contributed a greater share to economic development, the contribution of local SMEs is no less significant. Drawing on their traditional strengths, they helped Singapore embark on three decades of export-led growth (Lee, 2000).

By 1999, local SMEs formed the base that supported the MNCs and larger companies in the economy accounting for 92% of establishments and 52% of the Singaporean workforce (about 583,000 workers), and contributed 35% of the Gross Domestic Product (SICC, 2000). In

2003, there were 103,000 SMEs in Singapore, which accounted for 92% of businesses and 51% of the total workforce. SMEs make a significant contribution to the economy in Singapore (AC-CADEMY, 2003): the manufacturing sector accounts for 15% of GDP; commerce accounts for 11% of GDP; and the service industry contributes 17% of GDP.

EDI Adoption

The business community's adoption of telecommunications applications has been delayed by a general lack of understanding of the potential strategic benefits that can accrue from their effective utilization (Dholakia & Kshetri, 2004). Indeed, many organizations appear to regard such technologies as providing only a faster mail service, rather than offering infrastructure suitable for strategic initiatives such as business re-engineering (Swatman, 1994).

The EDI literature has suggested a variety of decision factors that influence the adoption of EDI. Among those that have been identified as the most cited are perceived benefit, organizational readiness, competitive pressure, and pressure from trading partners ((Iacovou et al., 1995; Jun, Chai, & Peterson, 2000; Premkumar & Ramamurthy, 1995). Among the most commonly investigated EDI characteristics that promote the adoption of the technology are: relative advantage (i.e., perceived EDI benefits and impact), compatibility (both technical and organizational), and trial-ability (e.g., pilot tests, prototypes). Perceived relative advantage of EDI is the only variable that has been consistently identified as one of the most critical adoption decision factors in small firms (Cragg & King, 1993). Organizational readiness for EDI refers to available levels of financial resources, IS infrastructure, and organizational compatibility for EDI adoption (Iacocou, Benbasat, & Dexter, 1995). Competitive pressure is related to the level of EDI capability of a firm's industry competitors (Iacocou et al., 1995; Premkumar, Ramamurthy,

& Crum, 1997). As noted by Cunningham and Tynan (1993), while establishing electronic linkages with trading partners can be an important source of competitive advantage, lack of EDI systems may turn out to be a serious weakness. Small and mid-sized companies' primary rationale to implement EDI is the competitive advantage it can provide (Dholakia & Kshetri, 2004).

Pressure from trading partners who are EDI initiators plays a critical role in EDI adoption by small firms. Although many companies consider EDI a more efficient way of handling business communication than traditional methods, many small businesses resist adopting EDI, primarily due to perceived high cost and reliance on their paper-based system (Hart & Saunders, 1997). Indeed, more than 70% of the respondents in surveys identified customer pressure/mandate as one of the primary reasons for adopting EDI (Iacocou et al., 1995).

EDI adoption is not a one-dimensional construct. EDI adoption can be evaluated in terms of the number of transactions supported, the number of participating partners, the volume of business handled, and the level of integration with internal systems (Vijayasarathy & Tyler, 1997). In order to measure and analyze the degree of EDI adoption, this study identified from the literature four key dimensions of EDI usage. The four dimensions are EDI volume, diversity, depth, and breadth. EDI *volume* represents the extent to which an organization's document exchanges are handled through EDI connections. EDI *diversity* refers to the number of distinct document types that an organization handles via EDI. EDI *depth* refers to the degree of electronic consolidation that has been established between the business processes of two or more trading partners, and EDI *breadth* presents the extent to which an organization has established EDI connections with external organizations such as suppliers, customers, government agencies, and financial institutions (Hart & Saunder, 1998; Jun et al., 2000; Massetti & Zmud, 1996; Williams et al., 1998).

Size is generally believed to influence a firm's operations and performances. Larger firms are likely to have expanded capabilities because of their larger resource base. It has been shown that larger firms are more likely to have EDI capability (Rogers et al., 1992). Iacocou et al. (1995) also looked closely at the relationship between size and adoption behaviour in terms of sales volume. It appears that EDI adopters are on average, larger than nonadopters. Number of employees and total annual sales are the measures most frequently used as a measure of an organisation's size. Every firm knows precisely how many people it employs and its annual sales figures at any given time. Added value is directly linked to the firm's economic activities, and takes into account the level of internal activities because of the implementation of all production factors. Other measurements such as quantities produced, salaries, assets, capital and even profits have occasionally been used to determine an enterprise's size (d'Amboise, 1991). Stage of development could also influence the adoption as the longer and more mature the firm the more likely they may be to extensively adopt EDI. The adoption of EDI may support an advancement of a firm's maturity from one stage to another.

THE STUDY

Although many EDI articles have become available, there are very few studies on the effect of EDI on small firms, and those that do exist are contradictory. This research attempts to fill a number of gaps in the literature. First, there is little research on the relationship between decision factors to adopt EDI and the degree of EDI adoption in a holistic framework (Walton, 1994; Hart & Saunders, 1998; Jun et al., 2000). Second, there are few empirical research studies on EDI in SMEs conducted by survey (lack of quantitative research) (Bamfield, 1994a; Bytheway, 1994; Clarke, 2001; Holland, Lockett, & Blackman,

1992; Joseph & Engle, 1996; Jun et al., 2000; Massetti & Zmud, 1996; Mische, 1992; Ojala & Suomi, 1992; Ratnasingham, 1997; Ricks, 1997; Walton & Gupa, 1999). Finally, there were no identified studies of EDI adoption by Singaporean SMEs to date of completion of this study. The lack of EDI capability of small organizations is critical because of the important role they play in the economy (Iacovou et al., 1995).

In developing the conceptual model, the study explored the relationship between EDI decision factors and EDI adoption. It proposed that the decision factors to adopt EDI will initiate EDI adoption and the degree of EDI adoption. The model was developed to answer a number of research questions. This chapter reports on the following two questions.

Q1: Is firm size associated with the adoption of EDI?

Q2: What decision factor is significantly associated with EDI adoption?

To test part of the study's model, the following hypothesis was formulated with sub hypotheses. Hypothesis one (H1) tests the proposition that large firms have more of a propensity to adopt EDI. However, firm size can be measured in many ways—employee size or annual turnover are often used to classify firms as SMEs or large enterprises. Based on the literature, volume, diversity, depth, and breadth were used to examine the degree of EDI adoption (Massetti & Zmud, 1996). This hypothesis tested whether firm size is positively associated with EDI adoption and is significantly associated with all these four dimensions of EDI adoption.

H1: Firm size is positively associated with the degree of EDI adoption.

H1a: Firm size measured by employee numbers and turnover are significantly associated with EDI volume.

H1b: Firm size measured by employee numbers and turnover are significantly associated with EDI diversity.

H1c: Firm size measured by employee numbers and turnover are significantly associated with EDI depth.

H1d: Firm size measured by employee numbers and turnover are significantly associated with EDI breadth.

To answer the second research question, a proposition was posited that decision factors to adopt EDI will initiate EDI adoption. The study was concerned with assessing which EDI decision factors most significantly associated with the degree of EDI adoption. The decision factors identified from the literature were perceived benefit, organizational readiness, competitive pressure, and pressure from trading partners (Iacocou et al., 1995; Jun et al., 2000; Premkumar & Ramamurthy, 1995). Thus, proposition one was postulated as follows.

P1: All decision factors are significantly associated with all four dimensions of EDI adoption.

In order to explore the extent to which Singaporean SMEs adopted EDI, a survey-based study was undertaken and correlation analysis applied to investigate the relationships between specific variables (i.e., the firm's size and organization's life cycle) identified in the literature and the degree of EDI adoption (i.e., EDI volume, EDI diversity, EDI depth, and EDI breadth). An instrument was developed drawn from the literature that contained the above constructs as well as some demographic questions (Chen & Williams 1998; Hart & Saunders, 1998; Iacocou et al. 1995; Jun et al., 2000; Maingot & Quon 2001; Massetti & Zmud, 1996; Rebecca, Nath, & Hendon, 1998; Williams et al., 1998).

With the help of the Singapore EDI Committee, a sample of 445 SMEs which were currently using EDI were chosen from users of an EDI service provided in Singapore using nonrandom purposive sampling. The sample firms were within the study's definition of Singaporean SMEs as defined by ASME. During the follow-up phone calls to SMEs, 35 companies were found to no longer exist or not to be currently using EDI. Hence, 410 questionnaires were qualified for the survey based on the criteria of target organizations. A total of 94 questionnaires were returned after follow-up phone calls. Out of 94 responses, 3 cases were deleted because they had too much missing data (Tabachnick & Fidell, 2001). As a result, a total of 91 responses were used for the data analysis. The overall response rate was 22.2% (91/410). As indicated above, the United States is the world leader in the adoption of EDI (Clarke, 2001). Compared to the USA, Singapore is relatively immature and unsophisticated in terms of EDI usage. However, the response rate of 22.2% for this study implies that Singaporean SMEs had a fair level of EDI awareness despite its lower-level experience and sophistication.

RESULTS

Profile of Singaporean SMEs

Of 91 usable responses, 89% of respondents were private limited companies and only 11% were sole proprietorships. Respondents were from a broad range of industries and organizations. Approximately half of all respondents (42.9%) were in distribution, including wholesale, retail, and import/export. Respondents were also from transportation and communication (25.2%) and service (15.4%), as well as manufacturing (14.3%). Only 1.1% of respondents were from construction, and food and beverage. According to statistics, the majority of Singaporean SMEs are in the commerce and service sectors, accounting for 49% and 48% of the totals respectively (Ho, 2000). Hence, the majority of EDI users in Singaporean SMEs are in the distribution industry including wholesale, retail, and import/export. Thus respondents were representative on the SME population.

Over a quarter of the firms (27.5%) had been established more than 20 years. Some 24.2% of respondents had between 6 to 10 years, 23.1% had between 11 to 15 year and 14.2% of them had between 16 to 20 years. Employee size is one of the defining measures of firm size in this study (ASME, 2003). Close to three quarters of firms (71.4%) had less than 50 employees. Some 17.6% of them had 51–100 employees, 8.8% had 151–200 employees and only 2.2% had 101–150 employees. The annual sales/turnover for the last financial year is another measure of SMEs' size (ASME, 2003). Close to half of respondents (46.2%) have annual sales of less than S$10 million; on the other hand, more than half of respondents (53.8%) have annual sales between S$10 million and S$30 million. Thus all firms met the definition of a SME.

EDI Systems and Standards Adopted

Most SMEs (94.5%) are using microcomputers/ PCs to adopt EDI. More than half (65%) of SMEs were using EDIFACT as EDI message standard and 30.8% of them are using XML. Firms with a long EDI history used EDI more intensively than firms with a shorter history. A long history provides more time to establish EDI links with partners and more time to develop skills and standards to use EDI widely and deeply. Therefore, firms with a longer EDI history tend to use EDI more widely and deeply than firms with a shorter EDI history, because intensive use of EDI is normally found in firms that have a long history using EDI (Williams et al., 1998). However, this research did not support the Williams et al., (1998) study. There is not a significant relationship between EDI adoption (EDI volume, EDI diversity, EDI depth and EDI breadth) and years of using EDI. The reasons may be explained as:

- Over half of respondents (59.3%) had EDI links with the government customs department to declare import and (or) export permits only. Hence, they did not intend to use EDI more widely and deeply even though they had used EDI for a long time.
- A resistance to change is one of the major inhibitors of adopting EDI by small firms (Arunachalam, 1995; Ghobadian, Liu, & Stainer, 1994; Healy, 1991; Manus, 1993; Jun et al., 2000; Swatman, 1994).

Most responding firms had multiple EDI links with government, customers, suppliers, transportation, banks, or subcontractors. More than half of respondents (59.3%) had EDI links with government. Close to half (42.9%) of them were linked with their customers and 19.8% were linked with their suppliers. They were also linked with carrier/transportation (14.3%), banks (11%) and subcontractors (3.3%).

From the survey responses it appears that 65.9% of SMEs used EDIFCT and 1.1% of them use ANSI X.12 for VAN communication links (67%). Some 31% used XML for Web-based EDI. These figures may indicate that most Singaporean SMEs are still reliant on VAN-based EDI.

Summarising the finding from EDI system and standards:

- The extent of EDI use by Singaporean SMEs was regardless of length of time they had been using EDI. This finding did not provide support for the Williams et al. (1998) study which found that firms with a longer EDI history tend to use EDI more widely and deeply than firms with a shorter EDI history. It seems that most of them just treat EDI as a necessity for doing business.
- Singaporean SMEs had EDI links mostly with government. The next most important trading partners were their customers followed by their suppliers.

- A majority of Singaporean SMEs still relied on VAN-based EDI. They mainly used TradeNet service as well as EDIFACT message standard.

EDI Adoption by SME Size

In order to explore further the significance of the findings from the SMEs' profiles, correlation analysis was undertaken to analysis the relationship between some specific variables in the profile (i.e., the firm's size and organization's life cycle) and the degree of EDI adoption (i.e., EDI volume, EDI diversity, EDI depth, and EDI breadth). Some significant relationships between the firm's size and the degree of EDI adoption were found (Table 1).

Size is generally believed to influence a firm's operations and performances. For example, larger firms are likely to have expanded capabilities simply because of their larger resource base. Therefore, it may be hypothesized that larger firms are more likely to have EDI capability (Rogers et al., 1992).

Iacocou et al. (1995) also looked closely at the relationship between size (in terms of sales volume) and adoption behaviour. It appears that EDI adopters are on average, larger than nonadopters. In terms of the number of employees, however, Iacocou et al. (1995) found no relationship between a firm's size and EDI adoption. The

results of this study support the findings of Iacocou et al. It shows that EDI adoption is significantly associated with a firm's annual sales but is not significantly associated with employee size.

Some reasons can be postulated:

- The literature suggests that power and dependence are not the main driving forces in some organizations' decisions to adopt EDI. For these organizations, instituting electronic partnerships was driven by long-standing and trusting relationships to achieve mutual benefits (Sohel & Schroeder, 2001). Therefore, an organization's success with EDI can be independent of employee size.
- In the context of power and dependence, employee size as a measure of the size of an organization may not be the appropriate one. For example, Sohel and Schroeder (2001) believed that a high-tech organization may not have a large workforce yet could have captured substantial market share, making it powerful. The amount of annual sales is probably a better measure in this context.
- Organization size measured as annual sales/turnover showed a significant relationship with the volume and diversity of EDI use but not to the depth and breadth. This result is somewhat at odds with previous singledimension EDI adoption studies indicating

Table 1. EDI adoption – employee size and organization's annual sales

		Employee Size	Organization's Annual Sales
EDI Volume	-c	ns	.309**
	-dos		.003
EDI Diversity	-c	ns	.228*
	-dos		.030
EDI Depth		ns	ns
EDI Breadth		ns	ns

*c: coefficient   dos: degree of significance   ns: not significant   ** at 0.01 level   * at 0.05 level* a significant relationship between firm size (annual sales) and EDI depth (Williams et al., 1998). The influence of firm size on EDI volume and diversity seems logical, since large organizations would have a large set of business transactions and more distinct business transactions. Lack of a significant relationship between firm size and EDI breadth also seems logical, since having a large organization is not necessarily a prerequisite to having EDI links with many trading partners.

From the comparison of company stage before and after adoption of EDI, it would appear that firms have changed their position in terms of the stage of development after adopting EDI. Most respondents (76.9%) were at stable/maturity stage of their business life cycle (28.6% before adoption of EDI) and no company was at start up stage (30.8% before adoption). Some 17.6% of them were at the growth stage of their life cycle (39.6% before adoption) and 5.5% were at the declining stage after adoption of EDI.

Thus it can be concluded that H1 is partly supported in that organisation size (measured by sales turnover) is positively associated with EDI volume (H1a) and diversity (H1b) but not with depth (H1c) and breadth (H1d). Further support for this is evidenced below. However, only two of the dimensions (volume and diversity) were

significantly related to organisation size measured by annual turnover.

Reasons Why SMEs Adopt EDI

Not surprisingly, the most important reason for Singaporean SMEs to adopt EDI was "pressure from their trading partners." This result is consistent with previous studies (Hart & Saunders, 1997; Iacocou et al., 1995). Perceived benefit of EDI was ranked second and organizational readiness for EDI was ranked third. The least important reason was "pressure from competitor" (Table 2).

Thus the most important reason for Singaporean SMEs to adopt EDI was pressure from their EDI-capable trading partner (e.g., government, customer, and suppliers). However, they treated the pressure from their competitors as the least important reason to adopt EDI. When an analysis was undertaken of the degree of adoption of EDI the findings can be summarised as follows:

- **EDI volume:** Over 23% of Singaporean SMEs exchanged more than 50% of their business documents with their trading partners. Many of them used EDI not for sales/purchase processing but to declare permits with customs.
- **EDI diversity:** Only 13.2% of Singaporean SMEs processed more than 75% of business documents via EDI.

Table 2. Main reasons SMEs adopted EDI

	Rank	1st %	2nd %	3rd %	4th %	None* %	Total %
Perceived benefits of EDI	2	37.3	**41.8**	16.5	2.2	2.2	100
Organizational readiness for EDI	3	4.3	35.2	**42.9**	11.0	6.6	100
Pressure from competitor	4	2.2	5.5	11.0	**50.5**	30.8	100
Pressure from trading partner	1	**56.0**	16.5	19.8	0	7.7	100

* The respondents did not answer the questions

- **EDI depth:** A majority of Singaporean SMEs (72.5%) adopted application-to-application connections (third level of EDI depth) but the deepest EDI connection (system-to-system) still had very low usage (4.4%).

- **EDI breadth:** A majority of Singaporean SMEs (74%) had established EDI links with less than 6 EDI partners and only 6.6% of them had more than 20 EDI partners.

Correlation analysis was used to identify relationships between specific variables of EDI decision factor and EDI adoption. Correlations indicate that there are moderate to strong relationships between items proposed to measure a given construct. This suggests that the items exhibit moderate to strong convergent validity (Hair, Anderson, Tatham, & Black, 1992).

The results show the significant relationship between key variables of EDI decision factor to the four dimensions of EDI adoption—volume, diversity, depth, and breadth (Table 3). Note, the decision factor "pressure from trading partners" was represented by four significant variables. EDI depth was weakly correlated with the variables of decision factor compared to EDI volume, EDI diversity, and EDI breadth. Another interesting result is that the indicator of pressure from government was negatively correlated to EDI volume, EDI diversity, and EDI breadth but there was no significant relationship to EDI depth. This may be explained as (1) a majority of SMEs (59.3%) had EDI links with government (e.g., customs) to declare import and/or export permits only leading to low EDI volume, low EDI diversity, and low EDI breadth; but (2) most SMEs (72.5%) adopted the third level of EDI communication connection (application-to-application connection) regardless of the decision factor to adopt EDI. Hence, the results from this sample show that higher pressure from government leads to lower EDI adoption degree in terms of EDI volume, EDI diversity, and EDI breadth but not EDI depth.

It would appear that the proposition mainly supported is that EDI decision factor has a significant positive association on degree of EDI adoption in terms of EDI volume, EDI diversity, and EDI breadth but not EDI depth. The only negative association was with pressure from government. However further analysis would need to be undertaken to determine if there is a causal relationship (this was undertaken by factor analysis and regression analysis but is not discussed in this chapter).

CONCLUSION

The results show that the most significant contributor to the degree of EDI adoption is pressure from trading partners. In other words, it would seem that Singaporean SMEs lack organizational readiness and awareness of competition. Three dimensions (volume, diversity, and breadth) of EDI adoption are significantly related to the decision factor.

The survey results appear to provide some insights on decision factor for Singaporean SMEs to adopt EDI. The findings indicate that:

- Most Singaporean SMEs (43%) were asked by their EDI-capable trading partner to adopt EDI to do business;
- Singaporean SMEs are at a relatively low level of EDI adoption—this finding is supported by the Iacocou et al. (1995) study and Williams, Hood, and Chen (1997) study that SMEs are still at an immature and unsophisticated stage of EDI usage.

As this is a preliminary study to quantify the adoption of EDI in Singapore, these results need to be treated with caution. Given that the sample was obtained from a small nation, the conclusions may not be applicable to larger countries. A study that includes cross country representation may

Table 3. Correlation analysis – external pressure associated with EDI adoption

Decision Factors		EDI Volume	EDI Diversity	EDI Depth	EDI Breadth
Pressure from Competitor					
Percent of EDI capable competitor	-c	.295**	ns	ns	.301**
	-dos	.005			.004
Pressure from Trading Partner					
No. of trading partners	-c	.511**	.375**	.310**	.470**
	-dos	.000	.000	.003	.000
No. of large trading partners	-c	.519**	.424**	ns	.506**
	-dos	.000	.000		.000
Percent of sales and purchase	-c	.691**	.426**	ns	.456**
	-dos	.000	.000		.000
Percent of EDI capable trading partners	-c	.292**	ns	ns	ns
	-dos	.005			
Pressure from customers	-c	.227**	.353**	ns	ns
	-dos	.031	.001		
Pressure from government	-c	-.396**	-.302**	ns	-.273**
	-dos	.000	.004		.009

c: coefficient dos: degree of significance ns: not significant ** at 0.01 level * at 0.05 level

provide evidence for the generalization of the findings to other Asian countries.

REFERENCES

ACCADEMY. (2003). *The economic environment and the SME, ACCA.* Retrieved June 10, 2008, from http://www.accademy.com/pdfs/smallbusiness/EESME.doc

Arunachalam, V. (1995). EDI: And analysis of adoption, uses, benefits and barriers. *Journal of Systems Management, 46*(2), 60-65.

ASC X12 Group. (2002). ASC X12 accelerates XML: Standards convergence. *Electronic Commerce News, 7*(25), 10-18.

ASME (2003). *Terms and conditions of SME in Singapore, association of small and medium*

enterprises. Retrieved June 10, 2008, from http://www.asmes.org.sg

Bakos, J.Y., & Tracy, M.E. (1986). Information technology and corporate strategy: A research perspective. *MIS Quarterly, 10*(2), 23-38.

Bamfield, J. (1994a). Learning by doing: Electronic data interchange adoption by retailers. *Logistics Information Management, 7*(6), 32-38.

Bamfield, J. (1994b). Technological management learning: The adoption of electronic data interchange by retailer. *International Journal of Retail & Distribution Management, 22*(2), 3-11.

Banerjee, S., & Golhar, D.Y. (1995). Security issues in the EDI environment. *Information Management & Computer Security, 26*(2), 27-33.

Bytheway, A. (1994). A concept model and checklist for EDI planning. *Logistics Information Management, 7*(2), 32-46.

288

Chakrabarti, R., & Kardile, V. (2002). *The Asian managers handbook of e-commerce.* New Delhi, India: Tata McGraw-Hill Publishing Company Limited.

Chan, B., & Hawamdeh S.A. (2002). The development of e-commerce in Singapore: The impact of government initiatives. *Business Process Management Journal, 8*(3), 278-288.

Chen, J.C., & Williams, B.C. (1998). The impact of electronic data interchange (EDI) on SMEs: Summary of eight British case. *Journal of Small Business Management, 36*(4), 68-72.

Chong, C.W., Lim, K.S., & Wong, W.H. (1998). *How some Singapore small and medium enterprises are using the Internet.* In Nanyang Business School (School of Accountancy and Business), Nanyang Technology University.

Clarke, R. (2001), Electronic data interchange (EDI): An introduction. *Business Credit, 103*(9), 23-25.

Colberg, T.P. (1990). The compelling case for EDI. *The Financial Manager, 20,* 20-26.

Cragg, P., & King, M. (1993). Small firm computing motivators and inhibitors. *MIS Quarterly, 17*(1), 47-60.

Cunningham, C., & Tynan, C. (1993). Electronic trading, inter-organizational systems and the nature of buy-seller relationships: The need for a network perspective. *International Journal of Information Management, 13,* 3-28.

d'Amboise, G. (1991). *The Canadian small and medium-sized enterprise.* Canada: The Institute for Research on Public Policy.

Dholakia, R.R., & Kshetri, N. (2004). Factors impacting the adoption of the Internet among SMEs. *Small Business Economics, 23*(4), 311-322.

Drickhamer, D. (2003). EDI is dead! Long live EDI. *Industry Week.*

E-Marketer (2008). Asia-Pacific B2C e-commerce awakens. Retrieved June 10, 2008, from www.emarketer.com/articles

Emmelhainz, M.A. (1987). Electronic data interchange: Does it change the purchasing process. *Journal of Purchasing and Materials Management, 2*(8), 2-8.

Gartner Group. (2000). Gartner group forecasts regional B2B outlook through 2004. Retrieved June 10, 2008, from http://gartner5.gartnerweb.com/public/static/aboutgg/pressrel/pr021600.html

Ghobadian, A., Liu, J., & Stainer, A.I. (1994). Case studies on EDI implementation. *Logistics Information Management, 7*(1), 24-30.

Gwee, S.K. (2001). E-commerce for SMEs – Singapore's perspectives. In T. Takashi (Ed.), *E-commerce, opportunities and challenges for SMEs* (pp. 13-17). Asian Productivity Organization.

Hair, J.F.J., Anderson, R.E.A., Tatham, R.L., & Black, W.C. (1992). *Multivariate data analysis* (3rd ed.). New York: MacMillan Publishing Co.

Han, S.L. (1992). *Antecedents of buyer-seller long-term relationships: An exploratory model of structural bonding and social bonding.* University Park, PA: Institute for the Study of Business Markets Report.

Hart, P.J., & Saunders, C. (1997). Power and trust: Critical factors in the adoption use of electronic data interchange. *Organization Science, 8*(1), 23-42.

Hart, P.J., & Saunders, C.S. (1998). Emerging electronic partnership: Antecedents and dimensions of EDI use from the supplier's perspective. *Journal of Management Information System, 14*(4), 87-111.

Healy, T. (1991). EDI in Australia: Still making haste slowly. *Australian Communications,* 63-70.

Ho, N.K. (2000). *Impact of CPA intervention on the business performance of Singaporean Chinese SMEs*. Unpublished Ph.D. Thesis, University of South Australia Division of International Business and Management.

Holland, C., Lockett, G., & Blackman, I. (1992). Planning for electronic data interchange. *Strategic Management Journal, 13*(7), 539-550.

Huff, S.L., Schneberger S., & Newson P. (2000). *Cases in electronic commerce*. Irwin McGraw-Hill.

Iacocou, C.L., Benbasat, I., & Dexter, A.S. (1995). Electronic data interchange and small organizations: Adoption and impact of technology. *MIS Quarterly, 19*(4), 85-486.

IDA. (1997). Press statement, infocomm development authority of Singapore. Retrieved June 10, 2008, from http://www.ncb.gov.sg/ncb/press/3307.asp

Johnston, H.R., & Vitale, M.R. (1998). Creating competitive advantage with inter-organizational systems. *MIS Quarterly, 12*(1), 37-48.

Jones, M.C., & Beatty, R.C. (2001). User satisfaction with EDI: An empirical investigation. *Information Resources Management Journal, 14*(2), 17-26.

Joseph, G.W., & Engle, T.J. (1996). Controlling an EDI environment. *Journal of Systems Management, 47*(4), 42-68.

Jun M.J., Cai, S.H., & Peterson, R.T. (2000). EDI use and participation models: From the inter-organization relationship perspective. *Industrial Management + Data Systems, 100*(9), 412-420.

Kimberley, P. (1994). EDI: Status in the Asia – Pacific Region. *Telecommunications, 28*(1), 39-32.

Lambert, D.M., Emmelhainz, M.A., & Gardner, J.T. (1996). So you want a partner? *Marketing Management, 5*(2) 9-24.

Lankford, W.M., & Riggs, W.E. (1996). Electronic data interchange: Where are we today. *Journal of Systems Management, 47*(2), 58-61.

Lee, Y.J. (2000). *Role and experience of SMEs in South Korea*. Huntington, NY: Nova Science Publisher, Inc.

Li, P. (2005). *The impact of adopting electronic data interchange on small and medium enterprise performance: A preliminary model of EDI adoption process in Singapore*. Unpublished Ph.D. Thesis, University of South Australia Division of International Business and Management.

Lim, K., & Kamarudin, B.T. (2002). The coming dawn of ebXML in Asia, Singapore EDI Committee. Retrieved June 10, 2008, from http://www.sec-edi.org/res_articles.htm

Mackay, D., & Rosier, M. (1996). Measuring organizational benefits of EDI diffusion: A case of the Australian automotive industry. *International Journal of Physical Distribution & Logistics Management, 26*(10), 60-66.

Maingot, M., & Quon, T. (2001). A survey of electronic data interchange (EDI) in the top public companies in Canada. *INFOR, 39*(3), 314-332.

Manus, P. (1993). EDI: Simple, but not easy. *Healthcare Financial Management, 47*(1), 2-30.

Massetti, B., & Zmud, R.W. (1996). Measuring the extent of EDI usage in complex organizations: Strategies and illustrative examples. *MIS Quarterly, 20*(3), 331-345.

Mische, M. (1992). EDI strategy: Business shift from technical to business goals. *Chief Information Officer Journal, 5*(1), 18-45.

National Computer Board. (1992). *A vision of an intelligent island: The IT 2000 report*. Singapore: National Computer Board.

OECD. (1998). *SMEs and electronic commerce*. Ottawa: Working Party on Small and Medium-sized Enterprises, The Directorate for Science,

Technology and Industry, Industry Committee, DSTL/IND/PME (1998) 18/REV1.

Ojala, L., & Suomi (1992). EDI: An advantage or disadvantage for remotely-situated countries? *International Journal of Physical Distribution & Logistics Management, 22*(8), 35-68.

Pfeiffer, H.K.C. (1992). *The diffusion of electronic data interchange.* Heidelberg, Germany: Physica-Verlag.

Premkumar, G., & Ramamurthy, K. (1995). The role of inter-organizational and organizational factors on the decision mode for adoption of inter-organizational systems. *Decision Science, 26*(3), 37-303.

Premkumar, G., Ramamurthy, K., & Crum, M. (1997). Determinants of EDI adoption in the transportation industry. *European Journal of Information Systems, 6*(2), 21-107.

Rajesh, C., & Vikas, K. (2002). *The Asian managers handbook of e-commerce.* New Delhi, India: Tata McGraw-Hill Publishing Company Limited.

Ratnasingham, P. (1997). EDI security: A model of EDI risks and associated controls. *Information Management & Computer Security, 5*(2), 63-71.

Rebecca, A., Nath, R., & Hendon, D.W. (1998). An empirical investigation of the level of electronic data interchange (EDI) implementation and its ability to predict EDI system success measures and EDI implementation factors. *International Journal of Physical Distribution & Logistics Management, 28*(9/10), 773-780.

Ricks, J.E. (1997). Electronically developed theory and procedure for distribution channel management via electronic data interchange linkage. *Logistics Information Management, 10*(1), 20-27.

Robson, L. (1994). EDI-changing business practice. *Logistics Information Management, 7*(4), 35-42.

Rogers, D.S., Daugherty, P.J., & Stank, T.P. (1992). Enhancing service responsiveness: The strategic potential of EDI. *International Journal of Physical Distribution and Logistics Management, 22*(8), 15-22.

SEC. (2001). *Singapore EDI committee (SEC) progress report.* Singapore: EDI Committee.

Shapiro, J. (1999). *SME electronic commerce study.* Singapore: PricewaterhouseCoopers.

SICC. (2000). *The investor's guide to Singapore* (2000 ed.). Singapore International Chamber of Commerce.

Sohel, A., & Schroeder, R.G. (2001). The impact of electronic data interchange on delivery performance. *Production and Operations Management, 10*(1), 16-30.

Swatman, P.M.C. (1994). Business process redesign using EDI: The BHP steel experience. *Australian Journal of Information Systems, 1*(2), 55-73.

Tabachnick, B.G., & Fidell, L.S. (2001). *Using mltivariate statistics* (4th ed.). Allyn & Bacon.

Takashi, T. (2001). *E-Commerce, opportunities and challenges for SMEs.* Asian Productivity Organization.

Takeaki, K. (2001). IT applications in Japanese SMEs. In T. Takashi (Ed.), *E-commerce, opportunities and challenges for SMEs* (pp. 109-110). Asian Productivity Organization.

Tan, C.Y., Thio, F.W., & Ser, T.H. (2003). *Facilitating cross-border trade with PKI and ebXML.* Singapore EDI Committee. Retrieved June 10, 2008, from http://www.sec-edi.org/res_articles.htm

Teo, H.H., Tan, B.C.Y., & Wei, K.K. (1997). Organizational transformation using electronic data interchange: The case of TradeNet in Singapore. *Journal of Management Information Systems, 13*(4), 139-165.

Tingle, A. (2000). EDI: Antiquated or ready for a rebirth? *Apparel Industry Magazine, 61*(1), 67-85.

Vijayasarathy, L.R., & Tyler, M.L. (1997). Adoption factors and electronic data interchange use: A survey of retail companies. *International Journal of Retail & Distribution Management, 25*(9), 286-292.

Walton, L.W. (1994). Electronic data interchange (EDI): A study of its usage and adoption within marketing and logistics channels. *Transportation Journal, 34*(2), 37-45.

Walton, S.V., & Gupta, J.N.D. (1999). Electronic data interchange for process change in an integrated supply chain. *International Journal of Operational & Production Management, 19*(4), 372-388.

Walton, S.V., & Marucheck, A.S. (1997). The relationship between EDI and supplier reliability. *International Journal of Purchasing and Materials Management, 33*(3), 37-76.

Williams, B.C., Hood, K.L., & Chen, J.C. (1997). Understanding changes in system, accounting and auditing: The impact of EDI. *Managerial Auditing Journal, 12*(6), 298-304.

Williams, L.R., Magee, G.D., & Suzuki, Y. (1998). A multidimensional view of EDI: Testing the value of EDI participation to firms. *Journal of Business Logistics, 9*(2), 73-87.

Wong, J., & Lam, E. (1999). *Measuring electronic commerce in Singapore: Methodological issues and survey findings.* Singapore: E-Commerce and Official Statistics, Singapore Department of Statistics.

Yang, J., & Miao, G. (2005). The estimates and forecasts of worldwide e-commerce. In *Proceedings of 7th International Conference on Electronic Commerce (ICEC'05)*, Xi'an, China, August (ACM 1-59593-112-0/05/08).

Zwass, V. (1996). Electronic commerce: Structures and issues. *International Journal of Electronic Commerce, 1*(1), 3-23.

ENDNOTES

[1] Australia, China, India, Japan, and South Korea

[2] ebXML is electronic business using eXtensible Markup Language which enables business to be conducted electronically between business partners in a secure, consistent, and interoperable manner.

Section 2.3
Web Services

Chapter XVI
Towards Google Earth:
A History of Earth Geography

Hatem F. Halaoui
Haigazian University, Lebanon

ABSTRACT

Using geographical information systems (GIS) has been of great interest lately. A lot of GIS applications are being introduced to regular and noncomputer-expert people through their everyday used machines such as cars (GPS), mobile (location systems), Internet (locating systems and direction guiders), and others. "Google Earth," a free online application, is one of those online geographical systems that provide users with a variety of functionalities towards exploring any place on the earth. The software uses Internet to connect to the online world database and travel in seconds between cities. This chapter briefly explores "Google Earth" and presents a possible future view and an extension of this GIS application by adding a time feature that gives "Google Earth" the ability to store the history of the geographical information that leads towards a new "Google Earth: A History of Earth Geography." For this purpose, the chapter presents storage and indexing approaches to be used for the storage, indexing, retrieval, and manipulation of geographical data used by the geographical database of the world used by "Google Earth."

INTRODUCTION

This chapter explores "Google Earth" and presents a possible future view of this geographical information systems (GIS) application by extending it with a temporal (from time) feature that gives "Google Earth" the ability to store the history of the spatial (from space) and geographical information that leads towards a new "Google Earth: A History of Earth Geography."

There are many reasons for ranking "Google Earth" as one of the most professional and well done works in the field of geographical information systems. This section briefly presents the four important reasons for considering "Google Earth" as a revolution in the world of Internet GIS:

1. **Easy use of the software:** The software is designed for any Internet user who does not know anything about how GIS systems behave. Spending 30 minutes to 1 hour exploring the software makes the user able to use most if not all the basic functionalities of the software.
2. **Availability of the software:** The software is available for free to be used by any Internet user. It is self-connected to the online database that is also available to everybody, through "Google Earth" (anyone having an Internet connection).
3. **Performance of the software:** The software interacts relatively very quickly with the user. If we consider the huge number of raster and other kinds of spatial and nonspatial data in the database, we can appreciate how fast "Google Earth" process the user input. The high performance is the result of using efficient spatial indexing structures and others. Such structures aim to index and categorize spatial data according to their position and use when the user asks a query. They consider the spatial information (location) in the query and go efficiently (in a tree structures, such as KD-trees, R-trees, or others) to the place asked in the query.
4. **Variety of data:** "Google Earth" offers different kinds of data. Here is a list of the most important:
    a. *Raster data:* Images with surfaces, elevation, and others.
    b. *Spatial data:* Geometries of spatial objects such as shapes, boundaries, directions, positions, distances, coordinates, and so forth.
    c. *Nonspatial data*: Information about the geography such as city names, country names, villages, businesses, and so forth.

d. *Video:* online satellite camera showing movement (with delay).

Introducing all these features to non-GIS users in a user-friendly layout is a revolution in the field of spatial information science. "Google Earth" made it so easy to explore the Earth in a mouse click.

It will be useful to introduce the following definitions before going on with this section:

*   **Spatial databases:** Database that deal with space and this includes geometries of objects, location of objects, and others
*   **Temporal databases or historical database:** Databases that deal with the history of changes where old, current, and sometime future (estimates) data are stored in the database. In this case, time is involved in two common ways:
    1. *Time stamp:* One attribute is used to save the time of the validity
    2. *Time interval:* Two attributes are used to indicate the interval of validity (start time and end time).
*   **Spatio-temporal databases:** A combination of spatial and temporal databases where changes occur on databases dealing with spatial information. Such databases are categorized in three main categories:
    1. *Discretely changing spatio-temporal databases:* Like the changes of the geometry of land parcels where it could occur once every year or more.
    2. *Continuously changing spatio-temporal databases:* Mostly deal with moving objects like plane or cars where the position of the object is changing continuously with time.
    3. A third category that is a combination of the above two.

The chapter is organized as follows: the next section presents the background of "Google

Earth," its functionalities, as well as background of spatial, temporal, and spatio-temporal indexing approaches and their use in spatio-temporal databases. The next section presents the possible future view of "Google Earth" by introducing a design for storing the history of the geographical data as well as a model for storing and indexing such huge number of data. We then discuss some conclusions of the work done and finally suggest some of the ideas that could be implemented in the future.

BACKGROUND

This section briefly presents "Google Earth" and its main functionalities. This information was collected when exploring and executing "Google Earth" as well as documentations, articles, and literature about the software (Google Earth, 2007). Moreover, the section provides some work done in the field of spatial, temporal, and spatio-temporal indexing. Some of these indexing structures could be used in "Google Earth" and give it the ability to store a history of the spatial data.

Google Earth: An Overview

Google Earth is a geographical system that offers the user satellite images of the locations along with spatial information (coordinates, elevation, etc.). It contains about 70.5 TB of Data (Google Earth Blog, 2006). As mentioned before, it provides the user with three main kinds of data: raster data, spatial, nonspatial data, and video.

Moreover, "Google Earth" offers a set of functionalities, and here is an important subset of them:

- **Answer location queries:** The user gives a location (New York, USA) as an input and gets a geographical image as an output. The image can explored in details

  i. ***This feature includes:*** Cities, businesses, public places (museums, etc.), and others.

- **Show directions:** The user gives a source and destination as inputs and gets a map (output) showing the directions with driving hints written on the map.

- **Displays spatial information:** Google Earth shows spatial information like coordinates, elevations, altitude, and others.

- **Has learning abilities:** Google Earth saves recently and regularly visited locations and queries so that the user avoids delays the next time these locations or queries asked.

- **Includes pre-known locations:** Google Earth offers a list of most used locations like government offices, schools, and others.

- **Provides user interaction:** The user is able to put place marks on the maps so can avoid delays the next time visits the same place.

- A prepaid online service that provides the customer with live video (with restriction and delay due to security) of any place in the world.

- **Other products like Google Earth PRO:** It is a paid service that makes it very easy to research locations and present discoveries. In just a few clicks, the user can import site plans, property lists, or client sites and share the view with clients or colleagues. Moreover, the user can export high-quality images to documents or the Web.

In this subsection, "Google Earth" will be briefly presented from two aspects: (1) User view and (2) Google Earth Enterprise.

Google Earth: User Solution

This subsection presents the main layout of "Google Earth" and the result of some common user queries that present the power of "Google Earth." Figure 1 presents the main layout displayed when the user execute "Google Earth." Figure 1

Figure 1. The main layout of Google Earth with brief description of some fields

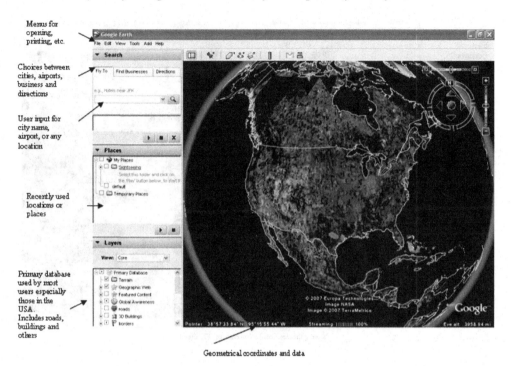

briefly explains some of the main graphical user interfaces and their use in the "Google Earth" Software.

The rest of this subsection will be a presentation of some sample queries executed using "Google Earth."

Example Query 1: JFK Airport

Figure 2 presents the result of running the "JFK, New York" as a query input given to "Google Earth." Figure 2 shows the text area where the query is written, the main zoom out map of JFK Airport, and the directional coordinates of the location. In order to view special places in this map, we have to zoom into the map which will lead to a close satellite image taken at some time lately. For an annual fee, the user will be able to see a live video of the movements happening at the current moment of the query execution (one or two minute delay).

Example Query 2: 5th Avenue, New York, NY

Figure 3 presents the output of another kind of queries where the street, city, and state (in the USA) are being given as an input (shown in the input text area). The output shown in Figure 3 presents a zoom out of the query in question with a text near the place asked in the query. Again, to see specific places, users have to zoom in, which is done in the few seconds that the software needs to get the zoomed data from the server.

Using the result of the query showing in Figure 3 and clicking on the icon (⊗) near "5th Ave, New York, NY" on the result map will result into a snapshot photo taken at that place, which is shown in Figure 4.

Figure 2. JFK Airport in New York after passing "JFK, New York" and a query key

Showing the directional coordinates of JFK airport

Figure 3. Manhattan (NY) with 5ᵗʰAvenue showing in the middle

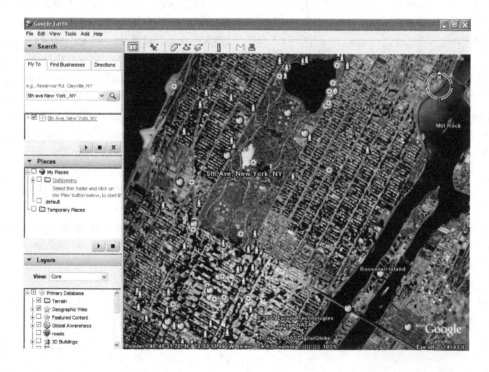

Figure 4. A central park picture after clicking on the "5ᵗʰ Ave, New York, NY"

Figure 5. Road and driving directions between New York, NY, and Jersey City, NJ

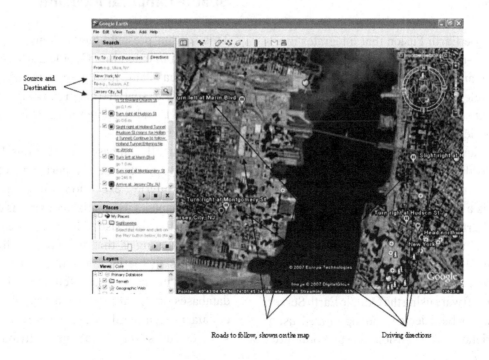

Example Query 3: Directions form "New York, NY" to "Jersey City, NJ"

Figure 5 shows the driving direction with a map image from New York, NY, to Jersey City, NJ. Figure 5 shows the inputs (source and destination) and outputs on the map (roads and driving direction). In such queries, "Google Earth" provides the user with some driving hints to be followed when driving from the source to the destination given in the query in question. The user can be more specific by passing a full address (building, street, city, state, and zip assuming the USA. is the country).

Google Earth: Enterprise Solution

This section presents some of the system aspects of Google Earth. The section is heavily dependent on the documentation provided by Google Earth official Web page (earth.google.com).

"Google Earth uses **70.5 TB of data**: 70 TB for the raw imagery and 500 GB for the index data" (Google Earth Blog, 2006). The Google Earth Enterprise Solution is composed of three main elements:

- Google Earth Fusion that integrates user's data—raster (imagery), GIS, terrain, point data, and others.
- Google Earth Server streams data to the client software (Google Earth EC).
- Google Earth EC (Enterprise Client) used for viewing, printing, data authoring, and so forth.

Here is a description of these three elements (Google Earth, 2007):

Google Earth Fusion integrates the user's geographical data into the Google Earth Enterprise system. When data is integrated, it is delivered to the client software using the Google Earth Server. Datasets can be selected and optimized using a user friendly GUI. Fusion can be configured to update data so that the user's Google Earth Enterprise system is synchronized to the latest available datasets.

The Google Earth Server sends the Google Earth database to the client software and includes some optional supporting services such as geocoding and others.

It uses Google Earth fusion to send data to the Google Earth Enterprise system. Google Earth Server can be configured as an overlay server or as a stand-alone server.

The overlay mode enables the user to benefit from Google's rich, multi-Terabyte basemap without the expense or hassle of licensing this data separately, updating, and hosting it.

Google Earth Enterprise Client (EC) is the part of the Google Earth client software designed to work in conjunction with Google Earth Fusion and Google Earth Server in stand-alone enterprise deployments. Google Earth EC contains all of the features of Google Earth PRO and adds support for connecting to multiple servers and for connecting to enterprise search servers.

Spatial, Temporal, and Spatio-Temporal Indexing

This section presents methods and approaches to be used in extending Google Earth to be able to historical data. It explores various methods for indexing spatial (geographical), temporal (historical), and spatiotemporal (history of geography) data.

Almost all databases use various kinds of indexing to maximize the performance of the database queries execution. Geographical or spatial databases use spatial indexing as the main index in the database. The main idea behind spatial indexing is that searching in the index is done using spatial information that could be locations in most cases. Temporal databases, databases designed to save a history or changes of data, use temporal indexes where the indexing structure uses time as the main attribute when searching in the index. In this sense, it will be obvious that spatiotemporal databases, which are a combination of spatial and temporal databases, use spatiotemporal indexes that use a combination of space and time attributes when searching in such index. This subsection, presents some of the proposed approaches in spatial, temporal, and spatiotemporal indexing. R-tree is presented as an example of spatial indexes, CTI is presented as an example of temporal indexes, whereas the Po-tree and AIRSTD are presented as examples of spatiotemporal indexes. The reason for such presentations is that a subset of these approaches will be proposed as part of the solution to reach our main goal proposed in this chapter that is "Google Earth: A History of Earth Geography."

Spatial Indexing: R-Tree

An R-tree is a hierarchical, height-balanced external memory data structure proposed by Guttman (1984). It is a general view of the B-tree for multidimensional spaces. Multidimensional objects are represented by what is called a Minimum Bounding Rectangle (MBR), where an MBR of an object is the smallest rectangle that encloses the object and has its sides parallel to the axes.

Figures 6 shows an example of a spatial object enclosed in a rectangle (MBR), section (a) of Figure 7 shows a group of MBRs, and section (b) of Figure 7 shows how these MBRs are indexed in an R-tree structure.

The R-tree (Guttman, 1984) consists of directory and leaf (data) nodes, each one corresponding to one disk page (secondary storage). Directory

Figure 6. An MBR enclosing geometry

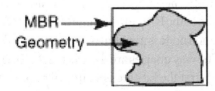

nodes contain entries of the form (container, ptr) where "ptr" is a pointer to a successor node in the next level of the tree, and "container" is the MBR of all the entries in the descendant node. Leaf nodes contain entries of the form (container, oid), where "oid" is an object-identifier used as a pointer to the real object, and it is the MBR of the corresponding object. Each page can hold up to "B" entries and all the nodes except the root must have at least "m" records (usually m=B/2). Thus the height of the tree is at most $\log_m N$ where N is the total number of objects.

Searching an R-tree is similar to searching a B-tree. At each directory node, we test all entries against the query, and then we visit all child nodes that satisfy the query. However, MBRs in a node are allowed to overlap. This is a potential problem with the R-tree, since, unlike B-trees, we may have to follow multiple paths when answering a query, although some of the paths may not contribute to the answer at all. In the worst case we may have to visit all leaf nodes.

Temporal Indexing: Changes Temporal Index

Halaoui (2005) presents the idea of "Changes Temporal Index" (CTI). The main definition used in this index can be declared as follows: "A database version at time T is the current version with some changes." The main idea behind this simple definition is that we will always use the current version (called "Now" version) as our main database and apply few changes to get the old ones. These changes are stored in minidatabases indexed by the temporal index CTI. The reason for not doing this the other way, that is the full version is the oldest one and all the rest are changes with respect to the oldest rather than the current, is that the most quires are done on the current and we do not want to construct the current version every time but have it ready all the time.

The indexing approach can be described as follows: Multiple versions are used to store the

Figure 7. (a) A collection of spatial objects in MBRs and (b) R-tree of MBRs

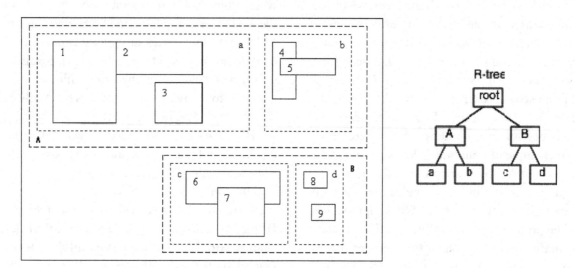

spatiotemporal database. Only the current version of the database contains information about all objects (or pointers to them). All old versions include objects (or pointers to them) that are valid at that version but not in the current version. In other words, these objects are the changes of the spatial information with respect to the current version. Figure 8 explains this idea, where the last version (current) includes the whole database that is available between some time n and now. All previous versions include only the tuples that are different at the time of their interval.

Moreover, Halaoui (2005) introduces some rules and algorithms for manipulating and querying the CTI structure. The following is a list of all the proposed algorithms:

- Updating tuples in the current database
- Adding a new tuple to the current database
- Deleting a tuple from the current database
- Querying, accessing, or building a snapshot of an old version
- Moving to a new version

Also we mention that since the CTI is ordered according to time, it is better to use an efficient structure like B-trees or Binary Search trees when indexing the versions according to time.

Spatio-Temporal Indexing: PoTree

This section presents recent work (Noel, Servigne, & Laurini, 2005) in spatial and temporal information structuring for natural (volcano) risk monitoring. In these papers, Noel, Servigne, and Laurini (2005) and Noel et al. (2004) discuss methods and approaches that they designed and applied for volcanic activity monitoring of a Mexican volcano. The project uses the PoTree as the spatiotemporal index used when querying the database with data describing the activity of the volcano.

The PoTree (Noel et al., 2005) is a spatiotemporal index with two kinds of structures: a Kd-tree and a B+ tree. The Kd-tree (a well-known spatial index structure for efficient access of spatial objects) is not a traditional tree. Instead, each leaf node in the tree points to a B+ tree. The B+ tree (also a well-known structure and considered as an extension of the B-tree) uses time to order its nodes, where each node is a spatial object associated with time. The way queries are done in the Po-Tree is as follows: first the kd-tree is searched according to

Figure 8. A time interval index pointing to the changes and the current databases

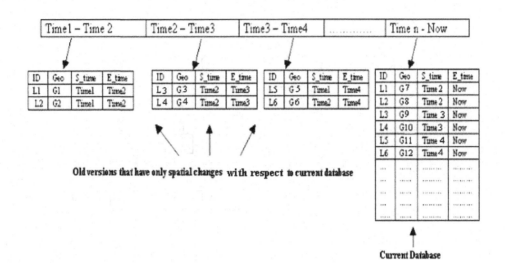

spatial attributes of the object then the B+ tree is also searched according the time attribute. Figure 9 represents the Po-Tree structure.

It is mentioned (Noel et al., 2005; Noel et al., 2004) that the Po-tree works the best when real time data is applied. Real-time data points to the data that changes so frequently, which is the case of the Mexican volcano example (Noel et al., 2005) each sensor send many data per minute.

Spatio-Temporal Indexing: AIRSTD Structure

AIRSTD structure (Halaoui, 2006) is a combination of CTI and R-Tree (Figures 6 and 7). All algorithms applied for CTI and R-tree can be applied to AIRSTD. Figure 10 illustrates the AIRSTD structure that is composed of the CTI (Figure 8) and R-tree (Figures 6 and 7). This proposal differentiate between the current version and the "Now" version. The current version is considered as the changes happened during the last period of time that last from some past time till the current time or what is called "Now." The "Now" version is the full database valid at the current time with all information spatially indexed by the R-tree spatial index.

As mentioned, only the "Now" version is a full version, where others point only to a list of changes with respect to the current node. The main goal behind this approach is that we want our "Now" version to be spatially indexed for better querying, especially when spatial information is used in the queries.

Halaoui (2006) presents the following algorithms that work of the AIRSTD structure:

- Updating tuples in the "Now" database
- Adding a new tuple to the "Now" database
- Deleting a tuple from the "Now" database
- Searching any version at any time
- Building a snapshot of any version at any time

As discussed in (Halaoui, 2006), AIRSTD works the best when applied to discretely changing data. Such data changes slowly (many times per year) like land parcels, cities structures as buildings, road networks, and others.

Figure 9. The PoTree

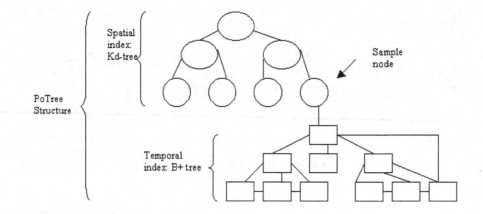

GOOGLE EARTH, A HISTORY OF EARTH GEOGRAPHY: ISSUES AND RECOMMENDATIONS

This section presents the issues and problems faced when extending "Google Earth" towards storing the history of Earth geography. As a solution, a model using previously discussed approaches is presented to be used when developing the future design of "Google Earth."

Issues, Controversies, Problems

The main issue that we raise in this chapter is the ability of "Google Earth" to present a history of that geographical information. An example of a simple query that "Google Earth" cannot answer (until the time of writing this chapter) is: what did JFK Airport look like on 1/3/1965. If we want to translate this English query as "Google Earth" query input, it will be summarized into two main inputs: (1) JFK, New York and (2) 1/3/1965 (or just 1965 if only the year is considered

Figure 10. AIRSTD structure

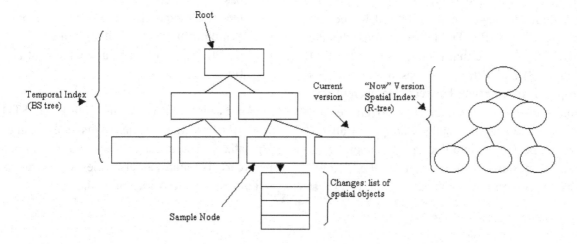

as the time period). Such a query cannot be done without having the old information stored in the database.

The following issues and functionalities are still missed by "Google Earth" in order to gain the ability of storing historical geographical data:

- **The time attribute:** To be able to store history, all databases must introduce time (or intervals) in their data structures or database relational model as a main attribute which most likely will be a part of the primary key in any database table.
- **The time operations:** After introducing the time attribute to the database, there must be operations and predicates that can be applied on data with time and consider time as an input of most queries.
- **The efficient storage:** Having time and time operations in the database will require changing the storage structure toward a better. The reason for such a step is that the database will be much bigger and could be huge when the database is changing so frequently. The storage structure will also need an index that considers time (temporal index) in addition to the spatial index that is already in use.

Solutions and Recommendations

This section proposes the main steps for a possible solution that gives "Google Earth" the ability to store a history of the world geographical database. For this reason, the section also presents some recommendations of some approaches to be used in such a solution. Note that the proposed solution does not include the videos (provided by satellite cameras) and their history.

Solution: Extending "Google Earth" Towards Storing and Presenting a History of Maps

The main steps towards this goal can be summarized in two steps:

1. **Time attribute:** Adding a time attribute (or interval) to the database.
   a. All objects (tables) that change with time must have two time attributes (start time and end time) representing a time interval validity of the object
   b. Example: City (ID, Name, Geometry, Stime, Etime) where Geometry represents the geometrical shape of the city, Stime and Etime represent the start and end times, which act as the time interval of validity.
2. **Efficient storage of historical and current data:** Using spatial, temporal, and spatiotemporal indexing in order to index the old and current data and hence be able to access them efficiently.
   a. We keep the same spatial index being used currently by "Google Earth." This index will be used for indexing the "Now" version that represent the data valid at the current time (now).
   b. We use an additional spatiotemporal index to index the changes with respect to the "Now" database. Such index will be used when historical queries are asked.

Moreover, the layout of "Google Earth" has to include an optional input area that allows the user to input time as an attribute of the query in case the user is interested in the history. Figure 11 simply shows a possible view of such a layout where only an additional input area used for dates is added under the query input field.

Figure 11. New "Google Earth" with only additional input representing the time

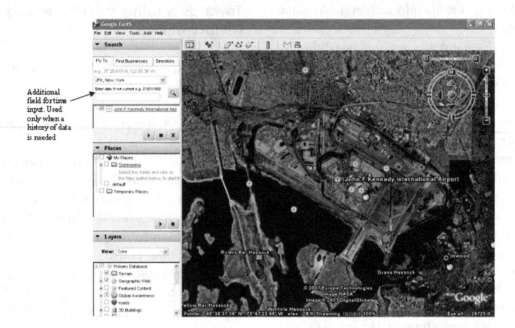

Recommendations: A Data Storage Model to Store Historical and Current Data

For the sake of reaching the goals mentioned in the "Solutions" section, a storage model is recommended. The choice of the spatial index in the model will be kept open for the software analysts to recommend. The reason for such a decision is that each kind of spatial indexing has positives and negatives that depend on the kind of queries that are frequently asked; most which are beyond the knowledge of this chapter.

The model is presented in Figure 12, which shows two indexing structures used to store the world geographical database and its history:

1. The B-tree (on the left) used to store the changes that describe the difference between the old versions at some past times and the current version named the "Now" version. This part use the idea of the temporal index CTI (Figure 8) described earlier in this chapter.

2. The spatial index (could be any spatial index like R-tree (Guttman, 1984), Kd-tree or any other used by "Google Earth") used to index the "Now" database that is the latest updated data. This is usually the database used currently by Google Earth.

The main idea is to have a ready database (which is the "Now database") where most user queries are asked and a set of minidatabases. These minidatabases are ordered and indexed according to their time interval (TI) of validity and each include the changes that should be done on the "Now database" to get the database at the period TI.

It is useful to mention that the model in Figure 12 is similar some how to the AIRSTD model (Figure 10) presented earlier in the "Background" section. In that sense, we can take advantage of all algorithms offered in that approach with few changes due to the choice of the spatial index. Again, here is a list of the algorithms proposed in the AIRSTD (Halaoui, 2006) approach:

Figure 12. The mdel towards Google Earth: A history of geography

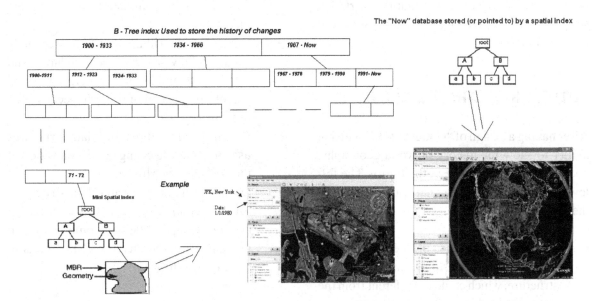

- Updating tuples in the "Now" database
- Adding a new tuple to the "Now" database
- Deleting a tuple from the "Now" database
- Searching any version at any time
- Building a snapshot of any version at any time

The reason of choosing AIRSTD as an idea to be used in "Google Earth" is that AIRSTD has been proven to be efficient with discretely changing databases, which is the case in "Google Earth." However, it could be the case that others like Po-Tree work better or could work together. This conclusion can be done after research and studies on the kinds of data, rate of change, and queries asked.

CONCLUSION

This chapter presents one of the recent popular online geographical information systems "Google Earth," its background, its functionalities, and a future view towards "Google Earth: A History of Geography." The chapter can be summarized in the following points:

- Briefly presents "Google Earth."
- Presents the execution of some sample queries to give an idea about "Google Earth" functionalities.
- Introduces spatial, temporal, and spatiotemporal indexing as structures used or could be used in future to store data used by "Google Earth."
- Proposes a solution to be used by "Google Earth" to be able to store history.
- And finally recommends some structures to be used in this solution by presenting a model describing the proposed solution.

It is useful to mention again that this could be done with just extending the current system of "Google Earth." It can happen by keeping all currently used structures in the system and add indexed minidatabases to store the history. These minidatabases (discussed in the "Solutions" section) will be only accessed when time (history) is involved. All approaches presented in this chapter have been implemented and tested and hence can be used. The only concern is that the work that should be done when adding the time attributes to the databases.

FUTURE RESEARCH DIRECTIONS

After having a design of "Google Earth" with the ability to show the history of world geography, a lot of work can be done in the future. The following is a group of ideas that could be done in the future:

- Analysis on the kinds of queries asked by a user to find the best indexing and storage structure, which could be different from the ones proposed in this chapter. For example, it has been shown in many studies that the kd-tree spatial index works the best when dynamic systems are involved where databases are updated almost continuously while the system is running. This could not be the case in most of the geographical information of "Google Earth" but could be the case if the movements of objects were part of the history. In that sense, studies should be done in order to choose the best kinds of indexing for the different kinds of data.
- Extend "Google Earth" to be able to store a history of the movement (coordinates and not just videos) of objects over time (planes, cars, land, etc.). In this case, "Google Earth" will be dealing with another kind of spatiotemporal database called continuously changing spatiotemporal databases. For this purpose, different and more suitable spatiotemporal indexing structures and database models will be needed.
- Extend "Google Earth" with purely temporal indexes (like CTI) to store a history of the video recordings (by satellite cameras). However, such a step is very huge due to the huge space it needs to store such data.

- Design of algorithms and data structures used to compare and analyze current and old versions.
- Design of algorithms and data structures used to show the evolution of lands and surfaces (Example: split or merging of land parcels, movement of water in oceans, etc.) over history.
- Design of algorithms and data structures used to show the change of the elevation of the surfaces over history.
- Design of algorithms and data structures used for computing statistical information about city population that could be known by comparing the increase of buildings in the city over history.

REFERENCES

Abdelguerfi, M., & Givaudan, J. (2002). Advances in spatio-temporal r-tree based structures (Tech. Rep. TR012-02). Computer Science Department, University of New Orleans.

Abdelguerfi, M., Julie, G., Kevin, S., & Ladner, R. (2002). Spatio-temporal data handling: The 2-3TR-tree, a trajectory-oriented index structure for fully evolving valid-time spatio-temporal datasets. In *Proceedings of the 10th ACM International Symposium on Advances in Geographic Information Systems*.

Google Earth. (2007). *Explore, search and discover.* Retrieved June 12, 2008, from http://earth.google.com/tour/index.html

Google Earth Blog. (2006). *Google Earth data size, live local, new languages coming.* Retrieved June 12, 2008, from http://www.gearthblog.com/blog/archives/2006/09/news_roundup_google.html

Guttman, A. (1984). R-tree: A dynamic index structure for spatial searching. In *Proc. of the 1984 ACM SIGMOND International Conference on Management Data,* Boston, MA (pp. 47-57).

Halaoui, H. (2005). Spatio-temporal data model: Data model and temporal index using versions for spatio-temporal databases. In *Proceedings of the GIS Planet 2005*, Estoril, Portugal.

Halaoui, H. (2006) AIRSTD: An approach for indexing and retrieving spatio-temporal data. In *Proceedings of the ACM/IEEE SITIS06*, Hammamet, Tunisia.

Nascimento, M., & Silva, J. (1998). Towards historical r-trees. In *Proceedings of the ACM Symposium on Applied Computing* (pp. 235-240).

Noel, G., et al. (2004). The po-tree, a real-time spatio-temporal data indexing structure. In *Proc. of Development in Spatial Data Handling SDH2004*, Leicester (pp. 259-270).

Noel, G., Servigne, S., & Laurini, R. (2005). Spatial and temporal information structuring for natural risk monitoring. In *Proc. GIS Planet 2005*, Estoril, Portugal.

Procopiuc, C., Agarwal, P., & Har-Peled, S. (2000). Star-tree: An efficient self-adjusting index for moving points. In *Proc. ALENEX*.

Saltenis, S., et al. (2000). Indexing the positions of continuously moving objects. In *the Proceedings of ACM SIGMOD2000*.

Schreck, T., & Chen, Z. (2000). R-tree implementation using branch-grafting method. In *Proc. of 2000 ACM Symposium*.

Shekhar, S., & Chawla, S. (2003). *Spatial databases: A tour*. Upper Saddle River, NJ: Prentice Hall.

Theodoridis, Y., Sellis, Papadopoulos, T A., & Manolopoulos, Y. (1998). Specifications for efficient indexing in spatio-temporal databases. In *Proc. SSDBM* (pp. 123-132).

Tsotras, V.J., Jensen, C.S., & Snodgrass, R.T. (1998). An extensible notation for spatio-temporal index queries. *ACM SIGMOND Record,* 47-53.

Tsotras, V.J., & Kangelaris, N. (1995). The snapshot index, an I/O-optimal access method for time-slice queries. *Information Systems, 20*(3).

ADDITIONAL READING

Al-Taha, K., et al. (1994). Bibliography on spatio-tempoal databases. *ACM SIGMOND Record, 22,* 59-67.

Antonio, J. C., & Güting, R.H. (2000). Dual grid: A new approach for robust spatial algebra implementation. In *CHOROCHRONOS Project*.

Bodolay, M., & Escobar-Molano, M. (2000). A schema-less spatio-temporal database system. In *Proc. SAC00 ACM*.

Davis Jr., et al. (1999). Multiple representations in GIS: Materialization through map generalization, geometric and spatial analysis operations. In *ACM GIS'99*, (pp. 60-65).

Dayal, G., & Wuu, T.J. (1992). A uniform approach to processing temporal queries. In *Proc. of the ACM 18th International Conference on Very Large Data Bases*.

Djafri, N., et al. (2002). Spatio-temporal evolution: Querying patterns of change in databases. In *Proceedings of ACM GIS2002 Conference*.

Egenhofer, J. (1994). Spatial SQL: A query and presentation language. *IEEE Transactions on Knowledge and Data Engineering, 6,* 86-95.

Fuhrmann, S., & Pike, W. (2004). User-centered design of collaborative geovisualization tools. In J. Dykes, A. MacEachren, & M. J. Kraak (Eds.), *Exploring geovisualization* (pp. 591-609). Elsevier.

Garnett, & Tansel, A.U. (1992). Equivalence of the relational algebra and calculus for nested relations. *Computers Math. Applic. 23*(10), 3-25.

Google. (2007). Hurricane Katrina imagery. Retrieved June 12, 2008, from http://earth.google.com/katrina.html2

Google Earth Blog. (2005). Hurricane Katrina archives. Retrieved June 12, 2008, from http://www.gearthblog.com/blog/archives/hurricane_katrina/2

Griffiths, T., et al. (2001). Triod: A comprehensive system for the management of spatial and aspatial historical objects. In *Proceeding of ACM Conference GIS'01*.

Güting, R.H. (1989). Gral: An extensible relational database system for geometric applications. In *Proceeding of the 15th Conference on Very Large Databases*.

Güting, R.H., et al. (1995). Implementation of the ROSE aAlgebra: Efficient algorithms for realm-based spatial data types. In *Proc. of the 14th Intl. Symposium on Large Databases* (pp. 216-239).

Koubarakis, M. (Ed.). (2003). *Spatio-temporal databases: The CHOROCHRONOS approach.* Springer.

Lander, R., Kevin, S., & Abdelguerfi, M. (Eds.). (2002). Mining spatio-temporal information systems. Kluwer Academic Press.

Nascimento, M. & Silva, J. (1998). Towards historical r-trees. In *Proc. of ACM Symposium on Applied Computing* (pp. 235-240).

National Research Council. (2007). *Successful response starts with a map: Improving geospatial support for disaster management.* Washington, DC: National Academies Press.

Nourbakhsh I. (2006). Mapping Disaster Zones. *Nature, 439.*

Open Geospatial Consortium. (2005). OGC announces risk and crisis management working group. Retrieved June 12, 2008, from http://www.opengeospatial.org/pressroom/pressreleases/4223

Papadimitriou, H., Suciu, D., & Vianu, V. (1996). Topological queries in spatial databases. In *ACM PODS*, (pp. 81-92).

Robinson, A.C., & Weaver, C. (2006). Re-visualization: Interactive visualization of the process of visual analysis. In *Workshop on Visualization, Analytics & Spatial Decision Support at the GIScience Conference*, Münster, Germany.

Snodgrass, R.T. (1987). The temporal query language tquel. *ACM Trans. Database Systems, 12*(2), 247-298.

Tansel, A.U. (1986). Adding time dimension to relational model and extending relational algebra. *Information Systems, 11*(4), 343-355.

Tansel, A.U. (1991). A historical query language. *Information Sciences Journal, 53,* 101-133.

Tansel, A.U. (1993). Temporal data modeling and integrity constraints in relational databases. In *ISCIS 2004*, (pp. 459-469).

Worboys, M.F. (1992). A generic model for planar geographic objects. *International Journal of Geographical Information Systems, 6*(5), 353-372.

Worboys, M. (1994). A unified model for spatial and temporal information. *The Computer Journal, 37*(1), 27-34.

Worboys, M.F. (1994). Object-oriented approaches to geo-referenced information. *International Journal of Geographical Information Systems, 8*(4), 385-399.

Zeiler, M. (1999). *Modeling our world.* New York: ESRI Press.

Chapter XVII
Empirical Studies for Web Effort Estimation

Sergio Di Martino
Università di Salerno, Italy
Università degli Studi di Napoli "Federico II", Italy

Filomena Ferrucci
Università di Salerno, Italy

Carmine Gravino
Università di Salerno, Italy

ABSTRACT

Web technologies are being even more adopted for the development of public and private applications, due to the many intrinsic advantages. Due to this diffusion, estimating the effort required to develop Web applications represents an emerging issue in the field of Web engineering since it can deeply affect the competitiveness of a software company. To this aim, in the last years, several estimation techniques have been proposed. Moreover, many empirical studies have been carried out so far to assess their effectiveness in predicting Web application development effort. In the chapter, we report on and discuss the results of the most significant empirical studies undertaken in this field.

INTRODUCTION

The availability of powerful server-side, Web-oriented component technologies, such as J2EE, ASP.NET, and so forth, has led to profound changes in the scenario of software systems, al-

lowing developers to create "Web applications," that is, highly-dynamic systems able to deliver a complex amount of functionalities, while running in a Web browser. The approach provides many advantages. In particular, it permits deployment of applications without caring of the client platform, it fully exploits the MVC architecture, and it allows different applications to easily interoperate, by using standard communication protocols and languages, such as XML. As a result, Web applications are becoming an essential support for the every-day activities of both public and private organizations. For instance, to date, most intranet applications, such as document management systems, workflow, and business organization, and B2B solutions are developed with this approach.

On the other hand, the development of these applications has introduced a set of unique features and characteristics, quite different from traditional software construction (Deshpande, 2002; Ginige & Murugesan, 2001). The main issues can be summarized as follows: the requirements are instable, their development is usually characterized by pressure time and compressed schedule; the employed technologies rapidly changes (technology instability), they are usually developed by a small team including young developers, with different backgrounds and knowledge, compared to a traditional software development team. So, a lot of research is needed to provide software engineers with tools and methodologies able to ensure a cost-effective development of this kind of systems. In particular, the traditional approaches for software cost estimation need to be adequately modified to take into account the specific characteristics of these applications. To this aim, currently, many researchers are addressing the crucial problem of estimating the effort required to develop Web applications. Indeed, development effort, meant as the work carried out by software engineers, is the dominant project cost, being also the most difficult to estimate and control, with significant effects on the overall costs. So, effort estimation is a critical activity for planning and monitoring software project development and for delivering the product on time and within budget. Significant over or under-estimates can be very expensive and deleterious for a company. Thus, it is paramount for the competitiveness of a company to be able to

effectively predict in advance the effort required to develop a Web-based project (Baresi, Morasca, & Paolini, 2003; Costagliola, Di Martino, Ferrucci, Gravino, Tortora, & Vitiello, 2006a; Mendes, Counsell, & Mosley, 2003b; Reifer, 2000; Ruhe, Jeffery, & Wieczorek, 2003b), and Web effort estimation is an important topic in the field of Web engineering. In this context, special attention is devoted to identifying suitable tools and approaches and to proving by empirical studies that the proposals can be effectively and affordably used in the industrial context.

Goal of the Chapter

The objective of this chapter is to report on the most significant empirical studies undertaken so far and aimed at assessing the effectiveness of measures and techniques for estimating Web application development effort.

BACKGROUND

In the literature, a lot of different methods to estimate software development effort have been proposed. A widely accepted taxonomy of estimation methods classified them in *Non-Model Based* and *Model Methods* (Briand & Wieczorek, 2002).

While *Non-Model Based Methods* mainly take into account expert judgments (thus with highly subjective factors), *Model Based Methods* involve the application of some algorithms to a number of inputs to produce an effort estimation. The inputs for these algorithms are the factors that heavily influence the resulting development effort of a software project. Among these, *Software Size* is accepted as a key cost driver, since it deeply affects total development effort, and thus total project cost (Bohem et al., 2000). Consequently, being able to obtain an early *size measure* for a project can provide a significant estimation of the overall development cost.

In the context of Software Engineering, widely employed *Model Based* estimation methods are Linear Regression (LR), Case Based-Reasoning (CBR), and Regression Tree (RT) (see, for example, Briand, El-Emam, Surmann, Wiekzorek, & Maxwell, 1999b; Briand, El-Emam, & Wiekzorek, 2000; Shepperd & Schofield, 2000). These approaches use data from past projects, characterized by attributes that are related to effort (e.g., the size), and the actual effort to develop the projects, to estimate effort for a new project under development. In the last years, many researchers and practitioners tried to apply these methods to Web applications. In particular, in the literature there are several works that address the problem of estimating the effort required to develop Web applications (Baresi et al., 2003; Costagliola et al., 2006a, 2006b; Mendes, Counsell, & Mosley, 2002a, 2003a, 2003b; Mendes, Counsell, Mosley, Triggs, & Watson, 2002, 2003; Reifer, 2000; Ruhe, Jeffery, & Wieczorek, 2003a) by identifying measures related to effort and validating them by empirical studies. Indeed, it is largely acknowledged that a software measure and/or estimation method or technique can be acceptable and effectively usable only if it has been validated through several empirical studies proving its usefulness (Basili, Briand, & Melo, 1996; Basili, Shull, & Lanubile, 1999; Briand et al., 1999b; Genero & Piattini, 2001; Mendes, Counsell, & Mosley, 2003b; Myrtveit, Shepperd, & Stensrud, 2005; Schneidewind, 1992).

A crucial aspect in performing empirical studies concerns the availability of a data set of past projects. Indeed, in order to build a model to estimate the effort of a new project, *Model Based Methods* exploit information of past projects on the actual development effort and on the factors that can influence the effort (e.g., the software size). Recently, some researchers have addressed the issue to understand whether a cross-company data set (i.e., a data set containing project data from several software companies) can provide estimates for the new projects comparable to

the one obtained from single-company data sets (i.e., data sets containing project data from a single company). Several empirical studies have addressed this issue (see, for example, Briand, El-Eman, Maxwell, Surmann, & Wieczorek, 1999; Jeffery, Ruhe, & Wieczorek, 2000, 2001; Lefley & Shepperd, 2003; Mendes, Lokan, Harrison, & Triggs, 2005; Ruhe & Wieczorek, 2002).

Estimation Techniques

Linear Regression (LR) is a statistical technique that explores the relationship between a dependent variable and one or more independent variables, providing a prediction model described by an equation

$$y = b_1 x_1 + b_2 x_2 + \dots + b_n x_n + c$$

where y is the dependent variable, x_1, x_2, ..., x_n are the independent variables, for i=1,..,n, b_i is the coefficient that represents the amount the variable y changes when the variables x changes 1 unit, and c is the intercept (Montgomery, Peck, & Vining, 2001).

In effort estimation, LR is usually exploited to obtain linear regression models that use the variable representing the effort as dependent and the variables denoting the employed size measures (e.g., number of Web pages, number of *Web Objects*, number of *COSMIC-FFP*, etc.) as independent. Once the prediction model has been constructed (i.e., an instance of the previous equation), the effort estimation for a new project can be obtained by substituting in this equation the project size, expressed in terms of the employed measure.

The idea behind the use of the Case-Based Reasoning (CBR) technique is to predict the effort of a new project by considering data on similar projects previously developed. In particular, the completed projects are characterized in terms of a set of *p* features, forming the *case base*. The new project is also characterized in terms of the same *p* attributes and it is referred as the *target case*. Then, the similarity between the target case and the other cases in the *p*-dimensional feature space is measured, and the most similar cases (or projects) are used, possibly with adaptations to obtain a prediction for the target case (Aamodt & Plaza, 1994; Myrtveit & Stensrud, 1999; Shepperd & Schofield, 2000). To apply the CBR technique, a Measurer has to select: the relevant project features, the appropriate similarity function, the number of analogies to select the similar projects to consider for estimation, and the analogy adaptation strategy for generating the estimation. In the effort estimation, usually the size measures have been exploited as the set of features characterizing the projects. It is worthwhile to point out that the selection of the similarity function and the number of analogies is a crucial decision. Many researchers suggested use of Euclidean distance as similarity measure and 1, 2, and 3 analogies to identify similar projects (Briand et al., 2000; Briand, El-Emam, Surmann, et al., 1999; Mendes, Counsell, & Mosley, 2002a; Mendes, Counsell, Mosley, Triggs et al., 2003). The analogy adaptation step allows for deciding how to obtain estimation after the most similar cases have been determined. Widely used adaptation techniques are the *nearest neighbour* (Briand, El-Emam, Surmann, et al., 1999; Mendes, Counsell, & Mosley, 2002a) the *mean of the closest analogies* (Mendes, Counsell, & Mosley, 2002a; Mendes, Counsell, Mosley, Triggs, et al., 2003; Myrtveit & Stensrud, 1999), the *inverse distance weighted mean*, and *inverse rank weighted mean* (Shepperd & Schofield, 2000).

Regression Tree (RT) is a variant of decision trees that can be used to approximate real-valued functions (Briand et al., 2000; Briand, El-Emam, Surmann, et al., 1999b; Mendes, Counsell, Mosley, Triggs et al., 2003). This technique takes as input a set of numerical variables (usually the size measures) and generates a binary tree predicting the value of the target variable (the development effort). In particular, the leaves of the binary tree

suggest the values for the target variable on the base of the values of the predicting variables. The binary tree is built by recursively splitting the input data (i.e., the values of the predicting variables) into partitions. At the beginning, all data are associated to the root. Then, they are split in two parts, minimizing the sum of the squared deviations from the mean in the separated parts. At each split, the process determines the input variable to be used for splitting, and its values to associate to the left and right child nodes, respectively. Let us observe that each node has associated the mean value of the target variable. The process ends when, for each node, a minimum size, specified for the node by the user, is obtained. Subsequently, to determine the predicted value for the target variable, we start from the root node and then follow the right or left branch, based on the value of the splitting variable. We continue until a leaf node is reached, which contains the predicted value.

Validation Method and Evaluation Criteria

Validation is a crucial step in the empirical studies in order to verify whether or not the predicted efforts are useful estimations of the actual development efforts. A *cross validation* is widely employed to address it. In particular, this method partitions the data set into two randomly selected sets: the *training set* for model building and the *test set* for model evaluation.

To assess the acceptability of the derived estimations, summary measures, like *MMRE* and *Pred*(0.25) (Conte, Dunsmore, & Shen, 1986), together with *boxplots of (absolute) residuals* (Kitchenham, Pickard, MacDonnell, & Shepperd, 2001; Mendes, Counsell, & Mosley, 2005b). *MMRE* and *Pred*(0.25) are widely employed in the literature to assess the accuracy of effort estimation (see, for example, Briand, El-Emam, Surmann, et al., 1999; Briand, El-Emam, & Wieczorek, 1999, 2000; Briand & Wieczorek, 2002;

Costagliola et al., 2006a; Costagliola, Martino, Ferrucci, Gravino, Tortora, & Vitiello, 2006b; Mendes, Counsell, & Mosley, 2003a, 2003b, 2003c; Mendes, Counsell, Mosley, Triggs, et al., 2003; Mendes & Kitchenham, 2004a, 2004b; Myrtveit. & Stensrud, 1999; Ruhe et al., 2003a, 2003b). In the following, we will briefly recall the main concepts underlying *MMRE* and *Pred*(0.25), and boxplots.

The *Magnitude of Relative Error* (Conte et al., 1986) is defined as

MRE = |EFHreal — EFHpred | / EFHreal

where *EFHreal* and *EFHpred* are the actual and the predicted efforts, respectively. MRE has to be calculated for each observation in the data set. To have a cumulative measure of the error, all the MRE values are aggregated across all the observations using the mean and the median, thus obtaining two measures of the central tendency, known as Mean of *MRE* (*MMRE*), and Median MRE (*MdMRE*), where the latter is less sensitive to extreme values (Mendes, Counsell, Mosley, Triggs, et al., 2003).

The Prediction at level 0.25 (Conte et al., 1986) is defined as

Pred (0.25) = k /N

where k is the number of observations whose *MRE* is less than or equal to 0.25, and N is the total number of observations. In other words, *Pred*(0.25) is a quantification of the predictions whose error is less than 25%. According to Conte et al. (1986), a good effort prediction model should have a *MMRE*≤0.25 and *Pred*(0.25)≥0.75, meaning that at least 75% of the predicted values should fall within 25% of their actual values.

Boxplots are widely employed in exploratory data analysis since they provide a quick visual representation to summarize the data using five numbers: the median, upper and lower quartiles, minimum and maximum values, and outliers (Kitchenham et al., 2001). The box of the plot is a rectangle with an end at each quartile and a line is drawn across the box at the sample median (*m* in Figure 1). The lower quartile (*l* in Figure 1) is determined considering the bottom half of the data, below the median, for example, by finding the median of this bottom data, while the upper quartile (*u* in Figure 1) is the median of the upper half of the data, above the median. The length of the box *d* is the interquartile range of the statistical sample. Lower tail is *u*+1.5*d while *u*-1.5*d is the Upper tail. Points at a distance from the median greater than 1.5 times the interquartile range represent potential outliers and are plotted individually.

In recent studies (see, for example, Costagliola et al., 2006b; Kitchenham et al., 2001; Mendes, Counsell, Mosley, Triggs, et al., 2003; Mendes, Counsell, & Mosley, 2005a, 2005b; Mendes & Kitchenham, 2004b; Ruhe et al., 2003b), the effectiveness of the obtained estimations of effort have been assessed by taking into account first the summary statistics and then the boxplots of absolute residuals, where residuals are calculated as (*EFHreal — EFHpred*).

Figure 1. The boxplot

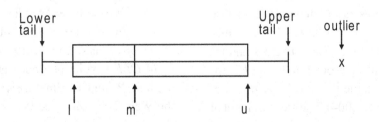

315

In the following, we recall the main concepts of LR, CBR, and RT, and the methods widely adopted in the literature to validate the obtained estimations. Then, we will report on and discuss the most important empirical studies dealing with the estimation of Web development effort.

EMPIRICAL STUDIES

In the context of Web effort estimation, many empirical studies have been carried out aiming to address one of the following research issues:

- Verify the usefulness of size measures and cost factors for estimating Web application development effort.
- Verify the appropriateness of methods and techniques to provide effective effort estimations for Web applications.
- Verify the usefulness of cross-company data set for estimating Web application development effort.

In the following, we report on and discuss the empirical studies provided in the literature, taking into account the above research directions.

Empirical Studies Focused on Size Measures

In the last years some measures have been proposed to size Web Applications, such as *Web Objects* defined by Reifer (2000), *COSMIC-FFP* (COSMIC, 2005), the measures defined in the *Tukutuku* database by Mendes, Counsell, and Mosley (2003c), and *Length* and *Functional* measures investigated by Costagliola et al. (2006b)

Web Objects represent an extension of Function Points (FPs) (Albrecht, 1979), which are briefly recalled in the following. The current standard definition and counting procedure of the *FP* approach is reported in the IFPUG Counting Practices Manual (IFPUG, 2004). The measurement of

the system size starts with the identification of all the functions, which can be of the following types: *external input, external output, external inquiry, internal logical file* and *external interface file*. The first three classes are considered transaction function types while the last two are considered data function types. Then, these identified functions are weighted in agreement with standard values specified in the Counting Practices Manual, by using their types and the level of their complexity. The *Web Objects* approach extends FPs by introducing four new Web-related components (*multimedia files, Web building blocks, scripts* and *links*), used as predictors together with the five traditional function types of FPs.

Ruhe et al. (2003a) were the first to investigate *Web Objects* by performing an empirical study based on a data set of 12 Web projects from industrial world, in order to establish whether or not this measure can be used to predict the development effort of Web applications in terms of person-hours, gathering interesting prediction results. In particular, these authors compared *Web Objects* with FPs and the results of the empirical analysis revealed that the model based on *Web Objects* presented significantly better prediction accuracy. In particular, they used LR as estimation technique and obtained an MMRE=0.24 and Pred(0.25)=0.67 for *Web Objects*, while the FPs produced a MMRE=0.33 and Pred(0.25)=0.42. These authors exploited 12 Web projects developed by a small-sized Australian software development company, which were very typical application in Web domain, for example, one for analysing and managing stock or transactions, several Web-based content management systems.

Successively, *Web Objects* measure has been investigated in other two studies (Di Martino, Ferrucci, Gravino, & Mendes, 2007; Ruhe et al., 2003b). In particular, Ruhe et al. (2003b) used *Web Objects* as size measure in the application of *WebCOBRA*, which is an adaptation of the *COBRA* method (Briand, El-Emam, & Bomarius, 1998) for the Web. They obtained better results than with

LR, in particular MMRE=0.17, MdMRE=0.15, and Pred(0.25)=0.75. More details on *WebCOBRA* are reported in the next section. The empirical study performed by Di Martino et al. (2007) was aimed at comparing several size measures. By employing LR technique they obtained good results with *Web Objects*, in particular MMRE=0.17, MdMRE=0.11, and Pred(0.25)=0.80.

Common Software Metrics Consortium - Full Function Points (COSMIC-FFP) is a widely adopted method for sizing software, approved as an International Standard (ISO/IEC 19761:2003). It turns out to be particularly suited for real-time and/or multilayered software, whose complexity is mostly dominated by the need to manage large amounts of data (COSMIC, 2005). The basic idea underlying this approach is that, for many kinds of software, the biggest programming efforts are devoted to handle data movements, and thus their number can provide a meaningful sight of the system size. With the COSMIC-FFP method, a set of models, rules, and procedures have to be applied to the Functional User requirements (FUR) to obtain a numerical value, which represents the functional size of the software, expressed in terms of *Cosmic Functional Size Unit* (CFSU) (COSMIC, 2005). To apply the method "the COSMIC-FFP model [...] requires FUR to be broken down into functional processes, each consisting of *data movements*, where a data movement moves a data group containing attributes of a single *object of interest*" (COSMIC, 2005).

Mendes, Counsell, and Mosley (2002a) applied the *COSMIC-FFP* measurement to Web hypermedia systems. Using data about 37 Web projects developed by academic students, they constructed an effort prediction model by applying LR. However, the derived model did not present reasonable prediction accuracy (MMRE < 0.50), and replications of the empirical study were highly recommended by authors to find possible biases in the collection of the data and/or in the application of the *COSMIC-FFP* method. Successively, Costagliola et al. (2006a) applied

COSMIC-FFP taking into account dynamic aspects of Web applications. The *COSMIC-FFP* method was evaluated by using 44 Web projects (mainly Web portals, e-commerce sites, etc.), developed by academic students. The prediction models obtained by applying LR provided a good level of accuracy (MMRE=0.15, MdMRE=0.10, and Pred(0.25)= 0.75).

Tukutuku database is part of the Tukutuku project, which aims to collect data about Web applications to be used to develop Web effort estimation models and to benchmark productivity across and within Web Companies (Mendes, Counsell, & Mosley, 2003c). Each Web project is characterized by 25 variables related to the application and its development process, such as *Web pages, Images, Features reused without any adaptation*, and so forth. The complete list can be found in Mendes, Counsell, and Mosley (2005a). These size measures have been obtained from several empirical investigations performed by Mendes, Counsell, and Mosley (2001, 2002a, 2003a, 2003b, 2003c) and Mendes, Counsell, Mosley, Triggs et al. (2002, 2003). These studies highlighted that the employed measures can be profitably exploited to predict effort since the best estimations (obtained with LR and CBR) were characterized by MMRE values less than 0.25 and Pred(0.25) values greater than 0.75. In particular, the final set of size measures and cost drivers included in the Tukutuku database have been defined from the results of a survey investigation (Mendes, Counsell, & Mosley, 2005a), using data from 133 online Web forms aimed at giving quotes on Web development projects. In addition, these measures and cost drivers have also been confirmed by an established Web company and a second survey involving 33 Web companies in New Zealand. Several empirical studies have been carried out to assess the effectiveness of these size measures (Mendes & Kitchenham, 2004a; Mendes, Counsell, & Mosley, 2005a; Mendes, Di Martino, Ferrucci, & Gravino, 2007). Mendes Counsell, and Mosley (2005c) also presented a survey literature of hypermedia and Web size measures proposed in recent papers and classifies the analyzed studies according to a proposed taxonomy. The aim was to provide a mean for classifying and understanding the body of knowledge about Web size measures and their employing for effort estimation.

Costagliola et al. (2006b) investigated two sets of size measures: *Length* and *Functional* measures. *Length* measures were derived from both previous research (Mendes, Counsell, & Mosley, 2001, 2002a) and interviews with the company's project managers. The set of *Length* measures includes *Web Pages, Media, Scripts and Application*, and so forth (the complete list can be found in Costagliola et al., 2006b). As for the *Functional* measures, Costagliola et al. (2006b) used the nine components that are part of *Web Objects*. These size measures were compared by exploiting data from 15 Web projects provided by an Italian small-medium sized company whose core business is the development of enterprise information systems, mainly for local and central government. The company is highly specialized in the design, development and management of solutions for Web portals, enterprise intranet/extranet applications (such as content-ware, e-commerce, work-flow managers, etc.), and Geographical Information Systems. The 15 Web applications employed in that case study are in several domains, such as e-government, e-banking, Web portals, and intranet applications. The results of the empirical study revealed that *Length* measures provided better estimates when using CBR (i.e., *MMRE*=0.15 and *Pred*(0.25)=0.73), while *Functional* measures provided better estimates when using LR (*MMRE*=0.21 and *Pred*(0.25)=0.73). However, their analysis suggested that there were no significant differences in the estimations and the residuals obtained with *Length* measures and *Functional* measures. Successively, Di Martino et al. (2007) compared the following size measures: *Web Objects* proposed by Reifer (2000), the *Length*

and *Functional* measures used by Costagliola et al. (2006b), the *Tukutuku* measures proposed by Mendes, Counsell, and Mosley (2003c). As a data set, they exploited the Web projects employed in Costagliola et al. (2006b). The empirical results showed that all the measures provided good predictions in terms of *MMRE, MdMRE*, and *Pred*(0.25) and the study largely confirmed the results of previous work (Costagliola et al., 2006b). Moreover, the analysis of residuals suggested that *Length* measures and *Web Objects* presented significantly superior predictions than *Functional measures* when estimates are obtained using LR; however all presented similar predictions to the *Tukutuku* measures.

Finally, we would recall other two works. Abrahão and Pastor (2003) proposed the *OOmF-PWeb* method, which maps the *FP* concepts into the primitives used in the conceptual modeling phase of *OOWS*, a method for producing software for the Web (Abrahão, Fons, & Pastor, 2001). In a recent work (Abrahão, Pastor, & Poels, 2004), a preliminary evaluation of the *OOmFPWeb* has been provided.

Baresi and Morasca (2003) focused their attention on Web applications automatically generated from a design model expressed in terms of W2000. They defined several measures on the basis of attributes obtained from design artifacts, and conducted empirical studies aiming to identify the attributes that may be related to the effort required for designing Web applications. This empirical study involved the students of an advanced university class on modeling Web applications, enrolled in engineering curricula, and employed Linear Regression. The empirical results suggested that the size of the information model, as well as the reuse level and the characteristics of the navigation model, influence the total design effort. It is worth noting that these studies differ from the ones presented above since Baresi and Morasca (2003) focused on design effort and not on the total effort.

Empirical Studies Focused on Estimation Techniques

Several empirical studies have been carried out to analyze the effectiveness of LR, CBR, and RT in the case of desktop applications. In particular, Briand, El-Emam, Surmann, et al. (1999) and Briand, El-Emam, and Wieczorek (2000) applied LR, RT, and CBR, using 1 and 2 analogies, and combinations of these techniques. Their results pointed out that LR is better than CBR in predicting efforts. To date, numerous studies have investigated these estimation techniques for Web effort estimation (e.g., Costagliola et al., 2006a, 2006b; Di Martino et al., 2007; Mendes, Counsell, & Mosley, 2001, 2002a, 2003a, 2003c, 2005b; Mendes, Counsell, Mosley, Triggs et al., 2002, 2003; Mendes & Kitchenham, 2004a, 2004b, Mendes & Mosley, 2002; Ruhe et al., 2003a;).

In the following, we focus our attention on the studies that have employed LR, CBR, and RT (Costagliola et al., 2006b; Di Martino et al., 2007; Mendes, Counsell, Mosley, Triggs et al., 2002, 2003; Mendes & Mosley, 2002;).

Costagliola et al. (2006b) performed an empirical analysis employing LR, CBR, and RT and exploiting *Length* and *Functional* measures (described in the previous section). They found that none of the effort estimation techniques used in their study was statistically significantly superior to others; however, the three accuracy measures used (i.e., MMRE, MdMRE, and Pred(0.25)) suggested that LR presented overall the best and the worst accuracy using elements of *Functional* and *Length* size measures, respectively. The study conducted by Di Martino et al. (2007) largely confirmed the above results, revealing that both LR and CBR can be profitably exploited to predict Web application development effort. Mendes, Counsell, Mosley, Triggs et al. (2002, 2003) exploited a data set of 37 Web projects developed by academic students and highlighted that LR models generally gave statistically significant better results than CBR. On the contrary, the case study carried out by Di Martino et al. (2007) revealed that there is no significant difference between estimations obtained with CBR and those obtained with the LR. As for CBR Mendes, Counsell, Mosley, Triggs et al. (2003) considered three choices for number of analogies (1, 2, and 3) and three choices for the analogy adaptation (mean of k analogies, inverse rank weighted mean, and median of k analogies). The best result was achieved by using weighted distance and 1 analogy. Moreover, in another work on the analysis of the CBR, Mendes and Mosley (2002) proved that the use of adaptation rules presented statistically better prediction accuracy than their counterparts than did not use adaptation. Costagliola et al. (2006b) obtained the best results with CBR using 2 analogies and inverse distance weighted mean as adaptation strategy (employing *Functional* measures), while Di Martino et al. (2007) obtained the best results with CBR using 2 analogies and the mean of 2 analogies as adaptation strategy (with *Web Objects* as size measure) and 2 analogies and the inverse distance weighted mean as adaptation strategy (for *COSMIC-FFP* as size measure).

Morever, we want to recall two works that have proposed cost estimation models specific for the Web, namely *WebMO* (Reifer, 2000) and *WebCOBRA* (Ruhe et al., 2003b).

WebMO is a direct extension of the COCOMO II Early Design model (Bohem, 1981). The idea underlying the approach is to adapt the existing effort estimation methods in order to use them in the context of Web applications. As an extension of the Early Design of the COCOMO II method, *WebMO* does not require a deep knowledge about the influence of cost drivers on the development process, and generic cost drivers can be defined in order to estimate in the early phase of the development process those features which will be more influent on the final development effort (Reifer, 2000). Except the empirical analysis performed by Reifer in order to calibrate the *WebMO*, to the best of our knowledge no empirical studies have been carried out employing this method.

WebCOBRA is an adaptation to the Web domain of the COBRA (COst estimation, Benchmarking and Risk Analysis) method (Briand et al., 1998). The key issue of this method is to use both expert knowledge and few past project data to obtain a COBRA instance, named COBRA model, which results specifically tailored for the intended software development context. In order to obtain a COBRA model, information about Project Characteristics, such as project type, application domain, and so forth, the Size Measure, calculated in a consistent way among all projects, and some Cost Drivers, specifying the resources expected to influence the development effort have to be determined. These three factors form the causal model, which is intended to describe all the cost factors involved in the project development. The causal model, together with the past project data, define a resulting COBRA model. The past project data are used to define the relationships between cost overhead and cost, for the considered software development context. Ruhe et al. (2003b) derived the *WebCOBRA* approach by modifying the causal model, and by adopting the *Web Objects* method to measure the size of the software. Furthermore, to evaluate the prediction accuracy of the *WebCOBRA* model, they performed an empirical study by exploiting the 12 Web projects developed by an Australian software development company and obtained *MMRE*=0.17, *MdMRE*=0.15, and *Pred*(0.25)=0.75. These results are better than those they obtained in Ruhe et al. (2003a) by employing as estimation technique LR (see the previous section). In the future, it could be interesting to exploit both *COSMIC-FFP* and *Web Objects* measures in the application of the *WebCOBRA* method using a larger industrial data set and compare the obtained results.

Empirical Studies Focused on Cross-Company Data Set

Recently, in the context of the Web, few studies have investigated whether a cross-company data set (i.e., a data set containing project data from several software companies) can provide estimates for the new projects comparable to the one obtained from single-company data sets (i.e., data sets containing project data from a single company), which deals with the generalization of the results achieved in a given context (Mendes et al., 2007; Mendes & Kitchenham, 2004a, 2004b).

The use of a cross-company data set seems particularly useful for companies that do not have their own data on past projects from which to obtain their estimates, or that have data on projects developed in different application domains and/or technologies (Mendes et al., 2007; Mendes & Kitchenham, 2004a, 2004b). The goal of these studies is to investigate how successful is a cross-company effort model to estimate effort for Web projects that belong to a single company and were not used to build the cross-company model, and compared to a single-company effort model. The data sets employed in these three studies were obtained from the Tukutuku database, and the effort estimates were obtained by means of LR and CBR. About the results, these empirical studies have revealed that the predictions based on the single-company model were significantly more accurate than those based on the cross-company ones. In particular, in the study presented by Mendes et al. (2007), the accuracy of estimates obtained using the cross-company model obtained with LR shows low prediction accuracy, with a quite high MMRE (85.86%), and an extremely poor Pred(25) (6.67%), far from the thresholds suggested by Conte et al. (1986). The same pattern was present for predictions obtained using CBR: MMRE is 92.54% and Pred(25) is 0%, both really poor. These results corroborate those obtained by Mendes and Kitchenham (2004b).

It is worth noting that the majority of the empirical studies provided in the literature, and reported in the previous sections, exploited data coming from a single company. On one hand, this can lead to more accurate results, since the data collection task can be carried out in a more controlled fashion than in a cross-company scenario, as recognized by Kitchenham, Mendes, Travassos, and Guilherme (2007). But, on the other hand, the obtained results might not hold in other industrial contexts. In particular, the models obtained with data coming from a given company/domain might not supply accurate predictions when used in different companies/domains, where some recalibrations could be necessary as suggested by Mendes and Kitchenham (2004b).

CONCLUSION

In this chapter, we have reported on and discussed the most significant empirical studies undertaken so far and aimed at verifying:

- The usefulness of size measures and cost factors for estimating Web application development effort.
- The appropriateness of methods and techniques to provide effective effort estimations for Web applications.
- The usefulness of cross-company data set for estimating Web application development effort.

The analysis has revealed that several size measures have been successfully employed to estimate the size and the effort of Web applications. However, further empirical investigations are needed to achieve widely accepted size measures for the Web. Regarding the employed estimation techniques, LR and CBR, widely adopted in Software Engineering to estimate effort of software projects, have also obtained interesting results in the context of Web.

FUTURE RESEARCH DIRECTIONS

It is worth noting that only few empirical studies in the field of Web effort estimation exploited industrial data sets (Costagliola et al., 2006b; Di Martino et al., 2007; Mendes, Counsell, & Mosley, 2005a, 2005b, 2005c; Mendes & Kitchenham, 2004a, 2004b; Ruhe et al., 2003a, 2003b). This is partly due to the lack of "meaningful" data sets publicly available that allow researchers to perform investigations. It is worth noting that the "quality" of the data set used can deeply influence the results of the study. Indeed, if data is not properly collected, or if it is not representative of a wider context, the effectiveness of the empirical study is heavily reduced. In the field of software engineering, these recommendations are usually fitted by using data coming from the industrial world, collected in a correct and consistent way (see, for example, Briand et al., 2000; Briand, El-Emam, & Surmann, et al., 1999; Greves & Schreiber, 1996; Jeffery et al., 2000; Mendes, Lokan et al., 2005). However, in the Web domain, it may be difficult to obtain large and significant data sets from the industrial world, since the time required to accumulate enough data on past projects may be very high, as well as the fact that technologies evolve very quickly, making old data useless (Mendes & Kitchenham, 2004b). Thus, in the future, Web companies should pay more attention to cope with the problem of collecting data from past projects in order to exploit them for effort estimation in several and different contexts.

Moreover, the research in the future should also focus on designing and developing tools able to automatically obtain information on cost factors and size measures. In particular, these tools should allow researchers to collect past projects data from companies developing Web applications employing different methods, techniques, and technologies with the aim of supporting managers in the identification of the most effective measures and estimation techniques to be applied in several and different contexts. Other techniques should also be investigated for effort estimation, such as fuzzy strategies, and the achieved results should be compared with those obtained by employing

LR and CBR. Finally, future work should also cover the identification and investigation of size measures to be used not only in the early phase of development process but also in other phases, such as testing and maintenance.

REFERENCES

Aamodt, A., & Plaza, E. (1994). Case-based reasoning: Foundational issues, methodological variations, and system approaches. *AI Communication*, 7(1), 39-59. IOS Press.

Abrahão, S.M., Fons, J.J., & Pastor, O. (2001). Object-oriented approach to automate Web applications development. In *Proceedings of International Conference on Electronic Commerce and Web Technologies* (EC-Web '01) (pp. 16-28). Springer Verlag.

Abrahão, S.M., & Pastor, O. (2003). Measuring the functional size of Web applications. *International Journal of Web Engineering and Technology*, 1(1), 5-16.

Abrahão, S.M., Pastor, O., & Poels, G. (2004). Evaluating a functional size measurement method for Web applications: An empirical analysis. In *Proceedings of International Software Metrics Symposium* (METRICS'04) (pp. 358-369).

Albrecht, A.J. (1979). Measuring application development productivity. In *Proceedings of the Joint SHARE/GUIDE/IBM Application Development Symposium* (pp. 83-92).

Baresi, L., & Morasca, S. (in press). Three empirical studies on estimating the design effort of Web applications. *ACM Transactions on Software Engineering and Methodology*.

Baresi, L., Morasca, S., & Paolini, P. (2003). Estimating the design effort of Web applications. In *Proceedings of the International Software Metrics Symposium* (METRICS'03) (pp. 62-72).

Basili, V.R., Briand, L.C., & Melo, W.L. (1996). A validation of object-oriented design metrics as quality indicators. *IEEE Transactions on Software Engineering*, 22(10), 751-761.

Basili, V.R., Shull, F., & Lanubile, F. (1999). Building knowledge through families of experiments. *IEEE Transactions on Software Engineering*, 25(4), 456-473.

Bohem, B. (1981). *Software engineering economics*. Englewood Cliffs, NJ: Prentice-Hall.

Bohem, B.W., Abts, C., Brown, A.W., Chulani, S., Clark, B.K., Horowitz, W., et al. (2000). *Software cost estimation with COCOMO II*. Englewood Cliffs, NJ: Prentice Hall.

Briand, L., El Emam, K., & Bomarius, F. (1998). COBRA: A hybrid method for software cost estimation, benchmarking, and risk assessment. In *Proceedings of International Conference on Software Engineering (ICSE'98)*, (pp. 390-399).

Briand, L.C., El-Emam, K., Maxwell, K., Surmann, D., & Wieczorek, I., (1999). An assessment and comparison of common cost estimation models. In *Proceedings of the International Conference on Software Engineering (ICSE'99)*, (pp. 313-322).

Briand, L., El. Emam, K., Surmann, D., Wiekzorek, I., & Maxwell, K. (1999). An assessment and comparison of common software cost estimation modeling techniques. In *Proceedings of International Conference on Software Engineering, (ICSE'99)*, (pp. 313-322).

Briand, L., El Emam, K., & Wieczorek, I., (1999). Explaining the cost of European space and military projects. In *Proceedings of International Conference on Software Engineering (ICSE'99)*, (pp. 303-312).

Briand, L., El. Emam, K., & Wiekzorek, I. (2000). A replicated assessment and comparison of common software cost modeling techniques.

In *Proceedings of the International Conference on Software Engineering, (ICSE'00),* (pp. 377-386).

Briand, L., & Wieczorek, I. (2002). Software resource estimation. In J.J. Marciniak (Ed.), *Encyclopedia of software engineering* (Vol. 2, pp. 1160-1196) (2nd ed.). New York: John Wiley & Sons.

Conte, D., Dunsmore, H.E., & Shen, V.Y. (1986). *Software engineering metrics and models.* The Benjamin/Cummings Publishing Company, Inc.

COSMIC. (2005, December). *Guideline for sizing business application software using COSMIC-FFP, Version 1.0.* Retrieved June 13, 2008, from http://www.lrgl.uqam.ca/cosmic-ffp/manual.html

Costagliola, G., Di Martino, S., Ferrucci, F., Gravino, C., Tortora, G., & Vitiello G. (2006a). A COSMIC-FFP: Approach to predict Web application development effort. *Journal of Web Engineering, 5*(2), 93-120.

Costagliola, G., Di Martino, S., Ferrucci, F., Gravino, C., Tortora, G., & Vitiello, G. (2006b). Effort estimation modeling techniques: A case study for Web applications. In *ACM Proceedings of the 6th International Conference on Web Engineering* (ICWE 2006), (pp. 9-16).

Deshpande, Y. (2002). Consolidating Web engineering as a discipline. *Software Engineering Australia,* 31-34.

Di Martino, S., Ferrucci, F., Gravino, C., & Mendes, E. (2007). Comparing size measures for predicting Web application development effort: A case study. In *Proceedings of Empirical Software Engineering and Measurement* (ESEM'07).

Genero, M., & Piattini, M. (2001). Empirical validation of measures for class diagram structural complexity through controlled experiments. In *Proceedings of International ECOOP Workshop on Quantitative Approaches in Object-Oriented Software Engineering* (QAOOSE 2001).

Ginige, A., & Murugesan, S. (2001). Web engineering: An introduction. *IEEE Multimedia, 8*(2), 14-18.

Greves, D., & Schreiber, B, (1996). The ESA initiative for software productivity benchmarking and effort estimation. ESA Bulletin, 87. Retrieved June 13, 2008, from <http://esapub.esrin.esa.it/bulletin/bulett87/greves87.htm>

International Function Point Users Group (IFPUG). (2004). *Function point counting practices manual.* Release 4.2.1, 2004.

Jeffery, R., Ruhe, M., & Wieczorek, I., (2000). A comparative study of two software development cost modeling techniques using multi-organizational and company-specific data. *Information and Software Technology, 42,* 1009-1016.

Jeffery, R., Ruhe. M., &Wieczorek, I., (2001). Using public domain metrics to estimate software development effort. In *Proceedings of International Software Metrics Symposium (METRICS'01),* (pp. 16-27).

Kitchenham, B., Mendes, E., Travassos, G.H., & Guilherme, H. (2007). Cross versus within-company cost estimation studies: A systematic review. *IEEE Transactions on Software Engineering, 33*(5), 316-329.

Kitchenham, B., Pickard, L.M., MacDonell, S.G., & Shepperd, M.J. (2001). What accuracy statistics really measure. *IEE Proceedings – Software, 148*(3), 81-85.

Lefley, M., & Shepperd, M.J. (2003). Using genetic programming to improve software effort estimation based on general data sets. In *Proceedings of GECCO'03,* (LNCS 2724, pp. 2477-2487). Springer-Verlag.

Mendes, E., Counsell, S., & Mosley, N. (2001). Web metrics – estimating design and authoring effort [Special issue on Web engineering]. *IEEE Multimedia,* 50-57.

Mendes, E., Counsell, S., & Mosley, N. (2002a). Comparison of Web size measures for predicting Web design and authoring effort. *IEE Proceedings-Software, 149*(3), 86-92.

Mendes, E., Counsell, S., & Mosley, N. (2003a). Early Web size measures and effort prediction for Web costimation. In *Proceedings of International Software Metrics Symposium (METRICS'03),* (pp. 18-39).

Mendes, E., Counsell, S., & Mosley, N. (2003b). A replicated assessment of the use of adaptation rules to improve Web cost estimation. In *Proceedings of International Symposium on Empirical Software Engineering (ISESE'03),* (pp. 100-109).

Mendes, E., Counsell, S., & Mosley, N. (2003c). Investigating early Web size measures for Web cost estimation. In *Proceedings of (EASE '03),* (pp. 1-22).

Mendes, E., Counsell, S., & Mosley, N. (2005a). Investigating Web size metrics for early Web cost estimation. *Journal of Systems and Software, 77*(2), 157-172.

Mendes, E., Counsell, S., & Mosley, N. (2005b). Exploring case-based reasoning for Web hypermedia project cost estimation. *International Journal of Web Engineering and Technology, 2*(1), 117-143.

Mendes, E., Counsell, S., & Mosley, N. (2005c). Towards a taxonomy of hypermedia and Web application size metrics. In *Proceedings of the International Conference on Web Engineering (ICWE'05),* (LNCS 3579, pp. 110-123). Springer.

Mendes, E., Counsell, S., Mosley, N., Triggs, C., & Watson I. (2002). A comparison of development effort estimation techniques for Web hypermedia applications. In *Proceedings of International Software Metrics Symposium (METRICS'02),* (pp. 131-140).

Mendes, E., Counsell, S., Mosley, N., Triggs, C., & Watson, I. (2003). A comparative study of cost estimation models for Web hypermedia applications. *Empirical Software Engineering, 8*(2), 163-196.

Mendes, E., Di Martino, S., Ferrucci, F., & Gravino, C. (2007). Effort estimation: How valuable is it for a Web company to use a cross-company data set, compared to using its own single-company data set?" In *ACM Proceedings of the International World Wide Web Conference (WWW2007),* (pp. 963-972).

Mendes, E., & Kitchenham, B. (2004a). A comparison of cross-company and single-company effort estimation models for Web applications. In *Proceedings EASE 2004,* (pp. 47-55).

Mendes, E., & Kitchenham, B. (2004b). Further comparison of cross-company and within-company effort estimation models for Web applications. In *Proceedings of International Software Metrics Symposium (METRICS'04),* (pp. 348-357).

Mendes, E., Lokan, C., Harrison, R., & Triggs, C. (2005). A replicated comparison of cross-company and within-company effort estimation models using the ISBSG database. In *Proceedings of International Software Metrics Symposium (METRICS'05),* (p. 36).

Mendes, E., & Mosley, N. (2002). Further investigation into the use of CBR and stepwise regression to predict development effort for Web hypermedia applications. In *Proceedings of International Symposium on Empirical Software Engineering (IESE'02),* (pp. 79-90).

Montgomery, D., Peck, E., & Vining, G. (2001). Introduction to linear regression analysis (3rd ed.). John Wiley & Sons, Inc.

Myrtveit, I., Shepperd, M., & Stensrud, E. (2005). Reliability and validity in comparative studies of software prediction models. *IEEE Transactions on Software Engineering, 31*(5), 380-391.

Myrtveit, I., & Stensrud, E. (1999). A controlled experiment to assess the benefits of estimating with analogy and regression models. *IEEE Transactions on Software Engineering, 25*(4), 510-525.

Reifer, D. (2000). Web-development: Estimating quick-time-to-market software. *IEEE Software, 17*(8), 57-64.

Ruhe, M., Jeffery, R., & Wieczorek, I. (2003a). Using Web objects for estimating software development effort for Web applications. In *Proceedings of the IEEE International Software Metrics Symposium (METRICS'03),* (pp. 30-37).

Ruhe, M., Jeffery, R., & Wieczorek, I. (2003b). Cost estimation for Web applications. In *Proceedings of International Conference on Software Engineering (ICSE'03),* (pp. 285-294).

Ruhe, M., & Wieczorek, I. (2002). How valuable is company-specific data compared to multi-company data for software cost estimation? In *Proceedings of the IEEE Symposium on Software Metrics (METRICS'02),* (pp. 237-246).

Schneidewind, N. (1992). Methodology for validating software metrics. *IEEE Transaction on Software Engineering, 18*(5), 410-422.

Shepperd, M., & Schofield, C. (2000). Estimating software project effort using analogies. *IEEE Transaction on Software Engineering, 23*(11), 736-743.

ADDITIONAL READING

Albrecht, A.J. (1979). Measuring application development productivity. In *Proceedings of the Joint SHARE/GUIDE/IBM Application Development Symposium* (pp. 83-92).

Boehm-Davis, D.A., & Ross, L.S. (1992). Program design methodologies and the software development process. *International Journal of Man-Machine Studies, 36*(1), 1-19.

Carver, J., Jaccheri, L., Morasca, S., & Shull, F. (2003). Issues in using students in empirical studies in software engineering education. In *Proceedings of International Software Metrics Symposium (METRICS'03),* (pp. 239-249).

Costagliola, G., Ferrucci, F., Gravino, C., Tortora, G., & Vitiello, G. (2004). A COSMIC-FFP based method to estimate Web application development effort. In *Proceedings of International Conference on Web Engineering (ICWE'04),* (LNCS 3140, pp. 161-165). Springer Verlag.

Costagliola, G., Ferrucci, F., Tortora, G., & Vitiello, G. (2005). Class point: An approach for the size estimation of object-oriented systems. *IEEE Transsctions on Software Engineering, 31*(1), 52-74.

Dawson, R., Bones, P., Oates, B.J., Brereton, P., Azuma, M., & Jackson, M.L. (2003). Empirical methodologies in software engineering. In *Annual International Workshop on Software Technology and Engineering Practice (STEP'03),* (pp. 52-58).

Dolado, J.J. (2000). A validation of component-based method for software size estimation. *IEEE Transactions on Software Engineering, 26*(10), 61-72.

El Emam, K. (2001). A primer on object-oriented measurement. In *Proceedings of IEEE International Software Metrics Symposium (METRICS'01),* (pp. 185-188).

Finnie, G.R., Wittig, G.E., & Desharnais, J.M. (1997). A comparison of software effort estimation techniques: Using function points with neural networks, case-based reasoning and regression models. *Journal of Systems and Software, 39,* 281-289.

Jørgensen, M., & Sjøberg, D.I.K. (2001). Impact of effort estimation on software project work. *Information and Software Technology, 43,* 939-948.

Kadoba, G., Cartwright, M., Chen, L., & Shepperd, M. (2000). Experiences using case-based reasoning to predict software project effort. In *Proceedings of Evaluation and Assessment in Software Engineering (EASE'00)*.

Kadoba, G., & Shepperd, M. (2001). Using simulation to evaluate predictions systems. In *Proceedings of International Software Metrics Symposium (METRICS'01)*, (pp. 349-358).

Kemerer, C.F. (1987). An empirical validation of software cost estimation models. *Communications of the ACM, 30*(5).

Kitchenham, B. (1998). A procedure for analyzing unbalanced datasets. *IEEE Transactions on Software Engineering, 24*(4), 278-301.

Kitchenham, B., Foss, T., Stensrud, E., & Myrtveit, I. (2003). A simulation study of the model evaluation criterion MMRE. *IEEE Transactions on Software Engineering, 29*(11), 985-995.

Kitchenham, B., Pfleeger, S.L., Pickard, L.M., Jones, P.W., Hoaglin, D.C., El Emam, K., et al. (2002). Preliminary guidelines for empirical research in software engineering. *IEEE Transactions on Software Engineering, 28*(8), 721-734.

Kitchenham, B., & Taylor, N.R. (1984). Software cost models. *ICL Technical Journal*, 73-102.

Lokan, C., & Mendes, E. (2006). Cross-company and single-company effort models using the ISBSG database: A further replicated study. In *Proceedings of International Symposium on Empirical Software Engineering (ISESE'06)*, (pp. 75-84).

Maxwell, K. (2002). *Applied statistics for software managers*. Prentice Hall, NJ: Software Quality Institute Series.

Maxwell, K., Wassenhove, L.V., & Dutta, S. (1999). Performance evaluation of general and company specific models in software development effort estimation. *Management Science, 45*(6), 787-803.

Mendes, E., & Mosley, N. (2006). *Web engineering 2006, XIX 438* (p. 143) (ISBN: 978-3-540-28196-2).

Morisio, M., Stamelos, I., Spahos, V., & Romano, D. (1999). Measuring functionality and productivity in Web-based applications: A case study. In *Proceedings of the International Software Metrics Symposium* (pp. 111-118).

Musilek, P., Pedrycz, W., Sun, N., & Succi, G. (2002). On the sensitivity of COCOMO II software cost estimation model. In *Proceedings of International Software Metrics Symposium (METRICS'02)*, (pp. 13-20).

Pfleeger, S. (1991). Model of software effort and productivity. *Information and Software Technology, 33*(3), 224-231.

Putnam, L.H. (1978). A general empirical solution to the macro software sizing and estimating problem. *IEEE Transactions on Software Engineering, 4*, 345-361.

Shepperd, M., & Cartwright, M. (2001). Predicting with sparse data. *IEEE Transactions on Software Engineering, 27*(11), 987-998.

Shepperd, M., Schofield, C., & Kitchenham, B. (1996). Effort estimation using analogy. In *Proceedings of International Conference on Software Engineering (ICSE'96)*, (pp. 170-178).

Section 2.4
e–Marketing

Chapter XVIII
Mobile Marketing

Kazuhiro Takeyasu
Osaka Prefecture University, Japan

ABSTRACT

Recently, cellular phones capable of accessing the Internet are prevailing rapidly in Japan. First, their functions and features are examined: Classification of services offered at i-mode; Characteristics of cyberspace communication tools and their comparisons with mobile instrument; Strengths and weaknesses of mobile phones. Then, mobile marketing is discussed on from the following perspectives. (1)Ability to use real-time marketing, (2) Ability to use online coupon marketing, (3) Ability to navigate customer easily to shop, (4) Ability to make purchase procedures seamless—from the notification of special offers (by retailers) to the payment (by customers), (5) Retrieval and utilization of information without time and spatial restriction. Third, we analyze the differences in meaning between so-called four Ps in real commerce marketing and those in cyberspace marketing. Finally, several cases using cellular phones are analyzed: coupon marketing, production/construction status control, and distribution control.

INTRODUCTION

NTT DoCoMo's launching of i-mode service in December of 1999 has drastically changed the landscape of Web business because it enables wireless Internet access. Mobile phone operators now offer a wide range of services using wireless Internet access technology. As of June 30, 2007, there were about 98.1 million mobile phone users, including 74.7 million 3G mobile phone users.

Wireless Internet access technology has created new, innovative services, such as the production status control using mobile handsets. This chapter examines potentials of marketing techniques using mobile Internet technology.

So far, many researches and writings have been made on mobile phone such as the theme of technology (Raina & Harsh, 2001), competition in mobile market (Steinbock, 2002), communication (Garrard, 1997), marketing (Haig, 2002), and so forth.

The abundant applications with wireless Internet access are first developed by i-mode. But the papers of the analysis of the application and its influence of i-mode are few. Some of them are executed by Tsukuda, Takeyasu, and Ono (2001) and Takeyasu, Ono, and Ueda (2003). In this chapter, overall analysis is executed for the mobile marketing focused on the application of i-mode.

BACKGROUND

In this chapter, mobile marketing means marketing on or with a mobile phone. Marketing on a mobile phone has increasingly become popular, especially in Japan (Takeyasu, 2006; Takeyasu et al., 2003; Tsukuda et al., 2001). After the development of i-mode service by NTT DoCoMo, which is well known world-wide (Matsunaga, 2000), other carriers also developed services similar to i-mode. We survey these services and evaluate the characteristics of Mobile Technologies and then the meaning and the characteristics of mobile marketing is investigated. Case studies are executed, followed by the conclusion.

CHARACTERISTICS OF MOBILE TECHNOLOGIES

Mobile communication instruments in a broader sense include hand-carry personal computers (PCs), personal digital assistants (PDAs), and so forth. This chapter, however, focuses primarily on cellular phones capable of Web browsing. We call this "*keitai*."

While data input on *keitai* is not as easy as on PCs, *keitai* has several advantages—very light, portable, and capable of transmitting voice/sound (Table 1, Table 2).

The characteristics of cyberspace technologies are described precisely by Takeyasu in Tsukuda et al. (2001).

Because *keitai* has unique characteristics as described in Table 2, it will be effective in the following use:

1. Simple and easy retrieval and input of information without restriction of location and time
    - Search train timetables, cooking recipes, and map information
    - Check bank account balance and money transfer.

Table 1. Comparing characteristics of cyberspace technologies with those of mobile telephone

Cyberspace technology		Mobile telephone (*keitai*)
Bilateral communication	○	Difficulty in data inputs Strong in voice/sound system
Borderless—beyond time, space, national borders	○	Two separate protocols—European and U.S. standard. Both protocols are adopted by Japanese carriers
Dual Phase communication by word of mouth and mass media	○	Difficulty in data inputs
Virtual nature	○	
Digital nature	○	
Real-time	◎	Compact and easy to carry, anytime, anywhere
Database involvement	○	

*○···characteristics recognized ◎···keitai is better than cyberspace

Table 2. Strength and weakness of mobile telephone

Strength	Weakness

-Light in weight
-Compact
-Inexpensive (initial cost and access charges)
-Easy to send voice message
-Access to the Internet
 i-mode uses "Packet" switched system, so relatively low fees
 -i-mode uses c-HTML,* which makes it easy for developers to
    develop Web content.
-Easy to connect *keitai* with PCs
-Capable of using GPS(Global Positioning System) and IC Card
    technologies.
-Easy to download software
	- Unsuitable for complicated data input
	- Unsuitable for sending a large volume of data
	- Absence of standardized operation protocol

* cHTML stands for "compact HTML" and is the content description language used in i-mode. cHTML is a subset of HTML, plus some additional tags, characters, and features.

2. Retrieval and input of ever-changing or timely information
   - Check prices and place selling or buying orders of stock
   - Look for and make reservations for restaurant, air tickets and hotel rooms.
3. New marketing techniques that utilize *keitai*
   - "Real-time" marketing
   - Online coupon marketing
   - Sending information through a trigger mail*
   - Navigating customers to shops
   - * Users are informed by e-mail of matters prescribed in advance by themselves whenever the conditions preset likewise are met.
4. Download software—games, music, and Application Service Provider (ASP)
5. User-friendly e-commerce
   Purchase procedures become more seamless—from the notification of offers to the payment

These are the summaries of many existing cases. In detail, see Takeyasu et al. (2003). I-mode is the first development of versatile full service of wireless Internet access, which service is arranged in Table 3.

MOBILE MARKETING

The basic characteristics of *keitai* are similar to those of other cyberspace technologies. However, because of its portability and ability to transmit sound and voice, the following marketing techniques are considered particularly useful in mobile marketing (Takeyasu, 2006).

- Real-time marketing
- Online coupon marketing
- Navigate customers easily to shops/stores
- Make purchase procedures seamless—from the notification of special offers to the payment
- Retrieval of information, irrespective of time and location

Next these are explained in specific.

"Real-Time" Marketing

Real-time marketing is effective on *keitai*. For instance, bar owner can send e-mail on special evening offers—a glass of beer free for each customer of a group of four or more. During lunch hour or in the evening, information on new video can be sent to customers' handsets so that they can drop by the store on their way home. General

Table 3. Classification of the i-mode service

Classification	Service contents
Transaction-related	Web banking, online stock trading, air tickets reservation/purchase
Lifestyle-related	News, weather forecast, and sports results
Database-related	Train transit information, restaurant information, cooking recipe, dictionary
Entertainment-related	Load ringing melodies into handsets, download cartoon characters, play Web games, watch TV program

Merchandise Store (GMSs) can send e-mail ad to housewives for limited-hour special sales.

Online Coupon Marketing

Culture Convenience Club Co. Ltd. operates video/CD rental chains called "Tsutaya." It started online services for i-mode users in August of 1999. Customers can purchase videos and CDs online with mobile phones. The firm distributes electronic code coupons onto the customers' handsets. They present such coupons to a store clerk to enjoy special offers/discounts. This is an epoch-making marketing technique, with a substantial impact on sales promotion (Table 4).

Navigate Customers Easily to Shops

With mobile Internet access, for example, one can receiver directions to a shop while driving. Route guidance by *keitai* in a crowded urban district is especially effective.

Make Purchase Procedures Seamless—From the Notification of Offers to the Payment

When a customer makes an online purchase, the customer can select from the following payment methods.

Table 4. Examples of keitai coupon marketing

Items	Contents	Notes
i-size discount gourmet	Presenting online coupon on i-mode would enable users to get a 10% discount. Monthly membership fee of 300 yen Free trial use for 30 days	
Gournavi	Digital discount/special offer coupons offer from 4,000 stores on i-mode	
E-fuel Auto-Backs discount coupon	Customers purchasing goods worth 3,000 yen or more at Auto Backs car accessories outlets could enjoy a 500-yen discount if they show a discount digital coupon on i-mode.	
Culture Convenience Club	Online coupon is shown in the shop (i-mode and other carriers' services)	First, a 50-yen discount for each CD or video rental. From next time and on, a 50% discount for each CD or video rental.

1. Purchase order → payment at bank or post office → product delivery upon confirmation of money transactions
2. Purchase order → parcel delivery service →payment to the parcel delivery service at the time of receiving products
3. Purchase order → make payment and receive products at convenience store
4. Purchase order → parcel delivery → receive products → payment at bank or post office

With *keitai*, one can process online all the procedures from order to payment. This is easy and convenient. In addition, the shortest lead time—time required from the placement of an order to the receipt of products—will be attained. Purchase procedures would become seamless, irrespective of time and location as described in Figure 1. No other Web marketing tools can offer convenience of this magnitude.

Retrieval and Use of Information, Irrespective of Time and Location

The advent of the Internet has made it dramatically easy to communicate with each other without physical constraints. However, if people access the Internet on PCs, it is indeed difficult to communicate at anytime, anywhere. Although PCs are available, they are not compact enough to carry everywhere. Moreover, a technical setup of PCs for Internet is also not easy. Many people use *keitai* while not knowing that their handsets are connected to the Internet. Carrying *keitai* is the same as carrying an enormous database with little weight. As the mobile Internet enables communication at anytime, anywhere, *Keitai* is becoming a "wearable" computer with an easy access to a huge database.

"Opt-in mail," one of the e-mail marketing systems, is prevailing at a high speed. It sends by e-mail such information as shopping, products, and services that the receivers of "opt-in mails" have selected as their favorite in advance. It is permission marketing. For example, people at

Figure 1. Seamless purchase procedures from the notification to the payment on cellular phone

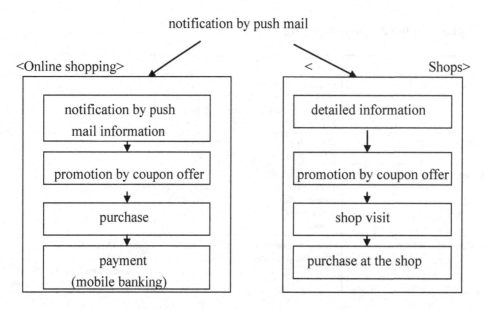

the office get an e-mail message on their *keitai* from a pub or a CD shop in the evening. They may visit there after work. If there are only a few customers in the shop, the shop manager can take quick action by sending e-mail discount coupon to potential customers' *keitai*. Thanks to portability, customers are able to receive information even if they are not sitting in front of PC desk. *Keitai* "opt-in mail" provides smooth and quick visits of customers to the shop.

Keitai users can collect e-brochures from several shops to compare the prices of products before they make purchases. A trigger mail service is also possible, for example, in order to inform *keitai* users of the fact that the price has gone down into the range preset by themselves.

Research Rresults of Usage Status of Mobile Phone

Now, we confirm the research results of usage status of mobile phone. Figure 2 shows i-mode users' share by the cluster of ages. It is prevailing for nearly every cluster of ages.

Figure 3 shows the frequently used Internet site by genre for mobile phone. The number of e-mails received for i-mode users is 5.6 on average for one day. The number of Internet access sites is 9.5 page views on average for one day. Information site for daily confirmation such as weather forecasting and general news are often used.

From the research results, we can see that many people often view the i-mode site at the time before going to bed, after coming home, during lunch, and so forth (Figure 4).

FOUR Ps IN MARKETING

In real commerce, four Ps—product, price, place, and promotion—are critical factors to develop marketing strategies. In a cyberspace marketplace, these four Ps have somewhat different meanings (Table 5). These are precisely described by Takeyasu in Tsukuda et al. (2001).

1. Product—products with the following features are suitable in cyberspace marketing
2. Precious products, products produced in only specific area or district, products with established brand name, or heavy and bulky products

Figure 2. I-mode users' share by the cluster of ages (NTT DoCoMo's Home Page, 2002, February)

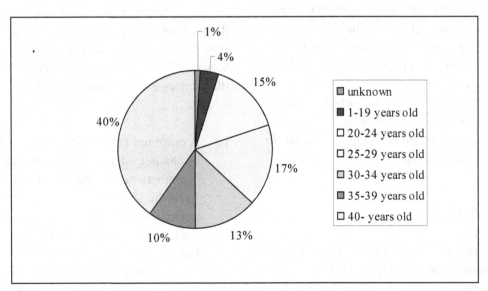

Figure 3. Frequently used Internet site by genre for mobile phone (Video Research, "Actual Usage Condition of Mobile Phone" (2001, February 16-February 26)

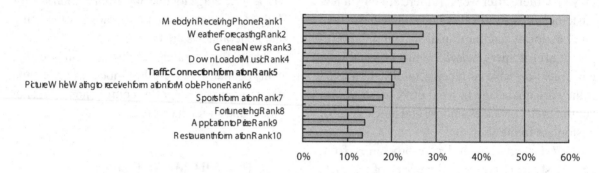

Figure 4. Viewing time of i-mode site (Research Result by Info-Plant, "Beneficial Menu", 2002 March)

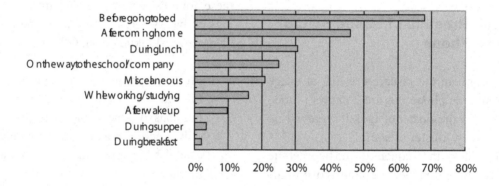

3. Price—In cyberspace, product prices of the similar products can be listed and put on databases. One can easily find the cheapest price by using "Bargain Finder" software.

4. One can easily create a portal site that attracts more visitors, no matter where he or she lives.

5. Promotion—One-to-one marketing is easier to be adopted in cyberspace. Enhanced interactive communications is possible in mobile marketing.

CASE STUDIES

Here, we introduce four case studies in three themes. Some cases are restricted in opening the detailed data.

Coupon Marketing

A Tokyo-based business systems developer, Ryoyu Keisan Co., Ltd., launched a new mobile Web coupon service at a local bakery shop in May of 2001 (Figure 5). The service, called "b-BOX," uses a coupon codes system. It works as follows:

1. A customer browses the bakery's Web site on handset, which flashes advertisements for "members-only" special campaigns/deals from the shop. The user registers his/her name, address, age, phone number, e-mail address, and so forth to enjoy special offers.

2. An electronic "membership" code coupon is automatically distributed on the Web site,

from which the customer can download it to keep it in his/her handsets.

3. The customer presents to the retailer a membership coupon on the handset to receive special offers, for example, a "buy-one, get-one-free" deal or discount. A bakery clerk scans the online code by using a bar code reader.

The system enables the bakery to collect such customer information as the user age, the visit frequency, and the amount of purchase, which can be used for developing marketing and sales promotion strategies. It also automatically awards customers redeemable points for purchase. The customer can easily view the updated total points on his/her cellular phone screen. It also flashes "members-only" banner ads notifying the time for selling fresh-baked bread. The firm trumpets this mobile Web coupon marketing system as a tool for retailers to be "with customers anytime, anywhere." Ryoyu Keisan hopes to enhance the service in the near future by exploiting GPS technology, the ability to discern the geographical location of mobile Web users. It should make the coupon offering more attractive, by letting

Table 5. Characteristics of mobile marketing vs. traditional marketing in terms of 4Ps as they relate to features of cyberspace

	Traditional marketing Ex. sales at shops (real world)	Mobile marketing sales at Web network (cyberspace)	Features of cyberspace as they relate to characteristics of mobile marketing
Product	All kinds of goods and services Ex. sales at stores < no limitation >	Goods with low availability Precious, in-ubiquitous & remote No anxiety—brandname; standardized Against self-purchase Weight, bulk and Psychological factor	Border-less nature Virtual nature (not real) Virtual nature (not real) delivery--outsourcing
Price	Possible pricing--- ①Fixed price (by seller) ②Auction (by buyer) Less comparable With some costs	Possible pricing --- selectable ①Fixed price (by seller) ②Auction (by buyer) ③Reverse auction (by seller) ④Bidding (by buyer) Prices widely comparable With low cost	Border-less, 2way communication Border-less, 2way communication Border-less, 2way communication Database involvement Virtual nature
Place	Real fixed place—Stores fully visible, touchable trials possible Multi-stage distribution channel manufacturer- wholesaler- retailer - consumer	Websites partly visible, untouchable trials impossible Single-stage distribution channel Direct sales	Virtual nature Virtual nature Virtual nature, 2way communication
Promo- tion	Advertisement Mass communication Wave & Printed matters Mass marketing with segmenta- tion	Real time marketing Coupon Route guidance Seamless processing - from notice to payment One to one marketing	Real-timeliness 2way communication 2way communication、Real-timeli- ness, 2way communication、Real-timeli- ness, Database involvement

Figure 5. Coupon marketing system of bakery shop

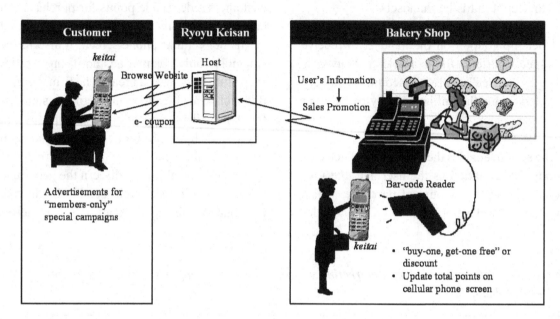

the bakery distribute special discounts, for instance, only when the registered members are near the shops.

Production/Construction Status Control

The Case of Sumitomo Forestry

Sumitomo Forestry developed Construction Process Management System for Detached House Using Browser Phones (Toyoda, 2006). The background of this is as follows.

Today'' house building consists by the operation to assemble nearly 30,000 components served by the various traders who take charge of foundation work, construction, electrical work, plumbing, and others allotting each process. In addition, as the construction site is located in the town, building operations are influenced easily by the position with vicinity to houses, road conditions, the weather, and other environments. Therefore, in order to make the construction advance smoothly, the information of its progress is important, and it

is a severe issue for each building company to get the accurate information from the site timely.

In Sumitomo Forestry Co., about 3,500 houses are usually being constructed in Japan. Every 20 to 30 of these sites are managed by one construction person in charge of the branch office and each site is managed daily by the cooperating small builder. Usually, the full-time person in charge of management does not reside in the construction spot, but one of the on-site workers is acting as the person in charge for each process. They are not necessarily familiar with office procedure; therefore various troubles occur in the site such as neglecting a regular contact and/or mishearing in a report. Such problems are common to each housing company, though there may be some differences.

In order to solve the above subjects, Sumitomo Forestry Co., Ltd. Developed "Construction Progress Management System (CPMS)," and established the production management system by incorporating CPMS. Figure 6 shows the outline of the production management system including CPMS.

Figure 6. Outline of the production management system including "Construction Progress Management System"

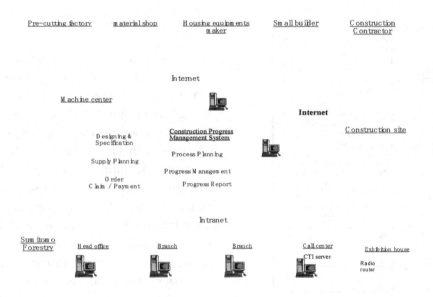

Figure 7. Outline of the progress reporting process

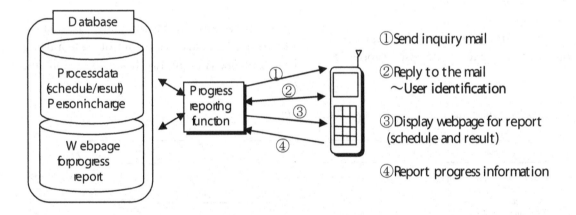

Figure 7 shows the outline of the progress reporting process.

Figure 8 shows the screen motion of the Web page for report.

In Sumitomo Forestry Co., Ltd., the production management system including CPMS has started in April, 2001, at some of branches and the cooperation small builders, and toward the end of that year, the system was expanded to all branches and the cooperation companies such as small builders, electrical work companies, and plumbing companies.

At present, approximately 10,000 users of 2,000 cooperative construction companies and the material makers have registered to the system, and the progress information is received from nearly 3,000 on-site workers using browser phones every day. Although the "support center" was organized

Figure 8. Screen motion of the Web page for report

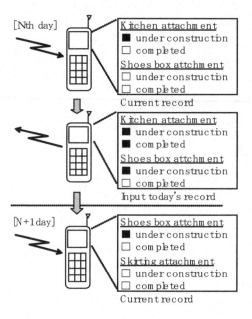

billion yen in 3 years in 2002 to 2004, and shortened the construction period by 10%.

The Case of Tokyu Home

A Tokyo-based housing manufacturer, Tokyu Home Co Ltd., introduced a system that can manage the construction process of a house by using *keitai* (Figure 9). A person responsible for the construction process inputs—by using cellular phones—such data as the date of the foundation work and the timing of materials delivery. Such information is stored at a host computer at its headquarters so that all employees can share the same information. By browsing data downloaded on their handsets, sales personnel could promptly answer queries from customers. The firm plans to enhance the service by allowing customers to have direct *keitai* access to its database in the near future.

Distribution Control

A Tokyo-based delivery company, DAT Japan Ltd., started a distribution control system using i-mode *keitai* (Figure 10). It works as follows:

in preparation for many inquiries from various users, there is almost no inquiry now and the system is working smoothly.

By using this production management system, Sumitomo Forestry reduced the cost by about 15

Figure 9. Production status control system of Tokyu Home

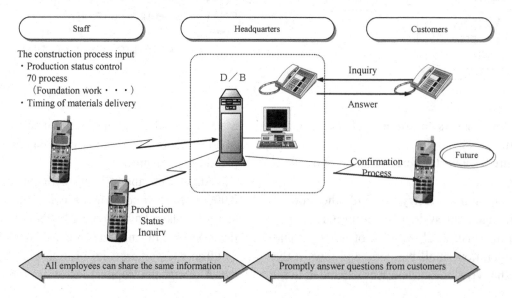

Figure 10. Distribution control of DAT Japan

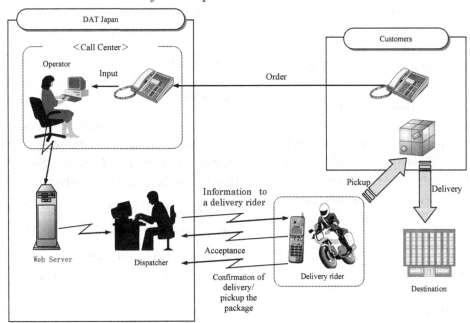

An operator inputs delivery/pickup orders into host computers, from which dispatchers retrieve such information to refer them to a delivery rider, located nearest to the destination. The rider checks the information on his handset to judge if he should deliver/pick up the package. The rider then contacts the dispatchers by *keitai* to confirm the delivery/pickup.

Because i-mode uses the Packet-switched system with fees charged not on usage time but the volume of information accessed, the firm, by adopting the new system, could reduce communication expense as much as by 85%. Previously, a delivery rider had to write down delivery information he received from an operator. However, under the new system, they can now confirm such data on their handsets. It can help prevent delivery errors, improve delivery efficiency and enrich customer satisfaction.

CONCLUSION

As shown in the cases above, the innovative use of *keitai* is beginning to emerge in the industrial sector. Such a trend is expected to continue. Take, for example, in equipment maintenance/control. Equipment control in a large factory is usually performed with maintenance workers moving around in the facility. However, predetermined schedule of equipment maintenance has to be changed when a breakdown occurs. In such an emergency, *keitai* can be used to issue instructions on how to cope with it. *Keitai* is also useful to confirm the inventory status of components needed to repair the equipment. *Keitai* can serve as a "liaison" between factory workers and staff in the head office. Using *keitai,* office staff can send to factory workers various messages such as a request for repairs and inventory management. Such data can be confirmed on PCs as well. *Keitai* is becoming a convenient tool to input and download data on intranetwork. Previously, handy terminals were used to input data on production or to check production process. They were in essence a "closed" system. However, because of its capability to access to the Internet, *keitai* can be used in an "open" environment. *Keitai* can be used to develop a system which is flexible and easy to be constructed and expanded. Mobile innovation will continue to evolve with potentials unlimited for new marketing and other technologies.

FUTURE RESEARCH DIRECTIONS

Mobile Marketing via Bluetooth may spread in the near future. Mobile tools are said to be a kind of ubiquitous computing tool. Users can handle them at any time and at any place and can communicate. Mobile tools would make much more development in the sense of ubiquitous computing tool.

REFERENCES

Garrard, G. A. (1997). *Cellular communications: Worldwide market development*. Boston, MA: Artech House.

Haig, M. (2002). *Mobile marketing: The message revolution*. London, UK: Kogan Page.

Hakuhodo Interactive Co. Ltd. (2000). *Keitai marketing*. Tokyo, Japan: Nihon Noritsu Kyokai Management Center.

Info-Plant. (2002). Beneficial, Menu. Tokyo: Info-Plant.

Matsunaga, M. (2000). *I-mode jiken*. Tokyo, Japan: Kadokawa Shoten.

Natsuno, T. (2000). *I-mode strategy*. Tokyo, Japan: Nikkei BP Kikaku.

Raina, K., & Harsh, A. (2001). M-*commerce security: A beginne's guide*. Berkley, CA: Mc-Graw-Hill.

Steinbock, D. (2002). *Wireless horizon: Strategy and competition in the worldwide mobile market-place*. New York: Amacom.

Strauss, J., & Frost, R. (1999). *Marketing on the Internet*. New Jersey: Prentice Hall.

Takeyasu, K. (2006). Mobile marketing. *The Journal of Economic Studies, 50*(2-4), 61-72. Osaka Prefecture University.

Takeyasu, K., Ono, A., & Ueda, M. (2003). *Current mobile business*. Tokyo, Japan: Chuo-Keizaisha.

Toyoda, J. (2006). Construction process management system for detached house using browser phones. *The Journal of Economic Studies, 52*(2), 155-169. Osaka Prefecture University.

Tsukuda, J., Takeyasu, K., & Ono, A. (2001). *Mobile e-business*. Tokyo, Japan: Chuo-Keizaishal.

Video Research. (2001). *Actual usage condition of mobile phone*. Tokyo, Japan: Video Research.

ADDITIONAL READING

Clarke, I., & Flaherty, T. (2005). *Advances in electronic marketing*. Hershey, PA: Idea Group Pub.

Crush, P. (2004). *The little book of mobile marketing*. London, UK: Haymarket Business Publications.

Davidson, J. (1999). *Fixed mobile convergence: Service integration and substitution*. London, UK: Ovum.

Funk, J. L. (2002). *Global competition between and within standards: The case of mobile phones*. New York: Palgrave Macmillan.

Hesselborn, O., & Fremuth, N. (2005). *The basic book of mobile marketing: Secrets of success*. Munich, Germany: Ocean Seven Consulting.

Jaokar, A., & Fish, T. (2006). *Mobile Web 2.0: The innovator's guide to developing and marketing next generation wireless/mobile applications*. London, UK: Futuretext.

Keen, P. G. W., Mackintosh, R., & Heikkonen, M. (2001). *The freedom economy: Gaining the m-commerce edge in the era of the wireless Internet.* California: McGraw-Hill.

Knott, P., Ablett, S., & Windle, L. (1998). *Mass marketing mobile telephony.* Cambridge, UK: Analysys.

Lamont, D. L. (2001). *Conquering the wireless world: The age of m-commerce.* Oxford: Capstone.

Lindgren, M., Jedbratt, J., & Svensson, E. (2002). *Beyond mobile: People, communications and marketing in a mobilized world.* New York: Palgrave Macmillan.

Louis, P. J. (2001). *M-commerce crash course: The technology and business of next generation Internet services.* New York: McGraw-Hill.

Mathieson, R. (2005). *Branding unbound: The future of advertising, sales, and the brand experience in the wireless age.* New York: Amacom.

Michael, A., & Salter, B. (2006). *Mobile marketing: Achieving competitive advantage through wireless technology.* Amsterdam, Holland: Butterworth-Heinemann.

Pinson, L. (2001). *Anatomy of a business plan: A step-by-step guide to building a business and securing your company's future.* Chicago: Dearborn Trade Pub.

Robson, J., Bond, K., Pow, R., & McKeon, S. (2001). *Successfully marketing mobile data services to SMEs.* Cambridge, UK: Analysys.

Shi, N., & Murthy, V. K. (2003). *Architectural issues of Web-enabled electronic business.* Hershey, PA: Idea Group Pub.

Stafford, M. R., & Faber, R. J. (2005). *Advertising, promotion, and new media.* Armonk, US: M.E.Sharpe.

Steinbock, D. (2005). *The mobile revolution: The making of mobile services worldwide.* London, UK: Kogan Page.

Takeyasu, K. (2007). Cyber marketing. *Journal of Economics, Business and Law, 9*, 45-56. Osaka Prefecture University.

Wakefield, T., McNally, D., Bowler, D., & Mayne, A. (2007). *Introduction to mobile communications: Technology, services, markets.* Boca Raton, FL: Auerbach.

Weiss, T. (2006). *Mobile strategies: Understanding Wireless business models, MVNos and the growth of mobile content.* London, UK: Futuretext.

Chapter XIX
The Retaliatory Feedback Problem:
Evidence from eBay and a Proposed Solution

Ross A. Malaga
Montclair State University, USA

ABSTRACT

Online auctions are an increasingly popular avenue for completing electronic transactions. Many online auction sites use some type of reputation (feedback) system—where parties to a transaction can rate each other. However, retaliatory feedback threatens to undermine these systems. Retaliatory feedback occurs when one party in a transaction believes that the other party will leave them a negative feedback if they do the same. This chapter examines data gathered from E-Bay in order to show that retaliatory feedback exists and to categorize the problem. A simple solution to the retaliatory feedback problem—feedback escrow—is described.

INTRODUCTION

The past few years have seen the explosive growth of online auction transactions. In 2005, E-Bay listed 1.9 billion items for auction, representing a 33% increase over the previous year. Those listing were responsible for $44 billion in transactions (a 29.6%) increase over 2004 (E-Bay, 2006). While E-Bay is the major player in this area, it is not the only one. Many other companies, such as Amazon, Yahoo, and Overstock, offer consumer-to-consumer (C2C) online auctions.

While online auction sites are an increasingly popular avenue for completing electronic transactions, they are characterized by a high degree of uncertainty. They face what Akerlof (1970) calls a "Lemons" market; that is, they have a high amount of uncertainty about the quality of the information and/or goods. Uncertainty primarily derives from the fact that buyers and sellers typically know little about each other, are involved in one-time transactions, and pictures and descriptions of goods provide the only means for assessing the quality of goods available for bidding (Montano, Porter, Malaga, & Ord, 2005). This lack of information available to auction bidders, termed information asymmetry, leads to a higher level of uncertainty about potential outcomes from an auction transaction than if a bidder were able to learn more about the auction seller and his product prior to bidding (Liang & Huang, 1998).

In order to reduce information asymmetry and increase the level of trust between auction participants, reputation systems have been developed. Wilson (1985, pp. 27-28) states, "in common usage, reputation is a characteristic or attribute ascribed to one person, industry, and so forth, by another (e.g., A has a reputation for courtesy)." This is typically represented as a prediction about likely future behavior (e.g., "A is likely to be courteous"). It is, however, primarily an empirical statement (e.g., "A has been observed in the past to be courteous"). The predictive power of reputation depends on the supposition that past behavior is indicative of future behavior. Reputation systems (sometimes called feedback systems) allow the participants in a transaction to rate each other. Individuals' ratings are aggregated and are available for everyone to see. These systems promote trust between buyers and sellers because they serve as a benchmark for seller reliability. Trust has been shown to serve as a key factor in the success of online transactions, including electronic auctions (Brynjolfsson & Smith, 2000; Resnick, Zeckhauser, Friedman, & Kuwabara, 2000; Hoffman & Novak, 1999).

This chapter proceeds as follows. The next section discusses the existing literature on trust and reputations systems. Following that, the retaliatory feedback problem is further defined. The research methodology is then discussed. Finally, future trends and conclusions are detailed.

BACKGROUND

Trust and Reputation Systems

A large body of research has shown that trust plays an important role in a consumer's decision to purchase a product in an electronic market (e.g., Jarvenpaa, Tractinsky, & Vitale, 2000; Lim, Sia, Lee, & Benbasat, 2006; McKnight, Choudhury, & Kacmar, 2002). In many contexts such as off-line auctions and stores, buyers have multiple clues that help them determine their level of trust in a seller (e.g., branding, location, past experience, visual observation). However, in online auctions there is no such context, and there is no guarantee that any pictures or descriptions provided are accurate. Thus, performance on past transactions (reputation) is typically the only factor that can contribute to the development of trust.

An important aspect of reputation is the dissemination of reputation information. Landon and Smith (1997, p. 313) concluded, "results suggest that consumers place considerable value on mechanisms that disseminate information on the past quality performance of firms." One way in which reputation information can be generated and disseminated in electronic markets and online communities is through the use of a reputation system (Nielsen, 1998). These systems allow participants in a transaction to rate each other, and the ratings are aggregated in order to provide an overall score. The overall score is provided to potential participants in future transactions.

As E-Bay is the dominant online auction site, we focus on its reputation system as an exemplar. In the E-Bay reputation system (which E-Bay calls feedback), any completed transaction may be rated by the winning bidder of an item and the seller of that item. The feedback scores are +1, representing a positive experience; 0, representing "neutral" feedback; and -1, meaning the purchasing experience was negative for some reason. These ratings are then used to calculate an overall reputation score (feedback score) as well as a percent positive feedback rating.

A number of researchers (Houser & Wooders, 2001; Lucking-Reiley, Bryan, Prasad, & Reeves, 2005; Resnick & Zeckhauser, 2002) have shown a correlation between higher reputation (feedback) scores on E-Bay and higher prices. Therefore, sellers have a strong incentive to achieve and maintain a high reputation score. Some sellers will go to great lengths to ensure a high score. For example, individuals with a negative reputation can easily open a new account (although E-Bay has taken measures to curtail this behavior). In addition, some sellers enter into agreements to purchase each other's goods and provide positive feedback (Gormley, 2004). However, mechanisms can be put in place to prevent this. On E-Bay, for example, a seller's reputation score only uses feedback from unique buyers. Therefore, multiple feedback from the same buyer is not counted.

It should be noted that sellers have a much greater incentive to attain positive feedback than buyers. This is due to the fact that it is buyers who chose whom to transact with. Sellers merely post their items and wait for buyers to bid on them.

Problem Definition

According to Bunnell (2000, p. 55) the E-Bay system, was founded on the belief that most people are trustworthy and committed to honorable dealings with each other. We are encouraging our community to think that basically 99% of the people out there are doing the right thing.

In fact, Resnick and Zeckhauser (2002) found that 99.1% of feedback left on E-Bay was positive, only 0.6% negative, and 0.3% neutral. While the empirical evidence seems to support the basic tenant that most people will behave correctly, we must consider the possibility that the underlying data is skewed due the problem of retaliation.

A number of researchers (Dellarocas, 2003; Resnick & Zeckhauser 2002) have suggested that the high level of positive feedback observed on E-Bay is the result of retaliatory feedback. Retaliatory feedback occurs when one party in a transaction believes that the other party will leave them a negative feedback if they do the same. In order to better understand this phenomenon we turn to game theory and anecdotal data gathered from E-Bay's feedback discussion forum.

The problem of retaliatory feedback on E-Bay was recently noted by Brian Burke, E-Bay's Director of Global Feedback Policy, who stated, "if you take this trend to its extreme we'll have 100% universal positive Feedback—which would make the Feedback system valueless" (Ninad, 2007).

Retaliatory Feedback and Game Theory

The theoretical basis for reputation systems is game theory (Resnick & Zeckhauser, 2000). The game theoretical approach views online auction transactions as a continuous Prisoner' Dilemma game (Fudenberg & Tirole, 1991; Tullock, 1997). In this game, if both players cooperate (provide each other with positive feedback) they will both receive a payoff of +1. If both players defect (provide each other with negative feedback) they will both receive a payoff of -1. However, if one player defects (provides a negative feedback) and the other player does not (provides positive feedback) then the payoffs are -1 for the player receiving the negative feedback, and +1 for the user receiving the positive feedback. These payoffs are summarized in Table 1. Neutral scores are not considered due to their low incidence and for the sake of simplicity. Therefore, if one person defects (in this case meaning provides a negative feedback) the best option for the other transaction participant is to also to defect. This is particularly true under E-Bay's revised feedback system, where transaction participants can agree to mutually withdraw feedback. Thus, the best possible payoff over time for both participants, under Nash equilibrium, is to cooperate (provide only positive feedback). This is in keeping with the findings of Bolton and Ockenfels (2000), who found that the second player in a Prisoner's Dilemma game will only cooperate when the first player has done likewise. With this in mind, many E-Bay participants have chosen to cooperate (never provide negative feedback) even when the circumstances dictate that they should not.

RESEARCH METHODOLOGY

We would not expect to see many instances of actual retaliation, since the fear of retaliation drives users to provide positive feedback. This tendency toward positive feedback has already been discussed above. Therefore, in order to find evidence to support the theory that users are concerned about retaliatory feedback, we monitored E-Bay's Feedback Discussion Forum during a one week period.

Data Analysis

During the period of observation there were 324 active threads. An active thread was defined a priori as either a new thread or a thread that contained a new reply. Each thread was reviewed to determine if the content was related to the retaliatory feedback problem. Of the 324 total threads, 51 or 15.7% concerned retaliatory feedback.

An example of a typical posting on this issues is I have to say this. I think it totally defeats the purpose of the feedback system if you don't leave feedback until the "other" person leaves it. In about fifty percent of my recent purchases, the sellers have said, "When I see you have left positive feedback, I will leave mine." No!, No!, No!. I have held up my end of the bargain by paying you within 30 seconds via PayPal, if you are happy with that, then the rest of the deal is up to you. Honestly, you have nothing else to base your feedback on for me. This is not a trade; it is FEEDBACK on how the transaction went. What if I am unhappy with your end of the deal, now if I leave negative feedback I have to worry about receiving negative feedback, when I did nothing wrong. Something has got to change. Do other E-Bayers out there face this same problem?

The 51 threads of interest were further examined in order to determine the exact nature of

Table 1. Prisoner's Dilemma Payoffs

Player A Provides Feedback

		Positive	Negative
Player B Provides Feedback	Positive	+1 +1	-1 +1
	Negative	+1 -1	-1 -1

the users' concerns. Based on this analysis, the retaliatory feedback problem can be broken into four main categories. Note, some threads fell into multiple categories resulting in the numbers below adding to more than 51.

First, 17 threads were primarily concerned with specific instances of retaliation. Many of the postings in this category discussed the problem of nonpaying winner bidders threatening to leave negative feedback for sellers who leave them a negative for nonpayment.

Second, a large number of threads (28) discussed the problem of who should leave feedback first after a completed transaction. Of course, most buyers believe that the seller should leave feedback first, and most sellers believe buyers are responsible for first feedback. The fact that both parties are waiting for the other to leave feedback first follows from game theory. If one party already knows that the other party either defected or cooperated then the best move is predefined. The impact of this waiting game is that many people do not leave feedback at all. This is in line with previous research by Resnick and Zeckhauser (2002) who found that only 52.1% of buyers leave feedback and 60.6% of sellers.

Third, 8 threads sought advice on whether and how to leave negative feedback. A number of posts recommend maintaining two E-Bay accounts—one only to sell and the other only to buy. This allows an individual who is unhappy with a purchase to leave negative feedback for a seller without fear that it will impact his or her own seller account. Since E-Bay allows 90 days to leave feedback, the other common advice is to wait until the last minute to post negative feedback. This would not allow enough time for the other party to the transaction to retaliate. However, a number of posts warn that this approach may backfire, as E-Bay does not always lock out feedback at exactly 90 days.

Fourth, some threads (5) discussed the problem of feedback extortion. This occurs when one party to a transaction demands something from

the other party and uses the threat of negative feedback as part of the demand. For example, in a recent posting a buyer complained that the seller had only shipped part of the purchase. After waiting 11 weeks for the rest of the purchase, the buyer posted negative feedback. At that point the seller told the buyer that he would not send the remainder of the purchase unless the negative feedback was withdrawn.

Retaliatory Feedback Solution

There is a very simple solution to the retaliatory feedback problem—feedback escrow. In a system with feedback escrow, parties to a transaction would be allowed to leave feedback only for a specified period of time (a few weeks perhaps). In addition, all feedback would be kept secret until both parties have left their feedback or until the time has expired. Finally, the option to mutually withdraw feedback would not exist.

In terms of game theory, feedback escrow changes the game from a Prisoner's Dilemma in which one party knows what the other party has already chosen, to one in which neither party has information about what the other has chosen. In this scenario there is essentially no first mover and thus no ability to retaliate. The elimination of mutual feedback withdrawal is an important aspect of this solution. If participants can withdraw feedback, then the optimal solution becomes defection.

It should be noted that feedback escrow addresses three of the categories of retaliation discussed above. Specific instances of retaliation would not occur. In addition, we would expect an increase in the amount of feedback and the speed with which it is left. Since feedback is kept secret until both parties have posted or until the time limit is reached, the concern about who should leave feedback first is eliminated.

The one area that feedback escrow cannot address is feedback extortion. If the system allows users to withdraw previously posted feedback, then some users will likely find ways to abuse the process.

FUTURE RESEARCH DIRECTIONS

While E-Bay is not the only auction site that uses a reputation system to provide user feedback, it is, by far, the largest. However, E-Bay has traditionally been reluctant to tinker with its feedback system. This is to be expected as millions of users have invested a considerable amount of time (and perhaps money) in building and protecting their E-Bay feedback scores. However, in 2007, it began pilot testing a revision to its feedback system, called Feedback 2.0. Under this new system auction, participants are able to leave detailed feedback. For example, a buyer will be able to rate a seller, using a five point Lickert scale, on certain aspects of the transaction, such as accuracy of the listing and shipping (E-Bay, 2007). As these detailed ratings are delayed, it should prove very difficult for participants to determine exactly who left feedback. However, E-Bay has simply added detailed feedback to its original feedback system. As Feedback 2.0 has only recently been rolled out, it provides a rich resource for future research in this area. For instance, how prevalent is the use of detailed feedback? Does the implementation of detailed feedback and the time delay increase the amount of negative feedback left on E-Bay?

CONCLUSION

The purpose of an online reputation system, such as E-Bay feedback, is to provide a level of trust between buyers and sellers. Game theory predicts, and comments from the E-Bay discussion board confirm, that retaliatory feedback likely occurs. In this situation, few users are likely to provide true feedback—guarding their own reputation against retaliation. Thus, less than one percent of all feedback left on E-Bay is negative (Resnick & Zeckhauser, 2002). If, as appears to be the case, almost everybody receives positive feedback, then the feedback system is ineffective in helping users determine with whom they should transact.

A simple solution to the retaliatory feedback problem, feedback escrow, has been proposed in this chapter. Feedback escrow alone would solve three of the four retaliation problems outlined above. Combined with the inability to retract previous feedback, the escrow system would also resolve the feedback extortion problem.

REFERENCES

Akerlof, G.A. (1970, August). The market for Lemons: Quality uncertainty and the market mechanism. *Quarterly Journal of Economics, 84,* 488-500.

Bolton, G., & Ockenfels, A. (2000). ERC: A theory of equity, reciprocity, and cooperation. *The American Economic Review, 90*(1), 166-193.

Brynjolfsson, E., & Smith, M. (2000). Frictionless commerce? A comparison of Internet and conventional retailers. *Management Science, 46*(4), 563-585.

Bunnell, D. (2000). *The E-bay phenomenon.* New York: John Wiley.

Dellarocas, C. (2003). The digitization of word of mouth: Promise and challenges of online feedback mechanisms. *Management Science, 49*(10), 1407-1424.

E-Bay. (2006). E-bay form 10-K, Feb. 24, 2006. Retrieved June 14, 2008, from http://investor. E-Bay.com/secfiling.cfm?filingID=950134-06-3678

E-Bay. (2007). Detailed seller ratings. Retrieved June 14, 2008, from http://pages.E-Bay.com/help/feedback/detailed-seller-ratings.html

Fudenberg, D., & Tirole, J. (1991). *Game theory.* Cambridge: MIT Press.

Gormley, M. (2004, November 8). E-Bay sellers admit to phony bids. *Associated Press.*

Hoffman, D.L., Novak, T.P., & Peralta, M. (1999). Building consumer's trust online. *Communications of the ACM, 42*(4), 80-86.

Houser, D., & Wooders, J. (2001). Reputation in Internet auctions: Theory and evidence from E-Bay, Working Paper, University of Arizona. Retrieved June 14, 2008, from *http://bpa.arizona.edu/~jwooders/E-Bay.pdf*

Jarvenpaa, S., Tractinsky, N., & Vitale, M (2000). Consumer trust in an Internet store. *Information Technology and Management, 1*(1-2), 45-71.

Landon, S., & Smith, C.E. (1997). The use of quality and reputation indicators by consumers: The case of Bordeaux wine. *Journal of Consumer Policy, 20,* 289-323.

Liang T.P., & Huang J.S. (1998). An empirical study on consumer acceptance of products in electronic markets: A transaction cost model. *Decision Support Systems, 24,* 29-43.

Lim, K, Sia, C., Lee, M., & Benbasat, I. (2006). Do I trust you online, and if so, will I buy? An empirical study of two trust-building strategies. *Journal of Management Information Systems, 23*(2), 233-266.

Lucking-Reiley, D., Bryan, D., Prasad, N., & Reeves, D. (2005). *Pennies from E-Bay: The determinants of price in online auctions.* Working Paper, Vanderbilt University. Retrieved June 14, 2008, from http://www.u.arizona.edu/~dreiley/papers/PenniesFromE-Bay.pdf

McAfee, R.P., & McMillan, J. (1987). Auctions and bidding. *Journal of Economic Literature, 25*(2), 699-738.

McKnight, D.H., Choudhury, V., & Kacmar, C. (2002). Developing and validating trust measures for e-commerce: An integrative typology. *Information Systems Research, 13*(3), 334-359.

Montano, B.R., Porter, D.C., Malaga, R.A., & Ord, J.K. (2005). Enhanced reputation scoring for online auctions. In *Twenty-sixth International Conference on Information Systems, Proceedings.*

Nielsen, J. (1998, February 8). The reputation manager. Retrieved June 14, 2008, from http://www.useit.com/alertbox/980208.html

Ninad. (2007). *Feedback 2.0 – a conversation with Brian Burke.* Retrieved June 14, 2008, from http://www.E-Baychatter.com/the_chatter/2007/02/feedback_20_a_c.html

Resnick, P., & Zeckhauser, R. (2002). Trust among strangers in Internet transactions: Empirical analysis of E-Bay's reputation system. In M.R. Baye (Ed.), *The economics of the Internet and e-commerce* (Vol. 11 of Advances in Applied Microeconomics). Amsterdam: Elsevier Science.

Resnick, P., Zeckhauser, R., Friedman, E., & Kuwabara, K. (2000). Reputation systems: Facilitating trust in Internet interactions. *Communications of the ACM, 43*(12), 45-48.

Tullock, G. (1997). Adam Smith and the prisoners' dilemma. In D.B. Klein (Ed.), *Reputation: Studies in the voluntary elicitation of good conduct* (pp. 21-28). Ann Arbor, MI: University of Michigan Press.

Wilson, R. (1985). Reputations in games and markets. In A. Roth (Ed.), *Game theoretic models of bargaining* (pp. 27-62). Cambridge: Cambridge University Press.

ADDITIONAL READINGS

Ba, S., & Pavlou, P.A. (2002(. Evidence of the effect of trust building technology in electronic markets: Price premiums and buyer behavior. *MIS Quarterly, 26*(3), 1-26.

Ba, S., Whinston, A.B., & Zhang, H. (2003). Building trust in online auction markets through an economic incentive mechanism. *Decision Support Systems, 35,* 273-286.

Bajari, P., & Hortacsu, A. (2004). Economic insights from Internet auctions. *Journal of Economic Literature, 42,* 457-486.

Dellarocas, C. (2003). The digitization of word of mouth: Promise and challenges of online feedback mechanisms. *Management Science, 49*(10), 1407-1424.

Fan, M., Tan, Y., & Whinston, A.B. (2005). Evaluation and design of online cooperative feedback mechanisms for reputation management. *IEEE Transactions on Knowledge and Data Engineering, 17*(2), 244-54.

Houser, D., & Wooders, J. (2001). Reputation in Internet auctions: Theory and evidence from E-Bay. Working Paper, University of Arizon. Retrieved June 14, 2008, from http://bpa.arizona.edu/~jwooders/E-Bay.pdf

Josang, A., Ismail, R., & Boyd, C. (2007). A survey of trust and reputation systems for online service provision. *Decision Support Systems, 43,* 618-644.

Lim, K, Sia, C., Lee, M., & Benbasat, I. (2006). Do I trust you online, and if so, will I buy? An empirical study of two trust-building strategies. *Journal of Management Information Systems, 23*(2), 233-266.

Lucking-Reiley, D., Bryan, D., Prasad, N., & Reeves, D. (2005). Pennies from E-Bay:

The determinants of price in online auctions. Working Paper, Vanderbilt University. Retrieved June 14, 2008, from http://www.u.arizona.edu/~dreiley/papers/PenniesFromE-Bay.pdf

Malaga, R.A. (2001). Web-based reputation management systems: Problems and suggested solutions. *Electronic Commerce Research, 1,* 403- 417

Melnik, M., & Alm, J. (2002). Does a seller's ecommerce reputation matter? Evidence from E-Bay auctions. *Journal of Industrial Economics, 50,* 337-349.

Yu, B., & Singh, M.P. (2002). Distributed reputation management for electronic commerce. *Computational Intelligence, 18*(4), 535-549.

Compilation of References

Aamodt, A., & Plaza, E. (1994). Case-based reasoning: Foundational issues, methodological variations, and system approaches. *AI Communication, 7*(1), 39-59. IOS Press.

Abdelguerfi, M., & Givaudan, J. (2002). Advances in spatio-temporal r-tree based structures (Tech. Rep. TR012-02). Computer Science Department, University of New Orleans.

Abdelguerfi, M., Julie, G., Kevin, S., & Ladner, R. (2002). Spatio-temporal data handling: The 2-3TR-tree, a trajectory-oriented index structure for fully evolving valid-time spatio-temporal datasets. In *Proceedings of the 10th ACM International Symposium on Advances in Geographic Information Systems*.

Abrahão, S.M., & Pastor, O. (2003). Measuring the functional size of Web applications. *International Journal of Web Engineering and Technology, 1*(1), 5-16.

Abrahão, S.M., Fons, J.J., & Pastor, O. (2001). Object-oriented approach to automate Web applications development. In *Proceedings of International Conference on Electronic Commerce and Web Technologies* (EC-Web '01) (pp. 16-28). Springer Verlag.

Abrahão, S.M., Pastor, O., & Poels, G. (2004). Evaluating a functional size measurement method for Web applications: An empirical analysis. In *Proceedings of International Software Metrics Symposium* (METRICS'04) (pp. 358-369).

ACCADEMY. (2003). *The economic environment and the SME, ACCA*. Retrieved June 10, 2008, from http://www.accademy.com/pdfs/smallbusiness/EESME.doc

Adorno, T. W. (1994). The stars down to earth. In S. Crook (Ed.), *The stars down to earth and other essays on the irrational in culture* (pp. 46-171). London and New York, NY: Taylor & Francis Group Routledge Classics.

Adorno, T. W. (1994). Theses against occultism. In S. Crook (Ed.), *The stars down to earth and other essays on the irrational in culture* (pp. 173-180). London and New York, NY: Taylor & Francis Group Routledge Classics.

Akerlof, G.A. (1970, August). The market for Lemons: Quality uncertainty and the market mechanism. *Quarterly Journal of Economics, 84,* 488-500.

Alawattage, C., & Wickramasinghe, D. (2006). Appearance of accounting in a political hegemony. *Critical Perspectives on Accounting.* Retrieved June 1, 2008, from www.sciencedirect.com

Albert, T.C., Goes, P.B., & Gupta, A. (2004). GIST: A model for design and management of content and interactivity of customer-centric Web sites. *MIS Quarterly 28*(2), 161-182.

Albrecht, A.J. (1979). Measuring application development productivity. In *Proceedings of the Joint SHARE/GUIDE/IBM Application Development Symposium* (pp. 83-92).

Allen, T. (1977). *Managing the flow of technology.* Cambridge, MA: MIT Press.

Al-Mabrouk, K., & Soar, J. (in press). A Delphi study on issues for successful information technology transfer in the Arab World. *The International Arab Journal of Information Technology.*

Al-Mashari, M. (2000). Constructs of process change management in ERP context: A focus on SAP R/3. In *Americas Conference on Information Systems,* Long Beach, California.

Althusser, L. (2005). On the young Marx. In *For Marx* (Chapter 2, pp. 49-86). London and New York, NY: Verso.

Althusser, L. (2005). The 1844 manuscripts of Karl Marx. In *For Marx* (Chapter 5, pp. 153-160). London and New York, NY: Verso.

Althusser, L. (2005). Marxism and humanism. In *For Marx* (Chapter 7, pp. 219-248). London and New York, NY: Verso.

Althusser, L. (2007). *Politics and history: Montesquieu, Rousseau, Marx*. London and New York, NY: Verso.

Andersen Consulting. (1998). *Logistics information system (LIS) study* (No. 4). Singapore National Computer Board.

Andersen, T. J. (2001). Information technology, strategic decision making approaches and organizational performance in different industrial settings. *Journal of Strategic Information Systems, 10*(2), 101-119.

Anderson, J.G., Aydin, C.E., & Jay, S.J. (1994). *Evaluating health care information systems: Methods and applications*. USA: Sage.

Anonymous. (2005). Review of NDA guidelines. Personal communication via e-mail. Simi Valley, CA.

Anquetil, N., de Oliveira, K.M., de Sousa, K.D., & Batista Dias, M.G. (2006). Software maintenance seen as a knowledge management issue. *Information and Software Technology, 49*(8), 515-529.

Archer, M., Bhaskar, R., Collier, A., Lawson, T., & Norrie, A. (Eds.). (1998). *Critical realism: Essential readings*. London: Routledge.

Argyris, C. (2004). *Reasons and Rationalizations: The Limits to Organizational Knowledge*. Oxford: Oxford University Press.

Argyris, C., & Schon, D.A. (1978). *Organizational learning: A theory of action perspective*. Reading, MA: Addison-Wesley.

Ariyachandra, T., & Watson, H. J. (2006). Which data warehouse architecture is most successful? *Business Intelligence, 11*(1).

Arnott, D. (2004). Decision support systems evolution: Framework, case study and research agenda. *European Journal of Information Systems, 13*, 247-259.

Arnott, D. (2006). Cognitive biases and decision support systems development: A design science approach. *Information Systems Journal, 16*(1), 55-78.

Arnott, D., & Pervan, G. (2005). A critical analysis of decision support systems research. *Journal of Information Technology, 20*(2), 67-87.

Arunachalam, V. (1995). EDI: And analysis of adoption, uses, benefits and barriers. *Journal of Systems Management, 46*(2), 60-65.

ASC X12 Group. (2002). ASC X12 accelerates XML: Standards convergence. *Electronic Commerce News, 7*(25), 10-18.

Asian Logistics Directory. Retrieved June 8, 2008, from http://www.schednet.com/

ASME (2003). *Terms and conditions of SME in Singapore, association of small and medium enterprises*. Retrieved June 10, 2008, from http://www.asmes.org.sg

Atkinson, C., Eldabi, T., & Paul, R. (2002). Integrated approaches to health informatics research and development. *Logistics Information Management, 15*(2), 138-152.

Au, Y.A. (2001). Design science I: The role of design science in electronic commerce research. *Communications of the Association for Information Systems (CAIS), 7*(1).

Augur, P., Barnir, A., & Gallaugher, J. M. (2003). Strategic orientation, competition, and Internet-based electronic commerce. *Information Technology and Management, 4*(2-3), 139-164.

Avgerou, C. (2000). Information systems: What sort of science is it? *Omega, 28*(5), 567-579.

Avgerou, C., Ciborra, C., & Land, F. (Eds.). (2004). *The social study of information and communication technology: Innovation, actors, and contexts*. Oxford: Oxford University Press.

Avison, D., Lau, F., Myers, M., & Nielsen, P.A. (1999). Action research. *Comm. of the ACM, 42*(1), 94-97.

Avison, D.E., & Wood-Harper, A.T. (1990). *Multiview: An exploration in information systems development*. Maidenhead: McGraw-Hill.

Avison, D.E., Baskerville, R., & Myers, M. (2001). Controlling action research projects. *Information Technology & People, 14*(1), 28-45.

Bakhshi, N., Versendaal, J., van den Berg, J., & van den Ende, D. (2007). Impact of the extensible business reporting language on the administrative burden of organizations: A case study at the Dutch water boards. In *Proceedings of the 4th International Conference on Enterprise Systems, Accounting & Logistics*.

Bakos, J.Y., & Tracy, M.E. (1986). Information technology and corporate strategy: A research perspective. *MIS Quarterly, 10*(2), 23-38.

Ball, R.K. (1987). *Annual software maintenance survey: Survey results* (working paper). Vallejo, CA: Software Maintenance Association.

Ballintijn, G. (2007). A case study of the release management of a health care information system. In *Proceedings of the IEEE International Conference on Software Maintenance, ICSM2005, Industrial Applications track*.

Balsiger, P. W. (2005). *Transdisziplinarität: Systematisch-vergleichende untersuchung disziplinenübergreifender wissenschaftspraxis.* München: Fink.

Bamfield, J. (1994). Learning by doing: Electronic data interchange adoption by retailers. *Logistics Information Management, 7*(6), 32-38.

Bamfield, J. (1994). Technological management learning: The adoption of electronic data interchange by retailer. *International Journal of Retail & Distribution Management, 22*(2), 3-11.

Bancroft, N., Seip, H., & Sprengel, A. (1998). *Implementing SAP R/3: How to introduce a large system into a large organisation.* Greenwich, CT: Manning Publications.

Banerjee, S., & Golhar, D.Y. (1993). EDI implementation in JIT and non-JIT manufacturing firms: A comparative study. *International Journal of Operations & Production Management, 13*(3), 13-403.

Banerjee, S., & Golhar, D.Y. (1995). Security issues in the EDI environment. *Information Management & Computer Security, 26*(2), 27-33.

Bannister, F. (2002). The dimension of time: Historiography in information systems research. *Electronic Journal of Business Research Methods, 1*(1), 1-10.

Banville, C., & Landry, M. (1989). Can the field of m-IS be disciplined? *Communications of the ACM, 32*(1), 48-61.

Bapat, J. (2005). *Development projects and critical theory of environment.* New Delhi, India: Sage Publications.

Baresi, L., & Morasca, S. (in press). Three empirical studies on estimating the design effort of Web applications. *ACM Transactions on Software Engineering and Methodology.*

Baresi, L., Morasca, S., & Paolini, P. (2003). Estimating the design effort of Web applications. In *Proceedings of the International Software Metrics Symposium* (METRICS'03) (pp. 62-72).

Barley, S. R. (1990). Images of imaging: Notes on doing longitudinal field work. *Organization Science, 1*(3), 220-247.

Basili, V.R., Briand, L.C., & Melo, W.L. (1996). A validation of object-oriented design metrics as quality indicators. *IEEE Transactions on Software Engineering, 22*(10), 751-761.

Basili, V.R., Shull, F., & Lanubile, F. (1999). Building knowledge through families of experiments. *IEEE Transactions on Software Engineering, 25*(4), 456-473.

Baskerville, R., & Myers, M. (2002). IS as a reference discipline. *M-IS Quarterly, 26*(1), 1-14.

Baskerville, R., & Myers, M. D. (Eds.). (2004). Special issue on action research in information systems: Making is research relevant to practice. *MIS Quarterly, 28*(3).

Baskerville, R.L., & Wood-Harper, A.T. (1996). A critical perspective on action research as a method for IS research. *Journal of Information Technology, 11*(3), 235-246.

Bates, A. W. (2000). Chapter ten: Avoiding the Faustian contract and meeting the technology challenge. In T. Bates (Ed.), *Managing technological change.* San Francisco: Jossey-Bass.

Bauman, Z. (1989). *Modernity and the holocaust.* Cambridge: Polity Press.

Bauman, Z. (2005). Afterthought: On writing; On writing sociology. In N. K. Denzin & Y. S. Lincoln (Eds.), *Handbook of Qualitative Research* (3rd ed., pp. 1089-1098). Thousand Oaks, CA: Sage Publications.

Becker, H., & Geer, B. (1969). Participant observation: A comparison. In G.J. McCall & J.L. Simmons (Eds.), *Issues in participant observation.* New York: Random House.

Becker, J., & Niehaves, B. (2007). Epistemological perspectives on IS research: A framework for analysing and systematizing epistemological assumptions. *IS Journal, 17*(2), 197-214.

Bell, J. (1992). *Doing your research project.* Open University Press, Milton Keynes

Benbasat, I., & Weber, R. (1996). Research commentary: Rethinking diversity in information system research. *IS Research, 7*(4), 389-399.

Benbasat, I., & Zmud, R. W. (2003). The identity crisis within the IS discipline: Defining and communicating the discipline's core properties. *MIS Quarterly, 27*(2), 183-194.

Benbasat, I., Goldstein, D. K., & Mead, M. (2002). The case research strategy in studies of information systems. In M. D. Myers & D. Avison (Eds.), *Qualitative Research in Information Systems: A Reader* (pp. 79-99). London: Sage Publications.

Benbasat, I., Goldstein, D. K., & Mead, M. (1987). The case research strategy in studies of information systems. *MIS Q., 11*(3), 369-386.

Benbasat, I., Goldstein, D., & Mead, M. (1987). The case research strategy in studies of information systems, *MIS Quarterly, 11*(3), 368-386.

Benbasat, I., Goldstein, D.K., & Mead, M. (1987). The case research strategy in studies of IS. *M-IS Quarterly, 11*(3), 369-386.

Berger, P.L. (1963). *Invitation to sociology: A humanistic perspective*. USA: Doubleday&Co. Hunt Barnard Printing Ltd. Great Britain: Aylesbury.

Berger, P.L., & Luckmann, T. (1966). *The social construction of reality: A tretise in the sociology of knowledge*. USA.

Bernstein, R.J. (1983). *Beyond objectivity and relativism*. Oxford, UK: Basil Blackwell.

Beyer, G. W. (2001). *Modern dictionary for the legal profession* (3rd ed.). Buffalo, NY: William S. Hein & Co., Inc.

Bhaskar, R. (1978). *A realist theory of science*. Hemel Hempstead: Harvester.

Bhaskar, R. (2002). *From Science to Emancipation: Alienation and the Actuality of Enlightenment*. Delhi: Sage Publications India Pvt Ltd.

Bhattacharjee, A., & Paul, R. (2004). Special issue on interpretive approaches to IS and computing. *European Journal of IS, 13*(3), 166.

Bhattacherjee, A. (2000). Beginning SAP R/3 implementation at Geneva Pharmaceuticals. *Communications of the AIS*.

Bischoff, J., & Alexander, T. (1997). *Data warehouse: Practical advice from the experts*. Upper Saddle River, NJ: Prentice Hall.

Blaikie, N. (2000). *Designing Social Research*. Cambridge: Polity.

Bloomfield, B. P., Coombs, R., Knights, D., & Littler, D. (2000). *Information Technology and Organisation*. Oxford University Press.

Bohem, B. (1981). *Software engineering economics*. Englewood Cliffs, NJ: Prentice-Hall.

Bohem, B.W., Abts, C., Brown, A.W., Chulani, S., Clark, B.K., Horowitz, W., et al. (2000). *Software cost estimation with COCOMO II*. Englewood Cliffs, NJ: Prentice Hall.

Boland, R.J. (1983). The in-formation of IS. In R.J. Boland & R.A. Hirschheim (Eds.), *Critical issues in IS research* (363-394). NY: John Wiley & Sons.

Boland, R.J. (1985). Phenomenology: A preferred approach to research on IS. In E. Mumford, R. Hirschheim, G. Fitzgerald, & T. Wood-Harper (Eds.), *Research methods in IS*. New York: North-Holland.

Boland, R.J. (1993). Accounting and the interpretive act. *Accounting, Organisations and Society, 18*(2/3), 125-146.

Boland, R.J., & Day, W.F. (1989). The experience of system design: A hermeneutic of organizational action. *Sc&inavian Journal of Management, 5*(2), 87-104.

Bolton, G., & Ockenfels, A. (2000). ERC: A theory of equity, reciprocity, and cooperation. *The American Economic Review, 90*(1), 166-193.

Boren, T., & Ramey, J. (2000). Thinking aloud: Reconciling theory and practice. *IEEE Transactions on Professional Communication, 43*(2), 261-278.

Boyce, G. (2006). The social relevance of ethics education in a global(ising) era: From individual dilemmas to systemic crises. *Critical Perspectives on Accounting*. Retrieved June 1, 2008, from www.sciencedirect.com

Briand, L., & Wieczorek, I. (2002). Software resource estimation. In J.J. Marciniak (Ed.), *Encyclopedia of software engineering* (Vol. 2, pp. 1160-1196) (2nd ed.). New York: John Wiley & Sons.

Briand, L., El Emam, K., & Bomarius, F. (1998). CO-BRA: A hybrid method for software cost estimation, benchmarking, and risk assessment. In *Proceedings of International Conference on Software Engineering (ICSE'98)*, (pp. 390-399).

Briand, L., El Emam, K., & Wieczorek, I., (1999). Explaining the cost of European space and military projects. In *Proceedings of International Conference on Software Engineering (ICSE'99)*, (pp. 303-312).

Briand, L., El. Emam, K., & Wiekzorek, I. (2000). A replicated assessment and comparison of common software cost modeling techniques. In *Proceedings of the International Conference on Software Engineering, (ICSE'00)*, (pp. 377-386).

Briand, L., El. Emam, K., Surmann, D., Wiekzorek, I., & Maxwell, K. (1999). An assessment and comparison of common software cost estimation modeling techniques. In *Proceedings of International Conference on Software Engineering, (ICSE'99)*, (pp. 313-322).

Briand, L.C., El-Emam, K., Maxwell, K., Surmann, D., & Wieczorek, I., (1999). An assessment and comparison of common cost estimation models. In *Proceedings of the International Conference on Software Engineering (ICSE'99)*, (pp. 313-322).

Brinkkemper, S., van Soest, I., & Jansen, S. (2007). Modeling of product software businesses: Investigation into industry product and channel typologies. In *The Inter-Networked World: ISD Theory, Practice, and Education,Proceedings of the Sixteenth International Conference on Information Systems Development (ISD 2007)*. Springer-Verlag.

Brown, C. V., & Vessey, I. (1999). ERP implementation approaches: Toward a contingency framework. In *International Conference on Information Systems (ICIS)*, Charlotte, North Carolina.

Bryant, A. (2002). Re-grounding grounded theory. *Journal of Information Technology Theory and Application, 4*(1), 25-42.

Bryer, R. A. (1999). A Marxist critique of the FASB's conceptual framework. *Critical Perspectives on Accounting, 10*(5), 551-589.

Bryer, R. A. (2006). Accounting and control of the labour process. *Critical Perspectives on Accounting, 17*(5), 551-598.

Bryman, A. (2001). *Social Research Methods*. Oxford: Oxford University Press.

Brynjolfsson, E., & Smith, M. (2000). Frictionless commerce? A comparison of Internet and conventional retailers. *Management Science, 46*(4), 563-585.

Buckland, M. (1998). *Overview of the history of science information systems*. Paper presented at the meeting of the American Heritage Foundation Conference on History and Heritage of Science information systems, Pittsburgh, PA. Retrieved June 3, 2008, from http://www.sims.berkeley.edu/~buckland/chfintr.htm

Bui, T. (2000). Decision support systems for sustainable development. In G. Kersten, Z. Mikolajuk, & A. Yeh (Eds.), *Decision support systems for sustainable development: A resource book of methods and applications*. MA: Kluwer Academic.

Bunge, M., (1977). *Treatise on basic philosophy (Vol. 3): Ontology 1: The furniture of the world*. Boston, MA: Reidel.

Bunge, M., (1979). *Treatise on basic philosophy: Volume 4: Ontology II: A world of systems*. Dordrecht: Reidel.

Bunnell, D. (2000). *The E-bay phenomenon*. New York: John Wiley.

Burrell, G. & Morgan, G. (2005). *Sociological Paradigms and Organisational Analysis: Elements of the Sociology of Corporate Life*. Ardershot: Ashgate Publishing Limited.

Burrell, G., & Morgan, G. (1979). *Sociological paradigms & organizational analysis*. London, UK: Heinemann Educational Publishers.

Burton, B., Geishecker, L., & Hostmann, B. (2006). *Organizational structure: Business intelligence and information management*: Gartner Research.

Butler, T. (1998). Towards a hermeneutic method for interpretive research in IS. *Journal of Information Technology, 13*(4), 285-300.

Byrd, T. A., & Davidson, N. C. (2003). Examining possible antecedents of IT impact on the supply chain and its effect on firm performance. *Information & Management, 41*(2), 243-255.

Bytheway, A. (1994). A concept model and checklist for EDI planning. *Logistics Information Management, 7*(2), 32-46.

Callo, V.N., & Packham, R.G. (1999). The use of soft systems methodology in emancipatory development. *System Research and Behavioral Science, 16*(4), 311-310.

Canals, J. (2000). *Managing Corporate Growth*. Oxford: Oxford University Press.

Carbonara, N. (2005). Information and communication technology and geographical clusters: Opportunities and spread. *Technovation, 25*(3), 213-222.

Carlsson, S.A. (2006, February). *Towards an IS design research framework: A critical realist perspective*. Claremont, CA: DESRIST.

Carr, L.T (1994). The strengths and weaknesses of qualitative and quantitative research; what method for nursing? *Journal of Advance Nursing, 20*(4), 716-721.

Carter P. (2007). Liberating usability testing. *Interactions, 14*(2), 18-22.

Chakrabarti, R., & Kardile, V. (2002). *The Asian managers handbook of e-commerce*. New Delhi, India: Tata McGraw-Hill Publishing Company Limited.

Chan, B., & Hawamdeh S.A. (2002). The development of e-commerce in Singapore: The impact of government initiatives. *Business Process Management Journal, 8*(3), 278-288.

Chapin, N. (1985). Software maintenance: A different view. In *AFIPS Conference Proceedings, 54th National Computer Conference* (pp. 509-513).

Chapin, N. (1993). Management problems seen in software maintenance: An empowerment study. In *IEEE 1993 Conference on Software Maintenance* (pp. 329-333).

Charmaz, K. (1983). The grounded theory method: An explication and interpretation. In R. Emerson (Ed.), *Contemporary field research: A collection of readings.* Boston, MA: Little Brown.

Chauduri, S., & Dayal, U. (1997). An overview of data warehousing and OLAP technology. *SIGMOD Record, 26*(1), 65-74.

Checkland, P. (1981). *Systems thinking, systems practice.* Chichester, UK: Wiley.

Checkland, P.B. (1972). Towards a system-based methodology for real-world problem solving. *Journal of Systems Engineering, 3*(2), 87-116.

Checkland, P.B. (1981). *Systems thinking, systems practice.* Chichester, UK: Wiley.

Checkland, P.B. (1992). From framework through experience to learning: The essential nature of action research. In C.J. Bruce & A.L. Russell (Eds.), *Transforming tomorrow today: Proceedings of the Second World Congress on Action Learning.* Nathan, Queensland: Action Learning, Action Research and Process Management Association Incorporated, Griffith University.

Checkland, P.B. (1995). Model validation in soft systems practice. *System Research, 12*(1), 47-54.

Checkland, P.B. (2001). Soft systems methodology in action: Participative creation of an information strategy for an acute hospital. In J. Rosenhead & J. Mingers (Eds.), *Rational analysis for a problematic world revisited: Problem structuring methods for complexity, uncertainty and conflict* (2nd ed.) (pp. 91-113). Chichester, West Sussex: John Wiley and Sons.

Checkland, P.B., & Holwell, S. (1998). *Information, systems and information systems.* Chichester, West Sussex: Wiley.

Checkland, P.B., & Scholes, J. (1990). *Soft systems methodology in action.* Chichester, West Sussex: Wiley.

Chen, C., & Stevenson, H. W., with Hayward, C., & Burgess, S. (1995). Culture and academic achievement: ethnic and cross-national differences. In M. L. Maehr and P. R. Pintrich (Eds.), *Advances in motivation and achievement: Culture, motivation and achievement* (Volume 9, pp. 119-151). Greenwich, CT: JAL Press.

Chen, J.C., & Williams, B.C. (1998). The impact of electronic data interchange (EDI) on SMEs: Summary of eight British case. *Journal of Small Business Management, 36*(4), 68-72.

Chen, P.P.-S., (1976). The entity-relationship model: Toward a unified view of data. *ACM Transactions on Database Systems, 1*(1), 9-36.

Chen, W. S., & Hirschheim, R. (2004). A paradigmatic and methodological examination of information systems research from 1991 to 2001. *Information Systems Journal, 14*(3), 197-235.

Chen, W., & Hirschheim, R. (2004). A paradigmatic and methodological examination of IS research from 1991 to 2001. *IS Journal, 14,* 197-235.

Chong, C.W., Lim, K.S., & Wong, W.H. (1998). *How some Singapore small and medium enterprises are using the Internet.* In Nanyang Business School (School of Accountancy and Business), Nanyang Technology University.

Chua, W.F. (1986). Radical developments in accounting thought. *The Accounting Review, 61*(4), 601-632.

Ciborra, C.U. (1998). Crisis and foundations: An inquiry into the nature and limits of models and methods in the IS discipline. *Journal of Strategic IS, 7,* 5-16.

Ciborra, C.U. (1998). From tool to gestell. *Information Technology and People, 11*(4), 305-327.

Clarke, R. (2001), Electronic data interchange (EDI): An introduction. *Business Credit, 103*(9), 23-25.

Clay, P. (2005). Response to NDA query. Personal communication via e-mail. Simi Valley, CA.

Closs, D. J., Goldsby, T. J., & Clinton, S. R. (1997). Information technology influences on world class logistics capability. *International Journal of Physical Distribution and Logistics Management, 27*(1), 4-17.

CMU. (2001, November). IP policy mark-up, including changes proposed by the University Research Council. Retrieved June 1, 2008, from http://www.andrew.cmu.edu/org/fac-senate/docsDec01/markedIPPol.pdf

Cohen, G., Salomon, I., & Nijkamp, P. (2002). Information-communication technology (ICT) and transport: Does knowledge underpin policy? *Telecommunications Policy, 26,* 31-52.

Colberg, T.P. (1990). The compelling case for EDI. *The Financial Manager, 20,* 20-26.

Cole, R., Purao, S., Rossi, M., & Sein, M.K. (2005). Being proactive: Where action research meets design research. In *Proceedings of the Twenty-Sixth International Conference on IS* (pp. 325-336).

Conte, D., Dunsmore, H.E., & Shen, V.Y. (1986). *Software engineering metrics and models.* The Benjamin/Cummings Publishing Company, Inc.

Copeland, D.G., & McKenney, J.L. (1988). Airline reservations systems: Lessons from history. *MIS Quarterly, 12*(3), 353-370.

Cordoba, J.-R. (2007). Developing inclusion and critical reflection in information systems planning. *Organization Connexions, 14*(6), 909-927.

Corey, M., Abbey, M., Abramson, I., & Taub, B. (2001). *Oracle data warehousing.* Osborne: McGraw-Hill.

CoSCo. (2000). *B-cource service.* Complex Computation Group, Department of Computer Science, University of Helsinki, Finland. Retrieved June 3, 2008, from http://b-cource.cs.helsinki.fi/

COSMIC. (2005, December). *Guideline for sizing business application software using COSMIC-FFP, Version 1.0.* Retrieved June 13, 2008, from http://www.lrgl.uqam.ca/cosmic-ffp/manual.html

Costagliola, G., Di Martino, S., Ferrucci, F., Gravino, C., Tortora, G., & Vitiello G. (2006a). A COSMIC-FFP: Approach to predict Web application development effort. *Journal of Web Engineering, 5*(2), 93-120.

Costagliola, G., Di Martino, S., Ferrucci, F., Gravino, C., Tortora, G., & Vitiello, G. (2006b). Effort estimation modeling techniques: A case study for Web applications. In *ACM Proceedings of the 6th International Conference on Web Engineering* (ICWE 2006), (pp. 9-16).

Cottrell, M. (1998). Theoretical aspects of the SOM algorithm. *Neurocomputing, 21,* 119-138.

Cragg, P., & King, M. (1993). Small firm computing motivators and inhibitors. *MIS Quarterly, 17*(1), 47-60.

Crook, S. (1994), Introduction: Adorno and authoritarian irrationalism. In S. Crook (Ed.), *The stars down to earth and other essays on the irrational in culture* (pp. 1-45). London and New York, NY: Taylor & Francis Group Routledge Classics.

Crowe, T.J., Zayas-Castro, J.L., & Vanichsenee, S. (2002). Readiness assessment for enterprise resource planning. In *the 11th International Conference on Management of Technology (IAMOT2002).*

Cunningham, C., & Tynan, C. (1993). Electronic trading, inter-organizational systems and the nature of buy-seller relationships: The need for a network perspective. *International Journal of Information Management, 13,* 3-28.

Curtis, B., Krasner, H., & Iscoe, N. (1988). A field study of the software design process for large systems. *Communications of ACM, 31*(11), 1268-1287.

d'Amboise, G. (1991). *The Canadian small and medium-sized enterprise.* Canada: The Institute for Research on Public Policy.

Darke, P., Shanks, G. G., & Broadbent, M. (1998). Successfully completing case study research: Combining rigour, relevance and pragmatism. *Information Systems Journal, 8*(4), 273-290.

Darke, P., Shanks, G., & Broadbent, M. (1998). Successfully completing case study research: Combining rigour, relevance and pragmatism. *IS Journal, 8*(4), 273-289

Dart, S.A., Christie, A.M., & Brown, A.W. (1993). *A case study in software maintenance* (SEI Tech. Rep. No. CMU/SEI-93-TR-08). Pittsburgh PA: Software Engineering Institute, Carnegie Mellon University.

Datta, A., & Thomas, H. (1999). The cube data model: A conceptual model and algebra for online analytical processing in data warehouses. *Decision Support Systems, 27*(3), 289-301.

Davenport, T. H. (2000). *Mission critical: Realizing the promise of enterprise systems.* Boston, MA: Harvard Business School Press.

Davies, I., Mason, R., & Lalwani, C. (2007). Assessing the impact of ICT on UK general haulage companies. *International Journal of Production Economics, 106*(1), 12-27.

Davies, R.B. (1994). From cross-sectional to longitudinal analysis. In A. Dale & R.B. Davies (Eds.), *Analyzing social & political change, a casebook of methods.* Sage Publications.

Dawe, R. L. (1994). An investigation of the pace and determination of information technology use in the manufacturing materials logistics system: A case study of Northern California's electronics manufacturers. *Journal of Business Logistics, 15*(1), 229-259.

Dawson, P. (2003). *Reshaping change: A processual perspective. Understanding organizational change.* Routledge, Taylor and Francis Group.

Dekleva, S.M. (1992). Delphi study of software maintenance problems. In *IEEE 1992 Conference on Software Maintenance* (pp. 10-17).

Dellarocas, C. (2003). The digitization of word of mouth: Promise and challenges of online feedback mechanisms. *Management Science, 49*(10), 1407-1424.

Deloitte & Touche (2001, June). *Value for money audit of the Irish health system*. Government of Ireland.

Delone, W., & McLean, E. (1992). Information systems success: The quest for the dependent variable. *Information System Research, 3*(1), 60-95.

Delone, W., & McLean, E. (2003). The DeLone and McLean model of information systems success: A ten-year update. *Management Information Systems, 19*(4), 9-30.

Denzin, N. K. & Lincoln, Y. S. (2005). The eight and ninth moments: Qualitative research in/and the fractured future. In N. K. Denzin & Y. S. Lincoln (Eds.), *Handbook of Qualitative Research* (3rd ed., pp. 1115-1126). Thousand Oaks, CA: Sage Publications.

Denzin, N. K. & Lincoln, Y. S. (2005). Introduction: The discipline and practice of qualitative research. In N. K. Denzin & Y. S. Lincoln (Eds.), *Handbook of Qualitative Research* (3rd ed., pp. 1-32). Thousand Oaks, CA: Sage Publications.

Denzin, N. K. & Lincoln, Y. S. (2005). Paradigms and perspectives in contention. In N. K. Denzin & Y. S. Lincoln (Eds.), *Handbook of Qualitative Research* (3rd ed., pp. 183-190). Thousand Oaks, CA: Sage Publications.

Denzin, N.K. (Ed.). (1978). *The research act: A theoretical introduction to sociological methods*. New York: McGraw-Hill.

DeSanctis, G. (1993). Theory and research: Goals, priorities and approaches. *M-IS Quarterly, 17*(1), 6-7.

Deshpande, Y. (2002). Consolidating Web engineering as a discipline. *Software Engineering Australia*, 31-34.

Devers, K.J. (1999). How will we know "good" qualitative research when we see it? Beginning the dialogue in health services research. *Health Services Research, 34*(5), 1153-1188.

Dholakia, R.R., & Kshetri, N. (2004). Factors impacting the adoption of the Internet among SMEs. *Small Business Economics, 23*(4), 311-322.

Di Martino, S., Ferrucci, F., Gravino, C., & Mendes, E. (2007). Comparing size measures for predicting Web application development effort: A case study. In *Proceedings of Empirical Software Engineering and Measurement* (ESEM'07).

Diamond, J. (2005). *Collapse: How societies choose to fail or survive*. Camberwell: Penguin.

Dickson, G. W., Leitheiser, R. L., Wetherbe, J. C., & Nechis, M. (1984). Key information systems issues for the 1980's. *MIS Quarterly, 8*(3), 135-159.

Dickson, G., & DeSanctis, G. (1990). The management of IS: Research status and themes. In A.M. Jenkins, H.S. Siegle, W. Wojtkowski, & W.G. Wojtkowski (Eds.), *Research issues in IS: An agenda for the 1990s*. WMC Brown Publishers.

Dickson, G., Senn, J.A., & Chervany, N.L. (1977). Research in management IS: The Minnesota experiments. *Management Science, 23*(9), 913-923.

Diesing, P. (1991). *How does social science work? Reflections on practice*. Pittsburgh, PA: University of Pittsburgh.

diFazio, W. (1998). Poverty, the postmodern and the jobless future. *Critical Perspectives on Accounting, 9*(1), 57-74.

Dillon, A., Sweeney, M., & Maguire, M. (1993). A survey of usability evaluation practices and requirements in the European IT industry. In. J. Alty, S. Guest, & D. Diaper (Eds.), HCI'93, *People and Computers VII* (pp. 81-94). Cambridge: Cambridge University Press.

Djikstra, E. W. (1989). On the cruelty of really teaching computing science. In P. J. Denning (Ed.), A debate on teaching computing science. *Communications of ACM, 32*(12), 1397-1404.

Dougherty, V. (1999). Knowledge is about people, not databases. *Industrial and Commercial Training, 31*(7), 262-266

Drickhamer, D. (2003). EDI is dead! Long live EDI. *Industry Week*.

Drucker, P.F. (1994, September-October). The theory of business. *Harvard Business Review*, 95-104.

Dube, L., & Pare, G. (2003). Rigor in IS positivist case research: Current practices, trends, and recommendations. *M-IS Quarterly, 27*(4), 597-635.

Duncan, N. B. (1995). Capturing flexibility of information technology infrastructure: A study of resource characteristics and their measure. *Management Information Systems, 12*(2), 37-57.

Dutton, J., & Dukerich, J. (1997). Keeping an eye on the mirror: Image and identity in organizational adaptation. *Academy of Management Journal, 34*, 517-554.

E-Bay. (2006). E-bay form 10-K, Feb. 24, 2006. Retrieved June 14, 2008, from http://investor.E-Bay.com/secfiling.cfm?filingID=950134-06-3678

E-Bay. (2007). Detailed seller ratings. Retrieved June 14, 2008, from http://pages.E-Bay.com/help/feedback/detailed-seller-ratings.html

Eckerson, W. (2003). Evaluationg ETL and data integration platforms. *The Data warehouse Institute Report Series*, 1-40.

Edgington, T. (2005). Response to NDA query. Personal communication via e-mail. Simi Valley, CA.

Efferin, S., & Hopper, T. (2007). Management control, culture and ethnicity in a Chinese Indonesian company. *Accounting, Organizations and Society, 32*, 223-262.

Ein-Dor, P., & Segev, E. (1993). A classification of information systems: Analysis and interpretation. *Information Systems Research, 4*(2), 166-204.

Eioerman, M.A., & Dishaw, M.T. (2007). The process of software maintenance: A comparison of object-oriented and third-generation development languages. *Journal of Software Maintenance and Evolution: Research and Practice, 19*(1), 33-47.

Eisenhardt, K. (1989). Building theories from case study research. *Academy of Management Review, 14*(4), 532-550.

Ellram, L. M., & Zsidisin, G. A. (2002). Factors that drive purchasing and supply management's use of information technology. *IEEE Transactions on Engineering Management, 49*(3), 269-281.

E-Marketer (2008). Asia-Pacific B2C e-commerce awakens. Retrieved June 10, 2008, from www.emarketer.com/articles

Emmelhainz, M.A. (1987). Electronic data interchange: Does it change the purchasing process. *Journal of Purchasing and Materials Management, 2*(8), 2-8.

Ericsson, K.A., & Simon, H.A. (1998). How to study thinking in everyday life: Contrasting think-aloud protocols with descriptions and explanations of thinking. *Mind, Culture, and Activity, 5*(3), 178-186.

Esposito, D., Aronowitz, S., Chancer, L., diFazio, W., & Yard, M. (1998). The (in)spectre returns! Global capital and the future of work. *Critical Perspectives on Accounting, 9*(1), 7-54.

European Logistics Association. Retrieved June 8, 2008, from http://www.elalog.org/

Everett, J. (2003). Globalisation and its new spaces for (alternative) accounting research. *Accounting Forum, 27*(4), 400-424.

Evermann, J., & Wand, Y. (2001). An ontological examination of object interaction in conceptual modeling. In *Proceedings of the 11th Workshop on Information Technologies and Systems, (WITS 2001),* New Orleans, Louisiana.

Falconer, D.J., & Mackay, D.R. (1999). *Ontological problems of pluralist research methodologies.* Paper presented at Americas' Conference on IS.

Ferrari, M., Fares, B., & Martinelli, P. (2002). The systemic approach of SSM: The case of a Brazilian company. *Systemic Practice and Action Research, 15*(1), 51-66.

Fetterman, D.M. (1989). *Ethnography step by step.* London, UK: Sage Publications.

Fettke, P., & Loos, P. (2003). Ontological evaluation of reference models using the Bunge Wand-Weber-model. In *Proceedings of the Ninth Americas Conference on Information Systems,* Tampa, FL (pp. 2944-2955).

Finck, M., Janneck, M., & Rolf, A. (2006). Techniknutzung zwischen kooperation und konkurrenz: Eine analyse von nutzungsproblemen. In F. Lehner, H. Nösekabel, & P. Kleinschmidt (Eds.), *Multikonferenz wirtschaftsinformatik 2006 - MKWI 2006, Buch 1, teilkonferenz collaborative business* (pp. 20-22, 363-376). Passau.

Firestone, W. (1993). Alternative arguments for generalizing from data as applied to qualitative research. *Educational researcher, 22*(4), 16-27.

Fisher, C. W., Lauria, E., Chengalur-Smith, I., & Wang, R. Y. (2006). *Introduction to information quality.* Cambridge, MA: MITIQ Press.

Fishman, C. (2006). *The Wal-Mart effect: How an out-of-town superstore became a superpower.* New York: Allen Lane.

Fitzgerald, G., Hirschheim, R., Mumford, E., & Wood-Harper, A.T. (1985). Information research methodology: An introduction to the debate. In E. Mumford, G. Fitzgerald, R. Hirschheim, & A.T. Wood-Harper (Eds), *Research methods in IS* (pp. 3-9), Proceedings of the IFIP (International Federation for Information Processing), WG 8.2 Colloquium, Manchester Business School.

Fleetwood, S., & Ackroyd, S. (Eds.). (2004). *Critical realist applications in organisation and management studies.* London: Routledge.

Flood, R.L., & Jackson, M.C. (1991). *Creative problem solving: Total systems intervention.* Chichester, West Sussex: Wiley.

Floyd, C. (1993). STEPS - a methodical approach to participatory design. *Communications of the ACM, 36*(6), 83.

Flyvbjerg, B. (2001). *Making social science matter: Why social inquiry fails and how it can succeed again* (S. Sampson, Trans.). Cambridge: Cambridge University Press.

Flyvbjerg, B. (2006). Five misunderstandings about case-study research. *Qualitative Inquiry, 12*(2), 219.

Foley, J. (2004). Bayh-Dole Act bad for computing research? *Computing Research News, 16*(1), 4, 7.

Foucault, M. (1979). *Discipline and punish: The birth of the prison*. London: Penguin Books.

Foucault, M. (1980). Prison talk: An interview with J.-J. Brochier. In C. Gordon (Ed.), *Power/Knowledge: Selected interviews and other writings, 1972-1977* (Chapter 3, pp. 37-54). New York: Random House.

Foucault, M. (1980). Two lectures. In C. Gordon (Ed.), *Power/ Knowledge: Selected interviews and other writings, 1972-1977* (Chapter 5, pp. 78-108). New York: Random House.

Foucault, M. (1986). *The care of the self: The history of sexuality volume 3*. London: Penguin Books.

Foucault, M. (1987). *The use of pleasure: The history of sexuality volume 2*. London: Penguin Books.

Francesconi, T. (1998). Transforming Lucent's CFO. *Management Accounting, 80*(1), 22-30.

Franz, C. R. & Robey, D. (1984). An investigation of user-led system design: Rational and political perspectives. *Communications of the ACM, 27*(12), 1202-1217.

Freedman, D.H. (1992, November-December). Is management still a science? *Harvard Business Review*, 26-38.

Friedman, A., & Cornford, D. (1989). *Computer systems development: History, organization and implementation*. New York: Information Systems Series; John Wiley & sons.

Friedman, T. (2005). *Gartner says more than 50 percent of data warehouse projects will have limited acceptance or will be failures through 2007*. Retrieved June 9, 2008, from http://www.gartner.com/it/page.jsp?id=492112

Frost, P.J., Morgan, G. (1983). Symbols of sensemaking: The realization of the framework. L. R. Pondy, P.J. Frost, G. Morgan & R.T.C. Dandrike (Eds.), *Organizational Symbolism* (pp. 419-437). New York: Wiley.

Fuchs, G. (2006). The vital BI maintenance process. In B. Sujatha (Ed.), *Business intelligence implementation: Issues and perspectives* (pp. 116-123). Hyderabad: The ICFAI University Press.

Fudenberg, D., & Tirole, J. (1991). *Game theory*. Cambridge: MIT Press.

Gable, G. G. (1994). Integrating case study and survey research methods: An example in information systems. *European Journal of Information Systems, 3*(2), 112-126.

Gadamer, H. (1976). *Philosophical hermeneutics*. Berkeley, CA: University of California Press.

Galliers, R. D. (2003). Change as crisis of growth? Toward a trans-disciplinary view of information systems as a field of study: A response to Benbasat and Zmud's call for returning to the IT artifact. *Journal of the Association for Information Systems, 4*(6), 337-351.

Galliers, R.D. (1992). Choosing IS research approaches. In R.D. Galliers (Ed.), *IS research: Issues, methods & practical guidelines* (pp. 144-162). Oxford, UK: Blackwell Scientific Publications.

Gangadharan, G. R., & Swami, S. N. (2004). *Business intelligence systems: Design and implementation strategies*. Paper presented at the 26th International Conference Information Technology Interfaces ITI.

Gardner, S. (1998). Kant. In A.C. Grayling (Ed.), *Philosophy 2: Further through the subject* (pp. 574-662). Oxford, UK: Oxford University Press.

Garner, B. A. (2004). *Black's law dictionary* (Vol. 1). St Paul, MN: Thomson/West.

Garrard, G. A. (1997). *Cellular communications: Worldwide market development*. Boston, MA: Artech House.

Gartner Group. (2000). Gartner group forecasts regional B2B outlook through 2004. Retrieved June 10, 2008, from http://gartner5.gartnerweb.com/public/static/aboutgg/pressrel/pr021600.html

Gasson, S. (2004). Rigor in grounded theory research: An interpretive perspective on generating theory from qualitative field studies. In M. E. Whitman & A. B. Woszczynski (Eds.), *The handbook of information systems research* (pp. 79-102). Idea Group Publishing.

Gattorna, J. L., & Berger, A. J. (2001). E-synchronized supply chain. *Supply Chain Management Review Global Supplement, 5*(1), 22-28.

Geertz, C. (1983). *Local knowledge: Further essays in interpretive anthropology.* New York: Basic Books.

Gemser, G., Jacobs, D., & Ten Cate, R. (2006). Design and competitive advantage in technology-driven sectors: The role of usability and aesthetics in Dutch IT companies. *Technology Analysis & Strategic Management, 18*(5), 561-580.

Genero, M., & Piattini, M. (2001). Empirical validation of measures for class diagram structural complexity through controlled experiments. In *Proceedings of International ECOOP Workshop on Quantitative Approaches in Object-Oriented Software Engineering* (QAOOSE 2001).

Ghobadian, A., Liu, J., & Stainer, A.I. (1994). Case studies on EDI implementation. *Logistics Information Management, 7*(1), 24-30.

Gibbons, M., Limoges, C., Nowotny, H., Schwartzman, S., Scott, P., & Trow, M. (1994). *The new production of knowledge: the dynamic of science and research in contemporary societies.* London: Sage Publications.

Gilbert, D. (2006). *Stumbling on happiness.* New York: Random House, Inc.

Ginige, A., & Murugesan, S. (2001). Web engineering: An introduction. *IEEE Multimedia, 8*(2), 14-18.

Glaser, B., & Strauss, A. (1967). *The discovery of the grounded theory: Strategies for qualitative research.* London: Wiedenfeld and Nicholson.

Glaser, B.G. (1992). *Emergence vs. forcing: Basics of grounded theory.* Mill Valley, CA: Sociology Press.

Glass, R. L., Ramesh, V., & Vessey, I. (2004). An analysis of research in computing disciplines. *Communications of ACM, 47*(6), 89-94.

Glass, R., Vessey, I., & Ramesh, V. (2002). Research in software engineering: An analysis of the literature. *Information and Software Technology, 44*(8), 491-506.

Goede, R. (2001). *A framework for the explicit use of specific systems thinking methodologies in data-driven decision support system development.* University of Pretoria.

Golicic, S. L. Davis, D. F., McCarthy, T.M., & Mentzer, J.T. (2002). The impact of e-commerce on supply chain relationships. *International Journal of Physical Distribution and Logistics Management, 32*(10), 851-871.

Google Earth Blog. (2006). *Google Earth data size, live local, new languages coming.* Retrieved June 12, 2008, from http://www.gearthblog.com/blog/archives/2006/09/news_roundup_google.html

Google Earth. (2007). *Explore, search and discover.* Retrieved June 12, 2008, from http://earth.google.com/tour/index.html

Gormley, M. (2004, November 8). E-Bay sellers admit to phony bids. *Associated Press.*

Goulding, C. (2002). *Grounded theory: A practical guide for management, business, and market researchers.* Thousand Oaks, CA, London: Sage Publications.

Graham, C., & Neu, D. (2003). Accounting for globalization. *Accounting Forum, 27*(4), 449-471.

Grant, R. M. & Baden-Fuller, C. (2004). A knowledge accessing theory of strategic alliances. *Journal of Management Studies, 41*(1), 61-84.

Grant, R. M. (1997). The knowledge-based view of the firm: Implications for management practices. *Long Range Planning, 30*(3), 450-454.

Gray, P., & Watson, H. J. (1998). *Decision support in the data warehouse.* Upper Saddle River, NJ: Prentice Hall.

Grayling, A.C. (1998). Modern philosophy II: The empiricists. In A.C. Grayling (Ed.), *Philosophy 1: A guide through the subject* (pp. 484-543). Oxford, UK: Oxford University Press.

Greatbatch, D., Murphy, E., & Dingwall, R. (2001). Evaluating medical information systems: Ethnomethodological and interactionist approaches. *Health Services Management Research, 14*(3), 181-191.

Greene, F., & Loughridge, B. (1996). Investigating the management information needs of academic heads of department: A critical success factors approach. *Information Research, 1*(3), 1-3.

Gregg, D.G., Kulkarni, U.R., & Vinze, A.S. (2001). Understanding the philosophical underpinnings of software engineering research in IS. *IS Frontiers, 3*(2), 169-183.

Gregor, S. (2006). The nature of theory in IS. *M-IS Quarterly, 30*(3), 611-642.

Gregory, R.L. (1987). *The Oxford companion to the mind.* Oxford, UK: Oxford University Press.

Greves, D., & Schreiber, B, (1996). The ESA initiative for software productivity benchmarking and effort estimation. ESA Bulletin, 87. Retrieved June 13, 2008, from <http://esapub.esrin.esa.it/bulletin/bulett87/greves87.htm>

Grix, J. (2002). Introducing students to the generic terminology of social research. *Politics, 22*(3), 175-186.

Grossman, M., Esq. (2004). *Technology law: What every business (and business-minded person) needs to know.* Lanham, MD: The Scarecrow Press, Inc.

Guba, E. G. (1990). The alternative paradigm dialog. In E. G. Guba (Ed.), *The paradigm dialog* (pp. 17-30). Newbury Park: California: Sage Publications.

Guba, E., & Lincoln, Y. (1989). *Fourth generation evaluation.* Newbury Park, CA: Sage Publications.

Guba, E.G., & Lincoln, Y.S. (1994). Competing paradigms in qualitative research. In N.K- Denzin & Y.S. Lincoln (Eds.), *Handbook of qualitative research. Thousand Oaks, CA:* Sage.

Guimaraes, T. (2000). The impact of competitive intelligence and IS support in changing small business organizations. *Logistics Information Management, 13*(3), 117-125.

GUIRR. (1997, October). *Openness and secrecy in research: Preserving openness in a competitive world.* Retrieved June 1, 2008, from http://www7.nationalacademies.org/guirr/Openness_and_Secrecy.html

Gummesson, E. (1991). *Qualitative methods in management research.* London, UK: Sage Publications.

Guttman, A. (1984). R-tree: A dynamic index structure for spatial searching. In *Proc. of the 1984 ACM SIGMOND International Conference on Management Data,* Boston, MA (pp. 47-57).

Gwee, S.K. (2001). E-commerce for SMEs – Singapore's perspectives. In T. Takashi (Ed.), *E-commerce, opportunities and challenges for SMEs* (pp. 13-17). Asian Productivity Organization.

Habermas, J. (1970). Knowledge and interest. In D. Emmet & A. MacIntyre (Eds.), *Sociological Theory and Philosophical Analysis* (pp. 36-54). London: Macmillan.

Habermas, J. (1974). *Theory and practice.* London: Heinemann.

Haider, A. (2007). *Information systems based engineering asset management evaluation: Operational interpretations.* University of South Australia, Adelaide.

Haider, A., & Koronios, A. (2003). *Managing engineering assets: A knowledge based approach through information quality.* Paper presented at the International Business Information Management Conference, Cairo.

Haig, M. (2002). *Mobile marketing: The message revolution.* London, UK: Kogan Page.

Hair, J.F.J., Anderson, R.E.A., Tatham, R.L., & Black, W.C. (1992). *Multivariate data analysis* (3rd ed.). New York: MacMillan Publishing Co.

Hakuhodo Interactive Co. Ltd. (2000). *Keitai marketing.* Tokyo, Japan: Nihon Noritsu Kyokai Management Center.

Halaoui, H. (2005). Spatio-temporal data model: Data model and temporal index using versions for spatio-temporal databases. In *Proceedings of the GIS Planet 2005,* Estoril, Portugal.

Halaoui, H. (2006) AIRSTD: An approach for indexing and retrieving spatio-temporal data. In *Proceedings of the ACM/IEEE SITIS06,* Hammamet, Tunisia.

Hammer, M. (1996). *Beyond reengineering: how the process-centered organization is changing our work and our lives.* New York: HarperCollins Publishers, Inc.

Hammersley, M., & Akinson, P. (1994). *Ethnography: Principles in practice* (2nd Edition). London, UK: Routlege.

Han, J., & Kamber, M. (2001). *Data mining: Concepts and techniques.* San Francisco: Morgan Kauffmann.

Han, S.L. (1992). *Antecedents of buyer-seller long-term relationships: An exploratory model of structural bonding and social bonding.* University Park, PA: Institute for the Study of Business Markets Report.

Hancock, J. C., & Toren, R. (2006). *Practical business intelligence with SQL server 2005 (Microsoft Windows server system series).* NJ: Addison-Wesley.

Handy, C. (1980, January-February). Through the organizational looking glass. *Harvard Business Review,* 115-121.

Hart, P.J., & Saunders, C. (1997). Power and trust: Critical factors in the adoption use of electronic data interchange. *Organization Science, 8*(1), 23-42.

Hart, P.J., & Saunders, C.S. (1998). Emerging electronic partnership: Antecedents and dimensions of EDI use from the supplier's perspective. *Journal of Management Information System, 14*(4), 87-111.

Hartley, J. (2004). Case study research. In C. Cassell & G. Symon (Eds.), *An essential guide to qualitative research methods in organizations* (pp. 323-333). London: Sage.

Hartson, H.R., Andre, T.W., & Williges, R.C. (2003). Criteria for evaluating usability evaluation methods. *International Journal of Human-Computer Interaction, 15*(1), 145-181.

Hay, C. (2002). *Political analysis: A critical introduction.* Basingstoke: Palgrave.

Healy, T. (1991). EDI in Australia: Still making haste slowly. *Australian Communications,* 63-70.

Heckerman, D. (1996). A *tutorial on learning with Bayesian networks* (Tech. Rep. No. MSR-TR-95-06). Redmond, WA: Microsoft Research: Advanced Technology Division.

Hegel, G.W.F. (1977). *Phenomenology of spirit.* Oxford: Oxford University Press.

Heidegger, M. (1962). *Being and time* (J. Macquarrie & E. Robinson, Trans.). New York: Harper.

Heidegger, M. (1976). *The piety of thinking* (translated by J. G. Hart and J. C. Maraldo). Bloomington: Indiana University Press.

Hein, S. J., & Lehman, D. R. (1999). Culture, self-discrepancies, and self-satisfaction. *Personality & Social Psychology Bulletin, 25*(8), 915-925.

Heinz, C., & Origgi, G. (2004). Rethinking interdisciplinarity. Emergent Issues. Seminar Rethinking Interdisciplinarity. Retrieved June 1, 2008, from http://www.interdisciplines.org/interdisciplinarity/papers/11/

Heiskanen, A. (1994). *Issues and factors affecting the success and failure of a student record system development process: A longitudinal investigation based on reflection-in-action.* Doctoral dissertation, University of Helsinki, Yliopistopaino, Helsinki.

Heitmeyer, D. (2004). It's not a race: Aboriginality and education. In J. Allen (Ed), *Sociology of education: Possibilities and practices* (3rd ed.) (Chapter 10, pp. 220-249). Southbank: Social Science Press.

Held, D., & McGrew, A. (2002). *Globalization/ anti-globalization.* Cambridge: Polity.

Helm, S., Hall, M., & Hall, C. (2003). Pre-implementation attitudes and organisational readiness for implementing an ERP system. *European Journal of Information Systems, 146.*

Herriott, R. E., & Firestone, W. A. (1983). Multisite qualitative policy research: Optimizing description and generalizability. *Educational Researcher, 12,* 14-19.

Hersleb, J.D., Mockus, A., Finholt, T.A., & Grinter, R.E. (2000). Distance, dependencies and delay in a global collaboration. *ACM Conference on Computer-Supported Cooperative Work.* Philadelphia (p. 319, 328), December 2-7.

Hertzum, M., & Jacobsen, N.E. (2003), The evaluator effect: A chilling fact about usability evaluation methods. *International Journal of Human-Computer Interaction, 15*(1), 183-204.

Hess, R. D., & Azuma, H. (1991). Cultural support for schooling: Contrasts between Japan and the United States. *Educational Researcher, 20*(9), 2-8, 12.

Hevner, A.R., March, S.T., Park, J., & Ram, S. (2004). Design research in information systems research. *MIS Quarterly, 28*(1), 75-105.

Hewitt-Taylor, J. (2001) Use of constant comparative analysis in qualitative research. *Nursing Standard, 15,* 42, 39-42.

Higgins, A.D. (1986). *Data structured software maintenance: The WARNIER/ORR approach.* New York: Dorset House Publishing Co.

Hirschheim, R. (1992). Information systems epistemology: An historical perspective. In R. Galliers (Ed.), *Information systems research: Issues, methods and practical guidelines.* Oxford: Blackwell Scientific Publications.

Hirschheim, R. (1992). IS epistemology: A historical perspective. In R.D. Galliers (Ed.), *IS research: Issues, methods & practical guidelines.* Oxford, UK: Blackwell Scientific Publications.

Hirschheim, R., & Klein, H.K. (1989). Four paradigms of IS development. *Communications of the ACM, 32,* 1199-1216.

Hirschheim, R., & Klein, H.K. (2003). Crisis in the IS field? A critical reflection on the state of the discipline. *Journal of the Association for IS, 4*(5), 237-293.

Hirschheim, R., & Newman, M. (2002). Symbolism and information systems development: Myth, metaphor, and magic. In M. D. Myers & D. Avison (Eds.), *Qualitative research in information systems: A reader.* Thousand Oaks, CA, London: Sage Publications.

Hirschheim, R., Klein, H.K., & Lyytinen, K. (1995). *IS development and data modelling: Conceptual and philosophical foundations.* Cambridge, UK: Cambridge University Press.

Hirschheim, R., Klein, H.K., & Newman, M. (1991). IS development as social action: Perspective and practice. *Omega, 19*(6), 587-608.

Ho, N.K. (2000). *Impact of CPA intervention on the business performance of Singaporean Chinese SMEs.* Unpublished Ph.D. Thesis, University of South Australia Division of International Business and Management.

Hoffman, D.L., Novak, T.P., & Peralta, M. (1999). Building consumer's trust online. *Communications of the ACM, 42*(4), 80-86.

Hofstede, G. (2001). *Culture's consequences: Comparing values, behaviors, institutions and organizations across nations* (2nd ed.). Thousand Oaks, CA: Sage Publications.

Hohmann, L. (2003). Usability: Happier users mean greater profits. *Information Systems Management, 20*(4), 66-76.

Holland, C., Lockett, G., & Blackman, I. (1992). Planning for electronic data interchange. *Strategic Management Journal, 13*(7), 539-550.

Holmes, D. R. & Marcus, G. E. (2005). Refunctioning ethnography: The challenge of an anthropology of the contemporary. In N. K. Denzin & Y. S. Lincoln (Eds.), *Handbook of Qualitative Research* (3rd ed., pp. 1099-1113). Thousand Oaks, CA: Sage Publications.

Hong Kong Logistics Association. Retrieved June 8, 2008, from http://www.hkla.org.hk/

Hoogvelt, A. (1997). *Globalisation and the post-colonial world; The new political economy of development.* London: Macmillan.

Houser, D., & Wooders, J. (2001). Reputation in Internet auctions: Theory and evidence from E-Bay, Working Paper, University of Arizona. Retrieved June 14, 2008, from *http://bpa.arizona.edu/~jwooders/E-Bay.pdf*

Houston, K., & Norris, D. (2001). Software component and the UML. In *Component based software engineering* (Chap. 14, pp. 243-263). Addison-Wesley.

Huber, G. P. (1990). A theory of the effects of advanced information technologies on organizational design, intelligence, and decision making. *Academy of Management Review, 15,* 47-71.

Huber, G.P., & Van de Ven, A.H. (1995). *Longitudinal field research methods: Studying process of organizational change.* Thousand Oaks, CA: Sage Publications.

Huberman, A.M. (1983). Improving social practice through the utilization of university-based knowledge. *Higher Education, 12,* 257-272.

Huff, S.L., Schneberger S., & Newson P. (2000). *Cases in electronic commerce.* Irwin McGraw-Hill.

Hugues, T. P. (1983). *Networks of power: Electrification in western society, 1880-1930.* Baltimore, MD: Johns Hopkins University Press.

Iacocou, C.L., Benbasat, I., & Dexter, A.S. (1995). Electronic data interchange and small organizations: Adoption and impact of technology. *MIS Quarterly, 19*(4), 85-486.

IDA. (1997). Press statement, infocomm development authority of Singapore. Retrieved June 10, 2008, from http://www.ncb.gov.sg/ncb/press/3307.asp

Iivari, J. (2003). The IS core -VII towards IS as a science of meta-artifacts. *Communications of the Association for IS, 12,* 568-581.

Ilharco, F. (2002) *Information technology as ontology.* Unpublished Ph.D. thesis. London School of Economics, London, UK.

Info-Plant. (2002). Beneficial, Menu. Tokyo: Info-Plant.

Inmon, W.H., & Hackathorn, R.D. (1994). *Using the data warehouse.* Somerset, NJ: Wiley-QED Publishing.

International Function Point Users Group (IFPUG). (2004). *Function point counting practices manual.* Release 4.2.1, 2004.

Introna, L. (1997) *Management, information and power.* London: Macmillan.

Introna, L., & Ilharco, F. (2004). Phenomenology, screens and the world: A journey with Hursell and Heidegger into phenomenology. In L. Willcocks & J. Mingers (Eds.), *Social theory and philosophy for IS* (pp. 56-102). Chichester: John Wiley & Sons.

Iversen, J.H., Mathiassen, L., & Nielsen, P.A. Managing risk in software process improvement: An action research approach. *MIS Quarterly, 28*(3), 395-433.

Ives, B., Hamilton, S., & Davis, G.B. (1980). A framework for research in computer-based management IS. *Management Science, 26*(9), 910-934.

Jackson, M. C. (1992). *Systems methodology for the management sciences.* New York: Plenum Press.

Jacobson, I., & Lindstrom, F. (1991). Re-engineering of old systems to an object-oriented approach. In *Proceedings of Conference on Object-Oriented Programming Systems, Languages and Applications OOPSLA 1991* (pp. 340-350).

Jacobson. I. (1987). Object oriented development in an industrial environment. In *Proceedings of OOPSLA,* Orlando, FL (pp. 183-191). ACM Press.

Jagielska, I., Darke, P., & Zagari, G. (2003). *Business intelligence systems for decision support: Concepts, processes and practice.* Paper presented at the 7th International Conference of the International Society for Decision Support Systems.

Jakobs, K. Pils, C., & Wallbaum, M. (2001). Using the Internet in transport logistics- the example of a track and trace system. *Lecture Notes in Computer Science, 2093,* 194-203.

James, K. (2007). A critical theory and postmodernist approach to the teaching of accounting theory. *Critical Perspectives on Accounting.* Retrieved June 1, 2008, from www.sciencedirect.com.

James, K., & Otsuka, S. (2007). International Chinese graduates and the Australian public accounting industry. Working Paper, University of Southern Queensland, Australia.

Janaway, C. (1998). Ancient Greek philosophy I: The pre-Socratics and Plato. In A.C. Grayling (Ed.), *Philosophy I: A guide through the subject* (pp. 336-397). Oxford, UK: Oxford University Press.

Janneck, M., & Finck, M. (2006). Making the community a hospitable place - identity, strong bounds, and self-organisation in Web-based communities. *International Journal of Web Based Communities, 2*(4), 458-473.

Jansen, S. (2005). Software release and deployment at Planon: A case study report. In *Technical Report SEN-E0504.* CWI.

Jansen, S. (2006). *Software release and deployment at a content management systems vendor: A case study report* (Tech. Rep. No. UU-CS-2006-044). Utrecht University: Institute of Computing and Information Sciences.

Jansen, S. (2006). *Software release and deployment at Stabiplan: A case study report* (Tech. Rep. No. UU-CS-2006-041). Utrecht University: Institute of Computing and Information Sciences.

Jansen, S. (2007). *Customer configuration updating in a software supply network.* Ph.D. Thesis, Utrecht University.

Jansen, S. (2007). Pheme: An infrastructure to enable any type of communication between a software vendor and an end-user. In *International Conference on Software Maintenance 2007, tool demonstration.*

Jansen, S., & Brinkkemper, S. (2007). Definition and validation of the key process areas of release, delivery and deployment of product software vendors: Turning the ugly duckling into a swan. In *Proceedings of the International Conference on Software Maintenance (ICSM2006, Research track).*

Jansen, S., & Brinkkemper, S. (2008). A benchmark survey into the customer configuration processes and practices of product software vendors in The Netherlands. In *Proceedings of the 7th IEEE International Conference on Composition-Based Software Systems (ICCBSS).* IEEE.

Jansen, S., & Rijsemus, W. (2006, September.). Balancing total cost of ownership and cost of maintenance within a software supply network. In *Proceedings of the IEEE International Conference on Software Maintenance,* Philadelphia, PA, USA.

Jansen, S., Ballintijn, G., & Brinkkemper, S. (2004). *Software release and deployment at exact: A case study report* (Tech. Rep. No. SEN-E0414). CWI.

Jansen, S., Ballintijn, G., Brinkkemper, S., & van Nieuwland, A. (2006). Integrated development and maintenance for the release, delivery, deployment, and customization of product software: A case study in mass-market ERP software. In *Journal of Software Maintenance and Evolution: Research and Practice, 18,* 133-151. John Wiley & Sons, Ltd.

Jansen, S., Brinkkemper, S., & Ballintijn, G. (2005). A process framework and typology for software product updaters. In *Ninth European Conference on Software Maintenance and Reengineering* (pp. 265-274). IEEE.

Jansen, S., Brinkkemper, S., Ballintijn, G., & van Nieuwland, A. (2005). Integrated development and maintenance of software products to support efficient updating of customer configurations: A case study in mass market ERP software. In *Proceedings of the 21st International Conference on Software Maintenance.* IEEE.

Jantsch, E. (1972). Towards interdisciplinarity and transdisciplinarity in education and innovation. In L. Apostel, G. Berger, A. Briggs, & G. Michaud (Eds.), *Interdisciplinarity. Problems of teaching and researching in universities* (pp. 97-121). Paris: Center for Educational Research and Innovation, Organization for Economic Cooperation and Development.

Järvenpää, S. (1991). Panning for gold in information systems research: Second-hand data. Information Systems research Arena in the 90's: Information Systems research: contemporary approaches and emergent traditions. In *Proceedings of the IFIP TC/WG 8.2 Working Conference,* Copenhagen, Denmark, (pp. 63-80).

Jarvenpaa, S., Tractinsky, N., & Vitale, M (2000). Consumer trust in an Internet store. *Information Technology and Management, 1*(1-2), 45-71.

Järvinen, P. (2004). *On research methods*. Opinpaja: Tampere.

Jayaratna, N. (1994). *Understanding and evaluating methodologies: NIMSAD a systematic framework*. New York, McGraw-Hill.

Jeffery, R., Ruhe, M., & Wieczorek, I., (2000). A comparative study of two software development cost modeling techniques using multi-organizational and company-specific data. *Information and Software Technology, 42,* 1009-1016.

Jeffery, R., Ruhe. M., &Wieczorek, I., (2001). Using public domain metrics to estimate software development effort. In *Proceedings of International Software Metrics Symposium (METRICS'01),* (pp. 16-27).

Jesitus, J. (1998). Even farmers get SAPed. *Industry Week, 247*(5), 32-36.

Johns, G. (1993). Constraints on the adoption of psychology-based personnel practices: Lessons from organizational innovation. *Personnel Psychology, 46,* 569-592.

Johnson, J.M. (1975). *Doing field research*. New York: The Free Press.

Johnston, H.R., & Vitale, M.R. (1998). Creating competitive advantage with inter-organizational systems. *MIS Quarterly, 12*(1), 37-48.

Jones, M. T., & Fleming, P. (2003). Unpacking complexity through critical stakeholder analysis: The case of globalization. *Business & Society, 42*(4), 430-454.

Jones, M.C., & Beatty, R.C. (2001). User satisfaction with EDI: An empirical investigation. *Information Resources Management Journal, 14*(2), 17-26.

Jorgensen, D.L. (1989). *Participant observation: Methodology for human studies*. Newbury, CA: Sage.

Joseph, G.W., & Engle, T.J. (1996). Controlling an EDI environment. *Journal of Systems Management, 47*(4), 42-68.

Joshi, M. P., Kathuria, R., & Porth, S. J. (2003). Alignment of strategic priorities and performance: An integration of operations and strategic management perspectives. *Journal of Operations Management, 21*(3), 353-369.

Jun M.J., Cai, S.H., & Peterson, R.T. (2000). EDI use and participation models: From the inter-organization relationship perspective. *Industrial Management + Data Systems, 100*(9), 412-420.

Kahen, G. (1995). Assessment of information technology for developing countries: Appropriateness, local constraints, IT characteristics and impacts. *International Journal of Computer and Applications Technology, 8*(5/6), 325-332.

Kahen, G. (1996). Building a framework for successful information technology transfer to developing countries: Requirements and effective integration to a viable IT transfer. *International Journal of Computer and Applications Technology, 9*(1), 1-8.

Kaiser, K. (2005). Response to NDA query. Personal communication via e-mail. Simi Valley, CA.

Kant, I. (1934). *The critique of pure reason* (J. M. D. Meiklejohn, Trans.). London: J M Dent.

Keen, P. G. W. (1987). MIS research: Current status, trends and needs. In R. A. Buckingham, R. A. Hirschheim, F. F. Land, & C. J. Tully (Eds.), *Information systems education: Recommendations and implementation* (pp. 1-13). Cambridge: Cambridge University Press.

Keen, P.G.W. (1991). Relevance and rigor in IS research: Improving quality, confidence, cohesion and impact. In H.E. Nissen, H. Klein, & R. Hirschheim (Eds.), *IS research: Contemporary approaches and emergent traditions* (pp. 27-49). Amsterdam, The Netherlands: Elsevier.

Kellner, D. (1991). Introduction to the second edition. In *One-dimensional man: Studies in the ideology of advanced industrial society* (pp. xi–xxxix). Boston, MA: Beacon Press.

Khandelwal, V. (2000). What the Australian CEOs want from IT. *Research and Practice in Information Technology, 32*(3), 151-167.

Khazanchi, D., & Munkvold, B. (2000). Is information systems a science? An inquiry into the nature of the information systems discipline. *The Database for Advances in Information Systems, 31*(3), 24-40.

Kieser, A. (1994). Why organization theory needs historical analyses - and how this should be performed. *Organizational Science, 5*(4), 608-620.

Kimberley, P. (1994). EDI: Status in the Asia – Pacific Region. *Telecommunications, 28*(1), 39-32.

Kitchenham, B., & Pfleeger, S. L. (2002) Principles of survey research part 3: Constructing a survey instrument. *ACM SIGSOFT Software Engineering Notes, 27*(2), 20-24.

Kitchenham, B., & Pfleeger, S. L. (2002) Principles of survey research part 4: Questionnaire evaluation. *ACM SIGSOFT Software Engineering Notes, 27*(3), 20-23.

Kitchenham, B., & Pfleeger, S. L. (2002) Principles of survey research part 5: Populations and samples. *ACM SIGSOFT Software Engineering Notes, 27*(5), 17-20.

Kitchenham, B., Mendes, E., Travassos, G.H., & Guilherme, H. (2007). Cross versus within-company cost estimation studies: A systematic review. *IEEE Transactions on Software Engineering, 33*(5), 316-329.

Kitchenham, B., Pickard, L., & Pfleeger, S. L. (1995). Case studies for method and tool evaluation. *IEEE Software, 12*(4), 52-62.

Kitchenham, B., Pickard, L.M., MacDonell, S.G., & Shepperd, M.J. (2001). What accuracy statistics really measure. *IEE Proceedings – Software, 148*(3), 81-85.

Kitchens, F. L. (2005). Response to NDA query. Personal communication via e-mail. Simi Valley, CA.

Klein, H. K., & Huynh, M. (2004). The critical social theory of Jurgen Habermas and its implications for IS research. In J. Mingers & L. Willcocks (Eds.), *Social theory and philosophy for information systems* (pp. 157-237). Chichester: John Wiley & Sons.

Klein, H. K., Nissen, H.-E., & Hirschheim, R. (1991). A pluralist perspective of the information systems arena. *Information Systems Reserch: Contemporary Approaches and Emergent Traditions*, 1-20.

Klein, H., & Lyytinen, K. (1985). The poverty of scientism in information systems. In E. Mumford, R. Hirschheim, B. Fitzgerald, & A. T. Wood-Harper (Eds.), *Research methods in information systems: Proceedings of the IFIP colloquium* (pp. 131-161). Amsterdam: New Holland.

Klein, H.K., & Myers, M.D. (1999). A set of principles for conducting and evaluating interpretive field studies in IS. *M-IS Quarterly, 23*(1), 67-94.

Klein, H.K., Hirschheim, R., & Nissen, H.E. (1991). A pluralist perspective of the IS research arena. In H.E. Nissen, H. Klein, & R. Hirschheim (Eds.), *IS research: Contemporary approaches and traditions*. Amsterdam, The Netherlands: Elsevier.

Klein, J. T. (1994). Notes toward a social epistemology of transdisciplinarity. In *Communication au Premier Congrès Mondial de la Transdisciplinarité*. Retrieved June 1, 2008, from http://nicol.club.fr/ciret/bulletin/b12/b12c2.htm

Klein, J. T. (2004). Prospects for transdisciplinarity. *Futures, 36*(2), 515-526.

Klein, R. (2007). Customization and real time information access in integrated e-business supply chain relationships. *Journal of Operations Management, 25*(6), 1366-1381.

Knights, D. (1992). Changing spaces: The disruptive impact of a new epistemological location for the study of management. *Academy of Management Review, 17*(3), 514-536.

Kohl, H. (1992). *From archetype to zeitgeist*. NewYork: Little Brown.

Kohonen, T. (1989). *Self-organization and associative memory*. Berlin: Springer-Verlag, Heidelberg.

Kohonen, T. (1995). *Self-organized maps*. Berlin, Germany: Springer-Verlag.

Korten, D. (2001). *When corporations rule the world*. Bloomfield: Kumarian Press and Berrett-Koehler.

Kraemmergaard, P., & Moller, C. (2000). *A research framework for studying the implementation of enterprise resource planning (ERP) systems*. IRIS 23. Laboratorium for Interaction Technology, University of Trollhattan Uddevalla.

Krahmer, E., & Ummelen, N. (2004). Thinking about thinking aloud: A comparison of two verbal protocols for usability testing. *IEEE Transactions on Professional Communication, 47*(2), 105-117.

Krause, D., Rolf, A., Christ, M., & Simon, E. (2006). Wissen, wie alles zusammenhängt – das mikropolismodell als orientierungswerkzeug für die gestaltung von informationstechnik in organisationen und gesellschaft. *Informatik Spektrum, 29*(4), 263-273.

Kraut, R.E., & Streeter, L.A. (1995). Coordination in software development. *Communications of the ACM, 38*(3), 69-81.

Krippendorff, K. (1980). *Content analysis: An introduction to its methods*. Beverly Hills, CA: Sage Publications.

Kuan, K. K. Y., & Chau, P. Y. K. (2001). A perception-based model for EDI adoption in small businesses using a technology-organization-environment framework. *Information and Management, 38*(8), 507-521.

Kuhn, T.S. (1970). *The structure of scientific revolutions*. Chicago, IL: University of Chicago Press.

Kulkarni, J., & King, R. (1997). *Business intelligence systems and data mining*. SAS Institute.

Lai, S.L. (2000). An integration of systems science methods and object-oriented analysis for determining organizational information requirements. *Systems Research and Behavioral Science, 17*(2), 205-228.

Lakoff, G., & Johson, M. (1980). *Metaphors we live by*. Chicago: The University of Chicago Press.

Lambert, D.M., Emmelhainz, M.A., & Gardner, J.T. (1996). So you want a partner? *Marketing Management, 5*(2) 9-24.

Lambert, P., & Gayle, V. (2004). Quantitative approaches to longitudinal research. *Session 2 of RCBN Training Workshop Longitudinal Research in Education*, University of York, England. Retrieved June 3, 2008, from http://www.cf.ac.uk/socsi/capacity/Activities/Themes/Secondary/Lambert.ppt

Lancioni, R. A., Smith, M. F., & Oliva, T. A. (2000). The role of the Internet in supply chain management. *Industrial Marketing Management, 29*(1), 45-56.

Land, F. F., & Kennedy-McGregor, M. (1981). Information and information systems: Concepts and perspectives. In R. D. Galliers (Ed.), *Information systems research: Issues, methods and practical guidelines* (pp. 63-91). Oxford: Blackwell.

Landon, S., & Smith, C.E. (1997). The use of quality and reputation indicators by consumers: The case of Bordeaux wine. *Journal of Consumer Policy, 20*, 289-323.

Landry, R., Amara, N., & Lamari, M. (2001). Utilization of social science research knowledge in Canada. *Research Policy, 30*, 333-349.

Langley, C. J., Allen, G. R., & Colombo, M. J. (2003). *Third party logistics study results and findings of the 2003 eighth annual study*. Georgia: Georgia Institute of Technology, Cap Gemini Ernest and Young, and FedEx Corporate Services.

Lankford, W.M., & Riggs, W.E. (1996). Electronic data interchange: Where are we today. *Journal of Systems Management, 47*(2), 58-61.

Latour, B. (1991). Materials of power: Technology is society made durable. In *A Sociology of Monsters: Essays on Power, Technology, and Domination, Sociological Review Monograph, 38*, 103-131.

Laudon, K. C. (1989). Design guidelines for choices involving time in qualitative research. In J. Cash & P. Lawrence (Ed.), *The Information systems research challenge: qualitative research methods* (pp. 1-12). Cambridge, MA: Harvard Business School.

Lawson, C.L. (1995). *Solving least squares problems*. Society of Industrial and Applied Mathematics.

Lawson-Tancred, H. (1998). Ancient Greek pilosophy II: Aristotle. In A.C. Grayling (Ed.), *Philosophy 1: A guide through the subject* (pp. 398-439). Oxford, UK: Oxford University Press.

Ledington, P.W.J., & Ledington, J. (1999). The problem of comparison in soft systems methodology. *Systems Research and Behavioral Science, 16*(4), 329-339.

Lee, A (1997). Integrating positivist and interpretivist approaches to organizational research. *Organization Science, 2*, 342-264.

Lee, A.S. (1989). Case studies as natural experiments. *Human Relations, 42*(2), 117-137.

Lee, Y.J. (2000). *Role and experience of SMEs in South Korea*. Huntington, NY: Nova Science Publisher, Inc.

Lefley, M., & Shepperd, M.J. (2003). Using genetic programming to improve software effort estimation based on general data sets. In *Proceedings of GECCO'03*, (LNCS 2724, pp. 2477-2487). Springer-Verlag.

Lehman, M.M. (1989). Uncertainty in computer application and its control through the engineering of software. *Journal of Software Maintenance: Research and Practice, 1*(1), 3-27.

LeMay, R. (2006). Sydney Water signs business intelligence vendor. Retrieved June 9, 2008, from http://www.zdnet.com.au/news/software/soa/Sydney-Water-signs-business-intelligence-vendor/0,130061733,139268270,00.htm

Leveson, N.G. (1995). *Safeware: System safety and computers*. Reading, MA: Addison-Wesley.

Lewin, K. (1951). Field theory in social science; selected theoretical papers. In D. Cartwright (Ed.). New York: Harper & Row.

Li, P. (2005). *The impact of adopting electronic data interchange on small and medium enterprise performance: A preliminary model of EDI adoption process in Singapore*. Unpublished Ph.D. Thesis, University of South Australia Division of International Business and Management.

Liang T.P., & Huang J.S. (1998). An empirical study on consumer acceptance of products in electronic markets: A transaction cost model. *Decision Support Systems, 24*, 29-43.

Liautaud, B., & Hammond, M. (2000). *E-business intelligence: Turning information into knowledge and profit*. New York: McGraw-Hill.

Lientz, B.P., & Swanson, E.B. (1980). *Software maintenance management*. Reading, MA: Addison-Wesley.

Lim, K, Sia, C., Lee, M., & Benbasat, I. (2006). Do I trust you online, and if so, will I buy? An empirical study of two trust-building strategies. *Journal of Management Information Systems, 23*(2), 233-266.

Lim, K., & Kamarudin, B.T. (2002). The coming dawn of ebXML in Asia, Singapore EDI Committee. Retrieved June 10, 2008, from http://www.sec-edi.org/res_articles.htm

Lin, S., Gao, J., Koronios, A., & Chanana, V. (2007). Developing a data quality framework for asset management in engineering organisations. *International Journal of Information Quality, 1*(1), 100-126.

Lincoln, Y. S. & Guba, E. G. (2000). Paradigmatic controversies, contradictions, and emerging confluences. In N. K. Denzin & Y. S. Lincoln (Eds.), *Handbook of Qualitative Research* (2nd ed., pp. 163-188). Thousand Oaks, CA: Sage Publications.

Lincoln, Y., & Guba, E. (1985). *Naturalistic inquiry.* New York: Sage.

Lindgren, R., Henfridsson, O., & Schultze, U. (2004). Design principles for competence management systems: A synthesis of an action research study. *M-IS Quarterly, 28*(3), 435-472.

Little, R. G. (1998). *Identification of factors affecting the implementation of data warehousing.* Auburn University.

Locke, K. (2003). *Grounded theory in management research.* London: Sage.

Locker, K., Miller, S., Richardson, M., Tebeaux, E., & Yates, J. (1996). Studying the history of business communication. *Business Communications Quarterly, 59*(2), 109-138.

Logan, D., & Buytendijk, F. (2003). *The Sarbanes-Oxley Act will impact your enterprise.* Gartner.

Logistics Association of Australia. Retrieved June 8, 2008, from http://www.laa.asn.au/home

Lomas, J. (2000). Connecting research and policy. *ISUMA, 1*(1), 140-144.

Lu, X. H., Huang, L. H., & Heng, M. S. H. (2006). Critical success factors of inter-organizational information systems—a case study of Cisco and Xiao Tong in China. *Information & Management, 43*(3), 395-408.

Luckett, S., Ngubane, S., & Memela, B. (2001). Designing a management system for a rural community development organization using a systemic action research

process. *Systemic Practice and Action Research, 14*(4), 517-542.

Lucking-Reiley, D., Bryan, D., Prasad, N., & Reeves, D. (2005). *Pennies from E-Bay: The determinants of price in online auctions.* Working Paper, Vanderbilt University. Retrieved June 14, 2008, from http://www.u.arizona.edu/~dreiley/papers/PenniesFromE-Bay.pdf

Luhmann, N. (2006). System as difference. *Organization, 13*(1), 37-57.

Lutters, W.G., & Seaman, C.B. (2007). Revealing actual documentation usage in software maintenance through war stories. *Information and Software Technology, 49*(6), 576-587.

Luttrell, S. P. (1989). Self-organization: A derivation from first principles of a class of learning algorithms. In *Proceedings of the IJCNN'89 International Joint Conference on Neural Networks* (Vol. 2. pp. 495-498).

Lyytinen, K. (1987). Different perspectives on information systems: Problems and solutions. *ACM Computing Surveys, 19*(1), 5-46.

Lyytinen, K., & King, J. L. (2004). Nothing at the center? Academic legitimacy in the information systems field. *Journal of the Association for Information Systems, 5*(6), 220-246.

Mackay, D., & Rosier, M. (1996). Measuring organizational benefits of EDI diffusion: A case of the Australian automotive industry. *International Journal of Physical Distribution & Logistics Management, 26*(10), 60-66.

Macredi, R.D., & Sandom, C. (1999). IT-enabled change: Evaluating an improvisational perspective. *European Journal of IS, 8,* 247-259.

Maingot, M., & Quon, T. (2001). A survey of electronic data interchange (EDI) in the top public companies in Canada. *INFOR, 39*(3), 314-332.

Major, M., & Hopper, T. (2005). Managers divided: Implementing ABC in a Portuguese telecommunications company. *Management Accounting Research, 16,* 205-229.

Malerba, F. (Ed.). (2004). *Sectoral systems of innovation: Concepts, issues and analyses of six major sectors in Europe.* Cambridge: Cambridge University Press.

Malone, T.W., & Crowston, K. (1990, October 7-10). What is coordination theory and how can it help design cooperative work systems? In *Conference on Computer Supported Cooperative Work (CSCW '90),* Los Angeles, (pp. 357-370). ACM Press.

Malone, T.W., & Crowston, K. (1994). The interdisciplinary study of coordination. *ACM Computing Surveys*, *26*(1), 87-110.

Manus, P. (1993). EDI: Simple, but not easy. *Healthcare Financial Management*, *47*(1), 2-30.

March, S.T., & Smith, G. (1995). Design and natural science research on information technology. *Decision Support Systems*, *15*(4), 251-266.

Marcus, A. D. (1999). Class struggle: MIT students, lured to new tech firms, get caught in a bind--they work for professors who may also oversee their academic careers--homework as nondisclosure. *Wall Street Journal (Eastern Edition)*, p. A1.

Marcuse, H. (1964). *One-dimensional man: Studies in the ideology of advanced industrial society*. Boston, MA: Beacon Press.

Marcuse, H. (1968). The struggle against liberalism in the totalitarian view of the state. In *Negations: Essays in Critical Theory* (Chapter 1, pp. 3-42). London: Allen Lane The Penguin Press.

Marcuse, H., & Neumann, F. (n.d.). *A history of the doctrine of social change*. Unpublished manuscript in the Marcuse Archive.

Markus, I. (1994). Electronic mail as the medium of managerial choice. *Organizational Science, 5*(4), 502-527.

Markus, K.L., & Robey, D. (1988). Information technology and organisational change: Causal structure in theory and research. *Management Science*, *34*(5), 583-598.

Markus, M.L., & Tanis, C. (2000). The enterprise systems experience-from adoption to success. In R. W. Zmud (Ed.), *Framing the domains of IT research: Glimpsing the future through the past* (pp. 173-207). Cincinnati, OH: Pinnaflex Educational Resources, Inc.

Markus, M.L. (1983). Power, politics and m-IS implementation. *Communications of the ACM, 26*(6), 430-445.

Markus, M.L., & Lee, A.S. (1999). Special issue on intensive research in IS: Using qualitative, interpretive, and case study methods to study information technology. *M-IS Quarterly, 23*(1), 35-38.

Markus, M.L., & Lee, A.S. (2000). Special issue on intensive research in IS: Using qualitative, interpretive, and case study methods to study information technology (2nd installment; foreword). *M-IS Quarterly, 24*(1), 1.

Markus, M.L., & Robey, D. (1988). Information technology and organizational change: Causal structure in theory and research. *Management Science*, *34*(5), 583-598.

Marshall, P., Kelder, J-A, & Perry, A. (2005). Social constructionism with a twist of pragmatism: A suitable cocktail for IS research. In *16th Australasian Conference on IS,* Sydney.

Martensson, P., & Lee, A.S. (2004). Dialogical action research at omega corporation. *M-IS Quarterly, 28*(3), 507-536.

Martin, J., & Osborne, W.M. (1983). *Guidance on software maintenance*. NBS Special Publication 500-106. Washington, DC: Institute for Computer Science and Technology, National Bureau of Standards.

Marx, K. H. (1976). *Capital: A critique of political economy volume 1*. London: Penguin Books.

Marx, K. H. (1994). Critique of the Gotha Program. In L. H. Simon (Ed.), *Selected writings* (pp. 315-332). Indianapolis, IN: Hackett Publishing.

Mason, R., McKenney, J., & Copeland, D.G. (1997a). A historical method for MIS

Mason, R., McKenney, J., & Copeland, D.G. (1997b). Developing an historical tradition in MIS research. *MIS Quarterly, 21*(3), 257-276.

Massetti, B., & Zmud, R.W. (1996). Measuring the extent of EDI usage in complex organizations: Strategies and illustrative examples. *MIS Quarterly, 20*(3), 331-345.

Mathew, J. (2003). *CIEAM business plan V1.0*. Brisbane, Australia: Centre for Integrated Engineering Asset Management (CIEAM).

Mathworks Inc. (1995). Matlab. Retrieved August 20, 2008 from http://www.mathworks.com

Matsunaga, M. (2000). *I-mode jiken*. Tokyo, Japan: Kadokawa Shoten.

McAfee, R.P., & McMillan, J. (1987). Auctions and bidding. *Journal of Economic Literature, 25*(2), 699-738.

McClure, C. (1992). *The three Rs of software automation*. Englewood Cliffs, NJ: Prentice Hall.

McCracken, G. (Ed.). (1988). *The long interview*. Beverly Hills, CA: Sage Publications.

McDermid, D.C. (1990). *Software engineering for information systems*. Oxford: Blackwell Scientific Publications.

McGrath, K. (2002). The golden circle: A way of arguing and acting about technology in the London ambulance service. *European Journal of IS, 11*(4), 251-266.

McKenney, J.L., Mason, R.O., & Copeland, D. (1997). Bank of America: The crest and trough of technological leadership. *MIS Quarterly, 21*(3), 321-353.

McKnight, D.H., Choudhury, V., & Kacmar, C. (2002). Developing and validating trust measures for e-commerce: An integrative typology. *Information Systems Research, 13*(3), 334-359.

McLaren, T. (2005). *Response to NDA query.* Personal communication via e-mail. Simi Valley, CA.

McPhail, K. (1999). The threat of ethical accountants: An application of Foucault's concept of ethics to accounting education and some thoughts on ethically educating for the other. *Critical Perspectives on Accounting, 10*(6), 833-866.

Melling, D. (1987). *Understanding Plato.* New York: Oxford University Press.

Menard, S.W. (2002). Longitudinal research. In *Series: Quantitative Applications in the Social Sciences.* USA: Sage Publications.

Mendes, E., & Kitchenham, B. (2004). A comparison of cross-company and single-company effort estimation models for Web applications. In *Proceedings EASE 2004,* (pp. 47-55).

Mendes, E., & Kitchenham, B. (2004). Further comparison of cross-company and within-company effort estimation models for Web applications. In *Proceedings of International Software Metrics Symposium (METRICS'04),* (pp. 348-357).

Mendes, E., & Mosley, N. (2002). Further investigation into the use of CBR and stepwise regression to predict development effort for Web hypermedia applications. In *Proceedings of International Symposium on Empirical Software Engineering (IESE'02),* (pp. 79-90).

Mendes, E., Counsell, S., & Mosley, N. (2001). Web metrics – estimating design and authoring effort [Special issue on Web engineering]. *IEEE Multimedia,* 50-57.

Mendes, E., Counsell, S., & Mosley, N. (2002). Comparison of Web size measures for predicting Web design and authoring effort. *IEE Proceedings-Software, 149*(3), 86-92.

Mendes, E., Counsell, S., & Mosley, N. (2003). Early Web size measures and effort prediction for Web costimation. In *Proceedings of International Software Metrics Symposium (METRICS'03),* (pp. 18-39).

Mendes, E., Counsell, S., & Mosley, N. (2003). A replicated assessment of the use of adaptation rules to improve Web cost estimation. In *Proceedings of International Symposium on Empirical Software Engineering (ISESE'03),* (pp. 100-109).

Mendes, E., Counsell, S., & Mosley, N. (2003). Investigating early Web size measures for Web cost estimation. In *Proceedings of (EASE '03),* (pp. 1-22).

Mendes, E., Counsell, S., & Mosley, N. (2005). Investigating Web size metrics for early Web cost estimation. *Journal of Systems and Software, 77*(2), 157-172.

Mendes, E., Counsell, S., & Mosley, N. (2005). Exploring case-based reasoning for Web hypermedia project cost estimation. *International Journal of Web Engineering and Technology, 2*(1), 117-143.

Mendes, E., Counsell, S., & Mosley, N. (2005). Towards a taxonomy of hypermedia and Web application size metrics. In *Proceedings of the International Conference on Web Engineering (ICWE'05),* (LNCS 3579, pp. 110-123). Springer.

Mendes, E., Counsell, S., Mosley, N., Triggs, C., & Watson I. (2002). A comparison of development effort estimation techniques for Web hypermedia applications. In *Proceedings of International Software Metrics Symposium (METRICS'02),* (pp. 131-140).

Mendes, E., Counsell, S., Mosley, N., Triggs, C., & Watson, I. (2003). A comparative study of cost estimation models for Web hypermedia applications. *Empirical Software Engineering, 8*(2), 163-196.

Mendes, E., Di Martino, S., Ferrucci, F., & Gravino, C. (2007). Effort estimation: How valuable is it for a Web company to use a cross-company data set, compared to using its own single-company data set?" In *ACM Proceedings of the International World Wide Web Conference (WWW2007),* (pp. 963-972).

Mendes, E., Lokan, C., Harrison, R., & Triggs, C. (2005). A replicated comparison of cross-company and within-company effort estimation models using the ISBSG database. In *Proceedings of International Software Metrics Symposium (METRICS'05),* (p. 36).

Miles, M., & Huberman, A. (1984). *A qualitative data analysis: A sourcebook of new methods.* Beverly Hills, CA: Sage Publications.

Miles, M., & Huberman, A. (1994). *Qualitative data analysis: An expanded sourcebook.* London: Sage.

Miles, M.B., & Huberman, A.M. (1984). *Qualitative data analysis: A sourcebook of a new methods.* Beverly Hills, CA: Sage.

Miles, M.B., & Huberman, A.M. (1994). *Qualitative data analysis*. Thousand Oaks, CA: Sage Publications.

Milgrim, M. R. (2006). *Milgrim on trade secrets* (Vol. 2). New York: Matthew Bender & Company.

Milgrim, M. R. (2006). *Milgrim on trade secrets* (Vol. 1). New York: Matthew Bender & Company.

Min, H., & Galle, W. P. (2003). E-purchasing: profiles of adopters and nonadopters. *Industrial Marketing Management, 32*(3), 227-233.

Mingers, J. (2001). Combining IS research methods: Towards a pluralist methodology. *Information Systems Research, 12*(3), 240-259.

Mingers, J. (2001). Embodying IS: The contribution of phenomenology. *Information and Organization, 11*(2), 103-128.

Mingers, J. (2003). The paucity of multimethod research: A review of the information systems literature. *Information Systems Journal, 13*, 233-249.

Mingers, J. (2004). Realizing IS: Critical realism as an underpinning philosophy for IS. *Information & Organization, 14*, 87-103.

Mische, M. (1992). EDI strategy: Business shift from technical to business goals. *Chief Information Officer Journal, 5*(1), 18-45.

Mitra, S., & Chaya, A.K. (1996). Analyzing cost-effectiveness of organizations: The impact of information technology spending. *Journal of Management Information Systems, 13*(2), 29-57.

Montano, B.R., Porter, D.C., Malaga, R.A., & Ord, J.K. (2005). Enhanced reputation scoring for online auctions. In *Twenty-sixth International Conference on Information Systems, Proceedings*.

Monteiro, E. (2004). Actor network theory and cultural aspects of interpretative studies. In C. Avgerou, C. Ciborra, & F. Land (Eds.), *The social study of information and communication technology: Innovation, actors, and contexts* (pp. 129-139). Oxford: Oxford University Press.

Monteiro, E., & Hanseth, O. (1996). Social shaping of information infrastructure: On being specific about technology. In W. J. Orlikowski, G. Walsham, M. J. Jones, & J. I. DeGross (Eds.), *Information technology and changes in organizational work* (pp. 325-343). London: Chapman & Hall.

Monteiro, L., & Macdonald, S. (1996). From efficiency to flexibility: The strategic use of information in airline industry, *Journal of Strategic Information Systems, 5*(3), 169-188.

Montgomery, D., Peck, E., & Vining, G. (2001). Introduction to linear regression analysis (3rd ed.). John Wiley & Sons, Inc.

Moss, L., & Atre, S. (2003). *Business intelligence roadmap: The complete lifecycle for decision-support applications.* Boston, MA: Addison-Wesley.

Moss, L., & Hoberman, S. (2004). *The importance of data modeling as a foundation for business insight.* Teradata.

Motulsky, H. (Ed.). (1995). *Intuitive biostatistics.* New York: Oxford University Press.

Mowschowitz, A. (1981). On approaches to the study of social issues in computing. *Communications of the ACM, 24*(3), 146-155.

Munro, I., & Mingers, J. (2002). The use of multimethodology in practice—Results of a survey of practitioners. *Journal of Operational Research Society, 53*, 369-378.

Mustoen-Ollila, E., & Heikkonen, J. (2002). Gatekeepers in information system process innovation adaptation: A longitudinal case study. In T. Terano & M.D. Myers (Ed.), *Proceedings of the 6th Pacific Asia Conference on Information System: The Next E-What? for Business and Communities* (pp. 1043-1047). Tokyo, Japan.

Mustonen-Ollila, E. (2003). How outsourcing impacts to decision-making over IS process innovations. In *Proceedings of the Computer Supported Scientific Collaboration (CSSC) Workshop, ECSCW '03 8th European Conference of Computer-Supported Cooperative Work*, Helsinki, Finland. (pp. 1-4).

Mustonen-Ollila, E. (2004). IS process innovation unlearning in organisations. In *Proceedings of the European Conference on Information Systems (ECIS), The European IS Profession in the Global Networking Environment*, Turku, Finland (pp. 1-12).

Mustonen-Ollila, E. (2005). *Information system process innovation adoption, adaptation, learning, and unlearning: A longitudinal case study.* Doctoral dissertation. Acta Universitatis Lappeenrantaensis 216, Lappeenranta University of Technology: Digipaino, Finland.

Mustonen-Ollila, E. (2007, December). Information system process innovation life cycle model. *Journal of Knowledge Management: In the Knowledge Garden, 8*(4), 1-12.

Mustonen-Ollila, E., & Heikkonen, J. (2003). IS process innovation knowledge acquisition and information distribution mechanisms. In *Proceedings of the United Kingdom Academy for Information Systems (UKAIS2003) Conference, Coordination and Coopetition: The IS role,* Warwick, England, (pp. 1-16).

Mustonen-Ollila, E., & Heikkonen, J. (2008). IS process innovation evolution in organizations. T*he Academy of Information and Management Sciences Journals* (AIMS), (Forthcoming).

Mustonen-Ollila, E., & Heikkonen, J. (2008). Information System process innovation evolution paths. Submitted for a review to the *10th International Conference on Enterprise Information Systems (ICEIS2008),* 12-16 June, 2008, Barcelona, Spain.

Mustonen-Ollila, E., & Heikkonen, J. (2008). *Actors' behaviour mechanisms in using and implementing information system process innovations: A longitudinal case study using actor-network theory and structuration theory.* (Under work).

Mustonen-Ollila, E., & Lyytinen, K. (2003). Why organisations adopt information system process innovations: A longitudinal study using diffusion of innovation theory. *Information Systems Journal, 13,* 279-297.

Mustonen-Ollila, E., & Lyytinen, K. (2004). How organizations adopt information system process innovations: A longitudinal analysis. *European Journal of Information Systems, 13,* 35-51.

Myers, M. (1997). Qualitative research in IS. *M-IS Quarterly, 21*(2), 241-242

Myers, M. (2004). Hermeneutics in IS research. In J. Mingers and L. Willcocks (Eds.), *Social theory and philosophy for IS* (pp. 103-128). Chichester: John Wiley & Sons.

Myers, M. D. (1997). Qualitative research in information systems. *MIS Quarterly, 21*(2), 241-242. Retrieved June 1, 2008, from http://www.misq.org/discovery/MISQD_isworld/

Myers, M. D., & Avison, D. (Eds.). (2002). *Qualitative research in information systems: A reader.* London: Sage Publications Ltd.

Myers, M.D. (1997, June). Qualitative research in information systems. *MIS Quarterly, 21*(2), 241-242.

Myles, B. (1990). *The Theaetetus of Plato* (M. J. Levett & M. Burnyeat, Trans.). Indianapolis: Hackett Publishing Company, Inc.

Myrdall, G. (1970). *Objectivity in social research.* London, UK: Gerald Duckworth & Co. Ltd.

Myrtveit, I., & Stensrud, E. (1999). A controlled experiment to assess the benefits of estimating with analogy and regression models. *IEEE Transactions on Software Engineering, 25*(4), 510-525.

Myrtveit, I., Shepperd, M., & Stensrud, E. (2005). Reliability and validity in comparative studies of software prediction models. *IEEE Transactions on Software Engineering, 31*(5), 380-391.

Nahar, N., Lyytinen, K., Huda, N., & Muravyov, S. V. (2006). Success factors for information technology supported information technology transfer: Finding expert consensus. *Information & Management, 43,* 663-677.

Nanang, D. D., Pokharel, S., & Jiao, J. (2003). Strategic use of information technology in warehouses: A Singapore case. *Conradi Research Review, 2*(1), 5-25.

Nandhakumar, J., & Avison, D. (1999). The fiction of methodology development: A field study of information systems development. *Information Technology & People, 12*(2), 176-191.

Nandhakumar, J., & Jones, M. (1997). Too close for comfort? Distance and engagement in interpretive information systems research. *Information Systems Journal, 7*(2), 109-131.

Nascimento, M., & Silva, J. (1998). Towards historical r-trees. In *Proceedings of the ACM Symposium on Applied Computing* (pp. 235-240).

National Computer Board, Gintic Institute of Manufacturing Technology and Singapore Confederation of Industries. (1996). *Survey on Information Technology in Supporting Supply Chain Management.* Singapore.

National Computer Board. (1992). *A vision of an intelligent island: The IT 2000 report.* Singapore: National Computer Board.

Natsuno, T. (2000). *I-mode strategy.* Tokyo, Japan: Nikkei BP Kikaku.

NCCUSL. (1985, August 9). Uniform Trade Secrets Act with 1985 Amendments. Retrieved June 1, 2008, from http://www.law.upenn.edu/bll/ulc/fnact99/1980s/utsa85.htm

Nederveen Pieterse, J. (2002). Globalization, kitsch and conflict: Technologies of work, war and politics. *Review of International Political Economy, 9*(1), 1-36.

Negash, S. (2004). Business iIntelligence. *Communications of the Association for Information Systems, 13,* 177-195.

Nelson, C., Treichler, P. A., & Grossberg, L. (1992). Cultural studies: An introduction. In L. Grossberg, C. Nelson & P. A. Treichler (Eds.), *Cultural Studies* (pp. 1-16). New York: Routledge.

Neuman, W.L. (1994). Sampling. In W.L. Neuman (Ed.), *Social research methods* (pp. 193-220). Boston, MA: Allyn and Bacon.

Newberg, J. A., & Dunn, R. L. (2002). Keeping secrets in the campus lab: Law, values and rules of engagement for industry-university R&D partnerships. *American Business Law Journal, 39*(2), 187-240.

Newman, J. (2005). Response to NDA query. Personal communication via e-mail. Simi Valley, CA.

Ngai, E. W. T., Lai, K. H., & Cheng, T. C. E. (2007). Logistics information systems: The Hong Kong experience. *International Journal of Production Economics.* Retrieved June 8, 2008, from doi:10.1016/j.ijpe.2007.05.018

Ngwenyama, O. K., & Lee, A. S. (1997). Communication richness in electronic mail: Critical social theory and the contextuality of meaning. *MIS Quarterly, 21*(2), 145-167.

Nielsen, J. (1998, February 8). The reputation manager. Retrieved June 14, 2008, from http://www.useit.com/alertbox/980208.html

Nietzsche, F. (1973). *Beyond good and evil.* London: Penguin Books.

Nietzsche, F. (1990). *Twilight of the idols.* London: Penguin Books.

Nietzsche, F. (1994). *Human, all too human.* London: Penguin Books.

Ninad. (2007). *Feedback 2.0 – a conversation with Brian Burke.* Retrieved June 14, 2008, from http://www. E-Baychatter.com/the_chatter/2007/02/feedback_20_a_c.html

Noel, G., et al. (2004). The po-tree, a real-time spatio-temporal data indexing structure. In *Proc. of Development in Spatial Data Handling SDH2004,* Leicester (pp. 259-270).

Noel, G., Servigne, S., & Laurini, R. (2005). Spatial and temporal information structuring for natural risk monitoring. In *Proc. GIS Planet 2005,* Estoril, Portugal.

Nolan, R.L. (1973). Managing the computer resource: A stage hypothesis. *Communications of the ACM, 16*(7), 399-405.

Nosek, J., & Palvia, P. (1990). Software maintenance management: Change in the last decade. *Journal of Software Maintenance: Research and Practice, 2*(3), 157-174.

Nunamaker, J., Chen, M., & Purdin, T. (1991). System development in IS research. *Journal of Management IS, 7*(3), 89-106.

Nunamaker, J.F., & Chen, M. (1990). Systems development in information systems research. In *The Proceedings of the Twenty-Third Hawaii International Conference on System Sciences* (pp. 631-640). IEEE Computer Society Press.

OECD. (1998). *SMEs and electronic commerce.* Ottawa: Working Party on Small and Medium-sized Enterprises, The Directorate for Science, Technology and Industry, Industry Committee, DSTL/IND/PME (1998) 18/REV1.

Ojala, L., & Suomi (1992). EDI: An advantage or disadvantage for remotely-situated countries? *International Journal of Physical Distribution & Logistics Management, 22*(8), 35-68.

Olszak, C., & Ziemba, E. (2007). Approach to building and implementing business intelligence systems. *Interdisciplinary Journal of Information, Knowledge, and Management, 2,* 135-148.

Opdahl, A.L., & Henderson-Sellers, B. (2002). Understanding and improving the UML metamodel through ontological analysis. *Journal of Software and Systems Modelling (SoSyM), 1*(1), 43-67. Springer.

Oppedahl & Larson LLP. (1995, June 29). Comparing patents and copyrights. Retrieved June 1, 2008, from http://www.patents.com/patents.htm#compare-copyright

Orlikowski, W. (2000). Using technology and constituting structures: A practice lens for studying technology in organizations. *Organization Science, 11*(4), 404-428.

Orlikowski, W. J. (1993). CASE tools as organisational change: Investigating incremental and radical changes in systems development. *Management Information Systems Quarterly, 17*(3), 309-340.

Orlikowski, W. J., & Baroudi, J. J. (1991). Studying information technology in organizations: Research approaches and assumptions. *Information Systems Research, 2*(1), 1-28.

Orlikowski, W.J. (1993). Case tools as organizational change: Investigating incremental and radical changes in systems development. *MIS Quarterly, 17*(3).

Orlikowski, W.J., & Gash, D.C. (1994). Technological frames: Making sense of information technology in organizations. *ACM Transactions on Information Systems*, *12*(2), 174-207.

Ormerod, P. (2005). *Why most things fail: Evolution, extinction and economics*. London: Faber and Faber Limited.

Ormerod, R. (1995). Putting soft OR methods to work: Information systems strategy development at Sainsbury's. *Journal of the Operational Research Society*, *46*(3), 277-293.

Ormerod, R.J. (1996). IS strategy development at Sainsbury's Supermarkets: Using soft OR. *Interfaces*, *26*(1), 102-130.

Otsuka, S. (2005). *Cultural influences on academic performance in Fiji: A case study in the Nadroga/Navosa Province*. Unpublished doctoral dissertation, University of Sydney, Australia.

Otsuka, S. (2006). Multicultural classroom in the 21st Century: A case of cross-cultural interaction between Australians and Japanese. In J. Zajda (Ed.), *Equity, access and democracy in education*. Melbourne, Australia: James Nicholas Publishers.

Otsuka, S., & Smith, I.D. (2005). Educational applications of the expectancy-value model of achievement motivation in the diverse cultural contexts of the west and east. *Change: Transformations in Education*, *8*(1), 91-109.

Ovaska, P. (2004, April 14-17). Measuring requirement evolution – a case study in the e-commerce domain. In *6th International Conference on Enterprise Information Systems (ICEIS(3))*, Porto, Portugal, INSTICC (pp. 669-673).

Ovaska, P. (2005). Working with methods: Observations on the role methods in systems development. O. Vasilegas, A. Capinskas, W. Wotjowski, W.G. Wotjowski, J. Zupneic, & S. Wrycza (Eds.), *Information systems development, advances in theory, practice and education, ISD 2004* (pp. 185-197). Springer.

Ovaska, P., & Bern, A. (2004, June 7-11). Architecture as a predictor of system size – a metaphor from construction projects. In *16th International Conference on Advanced Information Systems Engineering (CAISE '04 Forum)*, Riga, Latvia, Riga Technical University (pp. 193-203).

Ovaska, P., Rossi, M., & Marttiin, P. (2004). Architecture as a coordination tool in multi-site software development. *Software Process Improvement and Practice*, *8*(4), 233-248.

Ovaska, P., Rossi, M., & Smolander, K. (2005). Filtering, negotiating and shifting in the understanding of information systems requirements. *Scandinavian Journal of Information Systems*, *17*(1), 31-66.

Overby, E. (2005). Response to NDA query. Personal communication via e-mail. Simi Valley, CA.

Pan, Z. X. (Thomas), & Pokharel, S. (2007). Logistics in hospitals: A case study of some Singapore hospitals. *Leadership in Health Services* (Accepted for publication).

Pandit, N. (1996). The creation of theory: A recent application of the grounded theory method. *The Qualitative Report*, *2*(4).

Parr, A., & Shanks, G. (2000). A model of ERP project implementation. *Journal of Information Technology*, *15*, 289-303.

Pataki, T. (2007). *Against religion*. Melbourne, Australia: Scribe Publications.

Patton, M.Q. (1990). *Qualitative Evalution and Research Methods* (2nd ed.). Newbury Park, CA: Sage.

Patton, M.Q. (2002). *Qualitative research & evaluation methods* (3rd ed.). London: Sage Publications.

Pennings, J. & Buitendam, A. (Eds.). (1987). *New technology as organizational innovation*. Cambridge, Massachusetts: Ballinger.

Perry, C., Riege, A., & Brown, L. (1999). Realism's role among scientific paradigms in marketing research. *Irish Marketing Review*, *12*(2).

Peterson, I. (1985). Bits of ownership: Growing computer software sales are forcing universities to rethink their copyright and patent policies. *Science News*, *128*(12), 189-190.

Pettigrew, A. (1985). *The wakening giant, continuity and change in ICI*. Oxford and New York: Basil Blackwell.

Pettigrew, A. (1989). Issues of time and site selection in longitudinal research on change. *The Information Systems Research Challenge: Qualitative Research Methods*, *1*, 13-19. Boston, MA.

Pettigrew, A.M. (1990). Longitudinal field research on change: Theory and practice. *Organization Science*, *1*(3), 267-292.

Pettigrew, A.M. (1997). What is a processual analysis? *Scandinavian Journal of Management*, *13*(4), 337-348.

Pfeiffer, H.K.C. (1992). *The diffusion of electronic data interchange*. Heidelberg, Germany: Physica-Verlag.

Pierce, C.S. (1931). Collected papers. In C. Harshorne & P. Weiss (Eds). Cambridge, MA: Harvard University Press.

Platt, A., & Warwick, S. (1995). Review of soft systems methodology. *Industrial Management and Data Systems, 4*(1), 19-21.

Poe, V., Klauer, P., & Brobst, S. (1997). *Building a data warehouse for decision support* (2nd ed.). New Jersey: Prentice Hall.

Pokharel, S. (2005). Perception on information and communication technology perspectives in logistics: A study of transportation and warehouses sectors in Singapore. *The Journal of Enterprise Information Management, 18*(2), 136-149.

Polanyi, M. (1962). *Personal knowledge*. London: Routledge and Kegan Paul.

Ponniah, P. (2001). *Data warehousing fundamentals*. New York: Wiley-Interscience.

Popper, K. (1965). *Conjectures and refutations*. New York: Harper and Row.

Porto de Albuquerque, J., & Simon, E.J. (2007). Dealing with socio-technical complexity: Towards a transdisciplinary approach to IS research. In O. Hubert, J. Schelp, & R. Winter (Eds.), *Proceedings of the 15th European Conference on Information Systems (ECIS 2007)* (pp. 1458-1468).

Powell, W.W., & Owen-Smith, J. (1998). Universities and the market for intellectual property in the life sciences. *Journal of Policy Analysis and Management, 17*, 253-277.

Power, D. J. (2001). *Supporting decision-makers: An expanded framework*. Paper presented at the Informing Science and IT Education, Krakow, Poland.

Powers, R., & Dickson, G.W. (1973). M-IS project management. *California Management Review, 15*(3), 127-56

Pratt, V. (1978). *The philosophy of the social sciences*. London, UK: Methuen & Co. Ltd.

Premkumar, G., & Ramamurthy, K. (1995). The role of inter-organizational and organizational factors on the decision mode for adoption of inter-organizational systems. *Decision Science, 26*(3), 37-303.

Premkumar, G., Ramamurthy, K., & Crum, M. (1997). Determinants of EDI adoption in the transportation industry. *European Journal of Information Systems, 6*(2), 21-107.

Procopiuc, C., Agarwal, P., & Har-Peled, S. (2000). Startree: An efficient self-adjusting index for moving points. In *Proc. ALENEX*.

Proudlock, M., Phelps, B., & Gamble, P. (1999). IT adoption strategies: Best practice guidelines for professional SMEs enterprise development. *Journal of Small Business and 6*(3), 240-252.

Purao, S. (2002). *Design research in technology and IS: Truth or dare*. Unpublished paper, School of Information Sciences and Technology, The Pennsylvania State University, University Park, State College, PA.

Quattrone, P., & Hopper, T. (2005). A time-space odyssey: Management control systems in two multinational organizations. *Accounting Organizations and Society, 30*(7/8), 735-764.

Radford, M. L., & Kern, M. K. (2006). A multiple-case study investigation of the discontinuation of nine chat reference services. *Library and Information Science Research, 28*(4), 521-547.

Raina, K., & Harsh, A. (2001). M-*commerce security: A beginne's guide*. Berkley, CA: McGraw-Hill.

Rajesh, C., & Vikas, K. (2002). *The Asian managers handbook of e-commerce*. New Delhi, India: Tata McGraw-Hill Publishing Company Limited.

Rapoport, R.N. (1970). Three dilemmas of action research. *Human Relations, 23*(6), 499-513.

Ratnasingham, P. (1997). EDI security: A model of EDI risks and associated controls. *Information Management & Computer Security, 5*(2), 63-71.

Rebecca, A., Nath, R., & Hendon, D.W. (1998). An empirical investigation of the level of electronic data interchange (EDI) implementation and its ability to predict EDI system success measures and EDI implementation factors. *International Journal of Physical Distribution & Logistics Management, 28*(9/10), 773-780.

Reid, D. (2002). Employing normative stakeholder theory in developing countries. *Business & Society, 41*(2), 166-207.

Reifer, D. (2000). Web-development: Estimating quicktime-to-market software. *IEEE Software, 17*(8), 57-64.

Reinschmidt, J., & Francoise, A. (2000). *Business intelligence certification guide*. San Jose, CA: IBM Corporation, International Technical Support Organization.

Resnick, P., & Zeckhauser, R. (2002). Trust among strangers in Internet transactions: Empirical analysis of E-Bay's reputation system. In M.R. Baye (Ed.), *The economics of the Internet and e-commerce* (Vol. 11 of Advances in Applied Microeconomics). Amsterdam: Elsevier Science.

Resnick, P., Zeckhauser, R., Friedman, E., & Kuwabara, K. (2000). Reputation systems: Facilitating trust in Internet interactions. *Communications of the ACM, 43*(12), 45-48.

Ricks, J.E. (1997). Electronically developed theory and procedure for distribution channel management via electronic data interchange linkage. *Logistics Information Management, 10*(1), 20-27.

Riihimaa, J. (2004). *Taxonomy of information and communication technology system innovations adopted by small and medium sized enterprises*. Doctoral dissertation, University of Tampere, Tampere University Press, Tampere.

Ritzer, G. (1975). *Sociology: A multiple paradigm science*. Boston, MA: Allyn & Bacon.

Roberts, D., Cater-Steel, A., & Toleman, M. (2006). Factors influencing the decisions of SMEs to purchase software package upgrades. In *Proceedings of the 17th Australasian Conference on Information Systems (ACIS 2006)*.

Roberts, V.L., & Fels, D.I. (2006). Methods for inclusion: Employing think aloud protocols in software usability studies with individuals who are deaf. *International Journal of Human-Computer Studies, 64*, 489-501.

Robey, D., & Newman, M. (1996). Sequential patterns in IS development: An application of a social process model. *ACM Transactions on IS, 14*(1), 30-63.

Robson, C. (1993). *Real world research*. Oxford: Blackwell Science.

Robson, L. (1994). EDI-changing business practice. *Logistics Information Management, 7*(4), 35-42.

Rockart, J. F. (1979). Chief executives define their own data needs. *Harvard Business Review, 57*(2), 81-93.

Rockart, J. F., & DeLong, D. W. (1988). *Executive support systems: The emergence of top management computer use*. Homewood, IL: Dow Jones-Irwin.

Rogers, D.S., Daugherty, P.J., & Stank, T.P. (1992). Enhancing service responsiveness: The strategic potential of EDI. *International Journal of Physical Distribution and Logistics Management, 22*(8), 15-22.

Rogers, E. M. (2003). Diffusion of Innovations (5th ed.). New York: Free Press/Simon & Schuster, Inc.

Rolf, A. (2004). Von der theoriearbeit zur gestaltung. In H.-D. Kübler & E. Elling (Eds.), *Wissensgesellschaft. Neue medien und ihre konsequenzen*. Bonn: Bundeszentrale für politische Bildung.

Rolf, A., Janneck, M., & Finck, M. (2006). Soziotechnische gestaltung von freelancer-netzwerken – eine exemplarische analyse mit dem mikropolis-modell. *WISU – Das Wirtschaftsinformatikstudium, 9*(06), 1089-1095.

Rorty, R. (1982). *Consequences of pragmatism*. Brighton, UK: Harvester Press.

Rose, J. (2007). Interaction, transformation and information systems development – an extended application of SSM. *Information Technology & People, 15*(3), 242-268.

Rosemann, M., & Green, P. (2002). Developing a meta model for the Bunge-Wand-Weber ontological constructs. *Information Systems, 27*, 75-91.

Rosen, M. (1991). Coming to terms with the field: Understanding and doing organizational ethnography. *Journal of Management Studies, 28*, 7-24.

Rosen, M. (1998). Continental philosophy from Hegel. In A.C. Grayling (Ed.), *Philosophy 2: Further through the subject* (pp. 663-704). Oxford, UK: Oxford University Press.

Ruddin, L P. (2006). You Can Generalize Stupid! Social Scientists, Bent Flyvbjerg, and Case Study Methodology. *Qualitative Inquiry, 12*(4), 797-812.

Ruhe, M., & Wieczorek, I. (2002). How valuable is company-specific data compared to multi-company data for software cost estimation? In *Proceedings of the IEEE Symposium on Software Metrics (METRICS'02)*, (pp. 237-246).

Ruhe, M., Jeffery, R., & Wieczorek, I. (2003). Using Web objects for estimating software development effort for Web applications. In *Proceedings of the IEEE International Software Metrics Symposium (METRICS'03)*, (pp. 30-37).

Ruhe, M., Jeffery, R., & Wieczorek, I. (2003). Cost estimation for Web applications. In *Proceedings of International Conference on Software Engineering (ICSE'03)*, (pp. 285-294).

Rumelhart, D. E., & Ortony, A. (1977). *The representation of knowledge in memory*. In R. C. Anderson, R. J.

Shapiro & W. E. Montague (Eds.), (pp. 99-135). Hillsdale, NJ: Erlbaum Publishing.

Ruspini, E. (1999). Longitudinal research and the analysis of social change. *Quality & Quantity, 33*(3), 219-227.

Rutter, M., Maughan, B., Pickles, A., & Simonoff, E. (1998). Retrospective recall recalled. In R.B. Cairns, L.B. Bergman, & J. Kagan (Ed.), *Methods and models for studying the individual* (pp. 219-242). Thousand Oaks, CA: Sage Publications.

Rynes, S.L., Bartunek, J.M., & Daft, R.L. (2001). Across the great divide: Knowledge creation and transfer between practitioners and academics. *Academy of Management Journal, 44*(2), 340-355

Saeki, M. (1994). Software specification and design methods and method engineering. *International Journal of Software Engineering and Knowledge Engineering.*

Saltenis, S., et al. (2000). Indexing the positions of continuously moving objects. In *the Proceedings of ACM SIGMOD2000.*

Sammon, D., Adam, F., & Elichirigoity, F. (2001). ERP dreams and sound business rationale. In *Seventh Americas Conference on Information Systems.*

Sandberg, B. (2005). *The hidden market-even for those who create it? Customer-related proactiveness in developing radical innovations.* Publications of the Turku School of Economics and Business Administration Series, doctoral dissertation, Turku, Finland.

Santas, G. X. (Ed.). (2006). *The Blackwell Guide to Plato's Republic.* Malden, MA: Blackwell Publishing Ltd.

Saravanamuthu, K., & Tinker, T. (2003). Politics of managing: The dialectic of control. *Accounting, Organizations and Society, 28*(1), 37-64.

Scheer, A.-W. (1998). *ARIS-business process frameworks* (2nd ed.). Berlin, Germany: Springer-Verlag.

Schlosser, E. (2002). *Fast food nation: What the all-American meal is doing to the world.* London: Penguin Books.

Schneberger, S., & Wade, M. (Eds.). (2006). Theories used in IS research. Retrieved June 1, 2008, from http://www.istheory.yorku.ca

Schneidewind, N. (1992). Methodology for validating software metrics. *IEEE Transaction on Software Engineering, 18*(5), 410-422.

Schneidewind, N.T. (1987). The state of software maintenance. *IEEE Transactions on Software Engineering, 13*(3), 303-310.

Schreck, T., & Chen, Z. (2000). R-tree implementation using branch-grafting method. In *Proc. of 2000 ACM Symposium.*

Schreyögg, G., Sydow, J., & Koch, J. (2003). Organisatorische pfade — von der pfadabhängigkeit zur pfadreaktion? In G. Schreyögg & J. Sydow (Eds.), *Managementforschung 13: Strategische prozesse und pPfad* (pp. 257-294). Wiesbaden: Gabler.

Schultze, U., & Orlikowski, W.J. (2001). Metaphors of virtuality: Shaping an emergent reality. *Information and Organization, 11*(1), 45-77.

Scientific Software. (2001). Atlas.ti-the knowledge workbench. Retrieved June 3, 2008, from http://www.atlasti.de/

Scruton, R. (1998). Modern philosophy I: The rationalists and Kant. In A.C. Grayling (Ed.), *Philosophy 1: A guide through the subject* (pp. 440-483). Oxford, UK: Oxford University Press.

SEC. (2001). *Singapore EDI committee (SEC) progress report.* Singapore: EDI Committee.

Sen, A., & Jacob, V. (1998). Industrial-strength data warehousing. *Communications of the ACM, 41*(9), 28-31.

Shafer, G. (1988). *Functional analysis of office requirements: A multiperspective approach.* Chichester: John Wiley & Sons.

Shapiro, J. (1999). *SME electronic commerce study.* Singapore: PricewaterhouseCoopers.

Shekhar, S., & Chawla, S. (2003). *Spatial databases: A tour.* Upper Saddle River, NJ: Prentice Hall.

Shepperd, M., & Schofield, C. (2000). Estimating software project effort using analogies. *IEEE Transaction on Software Engineering, 23*(11), 736-743.

Shin, B. (2003). An exploratory investigation of system success factors in data warehousing. *Journal of the Association for Information Systems, 14*(1).

Shippey, K. C. (2002). *A short course in international intellectual property rights: Protecting your brands, marks, copyrights, patents, designs, and related rights worldwide.* Novato, CA: World Trade Press.

Shrivastava, P., & Mitroff, 1.1. (1984). Enhancing organizational research utilization: The role of decision makers' assumptions. *Academy of Management Review, 9,* 18-26.

Sian, S. (2006). Inclusion, exclusion and control: The case of the Kenyan accounting professionalisation project. *Accounting, Organizations and Society, 31*(3), 295-322.

SICC. (2000). *The investor's guide to Singapore* (2000 ed.). Singapore International Chamber of Commerce.

Simon, E., Janneck, M., & Gumm, D. (2006, September 21-23). Understanding socio-technical change: Towards a multidisciplinary approach. In J. Berleur, M. I. Nurminen, & J. Impagliazzo (Eds.), *Social informatics: An information xociety for all? In Remembrance of Rob Kling, Proceedings of the Seventh International Conference on Human Choice and Computers (HCC7), IFIP TC 9,* Maribor, Slovenia (pp. 232-243). New York: Springer.

Singapore Logistics Association. Retrieved June 8, 2008, from http://www.sla.org.sg/index.shtm

Singh, M. (2004). Enabling Australia: Responsive education and global movements of people. In J. Allen (Ed), *Sociology of education: Possibilities and practices* (3rd ed.) (Chapter 9, pp. 197-219). Southbank: Social Science Press.

Sjoberg, G., Williams, N., Vaughn, T. R., & Sjoberg, A. F. (1991). The case study approach in social research: Basic methodological issues. In J. R. Feagin & A. M. Orum (Eds.), *A Case for the Case Study* (pp. 27-79). Chapel Hill: University of North Carolina Press.

Skok, W., & Legge, M. (2002). Evaluating enterprise resource planning (ERP) systems using an interpretive approach. *Knowledge and Process Management, 9*(2), 72-82.

Smaling, A. (1987). *Methodological objectivity and qualitative research.* Lisse, the Netherlands: Swets & Zeitlinger.

Smit, J., & Bryant, A. (2000). Grounded theory method in IS research: Glaser vs. Strauss. Research in Progress Working Papers, 2000-2007.

Smith, D.D. (1999). *Designing maintainable software.* Berlin, Heidelberg, New York: Springer-Verlag.

Smith, M. L. (2006). Overcoming theory-practice inconsistencies: Critical realism and information systems research. *Information and Organization, 16,* 191-211.

Smith, N.G. (1990). The case study: A useful research method for information management. *Journal of Information Technology, 5,* 123-133.

Snow, D. A., & Anderson, L. (1991). Researching the homeless: The characteristic features and virtues of the case study. In G. R. Ferris & A. M. Orum (Eds.), *A Case for the Case Study* (pp. 143-173). Chapel Hill: University of North Carolina Press.

Sohel, A., & Schroeder, R.G. (2001). The impact of electronic data interchange on delivery performance. *Production and Operations Management, 10*(1), 16-30.

Somers, T., & Nelson, K. (2001). The impact of critical success factors across the stages of enterprise resource planning implementations. In *Hawaii International Conference on Systems Sciences.*

Spanos, Y. E., Prastacos, G. P., & Poulymenakou, A. (2002). The relationship between information and communication technologies adoption and management. *Information and Management, 39*(8), 659-675.

Spradley, J.P. (1979). *The ethnographic interview.* New York: Holt, Rinehart and Winston.

Stake, R. E. (1995). *The art of case study research.* London: Sage Publications, Inc.

Stake, R. E. (2005). Qualitative case studies. In N. K. Denzin & Y. S. Lincoln (Eds.), *The Sage Handbook of Qualitative Research* (3rd ed., pp. 443-466).

Stake, R. E. (2005). *Multiple case study analysis.* The Guilford Press.

Stake, R.E. (1995). *The art of case study research.* CA: Sage.

Steinbock, D. (2002). *Wireless horizon: Strategy and competition in the worldwide mobile marketplace.* New York: Amacom.

Stim, R., & Fishman, S. (2001). *Nondisclosure agreements: Protect your trade secrets and more* (1st ed.). Berkeley, CA: Nolo Press.

Stowell, F., & Mingers, J. (1997). Introduction. In J. Mingers, & F. Stowell (Eds.), *IS: An emerging discipline?* London: McGraw-Hill.

Stratton, J. (1998). *Race daze: Australia in identity crisis.* Annandale: Pluto Press.

Straub, D. (2005). Response to NDA query. Personal communication via e-mail. Simi Valley, CA.

Straub, D. W., Loch, K. D., & Hill, C. E. (2001, October-December). Transfer of information technology to the Arab world: A test of cultural influence modelling. *Journal of Global Information Management,* 6-28.

Straub, D.W., Ang, S., & Evaristo, R. (1984, February). Normative standards for IS research. *Database,* 21-34.

Strauss, A. L., & Corbin, J. (1990). *Basics of qualitative research: Grounded theory procedures and techniques.* Newbury Park, CA: Sage Publications.

Strauss, A. L., & Corbin, J. (1994). Grounded theory methodology: An overview. In N. K. Denzin & Y. S. Lincoln (Eds.), *Handbook of qualitative research*. Thousand Oaks, CA: Sage Publications.

Strauss, A. L., & Corbin, J. (1998). Basics of qualitative research: Techniques and procedures for developing grounded theory (2nd ed.). London, Thousand Oaks, CA: Sage Publications.

Strauss, A., & Corbin, J. (1990). *Basics of qualitative research: Grounded theory procedures and applications*. Newbury Park, CA: Sage.

Strauss, J., & Frost, R. (1999). *Marketing on the Internet*. New Jersey: Prentice Hall.

Street, C., & Meister, D.B. (2004). Small business growth and internal transparency: The role of IS. *M-IS Quarterly, 28*(3), 473-506.

Sturgeon, S., Martin, M.G.F., & Grayling, A.C. (1998). Epistemology. In A.C. Grayling (Ed.), *Philosophy 1: A guide through the subject* (pp. 7-60). Oxford, UK: Oxford University Press.

Sullivan P. (1989). Beyond a narrow conception of usability testing. *IEEE Transactions on Professional Communication, 32*(4), 256-264.

Sum, C. C., & Teo, C. B. (1999). Strategic postures of logistics service providers in Singapore. *International Journal of Physical Distribution and Logistics Management, 29*(9), 588-605.

Supply Chain & Logistics Association Canada. Retrieved June 8, 2008, from http://www.sclcanada.org/index.php?id=10

Swanson E.B., & Ramiller, N.C. (1993). Information systems research thematics: Submissions to a new journal, 1987-1992. *Information Systems Research, 4*(4), 299-330.

Swanson, E.B. (1994). Information systems innovation among organizations. *Management Science, 40*(9), 1069-1088.

Swanson, E.B., & Beath, C.M. (1989). *Maintaining information systems in organizations*. Great Britain: John Wiley & Sons.

Swanson, E.B., & Ramiller, N.C. (1993). IS research thematics: Submission to a new journal, 1987-1992. *IS Research, 4*(4), 299-329.

Swanson, E.B., & Ramiller, N.C. (1997). The organizing vision in information systems innovation. *Organization Science, 8*(5), 458-274.

Swatman, P.M.C. (1994). Business process redesign using EDI: The BHP steel experience. *Australian Journal of Information Systems, 1*(2), 55-73.

Swenseth, S. R., & Godfrey, M. R. (2002). Incorporating transportation costs into inventory replenishment decisions. *International Journal of Production Economics, 77*(2), 113-130.

Sy, A., & Tinker, T. (2006). Bury Pacioli in Africa: A bookkeeper's reification of accountancy. *Abacus, 42*(1), 105-127.

Tabachnick, B.G., & Fidell, L.S. (2001). *Using mltivariate statistics* (4th ed.). Allyn & Bacon.

Tajino, A., & Smith, C. (2005). Exploratory practice and soft systems methodology. *Language Teaching Research, 9*(4), 448-469.

Takashi, T. (2001). *E-Commerce, opportunities and challenges for SMEs*. Asian Productivity Organization.

Takeaki, K. (2001). IT applications in Japanese SMEs. In T. Takashi (Ed.), *E-commerce, opportunities and challenges for SMEs* (pp. 109-110). Asian Productivity Organization.

Takeda, H., Veerkamp, P., Tomiyama, T., & Yoshikawam, H. (1990, Winter). Modeling design processes. *AI Magazine*, 37-48.

Takeyasu, K. (2006). Mobile marketing. *The Journal of Economic Studies, 50*(2-4), 61-72. Osaka Prefecture University.

Takeyasu, K., Ono, A., & Ueda, M. (2003). *Current mobile business*. Tokyo, Japan: Chuo-Keizaisha.

Taleb, N. N. (2007). *The Black Swan: The impact of the highly improbable*. London: Penguine Books Ltd.

Tan, C.Y., Thio, F.W., & Ser, T.H. (2003). *Facilitating cross-border trade with PKI and ebXML*. Singapore EDI Committee. Retrieved June 10, 2008, from http://www.sec-edi.org/res_articles.htm

Tan, W.G., & Gable, G.G. (1998). Attitude of maintenance personnel towards maintenance work: A comparative analysis. *Software Maintenance: Research and Practice, 10*(1), 59-74.

Tay, B. S., & Kam, B. C. (2001). Information technology in logistics: Issues and development. In *Proceedings of the first International Conference on Integrated Logistics: Logistics 2001*. Singapore: Nanyang Technological University.

Taylor, M.J., & DaCosta, J.L. (1999). Software issues in IS projects: Lessons from an SME case study. *System Research and Behavioral Science, 16*(3), 263-272.

Teo, H.H., Tan, B.C.Y., & Wei, K.K. (1997). Organizational transformation using electronic data interchange: The case of TradeNet in Singapore. *Journal of Management Information Systems, 13*(4), 139-165.

The Green Book, Singapore. Retrieved June 8, 2008, from http://www.thegreenbook.com

Theodoridis, Y., Sellis, Papadopoulos, T A., & Manolopoulos, Y. (1998). Specifications for efficient indexing in spatio-temporal databases. In *Proc. SSDBM* (pp. 123-132).

Thomas, K.W., & Tymon, W.G. (1982). Necessary properties of relevant research: Lessons from recent criticisms of the organizational sciences. *Academy of Management Review, 7,* 345-352.

Thomas, P. (1996). The devil is in the detail: Revealing the social and political processes of technology management. *Technology Analysis & Strategic Management, 8*(1), 71-84.

Thull, J. (2005). *The Prime Solution.* Dearborn Trade Publishing.

Tingle, A. (2000). EDI: Antiquated or ready for a rebirth? *Apparel Industry Magazine, 61*(1), 67-85.

Tinker, A. M., Merino, B. D., & Neimark, M. D. (1982). The normative origins of positive theories: ideology and accounting thought. *Accounting, Organizations and Society, 7*(2), 167-200.

Tinker, T. (1999). Mickey Marxism rides again! *Critical Perspectives on Accounting, 10*(5), 643-670.

Tinker, T. (2005). The withering of criticism: A review of professional, Foucauldian, ethnographic, and epistemic studies in accounting. *Accounting, Auditing & Accountability Journal, 18*(1), 100-135.

Tinker, T., Neimark, M., & Lehman, C. (1991). Falling down the hole in the middle of the road: political quietism in corporate social reporting. *Accounting, Auditing & Accountability Journal, 4*(2).

Toyoda, J. (2006). Construction process management system for detached house using browser phones. *The Journal of Economic Studies, 52*(2), 155-169. Osaka Prefecture University.

Trauth, E.M., & Jessup, L. (2000). Understanding computer-mediated discussions: positivist and interpretive analyses of group support system use [Special issue on intensive research]. *MIS Quarterly, 24*(1), 43-79.

Trist, E. (1976). N-gaging with large-scale systems. In A. Clark (Ed.), *Experimenting with organizational life: The action research approach* (pp. 43-75). New York: Plenum.

Tsotras,V.J., & Kangelaris, N. (1995). The snapshot index, an I/O-optimal access method for time-slice queries. *Information Systems, 20*(3).

Tsotras, V.J., Jensen, C.S., & Snodgrass, R.T. (1998). An extensible notation for spatio-temporal index queries. *ACM SIGMOND Record,* 47-53.

Tsoukas, H. (1994). From social engineering to reflective action in organizational behaviour. In H. Tsoukas (Ed.), *New thinking in organizational behaviour* (pp. 1-22). Oxford, UK: Butterworth-Heinemann.

Tsouvalis, C., & Checkland, P.B. (1996). Reflecting on SSM: The dividing line between real world and system thinking world. *Systems Research, 13*(1), 33-45.

Tsukuda, J., Takeyasu, K., & Ono, A. (2001). *Mobile e-business.* Tokyo, Japan: Chuo-Keizaishal.

Tull, D.S., & Hawkins, D.I. (1993). *Marketing research.* New York: McMillan.

Tullock, G. (1997). Adam Smith and the prisoners' dilemma. In D.B. Klein (Ed.), *Reputation: Studies in the voluntary elicitation of good conduct* (pp. 21-28). Ann Arbor, MI: University of Michigan Press.

Turban, E., Sharda, R., Aronson, J., & King, D. (2007). *Business intelligence* (1st ed.). New Jersey: Prentice Hall.

Turner, B. (1983). The use of grounded theory for the qualitative analysis of organisational behaviour. *Journal of Management Studies, 20,* 333-348.

Turner, J.A., Bikson, T.K., Lyytinen, K., Mathiassen, L., & Orlikowski, W. (1991). Relevance vs. rigor in IS research: An issue of quality. In H.E. Nissen, H.K. Klein, & R. Hirschheim (Eds.), *IS research: Contemporary approaches & emergent traditions* (pp. 715-745). Amsterdam, The Netherlands: Elsevier

Uche, C. U. (2002). Professional accounting development in Nigeria: Threats from the inside and outside. *Accounting, Organizations and Society, 27,* 471-496.

Udo, G. J., & Edoho, F. M. (2000). Information technology transfer to African nations: An economic development mandate. *Journal of Technology Transfer, 25,* 329-342.

Ultsch, A., & Siemon, H.P. (1990) Kohonen's self organizing feature maps for exploratory data analysis. In *Proceeding of the INNC'90, Internal Neural Network Conference* (pp. 305-308). Dordrecht, Netherlands: Kluwer.

Umble, E. J., Haft, J., & Umble, M. (2003). Enterprise resource planning: Implementation procedures and critical success factors. *European Journal of Operational Research, 146,* 241-257.

Urquhart, C. (2000, January). Strategies for conversion and systems analysis in requirements gathering: Qualitative view of analyst-client communications. *The Qualitative Report 4*(1/2).

USPTO. (2006, November 6, 2006). General information concerning patents - what is a Copyright? Retrieved June 1, 2008, from http://www.uspto.gov/web/offices/pac/doc/general/index.html#copyright

USPTO. (2006, November 6, 2006). General information concerning patents - what is a patent? Retrieved June 1, 2008, from http://www.uspto.gov/web/offices/pac/doc/general/index.html#patent

USPTO. (2006, November 6, 2006). General information concerning patents - what is a trademark or servicemark? Retrieved June 1, 2008, from http://www.uspto.gov/web/offices/pac/doc/general/index.html#mark

Vaishnavi, V., & Kuechler, W. (2005). Design research in IS. Retrieved May 29, 2008, from http://www.Vaishnavi and Kuechler, 2005.org/Researchdesign/drisVaishnavi and Kuechler, 2005.htm

Valverde, R., & Toleman, M. (2007). Ontological evaluation of business models: Comparing traditional and component-based paradigms in information systems re-engineering. In R. Kishore, R. Ramesh, & R. Sharman (Eds), *Ontologies in the context of information systems.* Berlin, Germany: Springer-Verlag.

Van Aken, J.E. (2004). Management research based on the paradigm of design sciences: The quest for field-tested and grounded technological rules. *Journal of Management Studies, 41*(2), 219-246.

Van Maanen, J. (1995). *Representation in ethnography.* London, UK: Sage Publications

van de Weerd, I., Brinkkemper, S., & Versendaal, J. (2007). Concepts for incremental method evolution: Empirical exploration and validation in requirements management. In *Proceedings of the 19th Conference on Advanced Information Systems Engineering.*

van de Weerd, I., Brinkkemper, S., Souer, J., & Versendaal, J. (2006). A situational implementation method for Web-based content management system-applications: Method engineering and validation in practice. *Software Process: Improvement and Practice, 11*(5), 521-538.

van der Storm, T., (2007). The Sisyphus continuous integration system. In *Proceedings of the Conference on Software Maintenance and Reengineering.* IEEE Computer Society Press.

Venkatesh, A., & Vitalari, N.P. (1991). Longitudinal surveys in information systems research: An examination of issues, methods, and applications. In K. Kramer (Ed.), *The information systems challenge: Survey research methods* (pp. 115-144). Harvard University Press.

Video Research. (2001). *Actual usage condition of mobile phone.* Tokyo, Japan: Video Research.

Vijayasarathy, L.R., & Tyler, M.L. (1997). Adoption factors and electronic data interchange use: A survey of retail companies. *International Journal of Retail & Distribution Management, 25*(9), 286-292.

Volonino, L. (2005). Editing feedback on manuscript. Personal communication via e-mail. Simi Valley, CA.

Von Mayrhauser, A., Vans, A.M., & Howe, A.E. (1997). Program understanding behaviour during enhancement of large-scale software. *Journal of Software Maintenance: Research and Practice, 9*(5), 299-327.

von Wright, G. H. (1971). A new system of deontic logic. *Danish Yearbook of Philosophy, 1,* 173-182.

Wade, M., & Hulland, J. (2004) Review: The resource-based view and information system research: Review, extension, and suggestions for future research. *M-IS Quarterly, 28*(1), 107-142.

Wallace, R. A., & Wolf, A. (2006). *Contemporary sociological theory: Expanding the classical tradition* (6th ed.). Upper Saddle River, NJ: Pearson Prentice-Hall.

Walls, J.G., Widmeyer, G.R., & El Sawy, O.A. (1992). Building an IS design theory for vigilant e-IS. *IS Research, 3*(1), 36-59.

Walls, J.G., Widmeyer, G.R., & El Sawy, O.A. (2004). Assessing information system design theory in perspective: How useful was our 1992 initial rendition? *Journal of Information Technology Theory and Application, 6*(2), 43-58.

Walsham, G. (1993). *Interpreting IS in organizations.* Chichester, UK: Wiley.

Walsham, G. (1995). Interpretive case studies in IS research. *European Journal of Information Systems, 4,* 74-81.

Walsham, G. (1995). Interpretive case studies in IS research: Nature and method. *European Journal of Information Systems, 4*(2), 74-81.

Walsham, G. (1995). Interpretive case studies in IS research: Nature and method. *European Journal of IS, 4,* 74-81.

Walsham, G. (1995). The emergence of interpetivism in IS research. *IS Research, 6*(4), 376-394.

Walsham, G. (1995). Interpetive case studies in IS research: Nature and method. *European Journal of IS, 4,* 74-81.

Walsham, G. (2006). Doing interpretive research. *European Journal of IS, 15,* 320-330.

Walsham, G. (1993). *Interpreting information systems in organizations.* New York: John Wiley & Sons, Inc.

Walton, L.W. (1994). Electronic data interchange (EDI): A study of its usage and adoption within marketing and logistics channels. *Transportation Journal, 34*(2), 37-45.

Walton, S.V., & Gupta, J.N.D. (1999). Electronic data interchange for process change in an integrated supply chain. *International Journal of Operational & Production Management, 19*(4), 372-388.

Walton, S.V., & Marucheck, A.S. (1997). The relationship between EDI and supplier reliability. *International Journal of Purchasing and Materials Management, 33*(3), 37-76.

Wand, Y., & Weber, R. (1989). An ontological evaluation of systems analysis and design methods. In E. Falkenberg & P. Lindgreen (Eds.), *Proceedings of the IFIP WG8.1 working conference on information systems concepts: An in-depth analysis,* Namur, Belgium (pp.79-107). North-Holland, Amsterdam.

Wand, Y., & Weber, R. (1993). On the ontological expressiveness of information systems analysis and design grammars. *Information Systems Journal, 3*(2), 217-237.

Wand, Y., & Weber, R. (1995). On the deep structure of information systems. *Information Systems Journal, 5*(2), 203-223.

Wania, C.E., Atwood, M.E., & McCain, K.W. (2006). How do design and evaluation interrelate in HCI re-

search? In *Proceedings of the 6th ACM conference on Designing Interactive Systems,* University Park, PA, USA (pp. 90-98).

Waterson, S., Landay, J.A., & Matthews, T. (2002). In the lab and out in the wild: Remote Web usability testing for mobile devices. In *Conference on Human Factors in Computing Systems (CHI '02 extended abstracts on human factors in computing systems),* Minneapolis, MN, USA, (pp. 796-797).

Watson, H. J., & Haley, B. J. (1997). Data warehousing: A framework and survey of current practices. *Journal of Data Warehousing, 2*(1), 10-17.

Watson, H. J., Gerard, J. G., Gonzalez, L. E., Haywood, M. E., & Fenton, D. (1999). Data warehousing failures: Case studies and findings. *Journal of Data Warehousing, 4*(1), 44-55.

Watson, R. (2001). Research in IS: What we haven't learned. *M-IS Quarterly, 25*(4), 5-15.

Weber, M. (1968). *Economy and society, volumes I, II and III.* New York: Bedminster.

Weber, R. (1997). *Ontological foundations of information systems. Coopers and Lybrand accounting research methodology.* Melbourne, Australia: Monograph No. 4.

Weber, R. (2003). Editor's comment: Theoretically speaking. *M-IS Quarterly, 27*(3), 3-13.

Weber, R. (2004). The rhetoric of positivism versus interpretivism: A personal view. *MIS Quarterly, 28*(1), iii-xii.

Weber, R. (2004). The rhetoric of positivism vs. interpretivism. *M-IS Quarterly, 28*(1), 3-12.

Weber, R., & Zhang, Y. (1996). An analytical evaluation of NIAM's grammar for conceptual schema diagrams. *Information Systems Journal, 6*(2), 147-170.

Webster, J., & Watson, R.T. (2002). Analyzing the past to prepare for the future: Writing a literature review. *MIS Quaterly, 26*(2), xii-xxii.

Weiss, C.H. (1979). The many meanings of research utilization. *Public Administration Review, 39,* 426-431.

Westerman, G. (2005). Response to NDA query. Personal communication via e-mail. Simi Valley, CA.

Wheen, F. (2006). *Marx's das kapital: A biography.* Crows Nest: Allen & Unwin.

Whitten, J.L., Bentley, D.L., & Dittman, K.V. (2001). *Systems analysis and design methods.* New York: Mc-Graw-Hill.

Wickramasinghe, D., & Hopper, T. (2005). A cultural political economy of management accounting controls: A case study of a textile mill in a traditional Sinhalese village. *Critical Perspectives on Accounting, 16*(4), 473-503.

Wicks, A.C., & Freeman, R.E. (1998). Organization studies and the new pragmatism: Positivism, anti-positivism, and the search for ethics. *Organization Science, 9*(2), 123-140.

Willett, J.B., & Singer, J.D. (2006). *In longitudinal research: Present status and future prospects.* Harvard University, Graduate School of Education. Retrieved June 3, 2008, from http://www.ats.ucla.edu/stat/seminars/alda/alda.ppt

Williams, B. (1995). Ethics. In A.C. Grayling (Ed.), *Philosophy.* Oxford UK: Oxford University Press.

Williams, B.C., Hood, K.L., & Chen, J.C. (1997). Understanding changes in system, accounting and auditing: The impact of EDI. *Managerial Auditing Journal, 12*(6), 298-304.

Williams, L.R., Magee, G.D., & Suzuki, Y. (1998). A multidimensional view of EDI: Testing the value of EDI participation to firms. *Journal of Business Logistics, 9*(2), 73-87.

Wilson, R. (1985). Reputations in games and markets. In A. Roth (Ed.), *Game theoretic models of bargaining* (pp. 27-62). Cambridge: Cambridge University Press.

Witman, P. (2005). The art and science of non-disclosure agreements. *Communications of the AIS, 16*(11), 260-269.

Wixom, B., & Watson, H. (2001). An empirical investigation of the factors affecting data-warehousing success. *MIS Quarterly, 25*(1), 17-41.

Wolfe, R.A. (1994). Organizational innovation: Review, critique and suggested research directions. *Journal of Management Studies, 3.* University of Alberta.

Wong, J., & Lam, E. (1999). *Measuring electronic commerce in Singapore: Methodological issues and survey findings.* Singapore: E-Commerce and Official Statistics, Singapore Department of Statistics.

Worthington, R. (2000). *Rethinking globalization: Production, politics, actions.* New York: Peter Lang.

Wynekoop, J., & Russo, N. (1997). Studying system development methodologies: An examination of research methods. *Information Systems Journal, 7*(1), 47-65.

Wyssusek, B. & Schwartz, M. (2003). *Towards a socio-pragmatic-constructivist understanding of information systems.* Hershey, PA: IRM Press.

Xu, L., & Brinkkemper, S. (2005). Concepts of product software: Paving the road for urgently needed research. In *First International Workshop on Philosophical Foundations of Information Systems Engineering* (LNCS). Springer-Verlag.

Xu, L.D. (2000). The contribution of systems science to information systems rersearch. *Systems Research and Behavioral Science, 17*(2), 105-116.

Yang, J., & Miao, G. (2005). The estimates and forecasts of worldwide e-commerce. In *Proceedings of 7th International Conference on Electronic Commerce (ICEC'05),* Xi'an, China, August (ACM 1-59593-112-0/05/08).

Yee, C. S.-L., Otsuka, S., James, K., & Leung J. K.-S. (2007). *How does Japanese culture affect budgeting? A pilot study and research agenda.* Working Paper, University of Southern Queensland, Australia.

Yeoh, W., Gao, J., & Koronios, A. (2006). *Exploring critical success factors for implementation of business intelligence systems.* Paper presented at the 6th International Business Information Management Conference Bonn, Germany.

Yeoh, W., Gao, J., & Koronios, A. (2007). Towards a critical success factors framework for implementing business intelligence system: A Delphi study in engineering asset management organisations. In L. Xu; A. Tjoa, & S. Chaudhry (Eds.), *IFIP Series Vol. 255, research and practical issues of enterprise information systems II* (Vol. 2). Boston, MA: Springer.

Yin, R K (2003). *Applications of case study research.* Thousand Oaks, CA: Sage Publications.

Yin, R. (1994). *Case study research – design and methods.* London: Sage Publications.

Yin, R. (2003). *Case study research: Design and methods* (3rd ed.). Thousand Oaks, CA: Sage.

Yin, R. K. (1993). *Applications of case study research.* Newbury Park: Sage Publications.

Yin, R. K. (2003). *Case study research - design and methods* (3rd ed.). SAGE Publications.

Yin, R.K. (1981). Life histories of innovations: How new practices become routinized. *Public Administration Review, 41,* 21-28.

Yin, R.K. (1981, March). The case study crisis: Some answers. *Administrative Science Quarterly, 26,* 58-65.

Yin, R.K. (1989). Research design issues in using the case study method to study management IS. In J.I.a.L. Cash (Ed.), *The IS research challenge: Qualitative research methods* (pp. 1-6). Boston MA: Harvard Business School Press.

Yin, R.K. (1994). *Case study research, design and methods* (2nd ed.). Newbury Park: Sage Publications.

Zimmerman, D.E., Akerelrea, C.Z., Buller, D.B., Hau, B., & Leblanc, M. (2003). Integrating usability testing into the development of a 5 a day nutrition Web site for at-risk populations in the American southwest. *Journal of Health Psychology, 8,* 119-134.

Zuboff, S. (1988). *In the age of the smart machine.* New York: Basic Books.

Zwass, V. (1996). Electronic commerce: Structures and issues. *International Journal of Electronic Commerce, 1*(1), 3-23.

About the Contributors

Aileen Cater-Steel is a senior lecturer in Information Systems at USQ. Her current research interests include IT governance, IT service management, and software process improvement. She has also published research related to software engineering standards, organisational and national culture, and electronic commerce. Aileen's PhD thesis was awarded the ACPHIS medal in 2005. Prior to her academic appointment, Aileen worked in private and government organisations where her career progressed from programmer, systems analyst, and project manager to IT manager.

Latif Al-Hakim lectures in management in the Faculty of Business at the University of Southern Queensland, Australia. His experience spans industry, research and development and academic institutions. Latif was awarded his undergraduate degree in 1968. His masters (1978) and PhD (1983) were awarded by the University of Wales (UK). Dr. Hakim has published extensively in information management and systems modelling. He is the author and editor of seven books, more than 10 chapters in books and more than 60 papers in various journals and conference proceedings. He is the editor-in-chief of *International Journal of Information Quality* and associate editor *International journal of Networking and Virtual Organisations*. Latif has also consulted to a number of major industrial organisations in Australia.

* * *

Khalid Al-Mabrouk is a PhD candidate at the University of Southern Queensland, Australia. He received his bachelor's degree in accounting from the University of Gar Younis, Libya and master's in accounting from the University of Al-Fatah – Academy of Higher Studies, Libya, and Graduate Certificate in Technology Management and MBA from Central Queensland University, Australia. His current research is focused on technology transfer and technological innovation, with particular emphasis on the issues, challenges, and benefits associated with technology adoption in the Arab countries. His expertise encompasses the area of technology transfer process, technological innovation, and development environment, stakeholder issues, and technology project management. He also has a methodological interest in the Delphi method. He is a member of number of associations. He has presented and published a number of papers at conferences and in journals.

Sjaak Brinkkemper is full professor of organization and information at the Institute of Information and Computing Sciences of the Utrecht University, The Netherlands. He leads a group of about 10 researchers specialized in product software entrepreneurship. The main research themes of the group are methodology of product software development, implementation and adoption, and business-economic aspects of the product software industry. He is chairman of the Platform for Product Software, a knowledge exchange forum for product software companies in The Netherlands. He also established Netherware, the incubator supporting students starting their own software company. Before, he was a consultant at the Vanenburg Group and a Chief Architect at Baan Development where he conducted software process improvement initiatives in Requirements Management, Architecture, and Design for various companies. Before Baan, he held academic positions at the University of Twente and the University of Nijmegen, both in The Netherlands, and visiting positions at the University of Texas at Austin (USA) and Tokyo Institute of Technology (Japan). He served on the program committees of numerous conferences and workshops (CAiSE, ICSOC, ECIS, WITS, OOIS, REFSQ, WICSA). He is a member of the Editorial Board of the *Requirements Engineering Journal, Journal of Database Management*, and *Journal on Information Systems and e-Business Management*. He is a member of IFIP Working Group 8.1 on the "Design and Evaluation of Information Systems," of the ACM, of the Computer Society of the IEEE, and of The Netherlands Society for Informatics.

Andrew Connor is a senior lecturer and associate director of the Software Engineering Research Lab in the School of Computing & Mathematical Sciences at Auckland University of Technology. His career has bridged the domains of Mechanical and Software Engineering; he has held a number of academic research positions in the UK and has worked for several years in technology consultancy. Andy's research interests relate to product and process improvement, with particular emphasis on both the management of software engineering projects and the application of artificial intelligence techniques in improving product design.

Francisco Chia Cua (CPA, ACA) (MEntr, University of Otago, New Zealand) is a senior lecturer at Otago Polytechnic. His extensive experience in accountancy and information systems includes International Consultant of the Asian Development Bank, Oracle systems administrator, and education consultant of the leading universities in New Zealand. He received the Best PhD Colloquium Presentation award in the 2006 UK Academy of Information Systems Conference, 2006 Excellence in Research Award from Otago Polytechnic, and 2007 Outstanding Alumni Award from Far Eastern University, Philippines. His current research concerns business case, business model, IAS, IFRS, and enterprise information systems.

Sergio Di Martino has been post-doc at University of Salerno. He currently is assistant professor in Computer Science at the University of Naples "Federico II." His research interests include software engineering, human-computer interaction, and Web metrics.

Filomena Ferrucci is an associate professor in Computer Science at the University of Salerno. Her research interests include human-computer interaction, software-development environments, visual languages, software metrics, and e-learning.

Jing Gao received his PhD from the University of South Australia. He is currently working as a full-time research fellow/lecturer for the School of Computer and Information Science at University of South Australia. He has also been working as a professional trainer/consultant for many Australian leading organisations including the Defence Science and Technology Organisation (DSTO) of Australia,

SA Water, and so forth. His research interest is about how to obtain an alternative view to appreciate complex social and technical problems.

Tony C. Garrett (PhD, University of Otago, New Zealand) is an Assistant Professor in Marketing at Korea University Business School, Korea University. His research has centered on culture and marketing management behaviour, new product/service development and innovation. He teaches in these areas as well. His work has been published in such journals as *Industrial Marketing Management*, *Journal of Product Innovation Management*, and the *European Journal of Marketing*.

Carmine Gravino is an assistant professor in Computer Science at the University of Salerno. His research interests include software engineering, human-computer interaction, and Web metrics.

Hatem F. Halaoui is an assistant professor in Computer Science at Haigazian University. His research interests include geographical information systems, spatial databases, temporal databases, spatial data indexing, and temporal data indexing.

Jukka Heikkonen received the MSc and Dr.Tech. in Information Technology at the Lappeenranta University of Technology, Finland, in 1991 and 1994, respectively. Since 1996, he has been working at the Laboratory of Computational Engineering of Helsinki University of Technology, Finland, where he is currently acting as senior research scientist. Currently he is on sabbatical in Italy where he is working at the Joint Research Center of European Commission. His research interest include statistical modelling, information theory, and data analysis in wide variety of application fields.

Kieran James is a senior lecturer in Accounting at University of Southern Queensland (Toowoomba, Australia). He has 16 years experience teaching in Australia and Singapore and has published in leading international and national journals including *Accounting Forum*, *Accounting and Finance*, *Critical Perspectives on Accounting*, and *Pacific-Basin Finance Journal*. He is also a regular contributor to the Australian newspaper *Socialist Worker*. His main research interests are: accounting education, accounting for goodwill and identifiable intangible assets, African accounting and capital markets, critical and Marxist perspectives on accounting, employment prospects in accounting for minority groups, Information Technology Transfer to the developing world, workplace relations and conditions, and the sociology of popular music. Kieran and his wife Jenny and daughter Irvina live in Toowoomba, Australia.

Slinger Jansen is currently an assistant professor at the Institute for Information and Organization at Utrecht University, the Netherlands, where he recently finished his PhD entitled "Customer Configuration Updating in a Software Supply Network." His current focus is in the area of product software and software product management, with a strong entrepreneurial component. Furthermore, he is specializing in the area of software supply networks and researching the impact of changes in such a network on the software architecture of a product. Slinger loves being active in the academic community and is a committee member for a range of different conferences, all in the areas of software development and maintenance.

Kapp L. Johnson, Esq., is a senior lecturer in Law and Ethics in the School of Business at California Lutheran University. His practice focused on business transactions, litigation, and governance. He is member of the California Bar Association and his teaching and research interests include law and economics, business ethics, and the legal environment of business.

Panagiotis Kanellis is currently a programme manager with Information Society S.A. in Athens, Greece. Previous to that, he held senior consulting positions with Arthur Andersen and Ernst & Young. He was educated at Western International University in Business Administration (BSc), at the University of Ulster in Computing and information systems (Post-Graduate Diploma), and at Brunel University in data communication systems (MSc) and information systems (PhD). He is a research associate in the Department of Informatics and Telecommunications at the National and Kapodistrian University of Athens and an adjunct faculty member at the Athens University of Economics and Business, having published more than 50 papers in international peer-reviewed journals, books, and conferences. He is a member of the British Computer Society (BCS) and a chartered information technology professional (CITP). He is also a certified information systems auditor (CISA).

Andy Koronios received his PhD from the University of Queensland. He has extensive teaching experience both in the tertiary sector at undergraduate and postgraduate, MBA, DBA, and PhD levels, as well as in the provision of executive industry seminars. He has numerous research publications in a diverse area such as multimedia and online learning systems, information security and data quality, electronic commerce, and Web requirements engineering. His current research interests focus on data quality and the use of information in strategic decision making. He is currently a Professor and the Head of the School of Computer and Information Science at University of South Australia.

Ivan K.W. Lai is an assistant professor in the Faculty of Management and Administration at the Macau University of Science and Technology. He has over 20 years of industrial experience in the logistics and supply chain management. He has published many papers on the topics of ERP, IOS, and SCM. His current research focuses on Internet-based IOS, extended enterprise, ERP implementation, supply chain risk management, and action research in enterprise information systems.

Carman Ka Man Lee is an assistant professor in the Division of Systems and Engineering Management, School of Mechanical and Aerospace Engineering at the Nanyang Technological University, Singapore. She obtained her PhD from The Hong Kong Polytechnic University in 2004. After receiving her doctoral degree, she was a postdoctoral fellow at Industrial and Systems Engineering Department, The Hong Kong Polytechnic University. Her current research areas include logistics information management, manufacturing information systems, product development, and data mining techniques. She focuses on applying computational intelligence such as genetic algorithm and artificial neural network for supply and demand chain management.

John Loonam is a lecturer in management at Dublin City University Business School. He holds a Bachelor of Arts in European Studies and a Masters of Business Studies from the University of Limerick. He received his PhD in business studies at Trinity College, Dublin. John teaches in the fields of management and strategic management at both undergraduate and postgraduate level. His current research focuses on top management and information systems.

Ross A. Malaga received his PhD in 1998 from George Mason University. He is currently an associate professor of Management and Information Systems in the School of Business at Montclair State University. His research focuses on search engine optimization, online auctions, and electronic commerce. He has published articles in *Communications of the ACM, Decision Support Systems, Journal of Organizational Computing and Electronic Commerce, Electronic Commerce Research,* and the *Journal of Electronic Commerce in Organizations.* Dr. Malaga serves on the editorial review boards of the *Information Resources Management Journal* and the *Journal of Electronic Commerce in Organizations.*

Joe McDonagh is a senior lecturer at the School of Business, Trinity College Dublin, where he also serves as director of postgraduate teaching & learning. His work focuses on leading large-scale change in complex systems of organisations, particularly change enabled by modern ICT systems. He has extensive international experience and advises executive and ICT leaders in governments and large corporations on the effective integration of both technological and organisational change. Some recent government assignments include Ireland, United Kingdom, United States of America, and the United Nations while corporate assignments include large private sector organisations.

Joseph M. Mula, PhD, is a senior lecturer in the Faculty of Business at the University of Southern Queensland. He has over 40 years of industrial experience in the accounting, information systems, and management as well as over 30 years in education. A number of papers have been produced on topics of IS, accounting, family business, and econometric modeling of government policy. Joseph's current research focuses on sustainable systems, forensic business investigation, education technology, and information systems in virtual organisations.

Erja Mustonen-Ollila received the MSc (1984), and DSc (2005) degrees from the Lappeenranta University of Technology (LUT), Finland. In 1984-1991 she worked in industry in diverse IS positions. In 1992 she started working in LUT, and currently she is a working as a senior IS lecturer in IT department. Her research covers IS methodologies, agile development methods, diffusion of innovations, organisational learning and unlearning, IS evolution, and IS life cycles. Her research methods cover longitudinal historical case studies using diverse analysing methods from learning and intelligent systems. She has published in *ISJ, EJIS, Journal of Knowledge Management,* and many high qualified conferences.

Paivi Ovaska is a researcher and lecturer specializing in the fields of information systems development, implementation and adoption in organizations. She has degrees (MSc, Lis. Tech, and Dr. Tech) from Lappeenranta University of Technology in Finland. She has gained a long experience from software industry while working as a software designer, project manager and head of department in several software firms in Finland over 15 years. Now she is working in South Karelia University of Applied Sciences as a senior lecturer. She has been an associate editor and on programming committees in several conferences, such as European Conference on Information Systems and Information Systems Development. She is also actively writing of her research in top IS journals.

Thanos Papadopoulos is doctoral researcher at Information Systems & Management Group, Warwick Business School, The University of Warwick, UK. He holds a diploma (Dipl-Eng) in computer engineering and informatics from the School of Engineering, University of Patras, Greece, and an

MSc in information systems from the Department of Informatics, Athens University of Economics and Business, Greece. His research interests include information systems, innovation and change in public services, business transformation and networks, Information Systems' assessment strategies, and educational evaluation and technologies. He has published in international conferences and journals and is a member of the Technical Chamber of Greece.

Li Ping is a managing director at ROC Consulting International (ROC) in Singapore where she provides a series of customized and effective corporate advisory services covering B-B e-commerce, corporate finance, and executive education to Small and Medium Enterprises (SMEs) from around the world. Prior to ROC, she has experiences in IT and finance industries. She received her PhD from the University of South Australia Division of International Business and Management. Her research interests include the impact of adopting electronic data interchange (EDI) on SME performance, B-B e-commerce, and information system management.

Shaligram Pokharel is an associate professor in the Division of Systems and Engineering Management, School of Mechanical and Aerospace Engineering at the Nanyang Technological University, Singapore. He obtained his master's and PhD in systems engineering division from the University of Waterloo, Canada. His research area includes supply chain, reverse logistics, and energy planning and management.

João Porto de Albuquerque is assistant professor at the School of Arts, Sciences and Humanities of the University of Sao Paulo, Brazil. He studied computer science and social sciences at the State University of Campinas (Brazil), from which he holds a BSc (2002) and PhD in computer science (2006). Part of his PhD research was performed at University of Dortmund, Germany (2004-2006). He was a research fellow of the Alexander von Humboldt Foundation at the Department Informatics of the University of Hamburg (2007-2008). His research interests are concentrated around understanding the sociotechnical aspects of the development and use of information and communication technologies in organisations, building upon theories from science and technology studies and social studies of ICTs.

Arno Rolf has been, since 1986, a professor of Information Systems in Organisations and Society at the University of Hamburg, Department Informatics. Among other professional activities, he worked formerly as a corporate consultant for an international software company as well as system and organisation developer for a publishing house in Hamburg. His research areas encompass informatics in environmental protection, development of systems for the management of material flow, information systems in context, work in virtual organisations and Webs, and social-oriented design theory.

Edouard J. Simon studied political science and informatics at the Universities of Hamburg and Duisburg, Germany. He worked as a software developer before he was appointed in 2005 as a research assistant at the Department of Informatics, University of Hamburg. His research focuses on interdisciplinary approaches to innovation and technology studies. Further topics of interest include software development methodology, open source software development, and computer supported cooperative work and learning.

Judith Symonds is a senior lecturer at AUT University, Auckland, New Zealand. Judith serves as the editor-in-chief of the *International Journal of Advanced Pervasive and Ubiquitous Computing (IJAPUC)*. Judith holds a PhD in rural systems management from the University of Queensland (2005, Australia). Judith has published in international refereed journals, book chapters, and conferences, including the *Australian Journal of Information Systems* and the *Journal of Cases on Information Technology*. She currently serves on editorial boards for the *Journal of Electronic Commerce in Organisations* and the *International Journal of E-Business Research*. Her current research interests include data management in pervasive and ubiquitous computing environments.

Kazuhiro Takeyasu is a head of Research Institute for Management Information System and a professor of Osaka Prefecture University, Japan. He graduated Kyoto University and Over Graduate Course of Kyoto University. He received a Doctor of Engineering from Tokyo Metropolitan Institute of Technology in 2004. He has extensive experiences in the analysis of time series and system identification. He had worked for Sumitomo Metal Industries, Ltd., and Mitsui Bank. He was a general manager and a director of a large consulting firm, which is an affiliated company of the bank. His main research interests are time series analysis, system identification, and marketing.

Mark Toleman is professor and head of School of Information Systems at the University of Southern Queensland. His research interests are wide and include IT service management, IT governance, systems development methodologies, research-practitioner nexus, novice developers, and information systems education. He has published over 100 articles in books, refereed journals, and refereed conference proceedings.

Raul Valverde has been working in the IT field for almost 17 years in different roles as MIS manager, university professor, software engineer, software developer, technical specialist, computer security instructor, and product manager. He presently runs a consulting company where he specializes in Microsoft certification training and works as a part time lecturer for the Management Information Systems Department at Concordia University, and Computer Security Department at Champlain College. He finished a Master of Engineering in electrical and computer engineering from Concordia University, a post Master of Business Administration in information systems from McGill University, and a graduate certificate in computer security from Stanford University. He is currently working towards a Doctor of Business Administration in information systems at the University of Southern Queensland. His research interests are information security, systems analysis and design, databases, and computer networks.

Jan-Hendrik Wahoff received his diploma in Information Systems from the University of Hamburg in 2005. From 2005 to 2007 he spent 18 months in Japan on a scholarship provided by the German Academic Exchange Service (DAAD). Currently, he is a PhD student at the Department of Informatics of the University of Hamburg. His research interests are sociotechnical systems, organisational development, philosophical and epistemic foundations of Information Systems, and transdisciplinary research methodology.

Paul D. Witman is an assistant professor of Information Technology Management in the School of Business at California Lutheran University. Witman holds a PhD in information systems and technology from Claremont Graduate University. His research interests include information security, usability, technology adoption and continuance, and electronic banking and finance.

William Yeoh is currently completing his PhD that focuses on the critical success factors for implementing Business Intelligence systems in School of Computer and Information Science at University of South Australia. He holds B. Engineering (Hons) degree in telecommunications, and received his Master of E-Commerce from UniSA in 2003. During the course of his PhD studies, he published a couple of journal articles, a book chapter, and numerous conference papers, and was an invited speaker at 7th Business Intelligence Conference in Sydney.

Index